We Must Not Be Afraid to Be Free

Stories of Free Expression in America

RONALD K. L. COLLINS

SAM CHALTAIN

OXFORD
UNIVERSITY PRESS

OXFORD
UNIVERSITY PRESS

Oxford University Press, Inc., publishes works that further
Oxford University's objective of excellence
in research, scholarship, and education.

Oxford   New York
Auckland   Cape Town   Dar es Salaam   Hong Kong   Karachi
Kuala Lumpur   Madrid   Melbourne   Mexico City   Nairobi
New Delhi   Shanghai   Taipei   Toronto

With offices in
Argentina   Austria   Brazil   Chile   Czech Republic   France   Greece
Guatemala   Hungary   Italy   Japan   Poland   Portugal   Singapore
South Korea   Switzerland   Thailand   Turkey   Ukraine   Vietnam

Copyright © 2011 by Ronald K.L. Collins and Sam Chaltain

Published by Oxford University Press, Inc.
198 Madison Avenue, New York, New York 10016

www.oup.com

Oxford is a registered trademark of Oxford University Press

Library of Congress Cataloging-in-Publication Data
Collins, Ronald K.L.
 We must not be afraid to be free : stories of free expression in
America / by Ronald K.L. Collins & Sam Chaltain.
   p.   cm.
Includes bibliographical references and index.
ISBN 978-0-19-517572-1 (hardcover : alk. paper)
1. Freedom of speech—United States.   2. United States. Constitution. 1st Amendment.
3. Civil rights—United States.   I. Chaltain, Sam.   II. Title.
KF4772.C65 2011
342.7308′53—dc22   2010014506

1 3 5 7 9 8 6 4 2
Printed in the United States of America
on acid-free paper

to
Bunny Kolodner
—RC

&

Cornelia Spelman
—SC

Two women who, in different ways,
taught us what it means to be free.

Too many men are being driven to become government-fearing and time-serving because the Government is being permitted to strike out at those who are fearless enough to think as they please and say what they think. This trend must be halted if we are to keep faith with the Founders of our Nation and pass on to future generations of Americans the great heritage of freedom which they sacrificed so much to leave to us. The choice is clear to me. If we are to pass on that great heritage of freedom, we must return to the original language of the Bill of Rights. We must not be afraid to be free.

—Justice Hugo L. Black
April 24, 1961

Contents

Prologue

Freedom and Fear: Justice Hugo Black

If we fight for freedom, we should maintain freedom.
—Walter Pollak (1940)

September 11 challenged our convictions. It defied our resolve for freedom, that dedication to let liberty be the default position in life and law. Times of crisis (1798, 1800, 1861, 1914, 1917, 1941, 1968, 2001), after all, test the "sunshine patriot" in each of us. They pit the need to defend our security against the desire to defend our liberty. Or so it seems. If history is any compass of the direction of things, liberty is too often lost in such times. Why? What is it in us—in all of us, liberal and conservative alike—that would trade away that very freedom that sets us apart from our adversaries?

This book speaks to that question by exploring how freedom and fear function in the context of free speech in America. The First Amendment[1] stories that follow—all true—are filtered through the lenses of freedom and fear. These stories are about select moments in the First Amendment's tortured evolution; they speak to its multiple meanings and what all this portends for the future of America.[2] Some of these stories or portions of them have been overlooked. Some are long forgotten. Others are more familiar. By telling the history of some of the people who have helped shape our law of freedom of expression—the litigants, lawyers, lawmakers, and judges—we hope to retell more than a few remarkable chapters in our nation's struggle for freedom of speech, press, petition, and assembly. At times, the struggles were honorable; at other times, they were shameful. But the common thread in our stories is the *people* who wove their way into the quilt of our nation's constitutional history.

Our aim is to inform Americans about First Amendment law by blending that discussion into rich narratives about some of those whose struggles came before the U.S. Supreme Court to be resolved. The characters range from avowed anarchists to devoted Jehovah's Witnesses. The controversies range from flag burning and cross burning to civil rights and national security, and from press freedoms and student speech to defamation. Our aim is to introduce our readers to core free speech doctrines (e.g., prior restraint, the clear and present danger test, fighting words) by way of real-life accounts of some colorful characters, such as a "Red" provocateur who first cheered Communists and later aided the government in rounding them up, or the Alabama judge who pledged to single-handedly cripple the NAACP. Each case narrative also serves as a starting point for introducing our readers to free expression as it existed then—and as it exists now.

We have chosen to bookend our particular narratives between considerations of the life and legacy of one of America's greatest champions of free speech, the late Justice Hugo L. Black (1886–1971). Given the title of this book, which comes from one of the justice's most notable lines, we thought the tension between freedom and fear could best be illustrated by recounting how Justice Black's own beliefs were tested in the flames of the proverbial fire. This perspective arches over all our stories—some of which predate or postdate Justice Black. Even so, we have tried not to let our (qualified) respect for Black color our explanation of the risks that arise when one sides, or claims to side, "absolutely" with the text and ideal of the First Amendment. While Black is not the most important jurist in the history of First Amendment law—that honor might well go to Oliver Wendell Holmes or perhaps Louis Brandeis followed by William Brennan—his constitutional boldness and trepidation nonetheless serve to illustrate the central, inextricably linked themes of this book. By that measure, he has no equal.

Freedom has its costs. That is precisely why we fear it. The freedom guaranteed by the First Amendment is no different. When liberals or libertarians applaud it, they can all too easily ignore the risks—indeed, the dangers—posed by unchecked expression. By the same token, when conservatives or conformists rally against it, they, too, can ignore the fact that unchecked demands for security lead all too often to tyranny. This is not an argument for a "happy medium." Rather, it is to say that those who love freedom or value security must be mindful of what they wish for.

Our passion for the First Amendment ought not to lead anyone to take our perspective as gospel. If it were, there would be little value in honoring the diversity of viewpoints on which the First Amendment is based. Still, we often side with the likes of Tom Paine, John Stuart Mill, Walt Whitman, and Justices Holmes, Brandeis, Black, Brennan, and John Paul Stevens—and sometimes Anthony Kennedy, Antonin Scalia, Clarence Thomas, and John Roberts, too—in affirming our commitment to a life rooted in James Madison's great contribution to constitutional government in America. Even as we praise (and criticize) their ideas, we try to keep an open mind and remain sensitive to the kind of nuance that can change views. (And then there are the newest justices—Sonia Sotomayor and Elena Kagan – for whom the vote is still out.)

Life, like liberty, is an experiment. For better or worse, America has committed itself to an unprecedented experiment in freedom, an experiment premised on the principle that more speech is better, that more information will produce better judgments, that more knowledge will make more self-realized persons, that more associations and beliefs will make us more open-minded, that more press freedom will benefit society, that more robust expression of all sorts will make us a freer people, and that the more we allow for all of this the better chances we will have to check government abuses, and also to discover truth, beauty, freedom, and something about ourselves as well. That, at any rate, is the operative principle—call it a collective hunch? On that principle—a core First Amendment principle—we have banked everything.

A note on this book: The narratives that follow attempt to bring to life the law and history of the First Amendment. Our goal is to provide the reader with *both* the law of free expression and the life stories behind that law. In part, our narrative approach tracks that of others such as Fred Friendly, Anthony Lewis, and Peter Irons, to list but a few. In our view, too many scholarly accounts of the First Amendment leave its history lifeless, whereas too many narrative accounts treat the law and its complexities as something to be ignored. We've tried to strike a balance between engaging narratives and informed accounts. Moreover, our discussion of the state of the law relating to any given case narrative is not limited to that case. Rather, the applicable law, both prior to and after the highlighted case, is woven into the case narrative at hand. For example, the discussion of advocacy of violence is built around the 1949 *Dennis* case but extends in time both before it and after it to the Court's 1969 ruling in *Brandenburg v. Ohio.* By and large, we have confined our focus to political expression, except for chapter 9 (defamation), although even that has its political side. Admittedly, we would have liked to include other chapters on topics such as obscenity, indecency, campaign financing, commercial speech, religious speech, and Internet expression. But that would have made an already long book longer. Since our research is well along in those areas, we might one day publish a sequel devoted to such topics.

We hope you enjoy the book.

1

First Amendment Fundamentalism

George Anastaplo and Free-speech Absolutism

September 27, 1971, 2:00 P.M.: It was a Monday, partly cloudy, nearly eighty degrees. A thousand people filed reverently into the Washington National Cathedral. As the mourners entered, each received a pocketsize government-issued copy of the Constitution. Blue-collar and VIP alike traveled across the marble floor, past the magnificent stained-glass rose windows and below the lofty vaulting, to take a seat in this house of worship where Dr. Martin Luther King had preached his last Sunday sermon three years earlier. They had come to pay their respects to the memory of the man in the plain pine box, Hugo Lafayette Black of Clay County Alabama.

More than others, Justice Black had brought the Constitution back to the people. His populist spirit colored his constitutional vision. He had done much to make freedom respectable during his thirty-four years on the High Court. Now it was his legacy, his great contribution to America. As he had requested, the organ intoned "Swing Low, Sweet Chariot," the choir sang "Rock of Ages," and the minister read from the Bible (I Corinthians 13), Aeschylus, Cicero, Virgil, and Jefferson. The Justice had also asked that passages be read from some of his most inspiring opinions, including *In re Anastaplo* (1961), which closed with these words: "We must not be afraid to be free."[1]

They were the words of dissent. In that case, a bare majority of the justices voted against freedom and for a way of life where conformity and security often trump individuality and liberty. By that time, the justice born in a wooden farmhouse had become America's foremost champion of free speech. A majority of his colleagues feared such freedom, at least freedom in the absolutist sense that their Brother Black had counseled. But what was the Justice suggesting? Why, after all, would anyone "fear" freedom? Why would anyone fear *words?*

We fear what we do not know, what we do not like, and what is different from what we know and like. In other words, we fear that our world might fall apart, that the values we hold may collapse, just as the Colossus of Rhodes crumbled when the earth shook. After all, ideas can change minds. What was gospel yesterday may become heresy tomorrow, and vice-versa. Whenever we allow anyone the freedom to speak freely, to print freely, to associate freely, to petition freely, or to hold any belief freely, we jeopardize what we hold dear. For risk is the companion of freedom. Without it, there could be no freedom, even though with it freedom has suffered.

In re Anastaplo exemplifies the conflict between those who, like Justice Black, placed *absolute* faith in the First Amendment, and others who, like Justice John Harlan, felt that its freedoms had to be *balanced* against societal needs. That, at any rate, was how the debate was then cast in its boldest fashion. If truth be known, there was, of course, always a troublesome measure of wiggle room in both camps. Even so, *In re Anastaplo* reveals the debate in one of its most pristine forms.

In 1950 a man named George Anastaplo—a man of absolute tendencies—dared to step forward when others stepped back. For that, he sacrificed a lawyer's career, a loss Justice Black found symptomatic of a society fearful of freedom. Here is how it happened.

THE INCORRIGIBLE BAR APPLICANT

By his own admission, George Anastaplo was "incorrigible," a "hopeless case."[2] His behavior struck some as it did an irate Illinois bar examiner, as strange—and seeming "to border on the psychopathic." For others, like Justice Black, the "very most that can fairly be said against Anastaplo ... is that he took too much of the responsibility of preserving [this country's] freedom upon himself."[3] He was—and remains—a provocateur, a kind of modern-day Socratic gadfly. Still, he was not a radical, at least not in the contemporary political sense. There was something curiously conservative, quite old-fashioned, about him. In all of these respects and others, Anastaplo *got* to people—liberals, conservatives, and anyone else to the right, left, or in the center. George Anastaplo is, by any measure, a First Amendment figure, an American who speaks his mind frankly and fearlessly. Hence, his tendency to make some people irate.

He was born in Missouri, in 1925, to parents who were natives of Greece. When World War II broke out, Anastaplo was barely seventeen. He volunteered and performed thirty-eight months of military service in the Pacific, North Africa, Middle East, and various European theatres of operation. Then he went to the University of Chicago where he received his B.A., J.D., and Ph.D.[4] At the Law School, he graduated first in his class and readily passed the Illinois bar examination. A proud, patriotic, and highly intelligent young man of twenty-five, he seemed the ideal candidate for admission to the bar. That is, until he started talking about revolution and quoting from a "subversive" document—the Declaration of Independence.

In those days—the dark days of McCarthyism and the notorious Smith Act[5]—it didn't pay to step out of line, to say anything beyond what those in "patriotic" power wanted to hear. So when in 1950 the Illinois Committee on Character and Fitness asked bar applicants to fill out routine forms and state their views on the Constitution, they were looking for nothing more than the usual answers.

When George Anastaplo went down to the committee's offices on LaSalle Street, he either did not know the routine or simply would not follow it during the course of the customary ten-minute interview. The committee members— two lawyers: John E. Baker, Jr., and Stephen A. Mitchell—began the process with the usual softball questions. Soon enough the topic turned to the question of whether Communists should be permitted to practice law.

"I see no reason," responded the bushy-eyebrowed applicant, "why membership in the Communist Party in itself should disqualify anyone from the practice of law." Since Communists believe in revolution, the questioners noted, did Anastaplo believe that a citizen had the right to overthrow the government? "Well, don't we all?" he responded. Pointing to the ideals of the Declaration of Independence and the realities of the Revolutionary War, Anastaplo was brash when he added, "Certainly Americans believe in revolution."[6]

Unaccustomed to such candor, the committee members were again surprised when the young man continued: "The most important" principle of constitutional government in America is that "government is constituted so as to secure certain inalienable rights, those rights to Life, Liberty, and the Pursuit of Happiness, and elements of those rights are explicitly set forth in...the Bill of Rights." For good Jeffersonian measure, he then said: "And, of course, whenever that particular government in power becomes destructive of these ends, it is the right of the people to alter or abolish it and thereupon establish a new government." This, he concluded, "is how I view the Constitution."[7]

Such boldness did not sit well with the committee members. Soon enough they began to ask about his political beliefs and affiliations. Was he a radical? An anarchist? Was he a member of the Communist Party? Did he believe in God? Anastaplo respectfully declined to answer, not on Fifth Amendment self-incrimination grounds but on First Amendment grounds—they had no business prying into his political beliefs. By doing so, he argued, they infringed on his First

Amendment rights of freedom of belief and political association. Those rights ought not be violated absent at least some real and substantial evidence that he posed an imminent threat to his nation.

Fact: there was *no* evidence of anything unpatriotic in the detailed and extensive record before the committee. Indeed, the committee *admitted* that no evidence had been tendered that was "derogatory to Anastaplo's character or general reputation," and that it had "received no information from any outside source which would cast any doubt on [Anastaplo's] loyalty or which would tend to connect him in any manner with any subversive group."[8] Even so, the committee denied George Anastaplo's application for admission to the Illinois Bar. That he was *unwilling to cooperate* with them—to yield to their groundless fears—was enough. He was interfering with the Bar admission process; his stubbornness impeded that process. So ran the administrative argument against him.

On the human side of the ledger was a different set of concerns. What would be the cost—to his career, to his very livelihood—for what some saw as a stubborn or even silly refusal to comply with the bar committee's demands? By getting in an ideological row with the bar committee, Anastaplo risked the good chance he then had to join a prominent Chicago law firm, D'Ancona & Pflaum. Given that, even if one granted that the committee's fears were baseless, how sensible was it to lock horns with the committee members if the consequence was to nullify three years of legal education and decades of future practice and income as a lawyer? Besides, George Anastaplo clearly was *not* a Communist.

And then there was the young applicant's wife, Sara, and their newborn daughter. Surely, George Anastaplo's decision not to oblige the bar committee would negatively affect them and their future. "There were times when we were almost down to our last dollar," recalled Sara Anastaplo years later. "I could not have endured the stress," she added, "if I had not agreed with his position. I trusted his political judgment; it coincided with mine. I was not angry with George. I was, however, extremely angry at the character and fitness committee."[9]

Like her husband, Sara Anastaplo was a believer, a woman of conviction: "If you really believe in something, you have to stand up for it," she said. By that measure, to allow the government to abridge the First Amendment was to allow it to turn free citizens into fearful ones—people afraid to speak openly about this or that idea or associate with this or that group, for fear that it might one day cost them their jobs. If such freedoms are to survive, someone had to defend them. In other words, someone had to be the "sacrificial lamb." George Anastaplo was just that proverbial figure. Then again, some saw this as no more than a case of a stubborn man making a mountain out of a molehill. If Anastaplo was indeed as patriotic as he seemed, then why not answer the committee's questions and be done with the matter? Sometimes there is a fine line between courage and foolhardiness.

Time passed, and Anastaplo's law career remained on hold as *In re Anastaplo* moved its way up and down the appellate courts. He lost in the Illinois Supreme Court in 1954 and then petitioned the Supreme Court in 1955; his petition was denied. In 1959, his case again came before the Illinois Supreme Court; again he lost. Thereafter, he repetitioned the U.S. Supreme Court.

Fortuitously, and after more than a decade of litigation, the U.S. Supreme Court agreed to review his case along with another First Amendment bar admission case, *Konigsberg v. State Bar of California*. Was this a good omen, a sign that the Court was prepared to invigorate the First Amendment?

Oral arguments were set for December 14, 1960. George Anastaplo would argue the case *pro se*, meaning he would represent himself. Incredibly, the very man who was seeking admission to the bar was about to argue a case in the highest court of the land. How good a "lawyer" could he be? Could he win over the more conservative wing of the Court, represented by Justice John Harlan and others? And could he count on the votes from all of the members of the liberal wing of the Court, represented by Justice Hugo Black and others? His future would very much be shaped by how much influence those two justices had on their colleagues—Earl Warren, William Brennan, Jr., Tom Clark, William O. Douglas, Felix Frankfurter, Potter Stewart, and Charles Whittaker.

TWO JUSTICES, TWO VIEWS OF THE FIRST AMENDMENT

Well-bred, well-mannered, and well-tailored, John Marshall Harlan II was a Brooks Brothers man. He was well educated, having received a B.A. and M.A. from Oxford. Perhaps that explained the trace of a British accent in his voice. A former prosecutor and corporate lawyer, Harlan was also an establishment man, someone who never veered too far from decent conventions.

When it came to constitutional law, Harlan was a deferential man; as a justice he believed in deferring to federal agencies, state officials, and the legislative will whenever possible. These qualities often made Justice Harlan the "great dissenter" on the Warren Court. He took thoughtful exception to many of the Warren Court's landmark rulings on federalism, criminal justice, reapportionment, and freedom of speech.[10]

Like George Anastaplo, John Harlan was an old-fashioned conservative, but one of a very different order. Justice Harlan saw self-restraint as the key virtue of any judge. Such restraint applied as well to his interpretation of the First Amendment. For it, too, should be read in such a way as to make it reasonably deferential to the government. He thus subscribed to a *balancing approach* to the First Amendment.

"Where First Amendment rights are asserted to bar governmental interrogation," he declared in a 1959 opinion for the Court, "resolution of the issue always involves a balancing by the courts of the competing private and public interests at stake in the particular circumstances shown."[11] Justice Harlan's balancing approach was very contextual, and very much disposed to retaining the balance first struck by federal, state, or local officials. Above all, John Harlan disdained constitutional absolutism, and any kind of judicial philosophy that was categorical and blind to valid governmental interests.

Judicial restraint would not allow him to second-guess a government call unless it was clearly arbitrary. This was especially true when it came to reviewing the judgments of bar committees. He would not read the First Amendment in a way that, he feared, might turn the Supreme Court into some kind of super–bar committee run by nine men in black robes. Bar committees were entitled to considerable deference in doing their job in looking into the fitness of applicants to practice law. As he rhetorically put it in a 1957 bar admission case: "Can it really be said that a bar-admissions committee could not reject an applicant because he refused to reveal his past addresses, or the names of his former employers, or his criminal record?"[12]

Justice Black liked the gentle and kindly Justice Harlan, even though they had little in common when it came to their constitutional view of things. Though Black, in his own way, could be deferential, he was far less inclined to be a "yes man" when it came to the Bill of Rights, particularly rights touching on freedom of expression. The First Amendment was his North Star, his constitutional compass. It informed his universe, at least as he defined that sphere.

"I have always believed that the First Amendment is the keystone of our Government, that the freedoms it guarantees provide the best insurance against destruction of all freedom" is how he put it in a 1951 case.[13] A decade later, in his dissent in *Wilkinson v. United States*, he added: "This country was not built by men who were afraid and it cannot be preserved by such men. Our Constitution, in unequivocal terms, gives the right to each of us to say what we think without fear of the power of the Government. That principle has served us so well for so long that I cannot believe it necessary to allow any governmental group to reject it in order to preserve its own existence."[14] He was not then afraid of change, at least not change wrought by words or beliefs.

Nominated to the Supreme Court in 1937 by Franklin Delano Roosevelt, Hugo Black[15] was one of the central figures in the constitutional revolution ushered in by the Warren Court (1953–1969). It was a curious legacy for a man who was once a member of the Ku Klux Klan. The populism that once guided his days as a politician from Alabama was redirected when he came onto the Court. Jeffersonian ideals of equality and Madisonian ideals of free expression now directed the path of his populist mission. He led the charge for the vigorous application of the Bill of Rights to the states, and for an "absolutist" conception of the First Amendment—as he famously stated, "'No law' means *no law*." No ifs, no buts, no qualifiers, no balancing. "I believe that the First Amendment's unequivocal command that there shall be no abridgment of the rights of free speech and assembly," he wrote in 1961, "shows that the men who drafted our Bill of Rights did all the 'balancing' that was to be done in this field."[16]

A few years before *In re Anastaplo* came before the Supreme Court, Hugo Black summed up his take on the First Amendment in his opinion in *Speiser v. Randall*. Here is what he wrote:

> [I believe] that the First Amendment grants an absolute right to believe in any governmental system, [to] discuss all governmental affairs, and [to] argue for desired changes in the existing order. This freedom is too dangerous for bad, tyrannical governments to permit. But those who wrote and adopted our First Amendment weighed those dangers against the dangers of censorship and deliberately chose the First Amendment's unequivocal command that freedom of assembly, petition, speech and press shall not be abridged. I happen to believe this was a wise choice and that our free way of life enlists such respect and love that our Nation cannot be imperiled by mere talk.[17]

It was pure Hugo Black—clear, concise, absolute, and of course, fearless. So when the *Anastaplo* case arrived at the Court for oral argument, George Anastaplo could be confident that he had Hugo Black in his corner. For Anastaplo embodied the fighting spirit and personal commitment to constitutional government that so much characterized Hugo Black's view of the First Amendment and his vision of America. But Black was one vote. And even with Warren, Brennan, and Douglas—the liberal wing—Anastaplo would still be one vote short of majority. Justices Frankfurter and Whittaker—two staunch conservatives—surely would vote against him. And Justice Harlan would probably do likewise. So would Justice Clark. That left Justice Potter Stewart, a centrist jurist not disposed to flights of judicial activism. To which side would he be persuaded? Absolutism? Balancing? Or perhaps something else?

DECISION DAY

In a sense, Potter Stewart was the Sandra Day O'Connor or the Anthony Kennedy of the Warren Court. Like them, he was often a tiebreaker. And as became evident on April 24, 1961, his vote would determine the future of George Anastaplo and two other applicants to the bar. That Monday, the nine justices entered the courtroom at 10:00 A.M. to announce their constitutional judgments. Among other cases, they were there for the formal announcement of the rulings in the latest round of bar admission cases: *Konigsberg v. State Bar of*

California, In re Anastaplo, and *Cohen v. Hurley* (a Fifth Amendment self-incrimination case).

It was a John Harlan day. Today, he would not be on the dissenting end of a constitutional precedent.[18] Instead, he held three aces—three majority opinions in three five-to-four cases. Felix Frankfurter—the Court's Harvard intellectual with a zealous faith in judicial restraint[19]—must have been delighted by this triumph over the liberal wing of the Warren Court.

As is the custom, the justices who authored the opinions (majority or separate) gave a short summary of their opinions in open court. Harlan, a tall man, leaned forward as he sketched the facts and holdings in the cases. It was a clean sweep: the constitutional claims had been denied in each and every one of the bar admission cases.

When it came time for Justice Black to summarize his dissent in *Anastaplo,* he added some editorial flare, stating that the applicant had "made the mistake of saying he believed fully in the Declaration of Independence." It was a bit unusual. Even more unusual was Justice Harlan's retort to Black's dissent. "It is clear from the opinion of the Illinois Supreme Court," declared Harlan, "that [Anastaplo] was denied admission not because he believes in the Declaration of Independence but because he refused to answer questions about his Communist Party membership."[20] Clearly, the facts of the cases divided these men...philosophically, jurisprudentially, and personally.

Back in Chicago, George Anastaplo was getting ready to teach an adult-education class when a colleague tracked him down and informed him that a *Chicago Tribune* reporter was on the phone and wanted to talk to him about the Court's ruling in his case. When he heard that Justice Harlan had written the majority opinion, he knew immediately he had lost. That informed hunch was officially confirmed a few days later when a printed copy of the bad news came in the U.S. mail.

Anastaplo knew what any good lawyer knew—that how a court characterizes an issue often determines how it will resolve that issue. "The denial was based," Harlan wrote, "upon his refusal to answer questions of the Committee on Character and Fitness as to whether he was a member of the Communist Party." In other words, the denial was *not* based on Anastaplo's political views or associations. Hence, the majority's conclusion: "it is not constitutionally impermissible for a State legislatively, or through court-made regulation as here...to adopt a rule that an applicant will not be admitted to the practice of law if, and so long as, by refusing to answer material questions, he obstructs a bar examining committee in its proper functions of interrogating and cross-examining him upon his qualifications."[21]

Since Anastaplo was, in Harlan's eyes, being punished *solely* because of his obstructionism, everything else was of no consequence. Thus Harlan could readily concede that the

Committee already had before it uncontroverted evidence as to Anastaplo's "good moral character," in the form of written statements or affidavits furnished by persons of standing acquainted with him, and the record on rehearing contains *nothing* which could properly be considered as reflecting adversely upon his character or reputation or on the sincerity of the beliefs he espoused before the Committee. (emphasis added)

What did matter was the following:

Where, as with membership in the bar, the State may withhold a privilege available only to those possessing the requisite qualifications, it is of no constitutional significance whether the State's interrogation of an applicant on matters relevant to these qualifications—in this case Communist Party membership—is prompted by information which it already has about him from other sources, or arises merely from a good faith belief in the need for exploratory or testing questioning of the applicant.... The Constitution does not so unreasonably fetter the States.[22]

The Bar, then, could deny admission to those who did not conform to its demands to inquire into their background, character, and fitness to practice law. And when it did, the Harlan majority stressed, the Court would not second-guess what local or state authorities decided. Thus the constitutional balance was struck...in favor of the government.

Hugo Black could hardly contain himself, so great was his opposition to how the majority characterized and then resolved the Anastaplo case. In dissent he wrote: "This case illustrates to me the serious consequences to the Bar itself of not affording the full protections of the First Amendment to its applicants for admission. For this record shows that Anastaplo has many of the qualities that are needed in the American Bar...." What the majority did, argued Justice Black, was contrary to the very spirit of the First Amendment. Moreover, such balancing away of First Amendment freedoms had the effect of turning courageous citizens into humble servants:

[T]his case provides...a striking illustration of the destruction that can be inflicted upon individual liberty when this Court fails to enforce the First Amendment to the full extent of its express and unequivocal terms.... The legal profession will lose much of its nobility and its glory if it is not constantly replenished with lawyers like these. To force the Bar to become a group of thoroughly orthodox, time-serving, government-fearing individuals is to humiliate and degrade it.

He then issued a warning:

> But that is the present trend, not only in the legal profession but also in almost every walk of life. Too many men are being driven to become government-fearing and time-serving because the Government is being permitted to strike out at those who are fearless enough to think as they please and say what they think. This trend must be halted if we are to keep faith with the Founders of our Nation and pass on to future generations of Americans the great heritage of freedom which they sacrificed so much to leave to us.[23]

Black ended on a yet more powerful note: "The choice is clear to me. If we are to pass on that great heritage of freedom, we must return to the original language of the Bill of Rights. We must not be afraid to be free."

Even the liberal Justice William Brennan, Jr. (1906–1997), was taken aback by Black's rhetoric. "You have immortalized George Anastaplo,"[24] he privately told his colleague.

Hugo Black, unlike John Harlan, was then willing to take chances in the name of freedom. He did not mind if the bar admission process was more cumbersome because of it; he did not mind if bar committees were sometimes hamstrung in what they could or could not ask about an applicant's fitness to practice law. Presumably, he would hold to this absolutist view even in times of war, even in times of terrorist attacks when other arms of the state inquired into a person's political beliefs.

Glorious as Black's dissent was, George Anastaplo was done. It was now official: he was deemed "unfit" to practice law. He could drive a cab (which he did), he could repeat and write a farewell letter (which he did), he could teach philosophy (which he did), he could author books on the First Amendment and the Constitution (which he has), he could even teach law (which he does), but he could not be a lawyer—he lacked the "good character" for that. So the case against him went.

Perhaps what his critics feared most was not any allegiance to a foreign government or ideology but his outspoken manner, his outright refusal to bend to their wills. Some saw it as character strength; others saw it as a character flaw. However viewed, could bar committees, even honorable ones, conduct meaningful inquiries into an applicant's character fitness if every time they sought to raise a question the applicant invoked his or her First Amendment right not to comply? In 1961, the Court was not about to allow any asserted First Amendment freedoms to interfere with the everyday workings of bar committees. That was the end of the matter... Or was it?

THE CONSTITUTION AND THE CONSTITUTIONALIST

A decade later, the world and the Court had changed. The wind was rife with political protest—seven thousand antiwar demonstrators were arrested in Washington, D.C., alone. The Supreme Court had just sustained Muhammad Ali's conscientious objector claim. And Motown singer Marvin Gaye asked Americans to reconsider their views and values in his song "What's Going On?" Predictably, those applying to the bar were more brazen than their predecessors. First Amendment issues lingered as applicants fiercely objected to government inquiries into their political beliefs and affiliations. The laws were thus challenged anew. One of those at the forefront of the litigation was John P. Frank (1918–2002), a bright and progressive lawyer who had served as law clerk to Black in 1943.

By 1971 three more bar-admission cases—out of Arizona, New York, and Ohio—found their way to the "cert. granted" docket of the Supreme Court. These cases would, like their 1961 counterparts, all produce five-to-four rulings. The issues were also similar in two of the cases: they involved First Amendment challenges to bar committee inquiries into membership in political organizations, in the Communist Party, or in groups that purportedly advocated the violent overthrow of the government. In the third case, out of New York, the First Amendment challenge was to a rule that required an applicant to "furnish proof he 'believes in the form of government of the United States and is loyal to such government.'" In the first two cases, Justice Black led the charge while Justice Harlan trailed in dissent; this time, the First Amendment claim prevailed. The third case pitted Justice Stewart for the majority (joined by Justice Harlan) against Justice Black in dissent; the First Amendment claim lost.

Admittedly, the 1971 cases were splintered precedents with various opinions by multiple justices, with Justice Stewart again tipping the scales. And while the *Anastaplo* precedent was not formally reversed, the wind of its constitutional logic had been depleted from its jurisprudential sails. In the decades-long contest between liberty and conformity, this time freedom prevailed over fear. Hugo Black had been vindicated, or at least largely so. All future Anastaplos need not suffer as he did. Henceforth, bar committees would be constrained about what they could or could not ask about an applicant's background.

Meanwhile, as noted, George Anastaplo never practiced law, though he did teach young women and men about life, law, literature and the First Amendment. He also wrote many books, including *The Constitutionalist: Notes on the First Amendment.* It bore the following "revolutionary" but nonetheless constitutional dedication:

To My Children
and to my Children's Children
with the Reminder that their Revolutionary Forefathers
not only made the American, Greek, and Texas Wars of Independence
but thereafter instituted and maintained new Governments of their own.

CATEGORICAL IMPERATIVES

In re Anastaplo was a colorful case that pitted Black's categorical absolutism against Harlan's subjective balancing test. Law is nuance, yet nuance seemed lacking in the Black-Harlan debate. Was there nothing in between? Was there not some way to navigate the waters between an approach that protected too much and one that protected too little?

There was an alternative approach, namely, *categorizing* speech into classes of expression that determined the measure of constitutional protection to be provided. Five years after Justice Black accepted his judicial robes, the Supreme Court handed down its ruling in *Chaplinsky v. New Hampshire* (1942). Without elaborating, it is enough to quote from the seminal language of the author of that unanimous opinion, Justice Frank Murphy (1890–1949). Here is how Justice Murphy articulated his approach to First Amendment decision-making, an approach to which Justice Black curiously took no exception:

> There are certain well-defined and narrowly limited classes of speech, the prevention and punishment of which has never been thought to raise any Constitutional problem. These include the lewd and obscene, the profane, the libelous, and the insulting or "fighting" words—those which by their very utterance inflict injury or tend to incite an immediate breach of the peace. It has been well observed that such utterances are no essential part of any exposition of ideas, and are of such slight social value as a step to truth that any benefit that may be derived from them is clearly outweighed by the social interest in order and morality.[25]

In other words, there are:

- Categories of expression that are entitled to *no* First Amendment protection
- Categories that are entitled to *considerable* protection
- Categories that are entitled to *limited* protection

Hence, obscenity (and today child pornography) received no protection, political expression received nearly absolute protection, and commercial speech received qualified protection. As we will show in subsequent chapters, this approach of classifying expression along a spectrum of high- to low-value speech depends heavily on exactly how a particular kind of expression is *defined*. If expression can be defined one way or another, it can be protected or punished accordingly.

Such classifying was a variation on Black's absolutism, for it assumed that black-letter rules could hold fast in all contexts. No flexibility here. Justice John Paul Stevens, the High Court's most recent reitree, expressed his disapproval of such inflexible approaches to First Amendment interpretation. In a 1992 lecture at the Yale Law School, he announced: "While black-letter rules have their appeals as a means of deciding cases, they also carry the risk that specific facts may be discounted and, as a result, that deserving speech may be left unprotected while unimportant speech is overprotected."[26]

The Court would struggle with such concerns as it developed its First Amendment jurisprudence. It would continue to use *Chaplinsky's* classifications, though it would alter them, and it would use other tests and procedural rules to buttress free-speech freedoms. Even so, the Black-Harlan debate continued during the reign of the Warren Court.

In 1961, however, the *Chaplinsky* approach to the First Amendment took a back seat to the absolutism-versus-balancing debate. Perhaps that is because a majority of the Court was hesitant to classify George Anastaplo's expression (which was clearly political) for fear that if they did so it would be entitled to First Amendment protection and thus be beyond the pale of regulation by bar committees.

Doctrine had failed him, a majority had opposed him, and the times were not ripe for him. True, the 1971 bar admission cases would vindicate him in principle, though not in deed. But clearly George Anastaplo was ahead of his time—a time that still clung to the past as the wave of a new future emerged.

When Justice Black unleashed his forceful dissent in *Anastaplo*, the nation was veering toward a social revolution that would change the face and future of America. The civil rights movement was burgeoning, the counterculture was blossoming, opposition to the Vietnam War was looming, and virtually every aspect of American life was about to be called into question. As Bob Dylan put it, "'The times, they are a-changin.'" How, if at all, would that revolution—and what followed it—affect Justice Black's absolutism? Would it embolden him, or would it cause him to retreat from his principles in fear? What about national security, defamation, draft card burning, flag burning, student protests, and mass and unruly rallies in the streets? Would Justice Black come to fear the very measure of freedom he once so boldly championed? In the chapters ahead, we will explore such questions, and how and why the First Amendment evolved in the days before and after Justice Black's thirty-four year tenure on the Court.

"Everybody Is against the Reds"

Benjamin Gitlow and the First and Fourteenth Amendments

This is a story about a man with incredible luck. It was made possible by some remarkable lawyers and judges, though it ends in an unpredictable way. It is the story of Benjamin Gitlow, a man who loved a freedom others feared, but then came to fear that freedom himself. It is also the story of the *history* of the First Amendment, a history that *Gitlow v. New York* (1925) helped to shape.

BAD ASSOCIATIONS

For each new arrival to New York's Sing Sing prison in 1920, the questions were the same: parents' names, places of birth, religion, occupation, and level of education. The last question was more psychological: "What made you do this?"

There were, of course, many possible answers. But Lewis Lawes, Sing Sing's new warden, wanted just one. The "experienced prisoner," Lawes said, knew what his answer had to be: " 'Bad associations.' . . . 'Bad associations.' "[1]

Born in 1891 in Elizabethport, New Jersey, Benjamin Gitlow was not your typical prisoner. Unlike his cellmates, he was not there for murder, rape, robbery, burglary, arson, or grand larceny. He was there for word crimes. Still, of Sing Sing's newest arrivals on February 11, 1920, Gitlow's "bad associations" were the worst of all.

The first Communist prisoner in the history of Sing Sing, Gitlow was also the first man to be tried and convicted under New York's Criminal Anarchy Act. Passed in 1902 after the assassination of President William McKinley[2] in Buffalo, the Act made it a crime to "print, publish, edit, issue or knowingly circulate" anything that advocated, advised, or taught "the doctrine that organized government should be overthrown by force, violence and unlawful means."[3] His fellow prisoners had little need for or like of him. Whatever else, prisoners are patriotic.

At the time of Gitlow's arrest, Americans nationwide became increasingly concerned, and increasingly vocal, about the extent to which the country was at risk. "The more of these dangerous anarchists are arrested," declared a *New York Times* editorial, "the better for the United States." A *Washington Post* banner read: "A Terrorist Plot." The editorial asserted that "every known radical with a tendency toward terrorism should be rounded up and kept under surveillance."[4] In one of the more bizarre incidents, a Communist sympathizer was arrested and jailed. Then a mob took matters into its own hands and beat, castrated, shot, and hanged him three times "on a rope that was too short." The assailants found a friend in the coroner, who reported that the Communist prisoner broke out of jail, shot himself, and then jumped off a bridge with a rope tied around his neck.[5]

In this climate, Gitlow had few known friends and many unknown enemies. Yet by the time his case concluded its long and agonizing path through the legal system, after years lost to the "rattling of locks and the clang of steel on steel,"[6] Benjamin Gitlow emerged an unlikely American hero. His case would revolutionize modern First Amendment law. In Zechariah Chafee's[7] words, it would place "forever in the hands of the Supreme Court [a] sharp sword with which to defend the ideals of [Thomas] Jefferson and [James] Madison against local intolerance."

WHAT MIGHT HAVE BEEN

Tellingly, Gitlow's troubles might have been mitigated if James Madison had just gotten his way 140 years earlier. It was June 1789, the first session of the first Congress, and the first order of business was the question of which rights to add to the Constitution. In some sense, the idea of constitutional *rights* was not central to the Constitution of 1787. What was central was the idea of *limits* on federal power. That is, the national government had only those powers given to it either by the Constitution directly or by particular laws enacted by Congress. Thus, the national government could not abridge freedom of speech, press, assembly, petition, or religion because it was not *authorized* by law to do so. Alexander Hamilton put it succinctly in *Federalist* no. 84:

[A Bill of Rights] would contain various exceptions to powers which are not granted; and, on this very account, would afford a colorable pretext to claim more than were granted. For why declare that things shall not be done which there is no power to do? Why for instance, should it be said, that the liberty of the press shall not be restrained, when no power is given by which restrictions may be imposed?

Moreover, Hamilton added, such an attempt to spell out the specific rights of the people would be counterproductive. For example, "What is liberty of the press? Who can give it any definition which would not leave the utmost latitude for evasion?" Hence, Hamilton and others believed it was best to omit a bill of rights and simply limit government power by granting it particular powers and none other.

However adequate this approach was or was not in safeguarding freedom of expression and religion, it did not envision any limitation on the power of the *states* to curtail civil liberties and civil rights, including the right to speak and print freely.

In anticipation of a June 1789 meeting to amend the Constitution, Madison compiled a dizzying list of recommendations collected from the thirteen state conventions—more than two hundred different amendments, to be precise, covering eighty different areas. By the time he presented the final draft to the House, Madison had reduced the original long list of amendments to nine. In the language of three, we can see the precursors to the five freedoms of our First Amendment. They read:

- The civil rights of none shall be abridged on account of religious belief or worship, nor shall any national religion be established, nor shall the full and equal rights of conscience be in any manner, or on any pretext infringed.
- The people shall not be deprived or abridged of their right to speak, to write, or to publish their sentiments; and the freedom of the press, as one of the great bulwarks of liberty, shall be inviolable.
- The people shall not be restrained from peaceably assembling and consulting for their common good; nor from applying to the Legislature by petitions, or remonstrances for redress of their grievances.

When Madison's list was considered, the senators eventually streamlined those three amendments into a more manageable forty-five words—"Congress shall make no law respecting an establishment of religion, or prohibiting the free exercise thereof; or abridging the freedom of speech, or of the press; or the right of the people peaceably to assemble, and to petition the Government for a redress of grievances."

Originally, this proposed amendment and the other nine were to be situated under article 1 of the Constitution, the legislative article. What became the First Amendment was at first to be listed among the limitations on legislative power set forth in Article I, section 9. Those limitations related to matters such as the suspension of the writ of habeas corpus and restrictions on bills of attainder. The reason the guarantee that ultimately became the First Amendment was addressed to Congress and did not refer either to the executive[8] or judicial branches,[9] or to the states either, is that the founding generation was concerned with the arm of government that was granted the most power under the Constitution of 1787. By far, that branch was Congress. It was that mammoth grant of constitutional power conferred on Congress that struck fear into Republican hearts of the likes of Thomas Jefferson, James Madison, and others of similar beliefs. Hence, the constitutional limitation was on that power: "*Congress* shall make no law..."

There was also a constitutional logic to that wording. The power to make laws is vested in the Congress; the power to enforce laws in the executive; and the power to interpret laws in the judiciary. By that constitutional measure, the executive could never enforce a law abridging any of the five freedoms protected by the First Amendment if Congress was barred from making such a law in the first place. Similarly, the judiciary could never interpret and thereafter apply a law abridging such rights for the same reason. Consequently, a restriction on Congress' lawmaking powers was seen as a limitation on the powers of the other two branches of the federal government as well.

Another argument, among others, was this: The Anti-Federalist objections to the Constitution of 1787 reveal that *if* any branch of government had the constitutional power to abridge citizens' expressive and religious freedoms, then Congress with its vast powers would be that branch, the *sole* branch. Thus, only its powers were limited when it came to our First Amendment freedoms. The Federalists thought Congress had no such power; the Anti-Federalists thought it did; but both would have agreed that neither the executive nor the judicial branches had any such delegated authority in need of restriction by way of constitutional amendment.[10] For the executive or judiciary to take any such actions, then, would be to act in contempt of the Constitution, or so the old-fashioned line of constitutional thinking might have it. (Whatever the soundness of such arguments, the First Amendment has since been held applicable to both the executive and judicial branches.)

While Madison continued to press for a national Bill of Rights that included protections for freedom of speech, press, and assembly, he also pushed for a bill that would restrict *state* encroachments on such freedoms and others. He proposed that no "*state* should infringe on the right of trial by jury in criminal cases, nor the right of conscience, nor the freedom of speech or of the press." (emphasis added). Madison insisted this amendment was essential because it bound the states to abide by freedoms that were outlined in the federal Bill of Rights. Without it, he argued, citizens of certain states would be powerless against the "oppressive majority" he had always feared. And that majority will, exercised most dangerously at the state and local levels, presented a greater threat to liberty than any act of the national legislature. Said Madison on June 8, 1879:

> But I confess that I do conceive that in a Government modified like this of the United States, the greater danger lies rather in the abuse of the community than in the legislative body. The prescriptions in favor of liberty ought to be leveled against that quarter where the greater danger lies, namely, that which possesses the highest prerogative of power. But this is not found in either the executive or legislative departments of Government, but in the body of people, operating by the majority against the minority.

For Madison, this proposal to limit the power of the states was seen as "the most valuable amendment in the whole list," he wrote in a letter on August 17, 1789, continuing, "If there is any reason to restrain the Government of the United States from infringing upon these essential rights, it was equally necessary that they should be secured against the State Governments."

The proposal, however, had its opponents—chief among them Thomas Tucker of South Carolina. "It will be much better," Tucker stressed, "to leave the State Governments to themselves, and not interfere with them more than we already do, and that is thought by many to be much too much."

The proposed amendment was subsequently reworded: "The equal rights of conscience, the freedom of speech or of the press, and the right of trial by jury in criminal cases, shall not be infringed by any State." While the amendment passed the House, it failed in the Senate; the House later agreed with the Senate's action.[11] Meanwhile, the text of what we now know of as the First Amendment became the law of the land, along with nine other amendments, on December 15, 1791, when Virginia cast the last vote needed to ratify the Bill of Rights.

And so, at the time of Gitlow's arrest in November 1919, the First Amendment right to freedom of speech applied to the federal government, and *not* to the states. As a result, dissidents like Gitlow received far less constitutional protection for freedom of speech than Americans have come to expect today. By 1920, in fact, thirty-five of the nation's forty-eight states had passed "antirevolution" laws, which forbade people from publicly calling for violent revolution in the United States. At the time, all of these state laws were beyond the reach of the First Amendment, which meant that the only express constitutional protection for free speech had to come from the state constitutions.

"THE VOICE OF DYNAMITE"

The new syndicalism laws had no shortage of potential targets, either, thanks to a series of events that put the nation on alert and culminated indirectly in Gitlow's arrest. In March 1919, the same month the U.S. Supreme Court handed down its unanimous decision in *Schenck v. United States* and upheld the suppression of dissident speech, Bolshevik agitators announced they would begin exporting the ideals of the Soviet Revolution. One month later, thirty-six bombs, each addressed to a different public figure—including *Schenck*'s author, Justice Oliver Wendell Holmes, Jr.—were discovered in various post offices across the country. (Calamity and mayhem were avoided thanks only to luck and insufficient postage.) And on May 1, riots broke out in various American cities as "radicals" attempted to publicly celebrate International Labor Day. In several locations, according to Margaret Blanchard, "police joined bystanders to put a bloody end to the marches."[12]

Then more bombs went off in early June. One exploded in front of the home of the U.S. attorney general, A. Mitchell Palmer. Palmer and his family escaped serious injury; the attacker was less fortunate. In fact, his head was blown across the street, in the direction of the home of then assistant secretary of the Navy Franklin D. Roosevelt, whose home had also been bombed. Among the debris was a leaflet, "PLAIN WORDS," that threatened yet more violence:

> The powers that be make no secret of their will to stop here in America the worldwide spread of revolution. The powers that be must reckon that they will have to accept the fight they have provoked.... We have been dreaming of freedom, we have talked of liberty, we have aspired to a better world, and you jailed us, you clubbed us, you deported us, you murdered us whenever you could.... We know that all you do is for your defense as a class. We know also that the proletariat has the same right to protect itself. Since their press has been suffocated, their mouths muzzled, we mean to speak for them the voice of dynamite, through the mouths of guns.[13]

All in all, there were ten bombings on that terror-filled day alone. The homes of judges, mayors, state legislators, and industrial giants were bombed in Boston, Cleveland, New York, Philadelphia, and Pittsburgh. According to Kenneth Ackerman, "all fingers pointed to the same familiar culprit: radical anarchists."

The next day, June 4, Attorney General Palmer announced that "the outrages of last night indicate nothing but the lawless attempt of an anarchistic element in the population to terrorize the country and thus stay the hand of the government. This they have utterly failed to do." Later that month, while addressing Congress, Palmer warned of more difficult days ahead. "It has almost come to be accepted as a fact," he said, "that on a certain day in the future, which we have been advised of, there will be another serious and probably much larger effort of the same character which the wild fellows of this movement describe as a revolution, a proposition to use up and destroy the Government at one fell swoop."[14]

With pressure mounting for Palmer to do *something*, the Department of Justice conducted the infamous "Palmer Raids," first in November 1919, and then again in January 1920. Thousands of Russian immigrants, along with members of the Communist Party and the Communist Labor Party, were hunted down. With the aid of his young twenty-four-year old assistant, J. Edgar Hoover, Palmer "directed federal agents and local police to go and round up between 5,000 and 10,000 people in a three month orgy of government bullying," Ackerman has recounted. Ironically, many of those rounded up were detained in the reception room at Ellis Island.

This was a breathtaking exercise of raw power. As Christopher Finan reports, "many were held for months in cramped, filthy, makeshift prisons, beaten, brutalized, railroaded, denied lawyers or access to family members, then released with no explanation, never charged with a crime." Additionally, there were hundreds of thousands of government files—450,000 by 1921. Notably, one of those files bore the name of Louis Brandeis, a sitting Supreme Court justice.

"Although the Palmer Raids generated a lot of good publicity for the Department of Justice," Finan has noted, "they accomplished little. The government never discovered who was behind the June bombings. The radicals who were arrested in November and January were not charged with any crime." Still, most Americans didn't mind, so great was the hostility toward the "Reds."[15]

"EVERYBODY IS AGAINST THE REDS"

Against that historical backdrop, Benjamin Gitlow and his ideological comrades preached their Marxist gospel. A week after Palmer's rousing address to the House, Gitlow and others broke ideological ranks with the Socialist Party. It was too timid for their revolutionary tastes. Their new group, tagged the Left Wing Section, rhetorically boasted of a more aggressive form of revolution, including— if necessary—violence.

The Left Wing Section appointed a National Council and charged it to produce a text capable of galvanizing people the way Marx's and Engel's *Communist Manifesto* had when it was published in 1848. During this time, Ben Gitlow was both a member of the Section and its business manager. It took a summer of feverish work to hammer out the manifesto. It called for "revolutionary Socialism" and "revolutionary mass action." True to its provocative title, the document declared, "it is necessary to destroy the parliamentary state, deprive the bourgeoisie of political power, and function as a revolutionary dictatorship." The proposed means to that revolutionary end: "The revolution starts with strikes of protest, and then into revolutionary mass action for the conquest of the power of the state."

That radical message, Ackerman has observed, was published in *"The Revolutionary Age* as a feature for its July 15, 1919, edition, with a record print of 16,000 copies." By November 1919, the radical Socialist message was taking hold—there were police strikes in Boston, steelworker strikes in fifty cities, and a United Mine Workers walkout. Yet when it came to the *Left Wing Manifesto*, some considered its message so boring as to be unable to move anyone to do anything. Harvard law professor Zechariah Chafee, the noted First Amendment scholar, was one such person. "Any agitator who read these thirty-four pages to a mob would not stir them to violence, except possibly against himself," he wrote. "This Manifesto would disperse them faster than the Riot Act."[16]

Dull prose or not, Gitlow's fellow Socialists shied away from the Left Wing Section's highly exaggerated rhetoric. More and more came to think that the Section was a menace to public safety. In a June 24 statement to the press, the National Executive Committee of the Socialist Party spoke of "an opera bouffe reign of terror," and warned that the group was planning "an incredible series of acts hitherto unknown in the Socialist party in this country."[17] That was more than enough for Attorney General Palmer. He set up a "Radical Division" within the Justice Department and appointed the ambitious Hoover as its head. And then, on November 7, 1919—the second anniversary of the Bolshevik revolution—government officials, federal and state, raided dissident meeting places in twelve different cities. New York was among the cities, and Benjamin Gitlow was among those jailed.

It was a bad omen. As Ackerman has noted, "federal prosecutors had [already] won more than five hundred Espionage Act convictions during the [First] World War." If Gitlow had wondered about his legal prospects, his criminal arraignment hearing clarified matters. "I hold that the Communist Party has declared a state of war against the United States," said the magistrate assigned to his bail hearing. "[T]he establishment of the Communist Party in the State of New York," he added, "is the highest crime known to our law. I will not reduce the bail one dollar." When defense counsel pointed out that the United States was not legally at war with Russia, the magistrate shot back: "'Who killed the 111 American soldiers whose bodies are being brought back from Russia?" The defense attorney shrugged his shoulders. "'I don't know,' he said. 'Well,' said the magistrate, 'it was the Soviet guards of Russia. Now let's get back to the law.'"[18]

Not everyone agreed with the new law and how it was being enforced. Editors of the *San Francisco Examiner* charged government officials with "trying to change our laws so that any American citizen who disagrees with their ideas or advocates a change in government may be sent to jail for twenty years." In New York, Governor Al Smith vetoed legislation that would have mandated loyalty tests for teachers, regulation of all school curricula, and special investigations to detect revolutionary conspirators. Eventually, Smith's willingness to stand up for constitutional principles would link his fate to Gitlow's, though in a curious way. For now, those principles cost him the 1920 election.

By contrast, far more Americans supported mass arrests of Communists, Socialists, anarchists, and any other *ists* hell-bent on empowering the proletariat. It was that mindset that led Gitlow to be indicted by state prosecutors on November 26, 1919. He was charged with three counts of violating New York's Criminal Anarchy Act:

- He "feloniously advocated, advised, and taught...the necessity and propriety of overthrowing and overturning organized government by force."
- He printed *The Revolutionary Age*, which urged the overthrow of the government.
- He was an "evil-disposed and pernicious person...of most wicked and turbulent dispositions" (this count was later withdrawn at the trial).

Ben Gitlow, the pudgy, round-faced radical, was in big trouble, and he needed a big-time lawyer to defend him. He found just such counsel in *three* lawyers. Charles Recht and Walter Nelles, a pair of seasoned lawyers from the National Civil Liberties Bureau, conducted the lion's share of the trial.[19] But for the jury argument portion, an even more accomplished criminal defense lawyer was recruited—someone who would argue for the defense in more than two thousand cases during the course of his career: Clarence Darrow (1857–1938). The great defender of the underdog, the staunch opponent of capital punishment, the man who famously debated William Jennings Bryan in the 1925 Scopes trial involving the teaching of evolution, Darrow was so dedicated to free-speech issues that he accepted Gitlow as a client even before the two had personally met. That occasion was reserved until the eve of the trial, in January 1920. "Oh, I know you are innocent," Darrow then told Gitlow, "but they have the country steamed up. Everybody is against the Reds."[20]

The lead prosecutor, Alexander I. Rorke, spent two days making the state's case against Gitlow. He called eight witnesses, including a federal undercover agent. Predictably, the picture he painted of Gitlow was of a man irreparably wed to violent revolution.

By contrast, Darrow offered no opening statement. He barely made an objection when the prosecution offered its case, and throughout the trial he did not call a single witness. (Such inaction, not surprisingly, infuriated his client.) When Darrow did speak, albeit briefly, he spoke in a slow drawl. "My client was the business manager and on the board of this paper and there will be no attempt on

his part to deny legal responsibility for it," he said. "He was on the board of man-
agers, he knew of the publication, in a general way and he knew of its publication
afterwards, and is responsible for its circulation."

Darrow's argument was twofold: first, the *Manifesto* was not a revolutionary
call for violence; and second, if the statute were allowed to be applied to such
expression, it would be unconstitutional. As to the first argument, he told the
jury that the *Manifesto* was the "tamest, the dullest, the most uninteresting document ever submitted." Surely, its publication and distribution could not fall
within the purview of New York's Criminal Anarchy Act. As for the second
argument, Darrow told the jury that any advocate of freedom of speech and of
the press would want "no fetters on the thoughts and actions and dreams and
ideals of men, even the most despised of them. Whatever I think of their prudence, whatever I may think of their judgment, I am for the dreamers," he said.
"I would rather that every practical man shall die if the dreamer be saved."

Consistent with that, and per Gitlow's request, Darrow lectured the jury on
the splendor of revolution: "For a man to be afraid of revolution in America
would be to be ashamed of your mother. Nothing else. Revolution? There is not
a drop of honest blood in a single man that does not look back to some revolution
for which he would thank his God that those who revolted won."[21]

Grudgingly, Darrow also allowed Gitlow to address the jury on his own
behalf. "I suppose a revolutionist must have his say in court even if it kills him,"
the compassionate yet cynical lawyer remarked. Faithful to Darrow's prediction, Gitlow, who spoke for nearly an hour—sometimes in rambling fashion—
told the court: "In the eyes of the present day society I am a revolutionist" and
proud of it. Frequently, Gitlow bickered and exchanged barbs with an impatient judge by the name of Bartow S. Weeks. But the self-righteous defendant
refused to sacrifice his opinion for his liberty. "I am not going to evade the
issue," he told the jury. "My whole life has been dedicated to the movement in
which I am in. No jails will change my opinion in that respect. I ask no
clemency."[22] Passionate—yes. Principled—yes. Prudent—no. Despite Darrow's
bold three-hour summation, Gitlow was convicted on February 5, 1920, in the
Criminal Branch of the New York Supreme Court. In thanking the jury, which
reached its decision in less than three hours, Judge Weeks said: "Your verdict
reflects credit on your sincerity and intelligence and is one of distinct benefit to
the country and the State. There must be a right in this organized State to protect itself....I hope this verdict will reach out and act as a deterrent to
others."[23]

Six days later, Judge Weeks gave Gitlow the maximum—five to ten years.
Shortly thereafter, the still-proud revolutionist boarded a train bound for Sing
Sing to begin his sentence in a prison cell seven feet deep, three feet wide, and six
feet seven inches high.

"MERE ADVOCACY WAS ENOUGH"

If a prison has a soul, Warden Lawes once said, "it is up there in those cells, suffering all the torments of an age-old and unsolved problem of life."[24] Looking back to the day he arrived at Sing Sing, Ben Gitlow remembered only the natural beauty surrounding it. The Hudson River, its frozen mass reflecting the rays of the retreating sun. The Palisades rising in the distance to encircle the stark prison at the top of the hill. Acres of snow, providing the landscape with its winter blanket. As he remarked, "I felt no fear in approaching the place. I confess, it appealed to me. I began to wonder what was in store for me. Perfectly calm, I took a fatalistic attitude and was prepared for anything that was to follow."[25]

More bad news followed. On April 1, 1921, the Appellate Division of the New York Supreme Court (an intermediate appellate court) unanimously affirmed Gitlow's conviction. "It behooves Americans to be on their guard," wrote the court, "to meet and combat the movement which, if permitted to progress as contemplated, may undermine and endanger our cherished institutions of liberty and equality."

So Gitlow remained in jail, imprisoned but not disillusioned. In fact, the ever-idealistic Socialist behind bars ran (unsuccessfully) for mayor of New York City. Then, a year after his first failed appeal, he received his first good news: after twenty-six consecutive months in a cell, he was to be released pending his next appeal. Gitlow's good fortune was the handiwork of Benjamin N. Cardozo, then a member of New York's high court and later the successor to Justice Oliver Wendell Holmes on the U.S. Supreme Court. Cardozo issued the order because he surmised the criminal anarchy statute might well be inapplicable to the facts of the case.

Benjamin Gitlow was again free to revel with his revolutionary friends. Or so he thought, until he was rearrested a short time later for a separate warrant relating to criminal anarchy. The next morning he found himself back in a line-up of prisoners, awaiting arraignment. Meanwhile, Gitlow's lead appellate attorney, Walter Nelles, prepared his next state court appeal, this time to the seven judges of the Court of Appeals of New York, the state's highest tribunal. It would be Gitlow's last chance, short of the highly unlikely intervention of the U.S. Supreme Court, to have his First Amendment rights vindicated. But without some new legal angle, Nelles's prospects for victory were bleak. Absent a different interpretation of the state statute or some new constitutional defense, Gitlow would remain a resident of Sing Sing.

Predictably, the Court of Appeals was disinclined to render novel rulings on behalf of Communist agitators. On July 12, 1922, the judges voted five to two against Gitlow. Writing for the majority, Judge Frederick E. Crane declared: "The First Amendment to the United States Constitution and section 8 of article I of the New York State Constitution[26]...do not protect the violation of this liberty or permit attempts to destroy that freedom which the Constitutions have established." While the majority admitted "there is no advocacy in specific terms of the use of assassination or force of violence," it ruled, nonetheless, that "there was no need to be. Some things are so commonly incident to others that they do not need to be mentioned when the underlying purpose is described." Mere advocacy—or even something approximating it—was enough. Moreover, it didn't much matter if any threat it posed was not imminent.

Judge Cuthbert W. Pound, joined by Judge Cardozo, saw it differently in his dissent. For him, New York's criminal statute was not violated because Gitlow had not actually advocated violent anarchy. As Pound put it: "Although the defendant may be the worst of men; although Left Wing socialism is a menace to organized government; the rights of the best of men are secure only as the rights of the vilest and most abhorrent are protected."

Pound and Cardozo aside, Ben Gitlow had now lost before three different courts and thirteen different judges. His options were running out. With the sweltering summer months ahead—when his limestone-walled cell grew so wet that, as Gitlow would later write, "the moisture drips from the walls"[27]—it seemed he had no choice but to serve out his sentence.

A QUESTION OF "FUNDAMENTAL RIGHTS AND LIBERTIES"

Success in the U.S. Supreme Court is always a long shot. What were the chances of prevailing? After all, in the twenty freedom-of-expression cases the Court had ruled on by that time, it had decided *against* the free-speech claim nineteen times. Even the Court's two liberals, Justices Oliver Wendell Holmes and Louis Brandeis, had only sided with free-speech claims in a few cases.

As the case came to the High Court, Gitlow's legal team added yet another notable legal mind to the roster of his defense counsel: Walter Helprin Pollak, a bright, Harvard-educated lawyer, then thirty-five years old. In later years he would become one of the most celebrated civil liberties appellate lawyers in the land. For now, he had to deal with a formidable challenge to his somewhat novel argument that the First Amendment protected Benjamin Gitlow from prosecution under the New York Criminal Anarchy Act. In other words, he had to argue that the First Amendment, its text notwithstanding, applied to the states.

History was against him. No court up to that time had ever invalidated the Alien and Sedition Acts of 1798, in which seditious libel was deemed to be a crime.[28] Borrowing a page from the English common law of seditious libel, this early federal statute made it a crime to, among other things, disparage the government or government officials or to hold either up to ridicule in ways that might erode their authority. Indicative of its partisan slant, the original sedition act was written so as to expire when President John Adams ended his term in 1801.

While such eighteenth-century laws did have some few and notable protections not available under the old common law—truth was a defense and trial by jury was permitted—the Acts were seen by Jeffersonian Republicans and others as a blatant violation of the First Amendment. A mere seven years after the First Amendment became law, President Adams and his Federalist friends invoked the sedition provision to arrest the likes of Matthew Lyon (an outspoken Vermont congressman), James Thompson Callender (an Anti-Federalist satirical writer, reporter, and author of a book critical of Adams), Thomas Cooper (a British commentator and feisty Anti-Federalist also critical of Adams), Benjamin Bache (the spirited publisher of the infamous Anti-Federalist *Aurora*),[29] and twenty-two others, most of them newspaper editors. All but one of the eleven people tried were convicted. But when Thomas Jefferson, a Republican, took office in 1800, he denounced the sedition law as unconstitutional and violative of the First Amendment. Accordingly, he pardoned all those convicted under the law.[30]

Admittedly, the historical ending of the alien and sedition laws did offer some comfort to Gitlow's lawyers, even if it did not amount to binding judicial precedent. But even if his counsel could get past the precedent of the early sedition act prosecutions, there was another legal hurdle in their way. Whatever viability the First Amendment had—so one major historical school of thought maintained—was confined to prior restraints, which meant that the government could punish a person *after* the expression occurred. And that was what the state of New York had done with Gitlow.

Even if Pollak could overcome legal historical hurdles, how could he get the Court to set aside New York's Criminal Anarchy Act? Whatever constitutional relief Gitlow may have been entitled to, so the argument went, was limited to the protections afforded by the New York Constitution. Gitlow had already lost that argument on appeal, twice, and there was nothing the Supreme Court would do to change that interpretation of state law.

As for applying the First Amendment to the states, as early as 1833 the Court, in an opinion by Chief Justice Marshall, had held that the Bill of Rights restricts the power of the national government alone. Here is how John Marshall put it in *Barron v. The Mayor and City Council of Baltimore*:

> In almost every convention by which the constitution was adopted, amendments to guard against the abuse of power were recommended. These amendments demanded security against the apprehended encroachments of the general government—not against those of the local governments. In compliance with a sentiment thus generally expressed, to quiet fears thus

extensively entertained, amendments were proposed by the required majority in congress, and adopted by the states. These amendments contain no expression indicating an intention to apply them to the state governments. This court cannot so apply them.

Such a view of things held firmly until at least 1868, when the Fourteenth Amendment[31] was ratified. That historic amendment, a child of the Civil War, promised what Madison had sought unsuccessfully to guarantee—namely, a fundamental alteration of the balance of power between the national government and the states. For one thing, it suggested that the rights secured by the Bill of Rights might be interpreted as limits on *state* power, insofar as to abridge them would be to deny people "due process of law." So great was its potential that by 1897 the Court interpreted the Fourteenth Amendment's due process guarantee as restricting the power of the states to take property for public use without just compensation. Thus, some believed that if the promise of the Fifth Amendment could be applied to the states, then that of the First Amendment could likewise apply.

The Court's 1897 ruling, however pregnant with potential, did not formally apply to the states all of the guarantees of the Bill of Rights. Still, it offered Pollak and Nelles the main legal argument that had been missing in the earlier appeals cases—a hook on which to hang the petitioner's claim that freedom of speech was a "fundamental right" safeguarded under the due process clause of the Fourteenth Amendment.[32] If the argument could be presented convincingly enough, the Court might agree that the First Amendment's free-speech guarantee was "incorporated" into the Fourteenth Amendment. In other words, the due process protections of the Fourteenth Amendment included the protections of freedom of speech and association.[33] By that logic, the Court would have to concede that the First Amendment was incorporated into the Fourteenth Amendment. If so, the justices would have no choice but to apply the First Amendment to the states, and Madison's 150-year-old dream of advancing civil liberties by checking state power would then be realized.

Could such a defense carry the day? Granted, Holmes and Brandeis were then pushing the boundaries of First Amendment protections generally, though not against the states specifically. On that score, in 1907 in the case of *Patterson v. Colorado*, the great Holmes (Brandeis was not on the Court then) left open the question of whether the First Amendment applied to the states. "We leave undecided the question whether there is to be found in the 14th Amendment a prohibition similar to that in the 1st," declared Holmes. Justice John Marshall Harlan, however, disagreed. He believed that the Fourteenth Amendment's privileges and immunities clause protected freedom of expression:

> I go further and hold that the privileges of free speech and of a free press, belonging to every citizen of the United States, constitute essential parts of every man's liberty, and are protected against violation by that clause of the 14th Amendment forbidding a state to deprive any person of his liberty without due process of law. It is, I think, impossible to conceive of liberty, as secured by the Constitution against hostile action, whether by the nation or by the states, which does not embrace the right to enjoy free speech and the right to have a free press.

Again, in 1920, a majority of the Supreme Court (with Brandeis in dissent) declined to apply the liberty protected by the Fourteenth Amendment in such a way as to include freedom of speech. And as late as 1922, the Court, again with Holmes's approval, had ruled in *Prudential Insurance Co. v. Cheek* that the Fourteenth Amendment imposed no restrictions on the states when it came to matters of free speech. Yet even if Holmes were to change his mind and Brandeis were to join him, they were only two in number. Five votes were needed for a win. Besides, how kindly would Justice Holmes's perspective be on the likes of Benjamin Gitlow if his ilk were indeed the ones who had earlier attempted to murder Holmes with a mail bomb? For any variety of reasons, winning in the Supreme Court was unlikely.

Even if the First Amendment were to be held applicable to the states, and even if it were to apply the states in the same way it applied to the federal government, there was still a problem. Since 1919, the Court had heard four such criminal advocacy cases and had denied the First Amendment claims in all of them.[34] Even the Court's "clear and present danger test,"[35] first announced by Justice Holmes, had not convinced a majority of the Court to vindicate a First Amendment claim of right. So even if Gitlow's lawyers could convince the Court to apply the First Amendment to the state of New York, the chances were still slim that they could convince the justices to agree with them on the substantive merits of their claim.

When *Gitlow v. New York* came before the nine justices of the Supreme Court on April 12, 1923, Pollak and Nelles knew they could not count on the support of at least one of them—Justice Mahon Pitney. A lackluster and rather mediocre justice, Pitney had authored two opinions that were nonetheless of special interest to Pollak and Nelles. One was the decision in *Prudential Ins. Co. v. Cheek*, wherein Pitney announced that "the Constitution of the United States imposes on the states no obligation to confer upon those within their jurisdiction…the right of free speech." Phrased differently: The protections of the First Amendment did not apply to the states. The same year, Pitney again wrote for the Court, this time in *Pierce v. United States*, to uphold the convictions of three Socialists for distributing an antiwar pamphlet. (Brandeis and Holmes, of course, dissented.) Again, when it came to the states, the First Amendment had no real role to play. Not yet anyway.

Then, unexpectedly, Justice Pitney suffered a stroke and retired from the Court—after *Gitlow* was argued but before it was decided. It was a good omen for Pollak and Gitlow; one of their leading constitutional foes on the Court was now gone. As a result, the case was reargued later that year, on November 23rd, this time before the Court's newest member, Justice Edward T. Sanford.

When it came time for Pollak to deliver his opening remarks, he said: "If the Court please, this case is one of such complexity and importance that I feel I cannot do justice to my argument in the allotted hour.[36] I therefore respectfully request an additional 15 minutes of time." At that point Chief Justice William Howard Taft—the former president of the United States—leaned his big bulk toward the senior justice on his right, Justice Holmes, and asked his opinion. Holmes replied by way of a whisper that could be heard in open court: "I'll see him in Hell first." At that point, Taft turned to Pollak and said: "Mr. Pollak, it is the view of the Court that you should confine yourself to the allotted hour."[37]

For the next two hours the lawyers and the Court went back and forth over the merits of New York's Criminal Anarchy Act, the application of the First Amendment to the states, and the proper construction of a free speech test in light of the Court's more recent rulings. Nineteen long months later, on June 8, 1925, the Court issued its ruling in *Gitlow v. New York*. The vote was seven to two, with Holmes and Brandeis in dissent. Justice Sanford wrote for the majority.

A big man who smoked small cigars, Justice Sanford was highly educated, with a law degree and a M.A. from Harvard. He paid strict attention to legal detail, was conscientious in reading legal briefs, and was as open-minded and as attentive to civil liberties as any man born in Knoxville, Tennessee, just three months after the Confederate surrender at Appomattox, could be. The following statement from his majority opinion would be his greatest First Amendment legacy:[38]

> For present purposes, we may and do *assume* that freedom of speech and of the press—which are protected by the First Amendment from abridgment by Congress—are among the fundamental personal rights and "liberties" protected by the due process clause of the Fourteenth Amendment from impairment by the States. We do not regard the incidental statement in *Prudential Ins. Co. v. Cheek*…that the Fourteenth Amendment imposes no restrictions on the States concerning freedom of speech, as determinative of this question. (emphasis added)

It was just an assumption, not a legal holding. But it was an assumption that would ultimately change the course of constitutional history. For the first time, a majority of the Court was willing to *assume* that the First Amendment was incorporated into the protections of the Fourteenth Amendment, which were binding on the states. It was *dicta*—nonbinding legal language—that would help to change the law of the land.

For Charles Warren, a respected constitutional law scholar writing at the time, what the *Gitlow* Court had done with its *dicta* amounted to a major and unwarranted shift in the American constitutional scheme of things. He tagged it a "new conception of 'liberty.'" And he was highly critical of that "new conception": "this most recent development…may well awaken serious thoughts as to whether there is not danger that the 'liberty' of the States is being unduly sacrificed to this new conception of 'liberty' of the individual."

Warren feared that the *Gitlow* dicta would ignite a wildfire in constitutional law. "If the doctrine of the case is to be carried to its logical and inevitable conclusion," he wrote in 1925, every one of the rights contained in the Bill of Rights ought to be and must be included within the definition of 'liberty,' and must be guaranteed by the Fourteenth Amendment against deprivation by a State 'without due process of law.'"

SUBSTANTIVE EVILS

Such fears notwithstanding, the actual ruling in the case sealed Benjamin Gitlow's fate: "By enacting the present statute," wrote Justice Sanford,

> the State has determined, through its legislative body, that utterances advocating the overthrow of organized government by force, violence and unlawful means, are so inimical to the general welfare and involve such danger of substantive evil that they may be penalized in the exercise of its police power. That determination must be given great weight. Every presumption is to be indulged in favor of the validity of the statute.

Sanford stressed that the New York statute could be "constitutionally applied to the specific utterance of the defendant if its natural *tendency* and probable effect was to bring about the substantive evil which the legislative body might prevent."[39] The state, he added, "cannot reasonably be required to measure the danger from every such utterance in the nice balance of a jeweler's scale." But, importantly, he also noted: The law "does not restrain the advocacy of changes in the form of government by constitutional and lawful means." But if that were the actual measure, Professor Geoffrey Stone has observed, the "Court clearly implied that utterances that stopped short of criminal conduct would pose a *different* constitutional question." Even so, Sanford was not troubled; he had another argument. Further on in his opinion, and with a touch of literary flare, Justice Sanford wrote words that would come back to haunt him:

A single revolutionary spark may kindle a fire that, smouldering [*sic*] for a time, may burst into a sweeping and destructive conflagration. It cannot be said that the State is acting arbitrarily or unreasonably when in the exercise of its judgment as to the measures necessary to protect the public peace and safety, it seeks to extinguish the spark without waiting until it has enkindled the flame or blazed into the conflagration. It cannot reasonably be required to defer the adoption of measures for its own peace and safety until the revolutionary utterances lead to actual disturbances of the public peace or imminent and immediate danger of its own destruction; but it may, in the exercise of its judgment, suppress the threatened danger in its incipiency.

As he concluded, Sanford announced the bottom line: "We cannot hold that the present statute is an arbitrary or unreasonable exercise of the police power of the State unwarrantably infringing the freedom of speech or press; and we must and do sustain its constitutionality." In other words, even if the First Amendment applied to the states, New York's Criminal Anarchy Act had not abridged the First Amendment.

So Benjamin Gitlow's fate would stand—a fact that troubled the Court's two most respected members. Justice Holmes, issuing what the *New York Times* characterized as "the sharpest kind of divergence" on the case, began his dissent, joined by Justice Brandeis, by observing:

[T]his judgment should be reversed. The general principle of free speech, it seems to me, must be taken to be included in the Fourteenth Amendment, in view of the scope that has been given to the word "liberty" as there used, although perhaps it may be accepted with a somewhat larger latitude of interpretation than is allowed to Congress by the sweeping language that governs or ought to govern the laws of the United States.

In true Holmesian vernacular, he then turned Sanford's incitement language back on itself:

It is said that this manifesto was more than a theory, that it was an incitement. Every idea is an incitement. It offers itself for belief and if believed it is acted on unless some other belief outweighs it or some failure of energy stifles the movement at its birth. The only difference between the expression of an opinion and an incitement in the narrower sense is the speaker's enthusiasm for the result.

Holmes's *Gitlow* dissent suggested that he had become more liberal in his view of the First Amendment. He no longer applied it in quite the restricted way he had earlier in *Schenck, Frohwerk,* and *Debs*. Off the record, Holmes was less than flattering about men and women like Gitlow, who believed in a proletarian panacea to the ills of capitalism. About a month after the decision came down, Holmes said as much in a letter to his friend Lewis Einstein: "I regarded my view as simply upholding the right of a donkey to drool."[40]

But in his published dissent, Holmes concluded with a flourish on behalf of "donkeys" like Gitlow: "Eloquence may set fire to reason," he wrote. "But whatever may be thought of the redundant discourse before us it had no chance of starting a present conflagration." He then added a dose of social Darwinism—a survival-of-the-fittest approach to politics and free speech. "If in the long run the beliefs expressed in proletarian dictatorship are destined to be accepted by the dominant forces of the community," he stressed, "the only meaning of free speech is that they should be given their chance and have their way."

Holmes and Brandeis aside, the *Gitlow* opinion met with predictable acceptance. "The decision stands as a safeguard for sound government," editorialized the *Washington (DC) Evening Star*. Similarly, a *New York Times* editorial declared: "There is no denial of free speech. But the free speakers must be ready to face their responsibility to the law for what they say."

Writing in the *New Republic*, Holmes's friend Professor Zechariah Chafee took a longer view of things: "The victories of liberty of speech must be won in the mind before they are won in the courts. In that battle-field of reason we possess new and powerful weapons, the dissenting opinions of Justices Holmes and Brandeis. Out of this long series of legal defeat [starting with the 1919 cases]," added Chaffee, "has come a group of arguments for toleration that may fitly stand beside the *Areopagitica* and Mill's *Liberty*. The majority opinions determined the cases, but the dissenting opinions will determine the minds of the future."

Pollak and Nelles's work, too, would help shape those minds of the future. The good news was that the Court had assumed that the free-speech provision of the First Amendment applied to the states. Though not a formal victory, it was a symbolic one. *Gitlow v. New York* was a constitutional milestone; it would forever be hailed as the first case in which the Court applied the First Amendment to the states.

The formal victory came later, thanks largely to Chief Justice Charles Evans Hughes. First, in *Stromberg v. California* (1931) he wrote for the Court when it struck down a state "red-flag" law on First Amendment grounds. Relying on *Gitlow*, Hughes declared: "It has been determined that the conception of liberty under the due process clause of the Fourteenth Amendment embraces the right of free speech." Not long afterward, in *Near v. Minnesota* (1931), the First Amendment's press clause was applied to the states: "It is no longer open to doubt that the liberty of the press and of speech is within the liberty safeguarded by the due process clause of the Fourteenth Amendment from invasion by state action."

Then in *DeJonge v. Oregon* (1937), Hughes again wrote for the Court when it applied the First Amendment's assembly guarantee to the states: "Freedom of speech and of the press are fundamental rights which are safeguarded by the due process clause of the Fourteenth Amendment of the Federal Constitution.... The right of peaceable assembly is a right cognate to those of free speech and free press and is equally fundamental."[41]

By 1937 Pollak's former law office boss, Benjamin Cardozo, was also flying the incorporation banner. Writing for the Court in *Palko v. Connecticut*, Justice Cardozo ruled that *some* of the protections found in the Bill of Rights were so fundamental that the states must honor them. A decade later, in *Adamson v. California*, Justice Hugo Black further extended the Pollak and Nelles incorporation principle by arguing that the states must honor *all* of the rights specified in the Bill of Rights.

> My study of the historical events that culminated in the Fourteenth Amendment, and the expressions of those who sponsored and favored, as well as those who opposed its submission and passage, persuades me that one of the chief objects that the provisions of the Amendment's first section, separately, and as a whole, were intended to accomplish was to make the Bill of Rights, applicable to the states. With full knowledge of the import of the *Barron* decision, the framers and backers of the Fourteenth Amendment proclaimed its purpose to be to overturn the constitutional rule that case had announced.

While Black's historical conclusions were contested, and while the full Court never went quite that far, in time all of the provisions of the First Amendment were held applicable to the states, as were most of the provisions of the Bill of Rights. Charles Warren's 1925 prediction came to pass—though it was not an outcome he welcomed.

On the merits, Holmes's *Gitlow* dissent pointed to the future. Though his general view of the First Amendment would be vindicated in later opinions, that time was still decades away.

Walter Pollak and Walter Nelles had set the wheels of American constitutional law in motion.[42] Pollak's greatest professional satisfaction, in fact, came from having had, as he later expressed it, "some part in a number of legal battles on behalf of persons persecuted for their opinions." Even so, his client had lost. And grand as the symbolic victory was, the real and immediate consequence of the Court's handiwork was to require Gitlow to serve out the remainder of his five-to-ten year jail term.

Benjamin Gitlow's options had run out. If the Highest Court in the land would not spare him, who in the world would?

"TO ORGANIZE, TO SPEAK, TO STRIKE AND TO PICKET"

"Within a week after the decision," wrote Harold Josephson, "the American Civil Liberties Union petitioned Governor Al Smith for a pardon, arguing that Gitlow already had served thirty-four months and that his only offense was the expression of his political views." The International Labor Defense organization and several locals of the International Ladies Garment Workers Union echoed that call. But what were the chances?

Six months after the Supreme Court decision, on his first wedding anniversary, Ben Gitlow was resigned to accepting his status as a ward of Sing Sing. It was Friday, December 11, 1925, when the dark-curly-haired prisoner ventured to the visiting room to see his wife, Badonna Zeitlin. Together, they struggled with the real likelihood of him remaining in prison for years. About that time, a guard approached Badonna. She had a phone call. "Wouldn't it be funny if the call is on the matter of your pardon?" she quipped. Governor Al Smith, who had returned to the governor's mansion after his 1920 defeat, had recently pardoned one of Gitlow's fellow dissidents; might he now be willing to do the same for Gitlow? But that was too good to be true—it was fanciful revolutionary thinking.

When Badonna returned from the warden's office, she could barely contain her enthusiasm. "Don't be surprised if you will lose one of your steady guests soon," she said rather snidely to the guard. "I just got word that the Governor pardoned my husband."[43]

The next day, after accepting a cheap suit of clothes from the state and a gift of $10, Benjamin Gitlow left Sing Sing for good. As he watched Gitlow pull his brown cap down over his eyes and board a train for Grand Central Station, Lewis Lawes may well have wondered if this unusual prisoner had finally learned his lesson. Was he a man for whom "bad associations" would no longer be a problem?

An hour later, a group of twenty-five energized radical friends met Gitlow at Grand Central Station. Befitting the occasion, the general secretary of the Workers Party made a promise to a gathering of the press: Despite his personal hardships, Benjamin Gitlow "would continue to carry forward the fight for which he was imprisoned ... [for] the struggles with the employing class and for the defense of every right of the workers to organize, to speak, to strike and to picket."[44]

THE PLOT TWISTS

It's hard to comprehend what followed next. After all, who would believe that a man who sacrificed so much for the principles of freedom would later deny the same freedoms to others? Yet that's exactly what happened: Ben Gitlow—the man who twice ran (unsuccessfully) as a Socialist for vice president of the United

States, promising he would turn the White House into apartments for poor farmers—turned on his comrades and became a government informant.

In 1929, thanks to Joseph Stalin (whom he had once met), Gitlow was expelled from the Communist Party. Infuriated and feeling betrayed, Gitlow and others organized, unsuccessfully, the Communist Party, U.S.A. Meanwhile, the thirty-nine-year-old agitator became a man without an ideological anchor. He drifted. By the late 1930s and into the 1950s, he opposed those he had once embraced by testifying (sometimes as a paid government informant) before the House Un-American Activities Committee (HUAC), the Subversive Activities Control Board, and similar government commissions. Among others, he testified against Harry Bridges (a noted longshoreman leader)[45] and Stephen S. Wise (a revered American rabbi).[46]

"Mr. Gitlow was a favorite witness of the House Un-American Activities Committee, but his testimony became suspect in many quarters in 1953 when he said that" the Communists were highly successful at infiltrating the Methodist Church. That same *Washington Post* story added: "He and other defectors related that 600 clergymen in the country were secret Reds." A few years earlier, as recounted by Ackerman, Gitlow wrote a letter to FBI director J. Edgar Hoover "praising him for his anticommunist work and offering to meet with him in Washington to help him ferret out subversives."

Gitlow's critics—aging Socialists and young progressives—denounced him as a vengeful man bent on destroying the world he was forced to leave behind. Gitlow, no doubt still wounded by Stalin's rebuke of him, said he turned against Communism because of its "enslavement of the human mind." If true, Ben Gitlow came to that truth in the rough-and-tumble of ideas he first defended and then divorced. That process—of talking, debating, publishing, protesting, and thereafter reconsidering it all—represents one of the cornerstones of the First Amendment. If Gitlow had reflected long enough on that fact before he died on July 19, 1965, perhaps he would have realized that freedom changes minds; suppression changes nothing.

As for Walter Pollak,[47] the lead lawyer in Gitlow's Supreme Court case, he died years earlier, in 1940, at the age of fifty-three. Unlike the man he defended, Pollak's legacy was honorable. His son, Judge Louis H. Pollak, said this of his father: He lived a "life in the law with enterprise, courage, and utility, a life which affirms that law can be a worthy calling." And then there is Zechariah Chafee's assessment. As he put it in a tribute published in the *Nation* on October 12, 1940: "It is hard to realize that a person so much alive as Walter Pollak can be dead.... He radiated generous enthusiasm for justice; delight in mental activity, unexpected flashes of wit. We have lost him when we need him most."

Calling Dr. Meiklejohn

Alexander Meiklejohn and First Amendment Theories

Why do we protect speech? What values are furthered by the free-speech principle? Or to put it otherwise: what is the purpose of the First Amendment?

To raise such questions is to ask about *theories* of the First Amendment, those animating principles that "justify" the liberties taken in its name. Perhaps no American is more widely associated with First Amendment theory than Alexander Meiklejohn (1872–1964). His writings on the First Amendment captured the imagination of readers in a way most other such works never have. Surprisingly, few know of his colorful and controversial career, which points all too naturally to his theory of free speech. That theory prompted other free-speech theories that countered or complemented his. Together, they help us think about why we value freedom of expression.

A THEORY BORN IN LIFE

> Critical thinking is not comfortable to those who are criticized.
> —Cynthia Stokes Brown[1]

The stories in the *New York Times* set the stage for what unfolded on the days leading up to, on, and after an extraordinary commencement day in June 1923. There were many banners; the more foretelling ones read:

- "Amherst in Clash over Meiklejohn"
- "Trustees May Force Dr. Meiklejohn Out If He Won't Resign"
- "Expect Meiklejohn Will Resign Today"
- "Meiklejohn Quits Amherst"

Back then, he was not yet known as "Mr. Free Speech." That would come four decades later. Still, the audience at Amherst's 103rd commencement ceremony must have sensed something dramatic when Alexander Meiklejohn rose to speak. For on that graduation day, dissent was in the air. The college had fired President Meiklejohn, ignoring many students' objections. Twelve seniors had openly refused their diplomas. The nephew of the president of the board of trustees accepted his sheepskin in a fighting spirit: "I am taking this degree under protest..."[2] It was a day of drama, one like no other (then or now) at the venerated Massachusetts campus. It was the day a defiant Meiklejohn, then fifty-one years old, took to the podium to address friend and foe for the last time.

What happened on that Wednesday and thereafter was a real-life prelude to *Free Speech and Its Relation to Self-Government*, Meiklejohn's famous 1948 work on the First Amendment. It was a window into the mind of a man who practiced free speech before he penned any words about it. The life work that he started with the Amherst commencement ceremonies set the context and contours of a free-speech theory that came to be widely revered, rejected, and reincarnated in countless ways.

At various points during the 1923 graduation ceremonies, Amherst students booed and hissed to manifest their disapproval at what the college had done in firing President Meiklejohn. His turbulent differences with some of the faculty, his arguments with the trustees, his controversial educational objectives, and even certain alleged financial irregularities did not matter. This iconoclastic educator—this Socrates, if you will—was being given institutional hemlock. But his defenders would not stand for it, and many remained seated when it came time to accept their diplomas.

At the alumni luncheon the following day, the mood was tense in the college gymnasium where Meiklejohn delivered his presidential address. A tall and lean man of Scottish dissent, Meiklejohn took to the small stage beneath the flying rings and ropes and spoke extemporaneously: "I am no longer active President of this college," he proclaimed proudly. "I am no longer bound by that. I am myself free to say what may come into my mind and heart."[3] The stifling heat in the gym—it was the hottest day in thirty-five years—intensified the frenzy of it all. The temper during Meiklejohn's talk shifted back and forth from concentrated silence to wild outbursts. Half the audience, the elders and men of power in the front rows, remained as stiff as their white-starched collars. The other half, the young ones, waved and roared with boisterous approval.

An unrepentant Meiklejohn extolled the cause of the outsider, of the dissenter who parts from the unthinking herd. Generally speaking, this was the cause, albeit controversial, he had attempted to institutionalize while president of Amherst. It was, in classical terms, also a paean to Heraclitus, the great pre-Socratic philosopher and champion of change. Said Meiklejohn:

> I am a minority man. I am always wanting change. I am almost invariably in an issue against the larger number. That being the case, I am perfectly willing to take my medicine. . . . I am expected to be in the minority, and institutions must inevitably be in the hands of majorities. I am a believer in democracy, but my query is whether institutions of learning should be in the hands of majorities. May I place myself, as usual, somewhere at swords' points with my friend [John] Erskine. Mr. Erskine said to me: "Keep the best of the past, be sure of that"; and I said: "Yes, and the best of the past is change. For change is life. Life that does not change is death."[4]

Then came his parting shot at the heads of his adversaries and the hearts of his admirers: "I differ from most of you on most of the issues of life, and I am going to keep it up." The audience cheered, pounded tables. Some even cried. Amid thunderous chaos, a proud Meiklejohn made his exit.

Alexander Meiklejohn was in his element, in the thick of it. Then, as in the years to follow, he never dodged controversy. He preferred to meet it head on with fierce passion, engaging rhetoric and contested logic and with a view of life in which free speech was central. The same life logic would one day make him one of the great—but controversial—names in First Amendment history.

Meiklejohn always attracted (and repelled) people of power. Take, for example, Felix Frankfurter, then a noted Harvard law professor. The future Supreme Court justice, a close friend, saw Meiklejohn's firing as "a matter of national concern." According to Meiklejohn's biographer, Adam R. Nelson, Frankfurter expressed his sentiments in a letter to Meiklejohn: "I . . . feel terribly sad about the termination of your work at Amherst because it means certainly the temporary arrest of forces that are most precious and indispensable to the wise unfolding of our national life." Zechariah Chafee, then at Harvard, too, was equally supportive and upset. "The news of your resignation," wrote the man who would become a revered First Amendment scholar,[5] "comes as a real blow to many of us in Cambridge. You raised the American college to a new plane."[6] Personally and professionally he sided with Meiklejohn, one of his former teachers when he and Frankfurter were both at Brown University.

Two friends, two supporters, two men with futures—they stood tall with Alexander Meiklejohn and his cause. Times would change, as would their views about freedom, free speech, and the role of the First Amendment in American life. But those times had not yet arrived. Solidarity and silence were norms.

Meanwhile, Amherst was history. Meiklejohn had to move on, and move on he did to the University of Wisconsin, where he later taught philosophy and set up the Experimental College, which opened in 1927. Among other things, that college's students would study the ancients (Pericles and Plato) and the modern progressives (like Louis Brandeis). Meiklejohn championed a more "radical" curriculum, more education in civic participation, and more talk about the importance of public discourse. What he was doing in Wisconsin echoed what he had said in Providence in January 1923: "In the field of democracy, America is attempting something never before and seemingly impossible."[7] That "something" was building an *informed* democracy of men and women willing to come together to hash out the best course of life for a freedom-loving people. By 1928, Meiklejohn was drawing national attention, so much so that on October 1, his photograph appeared on the cover of *Time*.

As fate would have it, in 1932 the Experimental College fell on economic hard times and closed. The sixty-year-old England-born educator then moved to Berkeley, California. In time, he would join the School of Social Studies in San Francisco, where he was involved in adult education. From his base in Berkeley, Meiklejohn, now gray-haired, charted out a career of writing and activism. He was busy developing a theory of life, law, and freedom. The First Amendment was the axis point of it all.

WHY DO WE NEED A THEORY OF THE FIRST AMENDMENT?

As a professor of philosophy, Dr. Meiklejohn must have known this: We turn to theory when we doubt our moorings. If the *text* of the First Amendment were utterly decisive, there would be no use for a theory of the First Amendment. Like the Bible, the Constitution needs its interpretive priests and rabbis. For example, as already noted, the use of the term "Congress" in the text of the First Amendment has not been interpreted as confining it to constitutional restraints on a single branch of the federal government. Hence, in the *Pentagon Papers* case (see chapter 4), the First Amendment was applied as a limitation on the federal executive and judicial branches. Likewise, no one has been so tenacious a constitutional literalist as to apply the "no law" command categorically, in *all* instances. If the ultra-orthodox textualist were given free rein to apply the constitutional command literally, for example, it would be impossible for Congress to outlaw speech acts like perjury, consumer fraud, blackmail, and murder for hire. In such a word-free world, lying, cheating, thieving, and homicide would abound. Hence, qualifications, explanations, and justifications needed to be devised.

For similar reasons, there would be no need for theory if the *historical intent* was so patently obvious as to govern the future in all its unconceivable circumstances. If what the framers said in 1791 spoke directly to all of the issues of our time, then the very idea of a theory of free speech could be discarded. But the First Amendment's history—what the framers did, said, and meant—has not always been determinative. Theory thus allows the living to tinker with the past whenever a precise meaning can neither be readily discerned nor easily tolerated.

Enter the theorists. Alexander Meiklejohn's central thesis was rooted in the Enlightenment, in the idea that *reason* can set men and women free. The Bill of Rights, as the Supreme Court noted in a 1941 First Amendment opinion, "was the child of the Enlightenment." The "guaranty of free speech," added Justice Felix Frankfurter, was premised on a "faith in the power of an appeal to reason."[8] In that sense, Dr. Meiklejohn's theory of free speech derived some of its staying power from the likes of John Milton (1608–74) and John Stuart Mill (1806–73)—two philosophers who defended free speech as a *means* to discovering truth. As Milton put it in his famous tract *Areopagitica* (1644): Where "Truth and Falsehood grapple; who ever knew Truth put to the worse, in a free and open encounter?" Similarly, in *On Liberty* (1859), Mill defended the utilitarian value of free speech this way:

> The real advantage that truth has consists in this, that when an opinion is true, it may be extinguished once, twice, or many times, but in the course of ages there will generally be found persons to rediscover it, until some one of its reappearances falls on a time when from favourable circumstances it escapes persecution until it has made such head as to withstand all subsequent attempts to suppress it.

From such vantage points, the First Amendment is important precisely because of its value in ferreting out truth. "If the opinion is right," Mill added, humanity is "deprived of the opportunity of exchanging error for truth; if wrong, they lose, what is almost as great a benefit, the clearer perception and livelier impression of truth, produced by its collision with error." Or to phrase it as the pragmatist Justice Oliver Wendell Holmes did in his famous *Abrams* dissent (see chapter 5), "the ultimate good desired is better reached by free trade in ideas.... [T]he best *test* of truth is the power of the thought to get itself accepted in the competition of the market."[9]

This *marketplace of ideas*[10] theory of the First Amendment sees the Madisonian guaranty as a mechanism not so much for necessarily securing truth as for testing the truthfulness of various positions. "Certainty generally is illusion,"[11] is how the ever-skeptical Holmes couched it in an 1897 article. In this sense, truth is provisional and what is most important is the *quest*. Hence, the integrity of the *process* of truth-seeking must be maintained so that this or that "truth" may be tested anew.

For Meiklejohn, however, this truth-seeking mission of the First Amendment was not simply philosophic, at least not insofar as the thing to be cherished was the individual gain in discerning or testing truth. Rather, what he valued was the *collective* benefit in discovering truth, or at least the kind of truth that would make humankind better. That, above all else, was the utility of a system of free expression. In that regard, Meiklejohn's free-speech theory was political philosophy. That political component was the crown jewel in his thinking about the First Amendment.

THE BOOK AND ITS TIMES

Meiklejohn's *Free Speech and Its Relation to Self-Government* was published in 1948. It derived, most directly, from lectures he had given at the University of Chicago, Yale University, St. John's College, and Dartmouth College. Of course, the book was also informed by much of what he had done and said dating back to and for many years since his Amherst years. It was an evolving work.[12] Its first formal incarnation was a draft of the manuscript Meiklejohn sent to Ordway Tead, an editor at Harper and Brothers, in April 1946. The manuscript was then titled *Free Speech and Justice Holmes*. Its focus was quite limited, and overall the work wasn't ripe for publication. Besides, the political climate was not then conducive to a favorable public response. These, after all, were the times when the HUAC ruled the roost—when fear was the rule and free speech the exception.

To get a sense of the activist flavor of this famous paean to First Amendment freedoms, one must have some general impression of the times. They were, by and large, times very much out of sync with virtually every idea Alexander Meiklejohn had about education, government, politics, freedom, and the First Amendment. It was the Cold War era, that post–World War II period when military tensions between the United States and the Soviet Union were high. President Truman and Premier Stalin were at such loggerheads that the idea of full-scale war loomed as a real possibility. The HUAC had recently become a standing committee in Congress, and Attorney General Tom Clark[13] was busy doing his best to infiltrate "subversive" Communist cells in America. During this period, when prosecutions against alleged Communists were occurring, *Time* editor Whittaker Chambers accused Alger Hiss (a former Holmes law clerk and a former State Department official) of being a member of the Communist Party involved in clandestine activities.[14] By the summer of 1948, and buttressed by strong anti-Soviet public sentiment, the Justice Department issued indictments against

Eugene Dennis (see chapter 5) and eleven other Communist Party leaders for conspiring to "teach and advocate the overthrow and destruction of the government of the United States by force and violence." Such "enemies of the state," many thought, were not entitled to First Amendment protection, especially in such dangerous times.

Before, during, and after this time, the spectacled philosopher was busy publicly lambasting—in speeches, articles, and before government bodies—the anti-Red campaigns then being waged by the president, the Justice Department, the FBI, and federal and state legislative committees. Such campaigns, Meiklejohn argued, could not be reconciled with the First Amendment. Here is how he put it in an article he published in the *New York Times Magazine* in July 1948:

> The Government of the United States in the recent past has in many ways limited the freedom of public discussion. For example, the Federal Bureau of Investigation has built up, throughout the country, a system of espionage, of secret police, by which hundreds of thousands of our people have been listed as holding this or that set of opinions. The only conceivable justification of that listing is to provide a basis for action by the Government in dealing with those persons.

He then raised his rhetorical lance against the nation's lawmakers, whom he viewed as equally complicit in such "witch hunts":

> The legislative committees, Federal and State, which have been appointed to investigate un-American activities, have the same implicit purpose. All the inquiries and questionings of those committees are based upon the assumption that certain forms of political opinion and advocacy should be, and legitimately may be, suppressed.[15]

President Truman was likewise constitutionally culpable for his loyalty oath order of 1947, the first section of which declared: "There shall be a loyalty investigation of every person entering the civilian employment of any department or agency of the executive branch of the Federal Government." For Meiklejohn, it was a betrayal of constitutional principles: "[T]he President's loyalty order, moving with somewhat uncertain and wandering steps, follows the same road. In these and other ways, we are officially engaged in the suppression of 'dangerous speech.'"[16]

That left only the Supreme Court. Meiklejohn's contempt for the Court's "clear and present danger" test was no less apparent: "Whoever, today, wishes to suppress dangerous debate, turns to that phrase for his final justification. The time has come when, by action of the Supreme Court, the phrase should be eliminated from the interpretation of the First Amendment." He added, "That Amendment tells us that, when dangers arise from public discussion, the evils which they threaten must be endured if the only way of avoiding them is by abridging that freedom of speech upon which the entire structure of our free Government rests."[17]

To make his free-speech contentions more colorful, Meiklejohn proceeded to paint his constitutional argument in still bolder strokes: "The First Amendment, then, declares to us and to all men that Hitler's *Mein Kampf* or Lenin's *The State and Revolution* or the *Communist Manifesto* of Engels and Marx may be freely printed, freely sold, freely distributed, freely read, freely discussed, freely believed, freely denied, throughout the United States." He capped things with this: "The *unabridged* freedom of public discussion of public policy is the rock on which our Government stands. With that foundation beneath us, we shall not flinch in the face of any clear and present—or, even, terrific—danger."[18]

In what may be an unprecedented kind of editorial, published the same Sunday on which Meiklejohn's article ran, the editors of the *New York Times* said this to their readers:

> There must be many readers of this and other newspapers who are honestly worried about the guarantees of free speech and a free press which are written into the First Amendment to the Constitution. We would like to refer these readers to an article entitled "Everything Worth Saying Should be Said," written by Dr. Alexander Meiklejohn and published in today's issue of our Magazine.[19]

Here, then, was Meiklejohn, inspirationally flanked by the editors of the *New York Times*, making an argument for the First Amendment—an argument against all odds, all polls, and certainly the lion's share of public opinion. The logic of that argument would and did suggest that:

- Avowed Communists should be allowed to teach in public schools.
- The Justice Department should immediately cease and desist compiling lists of organizations deemed subversive.
- The FBI should stop its surveillance of political activists.
- The Immigration Service should ignore the political beliefs of immigrants.
- Federal and state lawmakers should end legislative hearings designed to ferret out citizens with "dangerous beliefs."

From Meiklejohn's First Amendment perspective, such measures were pure "idiocy," as he later complained. To continue down such a road, he told a New

York audience in 1950 at the tenth annual convention of the National Lawyers Guild, was to "stand in contempt" of the people.

ABSOLUTELY PROTECTED OR NOT?

Against that backdrop, *Free Speech and Its Relation to Self-Government* debuted in America in 1948 for $2 a copy. The 107-page book, which would become a free-speech benchmark, was divided into four parts:

I. "The Rulers and the Ruled"
II. "Clear and Present Danger"
III. "American Individualism and the Constitution"
IV. "Reflections"

Meiklejohn opened the first chapter with the proposition that "there are two different freedoms of speech, and hence two different guarantees of freedom rather than only one." One of these freedoms is "open to restriction by the government. The other is not open to such restriction." Given that dichotomy, the First Amendment is "not the guardian of unregulated talkativeness.... What is essential is not that everyone shall speak, but that everything worth saying shall be said." Hence, what is important was "not the words of the speakers, but the minds of the hearers." This hierarchy of free-speech freedoms was designed to serve the collective good in making "wise decisions."

"Public discussion" related to the public welfare, he continued, could *never* be abridged. By contrast, "private discussion" related to "individual self-seeking" could be regulated or "'balanced' against the public safety," subject only to the Constitution's "due process of law" commands. Phrased another way:

> The guarantee given by the First Amendment is not, then, assured to all speaking. It is assured only to speech which bears, directly, or *indirectly*, upon issues with which voters have to deal—only, therefore to the consideration of matters of public interest. Private speech, or private interest in speech, on the other hand, has *no* claim whatever to the protection of the First Amendment.[20] (emphasis added)

Put simply: *All* public-interest expression is entitled to *absolute* protection—even if there is a "clear and present danger" to some societal interest. If expression could not be lumped under that rubric (even "indirectly"), then the government might well be able to ban labor picketing, special-interest lobbying, product advertising, commercial broadcasting,[21] and sexual expression, subject only to minimum levels of due-process protection.

The animating idea behind this dichotomy was Meiklejohn's notion of self-government, of government actually *by* the people, albeit an *informed* electorate. This was less a call for direct democracy than a call for participatory and deliberative democracy, whereby citizens and their lawmakers discuss and debate all matters of public interest in the hope of improving the collective welfare. That town-meeting conception, with its "rules of order," is "self-government in its simplest, most obvious form," Meiklejohn noted.[22]

For Meiklejohn, self-government was premised on the people's right to know, to discuss and hear any and all ideas, subjects, ideologies, philosophies, or creeds. In the realm of public discussion, no philosophy or creed can be taboo; no idea can be kept out of the marketplace of ideas. Absolutely none! Or as Meiklejohn more eloquently offered it: "To be afraid of ideas, any idea, is to be unfit for self-government."[23] Given the absolutist tenor of his views on public expression, Meiklejohn, ever politically outspoken, was predictably critical of the "clear and present danger" test as formulated by Justice Holmes—the man whose First Amendment doctrines had long been in Meiklejohn's crosshairs. He thus devoted an entire chapter to critiquing the danger test as first formulated by Holmes in 1919 and revised by Zechariah Chafee. Under Meiklejohn's view of the First Amendment, "certain substantive evils" that in principle "Congress has a right to prevent" must nonetheless "be endured."

Not surprisingly, a few years later the former Amherst president blasted the Supreme Court's ruling in *Dennis v. United States* (1951), which invoked a variation of the "clear and present danger" test to sustain the imprisonment of American Communists. He fearlessly and unapologetically declared that the *Dennis* majority was responsible for the "destruction" of the very free-speech principle it was sworn to defend. Speaking at a conference of the Emergency Civil Liberties Committee in New York City, Meiklejohn drew thunderous response when he sought to "challenge and refute" the concurring opinion of "my old friend" Justice Frankfurter[24]—the same man who some three decades earlier had stood in defense of Meiklejohn and condemned those who fired him from Amherst (*Dennis* is discussed in Chapter 5).

During this general period, the always political Meiklejohn—who helped found the Northern California chapter of the ACLU in 1934—became ever more committed to defending the cause of the First Amendment in ways beyond the borders of scholarly print. For example, in October 1949, he joined Carey McWilliams, then editor of the *Nation*, in defending the Hollywood Ten.[25] The two submitted an amicus brief to the Supreme Court in *Parker et al v. City of Los Angeles* (1949), a loyalty oath case. And as Adam Nelson has documented, a year later Meiklejohn took exception to the kind of policies that then California governor Earl Warren (who would later become chief justice) supported when he signed the Levering Act, "which converted state employees into civil defense workers, giving them thirty days to swear under oath that they had not, in the previous five years, advocated the violent overthrow of the U.S. government."[26]

In December 1957, Meiklejohn petitioned the House of Representatives for a redress of grievances: "I...petition the House of Representatives either (1) to decide against continuing the mandate of the Committee of Un-American Activities or (2) to so modify that mandate as to deny the Committee any authority to 'compel testimony' concerning the 'beliefs, expressions or associations' of its witnesses."[27] Several years later, in 1962, the aging scholar became the chair of the National Committee to Abolish the House Un-American Activities Committee. Whatever else may be said of Dr. Meiklejohn, he was by no measure an armchair defender of freedom of expression.

While *Free Speech and Its Relation to Self-Government* may today seem, at least in some quarters, rather tame, it was in its day a firebrand philosophy dedicated to bolstering freedom under the First Amendment. Still, whatever unprecedented freedom it gave to public political expression it seemed to revoke from all sorts of other kinds of expression. And that, as we shall show, was precisely what worried many of those who believed that Meiklejohn's horizon needed to be expanded, both doctrinally and practically.

CLASHES AND CRITICISMS

When *Free Speech and Its Relation to Self-Government* came out, it was hailed in some circles, notwithstanding its provocative thesis. For example, biographer Adam Nelson has noted that the syndicated columnist Max Lerner[28] "applauded Meiklejohn's efforts." Wrote Lerner: " 'I count Alexander Meiklejohn's book...among the very small number of books published this year that will live.' "[29] Predictions of longevity aside, even Lerner had serious doubts about Meiklejohn's political/private speech distinction. To maintain the integrity of such a distinction, Lerner wrote in the *New Republic*, was like "trying to square the circle." In that respect, Lerner was not alone.

Zechariah Chafee was far more critical. The famous First Amendment authority from Harvard Law School respected Meiklejohn, who had been dean while Chafee attended Brown University in the early years. And when Meiklejohn was fired from Amherst, Chafee rallied to his defense. But Chafee could not respect some of the bold ideas his former teacher was now advancing. "The book," he told Felix Frankfurter, "has more errors of law per page than about any I have ever read."[30] Then, writing in the *Harvard Law Review*—the Bible of the legal academy—he wrote: "The most serious weakness of Mr. Meiklejohn's argument is that it rests on his supposed boundary between public speech and private speech. That line is extremely blurred." In his eleven-page review essay, which was scholastically detailed, Chafee argued that Meiklejohn's dichotomy actually diminished our First Amendment freedoms: "[T]he framers would hardly have relegated science, art, drama, and poetry to the obscure shelter" provided by the due process command of the Fifth Amendment, though Meiklejohn had done just that. By the same token, he added, Meiklejohn's thesis rendered too much protection to political speech: "[T]he freedom which Congress was forbidden to abridge was not, for [the framers], some absolute concept." All in all, Chafee argued, the Amherst philosopher "does not realize how unworkable his own views would prove when applied to litigation."[31]

Years later, Hugo Black registered a similar, though far more conciliatory, critique. Justice Black both liked and respected the feisty Meiklejohn. He surely must have admired the way this free-speech activist had stood up to power—to the likes of the Amherst establishment and the HUAC. And Black certainly liked the rhetorical broadsides Meiklejohn had launched against the "clear and present danger" test. Still, for Black the fly in the ointment of Meiklejohn's theory of free speech was that it was too narrow. "There is nothing," wrote Black, "in the language of the First Amendment to indicate that it protects only *political* speech, although to provide such protection was no doubt a strong reason for the Amendment's passage."[32]

As we have seen, the major criticism focused on the public/private speech dichotomy. The two main questions came to this: (1) Why, for speech to be protected under the First Amendment, must it be designated political speech, or public discussion, or speech about issues of public importance? (2) Why is self-governance so important that it trumps all other free-speech values? The following scenarios speak to such questions, which in turn raise further questions. They bear out the points raised by Meiklejohn's critics, then and now:

- What if Max Planck's writings on quantum physics irked local librarians in Lima, Ohio, so much so that they barred such works from their shelves?
- What if homophobic officials in Tuscaloosa, Alabama, outlawed public readings of Allen Ginsberg's poem "Howl" at the state community college there?
- What if the city fathers of Fort Worth, Texas, could not fathom the music of rappers like Lil Wayne and barred such artists from performing in their communities?
- What if a new, uncensored release of Radclyffe Hall's 1928 novel *The Well of Loneliness* was threatened with prosecution in Evansville, Indiana?
- What if Robert Mapplethorpe's photo art could not go on display in public galleries in New York?
- Finally, what if state lawmakers in Utah opted to ban all commercial messages about alcohol?

Such "what-ifs" point to the central problem—namely, that so much of what we as Americans value cannot be quartered under the tent of political speech linked solely to self-governance. If our free-speech freedoms were so confined, many would deem this tyrannical.

Dr. Meiklejohn saw the problem. But it took him thirteen years to amend his thesis. In a much-noticed 1961 article in the *Supreme Court Review*, he broadened his concept of protected speech to include "novels and dramas and paintings and poems" and the like, insofar as they may, in some slight way, contribute to the people's right to govern themselves. When he finally expanded his theory, he likewise watered down its logic. "Yet when the theory has been thus expanded," Professor Laurence Tribe rightfully observed, "it tells us disappointingly little."[33] There were many other criticisms that were leveled over time. Take those, for example, leveled decades later by Lee Bollinger, the current president of Columbia University. Bollinger was even harsher in his assessment of Meiklejohn's theories. "The work borders on the unsophisticated" is how he put it in *The Tolerant Society* (1986). For Bollinger, another law professor who has written extensively on free speech, "Meiklejohn's seminal [book] is a curious and deceptive work.... Its power is elusive." Beyond the public/private dichotomy, Professor Bollinger identified what he saw as "two fundamental problems" with Meiklejohn's thinking:

> The first is whether the theory has anything to say about speech restrictions that are the *product* of the democratic system, and not simply the imposition of censorship by a government acting outside of democratic procedures. The second is whether the theory has anything to say about why in particular we should protect speech that seeks to undermine the system itself—for example, by advocating the violation of concededly legitimate laws.[34]

There you have it—wings, warts, and all. Yet while his history, logic, jurisprudence, philosophy, and definitional formulas were challenged, several of Meiklejohn's core views survived the rhetorical storms. As we shall shortly show, none of the criticisms of his work was so strong as to remove him from the pantheon of great free-speech theorists. Still, there have been other theorists and theories that in one way or another enriched our conception of what free speech is and why we value it.

OTHER THEORIES (OR AWAY FROM A SINGLE THEORY)

Of course, even if one grants the need for theory (any theory), one might still question the adequacy of a single all-encompassing theory of the First Amendment. Is a general theory of free speech, like Meiklejohn's, ever capable of addressing the rich variety of cases that arise under the First Amendment? Can a lone organizing principle ever begin to explain why we should or should not protect this or that kind of expression?

In recent years, the Supreme Court has from time to time embraced Holmes's "marketplace of ideas" theory. At other times, the Court has championed Meiklejohn's self-governance rationale. At still other times, the Court has relied on the "liberty" model of self-expression. And sometimes the Court's rulings are not grounded in any theory. What the Court has not done is adopt any *single-value* theory of the First Amendment. This is because, as Daniel Farber has duly noted, "[t]he search for a foundational First Amendment 'brick' has been unavailing so far."[35] The reason it has been unavailing, stresses Tribe, is that "no satisfactory jurisprudence of free speech can be built upon...partial or compromised notions" of free expression. "Any adequate conception of freedom of speech," he adds, "must instead draw upon several strands of theory in order to protect a rich variety of expressional modes."[36]

In other words, any adequately protective view of First Amendment freedoms must look to diverse rationales in order to help explain why we do or do not value free expression in any given context. To quote Farber: "Instead of thinking of the First Amendment as a tower, built on a single sturdy foundation, we might do better to think of it as part of a web of mutually reinforcing values...that [help to] support both democracy and free speech." Ideally, such values would be mutual and would reinforce democracy and liberty. But there can be no guarantee, of course, that they will.

As we have already indicated (chapter 1), the Supreme Court has often employed a *balancing* approach to First Amendment adjudication. Ideally, that approach balances, with objective precision, the rights of the individual against the needs of society. Cases like *Anastaplo* (1961), however, reveal that such an approach can all but read the First Amendment out of existence, since societal interests can frequently, if not always, trump individual rights. The Court has likewise invoked the "marketplace of ideas" theory as a justification for protecting expression. This Enlightenment-based theory cannot adequately justify some of the positions the Court has taken in defending sexual expression, commercial speech, symbolic speech, and emotive expression. However much one may tout the importance of reason in the marketplace of ideas, the fact is that much freedom in modern America points in the opposite direction.[37] Hence, the "marketplace of ideas" theory has been discounted, ignored, or perverted as a comprehensive theory of free speech.

If balancing, self-governance, and the "marketplace of ideas" justifications for the First Amendment cannot adequately explain why we value speech, can any single approach or theory suffice? The consensus in today's First Amendment community is away from a single-value theory of free speech. We seem more conceptually comfortable with a *multiplicity of rationales*—a combination of truth seeking, self-government, self-fulfillment, checks on government abuse of power, diversity, and various other rationales (including balancing) to explain why we value free speech. Here is a sampling of the leading theories, starting with one of the more noted ones: the liberty model of free expression.

One of the main problems with Dr. Meiklejohn's self-governance theory of the First Amendment was that it was too narrow in its focus and therefore underprotective of too many kinds of valued American freedoms. Meiklejohn tried, in 1961, to remedy that problem by extending his theory to protect forms of expression like the literary and dramtic arts. The result, however, was that his self-governance theory began to seem artificial, too capable of manipulation, and too close to what is known as the *liberty model* of free expression.

The liberty model holds that free speech is an end in itself. That is, it has special intrinsic value to the speaker apart from any utilitarian value it may have to society. The individual in all of his or her potential splendor or squalor is the crown jewel of this theory. Freedom of expression is thus an *end* in itself rather than a *means* to some greater end, as in Meiklejohn's informed democracy. As Justice Lewis Powell, Jr. (1907–1998), put it in a 1974 opinion for the Court: "The First Amendment serves not only the needs of the polity but also those of the human spirit—a spirit that demands self-expression." That is the spirit of autonomy. From this vantage point the individual is the key beneficiary of the First Amendment's protections. In this way, the Court declared in 1971, the Constitution safeguards the values "of individual dignity and choice upon which our political system rests."[38]

This model of free expression permits the individual to *self-realize* or *self-fulfill* in any way he or she may see fit, so long as his or her actions do not directly and substantially harm other individuals. Societal values and moral codes typically take a back seat to this notion of freedom. The individual thus benefits both as speaker and listener. For example, this theory would protect the ribald expression of comics like Lenny Bruce, George Carlin, and Margaret Cho, notwithstanding the fact that their routines contain "indecent" expression. By the same token, this theory would protect the right of their audiences to hear such forms of expression. For that matter, the liberty/self-fulfillment model of free speech would protect much expression, ranging from mindless commercial TV entertainment (like the 1990s cable show *Beavis and Butthead*) to misogynist and violent rap music (like Niggaz With Attitude) to sexually explicit photographs (like Robert Mapplethorpe's) to revealing and erotic dancing in clubs (like the Pussy Cat Lounge). The theory invites individualistic indulgences of all kinds.

In that regard, the liberty model would not be the preferred choice of Plato or Aristotle. It would, however, be the choice of Henry David Thoreau (1817–62). Those who subscribe to this theory would protect expression even if it is irrational, emotive, or unrelated to the quest for truth. They would safeguard it even if unconnected to some collective good. By that measure, Holmes's *"marketplace of ideas" theory* and Meiklejohn's *self-governance theory* are both woefully inadequate. With their emphasis on the Enlightenment and collective values, they miss the mark: freedom is an end to be valued, not a means to some nobler end.

Critics of the liberty model maintain that it wars with core societal values like equality and public safety. Consider Farber's point: "[I]t is not clear that the [liberty model's] need for self-realization requires full protection for all ideas regardless of their social utility." He asked rhetorically, "Do we really want to preserve the possibility for people to 'find themselves' as bigots or as criminals?"[39] If theories like the liberty model of the First Amendment are not linked to some *social* good, the argument goes, then they must countenance the excesses that come with bigoted, criminal, and sexually deviant expression.

For Alexander Meiklejohn, the liberty model's potential for widespread abuse proved far too risky. It invited—or variations of it encouraged—precisely the kind of capitalistic and self-centered exploitation that could destroy any hope of an enlightened, truth-seeking, democratic, and self-governed people. By substituting the individual good for the collective one, and by turning the First Amendment into an end in itself rather than a means to a higher good, the liberty model turned collective freedom into individual license.

If the "marketplace of ideas" and self-governance theories proved underprotective of free speech, and if the liberty model proved overprotective of it, what other theories, then, could explain and thereby justify the freedoms we have come to enjoy under the First Amendment?

Professor Vincent Blasi has posited that one of the key purposes of free speech is its "checking value."[40] This is the value that "free speech, a free press, and free assembly serve in checking the abuse of power by public officials." This theory is "concerned not with the general process of selecting the best persons for office but with the narrower task of preventing the abuses of the public trust." The role of the press in exposing the abuses of the Clinton or Bush or Obama administrations, for example, exemplifies this justification for safeguarding First Amendment freedoms. Blasi's theory finds eloquent expression in Justice Black's concurring opinion in the *Pentagon Papers* case (see chapter 4):

> The Government's power to censor the press was abolished so that the press would remain forever free to censure the Government. The press was protected so that it could bare the secrets of government and inform the people. Only a free and unrestrained press can effectively expose deception in government. And paramount among the responsibilities of a free press is the duty to prevent any part of the government from deceiving the people

and sending them off to distant lands to die of foreign fevers and foreign shot and shell.[41]

The late Thomas I. Emerson advanced another notable theory.[42] Drawing on what Justice Brandeis argued in *Whitney v. California* (1927), Emerson emphasized the importance of what he called a "safety-valve theory" of free speech. According to this view, free speech provides a "framework in which the conflict necessary to the progress of a society can take place without destroying the society." Discussion is a safer course of action than repression. This theory has been described as the "flip-side" of the clear and present danger test. "Rather than representing an incitement, Harvey Zuckman and Robert Corn-Revere observe, "the ability to give voice to deep social resentments may dissipate the pressures that otherwise would lead to violence or revolt."[43] While the Supreme Court, most notably in a 1941 opinion, has recognized the value of this theory and the need to give the First Amendment a "generous scope,"[44] the Court has not always invoked it to uphold free-speech rights, especially where the threatened harm is impending and significant.

A related justification for protecting expression is the *tolerance theory*, propounded most notably by Lee Bollinger. In *The Tolerant Society: Freedom of Speech and Extremist Speech in America*, Bollinger maintained that one significant reason we value free speech is that it teaches us the importance of tolerance—an essential virtue in a diverse and democratic society. By tolerating those views that we detest (e.g., Stalinism) and by permitting the expression we loathe (e.g., Nazi rhetoric), we are better prepared to live in a conflict-based society such as our own. "This perspective," notes Bollinger, "sees the social benefits of free speech as involving not simply the acquisition of the truth, but the development of intellectual attitudes, which are important to the operation of a variety of social institutions— the spirit of compromise basic to our politics and the capacity to distance ourselves from our beliefs, which is so important to various disciplines and professional roles."[45]

Toleration permits dissent. And dissent, contends Professor Steven Shiffrin, is a key component of any theory of the First Amendment. Invoking a *romantic theory* of free expression, his general point in this: "If the First Amendment is to have any organizing symbol, ... let it be the image of the dissenter." Tracking the spirit of Ralph Waldo Emerson (1803–82), Shiffrin maintains that one of the essential purposes of the First Amendment is "to protect romantics—those who would break out of classical forms: the dissenters, the unorthodox, the outcast. The First Amendment's purpose and function in the American polity is not merely to protect negative liberty, but also affirmatively to sponsor the individualism, the rebelliousness, the antiauthoritarianism, the spirit of nonconformity within us all." From this vantage point, Shiffrin tells us, "Ralph Waldo Emerson and Walt Whitman have more to teach us about freedom of speech and democracy than do Alexander Meiklejohn or Oliver Wendell Holmes."[46]

These, then, are some of the other theories of, and justifications for, the freedoms we as Americans recognize under the First Amendment. There are, to be sure, yet other theories and justifications. Still, the larger point is that we value free-speech freedom for a variety of reasons. In that respect, it is well to repeat what Brandeis said in *Whitney*, for nowhere is there to be found a more comprehensive and stirring statement of the *various* reasons why we value free speech:

> Those who won our independence believed that the final end of the state was to make men free to develop their faculties, and that in its government the deliberative forces should prevail over the arbitrary. They valued liberty *both* as an end and as a means. They believed liberty to be the secret of happiness and courage to be the secret of liberty. They believed that freedom to think as you will and speak as you think are means indispensable to the discovery and spread of political truth; that without free speech and assembly discussion would be futile; that with them, discussion affords ordinarily adequate protection against the dissemination of noxious doctrine; that the greatest menace to freedom is an inert people; that public discussion is a political duty; and this should be a fundamental principle of the American government. They recognized the risks to which all human institutions are subject. But they knew that order cannot be secured merely through fear of punishment for its infraction; that it is hazardous to discourage thought, hope and imagination; that fear breeds repression; that repression breeds hate; that hate menaces stable government; that the path to safety lies in the opportunity to discuss freely supposed grievances and proposed remedies; and that the fitting remedy for evil counsels is good ones. Believing in the power of reason as applied through public discussion, they eschewed silence coerced by law—the argument of force in its worst form. Recognizing the occasional tyrannies of governing majorities, they amended the Constitution so that free speech and assembly should be guaranteed.[47]

Literally, that single statement says it all, or quite nearly all. Despite the multiplicity of rationales Justice Brandeis invoked, there was, nonetheless, much in his inspiring defense of free speech with which Dr. Meiklejohn would surely agree.

MEIKLEJOHN'S MOMENT

On April 14, 1965, Justice William Brennan spoke at Brown University, where Meiklejohn had been a student in 1889, a philosophy instructor in 1897, and

dean in 1901. Associate Justice Brennan was there to give the Alexander
Meiklejohn Lecture. He came to honor the life work of the then ninety-two-year-
old educator, that "militant champion of freedom" who bequeathed a "rich
legacy" to America, as Brennan put it. "He was not a lawyer," added Brennan, "yet
his views on the First Amendment are a significant contribution to the debate
over the limits that great keystone of our freedom places on governmental regulation of expression."[48]

By 1965, such kudos had become more commonplace as more and more people sought to pay homage to one of America's most famous dissidents. History
had come around to Meiklejohn's take on life and law—or came around as close
as it might ever get. Thus, in July 1963, President John F. Kennedy selected
Dr. Meiklejohn for the Medal of Freedom, the nation's highest civilian honor.
A year later, the Supreme Court, per Justice Brennan, handed down its landmark
opinion in *New York Times Co. v. Sullivan* (see chapter 8). The general spirit of the
opinion was vintage Meiklejohn. Little wonder, then, that Meiklejohn tagged it
as an "an occasion for dancing in the streets" when he registered his reaction with
his friend Professor Harry Kalven, Jr.[49] Shortly thereafter, the Court, in *Garrison
v. Louisiana*, struck down a criminal defamation statute on First Amendment
grounds. Portions of the opinion "echoe[d]" Meiklejohn's words. Essentially, as
Brennan also noted in his Brown lecture, "nearly [all of] Dr. Meiklejohn's hope
has been realized."[50]

For all the powerful criticisms of Alexander Meiklejohn's theory—from
Chafee's early critiques to Bollinger's more contemporary broadsides—the fact
remains: certain components of the Meiklejohnian view remain central to our
understanding of the First Amendment. Perhaps his idealized notion of a First
Amendment community—a nation of people discussing and debating ideas in a
town meeting—is what originally captured, and continues to capture, the imagination of those who still preach his free-speech gospel in one form or another. In
that sense, maybe, he is the Norman Rockwell[51] of First Amendment theory.

On December 17, 1964, Alexander Meiklejohn died while discoursing—discussing and debating the sit-ins at Berkeley's Sproul Hall. And so an era ended.
After his death, a *Washington Post* editorial declared: "He represented a great heritage. And he left a rich inheritance." He was, the editorial continued, "a figure
almost uniquely symbolic of [our] libertarian tradition."[52] A memorial tribute
was later held at the then new Senate Office Building. There to honor the fallen
philosopher was Justice Hugo Black, even though he had to miss one of the
Court's important conferences. George Anastaplo (see chapter 1), as fate had it,
was in Washington, D.C., that day and attended the memorial tribute. Though
Meiklejohn, Black, and Anastaplo had their differences, they were differences
within a spectrum of general agreement. Rhetorically and otherwise, an animating passion for freedom united them. Even after the many memorials,

Meiklejohn's followers still gathered to hail him years later. In 1972, some one hundred students, friends, admirers, relatives—and a few critics—turned up at the Cosmos Club in Washington, D.C., to honor the centennial anniversary of Meiklejohn's birth. It was as if they could not let go of the spirit of the "gentle iconoclast," as the New York Times once tagged him.[53]

References to Meiklejohn still dot scores and scores of federal and state court free-speech opinions. Even more citations can be found in the free-speech literature. Whatever the analytical merit of his views, Alexander Meiklejohn—the ramrod-straight philosopher who never shunned controversy—touched something in the American heart and mind. Like Hugo Black, and unlike most others, Meiklejohn made the First Amendment both politically respectable and politically powerful, despite the many criticisms of his views.

Key to Meiklejohn's view of the First Amendment was the notion that no idea can be held back from the citizenry. To reiterate: "If men are to be governed," he declared, "then the governing must be done not by others, but by themselves." No Platonic guardians, no benevolent paters, no government censors should decide what "We the People" do or do not hear, see, or read. There can, in other words, be no prior restraints when it comes to the information that a citizenry needs to be self-governing. By the time Meiklejohn ended his life journey, that principle had already started to take root in our First Amendment jurisprudence. But prior to Near v. Minnesota (1931), when the young Meiklejohn was still formulating his ideas about free speech, the principle had yet to find clear expression in the supreme law of the land. As we will show in the next chapter, the story of how that great principle of freedom came to be is as much a part of our First Amendment history as the theories offered to justify that freedom.

"The Final Jury of the Nation"

Daniel Ellsberg and National Security

The tension between government secrecy and press freedom is hardly new. Indeed, some might characterize it as one of the chief hallmarks of a democratic society. Yet understanding how best to put that tension to work in the service of both ideals is a riddle the United States is still struggling to solve.

When the nation is at war, this historic challenge—managing the delicate balance between our dual commitment to freedom and security—becomes even more charged. To what extent may a free press fully and adequately inform the citizenry about the government's conduct of the war without unduly jeopardizing military safety and national security? Must our commitment to an open society be muted during wartime? And if a line is to be drawn, where and why should it be drawn?

It is hard to say. On the one hand, as Justice Robert Jackson once wrote: "It is easy, by giving way to passion, intolerance, and suspicions in wartime, to reduce our liberties to a shadow, often in answer to exaggerated claims of security." On the other hand, the same Justice Jackson also thought that caution on such issues was sacrosanct, lest our "constitutional Bill of Rights" become a "suicide pact." Jackson's views on freedom underscore the challenge of reconciling security, which is not counterfeit, with liberty, which is not destructive. And when that challenge takes place against the backdrop of a steadily metastasizing, increasingly unpopular war—as it did back in the summer of 1971—we see one of the most emotionally charged, and legally significant, debates in the history of the First Amendment. In these times of seemingly endless war, there is more than one lesson to be learned here.

"MOST OF THE PRESS IS AGAINST US"

At first glance, one would have guessed that the big news in the June 13, 1971, edition of the *New York Times* was the wedding of the president's daughter. "After a tension-filled delay because of rain," the article read, "Tricia Nixon was married today in the Rose Garden of the White House to Edward Finch Cox, the man she has described as 'my first and last love.'" Accompanying the text was an oversized photo of the president, Richard M. Nixon, proudly walking his daughter down the aisle. Five other headlines shared above-the-fold status with the Nixon wedding that Sunday. Looking at that day's news today, one is struck by how little changes—"City to Disclose Budgetary Trims for Departments"; "U.S. Urges Indians and Pakistanis to Use Restraint."

But one headline was different. Within three days, its very appearance would cast an ever-encroaching shadow over the smiling father of the bride, a shadow that would not subside until he left the office of the presidency in disgrace. At the time, however, the headline itself was unspectacular:

Vietnam archive: Pentagon study traces 3

Decades of growing U.S. involvement

It was hardly the first time the government had been targeted by the press for its policy in Vietnam. More than three years earlier, then President Lyndon B. Johnson had bemoaned that fact to a gathering of high officials. "The leaks to [the newspapers] hurt us," he said. "Most of the press is against us."[1] But this was a different article, and a different kind of leak. It claimed that four successive presidential administrations had continued to support the non-Communist forces in Vietnam despite knowing that prospects for victory were bleak at best. At a time when growing numbers of Americans were taking to the streets to protest the war, the *Times*'s allegations were serious. And that was just the beginning, the editors promised—additional reports would appear in the coming days, complete with classified government documents to support their claims.

Or so the editors thought. Two days later, however, the *New York Times* was in court, temporarily restrained from publishing more "secrets" and accused by the U.S. government of breaching national security. It was one of the rare times since the Constitution's adoption that the federal government had legally challenged a newspaper's right to freedom of the press. It was also a new type of First Amendment fight—the clash between the doctrines of no prior restraints and of national security.

The *Times*'s source for the articles was a secret study prepared between June 1967 and January 1969 that became known as the Pentagon Papers. Only fifteen original copies of the report—which covered forty-seven volumes, spanned seven thousand pages, included 2.5 million words, and weighed sixty pounds—were produced. The Pentagon Papers were commissioned in the fall of 1966 by then U.S. defense secretary Robert McNamara,[2] who had hoped a comprehensive study of the war would clarify future U.S. policy decisions about Vietnam. But McNamara never told top administration officials, including the president, about the study, and he directed the project's staff to keep the work secret.

Everyone did, except for Daniel Ellsberg. A rising star in the Defense Department when McNamara ordered the report, Ellsberg was already thinking the United States might need to get out of the war. By the time the Pentagon Papers were completed, he was resolute. As he explained to a reporter in 1971: "The startling thing that came out of [the study] was how... [t]he decisions year after year were to continue the war, although all predictions pointed to a continued stalemate with this kind of approach and thus to prolong the war indefinitely."

It was a war, he said, "no American president had... the courage to turn down or to stay out of."[3] So Daniel Ellsberg would force their hand. He would give the Pentagon Papers to the *New York Times*, and let a free press tell the American people what was really happening behind closed doors.

"A PATRIOTIC AND CONSTRUCTIVE ACT"

For several years, though, Ellsberg kept largely silent about the entire matter. In fact, according to his 2002 memoir *Secrets*, Ellsberg spent several years helping to "prosecute a war I believed at the outset to be doomed." Reflecting back, Ellsberg came to realize why it took him so long to speak out: "You could not have the confidence of powerful men and be trusted with their confidences if there was any prospect that you would challenge their policies in public in any forum at all," he said. "That was the unbreakable rule of the executive branch. It was the sacred code of the insider, both the men of power and those, like me, privileged to access and help them. I knew that as well as anyone. I had lived by that code for the last decade; it was in my skin."[4]

Slowly, Daniel Ellsberg shed that skin. In 1965, he volunteered to serve in Vietnam as a State Department civilian. After two years of witnessing the results of U.S. policy, Ellsberg writes, the people and plight of Vietnam became real to him in a different way, "as real as the U.S. troops I walked with, as real as my own hands, in a way that made continuing the hopeless war intolerable." Yet the State Department civilian remained silent, still optimistic he might help influence U.S. policy from the inside. Then, on February 27, 1968, he saw a top secret memorandum from the chairman of the Joint Chiefs of Staff, General William

Westmoreland, to President Johnson. In the memo, Westmoreland requested an additional 206,000 troops—a 50 percent increase—saying they were needed to stave off a complete collapse in South Vietnam. It was a dramatic escalation of the U.S. commitment to the war, and a path, Ellsberg believed, down which "lay certain ruin." The path, however, was obstructed. Two weeks later, the General's request was leaked to the press and appeared in an article in the Sunday New York Times. "The request," wrote Times journalists Hedrick Smith and Neil Sheehan, "has touched off a divisive internal debate within high levels of the Johnson administration."[5]

The magnitude of the leak represented a massive breach of trust somewhere along the chain of command. But it was not yet Ellsberg's moment—he was not the source. To this day, he claims ignorance of who was. Yet as he watched members of Congress react to the news by increasing their criticisms of the president's war policy, Ellsberg recalls that the leak's effectiveness "opened my eyes to my responsibilities as a citizen....I had never questioned the assumption of many students of presidential power that secrecy is vital to preserve a president's range of options. But I now saw how the system of secrecy and lying could give him options he would be better off without, or it could dangerously prejudice his choice." Like everyone around him, Ellsberg had dutifully accepted the prevailing ethos of his profession, "the idea that leaking was always inherently bad." But from that point on, he began to feel differently. "I had been wrong," he said. "Obviously leaking could be a patriotic and constructive act."[6]

"SEVEN THOUSAND PAGES OF LYING"

Before long, Ellsberg had fully embraced his new calling. "What I had in mind was very simple," he wrote. "A leak a day of a closely held secret." Hence, in March 1968 he visited a newspaper office for the first time and gave a number of top-secret documents to Sheehan. Before long, the leaks had their desired effect. In a classified memo the same month, one senior official lamented to another: "Somewhere in the government there has obviously been a horrendous security violation, and it is my personal belief that this should be investigated, with prosecution, if appropriate."[7]

Despite his secret activism, Ellsberg, in those early months of 1968, was not without hope that the country could right itself in a more traditional way. Robert Kennedy, the senator from New York and former attorney general, had the inside track on the Democratic nomination for president. Ellsberg had already joined the campaign as Kennedy's "man on Vietnam." Looking back on those days, he remembers feeling as though "no other American had so impressed me with the depth and urgency of his concern, even anguish, about the war. I liked [Kennedy]. A lot." Three months later, though, Bobby Kennedy was dead, beckoned to eternity by an assassin's bullet in California. Ellsberg was devastated. "I realized at this moment that all my hopes had been on [Kennedy]," he said. "Not just for Vietnam, but for my country. I had a sudden vision that the war wasn't going to end. I was thinking: Maybe there's no way, no way, to change this country."[8]

Early in 1969, as the war continued to escalate, the Pentagon Papers study was finally completed. By the fall of that year, Ellsberg had read all seven thousand pages of the report. In the process, he reached several more disturbing conclusions about U.S. policy in Vietnam. Among them:

- Since at least the late 1940s, "there had probably never been a year when political violence in Vietnam would have reached or stayed at the scale of a 'war' had not the U.S. president, Congress, and citizens fueled it with money, weapons, and ultimately manpower."
- "A war in which one side (the South) was *entirely* equipped and paid by a foreign power—which dictated the nature of the local regime in its own interest—was not a civil war."

Ellsberg's disgust with the system worsened. It had become, he believed, "a system that lies automatically, at every level from bottom to top—from sergeant to commander in chief—to conceal murder." Then he thought of the Pentagon Papers. He was one of a small number of men who had a copy of the report. It then occurred to him, for the first time, "that what I had... was seven thousand pages of documentary evidence of lying, by four presidents and their administrations over twenty-three years."[9]

Ellsberg decided the Pentagon Papers had to be copied and, eventually, released to the public. But how? In 1969, even the fastest copying machine needed to be fed copies one by one. How could he do that and not arouse suspicion? He called his good friend Tony Russo, a fellow Washington insider who had also grown sick of the war, and told him of his plans. Russo loved the idea. Even better, his girlfriend owned a small advertising company. They could use her copy machine after hours, Russo explained. In fact, he said, they could start the next night. And so they did, one page at a time.

RUDE AWAKENING

When Richard Nixon opened his Sunday *New York Times* that June morning, he would have immediately noticed the photograph from his daughter's wedding. He might next have quickly skimmed the potentially troubling article "Nixon Criticized as Mayors Meet." But that didn't bother him much.

There was one headline that did catch his eye. At first blush, he was not too concerned with the Pentagon Papers article, even though he had had no idea the study even existed until he read about it that morning. In fact, according to Neil Rudenstine, author of *The Day the Presses Stopped*, Nixon "decided that his administration should do nothing to interfere with the *Times*'s publication plans and take no action to identify the source of the leak."[10]

Initially, Nixon surmised that he stood to benefit politically from the report—the study ended in 1968, after all, before his administration began, and it was highly critical of the previous two Democratic administrations. For Nixon, that was good news. So during a meeting that morning with his chief of staff, H. R. Haldeman, he stressed the "need to keep clear of the *Times'* series.... [the] key is to *keep out of it*." Later that day, however, after a conversation with Secretary of State Henry Kissinger, Nixon began to feel differently. As Rudenstine reports, Kissinger told Nixon "the fact that some idiot can publish all of the diplomatic secrets of the country on his own is damaging to your image, as far as the Soviets are concerned, and it could destroy our ability to conduct foreign policy. If other powers feel that we cannot control internal leaks, they will never agree to secret negotiations."[11]

By Monday morning Nixon, spurred by Kissinger, changed course completely and demanded that the *Times*'s criminal liability be evaluated. Attorney General John Mitchell said he knew just the man for the job. Mitchell's recommendation was a young assistant attorney general—first in his class at Stanford Law School and a former Supreme Court clerk—in charge of the Office of Legal Counsel. Although it was the ambitious attorney's first day back in the office following back surgery, Mitchell asked him to research the history of prior restraints and evaluate the government's chances of securing an injunction to prevent the *Times* from publishing any further installments in the series. And so, his back still aching, William Hubbs Rehnquist,[12] the future chief justice of the United States (and a Nixon appointee), agreed.

What the forty-six-year-old Rehnquist found was a mixture of discouraging, murky, and hopeful legal precedents. First, the discouraging news: many legal scholars believed then—and still believe now—that *any* system of prior restraints is incompatible with a free society. A "prior restraint," known originally as a "previous restraint," is a judicial order or administrative rule that forbids a certain type of expression from taking place. Typically, prior restraints required a publisher to acquire a license or permit before engaging in expression. Such orders were often issued in connection with expression that was allegedly seditious, defamatory, obscene, secret, or related to national security. Prior restraints might also, however, simply be judicial orders forbidding publication on pain of contempt. In a literal sense, of course, a prior restraint did not always prevent expression from occurring; it merely allowed for a subsequent punishment. As Laurence Tribe has observed: "The doctrine imposes a special bar on attempts to suppress speech prior to publication, a bar that is distinct from the scope of constitutional protection accorded the material *after* publication."[13]

BACK TO BRITISH HISTORY

Because of their clear connections to censorship, prior restraints are seen as antithetical to a free society. This was true in both England and the United States. The roots of the British system of censorship developed in the fifteenth century, shortly after the arrival in England of large-scale printing technology. To harness this dangerous new resource, Parliament developed some novel rules. They went like this: Before anything could officially be published, a government censor would need to review the material and decide whether or not to grant it a license. This system of prior restraints was a clever way for the government to regulate expression. "[T]o punish the crime of publishing without a license," Michael Kent Curtis has written, "the government did not need to prove that the book, pamphlet, or newspaper was treasonous or seditious. It needed only to prove that the defendant had published the book and that he lacked a license, just as a person may be punished for driving without a license although her driving might otherwise be perfect."[14]

Authors could still publish their works unofficially, but doing so subjected them to being punished for seditious libel. Technically, this term referred to false and malicious statements against the government. In reality, according to legal scholar Leonard Levy, seditious libel was an "accordion-like concept" that referred to "any comment about the government which could be construed to have the bad tendency of lowering it in the public's esteem."[15]

Such laws stunted the growth of true freedom of expression and the press, and prompted a generation of free-thinking men like John Locke (1632–1704), Benedict de Spinoza (1632–77), and John Milton (1608–74) to rail against the system and preach for change. Spinoza, for example, thought any wise ruler should allow freedom of speech simply to ensure that resistance would be out in the open, and "so that men may live together in harmony, however diverse, [however] openly contradictory their opinions may be."[16] And Milton demanded that all be given the "liberty to know, to utter, and to argue freely according to conscience, above all liberties."[17]

Many people, however, thought freedom of expression was the exclusive privilege of parliamentarians. Few felt that common people also deserved such rights. Even fewer believed they should tolerate freedom for the speech they despised. Yet when the English licensing laws expired in 1695, they were not renewed. And thereafter, according to Thomas Emerson, a new philosophy gradually emerged wherein "freedom of the press from licensing came to be recognized in England as a common law or natural right."[18]

No one better expressed this new attitude in England than Sir William Blackstone (1723–80). The son of a silk merchant, Blackstone was a member of Parliament and a law professor at Oxford University. He was also the author of the four-volume treatise *Commentaries on the Laws of England*. Written in the middle of the eighteenth century, the *Commentaries* were a guide for the British elite to English public and private law. Organizing his thoughts into two simple categories—"Rights" and "Wrongs"—Blackstone aimed to show that the legacy of England's unwritten, customary law had evolved into a masterful, complex scheme for protecting liberty.

One of the main areas in which Blackstone helped shape the law's future concerned the doctrine of prior restraints. In the following famous passage from the *Commentaries*, Blackstone outlined his own view of this:

> The *liberty of the press* is indeed essential to the nature of a free state; but this consists in laying no *previous* restraint upon publications, and not in freedom from censure for criminal matter when published. Every freeman has an undoubted right to lay what sentiments he pleases before the public: to forbid this is to destroy the freedom of the press: but if he publishes what is improper, mischievous, or illegal, he must take the consequence of his own temerity.[19]

These were basic principles that came to bear the weighty imprimatur of truth, shaping generations of scholars and lawmakers that followed, including the men who drafted the First Amendment and the various state constitutional free speech and press provisions. As Thomas Emerson once wrote, a prior restraint is thought to be so dangerous because it is "likely to bring under government scrutiny a far wider range of expression [than a system of subsequent punishment]; it shuts off communication before it takes place; suppression by a stroke of the pen is more likely to be applied than suppression through a criminal process…[and] the dynamics of the system drive toward excesses, as the history of all censorship shows."[20]

Rehnquist knew that prior restraint law in the United States began with the 1931 case, *Near v. Minnesota*, in which the U.S. Supreme Court—in forceful yet cautionary language—declared a Minnesota injunction against a newspaper to be unconstitutional. "It has been generally, if not universally, considered," wrote Chief Justice Charles Evans Hughes, on behalf of the narrow five-justice majority, "that it is the chief purpose of the guaranty to prevent previous restraints upon publication.... The fact that for approximately one hundred-and-fifty years there has been almost an entire absence of attempts to impose previous restraints upon publications…is significant of the deep-seated conviction that such restraints would violate constitutional rights."

Notably, the path the Court took to reach its decision in *Near* was hardly straightforward. In the spring of 1930, in fact, the relationship between the freedoms of the First Amendment and the due process clause of the Fourteenth Amendment ("No state shall...deprive any person of life, liberty, or property, without due process of law.") was an unresolved legal issue. What divided the justices was how they felt the word "liberty" in the Fourteenth Amendment should be interpreted. Some believed the Bill of Rights, with its detailed emphasis on individual liberty, should be their guide. Others defined liberty to mean "liberty of contract"—an interpretation that became known as *substantive due process*—and argued that a broader legal understanding of the word was, as Fred Friendly observed in *Minnesota Rag*, "a means of preserving a way of life, [and] a way of organizing society by which the establishment retained control of the institutions of business and government."[21]

In the Court's decisions leading up to its announcement of the ruling in *Near*, the justices—two of whom, Chief Justice Hughes and Associate Justice Owen Roberts, were brand new to the Court—gave mixed signals as to how they would rule on a First Amendment claim involving a state. In the case of *Stromberg v. California* (1931), for example, the Court voted seven to two to overturn a California law that made it a felony to display a red flag in any public assembly. Writing for the majority, Chief Justice Hughes stated that the "maintenance of the opportunity for free political discussion...is a fundamental principle of our constitutional system." Yet just a week later, in the case of *U.S. v. Macintosh* (1931), the Court sustained a lower court's decision to deny citizenship to a Canadian chaplain at Yale Divinity School because he would not swear military allegiance to the United States. It was a five-to-four ruling, with Justice Roberts in the majority.

On June 1, 1931, the last day of its term, the Court announced its decision in *Near v. Minnesota*. Speaking on behalf of the five-to-four majority, Chief Justice Hughes attempted to settle the debate about how to interpret the legal meaning of the word "liberty" and the proper relationship between the First and Fourteenth amendments: "It is no longer open to doubt that the liberty of the press and of speech is within the liberty safeguarded by the due process clause of the 14th Amendment from invasion by state action," he said. "Some degree of abuse is inseparable from the proper use of everything, and in no instance is this more true than in that of the press." Dissenting Justice Pierce Butler was outraged. "It gives to freedom of the press a meaning and a scope not heretofore recognized," he wrote, "and construes 'liberty' in the due process clause of the 14th Amendment to put upon the states a Federal restriction that is without precedent."

For the first time in history, the U.S. Supreme Court had held a state law to violate the free press clause of the First Amendment. Hughes and Roberts had joined three other justices—Brandeis, Holmes, and Harlan Stone—in giving new staying power to James Madison's constitutional legacy. As if that were not enough, the majority secured another victory for freedom when it struck a decisive blow against the practice of prior restraints. Sometimes people make bad decisions about what makes good journalism, the justices opined, but that does not justify preventing them from printing those views in the first instance. As the chief justice put it in *Near:*

> If we cut through mere details of procedure, the operation and effect of the statute in substance is that public authorities may bring the owner or publisher of a newspaper or periodical before a judge upon a charge of conducting a business of publishing scandalous and defamatory matter—in particular that the matter consists of charges against public officers of official dereliction—and, unless the owner or publisher is able and disposed to bring competent evidence to satisfy the judge that the charges are true and are published with good motives and for justifiable ends, his newspaper or periodical is suppressed and further publication is made punishable as a contempt. This is of the essence of censorship.
>
> The question is whether a statute authorizing such proceedings in restraint of publication is consistent with the conception of the liberty of the press as historically conceived and guaranteed. In determining the extent of the constitutional protection, it has been generally, if not universally, considered that it is the chief purpose of the guaranty to prevent previous restraints upon publication.[22]

That portion of the opinion did not bode well for what the Nixon administration hoped to do. Worse still, in case after case since *Near*, Rehnquist found the same principles *against* prior restraints being extended across a wide variety of factual circumstances. In the 1938 case of *Lovell v. City of Griffin*, for example, the Court ruled that the government could not require a license or permit before speech could occur. "[T]he ordinance is invalid on its face," wrote Chief Justice Hughes. "Whatever the motive which induced its adoption, its character is such that it strikes at the very foundation of the freedom of the press by subjecting it to license and censorship."[23]

But what if, at least, the government sought to secure a temporary restraining order (TRO) against the *Times* rather than a full prior restraint? Would that be enough to delay the newspaper's publication of any more government "secrets" and thus allow Justice Department officials to investigate further and determine a more comprehensive course of action? Or could the *Times* simply disregard the TRO with impunity? This option may have led Rehnquist to believe that a court-ordered TRO might effectively tie the hands of the *Times*, for a while anyway. Just four years earlier, for example, in the 1967 case *Walker v. City of Birmingham*, the Court had upheld contempt convictions against several civil rights protestors—among them Dr. Martin Luther King, Jr.—for ignoring a court order that prevented them from demonstrating on the streets of Birmingham without a permit. "[R]espect for judicial process," wrote the Court, "is a small price to pay for the civilizing hand of law, which alone can give abiding meaning to constitutional freedom." But it wasn't that simple. Just two years later, in *Shuttlesworth v. City of Birmingham* (1969), the Court had overturned the convictions of protestors who had marched without a permit. In that case, the justices refused to apply the collateral bar rule, ruling that "a person faced with such an unconstitutional licensing law may ignore it and engage with impunity in the exercise of the right of free expression for which the law purports to require a license."[24]

Rehnquist realized he could not return to the attorney general without *any* recommended course of action, especially with the president so intent on stopping the presses. But what could be offered to counter the heavy presumption against prior restraints that the government would be forced to meet? The ever astute Rehnquist—a man with not one but two master's degrees in political science, one from Stanford and the other from Harvard—found an answer. Ironically, it was in *Near v. Minnesota*, the case long celebrated as the highwater mark for freedom of the press.

The quotation had been forgotten by many, and treated as gratuitous dicta by others. But it was the perfect hook on which to hang an argument against the *Times*. "[T]he protection even as to previous restraint is not absolutely unlimited," wrote Hughes. "But the limitation has been recognized only in exceptional cases." The chief justice then quoted from the 1919 *Schenck v. United States* "clear and present danger" wartime case to offer one such example. "When a nation is at war many things that might be said in time of peace are such a hindrance to its effort that their utterance will not be endured so long as men fight and…no Court could regard them as protected by any constitutional right." Hughes then offered a rhetorical comment. "No one would question," he began, "but that a government might prevent actual obstruction to its recruiting service or the publication of the sailing dates of transports or the number or location of troops."[25]

Chief Justice Hughes was unconcerned with those scenarios at the time of the *Near* case—"[t]hese limitations," he wrote, "are not applicable here."[26] But they were a saving grace for William Rehnquist. In fact, as Rudenstine has written, "what [Hughes] wrote allowed Rehnquist to emphasize that the ongoing war in Vietnam enhanced the administration's chances of securing" an injunction against the *Times*. It also allowed him to advise that "if the *Times* publication threatened national security in a way comparable to the examples offered by Hughes in *Near*, the administration might succeed in stopping the *Times* from further publishing the classified history."[27]

Did the Pentagon Papers threaten national security in any meaningful and urgent way? Rehnquist did not know—he had never even seen them. At that point, neither had anyone else in the Justice Department. But they had an appealing argument at least—and that was a good start. The government, however, was still missing something very important—a *law* under which to prosecute Ellsberg for what had done. Most countries, from China to Great Britain, have such laws, which make it a crime to release "classified" information without authorization to newspapers, to Congress, and to the "sovereign public." Daniel Ellsberg certainly believed that what he had done was a crime. "All of us assumed," he said, "that there was *some* equivalent of an official secrets act in the United States." Ellsberg was even convinced he would go to prison, "possibly for the rest of my life,"[28] for copying the Pentagon Papers and giving them to the press. Yet there was no direct law against it. The government decided to proceed anyway. It would, as legal scholar and retired justice Hans Linde has argued, ask the courts not to apply a law but to provide one. With that peculiar mindset, a day after Rehnquist's recommendations—Tuesday, June 15, 1971—Attorney General Mitchell asked the *New York Times* to suspend its publication of the Pentagon Papers, and to turn over its copy to the Justice Department.

Floyd Abrams[29] remembers the date well. Just thirty-four years old at the time, Abrams was already preparing a case for the U.S. Supreme Court, *Branzburg v. Hayes*, that had significant implications for free press rights. The day before Mitchell's request to the *Times*, June 14, Abrams and his former Yale Law School professor Alexander Bickel[30] had lunch with the *Times's* general counsel, James Goodale. The group, Abrams recalls in his book *Speaking Freely*, had intended to talk about the legal issues in the *Branzburg* case. But the bulk of the afternoon was spent talking about the Pentagon Papers article the *Times* had published the day before. "That's one," Bickel announced confidently to Goodale, "that you can't lose." The government would never be foolish enough, Abrams surmised, to try to restrain the *Times* from publishing its planned series—after all, the government had *never* tried to do so in the nation's long history. Supremely confident of their views, "as only lawyers without clients are," Abrams and Bickel "told the representatives of the *Times* that if the government went to court, the newspaper would obviously win."[31]

Goodale clearly remembered the conversation, which resulted in a phone call that awakened Abrams at 1:00 A.M. with the chance of a lifetime. Since Bickel was already in town, Goodale began, and since he and Abrams had spoken so confidently and persuasively at lunch, would the two men be willing to represent the *Times*? "It was all like a dream," Abrams recalled. "Was I really going to represent the *New York Times* against Richard Nixon's administration? Was I really going to do so in collaboration with Alexander Bickel, my own professor from Yale?"[32] Abrams woke up his mentor, picked him up in a taxi, and sped with him to Abrams's office to work through the night, even though, he—like William Rehnquist, and nearly every other person at the center of the controversy— knew almost nothing about the source of all the trouble: the secret study itself.

ALL THE NEWS THAT'S FIT TO PRINT?

What Abrams also did not then know was that the *Times* had nearly passed on publishing the Pentagon Papers in the first place. In fact, before the first article ever ran, a team of *Times* journalists spent three months in complete secrecy reviewing the documents, checking the summaries for accuracy, and deciding what (if any) sections might be legitimate violations of national security. One hundred years before, in the summer of 1871, a different set of editors at the *Times* had been faced with a comparable conundrum. Back then, the documents were concerned not with national security but with the criminal activities of Boss Tweed and his Tammany Hall political machine in New York City. And back then the *Times* decided to publish.

This time, however, the stakes were unquestionably higher. Lewis Loeb and Herbert Brownell, two of the newspaper's chief legal advisers,[33] warned that publishing classified government documents might trigger federal espionage laws. Brownell even told *Times* publisher Arthur "Punch" Sulzberger that his father and grandfather, both of whom had preceded Sulzberger as publisher, would never have considered publishing such sensitive material. Sulzberger asked Goodale to investigate these espionage laws. Goodale responded by underscoring two of the law's provisions.

First, section 794(a) made it a crime to disclose any information "relating to the national defense" to a foreign government, if the disclosure was done with intent to injure the United States. Goodale was little concerned with this section because of its emphasis on releasing information directly to a foreign enemy. That scenario did not apply here. He was more concerned with another provision, section 793(e). It prohibited anyone with "unauthorized possession" of information "relating to the national defense" from sharing it with an unauthorized audience, provided the person believed he or she was injuring the United States in the process. While this section did not specifically authorize prior restraint, it clearly carried criminal sanctions. Goodale was worried because the *Times* was unquestionably unauthorized to possess the documents. He wondered if the vagueness of the phrase "national defense" as applied to the facts of this case might provide some legal cover. Basic principles of due process, after all, require criminal statutes to be clear enough to allow people to determine what is and is not allowed under law. A court might thus rule that section 793(e) was too vague to be enforced. Then again, it might not. There was also some wiggle room in the language requiring an intent to injure the government by such disclosure.

At a minimum, the *Times's* lawyers predicted, the government would seek—even without statutory authorization—an injunction to bar the materials from being published. But there could be more than a minimum—Sulzberger could go to jail. "Punch had weighed all of these factors carefully," wrote Susan Tift and Alex Jones in their biography of the paper. "But once he finally made up his mind, he became immovable." Upholding the First Amendment right to freedom of the press, the *Times* publisher concluded, was more important than any potential legal fallout with the government. More significantly, the opportunity to publish the Pentagon Papers appealed to Sulzberger's sense of obligation as a journalist. A free press exists to serve as a check on government power. And before him was perhaps the greatest test of that constitutional principle in American history.

"On the night before the first installment," Tift and Jones report, Sulzberger "attended a family dinner party and was called away so many times to speak to the office that others began to suspect something was up. 'Tomorrow I'm doing something that the world is going to hate,' he whispered to his cousin Ellen Straus, 'but it's the right thing to do.'"[34] Sulzberger recognized he was taking a huge risk. Because the national government had never before tried to *enjoin*, or legally prohibit, the mainstream press from publishing sensitive information, there was no controlling judicial opinion about whether or not they could. This meant that any potential case between the government and the *Times* would be what's known as a case of *first impression*, which gives the courts substantial leeway in deciding how to rule. Knowing such a ruling would come at a time when the nation was at war raised the stakes even higher.

After working through the night, Abrams and Bickel arrived at the *Times* offices later that morning, June 15. They immediately received word that a government lawyer had informed the paper it should have an attorney present in court at noon. They would need to settle on a strategy quickly. Wispy and well dressed, Bickel was confident even though he was not a litigator. He was, however, arguably the preeminent constitutional law scholar in the country at that time, and a rumored future appointee to the Court. Rudenstine reports that Bickel presented the key question to *Times* editors and executives that morning—"Should the *New York Times* concede that the First Amendment to the constitution permitted the government to obtain a prior restraint in narrowly defined circumstances but insist that those circumstances were not presented by this case? Or, alternatively, should the newspaper argue that the First Amendment prohibited all prior restraints?"[35]

Bickel argued vehemently for the first strategy. To win, he explained, the *Times* needed five votes. That meant convincing the swing voters—either Potter Stewart or Byron White. Both would be more likely to rule in their favor if they weren't backed into Justice Hugo Black's absolutist corner. Reluctantly, the *Times* agreed—giving up its romantic attachment to Justice Black's passionate belief that "no law means NO LAW." In retrospect, it was the most important decision made by either side.

"WE ARE ALL PATRIOTIC AMERICANS"

The two sides arrived later that day at a lower Manhattan courthouse to square off for the first time. The courtroom was packed, the air thick with the knowledge that history was being made. Ironically, the scholarly Bickel had *never* appeared in any court as counsel. It was, as Abrams recalls, "a sobering thought. Here, I thought, was a landmark case, an enormous threat to the press and, more broadly, to the First Amendment, being litigated by an academic with no court-room experience, accompanied by a lawyer who had never even watched a Supreme Court argument. I hoped the thought would not occur to the executives, lawyers, and journalists at the *Times*."[36] As chance would have it, Abrams and Bickel were not alone in their inexperience. The presiding judge in the case, Murray Gurfein, had been sworn into the district court just days earlier. This was his first case.

The hearing involved no witnesses—only oral arguments for both sides. Representing the government was U.S. attorney Michael Hess, a talented thirty-year-old lawyer who had learned while shaving that morning that he would be arguing the case. As Goodale had suspected, Hess argued that by publishing the Pentagon Papers, the *Times* had violated federal espionage laws, and that Gurfein was therefore authorized to enjoin the newspaper from publishing any more of the document. Such a drastic step was necessary, he continued, because criminal proceedings would take months, by which time the country's national security would be irreparably harmed. Bickel countered with his concessionary argument that the First Amendment permits prior restraints in a few exceptional cases, but that this was not one of them. He also contended that the government's suit could proceed only if a law existed to forbid what the *Times* had done. And there was no such law.

Gurfein was in a difficult position. In his first ever case on the district bench, he was being asked to authorize the federal government's first ever request for a prior restraint. And he had to make his decision quickly—in a few hours, the *Times* would go to press with its fourth installment of the series. After inviting both sides into his chambers, Judge Gurfein—a former army colonel during World War II with a background in military intelligence—asked Bickel if the *Times* would voluntarily consent to a temporary restraining order, which would last until he could hold a longer hearing and properly consider the facts. Rudenstine reports that "Gurfein added—by way of pressure—that he assumed 'we are all patriotic Americans,' obviously implying that the *Times* would be unpatriotic if it refused."[37]

Bickel then applied his own gentle pressure, reminding Gurfein that if the judge entered a prior restraint enjoining the *Times* from publishing further stories, he would become the first judge in American history to do so. But the professor promised to check with his client, who, predictably, refused to voluntarily stop publishing the series. For Gurfein, a tough first day was getting tougher. Given the situation, the sixty-three-year-old jurist felt he had no choice but to grant the government a TRO. "Any temporary harm that may result from not publishing," he wrote, "is far outweighed by the irreparable harm that could be done to the interest of the United States Government if [the *Times*] should ultimately prevail" in the case.[38]

Gurfein scheduled another hearing for Friday morning. He did not, however, ask the government to provide a single sample of a document that would affect national security if released. Good thing, too, since Hess—like Rehnquist, Mitchell, and the rest of the Department of Justice—still did not know if there was such a document. Daniel Ellsberg, by contrast, was one of the few people who *did* know which of the documents in the Pentagon Papers might endanger national security, because he was one of the few people who had actually read the entire report. Even more important, only Ellsberg knew he had copied less than half of the report to begin with, omitting the volumes related to ongoing peacemaking efforts. Because those volumes included the names of people who were working in Communist countries, their release might have posed a significant security breach. But the *Times* didn't have those volumes, and the government didn't have time to find out what the newspaper *did* have.

A few days later, the situation grew more complicated. On the Friday that Judge Gurfein scheduled the second hearing in the *Times* case, another leak in the dam had sprung; the *Washington Post* published its own article about the Pentagon Papers. What had previously been an isolated rupture now portended to be a flood of classified information.

The *Post* secured its copy of the Pentagon Papers on Thursday, June 17, in a motel room in Cambridge, Massachusetts. The plan was for the *Post*'s then assistant managing editor, Ben Bagdikian,[39] to pick up a copy and return to Washington. Bagdikian had already made two first-class plane reservations—one for him and one for his suitcase. Shortly after he arrived, however, Bagdikian realized he was going to need a bigger bag. After assembling a makeshift cover for the Pentagon Papers out of cardboard and tying it together with a six-foot rope he found near the motel's swimming pool, Bagdikian left for the airport. Once back in Washington, he and four other *Post* employees, including executive editor Ben Bradlee, did in fourteen hours what the *Times*'s staff did in slightly less than three months—reviewed the study and prepared it for publication.

Meanwhile, shortly after Bagdikian left for the airport, Ellsberg decided to turn on the TV in his Cambridge motel room and watch the morning news. What he saw on the screen was the image of two FBI agents knocking on the door of his home. He was wanted for questioning, said the anchorman, in the investigation of the Pentagon Papers leak. For the next thirteen days, Daniel Ellsberg went underground. "We were in Cambridge the whole time," he later revealed, "in five different locations, moving sometimes after one night."[40] All along, the FBI kept looking, but always to no avail. It was, according to the press, the largest FBI manhunt since the Lindbergh kidnapping. It was also, with each passing day, a major embarrassment to the Bureau, made even worse when Ellsberg—still in hiding—was interviewed by Walter Cronkite for CBS News on June 23.

Cronkite asked Ellsberg to name the most important revelations he felt had resulted from the release of the Pentagon Papers. "What these studies tell me," he responded, "is we must remember this is a self-governing country. We are the government. And in terms of institutions, the Constitution provides for separation of powers, for Congress, for the courts, informally for the press, protected by the First Amendment....I think we cannot let the officials of the Executive Branch determine for us what it is that the public needs to know about how well and how they are discharging their functions."[41]

"THE REPUBLIC STANDS"

It was a hot, sunny June day for much of the East Coast on the Friday the *Post* story broke and the editors at the *Times* case reconvened. Before the day was over, the government had secured its second injunction against a major American newspaper. A week earlier, there had never been a federally ordered cessation of the press. Now it had happened twice, placing both papers in court—albeit in separate cases.

The *Times* received its ruling first, on Saturday, June 19, from Judge Gurfein. Although the former army colonel had openly questioned the patriotism of *Times* officials during the trial, Gurfein dissolved the TRO against the *Times* and denied the government the preliminary injunction it had sought. Beyond the legal fine points, Gurfein's four-thousand-word opinion was an eloquent, ringing endorsement of the First Amendment: "A cantankerous press, an obstinate press, a ubiquitous press must be suffered by those in authority to preserve the even greater values of freedom of expression and the right of the people to know," he wrote. "This has been the genius of our institutions throughout our history....It is one of the marked traits of our national life that distinguish us from other nations under different forms of government."[42]

Just two days later, in a parallel proceeding, federal district judge Gerhard Gesell agreed and ruled in favor of the *Post*. His logic: Because the ongoing war in

Vietnam had provoked such intense debate across the country, any order suppressing vital information about the government's method of handling the war
"would feed the fires of distrust." In fact, Gesell wrote, given the "growing antagonism between the executive branch and certain elements of the press,"[43] it was
even more important that the debate take place out in the open, for all to witness.
The government's legal team appealed both rulings. In a few days, with the two
cases on fast track, both sides reconvened for Round Two.

On Wednesday, June 23—the same day Ellsberg was interviewed in hiding by
Cronkite—Erwin Griswold, the U.S. solicitor general, argued the *Post's* case
before a nine-member en banc bench of the U.S. Court of Appeals for the District
of Columbia. Like Michael Hess before him, Griswold learned he would be
arguing the case just hours before the hearing. As he wrote in his memoir, "I [had]
never seen even the outside of the Pentagon Papers. I [did] not know what [was]
in them, and I [had] given no real study to the applicable law." Griswold, a former
dean of Harvard Law School, recalls arguing the case "in a rather feckless way,
since I did not know much about it."[44] Later that day, the D.C. Circuit, in a per
curiam opinion, voted to affirm Judge Gesell's order by a vote of seven to two and
to deny the injunction against the *Washington Post*.

It was a tough loss for the government, but it was countered by the news that
the Second Circuit Court of Appeals—which reviews all appeals in New York—
had ordered Judge Gurfein, by a vote of five to three, to hold additional hearings.
The conflicting circuit court rulings increased the already strong likelihood that
the U.S. Supreme Court would accept the case for review.

Meanwhile, by Thursday morning the coverage and investigation of the
Pentagon Papers had spread to eleven other papers. After just ten days, the secret
musings of government officials were now appearing everywhere, except, it
seemed, in the *New York Times* and the *Washington Post*. That fact, however, hurt
the government's case, as Alexander Bickel knew and relished. When he first
learned of the *Post* article, Bickel doubted the government's claim that "grave
danger to the national security would occur if another installment of a story that
the *Times* had were published." With a twist of irony, he said, "[a]nother
installment of that story has been published. [Yet] the republic stands."[45]

"THE FINAL JURY OF THE NATION"

On Friday morning, June 25, the Supreme Court announced it would hear the
case on an emergency basis—the next day. Lawyers for both sides had less than
twenty-four hours to prepare their arguments. Again, time was of the essence, but
this time Griswold was determined to learn something specific about Robert
McNamara's secret study. Griswold didn't have enough time to read the Pentagon
Papers in their entirety. So he arranged for three people—the director of the

National Security Agency, a deputy undersecretary of state, and the director of operations for the Joint Chiefs of Staff—to come to his office and debrief him on the study. As he recalls, "I asked each of these gentlemen to tell me what was really dangerous in the Pentagon Papers, and would cause irreparable harm to the interests or the security of the United States."[46]

The solicitor general, searching for something to buttress his argument for secrecy, envisioned one concern that might be compelling—namely, that publishing any decoded telegrams would reveal the nation's code-breaking process to its enemies. When he inquired about this, one of his security experts laughed at the thought. "That has not been true since about 1935," Griswold remembers the man saying, at which point Griswold thought "that about half of my case, as I had analyzed it so far, went out the window." Griswold worked through the night on his brief for the Court. Eventually, he identified eleven specific items "[t]he publication of [which]," he wrote, he thought was "likely to close up channels of communication which might otherwise have some opportunity of facilitating the closing of the Vietnam War."[47] Within a few hours, he would have to re-suit in the traditional swallowtails to present his argument before the highest Court in the land.

At precisely 11:00 A.M. on Saturday, June 26—just thirteen days after the first article ran in the *Times*—the nine justices emerged from behind the thick scarlet curtains of the nation's most hallowed courtroom to take their seats. Griswold had already filed a motion for the argument to be held *in camera*—privately, without the press or public present. The request was not without precedent; parts of all four lower court proceedings in this case had been held in camera. Armed guards had escorted the records of each lower court's proceedings to the Supreme Court. An army staff sergeant had attempted to deny Griswold's secretary "clearance" to assist him in preparing the brief. As Roger Newman observes in his biography of Justice Black, "[i]t was a theater of the absurd."[48]

It was also another moment in American history when freedom and fear were at war. On the freedom side of the divide, there was a bold attitude that virtually everything should be shared with the public—national security (potentially) be damned, at least in this case. On the other side was a fear that even the truth about the war should be withheld from the public in the name of national security. For two weeks, the battle between the press and the government had been front-page news across America. In the span of those two weeks, there had been a national manhunt, a rumored threat to the nation's security, and four closed-court sessions. And yet despite all this, very few people—including those prosecuting the case—had actually read the secret report. It was a fascinating, fearful period. And it was almost over.

Griswold's motion to argue the case in private was denied. He would have to give his argument in front of the press corps and the 174 fortunate spectators with courtroom seats—out of fifteen hundred who had tried to get them. As the burly solicitor general began to speak, recalled journalist Sanford Ungar, the distinguished Griswold "seemed almost part of the furnishings that make up a great institution, [and his] voice rose and fell with natural, precise punctuation."[49] Griswold remembers the morning less triumphantly. "Justices Black, Brennan, and Douglas were especially hostile," he said. "Justice Black, interrupting Justice Marshall, said 'Does not the First Amendment say 'no law' and do you not think that 'no law' means no law?' "[50]

Although his aged body was starting to fail—nagging headaches had plagued him for months—Hugo Black had long waited to offer his opinion on the case since he first read about the leak. In fact, according to Newman, "the case rejuvenated Black, firing him up as nothing else could.... All the old excitement of a case that *had* to be won was there." Newman reports that from the moment Black first heard about the government's injunction against the publication of the Pentagon Papers, the justice was stunned. " 'They're actually stopping it. What's happened to the idea of prior restraint?' he said, before returning to the neurologist who could find no further reason for his headaches except calcium deposits in the blood vessels; he gave Black vitamins and painkillers, and told him the headaches would wear off. 'Just like the Republicans,' Black said afterwards."[51]

But Griswold was ready for Black's absolutist attack. "It still seems to me," he later wrote, "that there was something to my answer." Griswold looked up at the Alabama-born Justice and declared: "Now, Mr. Justice, your construction of [the First Amendment] is well known, and I certainly respect it. You say that no law means no law, and that it should be obvious. I can only say, Mr. Justice, that to me it is equally clear and obvious that 'no law' does not mean 'no law,' and I would seek to persuade the Court that that is true."[52]

Much to Black's chagrin, it was a point on which counsel for both sides agreed. Bickel's and Abrams's argument, from the beginning, had been that there were certain circumstances in which prior restraints *could* be allowed. At one point this fact prompted a righteous Black to bemoan what he saw as their pusillanimity: "It's too bad the *Times* couldn't find someone who believes in the First Amendment." But Bickel and Griswold were unconcerned with Hugo Black. One side absolutely had his vote; the other side just as absolutely did not. They knew the real fight was for Potter Stewart[53] or Byron White.

After both sides presented their case, the justices immediately went into conference. They were, in the words of the chief justice, proceeding at a "feverish pace." They were also still split along familiar ideological lines. Warren Burger, Harry Blackmun, and John Harlan were for the government; as Blackmun wrote in his notes after the argument, "The alleged stakes are high—real lives—prolongation of war. Can anyone know the consequences?" Black, Brennan, Douglas, and Marshall, by contrast, were for the newspapers. During the court conference

Black argued: "We should not destroy the First Amendment by providing a 'loitering' ordinance that is vague and loose." He continued, "It is not a question of fact. It would be the worst blow to the First Amendment to enjoin these publications. The president has deluded the public on Vietnam. This is an abridgment of freedom of the press."[54]

Stewart and White were still undecided. "The First Amendment is not an absolute," said Stewart, echoing Griswold. "If I am satisfied that publication would result in immediate, grave, and irreparable harm to the United States…this Court, as a court of equity, would have the power to enjoin that sort of publication." Then Stewart again asked the question at the heart of the case, still, remarkably, with no clear answer at hand. "Is there any such threat here?"[55]

While the justices debated, one of Black's clerks heard on the radio that the government had secured *another* TRO, its fourth, this time against the *St. Louis Post-Dispatch*.[56] A total of nineteen newspapers had now reported on—and were still reporting on—parts of the Pentagon Papers. Griswold had claimed earlier that day that no further injunctions would be needed. Yet the news of the latest TRO made it clear to the justices that the Pentagon Papers had already been widely distributed among the press corps. That meant further injunctions against the *Times* and the *Post* were futile. The press, it was argued, was doing its job. It was serving, in the words of the great 19th century newspaper editor James Gordon Bennett, as "the final jury of the nation."[57]

As the conference continued, the discussion seemed to move more and more in a direction favorable to the *Times* and the *Post*. In the end, Byron White announced he would vote for the newspapers. So would Stewart. That made it six to three in favor of the right to publish.

"GET SOME CHAMPAGNE QUICK"

The majority agreed to issue a one-paragraph *per curiam* opinion. Every justice on the Court, however, authored a separate opinion. Black got to work on his immediately. His secretary, Frances Lamb, remembered the period well. "The mental anxiety he suffered about this potential threat, as he regarded it, to the freedom of the press was apparently more excruciating than the physical pain" of his wavering health. But, Lamb said, her boss "turned it off to write his opinion, staying up past midnight."[58]

On Wednesday, June 30, just seventeen days after the first reporting of the Pentagon Papers had appeared in the Sunday *Times*, the majority of the Court released its terse joint unsigned opinion.

We granted certiorari in these cases in which the United States seeks to enjoin *The New York Times* and the *Washington Post* from publishing the contents of a classified study entitled "History of U.S. Decision-Making Process on Viet Nam Policy."

"Any system of prior restraints of expression comes to this Court bearing a heavy presumption against its constitutional validity."...The Government "thus carries a heavy burden of showing justification for the enforcement of such a restraint."...The District Court for the Southern District of New York in the *New York Times* case and the District Court of the District of Columbia and the Court of Appeals for the District of Columbia Circuit in the *Washington Post* case held that the Government had not met that burden. We agree.[59]

Notably, five justices grounded their rights-affirming judgment in the First Amendment. They were joined by a sixth justice who argued that the federal government lacked statutory authority to proceed with the case. The *per curiam* thus revealed that a majority had rejected *Near's* military security exception to the bar against prior restraints. Professor Tribe summed up the *per curiam* this way:

> The Court held that the government had not met the heavy burden of justifying a prior restraint. While a majority of the Justices was prepared to believe that the publication of the documents would probably be harmful to the Nation, they were not persuaded that the publication of the Papers would *surely* cause the harm alleged by the government. Unlike the situation hypothesized by Chief Justice Hughes—the publication of "the sailing dates of transports or the number and location of troops"—the casual allegations in the Pentagon papers case plainly could not be established as a matter of substantial certainty rather than speculation. Only the actual publication of the documents could determine the issue.[60]

It was a major victory, and a new day in the history of freedom of the press in America. The *per curiam* statement was not eloquent, but it was decisive. For Punch Sulzberger, it was an occasion for grand celebration: "Get some champagne quick," he boasted, "because we're drinking it like mad here."[61]

Of greater interest to the future staying power of *New York Times Co. v. United States* as a persuasive precedent were the nine separate opinions of the justices. In particular, court watchers were most interested in the logic of White and Stewart—the two men who formed the block of six that resolved the controversy in favor of the newspapers. Yet of all the opinions, Justice Black's (joined by Justice Douglas) provided the most passionate, as well as the most uncompromising, legal argument.

"Guarding military and diplomatic secrets at the expense of informed representative government provides no real security for our Republic," Black wrote. But "strength and security [are guaranteed] by providing that freedom of speech, press, religion, and assembly should not be abridged." One of the passages Black originally drafted read as follows: "Paramount among the responsibilities of a free press is the duty to prevent any part of the government from deceiving the people and tricking them into a war where young Americans will be murdered on the battlefield."[62] Even for the aging absolutist, these were harsh words, and they troubled him.

Twice during the night after he wrote these lines, Black woke up his wife, Elizabeth, to ask her opinion. The first time, she told him she thought the language was too harsh. The second time, at four A.M., Black proposed an alternative phrase. It was an adaptation of the southern ballad "I Am a Good Old Rebel." Black had often sung the lyrics—about Yankees dying from "Southern fever, and Southern steel and shot"—with his clerks. When Alabama's segregationist George Wallace had started fighting integration, Black had stopped singing the song completely. On this occasion, though, the line seemed appropriate again. It entered his final draft:

> In the First Amendment the Founding Fathers gave the free press the protection it must have to fulfill its essential role in our democracy. The press was to serve the governed, not the governors. The Government's power to censor the press was abolished, so that the press would remain forever free to censure the Government. The press was protected so that it could bare the secrets of government and inform the people. Only a free and unrestrained press can effectively expose deception in government. And paramount among the responsibilities of a free press is the duty to prevent any part of the government from deceiving the people and sending them off to distant lands to die of foreign fevers and foreign shot and shell.[63]

It was Hugo Black at his rhetorical best—making his point in a powerful way that every citizen—liberal and conservative alike—could comprehend and champion. What it lacked in logical or doctrinal niceties it compensated for in popular appeal.

What of the other justices? Justice Brennan was a fellow traveler, up to a point. In his concurring opinion, he argued strongly against any presumption favoring prior restraints on the press: "I write separately...to emphasize what should be apparent: that our judgments in the present cases may not be taken to indicate the propriety, in the future, of issuing temporary stays and restraining orders to block the publication of material sought to be suppressed by the Government." Brennan was not a Hugo Black absolutist, though his constitutional view approximated such absolutism. Instead, for Brennan the First Amendment hurdle was a high one: The government had to allege *and* prove, at a time of war, that a particular publication must inevitably, directly, and immediately cause the occurrence of an event kindred to imperiling the safety of a transport already at sea [before the government's argument] can support even the issuance of an interim restraining order. In no event may mere conclusions be sufficient: for if the Executive Branch seeks judicial aid in preventing publication, it must inevitably submit the basis upon which that aid is sought to scrutiny by the judiciary." In other words, judicial review is key, and judicial relief by way of a prior restraint is not to be granted "[u]nless and until the Government has clearly made out its case."[64]

Justice Stewart (joined by White) was sympathetic to the petitioners' First Amendment claims, but in a qualified way. "I am convinced," he wrote, "that the Executive is correct with respect to some of the documents involved. But I cannot say that disclosure of any of them will *surely result in direct, immediate, and irreparable damage* to our Nation or its people. That being so, there can under the First Amendment be but one judicial resolution of the issues before us."[65] By that measure, if the government could tender such proof, then Stewart and White would allow a prior restraint to be issued.

Justice White (joined by Justice Stewart) concurred in the judgment, "but only because of the concededly extraordinary protection against prior restraints enjoyed by the press under our constitutional system." Clearly, White believed this was an exceptional case. But he equally believed that "in no circumstances would the First Amendment permit an injunction against publishing information about government plans or operations." Still, White supported the ruling because the United States had not satisfied "the very heavy burden that it must meet to warrant an injunction against publication in these cases, *at least in the absence of express and appropriately limited congressional authorization for prior restraints* in circumstances such as these."[66] In other words, had Congress expressly authorized a narrowly drawn law of prior restraints, such restraints on the press might then be constitutionally permissible. More notable still, Justice White suggested the propriety of what had not presented itself in these cases—namely, the possibility of criminal prosecution: "Prior restraints require an unusually heavy justification under the First Amendment," he granted, "but failure by the Government to justify prior restraints does not measure its constitutional entitlement to a conviction for criminal publication. That the Government mistakenly chose to proceed by injunction does not mean that it could not successfully proceed in another way." He then set out to cite chapter and verse from the federal criminal code. "The Criminal Code contains numerous provisions potentially relevant to these cases. If any of the material here at issue is of this nature, the newspapers are presumably now on full notice of the position of the United States and must face the consequences if they publish. I would have no difficulty in sustaining convictions under these sections on facts that would not justify the intervention of equity and the imposition of a prior restraint."[67]

Justice Thurgood Marshall took a different tack entirely in his opinion, refusing to even *mention* the First Amendment except to state that he thought the primary issues in the case were "more basic"—in other words, that the executive lacked any constitutional authority to act against the press. Along the way, he offered a stinging rebuke of the Nixon administration. "It may be more convenient for the Executive if it need only convince a judge to prohibit conduct rather than to ask for Congress to pass a law," wrote Marshall. "But convenience and political considerations of the moment do not justify a basic departure from the principles of our system of government."[68]

Next was Chief Justice Warren Burger (1907–1995), writing in dissent. Burger argued for restraint on the part of the press. "Would it have been unreasonable, since the newspaper could anticipate the Government's objections to release of secret material, to give the Government an opportunity to review the entire collection and determine whether agreement could be reached on publication? Stolen or not, if security was not in fact jeopardized, much of the material could no doubt have been declassified, since it spans a period ending in 1968." Such moderation, he emphasized, was salutary and could benefit all sides: "With such an approach—one that great newspapers have in the past practiced and stated editorially to be the duty of an honorable press—the newspapers and Government might well have narrowed the area of disagreement as to what was and was not publishable, leaving the remainder to be resolved in orderly litigation, if necessary. To me it is hardly believable that a newspaper long regarded as a great institution in American life would fail to perform one of the basic and simple duties of every citizen with respect to the discovery or possession of stolen property or secret government documents. That duty, I had thought—perhaps naively—was to report forthwith, to responsible public officers."[69]

For Justice John Harlan, also in dissent, the haste of the ruling and the rhetorical pronouncements tendered all made for muddled law devoid of the nuance essential to reasoned decision-making. Too many important factors had to be ignored in the Court's rush to judgment. "Pending further hearings in each case conducted under the appropriate ground rules," he wrote, "I would continue the restraints on publication. I cannot believe that the doctrine prohibiting prior restraints reaches to the point of preventing courts from maintaining the status quo long enough to act responsibly in matters of such national importance as those involved here."[70]

Finally, there was Justice Harry Blackmun,[71] the last dissenter. For him, the problem with the majority's handiwork was that it focused on the First Amendment to the exclusion of everything else in the federal Constitution. "The First Amendment," he wrote, "is only one part of an entire Constitution. Article II of the great document vests in the Executive Branch primary power over the conduct of foreign affairs and places in that branch the responsibility for the Nation's safety. Each provision of the Constitution is important, and I cannot subscribe to a doctrine of unlimited absolutism for the First Amendment at the cost of downgrading other provisions."[72]

In addition, Blackmun felt that the First Amendment absolutism favored by Black and Douglas, and hinted at by Brennan, was far too lopsided to win judicial approval—in the past, present, or future. "First Amendment absolutism has never commanded a majority of this Court. See, for example, *Near v. Minnesota* and *Schenck v. United States*. What is needed here is a weighing, upon properly developed standards, of the broad right of the press to print and of the very narrow right of the Government to prevent. Such standards are not yet developed."[73] This was a call to adopt the *balancing approach* championed by Justice John Harlan.

The *per curiam* opinion lacked both doctrinal breadth and rhetorical passion; the concurring opinions veered in different directions, sometimes warring with one another; and the dissenting opinions gave rather short shrift to First Amendment values. Yet in the end, the majority ruling was a beautiful paean to the First Amendment.

After the decision was announced, Newman reports, "Chief Justice Burger rose, turned to Justice Black, took him by the elbow, and smiled." As they exited beyond the scarlet drapes, Black's wife greeted him. "Honey," she told him, "if this is your swan song, it's a good one." It was, he believed, the most important First Amendment opinion of his career. It was also his last. The headaches continued, challenging Black's vow never to retire.

A few weeks after the decision in *New York Times v. United States* was announced, Justice Black spent four days at the Bethesda Naval Medical Center. Over those four days, he spoke with his old friend Louis Oberdorfer. According to Newman, the dying justice returned to the theme that mirrored both his career and the history of his nation—that battle between freedom and fear. And in those last days, Oberdorfer remembers, "Black was paranoid about the future, expressing fears of governmental collapse." The aging justice worried about the future of his beloved republic in a way he never had before. "Anything can happen here," he said.[74]

The same man who had so absolutely argued for freedom in American society was now expressing his fears that too much freedom could be American society's undoing. Still, in his final opinion he cast his lot with an abiding faith in the people, and in the government, to do the right thing. Fate, it turned out, favored his optimism, but the situation would get worse before it got better. Before the oral arguments were made in *New York Times v. United States*, Daniel Ellsberg was arrested and charged with espionage. Afterward, in December 1971, he was reindicted and the charges against him were greatly expanded, so much so that he faced twelve felony charges and a possible total of 115 years in prison.

The criminal trial began on January 3, 1973, even though, much to Ellsberg's initial surprise, there was no official secrets act that had criminalized his leak of the Pentagon Papers. The case dragged on for several months. Then, in its final week, a series of shocking disclosures unfolded. The *New York Times* described them as the kind no novelist could invent. First, federal district judge Matthew Byrne learned that the office of Ellsberg's psychiatrist had been broken into in an attempt to acquire damning information about him. Shortly thereafter, Nixon was directly linked to the break-in. Members of his cabinet began resigning in quick succession in an attempt to deflect unwanted attention away from the president. But it was too late. Then, in the midst of the unraveling of the Nixon presidency, the FBI informed Judge Byrne that, despite many previous denials, it had in fact at one point electronically surveiled Ellsberg. Byrne was furious—but his own hands were hardly clean—he had already admitted twice interviewing for the director's post at the FBI while the trial against Ellsberg was in process!

On May 11, 1973, Ellsberg's lawyers asked Judge Byrne to dismiss the case "with prejudice," meaning he could never be tried again for the charges. The next day, Byrne granted the dismissal. "I am of the opinion," he wrote, "that the only remedy available that would assure the due process and the fair administration of justice is that this trial be terminated." In an editorial the next day, the *New York Times* wrote: "Seldom has a Government-initiated criminal prosecution revealed such contempt for individual rights and lawful procedure by the Government itself.... [And] seldom has a case provided more dramatic proof of the importance of a free and independent judiciary operating as a check on the abuses of executive power."[75]

Hugo Black was not there to savor the *Times's* freedom-loving language. On Constitution Day, September 17, 1971, with great reluctance, he retired from the Court. And eight days later, he was gone.

POSTSCRIPT—THE LEGACY OF THE NO PRIOR RESTRAINTS RULE

Hugo Black's concurring opinion was a fitting tribute to the First Amendment freedoms he cherished. Yet President Nixon was not convinced. "It is the role of government," he said, "not *The New York Times*, to judge the impact of a top secret security document."[76]

Nixon's past problems foreshadowed his future ones. According to William Safire, one of his speech writers, Nixon's "overreaction" to the Pentagon Papers case "led him to his most fundamental mistakes."[77] Already, there had been the Nixon-ordered break-in of the office of Ellsberg's psychiatrist in September 1971. The next such incident occurred nine months later, when Nixon ordered *another* break-in, this time at the Watergate offices of the Democratic National Committee. Then, in the early months of 1973, as the criminal trial against Ellsberg unfolded on a national stage, the full extent of the president's transgressions were gradually exposed by the press and presented to the nation for judgment. Unable to withstand the press scrutiny and the public shame, Nixon resigned in disgrace on August 9, 1974.

By stark contrast, Hugo Black left the Supreme Court with a final flourish. He was viewed by many as the most passionate defender of First Amendment freedoms. Even so, as Dean Erwin Chemerinksy has observed, the Court's opinion in the Pentagon Papers case left unanswered some crucial questions: First, what circumstances, if any, would justify a court order preventing publication so as to protect national security? And second, what difference, if any, would it make if there were a statute authorizing a prior restraint?

Clearly, the Court agreed with Alexander Bickel: prior restraints are sometimes permissible, despite the "heavy presumption" against them. Notwithstanding the bold results in *Near v. Minnesota* and *New York Times v. United States*, the fact is that both cases contained *dicta* that limited the doctrine of no prior restraint. Some of those limitations pertained to national security; some pertained to authorizing legislation; and some pertained to categories of cases not involving national security. In short, the seeds for undermining such landmark opinions had been sown in the opinions themselves. But would that potential be realized? Would the freedom-affirming spirit of the two cases be diluted over time?

Yes and no. On the one hand, the Court has applied the no prior restraint doctrine to void governmental censorship of films,[78] books,[79] plays,[80] and permit requirements,[81] among other things. On the other hand, the Court and lower courts have delineated certain categories of expression where prior restraints are permissible. Consider, for example, the following categories:

- National security [82]
- Public employees[83]
- Catastrophic loss[84]
- Public safety and order[85]
- Obscene materials (including child pornography)[86]
- Content-neutral regulation of a public forum[87]
- Judicial proceedings[88]
- Attorney-client conversations[89]
- Commercial property rights[90]

The prohibition against prior restraints has been relaxed in each of these categories, though in different ways, for various reasons, and for designated periods of time. In all of the above situations, and yet other related ones, courts rarely, if ever, invoke arguments akin to Hugo Black's absolutism, if only because such a rule would wreak havoc on American law as we know it.

There is, to be sure, a heavy presumption against *nearly* any system of prior restraint. Generally speaking, a prior restraint is constitutionally taboo *unless* the government can demonstrate some overarching interest, like national security. Prior restraints are not to be tolerated *unless* the government can prove that it seeks to regulate harmful and unprotected expression, like a manual about how to build an A-bomb, or an obscene magazine or DVD. So, the argument continues, prior restraints are anathema to our system of freedom of expression *unless* they interfere with constitutional rights or property interests, such as the right to a fair trial or the right to keep trade secrets private. Of course, such qualified commitments challenge the very idea of the doctrine of no prior restraints, a doctrine otherwise heavily influenced by an absolutist or near absolutist view of the First Amendment. Where prior restraints are permitted, they are justified by way of something akin to a balancing approach to the First Amendment.

Which raises the question—to what extent do we really have a no prior restraints rule? John Calvin Jeffries, among others, wonders. Given that the rule is "so often deflective of sound understanding," he wrote, "it no longer warrants use as an independent category of First Amendment analysis."[91] One imagines Justice Black spinning in his grave at the thought. Yet Tribe agrees with Jeffries. "The Court has often used the cry of 'prior restraint' not as an independent analytical framework," he says, "but rather to signal conclusions that it has reached on other grounds."[92]

Still, the sum of Black's absolutist-like legacy as manifested in the Pentagon Papers case remains intact. Writes Rodney Smolla: "Although current First Amendment doctrine does not erect a *per se* prohibition against all prior restraints, as a practical matter the burdens that must be satisfied . . . are so onerous that in application the 'prior restraint doctrine' amounts to a nearly absolute prohibition."[93] And as Geoffrey Stone further explains, "as a practical matter, the standard used in *New York Times v. United States* is essentially the same as the standard the Court would use in a criminal prosecution of the press for publishing information about the activities of government."[94] "Indeed," Stone continues, "in the 35 years since the Pentagon Papers case, the Supreme Court has not once upheld a content-based criminal prosecution of truthful speech relating to the activities of government that did not involve some special circumstance, such as public employment."

For Murray Gurfein, the district judge whose legal reasoning on his first day of work helped shape those ensuing thirty-nine-plus years of law, it would likely be both comforting and troubling to know that the concluding words to his 1971 opinion still carry such resonance—and challenges—to the same issues today. "These are troubled times," Gurfein wrote. "There is no greater safety valve for discontent and cynicism about the affairs of Government than freedom of expression in any form. It has been the credo of all our Presidents. It is one of the marked traits of our national life that distinguish us from other nations under different forms of government."[95]

Fighting Times and Fighting Faiths

Eugene Dennis and the Clear and Present Danger Test

They were three very different men: Eugene Dennis was a scrapper; Harold Medina a believer; and Learned Hand a thinker. Yet their destinies (activist, trial judge, and appellate jurist) came together in a case about words—words that inspired and inflamed, and words that turned people toward a cause—and against one another.

They were *ist* and *ism* words—"Communist," "Communism," and the like. Such words and what they symbolized could not in times past coexist with other *ist* and *ism* words—"capitalist," "capitalism," and the like. For some, it was honorable to defend the latter and seditious to defend the former. Eugene Dennis championed Communism, Harold Medina valued capitalism, and Learned Hand tried to divine a way by which the teachings of Communists could be tolerated by capitalists, in the name of *the Law*. Could that be done? Or was the message preached by Marxist missionaries simply too dangerous?

Its "goal is the overthrow of our government."[1] That's how J. Edgar Hoover put it in late March of 1947 when he testified before the House Un-American Activities Committee. He was referring to the Communist Party, that "fifth column if ever there was one," he said. By Hoover's measure, to be a Communist was to be a "fifth-column" soldier, a secret enemy agent working inside the nation's borders to sabotage the American way of life and law.

And so a year later, Communists were rounded up and rushed off to jail. One night in July 1948, the FBI arrested twelve top-ranking leaders of the Communist

Party of the United States of America (CPUSA) and charged them with violating the Alien Registration Act of 1940. One of those arrested was a burly and bold guy, an ideological scrapper, who would make a big stink about all of this. Eugene Dennis (1905–1961) was his name.[2]

What followed was a long, nasty, and unruly legal fight that created bad blood, prompted bizarre behavior, and produced bad law. It is a story that left a lasting imprint on the history of free speech in America. It is the remarkable story of *Dennis v. United States.*

CHARACTER PROFILES

Devoted as he was to Communist ideals, Dennis pleaded full fidelity to his motherland, America. "We Communists are second to none in our devotion to our people and to our country,"[3] he said in his opening trial statement. America's real enemies, he declared in March 1947, were the "Fascist-minded"[4] types like those on the HUAC who would not tolerate views contrary to their own. When it came to such types, Dennis always welcomed a fierce fight.

Harold Raymond Medina (1888–1990), a newly appointed federal district court judge, had no real idea what he was in for when Eugene Dennis and his buddies strutted into his courtroom. True, Medina loved public attention—he dressed in dapper clothes, drove snazzy cars, and had a big ego. But he would not love the attention, at the outset anyway, that would come his way. The trial became a Sisyphean challenge for Judge Medina, whose courtroom became a theatre replete with real-world drama beyond all imagination.

For Billings Learned Hand (1872–1961), a respected appellate judge on the U.S. Court of Appeals for the Second Circuit, the drama was of a different order. By the time the *Dennis* case came to his court in 1950, the challenge was not in the courtroom; the atmosphere there, unlike that in Medina's quarters, was contemplative rather than contentious. In life and law, the barrel-chested, square-faced, and stiff-haired Hand was a perfectionist. His bushy brows and piercing spectacled eyes marked him as a man of distinction, particularly mental distinction. While Judge Hand possessed liberal instincts, his approach to judicial decision-making was decidedly restrained. So when the *Dennis* case came before him, it was more a legal riddle to be solved than a political controversy to be settled. It was a riddle, moreover, that had first confronted him in 1917, when he was a federal district court judge charged with overseeing a subversive-speech case, a "Communist case" somewhat like the *Dennis* one.

Dennis v. United States eventually made its way to the U.S. Supreme Court, where it was settled in 1951. Perhaps "settled" is not the right word, however, for little in the case was ever settling or entirely settled. In Justice Hugo Black's mind, it would take "calmer times, when present pressures, passions and fears subside,"[5] to vindicate and thereby settle the great First Amendment principle raised by the case. Meanwhile, it stood as one of the most controversial precedents in the history of American law. In time, the *Dennis* holding was ignored, though it was never expressly overruled.

It was an astonishing First Amendment controversy—played out in Eugene Dennis's life, Harold Medina's courtroom, Learned Hand's mind, and ultimately in the Supreme Court's ruling. No case, in fact, better exemplifies the long and convoluted history of the most famous (perhaps infamous) doctrine in American free-speech law, the legendary clear and present danger test, one first announced by Justice Holmes in 1919. It was that test that ushered in a new era in the history of the First Amendment; *Dennis v. United States* was a part of that history.

THE COURTROOM OF THE ABSURD

They were men accused of being enemies of the state. Their names and occupations were a part of the official record:

- Eugene Dennis (forty-four, general secretary, CPUSA)
- William Z. Foster (sixty-seven, national chairman, CPUSA)
- Benjamin J. Davis, Jr. (forty-three, chairman, legislative committee of the CPUSA)[6]
- John Gates (thirty-five, editor, the *Daily Worker*)
- Gilbert Green (forty- three, district chairman, Illinois Communist Party)
- Gus Hall (thirty- seven, chairman, Ohio Communist Party)[7]
- Irving Potash (forty-six, elected vice-president, Fur and Leather Workers Union)[8]
- Jacob Stachel (forty-nine, chairman, American Communist National Board)
- Robert Thompson (thirty- four, chairman, New York State Communist Party)
- John Beattie Williamson (forty-five, labor secretary, CPUSA)
- Henry Winston (thirty-eight, organizational secretary, CPUSA)[9]
- Carl Winter (forty-one, chairman, Communist Party, State of Michigan)

When the ever unrepentant Eugene Dennis and his Communist cohorts went on trial[10] on January 17, 1949, their lawyers complained bitterly about "an atmosphere of martial law." Their clients, they argued, were being subjected to a "police trial." Others made less generous charges: "another Scottsboro case,"[11] a "Hitler trial." They were complaining about what was transpiring outside the classic facade and Corinthian colonnaded entrance of the federal courthouse in Foley Square—the site of this historic trial.

That day, uniformed police and plainclothes detectives numbered four hundred strong inside and outside the courthouse. They marched in double file in their double-breasted long overcoats. Others sat high on mounted horses overseeing every move of the crowd. Assistant Chief Inspector Frank Fristensky, Jr., claimed that the reason for the large detail of armed police was that "the *Daily Worker* [a Communist Party paper] has been building this thing up for days. We are in charge of protecting life and property, keeping the streets clear for unobstructed use of pedestrians and to keep vehicular traffic moving."[12]

True to the assistant chief's will, the streets were kept clear, traffic flowed, and order was maintained. Meanwhile, some five hundred protestors, exercising their First Amendment right to peaceably assemble, marched up and down the courthouse sidewalk, albeit without chanting or displaying placards. There were no incidents to speak of, and Judge Medina proceeded cautiously, though there was no real threat to his safety. His fedora hat remained unsullied as he entered the courthouse and proceeded to his chambers on the twenty-second floor.

Still, Medina was in the presence of the "enemy." American Communists were then seen by many as agents of the Soviet Union. "They were supposedly submissive to Moscow's bidding and mindless as zombies in their dedication," observes William Wiecek. The members of the Communist Party of the United States, it was alleged, were "financed by the USSR and were completely under its control." Worse still, recounts Wiecek, they were believed to be dangerous revolutionaries; their views and actions constituted an obvious and urgent threat to American institutions, and to the nation's security." Worst of all, domestic "Communists were agents of a conspiracy orchestrated by the Kremlin."[13] Or so the rumors and fears of the day had it. Given such fears, the need for armed security could not be discounted. That, at any rate, was the perception of those charged with safeguarding Medina and his colleagues.

When things got under way at 10:43 A.M., defense counsel argued that the "armed camp, martial law and police trial" atmosphere prejudiced their clients' trial and intimidated the jurors. The judge replied that he had seen no such evidence as he passed through the police lines and into the courthouse. The defense lawyers then complained that the judge was biased; a transcript of his remarks at a pretrial hearing was offered as proof. The motion was denied. There were other defense motions, including some highly provocative and specious ones. Predictably, all were denied.

Sitting in his high-backed, leather-upholstered chair, the American flag furled at his right, Judge Medina made it clear that he intended to run things as "a trial, not a spectacle." That was his intention, though it was not the result. By the time it ended, the trial had in fact become a spectacle. As his patience was tested, his volatile temper sometimes won out as the proceedings almost veered out of control.

The trial went on for 275 days. The transcripts were massive, their pages speckled with five million words of evidence. The trial was long, voluminous, and contentious beyond belief. When the case was reviewed by the U.S. Court of Appeals for the Second Circuit in 1950, it took another twenty thousand words to explain the court's judgment. The story remained spectacular when it reached the Supreme Court the following year: there was no majority opinion, only a majority judgment; five of the nine justices wrote opinions—totaling 32,175 words. Precedents were ignored, and the law of the First Amendment was recast.

Such is the legacy—actually only a fragment of it—of *Dennis v. United States*. What follows is a sketch of that legacy and of the man who made First Amendment history, Eugene Dennis.

THE "CURSE" OF COMMUNISM

The times were rife with fear of Communism.

On October 1, 1949, the People's Republic of China was formally established. The very next day, China's Maoist government was officially recognized by the Soviet Union. Shortly thereafter China and the Soviet Union signed their Treaty of Friendship, Alliance, and Mutual Assistance. The two Communist super-powers shared a common hatred of the United States. Such hatred fueled American fears of the Soviet Union and its development and use of an atomic bomb. Those fears were compounded when, in 1950, the FBI arrested Julius Rosenberg, an electrical engineer who had once worked for the U.S. army signal corps, and his wife, Ethel. The two were charged with conspiracy to transmit clas-sified military information to the Soviets. In the course of their trial the following year, the government charged that the couple had unlawfully obtained top-secret data on nuclear weapons then being developed at the Los Alamos atomic bomb project.

Against that backdrop Eugene Dennis and his Communist cohorts would be judged. Even so, it is well to keep in mind that Dennis and his codefendants were *not* prosecuted for advocating the overthrow of the government, or for attempt-ing to overthrow the government, or even for conspiring to overthrow the government. They *were* being prosecuted for *conspiring to advocate* the overthrow of the government. The legal question, then, was whether there was a demon-strable link between their acts and a "clear and present danger" to the security of the nation.[14]

The law that triggered things was the Smith Act, a measure first proposed in 1939 by Congressman Howard Worth Smith (Democrat of Virginia), a former farmer, dairyman, and state judge. The Smith Act of 1940 (a.k.a. the Alien Registration Act) made it a crime, punishable by a $10,000 fine and ten years in jail, to advocate, teach, advise, or abet the forceful overthrow of the government or to knowingly belong to a group that did so. The law also prohibited the publication or distribution of printed matter that advocated the violent overthrow of the government. The Smith Act was the first peacetime federal sedition law since the Alien and Sedition Acts of 1798. It was patterned after the New York Criminal Anarchy Act of 1902, the same law that gave rise to the prosecution of Benjamin Gitlow (see chapter 2).

When Dennis and his codefendants entered the courtroom, history was against them. For one thing, there was a series of bad First Amendment precedents dating back to 1919, when the Supreme Court had rendered its first opinion concerning free speech and subversive advocacy. For another, there was the Smith Act trial of 1943, in which eighteen members of the Socialist Workers Party had been tried in federal court in Minneapolis. All of those "fifth columnists," as they were tagged, were convicted. They served twelve to eighteen months in prison during 1944–45.[15] What were the chances, if any, that fate and a jury of twelve patriotic Americans would be kinder to Dennis and his comrades?

Even before Dennis and his cohorts were indicted by a grand jury in late July 1948 for conspiring to advocate the overthrow of the government, the stocky Marxist had been arrested several times. He had even been held in contempt of Congress in 1947 for failing to respond to a subpoena issued by the HUAC. When given a choice between paying a $100 fine and spending a year in jail or returning to Congress and testifying, he chose the fine and incarceration. Those who knew him, and those who knew of him, also knew that the ruddy-faced, gray-haired general secretary of the CPUSA was a man who welcomed confrontation— and perhaps invited it. Aided and abetted by his codefendants, Eugene Dennis confronted, head on, the system that he was certain would convict him, unless their First Amendment claims could save them.

A HIGHLY UNUSUAL TRIAL

> I suddenly found myself in the midst of that trial of the Communists. It took me a long time to realize what they were trying to do to me. But as I got weaker and weaker and found the burden difficult to bear, I sought strength from the one Source that never fails.
> —Judge Harold Medina, address to Church Club of New York (1951)

> Hey judge, we won't budge until the twelve are free.[16]
> —Foley Square demonstrators (1949)

The chanting outside the courthouse never stopped, and the trial never seemed able to begin. On January 17, 1949, the eleven defendants—William Z. Foster was too ill to be present—now had to make their *legal* case,[17] namely, why under the law they did not deserve to be prosecuted as enemies of the state. Would the judge allow them the wide latitude they argued was due them under the First Amendment?

Harold Medina was of Mexican-American ancestry, Brooklyn born, a devoted Presbyterian, and well educated, having received his B.A. from Princeton and his J.D. from Columbia University. He was also an able and successful lawyer. Now he was a federal judge, a special honor for someone with his humble upbringings. In short, Medina was an American success story. Not surprisingly, he felt passionately about "America's love of justice," as he later assured lawyers in 1951 at a New York State Bar Association meeting. That "justice," as he perceived it, had to be preserved at all costs. It was at that definitional intersection that Harold Medina and Eugene Dennis would collide.

This was Judge Medina's first criminal trial. For a "hypersensitive jurist," as historian Michael Belknap describes him, the preliminary proceedings—replete with diatribes, delays, and bizarre deeds of all sorts—were challenging enough. There were motions and more motions—everything from motions challenging the constitutionality of the grand jury to motions for a postponement—resulting in weeks of delays. There were police in the courtroom and even a special bodyguard to protect the judge. There were demonstrations outside, theatrics inside, and bags of letters sent as asides to influence Judge Medina's decision. And this was *before* the trial proper began on March 7, 1949.

Once the contentious trial—there were ten lawyers (five for each side), twelve jurors, 140 members of the public and press, and countless objections—had gotten under way, it would take weeks on end for things to wind down. Before they did, the five principal lawyers for the defense[18] would have to submit their arguments. The prosecution was represented by U.S. District Attorney John F. X. McGohey, who was aided by a group of four government lawyers. The two teams of attorneys butted heads for some ten days until a jury was empanelled on March 17. The jurors included seven women and three African Americans— including the forewoman, Mrs. Thelma Dial—and they were housewives, secretaries, a beauty parlor operator, a beer salesman, a store clerk, and an industrial engineer. Even by radical standards, this was not too bad a "proletarian" jury. The law they had to apply to the facts was another matter altogether.

Prosecutor McGohey began to outline the government's case. As he did, he was careful not to reveal the kind of evidence the government *lacked:* For example, it had no hard proof of any kind that the defendants had themselves plotted the violent overthrow of the government; it had no real proof that any of the defendants was actually working to overthrow the government by force; and it lacked any proof, as Belknap has noted, of "serious wrongdoing by any of the defendants."[19] The proof John McGohey *could* tender was that the defendants were all officials of one kind or another of the CPUSA; and that the CPUSA had litera-ture, which the defendants taught and distributed, that advocated a system of government radically different from that of the United States.

But how could such proof be translated into a violation of law, and breach of the Smith Act? How could such evidence demonstrate that each and every one of the defendants knowingly conspired to advocate the overthrow of the nation's government by force and violence? That was John McGohey's charge—one he executed with great passion. The formula McGohey employed was simple in theory and effective in practice. It went like this:

1. Introduce old Communist literature into evidence—books or pamphlets or manifestos like Marx's and Engel's *Communist Manifesto* or Lenin's *State and Revolution* or *The Program of the Communist International* or *The Constitution of the Communist Party of the United States of America.*
2. Read select passages from that literature.
3. Call expert witnesses—e.g., informants and former CPUSA members—to "interpret" that literature so as to suggest some actual violent and hidden agenda of Communists.
4. Show that the defendants, by working together to teach the creed of the CPUSA, thereby conspired with one another to overthrow the government by violence.

Whether this formula was legally and analytically sound was irrelevant. What mattered was McGohey convincing the jury that the defendants had violated the Smith Act, regardless of how constitutionally problematic the Act might be. To that end, the prosecution introduced twelve witnesses (informants and former Communists) to "interpret" the supposedly subversive literature and expose its violent agenda. Once that was done, it would be clear that the defendants were subversive Communist ringleaders.

Judge Medina sat through it all, rocking, leaning back and forth, and trying to comfort his ailing frame. He had chronic back problems, the kind that prompted him to adjourn his court dutifully at 4:30 P.M., whereupon he often left the court-room for his health club, located in the nearby Woolworth Building. After that, Medina returned home to his apartment house at 14 East 75th Street. Before he retired at 9:30 P.M., he would reflect on the day's events—the troubling moments like the time when, during closing arguments, he jailed three of the defendants for contempt.[20]

Tensions escalated constantly. Every day was a new battle, and Medina became increasingly abrasive, even caustic at times. "Medina's resentment of the defense grew and grew," reports Belknap, "until he became more adversary than arbiter, with the result that many of the most spectacular scenes in the drama which unfolded at Foley Square involved battles between the Communist side and an antagonist on the bench."[21] The lawyers for the defense welcomed the fight and thus pleaded their case in ways that would astonish the average law-respecting, contempt-fearing attorney. Rather than rebutting the prosecution's case point by point, they painted their case with a broad philosophical brush, as if the jurors would acquit if only they heard the true gospel of the CPUSA. Thus, the defense called some of its own, like John Gates, one of the editors of the *Daily Worker*. But as the discussion moved more and more toward a review of Party ideology, Judge Medina became proportionately impatient and refused to admit much of the evidence the defense demanded be in the record. Much of the same kind of thing continued as the defense called defendants Gilbert Green, Benjamin Davis, Robert Thompson, and Henry Winston to the witness stand. And the defense called still other witnesses, who readily accused the accusers of the crimes of capitalism. For Medina, too much of this "evidence" was inadmissible propaganda. When he excluded the evidence, defense counsel objected repeatedly and forcefully, prompting "in chambers" meetings between the lawyers and the jurist.

The case was well into late August when the trial took another bizarre turn, one that invigorated the defense, irritated the prosecution, and infuriated the judge. The incident involved Russell Janney, one of the jurors. Had the defense done a better job of screening jurors, it would have discovered that Janney was a man with a past—he was a rabid anti-Communist who spoke his mind loudly and forcefully, as he had done several months earlier in a fiery address he had delivered in Macon, Georgia. But that wasn't all. It seems that even after he became a juror, Janney discussed the case at some length with a young and attractive reporter, Carol Nathenson, who had left leanings unknown to Janney. Once Janney's discussions with Nathenson were publicized, hell broke loose yet again. George Crockett submitted a detailed affidavit and moved for a mistrial. As was their style, the defense organized correspondence campaigns to pressure Judge Medina to declare a mistrial. Predictably, that tactic failed, and the judge denied the various defense motions.

As the case moved from summer to winter, the volume of evidence took its toll on everyone. Not until October 7, 1949 did the defense lawyers get around to their closing arguments. Abraham Isserman and Robert Gladstein took the lead, arguing that the real focus of the trial was the Communist Party and the *ideas* it espoused. It was those ideas that were being prosecuted. For, they noted, there was no evidence in the case that any of the defendants had taken any overt steps toward the overthrow of the government by violence. Harry Sacher followed, tracking some of the same ground. George Crockett came next; he told the jury that the prosecution had directed its case not against the defendants but against a strained interpretation of the teachings of Marx, Engels, and Stalin. Moreover, he continued, the jury must not place the sins of the Soviets on the backs of the defendants. That was a political matter, whereas the case before them was a legal matter—they should not confuse the two.

The defense ended with arguments by Eugene Dennis. In the spirit of the First Amendment, the general secretary urged the jurors to be tolerant of ideas and ideologies foreign to them. In that regard, Dennis never shied away from the teachings of Communism and the inevitable revolution of the proletariat. Dennis did stress, as Belknap has pointed out, that he and his comrades hoped to bring that revolution about by peaceful and democratic means consistent with the U.S. Constitution.

John McGohey, for the prosecution, approached the jury next. Some five days had passed since the defense had begun its closing arguments. McGohey reviewed the evidence the prosecution had offered and emphasized that this secret clan of Communists had conspired to realize the goals of its leaders by revolutionary and violent means. The Constitution, he insisted, did not grant the defendants any license to forcefully overthrow the government. Such a notion of liberty was bizarre, he argued. McGohey concluded by reminding the jurors that they could infer a measure of criminal culpability on the basis of the fact, among others, that several of the defense's witnesses declined to identify their Communists cohorts. If this group was as democratic and peace-loving as the defendants had argued, why, then, would they refuse to identify their fellow Communists? With that the prosecution rested.

Judge Medina proceeded next to instruct the jury about the law and how that law should be applied. His charge to the jury was long—fifteen thousand words. Part of it included the following complex instruction, which bore on the First Amendment issues to be considered:

> In further construction and interpretation of the statute, I charge you that it is not the abstract doctrine of overthrowing or destroying organized government by unlawful means which is denounced by this law, but the teaching and advocating of action for the accomplishment of that purpose, by language reasonably and ordinarily calculated to incite persons to such action.[22]

To the same effect, Judge Medina added:

> Accordingly, you cannot find the defendants or any of them guilty of the crime charged unless you are satisfied beyond a reasonable doubt that they conspired to organize a society, group and assembly of persons who teach and advocate the overthrow or destruction of the government...by force

and violence and to advocate and teach the duty and necessity of over-throwing or destroying the Government...by force and violence, with the intent that such teaching and advocacy be of a rule or principle of action and by language reasonably and ordinarily calculated to incite persons to such action, all with the intent to cause the overthrow or destruction of the Government...by force and violence as speedily as circumstances would permit.[23]

Despite the breadth, number, and complexity of these instructions, many of which were crafted by the prosecution, Medina was far less inclined to fulfill defense counsel's requests as to how he instruct the jury. For example, and as Belknap also notes, the "defense had asked Medina to require a finding that Communist teaching and advocacy had created a clear and present danger of forcible overthrow, but the judge refused to submit this matter to the jury."[24]

Could the lay jurors comprehend, recall, and respect the massive set of instructions the judge had given to them? Would the prosecution's formula of guilt convince them? Would the theatrics of the defendants and their lawyers bias them?

For the defense lawyers, victory did not require unanimity—a lone holdout juror could save their clients. Thus, while most court watchers who witnessed the *Dennis* trial probably thought it unlikely that the jury would acquit all the defendants, it was anyone's guess whether a single juror would buck his or her colleagues and take principled (or stubborn) exception. That prospect may have been the lone comforting thought for Harry Sacher and his co-counsel.

"MADAM FOREWOMAN, HAVE YOU AGREED UPON A VERDICT?"

Friday, October 14, 1949: It was a little after 11:00 A.M. when the official courier brought a note up to Judge Medina's chambers. The note was from Thelma Dial, the jury forewoman. The jury, she reported, had reached a verdict. As biographer Hawthorne Daniel tells it, at around that time a "few lawyers, newspapermen, and spectators were lounging in the courtroom, reading newspapers and talking. The defense lawyers, with eight of the defendants and groups of their relatives and friends, were standing in the corridor outside or pacing back and forth. Most of them "pretended confidence but were clearly under stress. Some moved restlessly about. Some smoked constantly, lighting one cigarette from another. Some talked nervously and found it difficult to listen. None of them had had any word of developments in the jury room or had been told of the note that had been sent to Judge Medina."[25]

The public, press, prosecutors, defense lawyers, and defendants then left the marbled entrance hall and reentered the courtroom with its dark-paneled walls and high, frescoed ceiling. The jury returned to the majestic jury box; the defendants and their lawyers returned to the area cordoned off by an oak rail that separated the principals from the press and public. Fifteen uniformed marshals stood firm in a row behind them. Prosecutor McGohey and his aides returned to their table. After several moments, Judge Medina arrived, whereupon the bailiff declared: "All rise!" Soon thereafter the language of the law filled the ears of all present.

> CLERK OF THE COURT: Madam forewoman, have you agreed upon a verdict?
> MRS. DIAL: We have.
> CLERK OF THE COURT: How say you?
> MRS. DIAL: The jury finds each of the defendants guilty.[26]

The fate of Eugene Dennis and his cohorts now rested in the hands of Harold Medina, a man for whom they had shown repeated contempt. Whatever restraint Judge Medina had exercised during the trial, his self-control was now over. He gave a five-year jail sentence and $10,000 fine to each of the defendants, except for the less culpable Robert Thompson, who was sentenced to three years in prison and a $10,000 fine.

There was complete silence in the courtroom as the defense lawyers moved that their clients be granted bail. Medina would have none of it. "These defendants," he stressed, "were not convicted merely for their political beliefs or for belonging to the Communist Party. I made it plain in my charge that the jury could not convict for anything like that, but they had to find there was specific intent to overthrow the government by force and violence." And then, in a telling moment, he added: "*It seems to me absurd on its face to say, as you do, that there must be a clear and present danger of immediate overthrow to justify prosecution. By any such test, the government would be overthrown before it could protect itself and the very important right of freedom of speech would be gone with all the other freedoms.*"[27] Did such instructions comport with existing First Amendment law? That was one question, among many, that would be taken up on appeal. But before the defense lawyers took any appeal on the merits, there was one other matter to address.

"Now I turn to some unfinished business," declared the Judge. He was about to issue sentences for contempt, for all those times that several of the defense lawyers, he claimed, had caused delay, provoked incidents, and even "impair[ed]" the judge's "health so that the trial could not continue." He recited over thirty-nine detailed instances of contempt. "I will now proceed to judgment,"[28] he said. With the lawyers standing, he sentenced some of them to serve sentences ranging from thirty days to six months in jail. Eugene Dennis was among those who received a six-month sentence—this in addition to the five-year jail term and $10,000 fine that had already been imposed.

The business of the court was now done. The eleven defendants were to be removed from the courtroom and duly cuffed and restrained. They were off to the Federal House of Detention. The defense lawyers were off to the federal court of appeals where, in time, they would file a 403-page brief. The rowdy crowd outside went off the wall, chanting "We want bail! We want bail! We want bail!" Meanwhile, Judge Medina and his wife soon fled to Bermuda for a vacation.

When it was over, Judge Medina became the man of the moment. *Time* featured him (replete with spectacles and moustache) on its cover. *Newsweek* reported on the facts and figures of the incredible proceedings. The trial record was over twenty thousand pages long. The trial had cost the government approximately $1 million to prosecute; the bill for the defense was somewhere between $250,000 and $500,000. But that was just for the trial phase of things. Now there would be new costs—economic, political, and personal. Would the eleven defendants fare any better before a new tribunal?

ENTER JUDGE LEARNED HAND

> We had no alternative. Many is the time that I have declared valid a law
> I should never voted to pass.
>
> —Judge Learned Hand (1952)[29]

When *Dennis v. United States* came before the three judges of the appellate panel—Learned Hand, Thomas Swan, and Harrie Chase—North Korean forces were busily invading South Korea. Communist troops were capturing and killing American servicemen. The Cold War was escalating out of control. The judges of the Court of Appeals for the Second Circuit were, like other Americans, well aware of that fact. Chief Judge Hand and his colleagues were also disturbingly aware of the *Dennis* case, if only because of all of the commotion in Foley Square during the long trial. Even so, the seventy-eight-year old jurist was cool toward what he viewed as prosecutorial overreach in demanding that bail be set at $1 million pending appeal. Hand disagreed and set the total amount at $260,000, enough to permit all of the defendants to be released.

Judge Hand's own sympathies were not with the government: "Personally I should never have prosecuted those birds," he wrote to Justice Frankfurter shortly after the Supreme Court handed down its ruling in the case. "So far as all this will do anything," he added, "it will encourage the faithful and maybe help the Committee on Propaganda."[30] For any variety of reasons, then, he thought it imprudent to go after Eugene Dennis and his like. But those were his *personal* views, which he claimed to keep at bay in deciding the case before him.

The first issue the appellate judges had to decide was whether there was sufficient evidence to sustain the defendants' convictions. "There was abundant evidence," wrote Judge Hand for the Court, "to show that they were all engaged in an extensive concerted action to teach what indeed they do not disavow—the doctrines of Marxism-Leninism." The transition period from capitalism to communism "involves the use of 'force and violence' . . . and, although it is impossible to predict when a propitious occasion will arise, one certainly will arise: as, for example, by financial crisis or other internal division. When the time comes the proletariat will find it necessary to establish its 'dictatorship' by violence."[31] By that measure, Judge Hand ruled, the evidence was duly sufficient.

What test, then, should the court apply to the facts? The direct incitement test he fashioned in 1917 in a case known as *The Masses* was neither a constitutional test nor one that had been formally adopted by the Supreme Court. It was a test, he lamented, that found "little professional support." He was thus compelled, reports biographer Gerald Gunther, "to bid a long farewell to my little toy ship which set out quite bravely on the shortest voyage ever made."[32] That left Hand with the clear and present danger and related tests employed by the Court between 1919 and 1951. Those were the tests he had to consider in rendering a judgment in *Dennis*. And so he turned the law's pages back in time to 1917, when he himself had written an opinion on free speech and subversive advocacy.

THE CLEAR AND PRESENT DANGER TEST: THE EARLY YEARS

The past was unlike the present. The freedom ordered by the First Amendment did not always garner the level of respect it enjoys today. For one thing, the trustees of the amendment were often lawmakers—the very people most likely to violate its freedoms. As for the judicial branch (federal and state), it showed little respect for safeguarding the speech, press, and assembly rights abridged by the other two branches of government.

As conventional history records it, the modern First Amendment was born around the time of World War I with the clear and present danger line of cases. Prior to that period, the Supreme Court had rendered no remarkable free-speech opinions. No theory or doctrine of freedom of expression that was very speech protective had been developed. The very idea of judicial review under the First Amendment was, by and large, then beyond the pale of practical litigation. By 1919, however, things started to change, albeit slowly, as more and more wartime free-speech cases worked their way to the High Court.

As we have seen with *Gitlow v. New York* (1925), the First Amendment owes much of its twentieth-century development to Karl Marx. But for Marx and his political and economic ideology, there would have been no free-speech controversies involving Charles Schenck, Jacob and Mary Abrams, Eugene Debs, Benjamin Gitlow, and Charlotte Anita Whitney—those followers of Marx who got tangled up with the law and in the process helped forge the clear and present danger doctrine when the Supreme Court ruled in their cases.

When Eugene Dennis's lawyers consulted the *United States Report*, those were the case names they studied as they developed their First Amendment arguments. Those cases and others contained the pre-*Dennis* law of free speech and unlawful advocacy. It is perhaps easiest to understand the relevant legal doctrines they examined by way of five formulations of free-speech law. They are:

- The direct incitement formulation
- The early clear and present danger formulation
- The imminent threat formulation
- The bad tendency formulation (revisited)
- The emergency formulation

These formulations of the law gave birth to the modern era of First Amendment-law—that period of early twentieth-century Supreme Court rulings that followed the largely dormant period[33] between 1791, when the First Amendment was ratified, and the passage of the Espionage Act in 1917. Three jurists—Learned Hand, Oliver Wendell Holmes, and Louis Brandeis— were the key players in this remarkable development of American free-speech law.

The Direct Incitement Formulation

Learned Hand—he hated his first name, Billings—had been on the federal district court for the Southern District of New York for eight years when *Masses Publishing Co. v. Patten* (1917) came to his docket. He knew, though only in an off-hand way, the central petitioner in the case, Max Eastman (1883–1969)—it seems that Hand's wife, Frances, traveled in the same women's suffrage circles.

The fair-haired Eastman (young, poetic, political, and with a Ph.D. from Columbia) edited the *Masses*, a radical—"revolutionary and not reform"—journal. True to its unorthodox creed, it was a magazine "directed against rigidity and dogma where it is found." Its declared policy: "to do as it pleases and conciliate nobody, not even its readers." The postmaster, one General Albert S. Burleson,[34] had no patience for the bright-colored magazine with oversize pages filled with radical poems, cartoons, satire, and political criticism.[35] As Geoffrey Stone put it: "*The Masses* was iconoclastic, impertinent and confrontational."[36] It was an incendiary work, seditious by some standards. Predictably, Burleson refused to mail the August issue. Eastman petitioned Judge Hand to order the postal officials to mail the *Masses* to its nearly thirty thousand readers. Eastman knew that Hand was no "revolutionary," though he hoped that the judge believed enough in political "reform" to realize the importance of free speech, even for radical types.

For the postmaster general, the threshold for violating the newly enacted Espionage Act was a low one, at least when it came to the kind of "revolutionary" materials Max Eastman hoped to circulate through the mails. It mattered not that Eastman offered to delete the objectionable passages. Why? In Burleson's view, virtually everything in the *Masses* gave aid and comfort to America's enemies, interfered with conscription, and therefore undermined the nation's war effort. The legal touchstone for the Post Office's claim was the Espionage Act of 1917. "For 120 years, from the expiration of the Sedition Act of 1798 until our entry into World War I," observes Stone, "the United States had no federal legislation against seditious expression."[37] But during this war era, there was now "immense pressure" on the Justice Department to prosecute war dissenters. It was, in the words of John Lord O'Brian (head of the War Emergency Division of the Department of Justice) in this atmosphere of frenzied patriotism that the laws "affecting 'free speech' received the severest test thus far placed upon them in our history." Mindful of that, Stone notes, the "Department of Justice invoked the Espionage Act of 1917 to prosecute more than 2,000 dissenters during the war for allegedly disloyal, seditious or incendiary speech."[38]

The Act made certain acts criminal in wartime. Violating the law could result in a twenty-year prison sentence. In relevant part, it was illegal to "make or convey false reports or false statements to interfere" with the war effort. Similarly, it was unlawful to "cause or attempt to cause insubordination, mutiny, or refusal of duty, in the military or naval forces." By the same measure, it was illegal to "obstruct the recruiting or enlistment service of the United States." This was the law the government tapped when it refused to mail the *Masses*.

On July 22, 1917, Judge Hand heard the evidence in open court. Gilbert E. Roe, a progressive lawyer who had worked with Louis Brandeis in the early years, was counsel for the *Masses*. Assistant U.S. Attorney Earl. B. Barnes represented the government. He argued for a sweeping interpretation of the Espionage Act, and claimed that one of the magazine's objectionable cartoons—"Making the World Safe for Capitalism"—could create great harm abroad. "But the cartoon merely expresses an opinion," said Judge Hand in his gruff manner. "It is not a violation of the law," he continued. "Are we to assume that in passing the Espionage Act Congress intended to close the mails to any letter or publication in which appeared any expression of opinion contrary to that held by the majority in Congress?"[39]

Barnes argued just that: "I am convinced that Congress had that in mind when it passed the Espionage Act."[40] Judge Hand could only close the exchange with a rhetorical question, one that signaled his view of the government's position: "If that is so, doesn't that prevent any agitation for the repeal of the conscription law,

and doesn't that interpretation prevent any political argument that might be contrary to the expressed opinion of the Congress?"[41]

After reviewing the evidence and studying the Espionage Act, Judge Hand
issued his ruling on July 24, 1917. He wrote—literally, on a writing board with an
eyedropper fountain pen—against a backdrop of little or no judicial precedent.
The opinion he subsequently rendered, which was based on an interpretation of
the statute and not, strictly speaking, on the First Amendment, would become a
landmark ruling in establishing a boundary line between lawful advocacy and
punishable speech. In time, even Supreme Court justices would study and draw
on what he wrote in his *Masses* opinion, though not always in ways consistent
with Hand's intent.

It was good news for Max Eastman—Judge Hand ruled in his favor and
enjoined the postmaster from excluding the *Masses* from the mail. Quite simply,
Hand concluded that the Espionage Act of 1917 was designed to punish those
who actually interfered with the conduct of the war. It was not, by contrast,
designed to punish young and passionate idealists who criticized the war or who
propagandized against capitalism and for communism. Absent a clear directive
from Congress, Hand ruled, it should not be presumed that the freedoms granted
by the First Amendment should be so readily set aside. Or, as the judge put it in
his own analytical way:

> Political agitation, by the passions it arouses or the convictions it engenders,
> may in fact stimulate men to the violation of the law. Detestation of existing
> policies is easily transformed into forcible resistance of the authority which
> puts them in execution, and it would be folly to disregard the causal relation
> between the two. Yet to assimilate agitation, legitimate as such, without
> *direct incitement to violence,* is to disregard the tolerance of all methods of
> political agitation which in normal times is a safeguard of free government.
> The distinction is not a scholastic subterfuge, but a hard-bought acquisition
> in the fight for freedom.[42]

Reading the Espionage Act narrowly, Judge Hand held that speech could only
be punished under the statute when it amounted to a "direct incitement to violent
resistance" to the law. By that generously speech-protective standard, what graced
the pages of the magazine was patently lawful. It was a glorious day for Eastman
and all his radical comrades—the *Masses* was back in the U.S. mail.

Both the opinion and judgment were also a cause for celebration for the young
Harvard Law School professor Zechariah Chafee, Jr.—the man who would become
one of the most influential scholars in the history of First Amendment jurisprudence. Writing in the November 16, 1918, issue of the *New Republic,* Chafee discussed Hand's *Masses* opinion and added his own perspective:

The true meaning of freedom of speech seems to be this. One of the most important purposes of society and government is the discovery and spread of truth on subjects of general concern. This is possible only through absolutely unlimited discussion, for … once force is thrown into the argument, it becomes a matter of chance whether it is thrown on the false side or the true, and truth loses all its natural advantage in the contest. Nevertheless, there are other purposes of government, such as order, the training of the young, [and] protection against external aggression. Unlimited discussion sometimes interferes with these purposes, which must then be balanced against freedom of speech, but freedom of speech ought to weigh very heavily in the scale. The First Amendment gives binding force to this principle of political wisdom.[43]

By this measure, speech ought not be abridged unless it caused a "direct and dangerous interference with the conduct of the war." They were words pregnant with meaning, one that drew from Judge Hand but went well beyond it. The future seemed bright.

The *Masses* victory, however, was short-circuited when the Court of Appeals for the Second Circuit reversed Hand's ruling,[44] rejecting both its logic and conclusion. With its mailing privileges ended, the *Masses* went out of business. Then things got worse: Eastman was criminally indicted on charges of conspiracy. The first time he was tried under the Espionage Act, the jury hung ten to two. The government retried him. This time the jury hung eight to four, again favoring conviction. Finally, after much litigation and the close of the war, the case was dismissed.[45]

Judge Hand's *Masses* opinion would play a notable role in the history of free speech in America. And as it would come to pass, Judge Hand himself would play a rather significant role in the *Dennis* case some three decades later. But that time had yet to be born—the law had first to be shaped by one of Judge Learned Hand's friends, Oliver Wendell Holmes, Jr.

The Early Clear and Present Danger Formulation

For all his fame as a great defender of freedom of speech, Justice Holmes (1841–1932) did not start out that way. Unlike Brandeis, he had no admiration for idealistic activists, and unlike Hand he had, prior to 1919, no special respect for the First Amendment. "Free speech stands," he once wrote to Hand, "no different than freedom from vaccination."[46] This thrice-wounded Civil War veteran held to the creed that "man's destiny is to fight." And when free speech interfered with that creed, the former was the loser. A March 17, 1917, letter from Holmes to then Harvard law professor Felix Frankfurter reveals the trifling degree of sympathy Holmes had for dissent:

Patriotism is the demand of the territorial club for priority, and as much priority as it needs for vital purposes, over such tribal groups as the churches and the trade unions. I go whole hog for the territorial club and I don't care a damn if it interferes with some of the spontaneities of the other groups. I think the Puritans were quite right when they wiped the Quakers and if it were conceivable—as every brutality is—that we should go back a century or two, the Catholics would be quite right, if they got the power, to make you and me shut our mouth. Which, being so, I think any nation perfectly justified in thinking whether it will have them or not in its territory.[47]

Those were not the words that the great Holmes—the celebrated champion of freedom of expression—would be remembered for in the annals of First Amendment history. Those views were, however, consistent with his first two First Amendment opinions issued while on the Supreme Court. In both of those cases—*Patterson v. Colorado* (1907) and *Fox v. Washington* (1915)—Holmes articulated a very cramped view of free speech.

If there was any pinpoint in time when Holmes *began* to reconsider his views, it was perhaps in June 1918 when he hooked up with Judge Hand by a chance encounter. The two friends met on a train leaving the newly built white granite Washington Union Station—Holmes en route to Beverly Farms, Massachusetts, and Hand en route to Cornish, New Hampshire. As they rode the boxy Pacific Rail Road cars, they began to talk about toleration and then, gradually, about free speech. Perhaps the two greatest judicial minds of their time, Justice Holmes and Judge Hand, spoke about First Amendment freedoms in wartime.

Holmes—a tall, angular man, who sported a white winged mustache and dressed in tall hats and morning coats—was passionate about the law but quite dispassionate about defending the rights of rogues bent on subverting that law. At the time of their train ride, Holmes had not yet read Hand's *Masses* opinion. But even if he had, it is likely the stiff-collared jurist would have sided with the appellate court that reversed Hand. The idea of national security, defined very broadly, was then foremost on his mind. That was his rule of life and law, the First Amendment notwithstanding. As Holmes daringly put it in his classic work *The Common Law:* "No society has ever admitted that it could not sacrifice individual welfare to its own existence. If conscripts are necessary for its armies, it seizes them, and marches them, with bayonets in their rear, to death."[48]

Judge Hand was nowhere as bold, either in temperament or philosophy. When Hand later mulled over his train conversation, the ever-guarded judge felt he had granted the justice too much conceptual ground. In a June 22, 1918, letter to Holmes, Hand wrote: "Opinions are the best provisional hypotheses, incompletely tested. The more they are tested, after the tests are well scrutinized, the more assurance we may assume, but they are never absolutes. So we must be tolerant of opposite opinions or varying opinions by the very fact of our incredulity of our own."[49] It was a skepticism born in a belief in rationalism, and in a trust in the Enlightenment. Truth had to tumble with falsehood before it could lay claim to certainty. Toleration was the grease that allowed the wheels of reason to turn. Such skepticism seemed well suited to Holmes, yet he was quite taken aback by Hand's letter. As Holmes's biographer Liva Baker recounts: " 'Rarely,' he told Hand, did a 'letter hit me so exactly where I live as yours.' "[50] Still, he was not yet convinced.

Early in 1919, the Supreme Court did something it had never done before: it heard four free-speech cases challenging the constitutionality of the government's power to censor and punish expression in time of war.[51] The very idea that the Court would limit the authority of the national government to wage and conduct war, in any way, was almost absurd. Nothing in the Court's history held out much hope for a First Amendment claim prevailing in such an atmosphere. Still, the justices heard the following four cases:

- *Schenck v. United States:* defendants Charles T. Schenck, general secretary of the Philadelphia Socialist Party, and Elizabeth Baer published 16,000 antiwar leaflets, some of which were distributed at the Party's bookshop and others of which were mailed to enlisted soldiers. The circulars[52] declared the draft to be unconstitutional and urged the recipients to assert their rights. Schenck and Baer were indicted under the Espionage Act for conspiring and attempting to cause insubordination in the armed forces, and for obstruction of military recruitment.
- *Sugarman v. United States:* Abraham L. Sugarman was prosecuted under the Espionage Act of 1917 for speaking critically of the draft at a Socialist meeting attended by many Selective Service registrants.
- *Frohwerk v. United States:* Jacob Frohwerk was the publisher of a pro-German newspaper in Missouri. Shortly after the commencement of the war, he printed a series of articles opposing it. Like Sugarman, he also was indicted under the Espionage Act.
- *Debs v. United States:* Eugene V. Debs, one of the leaders of the American Socialist Party, spoke at an antiwar rally in 1918. Debs praised other Socialist leaders who had previously been arrested for opposing the draft law. Before an audience that included draft-age men, he said: "You have your lives to lose.... You need to know that you are fit for something better than slavery and cannon fodder." He, too, was arrested for violating the Espionage Act.

After the briefing and oral arguments, the all-too-predictable result occurred in the spring of 1919—the claims in *all* four cases were *denied*, unanimously.

Justice Brandeis, writing for the Court, dispensed with the *Sugarman* case on jurisdictional grounds. What happened in the other three cases is aptly summarized by David Rabban in his book *Free Speech in Its Forgotten Years:* "Justice Holmes wrote for a unanimous Court in all three cases. He discussed the First Amendment in one paragraph in *Schenck,* and then relied on *Schenck* in dismissing similar claims in *Frohwerk* and *Debs.* He never mentioned the *Masses* litigation or other protective precedents and legal authorities cited in the defendants' briefs." In many ways, Holmes had treated these First Amendment cases as standard common-law cases, the kind he wrote about when he was a state appellate judge in Massachusetts. According to Rabban:

> Holmes concentrated on issues of criminal law and accepted most of the positions advocated by the government. Holmes approved punishment based on the *indirect tendency* of speech, upheld substantial judicial deference to jury evaluations of evidence, and supported greater restrictions on speech during times of war. In all three cases, his analysis bore a remarkable similarity to his pre-war decisions, [which were unsympathetic to First Amendment claims].[53]

Holmes's rulings in these three cases could hardly foreshadow the fame that would later come his way as *the* intellectual godfather of modern free-speech law. Two things he wrote did, however, signal that future—one had to do with a misleading metaphor, while the other concerned a First Amendment test that, at the time, promised far less than it appeared to on its face.

Key to his *Schenck* analysis was a metaphor, one that would be repeated (often mistakenly) for decades to come. Here is how Holmes put it: "But the character of every act depends upon the circumstances in which it is done.... The most stringent protection of free speech would not protect a man in *falsely* shouting fire in a theatre *and* causing a panic. It does not even protect a man from an injunction against uttering words that may have all the effect of force."[54] Famous as the metaphor became, it was analytically problematic. As the First Amendment scholar Harry Kalven, Jr., remarked decades later: "[T]he example is ... wholly apolitical, it lacks the requisite complexity for dealing with any serious speech problem likely to confront the legal system. The man shouting 'fire' does not offer premises resembling those underlying radical political rhetoric—premises that constitute criticism of government." But the metaphor was a literary device, not a legal test. And so Holmes set out his test for determining when advocacy was lawful or unlawful:

> The question in every case is whether the words used are used in such circumstances and are of such a nature as to create a *clear and present danger*

that they will bring about the substantive evils that Congress has a right to pre-vent. It is a question of proximity and degree. When a nation is at war many things that might be said in time of peace are such a hindrance to its effort that their utterance will not be endured so long as men fight and that no Court could regard them as protected by any constitutional right.[55]

If it was a constitutional test, it was a weak one *as applied.* Holmes's handiwork was "puzzling," observes Geoffrey Stone. After all, notes Stone, the pamphlet the defendants had circulated "expressly called upon readers to support the repeal of the draft through lawful political means. It did not expressly advocate obstruc-tion of the draft."[56] But Holmes, his test aside, nonetheless denied the First Amendment claims. As a result, Charles Schenck went to jail for ten years, and all of the other petitioners likewise had their convictions sustained.

What Holmes had done both alarmed Judge Hand and disappointed Professor Chafee. At the time, the Harvard law professor was busy trying to formulate a theory of free speech that could speak to the concerns of the Hands and Holmes of the judiciary *and* advance the cause of civil liberties. To that end, in 1919 he wrote an article in the *Harvard Law Review* entitled "Freedom of Speech in War Time." With some Machiavellian liberty, Chafee argued that Holmes's clear and present danger test, as set forth in *Schenck*, was in "substan-tial" agreement with what Hand had written in the *Masses* case and likewise amounted to a rejection of the bad tendency test. The problem, for Chafee, was that Holmes had deviated from his incitement test when he applied it in the various cases. This libertarian spin on Holmes's opinions tried to put this new jurisprudence in its most favorable light. But not all were as kind to Holmes. Ernest Freund (another noted law professor) was openly critical of Holmes's thinking. It was, in Freund's eyes, an "unsafe doctrine." While the "clear and present danger" formulation on its face smacked of a liberal free-speech stan-dard akin to what Hand had developed in the *Masses* case, virtually everything else in the opinion suggested that Holmes either treated the matter as a crimi-nal-law attempts case or as one governed by an old and not very speech protective test, the *bad tendency doctrine.*

Wrote Holmes in *Schenck:* "If the act (speaking, or circulating a paper), its ten-dency and the intent with which it is done are the same, we perceive no ground for saying that success alone warrants making the act a crime."[57] Put another way, if the mere tendency—direct or indirect—of the spoken or printed words was to undermine the war effort, then the expression could be punished. Using that standard, a considerable amount of antiwar expression could be outlawed. Thus, observes Rabban, did Holmes continue the "prewar judicial tradition of hostility to First Amendment values by using the bad tendency theory to reject free speech claims in *Schenck*, *Frohwerk*, and *Debs*."[58]

The bad tendency doctrine would resurface a few years later in another First Amendment case, *Gitlow v. New York* (1925). But before it did, Justice Holmes would fine-tune his clear and present danger test so as to make it far more speech protective. Meanwhile, the cerebrally curious Holmes retreated to his study and pondered over what the likes of Hand, Chafee, Freund, and others had written about his work. In his dignified red brick home on I Street in Washington, D.C., the justice considered his next move.

The Imminent Threat Formulation

That momentous year in the history of the First Amendment, 1919, had not run its course when the Court handed down yet another free-speech case, *Abrams v. United States*. "During the period between March and November" 1919, notes Rabban, "debate over the Versailles Peace Treaty prompted many Americans to realize that the war had failed to achieve the idealistic goals that justified their initial support of American intervention."[59] Meanwhile, the government's authoritarian hand against radical expression became an object of increasing concern for many Americans. And by the time the *Abrams* case came down, Holmes was under friendly fire from Hand, Chafee, and Freund; it was the sort of constructive criticism he took quite seriously. The combination of these and other factors would change judicial minds, though not enough to save the defendants in *Abrams*.

In August 1918, Jacob Abrams, Molly Steimer, Hyman Lachowsky, Samuel Lipman, and others were arrested in New York for violating the Sedition Act of 1918. The Act made it unlawful to "willfully utter, print, write or publish any disloyal, profane, scurrilous, or abusive language" about American government, or to "willfully urge, incite, or advocate any curtailment of production [of things] necessary or essential to the prosecution of the war." The Act also required evidence of intent to "cripple or hinder the United States in the prosecution of the war."

With his colleagues, Abrams, a Russian immigrant and anarchist, printed and distributed two antiwar leaflets, one in English and the other in Yiddish. The leaflets condemned President Woodrow Wilson's campaign of war and in the rhetoric of the movement declared: "WORKERS—WAKE UP!! Workers, our reply to the barbaric intervention has to be a general strike! An open challenge only will let the government know that not only the Russian worker fights for freedom, but also here in America lives the spirit of Revolution."[60] One of their comrades threw the leaflets out the open window of a hat maker's shop on Broadway. For that, they were all arrested, tried, convicted, and sentenced to fifteen to twenty years in prison.

The result in the Supreme Court was no less severe: the justices voted seven to two to affirm the convictions, with Justice John Clarke (1857–1945) writing for the majority. Clarke relied on *Schenck* and the other Holmes opinions to uphold the Espionage Act convictions. But now, for the first time, there was a dissenting opinion in a free-speech case, that of Justice Holmes, joined by Justice Brandeis. "In this case," wrote Holmes, "sentences of twenty years imprisonment have been imposed for the publishing of two leaflets that I believe the defendants had as much right to publish as the Government has to publish the Constitution of the United States now vainly invoked by them."[61]

A signpost in the history of the First Amendment had been erected—the two greatest jurists then sitting on the Court had broken ranks and urged a far more liberal approach to resolving free-speech claims in time of war. Furthermore, Holmes was pulling out all the metaphorical stops to craft a powerful argument *in favor* of the free-speech principle. Ratcheting up what he had said in *Schenck*, Holmes declared: "But as against dangers peculiar to war, as against others, the principle of the right to free speech is always the same. It is only the *present danger* of *immediate evil* or intent to bring it about that warrants Congress in setting a limit to the expression of opinion…where private rights are not concerned. Congress certainly cannot forbid all effort to change the mind of the country."[62] And then in words penned for generations to come, Holmes added:

Persecution for the expression of opinions seems to me perfectly logical. If you have no doubt of your premises or your power and want a certain result with all your heart you naturally express your wishes in law and sweep away all opposition. To allow opposition by speech seems to indicate that you think the speech impotent, as when a man says that he has squared the circle, or that you do not care whole heartedly for the result, or that you doubt either your power or your premises.[63]

Having set the analytical groundwork, he graced his opinion with a memorable metaphor:

But when men have realized that time has upset many fighting faiths, they may come to believe even more than they believe the very foundations of their own conduct that *the ultimate good desired is better reached by free trade in ideas—that the best test of truth is the power of the thought to get itself accepted in the competition of the market,* and that truth is the only ground upon which their wishes safely can be carried out. That at any rate is the theory of our Constitution. It is an experiment, as all life is an experiment.[64]

With that passage, Holmes ushered in the famous "marketplace of ideas" theory of free speech (see chapter 3)—an idea very much influenced by what Chafee, the father of modern free-speech scholarship, had written in "Freedom of Speech in Wartime." Consistent with that article, Holmes reinvigorated the clear and present danger standard; he breathed new analytical life into it:

> Every year if not every day we have to wager our salvation upon some prophecy based upon imperfect knowledge. While that experiment is part of our system I think that we should be eternally vigilant against attempts to check the expression of opinions that we loathe and believe to be fraught with death, unless they so *imminently threaten immediate interference with the lawful and pressing purposes of the law that an immediate check is required to save the country.* I wholly disagree with the argument of the Government that the First Amendment left the common law as to seditious libel in force. History seems to me against the notion.[65]

It was just a dissent; it thus lacked the authority of binding law. But it did have the authority of a forceful speech-protective argument. Chafee was charmed, though he still felt Hand's *direct incitement* test was preferable. Holmes's *imminent threat* test in *Abrams* was like Hand's test in its emphasis on the immediacy of any threat of unlawful action. In that respect, and as articulated and applied, it was heartier than the meager *clear and present danger* test formulated in *Schenck*. Holmes's reworked test, however, focused on the *context* in which words were spoken or printed, whereas Hand's statutory test focused on the *content* of such words. "Hand was critical of the Holmes approach," Daniel Farber has argued, "because he considered its contextual determination of danger too subjective to constrain lemming-like judges from banning speech in times of national crisis."[66]

Whatever one may make of the *Abrams* dissent, it was a new day for the First Amendment. But would that day live on? Would the Holmes dissent ever become the law of the land?

The Bad Tendency Formulation (Revisited)

The next significant First Amendment ruling rendered by the Court came in 1925 in the case of *Gitlow v. New York*. Benjamin Gitlow, you may recall, was a onetime leader of the CPUSA. After World War I, he published and distributed 16,000 copies of the *Left Wing Manifesto*. It argued for a communist revolution and urged labor strikes and class action. Its objective was "the conquest of the power of the state." Gitlow was arrested by New York authorities for violating that state's criminal anarchy law, which made it a crime to advocate overthrowing the government by force or violence.

Justice Edward T. Sanford (1865–1930) spoke for the Court, which was again divided along seven-to-two lines, with Holmes and Brandeis in dissent. For Sanford, the "general provisions of the statute may be constitutionally applied to the specific utterance of the defendant if its *natural tendency and probable effect* was to bring about the substantive evil which the legislative body might prevent."[67] He cited *Schenck* and other cases as support for that proposition. That standard, largely deferential to the government, was controlling in his mind. The *Abrams* dissent, by contrast, was of no moment to Sanford and his six robed colleagues.

The *Gitlow* majority gave wholesale deference to legislative determinations of danger. It was enough if the government considered the possibility of some danger, somewhere, some day: "A single revolutionary spark may kindle a fire," wrote Sanford, drawing on Holmes fire metaphor to make his rhetorical case. "[S]moldering for a time, [it] may burst into a sweeping and destructive conflagration."[68]

Holmes was left in the unenviable position of having to fight his own words and metaphors, the ones he laid down as law and logic in *Schenck*. "It is true," he wrote in *Gitlow*, "that in my opinion this criterion was departed from in *Abrams v. United States*, but the convictions that I expressed in that case are too deep for it to be possible for me as yet to believe that it and *Schaefer v. United States* (1920)[69] have settled the law." With verve, pragmatic logic, and yet another fire metaphor, he added:

> It is said that this manifesto was more than a theory, that it was an incitement. Every idea is an incitement. It offers itself for belief and if believed it is acted on unless some other belief outweighs it or some failure of energy stifles the movement at its birth. The only difference between the expression of an opinion and an incitement in the narrower sense is the speaker's enthusiasm for the result. Eloquence may set fire to reason. But whatever may be thought of the redundant discourse before us it had no chance of starting a present conflagration.[70]

Newly the defender of the misguided, Holmes added: "If in the long run the beliefs expressed in proletarian dictatorship are destined to be accepted by the dominant forces of the community, the only meaning of free speech is that they should be given their chance and have their way."[71]

By this Holmesian measure, no idea that could not win out in the "marketplace of ideas" deserved to endure. This survival-of-the-fittest approach to free speech was yet another indicator that Holmes had become more tolerant. Then again, there was a cynical way of looking at his handiwork. "It amused Holmes," quipped Yale University Professor Alexander Bickel, "to pretend that if his fellow citizens wanted to go to hell in a basket he would help them."[72] Such, if you will, was his Darwinian toleration. But at this point in time, it mattered not, for what Holmes was saying in *Abrams* and *Gitlow* was no more than a discourse of dissent, words not binding as a matter of law.

By contrast, *Schenck*, its 1919 progeny, and now *Gitlow* were the law. Under such law, warned Chafee, "freedom of speech means little more than the right to say what a considerable number of citizens regard as sound.... For novel unpopular ideas, where alone it is really needed, it would no longer exist as a legal right." Insofar as the bad tendency formula had won acceptance, it was a bad sign, indicating, as Chafee lamented, that "we had...lost vision and courage." Still, he held out hope: "The majority opinions determined the cases, but these dissenting opinions will determine the minds of the future."[73]

The next set of judicial minds to convince were those that had to decide the fate of one Charlotte Anita Whitney, a California progressive—and a Communist—who spoke her mind and associated with others who did likewise.

The Emergency Formulation

Surprisingly, Brandeis and Holmes joined in the judgment of the majority of the Court in *Whitney v. California* (1927). There, the justices upheld a California law prohibiting the advocacy of criminal anarchy and criminal syndicalism. To be convicted under that law, it was enough that Whitney attended a meeting of the Communist Labor Party Convention, which adopted a platform calling for revolutionary unionism. That Whitney took exception to the platform was of no legal consequence. Mere association with Communists was enough to trigger the law and its penalty.

Holmes and Brandeis did not, however, join in the logic of the *Whitney* majority. That is, they did not countenance the majority's reliance on *Schenck* or its great deference to legislative determinations or its willingness to permit innocent association in a group to trump First Amendment rights. This time, Justice Louis Brandeis (1856–1941) took the lead in writing for the two great jurists. In his first free-speech opinion, albeit a concurring one, Brandeis began with rhetorical flare: "Fear of serious injury cannot alone justify suppression of free speech and assembly. Men feared witches and burnt women. It is the function of speech to free men from the bondage of irrational fears." He then proceeded to articulate a remarkably liberal free-speech test: "To justify suppression of free speech there must be reasonable ground to fear that serious evil will result if free speech is practiced. There must be reasonable ground to believe that the *danger* apprehended is *imminent*. There must be reasonable ground to believe that the *evil* to be prevented is a *serious* one."[74] Upping the stakes even higher, Brandeis continued:

[E]ven advocacy of violence, however reprehensible morally, is not a justification for denying free speech where the advocacy falls short of incitement and there is nothing to indicate that the advocacy would be *immediately* acted on. The wide difference between advocacy and incitement, between preparation and attempt, between assembling and conspiracy, must be borne in mind. In order to support a finding of clear and present danger it must be shown either that *immediate* serious violence was to be expected or was advocated, or that the past conduct furnished reason to believe that such advocacy was then contemplated.[75]

In other words, Brandeis believed there must be an imminent danger of a serious evil or the real likelihood of immediate serious violence before speech could be abridged. And as if that were not enough, the ever progressive jurist added: "Only an *emergency* can justify repression. Such must be the rule if authority is to be reconciled with freedom.... Such, in my opinion, is the command of the Constitution. It is therefore always open to Americans to challenge a law abridging free speech and assembly by showing that there was no *emergency* justifying it."[76]

It seemed that Brandeis had pulled out nearly all the stops in his attempt to maximize free-speech protection. And then with rhetorical force he stressed:

Those who won our independence by revolution were not cowards. They did not fear political change. They did not exalt order at the cost of liberty. To courageous, self-reliant men, with confidence in the power of free and fearless reasoning applied through the processes of popular government, no danger flowing from speech can be deemed clear and present, unless the incidence of the evil apprehended is so imminent that it may befall before there is opportunity for full discussion. If there be time to expose through discussion the falsehood and fallacies, to avert the evil by the processes of education, the remedy to be applied is more speech, not enforced silence.[77]

That "more speech" concept was then an idea waiting to be born into the fold of the law of the land. In time, it would be. But for now, less speech was seen as better, as evidenced by the result in *Whitney*. That is, the great irony in the case was that Brandeis voted to *sustain* Charlotte Anita Whitney's conviction. The great defender had developed a great defense of free speech, but it was of no moment to Whitney. Why, exactly, Brandeis changed what he had originally penned as a dissent into a concurrence is a great mystery.[78] Even so, what he denied to Whitney (who was subsequently pardoned by the governor of California) he more than paid over to future generations of dissidents who stood to gain from the measure of freedom he so powerfully urged.

In the years following *Whitney*, the Court in *Herndon v. Lowry* (1937) and *Bridges v. California* (1941), among other cases, either moved away from the bad tendency test[79] or showed some sympathy for the test Brandeis articulated in his *Whitney* concurrence. Nonetheless, the rights-denying holdings in *Schenck*, *Abrams*, *Gitlow*, *Whitney* and other cases stood, if only in a formal sense. The formal rules, though not the logic or the trend of the law, remained on the side of the government in its effort to ferret out anarchists, radicals, Communists, and all like-minded troublemakers bent on speaking ill of American policies and values.

It is against that historical and doctrinal backdrop that Judge Learned Hand and his colleagues had to decide how to rule in *Dennis*. There were several doctrinal avenues open to them. Which one would they take, and why?

APPLYING THIRTY YEARS OF CONFUSING AND CONTRADICTORY LAW

Having conducted a "wearisome analysis of the decisions of the Supreme Court,"[80] Judge Hand, writing for the Second Circuit in *Dennis*, was ready to deliver his opinion. He concluded that the governing precedents pointed to the application of the following test by which to judge the defendants' actions: "In each case they must ask *whether the gravity of the 'evil,' discounted by its improbability, justifies such invasion of free speech as is necessary to avoid the danger.*"[81] Incredibly, the test had no "imminent" component. It was enough if the danger could kindle and in time ignite into fiery revolution.

Of course, there was ample precedent for Judge Hand to discern a far more speech-protective standard of review. But by August 1950, when this appellate decision was rendered, he was not about to second-guess a judgment call made by Congress. Like his friend Justice Frankfurter, Hand relished the idea of being a defender—nay, an absolute apostle—of "judicial restraint." Judge Hand thus applied his test to the facts of the case. In relevant part, his appellate opinion declared:

> The American Communist Party, of which the defendants are the controlling spirits, is a highly articulated, well contrived, far spread organization, numbering thousands of adherents, rigidly and ruthlessly disciplined, many of whom are infused with a passionate Utopian faith that is to redeem mankind. It has its Founder, its apostles, its sacred texts—perhaps even its martyrs. It seeks converts far and wide by an extensive system of schooling,

demanding of all an inflexible doctrinal orthodoxy. The violent capture of all existing governments is one article of the creed of that faith, which abjures the possibility of success by lawful means.

If American democracy were to endure, it had to insist on a level playing field in the tumble of ideological clashes between itself and its adversaries. Judge Hand put it artfully:

> Our democracy, like any other, must meet that faith and that creed on the merits, or it will perish; and we must not flinch at the challenge. Nevertheless, we may insist that the rules of the game be observed, and the rules confine the conflict to weapons drawn from the universe of discourse. The advocacy of violence may, or may not, fail; but in neither case can there be any "right" to use it.[82]

That was the end of the matter; the appellate ruling[83] was final: "Convictions affirmed."

The irony of Hand's *Dennis* opinion was apparent. Here, after all, was the same man who authored the broad speech-protective opinion in the 1917 *Masses* case; the same judge who chastised Justice Holmes for not going far enough in his *Schenck* opinion; and now, the same jurist who turned his mind away from all of that and more, and sent men to jail for little more than espousing hated ideologies. Judge Hand devised a test based on the least speech-protective precedents then available to him. He discounted altogether what Justice Brandeis (joined by Holmes) had urged in *Whitney*—that "even [the] advocacy of violence, however reprehensible morally, is not a justification for denying free speech where...there is nothing to indicate that the advocacy would be *immediately* acted on."[84]

"His *Dennis* opinion," William Wiecek has argued, "not only affirmed the results of a badly conducted trial below; it provided a speech-repressive precedent that undercut the libertarian potential of [the] clear-and-present-danger [test] and set back the First Amendment momentum by twenty years."[85] The editors of the *New York Times*, however, viewed the matter differently at the time; they applauded Hand's judgment in *Dennis*. "The nation can no longer treat with good humored tolerance groups or individuals whose admitted aim is to defeat the national purpose and aid the national enemies."[86]

The substantive law now settled, the question centered on bail, pending yet another round of appeals, this time for a rehearing in the Second Circuit followed by a petition to the Supreme Court. On that score, the U.S. attorney, Irving Saypol, moved to revoke the defendants' bail pending their appeal. This time the Circuit Court did revoke bail but with Learned Hand in dissent.

Judge Hand[87] was later vindicated when Justice Robert Jackson reinstated their bail.

Whatever chance Eugene Dennis and his fellow Communists had was now in the hands of the Supreme Court. On October 23, 1950, the justices agreed to hear case number 336—*Dennis v. United States.*[88]

THE SUPREME COURT: ARGUMENTS, CONFERENCE, JUDGMENT

Russell Porter, the *New York Times* journalist who had been assigned to the *Dennis* case since March 1949, was in the courtroom the day the matter was argued before the justices on December 4, 1950. It was one of twenty-five or so stories he filed before the case ran its final course.

Unlike those in the Medina trial, oral arguments in the Supreme Court were calm, except for the doctrinal clashes between the justices and the lawyers. "Justices Felix Frankfurter, William O. Douglas and Hugo L. Black questioned both sides persistently and sharply, especially on the clear and present danger doctrine,"[89] reported Porter. Except for questions from those three justices, the lawyers were free to deliver their prepared remarks.

It was "idle" for the defense counsel to challenge the constitutionality of the Smith Act, argued Solicitor General Philip B. Perlman (1890–1960). After all, the very provisions of the Act that Dennis and his cohorts were challenging were taken from the New York law upheld in *Gitlow v. New York*. "This Court has never overruled the *Gitlow* decision," Perlman went on, "and it would *never* say that what the people of New York can do, the people of the United States can not do." Perlman, a conservative Baltimore Democrat, could be somewhat progressive on civil rights issues,[90] but he had little sympathy for any view of the First Amendment that countenanced Communist propagandizing. With six of the eleven defendants sitting quietly in the front row of the spectators' seats, Perlman told the Court that "what these people have been doing has been on orders from Moscow." Given that, not even Holmes's clear and present danger test could spare them from incarceration. "When Justices Holmes and Brandeis talked about 'clear and present danger," he argued, "they were thinking about isolated agitators, not about these tightly organized, rigidly disciplined people, operating on orders from a foreign country."[91]

Harry Sacher, Abraham Isserman, and George W. Crockett, Jr., appeared on behalf of the defense. As the justices listened from their elevated mahogany bench, Sacher urged them to look beyond the petitioners and to consider what a negative resolution of their case could mean for the future of freedom in America. If the Court were to uphold the convictions, he argued, "drastic curtailment of the liberties of the whole American people will result." By sanctioning the prosecution of his clients, Sacher said, Solicitor Perlman was endorsing "an unabashed suppression of political ideas." Sacher argued for a stringent interpretation of the clear and present danger test; only in an emergency when the threatened danger was "immediate" could the government step in and abridge freedom of expression. If the government were to act otherwise, it would be dictating what political creeds could or could not be aired in the "marketplace of ideas." And "the First Amendment keeps open house for all ideas, even the revolutionary" ones, he stressed.

When his turn came, Abraham Isserman returned to the argument first advanced by Sacher. If the Smith Act is held constitutional, he predicted, it will be applied not only to Communists but to the "500,000 Americans who, according to J. Edgar Hoover, do the bidding of the Communist party." And, he added, "it will have an intimidating effect on millions of others who differ from the Government in any way. Already men in high places have suffered from McCarthyism and men holding moderate views have been persecuted under pressure of hysteria."[92]

There was more argument from the other government and defense lawyers. But it didn't seem to matter to any of the justices but the three asking questions. Had the other five made up their minds?[93] If so, which way? No one could be entirely sure of the vote or outcome. Then again, the Court of Chief Justice Frederick Vinson(1890–1953), as newly reconstituted,[94] was unlikely to be very sympathetic to civil liberties claims. The odds had to be against Dennis and his codefendants. But *how* the Court would rule against them—what rationale it would invoke—was the more important question.

Eugene Dennis was not privy to any of it; he missed the oral arguments altogether. At the time, he was serving a jail sentence, at the Federal House of Detention, for contempt of Congress. (He would serve ten months of a one-year sentence.)

On December 9, 1950, the justices gathered in the oak-paneled conference room located directly behind the courtroom itself and next to the chambers of Chief Justice Vinson. After the customary shaking of hands, each took a seat at the large rectangular table, with the chief justice sitting at one end and Justice Hugo Black, the senior associate justice, sitting at the other. They were there to discuss the resolution of *Dennis v. United States* and the law related to it—from *Masses* to *Herndon v. Lowry* (1937) to *Bridges v. California* (1941) and beyond. What was the status of *Schenck*'s clear and present danger test as there applied? Was *Gitlow v. New York* controlling? What about *Whitney?* Or what about the nine cases the Court had handed down between 1940 and 1947 in which the *Gitlow-Whitney* approach seemed to yield to a formula approximating the far more liberal Holmes-Brandeis approach? Finally, how much deference, if any, would the justices give to legislative and judicial determinations? And quite apart from the trial record, could the

Court itself take judicial notice of the alleged danger posed by Dennis and his Communist colleagues?

As they sat at the table next to the fireplace, there was a smattering of discussion, mainly by Frankfurter, Jackson, and Burton. For the most part, there was little interaction. "The amazing thing about this conference on this important case," wrote Justice William O. Douglas in his conference notes, "was the brief nature of the discussion. Those wanting to affirm had their minds closed to argument or persuasion," he recalled. "The conference discussion was largely pro forma."[95]

By the end, the tentative vote count was six to two to affirm the convictions. Then as now, when the chief justice is in the majority, he or she assigns the opinion. This time, Vinson assigned the writing of the majority opinion to himself, something he seldom did. But what would he write? And how would he parse existing law to garner the votes necessary to retain a majority backing for his opinion?

Six months later, on June 4, 1951, the justices filed back into the courtroom to announce their judgment.[96] A few months earlier, the Australian high court had invalidated a law that outlawed membership in or activity with the Communist Party. But such thinking was foreign to this Court. In the end, the conference vote, six to two against the defendants, proved to be the final vote.

Try as he might, the chief justice could not get four other justices to sign on to his opinion. Thus he was left with announcing a plurality opinion, one joined by Justices Harold Burton, Stanley Reed (1884–1980), and Sherman Minton (1890–1965), one of the newest members of the Court. Frankfurter and Jackson wrote separate opinions, joining in the judgment. And Douglas and Black each wrote in dissent.

THE COLD WAR OPINION

> The Cold War generated unprecedented First Amendment activity for the Supreme Court....As a result of the Cold War, it handed down *sixty* such decisions. For roughly a decade, this was the dominant issue on the Court's docket....The key decision, the one that shaped the debate, was *Dennis v. United States.*
>
> —Geoffrey R. Stone[97]

Fred Vinson, the son of a Kentucky jailer, liked things simple. By no measure was he a profound thinker. While he liked the ceremonious robes and the title of chief justice of the United States, he didn't relish the cerebral work that came with the job. What mattered was the *result*—how to get there—and "crunching the cases" was the law clerks' work. The rumor among Court watchers was that the chief justice authored his opinions with his "hands in his pockets." He met with his clerks, outlined his take on things, and let them do the spadework. Then he made a few changes here and there to the draft, and that was the end of it.

His plurality opinion in *Dennis v. United States* is indicative of his approach to judicial opinion writing. Generally speaking, it was ill regarded by constitutional scholars, and had no strong precedential future.[98] The central question the plurality opinion had to address was the controlling law. "Although no case subsequent to *Whitney* and *Gitlow* has expressly overruled the majority opinions in those cases," Vinson declared, "there is little doubt that subsequent opinions have inclined toward the Holmes-Brandeis rationale."[99] Though those two cases were still on the books, their staying power had pretty much vanished. Even Vinson granted that. Hence, the justices were "squarely presented with the application of the 'clear and present danger' test, and [needed to] decide what that phrase imports." Would they use the deferential approach of that test as applied in *Schenck*? Would they tap the rigorous interpretation of it formulated by Holmes in his *Abrams* dissent? Or would they adopt the most fortified version of First Amendment liberty, as announced by Brandeis in his concurrence in *Whitney*?

In the end, the plurality opinion did none of the above. Instead, Vinson reached back in time and gave new meaning to an old test:

> Chief Judge Learned Hand, writing for the majority below, interpreted the phrase as follows: "In each case [courts] must ask *whether the gravity of the evil, discounted by its improbability, justifies such invasion of free speech as is necessary to avoid the danger.*" We adopt this statement of the rule. As articulated by Chief Judge Hand, it is as succinct and inclusive as any other we might devise at this time. It takes into consideration those factors which we deem relevant, and relates their significances. More we cannot expect from words.[100]

Just like that, the clear and present danger test, in its most liberal form, had been discounted. In considering the threat posed by subversive advocacy, Vinson had ruled that the danger no longer had to be obvious or "clear." Likewise, it need not even be "present"—it was enough if it could evolve. Meanwhile, the "direct incitement to violence" component of Hand's *Masses* opinion was ignored altogether.

The result was a test that butchered the best of the Hand-Brandeis-Holmes formula. As Professor Gunther observed, "it was viewed by many as a debacle for the First Amendment."[101] The new test resembled the old one in name only. "The words actually employed take all the starch out of the clear and present danger test,"[102] Yale law professor Thomas Emerson quipped. For Vinson, all that mattered was the seriousness of the evil. And that was an evil that the plurality could take notice of itself. Here, for example, Vinson felt that the "evil" was plain to see; it was the intended demise of capitalism, by revolution if necessary!—a grave evil by any American measure.

If the Vinson plurality opinion was an affront to the First Amendment, Justice Frankfurter's thirty-four-page concurring opinion was hardly any less so. The Vienna-born, Harvard-bred Brandeis protégé and FDR nominee staked out a First Amendment position that was entirely foreign to the progressive free-speech lessons of Holmes and Brandeis—two of his judicial heroes. Invoking his mantra of judicial restraint, Justice Frankfurter wrote:

> It is not for us to decide how we would adjust the clash of interests which this case presents were the primary responsibility for reconciling it ours. Congress has determined that the danger created by advocacy of overthrow justifies the ensuing restriction on freedom of speech. The determination was made after due deliberation, and the seriousness of the congressional purpose is attested by the volume of legislation passed to effectuate the same ends.[103]

He then asked, rhetorically, whether the judgment of Congress should be second-guessed: "Can we then say that the judgment Congress exercised was denied it by the Constitution? Can we establish a constitutional doctrine which forbids the elected representatives of the people to make this choice? Can we hold that the First Amendment deprives Congress of what it deemed necessary for the Government's protection?"[104] Granted, the First Amendment as Frankfurter construed it required that the interests of the state be *balanced* against those of the individual in order to determine if Congress might abridge freedom of speech. "But how are competing interests to be assessed?" he asked. With Frankfurtian deference he added: "Primary responsibility for adjusting the interests which compete in the situation before us of necessity belongs to the Congress."[105] Thus, unless Congress acted in a completely arbitrary way, its judgment was final even if there was some measure of bona fide doubt. Since the Smith Act was passed in 1940, and since Dennis and his codefendants were indicted in 1948, it must be assumed that the "balance" Congress struck in 1948 was a sufficient constitutional calculation to carry on almost ad infinitum.

Perhaps, as Professor Kalven has suggested, Justice Frankfurter voted and wrote as he did for two main reasons: First, he did not believe the clear and present danger test should be a constitutional test in any case. And second, if the Holmes-Brandeis formulation of that test had any constitutional credibility, that credibility was squandered in Vinson's plurality opinion. The only alternative, in his mind, was judicial restraint—due deference to lawmakers, even when such deference is hard to reconcile with progressive justice. In a passage that seems oddly out of character with his vote in *Dennis*, Frankfurter wrote:

A public interest is not wanting in granting freedom to speak their minds even to those who advocate the overthrow of the Government by force. For, as the evidence in this case abundantly illustrates, coupled with such advocacy is criticism of defects in our society. Criticism is the spur to reform; and Burke's admonition that a healthy society must reform in order to conserve has not lost its force.... Suppressing advocates of overthrow inevitably will also silence critics who do not advocate overthrow but fear that their criticism may be so construed.[106]

Even as he voted to sustain the convictions of the defendants, Frankfurter warned the nation that such prosecutions take a heavy toll on liberty:

No matter how clear we may be that the defendants now before us are preparing to overthrow our Government at the propitious moment, it is selfdelusion to think that we can punish them for their advocacy without adding to the risks run by loyal citizens who honestly believe in some of the reforms these defendants advance. It is a sobering fact that in sustaining the convictions before us we can hardly escape restriction on the interchange of ideas.[107]

For Hugo Black, all of this was constitutional heresy. In his eyes, the Smith Act was plainly unconstitutional, the defendants' actions were plainly within the purview of the First Amendment, the clear and present danger test plainly required a reversal of the defendants' convictions, and Frankfurter's balancing test was plainly an affront to the First Amendment. "Such a doctrine," he wrote, "waters down the First Amendment so that it amounts to little more than an admonition to Congress."[108]

Black, like Douglas writing in dissent, was addressing a future generation of judges. He was planting seeds, hoping that one day *Dennis* would be uprooted and in its place would blossom a new tree of liberty: "Public opinion being what it now is, few will protest the conviction of these Communist petitioners." But Black held out hope "that in calmer times, when present pressures, passions and fears subside, this or some later Court will restore the First Amendment liberties to the high preferred place where they belong in a free society."[109]

The *Dennis* ruling and the anti-Communist "hysteria" it countenanced outraged the Court's most maverick justice, William O. Douglas. Ten months later, he expressed that outrage in an article he wrote for the *Progressive* entitled "Frightened America." It began boldly: "The Communist threat inside the country has been magnified and exalted far beyond its realities. Irresponsible talk by irresponsible people has fanned the flames of fear. Accusations have been loosely made. Character assassinations have become common. Suspicion has taken the place of good will. Once we could debate with impunity along a wide range of inquiry. Once we could safely explore to the edges of a problem, challenge orthodoxy without qualms, and run the gamut of ideas in search of solutions to perplexing problems. Once we had confidence in each other." But those days, he argued, were past. "Now there is suspicion. Innocent acts become telltale marks of disloyalty. Suspicion grows until only the orthodox idea is the safe one. Good and honest men are pilloried. Fear runs rampant."[110]

WHAT BECAME OF HAROLD MEDINA?

Before and well after Harold Medina was on the October 24, 1949, cover of *Time*, he was in countless newsreels; his story was reported ad infinitum in newspapers, magazines, and tabloids; and every sort of pamphlet known to the radical Left carried reports of his fight and plight. Now, after the Supreme Court's ruling, he was back in the news. The news for Eugene Dennis, however, was not so good.

Federal District Court judge Sylvester J. Ryan presided over the July 2, 1951, proceeding during which the eleven defendants were to turn themselves over to a U.S. marshal for incarceration. Four of them—Henry Winston, Robert Thompson, Gus Hall, and Gilbert Green—failed to appear on time. They immediately became objects of a national FBI manhunt. Dennis asked that the sentences be suspended. Predictably, Judge Ryan declined. The time had come to pay for their crimes: $10,000 fines and five years in prison. And so the wavy-haired Communist "ringleader" was cuffed, shackled, and carted off to the Atlanta Penitentiary—the same prison the feds had sent Mafia mobster Al Capone to in 1932 for tax evasion. Unlike Capone, Dennis did not die in prison. He served three years and nine months of his sentence—from July 22, 1951, to March 1, 1955—having received time off for good behavior.[111]

Meanwhile, Judge Medina basked in the glow of his national celebrity. The majority will was clearly on his side—over 50,000 congratulatory letters came his way from all around the world. He was out and about, speaking on the "spiritual quality of justice." As on the occasion of a speech he gave before the Georgia Bar Association, whenever he spoke he wove the topics of God and good into his discussion of the *Dennis* trial. "I do not know why," he said in May 1953, "a judge should be ashamed to seek guidance and strength from Almighty God. According to my way of looking at things, that is precisely what a judge should do." Immediately thereafter, he referred to the "trial of the Communists." With religious fervor, he declared: "In some way, which will always remain a mystery to me, the spark had been fired and a great spiritual force had been released, and I was feeling it. I was the man who felt the impact of that force."[112]

A radically different spark continued to fire up Eugene Dennis. As national secretary of the CPUSA, Dennis continued to have his run-ins with legislative investigative committees. And he was still thumbing his nose and invoking his right to remain silent when he appeared before the Senate's Internal Security Subcommittee in December 1959. But on that occasion, his interrogators were less concerned about what he was doing than what was being done to him. Was it true that the Party was about to "dump" him as its leader? The answer came soon enough as the Party faithful gathered at the Hotel Theresa in Harlem for their national convention. Gus Hall, one of the original twelve codefendants, delivered the keynote address; Dennis was too ill to attend. No matter; the guard was being changed. Eugene Dennis was on his way out.

By June 1960, the veteran radical—a onetime electrician, teamster, carpenter, lumberjack, and longshoreman—had checked into Mount Sinai Hospital in New York to undergo an operation for lung cancer. He lived another eight months, dying on January 31, 1961. He was fifty-six.

The doctrinal and practical reach of the *Dennis* case was curbed somewhat in Eugene Dennis's own lifetime. Nonetheless, the *Dennis* precedent stood, replete with its affirmation of the majority opinions in *Gitlow* and *Whitney*. The more modern era of free speech had not yet arrived. Indeed, being a Marxist and preaching Communism could still be almost as hazardous to one's well-being as the cigarette smoking that killed Eugene Dennis.

THE ROAD AWAY FROM *DENNIS:* MODEST PRECEDENTS

In its majesty, the law moves slowly. Increment by increment by increment is its *modus operandi*. Swift and monumental changes are the rare exception. And so the rule of *Dennis v. United States* remained largely intact, though between 1957 and 1961 it was "refined" a bit in three Supreme Court cases that curbed some of its more oppressive applications.

All three majority opinions were authored by Justice John M. Harlan II—that grand defender of judicial restraint who approached the law on a case-by-case basis and thereafter *balanced* state interests against individual ones. Like Learned Hand in the *Masses* case, Justice Harlan's key rulings were *statutory* ones, interpretations of the Smith Act. Though two of Harlan's rulings certainly had important free-speech ramifications, they were not, strictly speaking, First Amendment pronouncements. And like the younger Hand, in those two cases Harlan construed the statute so as to make the prosecution of subversive advocacy and membership in subversive groups much more difficult than under the regime of *Dennis*.

Yates v. United States (1957) involved fourteen leaders of the Communist Party in California. They were indicted in 1951 under the Smith Act for conspiring to advocate and teach the duty and necessity of overthrowing the government by force and violence, and to organize as the CPUSA. It was alleged they did all this with the intent of causing the overthrow of the government by force and violence as speedily as circumstances would permit. The indictment charged that the conspiracy originated in 1940 and continued down to the date of the indictment. All fourteen defendants were convicted after a jury trial, and their convictions were sustained by the Court of Appeals. The Supreme Court disagreed. Under *Dennis*, "advocacy of violent action" in the abstract was enough to sustain a conviction, provided there was *some* proof of intent to overthrow the government. For Harlan, writing for a unanimous Court (seven to zero), such an interpretation of the Smith Act was too restrictive, too punitive. For the statute to apply, he wrote, "those to whom advocacy is addressed must be urged to *do* something, rather than merely to *believe* in something."[113]

In *Scales v. United States* (1961), Justice Harlan offered a similar "savings construction" to the Smith Act. This time he gave a somewhat narrow reading to the membership provision of the Act. The "savings" construction in *Scales*, however, was not enough to save the petitioner.

Junius Irving Scales, a former Communist leader in North Carolina, was convicted and sentenced to six years in jail for violating the membership clause of the Smith Act, which made it a crime to belong to any organization that advocated the overthrow of the government by force or violence, knowing the purposes thereof. The indictment charged that from January 1946 to the date of its filing in 1954, the CPUSA was such an organization and that, throughout that period, Scales was a member with knowledge of the Party's illegal purpose, and that he intended thereby to overthrow the government.

Writing for a divided Court (five to four), Harlan declared that the statute required "not only knowing membership, but active and purposive membership, purposive that is as to the organization's criminal ends."[114] In other words, one had to be *active* in the party, *know* of its illegal aims, and have a *specific intent* to bring about those aims. Thus narrowed, the statute did not run afoul of the First Amendment. Here, Harlan believed, those requirements were satisfied. Justice Douglas, in dissent, mocked Harlan's opinion: "When we allow petitioners to be sentenced to prison for six years for being a 'member' of the Communist Party, we make a sharp break with traditional concepts of First Amendment rights and make serious Mark Twain's light-hearted comment that 'It is by the goodness of God that in our country we have those three unspeakably precious things: freedom of speech, freedom of conscience, and the prudence never to practice either of them."[115] Years later, in his autobiography, Douglas was yet more critical: "*Dennis* and *Scales* mark the greatest decline in free speech in the history of the nation."[116]

For Black, also in dissent, Harlan's First Amendment balancing approach to save the Smith Act membership clause from constitutional attack proved too much. To begin with, the Court's constitutional focus was wrong:

This [case], I think, demonstrates the unlimited breadth and danger of the "balancing test" as it is currently being applied by a majority of this Court. Under that "test," the question in every case in which a First Amendment right is asserted is not whether there has been an abridgment of that right, not whether the abridgment of that right was intentional on the part of the Government, and not whether there is any other way in which the Government could accomplish a lawful aim without an invasion of the constitutionally guaranteed rights of the people.[117]

For Black, the test the majority employed would almost always favor the government, the First Amendment notwithstanding:

[The test is] simply whether the Government has an interest in abridging the right involved and, if so, whether that interest is of sufficient importance, in the opinion of a majority of this Court, to justify the Government's action in doing so. This doctrine, to say the very least, is capable of being used to justify almost any action Government may wish to take to suppress First Amendment freedoms.[118]

Finally, in *Noto v. United States* (1961), Harlan employed the same narrowing construction of the Smith Act's membership clause as in *Scales*. This time, however, the result was different and so was the vote (nine to zero).

John Francis Noto's conviction was set aside because the government failed to prove that the Communist Party in the Buffalo area presently advocated forcible overthrow of the government, not as an abstract doctrine but by the use of language reasonably and ordinarily calculated to incite persons to action, immediately or in the future.

While Justice Black joined in the judgment, he could not join in the logic of what Harlan had done: "I cannot join an opinion which implies that the existence of liberty is dependent upon the efficiency of the Government's informers. I prefer to rest my concurrence in the judgment reversing petitioner's conviction on what I regard as the more solid ground that the First Amendment forbids the Government to abridge the rights of freedom of speech, press and assembly."[119]

The bottom line in these cases was mixed news. "The Court's opinions were carefully limited and did not give the government a blank check," wrote Anthony Lewis for the *New York Times*. That was the first part of the news. "Nevertheless, the decisions," he added, "were substantial victories for the government—the most important legal victories it has had in the internal security field in many years."[120] That was the other part of the news.

By 1961, then, free-speech law concerning advocacy was all over the doctrinal map. There was the *Masses* statutory free-speech approach that had been ignored in *Schenck* and its progeny, and then adopted and reformulated in a less speech-protective way in *Dennis*. There was the bad tendency formula that seemed to have been killed in *Schenck* (but was not), only to be reborn in *Gitlow*. There was the reinvigorated clear and present danger test articulated by Holmes in his *Abrams* dissent but rejected by the majority of the Court in that case and others leading up to and including *Dennis*. The fact of mere association with Communists was enough to trump First Amendment rights under the *Whitney* rule, which was reaffirmed in *Scales* yet questioned in *Noto*. And Brandeis's "imminent danger"/ emergency formulation standard, as set forth in his *Whitney* concurrence, did not seem to be going anywhere.

Along the way, the Court often deferred to the arbitrary conclusions of juries and lawmakers concerning the dangers of a given type of expression. As if that were not enough, the Court could itself take judicial notice of what it perceived to be the dangers of a particular kind of expression. In addition, the Smith Act and Internal Security Act survived constitutional challenge, this at a time when government employees were losing their jobs because of their political beliefs, and bar applicants like George Anastaplo (see chapter 1) were being denied admission for the same reason. All in all, it was a rather bleak period in the history of free speech in America. It was, as some have come to see it, the final dark before the dawn. A new day was about to be born.

CHANGIN' TIMES: DEVALUING *DENNIS*

The members of the Emergency Civil Liberties Committee (ECLC) gathered at the Hotel Americana. They were there—every leftist one of them—to attend ECLC's annual dinner. On Friday, December 13, 1963, fourteen hundred paying guests arrived at the Grand Ballroom in New York City to celebrate the 172nd anniversary of the ratification of the Bill of Rights. That evening's Tom Paine Award would go to a young singer, song-writer, poet, and protestor, Bob Dylan. Back then, he had only two albums—*Bob Dylan* (1962) and *The Freewheelin' Bob Dylan* (1963). The latter included "Blowin' in the Wind," a protest song that would become a generational anthem.

Twelve years earlier, 150 clergy, educators, and professional people[121] had launched the ECLC. They were worried about increasing attacks on civil liberties, specifically under the Smith Act. The ECLC's purpose was to fill the void left by other civil liberties groups unwilling or unable to defend those targeted by the HUAC. Events like its annual Bill of Rights dinner helped fill the ECLC's coffers. There was, after all, never enough money to wage a full constitutional counterattack against Red-baiters determined to imprison Communists like Eugene Dennis. Besides, the *Yates* and *Noto* precedents notwithstanding, *Dennis* was still the supreme law of the land, which meant that the Smith Act could still be tapped to round up those who engaged in dissident expression.

"During the course of the evening," reports Mike Marquese, "Dylan drank heavily. When he got to the rostrum, he improvised a speech that managed to offend just about everyone in the house." But that sort of thing was to be expected in a crowd of free-speech enthusiasts. Still, there was a limit, one that the free-spirited troubadour crossed when, three weeks after the Kennedy assassination, he said: "I'll stand up and to get uncompromisable about it, which I have to be honest, I just got to be, as I got to admit that the man who shot President Kennedy, Lee Oswald, I don't know exactly where, what he thought he was doing, but I got to admit that I too—I saw something of myself in him."[122] Boos. Hisses. Anger. He had gone where neither liberal nor conservative dared to go, to the altar of the sacred memory of a just-slain American leader...and he defiled it. Then, with true outcast spirit, the young Dylan closed his rambling remarks with a remorse-less quip: "I do not apologize for being me nor any part of me."[123] It was this sort of speak-your-mind kind of thing that gave the ECLC a bad name. It confirmed the fear, true or not, that Communists and their defenders actually hated America and welcomed its destruction by any means, including assassination. And so, Smith Act prosecutions continued, though their numbers decreased as the Bob Dylan era came alive. The "times were a changin.' "

The Warren Court was also coming alive. Ever since Arthur Goldberg (1908–1990) had joined the Court in 1962, a "liberal" voting bloc had been developing, especially in constitutional cases. That bloc, which was often sympathetic to First Amendment claims, consisted of Chief Justice Earl Warren (1891–1974) and Justices Goldberg, Brennan, Black, and Douglas. By 1965, they would be joined by Justice Abe Fortas (1910–1982), another liberal vote.

In 1964, America finally turned a First Amendment corner with the ruling of New York Times v. Sullivan (see chapter 8). Its generous and rights-affirming com-mitment to "robust" expression set the tone for a new era of free-speech sensi-tivity. That commitment was fortified when Justice Brennan, the author of Sullivan, spoke for the Court in Keyishian v. Board of Regents (1967). There, the justices struck down, by a five-to-four vote, a New York teacher loyalty oath requirement. Mere knowing membership, the Court held, without a specific intent to further the unlawful aims of an organization, is not a constitutionally adequate basis for punishing someone. The Keyishian holding was yet another attack at the edifice of the Smith Act and Dennis v. United States, the case that but-tressed it.

One other attack, a major one, came on June 9, 1969. That day must have been one of delirious joy for the ECLC's members. For that was the day the Court handed down its unanimous ruling in Brandenburg v. Ohio and reversed Whitney v. California (1927), the case that had upheld a California criminal

syndicalism law that outlawed the advocacy of violence as a means of achieving political or industrial reform. Now, in a terse per curiam opinion, the justices struck down a similar Ohio law.[124] Equally remarkable, they struck a blow
at the constitutional structure of *Dennis.* A new First Amendment standard
had been erected. The Court, as professors Jerome Barron and Thomas
Dienes have observed, "achieved the feat of re-formulating the clear and present danger doctrine without mentioning the words 'clear and present
danger.'"[125]

The new test reinvigorated Judge Hand's *Masses* incitement formula,[126] fortified the old clear and present danger test, and abandoned the problematic gloss
placed on the latter by the *Dennis* Court. Even more incredibly, the *Brandenburg*
Court cited *Dennis* to support its holding. According to *Brandenburg's* per curiam[127] statement,

> later decisions have fashioned the principle that the constitutional guaran-
> tees of free speech and free press do not permit a State to forbid or proscribe
> advocacy of the use of force or of law violation except where such advocacy
> is directed to inciting or producing *imminent lawless* action and is *likely* to
> incite or produce such action....As we said in *Noto v. United States* "the
> mere abstract teaching...of the moral propriety or even moral necessity for
> a resort to force and violence, is not the same as preparing a group for violent
> action and steeling it to such action." A statute which fails to draw this dis-
> tinction impermissibly intrudes upon the freedoms guaranteed by the First
> and Fourteenth Amendments. It sweeps within its condemnation speech
> which our Constitution has immunized from governmental control.[128]

Under the *Brandenburg* test, then, advocating lawless action is not per se
unprotected expression. Rather, it can be prohibited *only* when the following
occur:

1. Expression is directed to inciting "imminent lawless action."
2. Expression is "likely" to produce such action.
3. There is a "specific intent" to bring about such results.

It was a feat akin to magic. "If *Dennis* stands for anything," Kent Greenawalt has
commented, "it is that lawless action need not be imminent, so that the Court's
citation of that case as a basis for the announced principle must be disingen-
uous."[129] Ironically, the *Brandenburg* Court took something of the same kind of
interpretative liberties with the *Dennis* precedent that the *Dennis* Court had taken
with the 1919–27 line of clear and present danger precedents. But this time, the
interpretive turn of the Court had ratcheted up free-speech freedoms. The

Brandenburg test is, as Professor Gunther has noted, "the most speech-protective standard yet evolved by the Supreme Court." Still, it was not enough for Justice Black. In his concurring opinion[130] in *Brandenburg*, the aging Alabama complained: "the 'clear and present danger' doctrine should have no place in the interpretation of the First Amendment."[131]

In Black's absolutist mind, not even this highly speech-protective variation of the clear and present danger test was sufficient to honor the command of the First Amendment. This line of cases reveal, then, just how absolutist Black's jurisprudence could be, insofar as he seemed, in some people's eyes, to throw concerns about danger to the wind. If Black was less than absolutist in other areas (see, e.g. chapter 7), he gave no dime when it came to political speech.

Gunther's approving nod at the level of free-speech protection offered under *Brandenburg* was shared by many First Amendment advocates who saw the faithful application of that standard as a way to maximize freedom, short of subjecting the political order to any and all sorts of imminent dangers. Consistent with that understanding, in *Watts v. United States* (1969) the Court invoked the First Amendment to protect the speech of a draft demonstrator who, at a public rally, said: "If they ever make me carry a rifle the first man I want to get my sights on is [President] L.B.J." Likewise, in *Hess v. Indiana* (1973), the Court set aside the disorderly-conduct conviction of an antiwar protestor who said: "We'll take the fucking street later." Finally, in *NAACP v. Claiborne Hardware Co.* (1982), the justices invoked *Brandenburg* to reverse an award of damages ($1,250,699, plus interest) arising out of remarks made during an NAACP boycott of white merchants in Claiborne, Mississippi. The boycott was largely supported by speeches encouraging nonparticipants to join it and by nonviolent picketing. Still, some acts and threats of violence did occur. For example, civil rights activist Charles Evers said: "If we catch any of you going in any of them racist stores, we're gonna break your damn neck."

For all the applause that Justice Holmes has garnered for his remarkable *Abrams* dissent, it is well to remember that the law he set in motion in, before, and after *Schenck* carried the day for a half-century, influencing along the way hostile First Amendment opinions in *Debs, Frohwerk, Gitlow, Whitney,* and *Dennis,* among other cases. Meanwhile, Judge Hand's conceptual spade work in the *Masses* case was ignored for decades, as were the dissenting opinions of Holmes and Brandeis. And neither Black's nor Douglas's absolutist stances could readily upset what Holmes had laid down as foundational in 1919. Admittedly, the constitutional test changed...and it was a long time coming.

The road from fear to freedom was a harsh one. Many starry-eyed rebels with their retinas fixed on the clouds of utopia either went to jail or were deported for their impassioned rhetoric, their imagined revolutionary might, or their membership in organizations that yearned to have the power their critics credited to them. Few were as fortunate as Benjamin Gitlow or Charlotte Anita Whitney in being pardoned by governors. In short, fear took its toll.

Since the Court announced the *Brandenburg* test some forty years ago, it has never applied that test to deny a First Amendment rights claim.[132] When the dust finally settled, the speech of Communists, radicals, and even revolutionaries was to be protected, at least so long as the present law is honored. The struggle from *Schenck* (1919) to *Brandenburg* (1969) and beyond shows the incredible lengths, albeit over a long period, to which the Court and the nation have gone to tolerate speech that threatens the nation's very survival.

And yet the holding in *Dennis* still stands, at least in a formal sense. Wiecek makes a telling point: "Perhaps, in some grave emergency, its core doctrine—that a group may suffer a diminution of First Amendment protections for its speech and associational rights because of its relationship to a foreign power and/or the content of its doctrines—might once again command the assent of American jurists." While *Brandenburg* seems to have superseded *Dennis*, the latter's "destructive potential," cautions Wiecek, "endures, having whatever persuasive force some future judiciary may assign it, moved by Hand's eloquence and Vinson's affecting sincerity."[133]

If indeed the balance has today tipped in favor of freedom—a balance approximating Black's fearless absolutism—is that a freedom we can afford in our post-9/11 world? In periods of war, cold war, or military "engagement," are we likely to wait up until that very moment when the danger is so *imminent* that it may be impossible to turn back? Given that, it is fair to ask: is *Brandenburg* a wise First Amendment policy? If so, what makes it so?

IDEAS "FRAUGHT WITH DEATH"

Justice Holmes admonished us to "be eternally vigilant against attempts to check the expression of opinions that we loathe and believe to be fraught with death."[134] One could have easily thought that his *Abrams* admonition would cut the other way. Why, after all, should we not rather be vigilant to *protect* ourselves against speech we believe to be "fraught with death"?

Why, as Daniel Farber duly asks, should we accept the *Brandenburg* rule that allows advocates—anarchists, Communists, Klanners, Nazis, homophobic bigots, right-wing extremists, and skinheads—"to spread evil so long as there is no proof of immediate physical danger"?[135] That question fairly well sums up Judge Medina's view of the *Dennis* case. And, it bears asking, is that such an intolerable view of life and law? The answer depends, in notable part, on why we value free speech (see chapter 3). The answer also depends on *how much* we value free speech over other values like security.

In sum, our values determine where and when we draw the line to limit expression. Then again, and pragmatically speaking, *context* very much matters—it can level the best of tests and theories. In all of this, it is important to recall something else Justice Holmes said in *Abrams*. Whatever values we invoke or tests we apply, they are merely "experiment[s], as all life is an experiment." In defending the First Amendment, we must sometimes wager our all in the name of this experiment in freedom. Whether we wager too much, when the risks are too high, remains to be seen. But freedom without risk is unattainable, just as freedom without limit is unworkable.

Saving the NAACP

Robert Carter and the (Civil) Right to Associate

By the time the sun had set on his career of three-plus decades on the Supreme Court, Hugo Black's name had become forever linked to freedom—especially the five freedoms of the First Amendment. Yet at the dawn of that career, Black's name had been synonymous with bigotry of the worst kind.

How the Alabama-born justice journeyed from one pole to the other—and then back again—is not only a fascinating story in the history of American constitutionalism; it is also part of the story about how the First Amendment was used to further the nation's promise of a society committed to liberty and justice for all.

That promise was also actualized, in no small measure, by the efforts of another great American: Robert L. Carter. Together, with the story of Hugo Black, Carter's story is also a partial history of free speech and civil rights, and how two men in particular responded to the challenge of creating a society that could honor both.

A CROSS TO BEAR

On October 1, 1937, at 9:30 P.M., Americans turned on their radios to hear if the rumor was true. On downtown streets, groups assembled around parked cars. In homes and apartments, friends gathered for listening parties. In poolrooms, the cues stopped clicking. As the *Washington Post* reported, "untold millions, from the highest officials in the land to bums sprawling in flop-houses," stopped what they were doing to listen to Supreme Court nominee Hugo Black fight for his professional life. White House officials were stunned and embarrassed by the story. Yet Roosevelt decided not to insist that his nominee withdraw. He did, however, want Hugo Black to make his case to the nation.

About two hours earlier, Black had arrived at a close friend's Washington home, forced to enter via a basement garage door to avoid the hundreds of photographers stationed outside. All the shades in the house were drawn. On a small table in the living room, just underneath an arched doorway, a battery of microphones sat beneath a large bridge lamp. The nominee, forced to cut short a European vacation with his wife when the story broke, appeared calm—his only movement being the repeated brushing back of a wisp of hair that fell across his forehead. Friends, family, and secret service agents huddled closely around him, largely obscuring the forest-print wallpaper that covered the living room's walls. As 9:30 neared, the room fell silent. Black took a final sip of water, returned the glass to the edge of the table, and waited for the engineer's final cue—"One minute. Thirty Seconds. Ten seconds. Okay." The radio broadcast began.

"Ladies and Gentlemen: The Constitution is the supreme law of our country. The Bill of Rights is the heart of the Constitution.... [And] any movement or action by any group that threatens to bring about a result inconsistent with this unrestricted individual right is a menace to freedom.... An effort is being made to convince the people of America that I am intolerant and that I am prejudiced against the people of the Jewish and Catholic faiths, and against members of the Negro race.... I believe that my record as a Senator refutes every implication of racial or religious intolerance."

Then the ex-senator addressed the issue that had brought his future into question. "The insinuations of racial and religious intolerance made concerning me are based on the fact that I joined the Ku Klux Klan about fifteen years ago. I did join the Klan. I later resigned. I never re-joined. What appeared then or what appears now on the records of the organization I do not know." Black concluded tersely: "When this statement is ended my discussion of the question is closed. I believe the character and conduct of every public servant, great and small, should be subject to the constant scrutiny of the people. This must be true if a democracy serves its purpose. It is in this spirit that I now bid those who have been listening to me goodnight."

Six weeks earlier, when the fifty-one-year-old Alabaman was FDR's surprise nomination to the Court, newspapers reported that Black's eleven-year tenure in the U.S. Senate had allegedly been made possible by Klan support. The NAACP, the interracial organization founded in 1909 "to end racial discrimination and segregation in all public aspects of American life," sent a protest letter to the chairman of the Senate Judiciary Committee. The news prompted several senators to oppose Black's nomination. Yet most Court watchers believed the Alabama native's confirmation was a foregone conclusion. The Senate, after all, fosters a clannish camaraderie of its own.

Then, on September 12, *Pittsburgh Post-Gazette* reporter Ray Sprigle published the first of six syndicated articles chronicling Black's undisputed involvement in the Klan. "The cloaked and hooded knights of the Klan," Sprigle reported, "have bestowed upon [Black] the solid gold passport that betokens life membership in the mysterious super-government that once ruled half a continent with terror and violence." Relying on the Klan's official records, Sprigle shared excerpts from a speech the nominee delivered at a special *klorero*—or state meeting—in Birmingham, Alabama, on September 2, 1926—just two months before his election to the U.S. Senate. "I swear," vowed Black, "that I will most zealously and valiantly shield and preserve by any and by all justifiable means and methods...white supremacy."

Reaction to Black's speech was mixed. Robert Carter, a twenty-year-old student at Howard University Law School who listened to the speech in his dorm room, believed such behavior was highly objectionable for a Supreme Court nominee. Similar sentiments sprang up in newspaper editorials across the country. "It is unthinkable that a man who held membership in that organization...should be permitted to take his seat on the bench of the United States Supreme Court," wrote the *St. Louis Globe-Democrat*. "One who associates with bigots...and then is so craven that he allows his friends in a crisis to deny it all can't clear himself...by asserting it was all contrary to his character," thundered the *Boston Post*. By contrast, railroad worker Reece Caton supported the nomination. "I thought he replied with the dignity of a Supreme Court Justice," he told a *Washington Post* reporter. Police detective Cy Embry had also heard enough to feel convinced. "I think he'll make a good Supreme Court Justice. Anyone has a right to join an organization."[1]

Nearly two decades later, long after Hugo Black joined the Court and any concerns about his past associations had disappeared into the rearview mirror of the nation's collective memory, that very issue—the right to join, or associate with, an organization—reappeared in state after state across the South. But the context for this new clash was entirely different.

The impetus for the conflict was the 1954 decision *Brown v. Board of Education*, in which the Court ruled that segregated public institutions were unconstitutional. What followed was a battle for the South itself. On one side were southern lawmakers, intent on resisting the push toward integration by any means necessary. On the other side were organizations like the NAACP, which had been steadily finding and arguing test cases across the former states of the Confederacy in order to cripple the last remaining defenses of the Jim Crow South.

The battlefield itself, at least at first, was a subtle question of law—whether one's right to associate was a constitutionally protected activity. Do the Constitution and Bill of Rights guarantee an individual's right to anonymous membership in an organization? Or is a state within its limits to demand the names and addresses of all individuals who belong to a certain group—say, the NAACP—even if the public release of those names might subject the group's members to racially fueled intimidation, attack, and even death?

Between 1958 and 1969, the U.S. Supreme Court would hear a steady stream of different cases—and consider a range of issues extending beyond the right of association—in which civil rights activists challenged the institutions of southern power. Hugo Black, the man whose nomination had been opposed by the NAACP, would vote on all of them. Robert Carter, the first-year Howard law student at the time of Black's famous radio address, and later the lead attorney for the NAACP, would argue—and win—eight of them. And fittingly, the first of those cases would take place in Black's birthplace, the state of Alabama.

THE LAWYER

Robert Carter was a child of the Great Migration. Born in a small town in Florida in 1917, he and his family moved to Newark, New Jersey, shortly thereafter. When he was just one year old, Carter's father died of a ruptured appendix, leaving Annie Martin Carter alone, at age thirty-three, to support her eight children.

While she worked by day as a domestic, by night Annie Carter worked to instill in her children a desire for a better life. "I told 'em I'd do my part and they had to do theirs," she said. "I felt a mother should live so her children wouldn't be ashamed of her—and the other way around."[2] At the age of sixteen, Annie Carter's youngest child, Robert, moved to Pennsylvania to attend Lincoln University. And in the fall of 1937, the same year Hugo Black admitted to his past life as a Klansman, Robert Carter enrolled in Howard University Law School. Not long after arriving in D.C., the quiet first-year student entered the halls of the U.S. Supreme Court for the first time. Howard Law School's dean, Charles Hamilton Houston, was arguing the NAACP's first case to reach the Court—a case revolving around an African American student's efforts to be admitted to the University of Missouri's law school[3]—and Carter was eager to experience the gallantry of the Court first-hand.

That experience left a lasting impression...for surprising reasons. When Houston rose to deliver his oral remarks, Justice James McReynolds—the Kentucky-born jurist and anti-Semite who refused to shake hands with his Jewish colleague, Louis Brandeis—spun his chair around and turned his back to the

African American attorney. "When it happened," Carter explained, years later, "what's most remarkable is that there was no reaction in the Court—even from me. But at that time, as far as Black people were concerned, we were all plagued by such low expectations of what to expect from white people in the public square."[4]

After graduating from Howard, the young scholar earned a fellowship to study at Columbia University. His intellectual focus was on America's founding principles and the nation's current struggles to better reflect the wisdom and justice of those founding documents. "In my judgment," Carter recalled, "the essential preservative of the democratic ingredients of our society was the First Amendment."[5] Intent on learning more, the young graduate applied for admission to Columbia's law school.

Despite Carter's having graduated magna cum laude from Howard, Columbia's dean tried to dissuade Carter from enrolling, so doubtful was he that a black student could handle the workload. Emboldened by their lack of faith that he could be successful, Carter entered Columbia in the fall of 1940. Bearing the burden that accompanied being the first African American enrolled in the graduate department, the slightly built scholar completed his thesis on the essentiality of the First Amendment for the preservation of a democratic society. Decades later, the ideas contained in that thesis would help Carter frame the arguments that expanded the legal protections of the First Amendment and helped the NAACP strike back against the segregationist impulses of the South. Back in 1941, however, he filed the paper away, and he didn't look at it again for some sixteen years. There was a war to fight, after all, and Robert Carter had been drafted. It proved to be a life-changing experience. "I thought I was pretty well balanced regarding the race problem," Carter recounted in Richard Kluger's *Simple Justice.* "But once I got in the Army, the thing was ground into my face everywhere I turned: blacks acting as lackeys to whites, and whites acting oppressively toward blacks." Carter's insistence on being treated the same as whites of equal rank led to a series of transfers and, eventually, an effort to get him discharged. In total, he says, the experiences "made a militant of me, [and] instilled in me a fierce determination to fight against racism with all my intellectual and physical strength."

In 1944, Carter obtained his release from the Army and joined the New York offices of the NAACP's Legal Defense Fund as chief legal assistant to its director, Thurgood Marshall. The great grandson of a slave and later the first African American to serve on the U.S. Supreme Court, Marshall, like Carter, received his B.A. at Lincoln University and his law degree at Howard. A giant of a man with a keen mind and a deep baritone voice, Marshall joined the NAACP immediately after graduating from Howard, largely at the urging of Charles Hamilton Houston, Howard's dean and the man forced to address Justice McReynolds' back in the first NAACP case to reach the Court.

THE BIRTH OF THE NAACP

It was an exciting time to work at the NAACP. As the celebrated poet Langston Hughes wrote in his 1962 book *Fight for Freedom*, "the most famous initials in America are N.A.A.C.P....Not a week goes by but that somewhere the lawyers of the NAACP are in court defending its members against arrest, fine or imprisonment."

It had taken a long time to reach that point. The roots of the interracial organization date back as far as 1830, the year of the first National Negro Convention in Philadelphia—home to the largest number of free blacks in the United States at the time. The purpose of that first convention was clear: to respond to "the oppression of our brethren in a country whose republican constitution declares 'that all men are born free and equal.'" Other ideas fundamental to the modern NAACP had aged roots. In 1847, well over a century before the *Brown* decision set the stage for the last great battle for the American South, Negro delegates in Troy, New York, urged students of color to seek admission to white colleges. And two years later, at a meeting in Ohio, attendees asked for educational rights "in common with others, for we pay school taxes in the same proportion [and we are] "entitled to all privileges—moral, mental, political and social—to which other men attain."[6]

It was not until 1905, however, that the call was made for a much more systematized response to the forces of white supremacy. It came from W. E. B. Du Bois, the Harvard-educated African American scholar who presciently predicted that the problem of the twentieth century in America would be "the problem of the color-line." Writing from his offices at Atlanta University, Dubois outlined his vision:

> The time seems more than ripe for organized, determined and aggressive action on the part of men who believe in Negro freedom and growth.... I write you to propose a conference during the coming summer for the following purposes: 1. to oppose firmly the present methods of strangling honest criticism, manipulating public opinion, and centralizing political power by means of the improper and corrupt use of money and influence. 2. To organize thoroughly the intelligent and honest Negroes throughout the United States for the purpose of insisting on manhood rights, industrial opportunity and spiritual freedom. 3. To establish and support proper organs of news and public opinion.[7]

In response to Du Bois's proposal, twenty-nine leading black scholars, ministers, editors, and community leaders from across the country met in Niagara Falls, New York, to map out a more far-reaching strategy, forming an organization called the Niagara Movement. By 1908, public rallies in support of the movement were being held in numerous American cities. And on February 12, 1909—the centenary of Abraham Lincoln's birth—sixty prominent Americans,[8] both black and white, urged more Americans to join the struggle. "The Celebration of the Centennial of the birth of Abraham Lincoln," the call read, "will fail to justify itself if it takes no note of and makes no recognition of the colored men and women for whom the Great Emancipator labored to assure freedom.... Hence we call upon all the believers in democracy to join in a National Conference for the discussion of present evils, the voicing of protests, and the renewal of the struggle for civil and political liberty."

The resulting conference began on May 30, 1909, and ended with the establishment of a new National Negro Committee. A year later, the committee chose a new name, the National Association for the Advancement of Colored People, or NAACP. Incorporated in the state of New York, the group announced its official purpose:

> To promote equality of rights and eradicate caste or race prejudice among the citizens of the United States; to advance the interest of colored citizens; to secure for them impartial suffrage; and to increase their opportunities for securing justice in the courts, education for their children, employment according to their ability, and complete equality before the law.[9]

By the time Robert Carter joined Thurgood Marshall's NAACP staff in 1944, a major internal policy debate was under way. On one side, key officials in the national NAACP office were seriously considering a frontal assault on the South's segregationist policies in public institutions, particularly its schools. On the other side, many local leaders were not so sure. Would white-dominated courts ever support such a significant cultural sea change? Furthermore, wouldn't desegregation destroy black institutions? With these reservations in mind, the issue became whether the NAACP's focus in the courts should be on contesting generalized systems of inequality or on particular cases of institutionalized segregation.

As early as 1946, the NAACP had explored the viability of pursuing the legal argument that segregation was unconstitutional.[10] But beginning in 1950, it shifted its strategy to a full frontal assault on institutionalized segregation. In April, Marshall and Carter argued separate cases before the U.S. Supreme Court on the same day.

The first case was brought by Herman Sweatt, a Houston mail carrier who, four years earlier, had been rejected from Texas's state law school on racial grounds. Sweatt was told he could attend an alternative black law school, housed in a basement, instead. In response, Sweatt challenged the state. By the time the Court heard the case, the bespectacled, balding mailman was in effect also challenging the laws of eleven southern and border states, all of which had filed amicus briefs supporting the Lone Star state's policy. Marshall argued the case before a packed courthouse.

Just two months later, the Court announced that, by a unanimous vote, it could not "find substantial equality in the educational facilities offered white and Negro law students by the state." The Court ordered that Sweatt be granted admission to the University of Texas Law School.[11] It was the first time the U.S. Supreme Court ordered a state to admit a black person to an all-white educational institution.

The same day in April, Carter argued the case of George McLaurin, an elderly black teacher who had applied for admission to the University of Oklahoma's doctoral program in education in 1948. Although the university admitted McLaurin in 1949, it forced him to occupy an anteroom separate from the regular classroom of the rest of the students. McLaurin was also made to sit at a solitary desk behind a pile of newspapers in the library, and he was assigned a different lunch hour—and a different lunchroom—from his white classmates. The NAACP felt the *McLaurin* case was significant because the facts of the case clearly isolated the segregation question. For Carter, the case also marked his first appearance before the justices. As he recalled in a November 2005 interview on C-SPAN, "I was frightened but arrogant."

The justices unanimously agreed with the young lawyer's argument. The university's actions, they ruled, "impair and inhibit [McLaurin's] ability to study, to engage in discussion and exchange views with other students, and, in general, to learn his profession."

Following the rulings in those two decisions, Carter, Marshall, and the other key lawyers of the Fund were jubilant. "The feeling had been that if we could win *McLaurin*," Carter said, "we could win it all." If the highest court in the land believed a state could not segregate anyone at a public institution because of his race, logic followed that it should also be illegal to segregate people in *separate* institutions. As Marshall said in a letter to a friend, "the decisions are replete with road markings telling us where to go next."[12]

On June 21, 1951, those road markings led Bob Carter to board a train to Topeka, Kansas, to learn more about the case of Linda Brown, a ten-year-old African American girl who was forced, like so many other young students of color in her hometown and across the South, to attend a separate black-only school.

THE BATTLE LINES ARE DRAWN

The Court announced its ruling in *Brown v. Board of Education* on May 17, 1954. After nearly sixty years of enduring the legal shame of *Plessy v. Ferguson*, the 1896 decision in which the Court ruled that separate facilities were constitutional so

long as they were equal, the nation learned that state-sponsored racial segregation no longer had a place in modern America.

"The Supreme Court decision is the greatest victory for the Negro people since the Emancipation Proclamation," wrote Harlem's *Amsterdam News*. "This means the beginning of the end of the dual society in American life and the system of…segregation that supports it," predicted the *Chicago Defender*. Thurgood Marshall, who argued the case, was even more to the point: "I was so happy I was numb."

While one side celebrated, the other mourned. May 17 became known across the South as "Black Monday." Herman Talmadge, the governor of Georgia, pre-dicted that the *Brown* decision would lead to "the mongrelization of the races." And thirty-four-year-old white citizen Bryant Bowles announced the formation of a new organization, the National Association for the Advancement of White People, warning that "my daughters will never attend a school with Negroes so long as there is breath in my body and gunpowder will burn."

As civil rights historian John Salmond has noted, "after *Brown*, nothing could ever be the same." A northern-based Supreme Court told southern states their policies of institutionalized racism could no longer exist in modern America. Yet southern states were not ready to give up their way of life.

With both sides entrenched, acts of extreme ugliness—and bravery—were sure to follow. Three months after the decision, a young Chicago-area boy named Emmett Till was brutally murdered in retaliation for whistling at a white woman in a Mississippi candy store. In December of that year, a young woman named Rosa Parks refused to give up her seat on the Cleveland Avenue bus of the Montgomery City Lines, igniting a public transportation boycott that further divided the first capital of the Confederacy along racial lines. And on March 12, 1956, nearly one hundred members of Congress presented a formal condemnation of the *Brown* decision that became known as the Southern Manifesto. "The unwarranted decision of the Supreme Court in the public school cases is now bearing the fruit always produced when men sub-stitute naked power for established law," it read. The *Plessy* decision, the sign-ers argued, was "founded on elemental humanity and commonsense, for parents should not be deprived by Government of the right to direct their lives and education of their own children. We reaffirm our reliance on the Constitution as the fundamental law of the land," they concluded. And "we pledge ourselves to use all lawful means to bring about a reversal of this decision which is contrary to the Constitution and to prevent the use of force in its implementation."[13]

One organization in particular drew the focus of the southern states' ire over *Brown*: the NAACP. Bob Carter, the skinny kid from New Jersey, was ready for the fight.

THE JUDGE

Whereas Robert Carter was a child of the Great Migration, Montgomery circuit judge Walter Burgwyn Jones was a child of the Old Confederacy. His father, a solider in General Robert E. Lee's army, had carried the flag of truce from Lee to Grant at Appomattox. When Montgomery staged a reenactment of the swearing-in of Jefferson Davis on the centennial of the Confederacy's founding, Judge Jones administered the oath of office. The youngest person in Alabama ever elected to the circuit court bench, by 1960 Jones had served almost forty years, long enough to author the state's seminal text on trial practice, and long enough to publicly proclaim his belief in the inherent inferiority of African Americans without fear of reprisal.

Walter Jones saw in the *Brown* decision the seeds of the South's undoing. Six months into the Montgomery boycott, he ruled that since the Supreme Court hadn't outlawed bus segregation *yet*, the city's bus company—crippled by the civil disobedience and eager to strike a compromise—must abandon its new integration plans. "A situation of tension and unrest has been created in the city of Montgomery," he wrote, "which is likely to explode into violence at any time, if not restrained."[14]

Less than a month later, on June 1, 1956, Walter Jones found a more effective way to fight back: instead of influencing local bus companies, he'd put the NAACP out of business. Bob Carter remembers: "A number of the segregating states reacted to *Brown* by threatening rebellion," he wrote in his memoir, *A Matter of Law*. "In addition to the empty bombast, a number began targeting the NAACP for destruction. . . . Many segregationists believed that getting rid of the NAACP would solve the problem."[15]

Walter Jones was one of them. So was Alabama's attorney general, John Patterson, who asked Jones for a temporary injunction against the NAACP, charging them with organizing and financing both the bus boycott in Montgomery and the attempts of two African American women to seek employment at the University of Alabama. "We cannot stand idly by and raise no hand to stay these forces of confusion," Patterson proclaimed, "who are trying to capitalize upon racial factors for private gain or advancement." Patterson's request outraged NAACP executive secretary Roy Wilkins, who remarked in the *Washington Post*: "These allegations appear to be efforts to deny the right of protest against intolerable and degrading treatment of citizens and to deny also the right of organized protest and legal action in the courts." Jones issued the order anyway, announcing that he "intend[ed] to deal the NAACP . . . a mortal blow from which they shall never recover."[16]

As a result of the injunction, the NAACP was barred from conducting business "of any description or kind" in the state; from soliciting new members or accepting contributions from old ones; and even from filing the necessary papers "for the purpose of qualifying to do business" in Alabama. There was, in fact, only one way the state of Alabama would let the New York–based organization continue: if its attorney general received from the NAACP a full list of the names and addresses of all its Alabama members.

Marshall, worried that resisting a direct legal order would do more harm than good to the NAACP's overall goals, planned to comply and turn over the lists. Carter persuaded him otherwise. "I was convinced to the point of passionate belief," he said, "that we could not give the names and addresses of our members to the state. To do so would expose our members to the threats of lost jobs, physical violence, even loss of life, and would risk serious danger to their families. Moreover, if we complied with the state's request, the organization would no longer be able to recruit members in the state. It would be finished in Alabama. All black people would be afraid to join for fear their names would be given to the local officials."[17]

The segregationist strategy was a clever counterpunch to *Brown*. And it caught on. At about the same time Robert Carter traveled south to appear for the first time before Judge Jones, the Florida legislature considered two new bills: one that would set up a committee to investigate the NAACP's activities in the state, and another that would grant local control to communities interested in setting up a private school system to preserve racial segregation. Although the second bill drooped and died, the first became Florida law on August 21, 1956.

The same summer, the Virginia legislature added a slightly different wrinkle to the legal assault, enacting a package of laws (or "chapters") that took aim at the NAACP's legal strategy. Carter has explained that strategy in his memoir, using the integration of state colleges as a model: "Typically, NAACP lawyers at the national level would announce that the organization was now prepared to sponsor litigation outlawing segregation in state colleges. The branches would be asked to recruit qualified applicants to apply for admission to a state college." When admission was refused, the NAACP would launch a lawsuit and undertake fund-raising drives to cover its costs. In this way, said Carter, "the NAACP conceived the action, secured the plaintiffs, provided the lawyers, prepared and filed the necessary court documents, and argued the matter before the court." Virginia's new laws challenged that approach, making it a crime to pay another person's legal expenses—unless the person paying the expenses was a relative or had a direct "pecuniary interest"—and ordering all groups that advocated racial integration to make broad disclosures of their contributors and membership rolls. The NAACP immediately contested the laws in federal court.

Meanwhile, other states forced the NAACP into court. In September 1956, Texas attorney general John Ben Shepperd obtained a preliminary order that barred the NAACP from operating in his state. Denouncing the organization for "peddl[ing] false hopes" and underwriting the financial needs of their clients, Shepperd said that the 'p' in NAACP did not stand for 'people,' but "Pick the Place, Prepare the setting, Procure the Plaintiffs, and Push them forward like Pawns." A week later he ordered armed Texas rangers to seize membership lists from the homes of NAACP officials. As Carter recalls, "the organization was under attack in almost all the eleven former Confederate states," most of which "passed legislation redefining barratry to cover and outlaw the NAACP litigation strategy."

Despite the breadth of attacks against its reason for being, the NAACP's primary battleground—both on the streets and in the courts—was Alabama. On July 25, 1966, Judge Jones denied the NAACP's request to dissolve the Alabama injunction and fined it $10,000 for contempt of court. The amount would grow to $100,000, he announced, unless the NAACP handed over the names and addresses of its 14,566 Alabama members within five days. Carter returned to Alabama to urge Judge Jones to hear the NAACP's argument before issuing such a judgment. Jones, predictably, refused and then abruptly left the bench. "For the first time ever," Carter recalls, "I lost my head in a courtroom"; he called the aging segregationist "incompetent and corrupt, among other choice derogatory terms." Jones could have used the young lawyer's emotional outburst against him. Carter believes he ignored the comments because the Alabama judge "had already achieved [his] objective of shutting down the NAACP in the state, thus freeing [him] ... from efforts to eliminate racial segregation."

Judge Jones's brazen actions drew the attention of the *New Republic*, which discussed the case in its August 6, 1956, issue. "This attack on the NAACP is a bushwhacking operation," wrote the editors. "One does not have to hold a brief for the NAACP to conclude that segregationists in the old Confederacy are engaged in the familiar tactic of using the law to defeat the law.... The NAACP is being harried to reveal names and transactions which have nothing to do with the issue of whether it is subject to state regulation but which have everything to do with putting its members and sympathizers at the mercy of White Citizens Council members and other racists who now dominate the life of Alabama as the Klan did 30 years ago."

Hugo Black still remembered those days, although by the time the Supreme Court agreed in May 1957 to hear the NAACP's case from his home state, nearly twenty years had passed since he had been forced to address the nation behind drawn curtains in a friend's living room. In nearly every regard, the black-robed justice had successfully shed the white robe of his past.

Yet despite a promising start to the year—on January 3, Congress passed its first civil rights legislation since Reconstruction—the country could not escape the ghosts of its own racist history. In fact, 1957 featured a full scorecard of injustice. On September 4, Arkansas governor Orval Faubus ordered the state's national guard to prevent nine black students from integrating Central High School in the state's capital city, Little Rock. A pulsing mob of angry whites gathered outside the school each morning to menace the young black students, while reporters and TV cameras recorded the drama. As the standoff intensified, the plight of the "Little Rock Nine" became, in the words of historian Taylor Branch, "the first on-site news extravaganza of the modern television era."

Later that fall, on Halloween, Little Rock officials expanded the fight, ordering the arrest of all NAACP officers for failing to comply with a recently enacted ordinance requiring certain organizations to make their confidential records available to the public. Just three days earlier, NAACP lawyers had filed a petition in U.S. district court seeking to enjoin the ordinance, which they claimed was a violation of the Fourteenth Amendment. "The action by the council," announced Marshall in a statement to the press, "is another instance of the efforts of the State of Arkansas to use judicial processes to thwart the Constitution of the United States of America." Fourteen other cities in Arkansas passed similar ordinances.

That left Robert Carter to, among other things, challenge the Arkansas ordinance, seek a declaratory judgment against the new Virginia statutes, and prepare for his argument before the U.S. Supreme Court in the Alabama case. By the end of 1957, the NAACP was involved in twenty-five different cases across the southern states, many of which, according to Carter, "began using a legislative-investigative-committee tactic, purportedly seeking information about our activities." Ironically, several states relied on extant laws originally passed to circumscribe the efforts of the Ku Klux Klan. The states even had Supreme Court precedent on their side—a 1928 decision, *Bryant v. Zimmerman*, in which the Court held that the state of New York could force the Klan to publicly file its membership lists. Such precedents and the tactics based on them, Carter thought, provided, ironically, both a useful legal argument and "a skillful technique to terrorize our unsophisticated members."

The battle was on. The matter came before the Supreme Court on January 15, 1958, in the case of *NAACP v. Alabama*.

THE COURT RECOGNIZES A NEW RIGHT

In addition to his other duties, Judge Walter Jones wrote a weekly column, "Off the Bench," that appeared in his hometown newspaper. Although the columns touched on a range of topics, two of his favorites were the need for segregation to prevent a mixing of the races, and the importance of state sovereignty to stave off the "unjust" assaults of "radical newspapers and magazines, communists and the federal judiciary." "Columnists and photographers," he wrote one week, "have been sent to the South to take back to the people of the North untrue and slanted tales about the South. Truly a massive campaign of super-brainwashing propaganda is now being directed against the white race, particularly those who envy its glory and greatness."

Jones believed his rulings against the NAACP were part of a cherished southern tradition—safeguarding individualism and state sovereignty. "And [that tradition] is a good thing," he explained in a 1955 speech,

> when the citizen is threatened and harassed on all sides by organizations, groups and federations which insist he be a pawn in the hands of their selfish leaders and associations and do no thinking of his own. The Southerner stands today as his Confederate fathers stood before him, independent and self-reliant and proud of the fact that he is a free American citizen and not a ward of his government.[18]

The judge was not alone in his thinking. Even after the NAACP's contempt fine ballooned to a shocking $100,000, the Alabama Supreme Court twice denied the NAACP's appeals, characterizing its refusal to turn over its membership lists as a "brazen defiance" of state law. Meanwhile, Jones refused to schedule a new trial on the merits of the case, leaving the original restraining order in effect, indefinitely. Carter, out of options in the state of Alabama, appealed the case to the nation's highest court.

Ordinarily, the Supreme Court will not consider cases in which a state court has refused to issue a ruling because the litigant failed to follow the proper procedural rules. But the clear lack of due process in the case[19] prompted the Court to accept Carter's appeal, and brought him before the justices for oral arguments on January 15, 1958. As Carter remarked later, "I argued that our rank-and-file members had the protection of the First Amendment to band together to agitate peacefully for the elimination of segregation and other forms of racial segregation. This right, I argued, could be theirs only if they could do so anonymously."[20]

It was the idea Carter had first developed years earlier, while writing his thesis at Columbia Law School. Two days later, when the justices met in private conference to discuss the case and take a preliminary vote, it was evident the young attorney had been persuasive. "The state has cut into the constitutional rights of NAACP members and put an end to them," began Chief Justice Earl Warren. Hugo Black agreed. "I reverse. The state...should not be allowed to defeat the federal courts. The petitioners were not given a fair trial." Similar votes followed. Frankfurter. Douglas. Burton. Clark. Harlan. Brennan. Whittaker. All agreed that the decision of the Alabama Supreme Court must be reversed.[21] Justice John Marshall Harlan would write for the Court.

"The effect of compelled disclosure of the membership lists," declared Harlan—whose father, also a Supreme Court justice, had provided the only voice of dissent in *Plessy v. Ferguson*—"will be to abridge the rights of its rank-and-file members to engage in lawful association in support of their common beliefs.... Effective advocacy of both public and private points of view, particularly controversial ones, is undeniably enhanced by group association.... It is beyond debate that freedom to engage in association for the advancement of beliefs and ideas is an inseparable aspect of the 'liberty' assured by the Due Process Clause of the Fourteenth Amendment, which embraces freedom of speech."

Although the Court had previously discussed the close connections between the freedoms of speech and assembly, particularly in the 1937 case *DeJonge v. Oregon*, never before had it suggested so emphatically that one's "right to association" was by implication a constitutionally protected form of behavior. By a unanimous vote, the Court had created new doctrine. Justice Harlan set out the two sides of the Court's new balancing test, writing: "state action which may have the effect of curtailing the freedom to associate is subject to the closest scrutiny."[22]

The young Columbia alum was thrilled that his thesis had found such a receptive audience. "I felt going in that I could depend on the votes of Black, Douglas, Brennan and Warren," Carter recalled. "So I directed my argument at Harlan. I believed he was the crucial fifth vote. As I spoke I remember that he got more and more interested. So I felt confident that we would win the case. But I never expected a unanimous ruling." Carter was equally thrilled that Justice Harlan distinguished in his opinion in *NAACP v. Alabama* from the 1928 Ku Klux Klan case, *Bryant v. Zimmerman*, that several southern states had been using as legal cover to cripple the NAACP. The key point, Harlan explained, was that whereas the NAACP's work focused on lawful advocacy, the KKK's activities "involved acts of unlawful intimidation and violence." Furthermore, the KKK "had made no effort to comply with any of the requirements of New York's statute but rather had refused to furnish the State with any information as to its local activities."

There was one small setback in the decision; the Court did not set aside Judge Jones's temporary restraining order. Since the state courts had never properly considered the merits of the NAACP's appeal, Harlan remanded the case to the Alabama Supreme Court "for proceedings not inconsistent with this opinion." Nonetheless, with the *Bryant* decision no longer an effective cover, and with the state supreme court ordered to hear the merits of his appeal, Robert Carter had good reason to feel optimistic. The only thing that could get in his way was outright insubordination from the state judges.

In the North, newspapers lauded the decision. "All Americans, no less than the members of the NAACP, can applaud this decision," editorialized the *Washington Post*. "It keeps open arteries of association and expression through

which the lifeblood of the democratic process can flow." The mood was less cel-
ebratory in Montgomery. Judge Jones announced he would refuse to disqualify
himself from hearing any cases that involved the NAACP, echoing his previous
promise to deliver the organization "a mortal blow...from which they shall
never recover." "No judge could handle a case if he were disbarred for social attitudes," Jones explained. "I am not biased toward the state and I do not show
prejudice toward the NAACP."

The Alabama Supreme Court was similarly straight-faced when, on February
12, 1959, it defied the U.S. Supreme Court's order and reaffirmed Judge Jones's
decision and his $100,000 fine. Claiming that the nine justices were "mistaken" in
their review of the facts, the state court explained that it "has never agreed, and
does not agree, that [the NAACP] has complied with the trial court's order to
produce with the exception of membership."

The assertion was astonishing, but Carter could do no more than wait for a
second ruling from the U.S. Supreme Court. In the meantime, much to the delight
of Judge Walter Jones and the effectiveness of the TRO, NAACP activity in the
state of Alabama essentially ceased to exist.

THE BATTLE FOR THE SOUTH CONTINUES

Even before Alabama's legal insubordination, Bob Carter was working hard to put
out several growing brushfires in other southern states. In September 1958, he
urged the Florida Supreme Court to block a legislative committee charged with
investigating the connections between the NAACP and the Communist Party. A
month later, Arkansas Attorney General Bruce Bennett proposed a "Southern Plan
for Peace" that included, among other things, a promise to emasculate the NAACP.
"The NAACP organizations are at the root of our racial problems," said Bennett.
"The only way I see to restore peace and tranquility to the South is to neutralize the
organizations." One way, he explained, would be to get Congress to withdraw the
NAACP's tax-exempt status. Another would be to prosecute "every lawyer and
individual" who filed integration suits. Bennett even urged the state to rethink its
welfare laws. "It is a matter of record," he alleged, "that some Negro mothers have six
illegitimate children, all by different fathers, and, at the same time, have taken these
welfare checks and paid NAACP dues with the charity money."[23]

By the end of 1958, the NAACP had been ordered to produce its membership
lists in both Florida and Arkansas. As the Supreme Court of Arkansas noted in its
ruling, "the Constitutional Amendments do not guarantee anonymity at all
events.... Other organizations have complied: why should this one have immunity as though it were a favored child?"

Then Carter got the news that, thanks to the Alabama high court's defiance,
the U.S. Supreme Court would rule *again* on *NAACP v. Alabama.* Carter and his

staff were already juggling another case, this one involving the new barratry stat-utes in Virginia. Two years earlier, in 1956, the Virginia legislature passed five statutes ("chapters") that directly impacted the NAACP's method of doing business in the state. Chapter 31 prevented anyone from raising funds to support litigation unless that person had a direct "pecuniary right or liability" or unless he or she had filed a detailed disclosure form; chapter 32 required any organization "whose activities are causing or may cause interracial tension and unrest" to reg-ister with the state; chapter 33 made the solicitation of legal business in which the solicitor was not a direct party a disciplinary offense; chapter 35 made it a misde-meanor to pay another person's legal expenses unless that person was a relative or had a direct pecuniary interest; and chapter 36 prohibited the advocacy of any suits against the state of Virginia.

As Professor Mark Tushnet[24] has written, key parts of the state's argument relied on the legal concept of abstention, a principle that "aimed at making it more difficult for federal courts to hold state statutes unconstitutional." The theory was that abstention would lessen the conflicts between federal courts and state legislatures, and a number of traditional progressive reformers—including Justice Frankfurter—were among the doctrine's loudest supporters. Abstention only made sense, of course, if the state laws in question were unclear. With that in mind, the three-judge federal court responding to the NAACP's appeal had no problem ruling on chapters 31, 32 and 35, which it found both clear…and invalid. The court found chapters 33 and 36 less coherent, however, prompting it to maintain the challenges in an inactive status in order to allow the NAACP some time to get a Virginia court to interpret them first.

Carter filed an action to establish that the two remaining laws were unconsti-tutional, while Virginia Attorney General Albertis Harrison appealed the invali-dation of the other three laws to the U.S. Supreme Court. Much to Carter's disappointment, a majority of the justices agreed in March 1959 that the lower court should have abstained from ruling on *any* of the laws. Justice William Orville Douglas—a 1939 Roosevelt appointee who, by the time he retired in 1975, had served longer than any other justice in the history of the Supreme Court—wrote a stinging dissent. Characterizing the use of abstention in a civil rights case as little more than a delaying tactic, Douglas wrote: "Where state laws make such an assault as these do on our decisions and a State has spoken defi-antly against the constitutional rights of the citizens, reasons for showing deference to local institutions vanish." It was an issue that would return to divide the Court again.

Meanwhile, a month after the U.S. Supreme Court's ruling on the Virginia laws, a new conflict emerged, again in Arkansas. The state legislature had passed a law requiring all public school teachers to take a "loyalty oath" and sign an affidavit listing all their organizational affiliations. It was clear to everyone which organization the state was targeting. As Attorney General Bennett claimed in one newspaper report, "the NAACP has been found to be a captive of the Communist conspiracy by a Special Education Committee of the Arkansas House of Representatives."[25] No such connections had been made. Even so, B. T. Shelton, a black teacher in the Little Rock public school system and a member of the NAACP, refused to sign the affidavit. When his contract was not renewed as a result, he filed suit in federal court on April 25, 1959.

Shelton's suit prompted the NAACP to file a second major case in Arkansas. About that time, the U.S. Supreme Court released a short *per curiam* opinion in which it politely—but firmly—chastised the Alabama Supreme Court for its refusal to abide by the Court's initial decision. Once again, however, the Court stopped short of settling the case itself, demanding instead that Alabama provide the NAACP due process in its appeal of the $100,000 contempt charge. "We assume," the Court tersely announced, "that the State Supreme Court...will not fail to proceed promptly with the disposition of the matters left open under our mandate for further proceedings."

But that good news hardly settled matters. In November 1959, Carter had a another concern—another appearance before the Court, this time to argue, in the case of *Bates v. City of Little Rock*, that Arkansas could not require the NAACP's state officers to turn over its membership lists. The oral arguments in the case seemed to favor him. On February 23, 1960, the Court delivered another unanimous decision. Citing *NAACP v. Alabama*, the justices reaffirmed in *Bates* that "it is now beyond dispute that freedom of association for the purpose of advancing ideas and airing grievances is protected by the Due Process Clause of the Fourteenth Amendment from invasion by the States." In a concurring opinion, Black and Douglas urged the Court to go further. Rejecting the balancing test that Justice Harlan proposed in *NAACP v. Alabama*, Black and Douglas suggested "First Amendment rights are beyond abridgment either by legislation that directly restrains their exercise or by suppression or impairment through harassment, humiliation, or exposure by government." Either way, it was clear that the newly recognized right of the freedom to associate was gaining strength among the members of the Warren Court.

Despite the Court's unequivocal language, the NAACP's right to associate—and the African American community's right to equal treatment—remained in dispute all over the South. Three weeks before the *Bates* decision was announced, four students from North Carolina A&T University sat down at a segregated lunch counter at a Woolworth's store in Greensboro, touching off several months of similar sit-ins and economic boycotts across the former states of the Confederacy. In the same month, Reverend Martin Luther King, Jr., was charged with felony tax evasion in his home state of Alabama.

While the national conflict escalated, Bob Carter and the Fund received some good news. On February 6, a three-judge panel in Louisiana ruled that the NAACP did not have to comply with a state law—originally drafted in 1924 to curb the Ku Klux Klan—requiring the submission of its membership lists. And in Virginia, a Richmond trial court held chapters 31, 32, and 35 to be unconstitutional while upholding chapters 33 and 36. On appeal, the state supreme court then struck down chapter 36 but upheld chapter 33—the law that made the solicitation of legal business in which the solicitor was not a direct party a disciplinary offense.

Virginia, Carter must have thought, was clearly a more hospitable place for justice than Alabama, where the NAACP could not even secure a fair day in court. But he also realized that even though just one statute remained on the books in Virginia, it still threatened the organization's mode of business. Carter appealed the decision to the U.S. Supreme Court. Oral arguments were scheduled for November 8, 1961.

RACISM AND THE LAW OF LIBEL[26]

While Bob Carter and the rest of the Fund staff juggled major cases in Alabama, Arkansas, Florida, Louisiana, and Virginia, Judge Walter Jones found another way to strike back against what he saw as the anti-segregation bias of the northern media. The opportunity came to him in the form of a full-page advertisement, titled "Heed Their Rising Voices," that appeared in the March 29, 1960, edition of the *New York Times*.

The advertisement was a direct solicitation for funds for Dr. King's legal defense against the tax evasion charges in Alabama. Although it mentioned no specific public officials in the state, the ad referred in general terms to "Southern violators of the Constitution" who were "determined to destroy the one man who, more than any other, symbolizes the new spirit now sweeping the South." Similar statements followed, along with the names of sixty-four people listed as the ad's sponsors. In the lower right-hand corner of the advertisement, readers were urged to cut out a coupon and send it with their contributions. The "inaccuracies prompted L. B. Sullivan, the elected Commissioner for Public Safety responsible for overseeing the police and public safety, to charge that the *Times* had defamed him. He was joined," reports Kermit Hall, "by the two other elected commissioners, Mayor Earl James and Frank Parks."

Although the *Times* sent just 394 of its 650,000 subscriptions to Alabama addresses in 1960, one of those copies ended up in the hands of M. Roland Nachman, Jr., who subscribed to the paper. Just thirty-seven at the time, Nachman had already become one of the preeminent libel lawyers in the state and had represented city commissioners recently in a libel suit against a New York magazine.

After receiving both his undergraduate and law degrees at Harvard, Nachman had returned home, where he served as assistant attorney general from 1949 to 1954. By the age of twenty-seven, he had already filed briefs in the U.S. Supreme Court.

As the young libel lawyer, a moderate southern Democrat, scanned the advertisement, he wondered if parts of it were false. He "clipped the page from the newspaper and delivered it to the three city commissioners. He indicated," adds Hall, "to Police Commissioner Sullivan that, even though he was not directly named in the ad, there could be little doubt that he could bring an action against the *Times*." Moreover, adds Hall, Nachman felt the ad was "mean-spirited…and it promised to contribute to an already high level of misunderstanding and distrust." Nachman knew that if parts of the ad *were* false, the *Times* could be sued for "libel per se" under Alabama law. Indeed, Alabama was one of seven southern states at the time that left all false statements unprotected by law; truth was the only available defense to a libel charge. As it turned out, there were several inaccuracies in the ad. The police, for example, had never "ringed" Alabama State's campus; students had been expelled for participating in lunch-counter protests, not for singing "My Country 'Tis of Thee" on the capitol steps; and King had been arrested four times, not six. The bottom line: It looked good for the commissioners and bad for the *Times*.

Around the same period, the *Times* published a two-part story by Harrison Salisbury in which the city of Birmingham was described as the "Johannesburg of America" and a place where press freedom did not exist. "Remember," one local businessman presciently warned Salisbury, "Birmingham is no place for irresponsible reporting. Be careful of what you say and who you mention. Lives are at stake."[27]

Rage spread in Montgomery. And plans for legal action were everywhere in the air. Throughout the months of April and May, the New York newspaper learned that an alarming number of Alabama officials, from small-town city commissioners to the governor himself—were suing for libel. In fact, by June 1960 the *New York Times* faced a total of over $6 million in potential damages—at a time when the paper was financially vulnerable. As *Times* counsel James Goodale put it, enough judgments against the newspaper would provoke "a reasonable question of whether the *Times*, then wracked by strikes and small profits, could survive."[28]

To make matters worse, *Times* lawyers lost a motion to move the trials out of Alabama. Ironically, the attorneys had relied on a leading legal text in the state, *Alabama Pleading and Practice at Law*, to ensure that proper protocols were followed. Yet presiding Judge Walter Jones ruled that the *Times* had committed a procedural mistake, even though Jones himself was the author of the book that had guided the attorneys' actions. It was a devastating blow. The *New York*

Times—the northern newspaper founded in 1851 as a political organ of the Republican Party and a tool in the cause of antislavery—was scheduled to defend against a libel action in an Alabama courthouse, before an Alabama judge and an Alabama jury. The trial was set to begin on November 1, 1960. And the presiding judge was none other than Walter Burgwyn Jones.

THE CAMPAIGN TO KILL THE NAACP CONTINUES

Throughout the summer and early fall of 1960, while presidential candidates John F. Kennedy and Richard M. Nixon raced toward a November vote that was still too close to call, Bob Carter continued to chip away at the southern assault on the NAACP. On June 20, he learned that the U.S. Supreme Court had accepted review of the *Shelton v. Tucker* case from Arkansas. And on August 5—the same day Judge Jones announced that the *Times* had conducted enough business in Alabama to warrant being sued there for libel—Carter learned that the state of Louisiana had requested that the U.S. Supreme Court hear its case seeking to compel the NAACP to turn over its membership lists. (The Court granted the state's request, scheduling oral arguments for the following spring.)

That very summer, Carter began a federal court action to bar Alabama from enforcing its "temporary" injunction against the NAACP. A federal district judge denied the NAACP's request, explaining that he wanted to see what the state courts did first. By this point, more than three years had passed since the NAACP had been able to conduct its business legally in Alabama. In November, Carter returned to Washington for the fourth time, now to argue the *Shelton* case. A month later, the Court announced that the young lawyer's unbeaten streak was still intact—albeit this time by a much narrower margin.

At issue, again, was how much each justice was willing to read between the lines of the state law requiring teachers to list their organizational affiliations. In the Court's private conference, Chief Justice Warren—whose tenure as chief was characterized by a degree of liberal-minded decisions that turned his name into a rallying cry for both the Left and the Right—thought "[t]he language of the statute is just too broad. The rights of association of the school teachers are invaded," he explained, and "requiring information on membership and contributions to church, political party, and social organizations goes too far." Justice Frankfurter disagreed. "The state may certainly search the thought processes of teachers. It is relevant to ask about the organizations to which teachers belong because it is relevant to know the associations teachers have if we are to appraise their fitness." Based on the facts of the case and nothing more, Frankfurter added, "the litigation is premature," a point on which Justice Harlan concurred. "There is no practical way to draw a line," he said. "If a state fires or refuses to hire for a reason having no rational relation to teaching fitness, then as applied the courts may strike it down." But "abuse … can't be assumed."[29]

In the end, Warren's argument prevailed. Justice Potter Stewart wrote the opinion for the five-man majority. "This controversy is not of a pattern with such cases as *NAACP v. Alabama* and *Bates v. Little Rock*," he began. "In those cases the Court held that there was no substantially relevant correlation between the governmental interest asserted and the State's effort to compel disclosure of the membership lists involved." By contrast, Stewart asserted, "there can be no question of the relevance of a State's inquiry into the fitness and competence of its teachers." Then Stewart explained why five justices had ruled against the state anyway. "The vigilant protection of constitutional freedoms is nowhere more vital than in the community of American schools. Such unwarranted inhibition upon the free spirit of teachers … has an unmistakable tendency to chill that free play of the spirit which all teachers ought especially to cultivate and practice."

In dissent, Justice Harlan explained why the Court had split so narrowly on the facts of the case. "It must be emphasized that neither of these cases[30] actually presents an issue of racial discrimination.… I need hardly say that if it turns out that this statute is abused, we would have a different kind of case than those presently before us. All that is now here is the validity of the statute on its face, and I am unable to agree that in this posture of things the enactment can be said to be unconstitutional."

Supreme Court rulings or not, it was clear that some southern states intended to resist any court order to integrate by legal means—unless the federal government forced them to do otherwise. Meanwhile, southern strategists looked for any loophole by which to circumvent integration efforts.

"HIT THEM IN THE POCKETBOOK"

As a new year began, other legal questions emerged. In Alabama, for example, the imbroglio between the *New York Times* and the state reached a new level of discomfort. During the initial libel trial in November 1960, Judge Jones had already proven, in the words of Professor Hall, to be "arbitrary, capricious, and paternalistic." He allowed the Sullivan team's three lawyers and their witnesses to describe blacks in derogatory terms. In the official written transcripts of the case, he made sure that the word "lawyer" appeared before the name of the black attorneys while the word "Mister" preceded the names of the white lawyers. And throughout the proceedings, he relished the stranglehold he had on the mighty northern newspaper. One of the plaintiff's lawyers articulated the central issue during his closing arguments: "Newspapers are very fine things," he said, "but newspapers have got to tell the truth. One way to get their attention and the attention of everybody else is to hit them in the pocketbook."

When it came time to instruct the jury of twelve white men on their duties, Jones told them they need not concern themselves with any questions of libel; the ad, he explained, was clearly libelous per se. That left the men, whose names and photographs had already been published in the city newspaper, just three issues to address: Had the defendants published the advertisement? Were the statements in the ad "of and concerning" L. B. Sullivan? If the answers to the first two questions were yes—as Jones well knew they would be—the only issue remaining for the jury to decide was how much money to award as damages.

Forty minutes later, the jury announced verdicts against both the *Times* and four black Alabama ministers—whose names had been added to the ad's list of signers at the last minute and without their consent—to the tune of $500,000, the full amount Sullivan demanded. When the parties asked for a new trial, Jones scheduled a hearing for February 1961. The *Times* then moved for a continuance, so Jones delayed the hearing another month. But when the ministers' lawyers did not make a separate motion for continuance, Jones—the man who knew the ins and outs of state law so well he had written the state's definitive procedural text— told them they had forfeited their right to a new trial.

Jones's legal maneuver meant that the defendants had to pay the $500,000 judgment against them as soon as it became final. Ralph Abernathy, one of the Alabama ministers and a close confidant of King, had his car impounded by the local sheriff. Later, local officials also auctioned off a small plot of land he owned, prompting Abernathy to seriously consider abandoning the fight and moving North. (When his congregation learned he was thinking of leaving, they took up a collection to buy him a new car. To guard against further seizures, Taylor Branch reports that the flock intended to register the car in "the name of Jesus.")

Then Jones denied the *Times*'s motion for a new trial, leaving the newspaper's fate in the hands of the Alabama Supreme Court. Had the *Times*'s lawyers asked, Robert Carter could have told them what to expect.

A NEW BODY OF FIRST AMENDMENT LAW

In the first few months of 1961, fresh conflicts emerged across the South, leaving the new president, John F. Kennedy, with little time to bask in the glow of his inauguration. On March 2, nearly two hundred black students from South Carolina were arrested for protesting segregation at the state capitol in Columbia. Earlier, police told the marchers "they had a right" to protest there "as long as they were peaceful." But as the crowd grew larger, officers moved in to arrest the pick-eters for breaching the peace.[31] On the same day, the Eighth Circuit Court of Appeals ordered school board officials in Little Rock to speed up their integration efforts, contending that the board had set up a "governmental framework to pre-vent desegregation." And in Mississippi, NAACP officials—including a young field secretary named Medgar Evers—announced an "all-out campaign" against the segregationist forces in that state.

By April, Bob Carter was back before the U.S. Supreme Court to defend the NAACP, this time for refusing to hand over its membership lists to Louisiana's secretary of state. Less than a month later, the Court announced its decision in *Louisiana ex rel. Gremillion v. NAACP*—providing the young civil rights attorney with not just another victory but also the latest addition to a growing body of First Amendment law by which to advance the cause of racial justice. "At one extreme," wrote Justice Douglas, "is criminal conduct which cannot have shelter in the First Amendment. At the other extreme are regulatory measures which, no matter how sophisticated, cannot be employed in purpose or in effect to stifle, penalize, or curb the exercise of First Amendment rights."

Throughout the spring and summer of 1961, while Robert Carter prepared for *two more* arguments before the Court that fall, scores of black and white "Freedom Riders" arrived in the South via interstate buses to test the 1960 Supreme Court decision, *Boynton v. Virginia*, in which the justices had outlawed racial segregation in interstate public facilities, including bus stations. Legally, thanks to the Court's ruling, the riders were not engaging in civil disobedience. Yet volunteers continually braved violent attacks while local police looked the other way. One of the worst cases of violence occurred in Montgomery, where a waiting mob was kept abreast via continual radio updates of the riders' whereabouts, and where Governor John Patterson—the man who, while attorney general, had asked Judge Jones to issue the restraining order against the NAACP—announced: "I refuse to guarantee their safe passage.... [T]he citizens of the state are so enraged that I cannot guarantee protection for this bunch of rabble-rousers."

Despite the intensity of the attacks against the Freedom Riders, President Kennedy failed to even mention them in his second State of the Union address on May 25, 1961. In fact, despite the growing racial revolution at home, Kennedy used his remarks to promote a new "freedom doctrine" in support of other revolutions abroad—in "Asia, Latin America, Africa and the Middle East, the lands of the rising peoples. Their revolution is the greatest in human history," he said, because "they seek an end to injustice, tyranny, and exploitation." Bob Carter and other Americans on the front lines of a second civil war found Kennedy's official disinterest puzzling. But as the executive branch ignored the nation's civil unrest, the judicial branch delivered its *third* ruling in *NAACP v. Alabama*. Once again, the justices debated just how involved in the fight they should be.

The conflict began when Justice Harlan, in the first draft of his opinion, set out to order the Alabama federal district judge to determine whether the state courts were purposely delaying the NAACP's hearing. At that point, Justice Tom Clark[32] cried foul. Robert Carter had not asked the Court to assess if there had been an unconstitutional delay, Clark argued—only whether Judge Jones's "temporary" injunction was unconstitutional. "Other litigants," he argued, "are held to the relief sought without benefit of *sua sponte* action." For Clark, this was no small distinction. If allowed to stand, he explained, Harlan's draft would "result in greater confusion and interminable legislation," proving "useless to the NAACP, improper for this Court and harmful to the administration of justice." Indeed, Clark continued, such an order would result in "two trials, one federal, one state. Why do this," he asked rhetorically, "unless it be to rebuff the State?"

Tom Clark's point troubled several other justices. To resolve the matter, the Court struck a compromise and released a *per curiam* opinion in which it ordered the federal district court to try the case no later than January 2, 1962.

THE SPECTER OF A FIRST AMENDMENT RETREAT

Before he could secure an actual trial date in Alabama, Carter addressed the Supreme Court again, this time in a Virginia case—*NAACP v. Button*. And by this point, the growing concern among some justices was that the Court had crossed the line into judicial activism. This concern made finding consensus in their private conferences even more difficult.

When it came time for a conference vote in the *Button* case, Chief Justice Warren, predictably, still voted to reverse. "The purpose of the statute is obviously to circumvent *Brown*," he said. Black agreed. "This is part of a scheme to defeat the Court's order," he added, and "sooner or later we will have to grapple with these problems in those terms. The NAACP is finished if this law stands." But Justice Frankfurter pushed back. "I can't imagine a worse disservice than to continue being the guardians of the Negroes.... There is nothing in the record to show that this statute is aimed at Negroes as such." Justices Clark and Whittaker agreed. "To strike this law down, we would have to discriminate in favor of Negroes," said Clark, to which Whittaker added: "We should be color blind on this law."[33]

Warren added up the votes. It was a five-to-four split, just as it had been in the Arkansas case—but this time the split was in favor of the state of Virginia. Justice Frankfurter began work on his majority opinion upholding Virginia's chapter 33—the statute that made the NAACP's brand of solicitation a disciplinary offense. At the same time, Black circulated drafts of a dissent in which he claimed, among other issues, that perhaps chapter 33 should be renamed "[a]n Act to make it difficult and dangerous for the [NAACP] and Virginia lawyers to assert the constitutional rights of Virginia Negroes in state and federal courts." Then Black wrote a passage revealing how far removed he was from his days as a hooded member of the Ku Klux Klan. "The job of lawyers under [the] Constitution is not to lead revolutions, but to lead their people in taking advantage of the American methods for correcting injustice." And courts, Black continued, had a responsibility to serve as "sanctuaries of justice." To ignore that role here, he concluded, was to leave the courts "a little less havens of refuge than they were before this Virginia law was sustained."

Black's words exposed just how wide the ideological chasm had grown between the members of this Court. But Robert Carter wouldn't get a chance to read them. Nor, for that matter, would anyone else. On April 1, 1962, before the Court could announce its decision in *NAACP v. Button*, Associate Justice Charles Evans Whittaker retired on the advice of his physician. He was sixty-one. The "great volume and continuous stresses of the court's work," he explained in a written statement, had brought him to the "point of physical exhaustion." That left a four-to-four split among the remaining jurists, who scheduled a rehearing of the case the following term. Then, a few days later, seventy-nine-year-old Felix Frankfurter collapsed at his desk from a stroke. He lived, but shortly afterward he announced his retirement. Just like that, President Kennedy could appoint two new justices—and Robert Carter could feel new hope.

TWO MORE WINS FOR THE NAACP

By the fall of 1962, President Kennedy had successfully appointed to the bench his top two choices—Byron White and Arthur Goldberg.[34] It promised to be a busy fall at the U.S. Supreme Court. On August 30, 1962—a day after Goldberg's nomination was announced—the Alabama Supreme Court again affirmed Judge Jones's judgments in the defamation cases against the *New York Times* and the ministers. "The First Amendment of the U.S. Constitution does not protect libelous publications," the Court announced curtly. Soon thereafter, the *Times* filed its petition for certiorari in Washington.

Meanwhile, aside from the *Times* case, Goldberg's confirmation hearings, and the customary docket of new cases to consider, the Court had already deferred a dozen cases from the previous term, presumably because the remaining justices were so evenly divided. Now two new voices would have a chance to weigh in. Of all the changes, Frankfurter's retirement was certain to have the largest impact on the fate of Carter's two deferred cases, *NAACP v. Button* and *Gibson v. Florida Legislative Investigation Committee*—the latest case concerning the NAACP's membership lists. Frankfurter had been the Court's most passionate defender of dispassion, and its most unbridled advocate for restraint. "The Court's authority—possessed neither of the purse nor the sword," Frankfurter wrote in dissent in the 1962 decision *Baker v. Carr*, "ultimately rests on sustained public confidence in its moral sanction. Such feeling," he continued, perhaps with the particular challenges of the civil rights cases in mind, "must be nourished by the Court's complete detachment, in fact and in appearance, from political entanglements and by abstention from injecting itself into the clash of political forces in political settlements."

By October 1962, Robert Carter had more than the unknown tendencies of Byron White and Arthur Goldberg to consider. The previous December, Louisiana police used tear gas to break up a large demonstration of students in downtown Baton Rouge. The decision of local authorities to arrest a black minister, Elton Cox, for disturbing the peace and "picket[ing] or parad[ing] in or near a building housing a court of the State of Louisiana" set in motion another case for Carter and his legal team to prepare. Then, less than two weeks later, on December 29, 1961, Judge Jones announced he was making permanent his "temporary" injunction against the NAACP. During the trial, Jones accused the NAACP of conspiring to prevent the University of Alabama football team from playing in a bowl game, and permitted Alabama secretary of state Bettye Frink, despite Carter's objections, to say that registering the NAACP to do business in her home state "would be like turning loose a pack of mad dogs."[35]

While the NAACP languished in Alabama, Robert Carter awaited news of its fate in both Florida and Virginia. After hearing rearguments, the justices met privately to discuss the cases on October 12, 1962. The split among them was particularly apparent in their conference discussion of *NAACP v. Button*—the Virginia case. Since first discussing the facts a year earlier, Chief Justice Warren had not changed his mind. "The NAACP has a right to be in business," he began. "If this suit goes against the NAACP, it is out of business." Justices Black, Douglas, and Clark—speaking in order of seniority, as is customary during Court conferences—also maintained their original opinions. So did the typically restrained Harlan, who continued to claim that Virginia's new law was "plainly constitutional.... *Brown v. Board of Education* will never work out if it is left in the federal domain. The states must do it. We have no reason to reverse Virginia on this law." Justice Potter Stewart, the Eisenhower appointee from Cincinnati with the unpredictable voting record, was the first of the veteran justices to suggest a possible change of heart. "I am not sure," he said, "but I am inclined to reverse." Justice White, the first of the two new members to speak at the private conference, was even less authoritative than Stewart. "I do not know where I stand." Goldberg was more certain. "There is a substantial equal protection point here and I could reverse on that," he said.

In the end, Bob Carter and the Virginia NAACP had come *that* close, as the chief justice had put it, to going out of business. But the loss of Frankfurter and Whittaker had produced a voting shift on the Court. Once the justices' final votes were tallied, last year's five-to-four defeat became this year's six-to-three victory. It was a new day for the NAACP. Justice William Brennan announced the decision on January 14, 1963. "We hold that the activities of the NAACP, its affiliates and legal staff shown on this record are modes of expression and association protected by the First and Fourteenth Amendments which Virginia may not prohibit, under its power to regulate the legal profession, as improper solicitation of legal business."

Brennan's opinion was notable, writes Thomas Emerson, because it "extend[ed] the concept of expression to a point that no decision of the Court had previously reached."[36] Litigation, Brennan ruled, is not just "a technique of resolving private differences; it is a means for achieving the lawful objectives of equality of treatment by all government, federal, state and local, for the members of the Negro community in this country. It is thus," Brennan concluded, "a form of political expression." In Carter's mind, the decision represented "a very vital civil rights victory. *Button* provided First Amendment protection for the activities of organizations such as the NAACP that engage in protest activities through the court process—those that use court litigation to fight racial or other forms of discrimination."[37]

Yet key considerations still divided the new Court. In a concurring opinion, Justice Douglas reasserted his belief that the Court should not tolerate laws like Virginia's. A number of key Virginia officials, he explained, made clear that "the purpose of the present law [was] to evade our prior decisions.... The facts that the contrivance used is subtle and indirect is not material to the question." In dissent, Justice Harlan again disagreed. "No worse setback could befall the great principles established by *Brown v. Board of Education*," he wrote, "than to give fair-minded persons reason to think otherwise. With all respect, I believe that the striking down of this Virginia statute cannot be squared with accepted constitutional doctrine in the domain of state regulatory power over the legal profession.... Neither the First Amendment nor the Fourteenth," Harlan argued, "constitutes an absolute bar to government regulation in the fields of free expression and association.[38]

Two months later, on March 25, 1963, the Court announced its decision in *Gibson v. Florida Legislative Investigation Committee*. Again, the justices split five to four—and again in favor of the NAACP. This time, the new justice, Arthur Goldberg, wrote the majority opinion. It was beyond dispute, Goldberg ceded, that the power to conduct investigations is essential to the legislative process. But "[t]o permit legislative inquiry to proceed on less than an adequate foundation would be to sanction unjustified and unwarranted intrusions into the very heart of the constitutional privilege to be secure in associations in legitimate organizations engaged in the exercise of First and Fourteenth Amendment rights; to impose a lesser standard would be inconsistent with the maintenance of those essential conditions basic to the preservation of our democracy."

Justices Black and Douglas felt Goldberg's opinion had not gone far enough. Both wrote concurring opinions in which they reemphasized their belief that the Court should be even *more* explicit in its rulings against the southern states.

Douglas even took direct aim at his dissenting colleagues by quoting a recent speech by Yale's president, A. Whitney Griswold, in which he asserted that America had become "a nation of lookers and listeners" and a place replete with "innumerable devices for avoiding or delegating personal responsibility for our opinions." Griswold, of course, was not thinking specifically of *judicial* opinions. But to his colleagues on the bench, Douglas's point was clear enough.

Through the months of another muggy Washington summer, as the president and Congress worked on drafting an acceptable piece of civil rights legislation, Martin Luther King and other civil rights leaders finalized their plans for an August 28 "March on Washington for Jobs and Freedom." It would be, planners hoped, the event in which nearly a decade of protest and activism would reach its symbolic pinnacle, and hundreds of thousands of Americans of all colors would gather in the shadow of Lincoln, in the centennial year of the Emancipation Proclamation, to petition Congress to establish 1963, in the words of organizer Roy Wilkins, as the year racial discrimination was ended.

For Bob Carter, the summer of 1963 was also a partial respite from the grueling pace of the past nineteen years at the NAACP and the Legal Defense Fund. Beginning with the 1951 *McLaurin* case, Carter had argued—and won—seven different First Amendment cases before the highest court in the land, helping ensure that the inexorable march toward civil rights legislation in the United States could continue. Before the era was over, he would argue—and win—one more. But that summer, Robert Carter was *still* waiting for the final ruling on the constitutionality of Judge Jones's restraining order from 1956. Three separate times the case had gone before the Supreme Court, and three separate times the Court had responded—the last time ordering the state to grant the NAACP a trial by no later than January 2, 1962.

Not surprisingly, Judge Jones had opted to ratchet things up. He permanently enjoined the NAACP from conducting business in the state on December 29—just four days before his Court-imposed deadline. At last, more than five years after Judge Jones's original order, Bob Carter would have a chance to appeal. But the Alabama Supreme Court—whose chief justice, J. Ed Livingston, once boasted that whereas Governor George Wallace had merely stood in the door, where he came from they burned the schools down—continued to stonewall the Fund. First, the Alabama court delayed its decision on the appeal for another year. Then, rather remarkably, it refused to consider the merits on an obscure procedural technicality. Robert Carter had no choice but to appeal to the Supreme Court a *fourth* time.

As he waited for the Court's decision in *NAACP v. Alabama,* and as the date for the March on Washington neared, Carter learned on August 1, 1963, that his chief nemesis, Judge Walter Burgwyn Jones, had died. "Listen to Mr. Lincoln,"

Jones told a northern audience years earlier, "if you want to understand the South's behavior. For it was Lincoln who said that 'any people, anywhere, being inclined and having the power, have the right to rise up and shake off the existing government, and form a new one that suits them better.' This is a most valuable, a most sacred right, a right which we hope and believe is to liberate the world."[39] He was seventy-four.

A MONUMENTAL SHIFT IN FIRST AMENDMENT LAW

Several months later, on January 6, 1964, the Supreme Court heard oral arguments in the case of *New York Times v. Sullivan*. Roland Nachman, the Alabama libel lawyer and chief architect of the lawsuits against the *Times*, argued for city commissioner L. B. Sullivan. Herbert Wechsler, a fifty-two-year-old Columbia law professor and constitutional scholar, argued on behalf of the *Times*. Seventy-seven-year-old former Klansman Hugo Black, by now the longest tenured member of the Court, sat to the left of Chief Justice Earl Warren in judgment. And the ghost of Walter Jones filled the halls.

On March 9, after Justice Brennan completed his eighth and final draft of the majority opinion, the Court announced its decision in the case—and broke with nearly 170 years of libel law precedent in the process. Brennan rested his opinion, as Professor Hall has observed, on a simple proposition: "that the nature of public discourse shaped the character of democratic self-governance."

"Brennan," says Hall, "constitutionalized" and "federalized" the law of political libel by establishing the doctrine of *actual malice*. More specifically, he brought civil libels against public officials like the *Sullivan* case under the protection of the First Amendment—by way of the due process clause of the Fourteenth—by prohibiting "a public official from recovering damages for a defamatory falsehood relating to his official conduct unless he proves that the statement was made with...knowledge that it was false or with reckless disregard of whether it was false or not."

It was a monumental shift, one made possible largely because of the civil rights component of this First Amendment case. The cause of equal justice combined with that of liberty produced a landmark ruling. The Warren Court, Hall writes, had "adopted a modern, northern conception of libel law designed to encourage a robust exchange of ideas...[and] rejected a competing vision of libel law, the [southern] notion that habits and manners of civility should govern public discourse."[40] In other words, Brennan's opinion was Walter Jones's worst nightmare. Roland Nachman was also shocked. "It never entered my head," he said years later, "that the case would come out the way it did."[41] Yet for Hugo Black, the Court had still not gone far enough. "An unconditional right to say what one pleases about public affairs is what I consider to be the minimum guarantee of the

First Amendment," he wrote in his concurrence. "I regret that the Court has stopped short of this holding indispensable to preserve our free press from destruction."[42]

Following the *Sullivan* ruling, the Court announced its fourth and final judgment in *NAACP v. Alabama* on June 1, 1964. State officials must vacate the permanent injunction against the NAACP, the Court ordered, and allow the organization to resume its business in the state. This time, the state capitulated. Eight long years after Judge Jones had first imposed the order, the NAACP was back in business in Alabama.

A JUSTICE RETURNS TO HIS ROOTS

By the beginning of 1965, the country's "Second Reconstruction" had almost reached its conclusion. President Lyndon Johnson had successfully championed sweeping new civil rights legislation, and Robert Carter's eighth and final Supreme Court victory on behalf of the NAACP and the First Amendment— *Henry v. Collins*—was just a few months away.[43] Recalling the hopefulness of the period, Carter said: "Everyone believed fundamental changes were ahead— changes that would permanently push the country closer to its initial vision and promise."[44] Decades earlier, a much younger Hugo Black, just starting down the path that eventually led him to the Supreme Court, had spoken of a similar ideal: "I see a vision of America honored by the nations of the world" and blessed by "a smile of the great God of the universe, beaming down upon it as it remains true to the principles of human liberty."[45] It was a vision the justice still believed in thirty-eight years later. Yet the contrast between then and now was hard to ignore. In 1926, after all, Hugo Black was not speaking out in defense of people of color; he was thanking his fellow Klansmen for their support.

But in early 1965, Black seemed less committed to civil rights and the First Amendment. In January, he dissented in part from both of the Court's judgments in favor of Elton Cox, a Louisiana minister arrested for organizing a rally at a Baton Rouge courthouse to object to the previous day's arrest of several students.[46] Perhaps reflecting his own growing fear of the direction his beloved nation was heading, Black's words took on a different tone. "Justice," he wrote in *Cox v. Louisiana II*, "cannot be rightly administered, nor are the lives and safety of prisoners secure, where throngs of people clamor against the processes of justice right outside the courthouse or jailhouse doors."

Black then delivered a message with civil rights activists in mind. "Minority groups in particular," he urged, "need always to bear in mind that the Constitution, while it requires States to treat all citizens equally and protect them in the exercise of rights granted by the Federal Constitution and laws, does not take away the State's power, indeed its duty, to keep order and to do justice according to law.

Those who encourage minority groups to believe that the United States Constitution and federal laws give them a right to patrol and picket in the streets whenever they choose," Black wrote, "do no service to those minority groups, their cause, or their country."[47]

Had Black really abandoned the First Amendment–fueled cause of the civil rights protesters down South? Or had the national mood of lawlessness finally pushed the anxious Alabaman to weaken his absolute defense of the right to free speech and free association? Fred Graham of the *New York Times* had a theory. On the occasion of Justice Black's eightieth birthday, Graham wrote that the aging Alabaman's career "has been marked by an unusual ebb and flow, and there are those who say he is breaking from the forward-looking philosophy he held as leader of the Court in recent years." Black now "dissent[ed] with increasing frequency along with the 'conservative' justices," Graham wrote. "As the Negroes' struggle has shifted from unequal laws to the more subtle demands for better jobs and educational opportunities, it seems clear that the pro–civil rights majority has left Justice Black behind."[48]

Such assessments, it might be argued, ignored Black's constitutional logic, the justifications he tendered to defend his position. For one thing, he thought that *speech*, which was entitled to absolute protection, differed from *conduct*, which could be regulated by the government. In that regard, James J. Magee has observed:

> [F]rom 1964 until his death in 1971, Justice Black grew increasingly less libertarian and more reflective of the conservative reaction to the Warren Court's onward march into the problems of...inequality. A major issue which impelled his alleged retreat was the spiraling use of symbolic conduct...as a means of communication and expression.[49]

"Justice Black's position," opined Thomas Emerson, "takes 'conduct,' as distinct from 'speech,' completely outside of the First Amendment. 'Conduct' is defined as including 'standing,' 'patrolling,' and 'marching.'"[50] This speech/conduct dichotomy increasingly became an integral part of Black's First Amendment jurisprudence as the Court waded through the troubled waters of the turbulent 1960s.

Even granting, at least *arguendo*, that dichotomy, the First Amendment rights of assembly and petition—rights grounded in expressive conduct—remain. What of those rights? How could Black explain his jurisprudential antagonism toward civil rights demonstrators given the express textual promise of the First Amendment?

His answer can be found in his dissent in *Cox v. Louisiana II*: Protesters have an absolute right of assembly, he wrote, but only "where people have a right to be for such purposes."[51] By that logic, if the government does not allow protesters to assemble in public places, then there is no First Amendment right. Of course, notes Magee, if that is the logic, then "the constitutional right of assembly evaporate[s]." To put it another way, again drawing on Magee, Black's absolute First Amendment right is one that can be "conditioned upon government's willingness to grant it."[52] Echoing that point, Emerson observed: "On [Justice Black's] formulation, there is very little left to the right of assembly or petition."[53]

But Black's logic, however problematic, was not confined to the rarified reasons of doctrinal jurisprudence. There were also practical reasons, he warned, for voting as he did. On that score, his fear was that the new champions of street justice would resurrect the world of the old champions of mob justice. Or as he put it in his *Cox v. Louisiana II* dissent:

> [M]inority groups, I venture to suggest, are the ones who always have suffered and always will suffer most when street multitudes are allowed to substitute their pressures for the less glamorous but more dependable and temperate processes of the law. Experience demonstrates that it is not a far step from what to many seems the earnest, honest, patriotic, kind-spirited multitude of today, to the fanatical, threatening, lawless mob of tomorrow. And the crowds that press in the streets for noble goals today can be supplanted tomorrow by street mobs pressuring the courts for precisely opposite ends.[54]

The First Amendment stretch of the 1950s and 1960s—from civil rights marches to antiwar demonstrations and from street marches to lunch counter sit-ins to courthouse picketing to library protests—proved too much for Hugo Black. First Amendment freedoms were, he worried, becoming the tools of anarchy. He said as much in dissent in *Brown v. Louisiana* (1966), the library sit-in case:

> It is an unhappy circumstance in my judgment that the group, which more than any other has needed a government of equal laws and equal justice, is now encouraged to believe that the best way for it to advance its cause, which is a worthy one, is by taking the law into its own hands from place to place and from time to time. Governments like ours were formed to substitute the rule of law for the rule of force. Illustrations may be given where crowds have gathered together peaceably by reason of extraordinarily good discipline reinforced by vigilant officers.[55]

Building on that point, Black felt compelled to give younger generations a lesson in political prudence: "'Demonstrations' have taken place without any manifestations of force at the time," he wrote. "But I say once more that the crowd moved by noble ideals today can become the mob ruled by hate and passion and greed and violence tomorrow. If we ever doubted that, we know it now. The peaceful songs of love can become as stirring and provocative as the Marseillaise did in the days when a noble revolution gave way to rule by successive mobs until chaos set in."[56]

Later that year, Black left no doubt that such concerns had prompted him to rearticulate his First Amendment jurisprudence by writing the majority opinion for the Court in *Adderley v. Florida*, a civil rights case in which the Court *denied* by a five-to-four vote the First Amendment claim of some students arrested for protesting in front of a jail where their friends were being held. "The United States Constitution does not forbid a State to control the use of its own property for its own lawful nondiscriminatory purpose,"[57] Black announced as he read from his opinion in open court. At that point, Justice Harlan—one of the Court's conservative voices—passed Black a private note: "Amen!"[58]

By contrast, Justice Douglas—Black's previous partner in the absolutist defense of the First Amendment—wrote a sharp dissent in *Adderley* in which his words could easily have been mistaken for the Hugo Black of just a few years earlier. "[W]hen a trespass law is used to bludgeon those who peacefully exercise a First Amendment right to protest," Douglas urged, "we only increase the forces of frustration which the conditions of second-class citizenship are generating against us."[59]

Was there merit to Black's charges? Were life and law then moving in that direction? Whatever the answer, one thing became certain—the First Amendment would soon enough be invoked by people with far less noble motives than Robert Carter and his NAACP colleagues.

LIBERTY VERSUS EQUALITY?

Justice Black's purported abandonment of the civil rights cause was surprisingly swift. Moreover, as if to compound the perceived problem, the Warren Court took the First Amendment to a new realm—a realm inhabited by racial bigots. This occurred on June 9, 1969, when the Court announced a unanimous decision in favor of Clarence Brandenburg. This First Amendment petitioner was not a civil rights activist; he was the Ohio leader of the organization that had first launched Hugo Black's career in public service: the Ku Klux Klan.

Brandenburg—a large man with a meaty, jowled face not unlike President Johnson's—had contacted a Cincinnati TV station. He wanted TV coverage of a Klan rally at which he and a handful of other hooded figures gathered around and burned a large wooden cross. According to court documents, Brandenburg concluded the rally, which received TV air time, with a short speech:

This is an organizers' meeting. We have had quite a few members here today which are—we have hundreds, hundreds of members throughout the State of Ohio. I can quote from a newspaper clipping from the Columbus, Ohio *Dispatch*, five weeks ago Sunday morning. The Klan has more members in the State of Ohio than does any other organization. We're not a revengent [*sic*] organization, but if our President, our Congress, our Supreme Court, continues to suppress the white, Caucasian race, it's possible that there might have to be some revengeance [*sic*] taken.[60]

On the basis of the TV footage, Brandenburg was arrested under a state law, originally passed in 1919, that made it illegal to "advocate...the duty, necessity, or propriety of crime, sabotage, violence, or unlawful methods of terrorism" or "voluntarily assemble with any society, group, or assemblage of persons formed to teach or advocate the doctrines of criminal syndicalism."[61] After his conviction, the Klan leader was fined $1,000 and sentenced to a one- to ten-year term of imprisonment. The Supreme Court of Ohio dismissed Brandenburg's appeal without comment on June 12, 1968.

Two months earlier, Martin Luther King's assassination had set off riots and escalated racial tensions in major cities across the country. If the rights of a cross-burning Klansman were upheld at that particular time, there were fears that it might ignite a new set of racial conflagrations. Furthermore, the Fourteenth Amendment—the constitutional device by which the First Amendment was made applicable to the states—had been originally passed to protect the rights of recently freed slaves in the post–Civil War South. Did Brandenburg's lawyers really expect the liberal Warren Court to validate the proposition that the First and Fourteenth Amendments provided their client with protective cover for his racist actions?

Yet in a short *per curiam* opinion in the case of *Brandenburg v. Ohio* (1969), the Court did exactly that—and revised First Amendment law in the process. Although in past decisions the Court had held that mere advocacy of violent means to effect political and economic change was sufficient grounds for prosecution, it used the facts in *Brandenburg* to revise its stance on the issue. "[T]he constitutional guarantees of free speech and free press do not permit a State to forbid or proscribe advocacy of the use of force or of law violation," the Court wrote, "except where such advocacy is directed to inciting or producing imminent lawless action and is likely to incite or produce such action."[62]

Although it was a unanimous decision, the Court's *Brandenburg* ruling signaled, for some civil rights activists, a worrisome change of course. Indeed, as Catharine MacKinnon wrote years later, what *Brandenburg* and other cases like it suggested to minority voices was that "the First Amendment has grown as if a commitment to speech were no part of a commitment to equality and as if a commitment to equality had no implications for the law of speech."[63] In her 1993 book, *Only Words*, MacKinnon imagined a different evolution. "If speech were seen through an equality lens," she explained, "cross burning prohibitions would be seen as the civil rights protections they are." Highly critical of the Court's ruling in *Brandenburg*, she declared: "Suppressed entirely in the piously evenhanded treatment of the Klan and the [protesters] was the fact that the Klan was promoting inequality and the civil rights leaders were resisting it, in a country that is supposedly not constitutionally neutral on the subject."[64]

In the eight First Amendment cases he argued before the Court between 1958 and 1965, Robert Carter had constructed a bridge between the liberty principle of the First Amendment and the equality principle of the Fourteenth Amendment. The former buttressed the latter, while the latter gave the former new and invigorated meaning. In all likelihood, all or many of the First Amendment victories scored by the NAACP during this period would not have occurred absent the organization's role in advancing racial justice. By contrast, the *Brandenburg* precedent was seen by MacKinnon and others as symbolizing the destruction of the bridge between liberty and equality. By that measure, it would not be surprising that a later Court—like the one in *R.A.V. v. City of St. Paul* (1992)—would once again find a First Amendment right in cross burning, even if such symbolic expression were otherwise prohibited by "race-hate" laws (see chapter 7).

It was almost as though the Court—with Hugo Black's blessing—had come full circle; the same First Amendment that had once been employed to defeat the southern tactics of resistance to *Brown* had now been used to undermine the spirit of that precedent by defending the rights of Klansmen. In the minds of many, liberty and equality now warred.

Had it indeed come to that? Was the First Amendment now the enemy of minorities? And had Robert Carter's First Amendment vision been blurred beyond all recognition?[65]

CIVIL RIGHTS, FREE SPEECH, AND THE NEXT GENERATION

> History teaches that a people's liberty is never preserved without vigilance.
>
> —ROBERT L. CARTER (1941)[66]

On the Monday following Thanksgiving, 2005, people filed into the National Archives auditorium in Washington to hear the latest in a series of public conversations about the First Amendment. The topic that day concerned freedom of association and assembly, past and present. The featured guests were Judge Robert L. Carter and University of Chicago Law School professor Geoffrey R. Stone. The format was a seventy-minute public interview[67] followed by questions. Judge Carter, then eighty-eight years old, reflected on the First Amendment cases he argued on behalf of the NAACP, while professor Stone commented on the role those cases played in resolving various contemporary First Amendment issues.

Near the end of the program, a young African American woman injected her voice into the conversation with a question: "Why do you feel the First Amendment is still not important today in the minority community, particularly among civil rights activists?" Stone took up the question and cut to the quick: "I think the question about the lack of appreciation of the First Amendment among civil rights activists really comes from the hate-speech issue," he said. "That's probably the core of it...what others would call political correctness. Many people, including women and minorities, have come to think of [certain kinds of] free speech...as a cause of harm and [that they] therefore should not be celebrated or protected in the way in which the strongest First Amendment advocates would demand."

Though openly mindful of the claims of free-speech critics, Stone nonetheless found such arguments problematic. "What happens," he continued, "is that too often they take for granted what's been achieved and see only the downside of a robust system of free speech and thus focus more on that. [Consequently,] the attitude to free speech becomes: 'this is not an unmixed blessing. Yes, it may have some value, but it's blown way out of proportion. [We] certainly shouldn't protect speech that makes women or minorities uncomfortable in work or university settings, and we need to curb it in order to prevent people from abusing that right in ways that lead to a sense of discrimination.' I think that's what creates the tension within those communities." In the end, Stone believed such critics would eventually come to regret any attempts to dilute First Amendment freedoms: "What it requires in my view," he concluded, "is for those who advocate hate speech codes...to recognize that their own long-term interests are much better protected by a strong and robust principle of free speech than by trying to fine tune what is protected and what is not. In the long run, they will not be the winners in that game."

Stone echoed several points the white-haired Carter had made earlier during the question-and-answer session. "When you look closely at the hate groups," Carter explained, "the tendency to restrict their hateful expression is understandably strong. But you can't have it that way. You've got to tolerate the whole business of allowing people in this country to be able to dissent. And it's hard. But you can't have it for one side and not have it for the other. That's why I don't accept the view that this business about hate speech, that somehow that it is the kind of speech we ought to curb."

As the C-SPAN cameras captured his words and body language, Carter leaned forward on his cane and, with vital vigor, added: "You don't curb speech, you curb action. When speech turns to action, then that's the time to stop it. But as long as it is speech, if you're going to have First Amendment rights in this country, then you've got to calm yourself down...you've got to breathe, breathe, breathe...and then say: 'Okay, I've got to let that go, too. Because I've got to allow that in order to have my rights.'"

Six decades earlier, in his Columbia dissertation, a much younger Robert Carter had made the same argument. A younger Hugo Black once held a similar sentiment. Yet only Carter had managed to survive the tumult of the 1960s with his commitment to the First Amendment unblemished. The contrast between the two men's stories—and the ongoing challenge to choose freedom over fear— would not have been lost on the aging civil rights champion. Indeed, one imagines him aware, as James Baldwin's protagonist in the classic story "Sonny's Blues" was aware, "that this was only a moment, that the world waited outside, as hungry as a tiger, and that trouble stretched above us, longer than the sky."[68]

Crosses and Crises

Edward Cleary and Hate Speech

Some messages and how they are conveyed are inherently offensive. Take the most iconic symbols of hate—the Nazi swastika, the burning cross, the Aryan Nations shield, and the three "sevens" of skinheads. Such communications are "speech" within the meaning of the First Amendment. But should they be protected speech? To what extent must an open society tolerate them? And when racists burn crosses in the dark of night, should the First Amendment be enlisted to help fuel the fire?

Almost every country in the world disallows any hate speech that is directed at racial, religious, or ethnic groups. By contrast, the United States has a tradition of striving to protect even the most offensive forms of expression. In the early 1990s, however, that "tradition" collided with a concatenation of racially charged events. Consider the following:

- Reports concerning noticeable rises in hate crimes
- Racially insensitive skits on college campuses
- National debates about "political correctness"
- A proposed act of Congress concerning hate speech
- Charges of a "high-tech lynching" by Supreme Court nominee Clarence Thomas
- A Klansman running for president of the United States

- Race riots in the streets of Los Angeles
- A Supreme Court ruling concerning a burning cross in a black family's yard

All of these incidents happened within the span of a few years. In each instance, Americans were challenged to recall their nation's historic efforts to balance freedom and fear. They were also asked to consider the social value, if any, of hate speech.

Is it possible to legislate tolerance? Is a free society obligated to protect its most vulnerable and victimized citizens from racist verbal and symbolic attacks? And must any American endure personal fear and intimidation in the name of a shared national commitment to freedom? Those were the questions. At least one important answer came in the landmark case *R.A.V. v. City of St. Paul* (1992)—a case that steered the First Amendment in a direction some celebrated, and others feared.

THE LAWYER

It was not even noon on June 25, 1990, and Edward J. Cleary was already tired. A young attorney with a thriving private practice, Cleary, who also served as a public defender in St. Paul, Minnesota, had already handled nearly twenty cases that morning. In his part-time work on behalf of the juvenile division of the Ramsey County court system, Cleary inherited cases involving defendants who were young and unable to secure legal representation on their own. Most were charged with misdemeanor offenses. It was hard work, and at 11:30 A.M. that day the Minnesota native received the file for his latest client—a seventeen-year-old charged with a "bias" assault crime.

Though tired of cases and case files, the young bearded attorney sensed the new case might be significant. The alleged crime—shocking to imagine anywhere in 1990, but particularly in Minnesota—involved the most reviled symbol in American history. The law in question was also obscure and legally dubious—in fact, as far as Cleary could tell, it had never been enforced. That combination of facts, he thought, could make for an incendiary and polarizing legal battle.

Two years later, almost to the day, the U.S. Supreme Court would prove him right. But first Edward Cleary would need to brave a social maelstrom of public scorn, professional ostracism, and repeated accusations of racism.

THE TARGETS

Russell and Laura Jones moved out of the inner city and into a neighborhood on the east side of St. Paul in search of the most fundamental right in a free

society—safety. After just two weeks, however, the tires on their station wagon—they were parents to five young children—were slashed. Later, a window
on their car was shattered. And the vandalism continued. The young thirty-
somethings were afraid, and they suspected the vandalism might have to do
with the color of their skin. The Dayton's Bluff area of St. Paul was experiencing
a spike in its nonwhite population, and not everyone was happy about African
American families like the Joneses moving into the neighborhood. But they
couldn't be certain.

Then, on June 21, 1990, awakened in the middle of the night by voices and
footsteps, the couple looked outside to see, in their small fenced-in yard, a
symbolic incantation of the injustice, hatred, and violence marking much of this
nation's history—a burning cross. "I looked out the...rear widow of the house
and I saw this glow," Russell Jones recalled on the *MacNeil/Lehrer NewsHour* in
February 1992. "The first thing that came to my mind was, well, what did they do
to my car, did they set it on fire, so I kind of jumped out of bed and went to the
window and looked out and I was quite shocked and surprised to see what they
did," he added.

Crudely fashioned out of pieces of a chair, wrapped in terry cloth and doused
with paint thinner, the cross was barely two feet high. Yet there was no longer any
mistaking what was happening to the Jones family; it was a campaign of intimidation. "If you're black and you see a cross burning," Laura Jones said, "you know it's
a threat, and you imagine all the church bombings and lynchings and rapes that
have gone before, not so long ago. A burning cross is a way of saying, 'We're going
to get you.'" In her mind, what was involved here was far more than free speech:
"If it was just a point of view, it would be fine. But we took this as a threat, and all
black people take cross-burning as a threat, just as all Jewish people take a swastika splattered across the wall as a threat."[1]

THE DEFENDANT

Robert Anthony Viktora was short, sullen, and seventeen. A neighbor of the
Jones family, he and one other boy were arrested in connection with the cross
burning within days of the incident.[2] Viktora was a high school dropout. His arms
were lined with tattoos, his garb consisted of combat boots, a t-shirt, and a leather
jacket, and he worked regularly as a manual laborer. He denied that he was a skinhead, or that he had any involvement in the incident. He did admit writing to and
visiting white power groups such as the White Aryan Resistance, the White
Christian Patriots League, and the National Socialists. Eventually, Viktora's father
would thank his son's court-appointed attorney for "marching into hell for a heavenly cause."[3] At the time, since Robert Viktora was a juvenile, he would simply be
identified in the official court records by his initials—R.A.V.

THE MOOD

In the early years of the 1990s, racial insensitivity and hatred among young Americans was front-page news, not just in St. Paul but also across the country. In cities and on campuses, there was a fear that the climate of hate was heating up, that racism was gradually working itself back into the more mainstream veins of the body politic.

In 1991, there were no fewer than three major reports from different groups documenting the rise of hate crimes in America. Klan Watch announced that the number of white supremacist groups had increased by 27 percent in a year—from 273 to 346. The Anti-Defamation League indicated there were a record number of anti-Semitic incidents that year. Another group reported a dramatic increase in hate crimes directed against Arab Americans as a result of the Gulf War. As Jack McDevitt, who was then preparing a report for the FBI, told his interviewer on the *MacNeil/Lehrer NewsHour* in early 1992: "There seems to be what some people describe as an ugliness out there that hasn't been seen for awhile, and I think it's prompting some additional hate-motivated behavior."

That "ugliness" also manifested itself on college campuses. A year earlier at the University of Wisconsin, students pledging a fraternity had dressed up in black-face to participate in a "slave auction." At George Mason University, a fraternity sponsored an "ugly woman contest," at which one student parodied the stereo-type of a black woman. And at Stanford University, two students turned a symphony recruiting poster into a Sambo caricature and posted it near the room of a black student. Similar acts of racist, sexist, or anti-Semitic intimidation or insensitivity emerged with seemingly renewed vigor across the country, prompting community officials, universities and students to wonder aloud how to stem the tide. "You have to set up something that tells [people] what the limits are, what they can do and what they can't," one Stanford student told a reporter. "We don't put as many restrictions on freedom of speech as we should."[4]

In response, scores of universities and local communities took steps to restrict forms of expression considered offensive. The University of Wisconsin system approved a proposal to prohibit discrimination based on sex, race, religion, color, creed, disability, sexual orientation, national origin, ancestry, or age if it posed "a clear threat to the educational environment." Stanford amended its student conduct code to prohibit "personal vilification of students on the basis of their sex, race, color, handicap, religion, sexual orientation or national and ethnic origin." By the end of 1990 alone, over a hundred colleges and universities had joined these institutions in enacting student speech codes.

That kind of thinking worried Geoffrey Stone, the constitutional scholar and then dean at the University of Chicago Law School: "The social climate is suddenly less tolerant to free expression across a wide range of issues,"[5] he said in a

1990 news story. Yet support for the speech codes could even be found in some unlikely places. The ACLU's three California affiliates adopted resolutions approving such codes, while its Massachusetts affiliate narrowly defeated a similar resolution. And although no such statement of public support was forthcoming from the national office, ACLU executive director Ira Glasser said he had established a committee to explore the issue.

It was the period of American history that launched the now ubiquitous phrase "political correctness,"[6] but advocates of the new laws were undeterred. As one Brown University student put it: "Yes, there is freedom of speech, but we've also got to take into consideration the rights of others to live in a comfortable and safe environment."[7] As the mood to fight "racist expression" fired up on the college campuses, local lawmakers also got involved. A model course of legislative action could be found in the law books of St. Paul, Minnesota. Years earlier, the city council of St. Paul had passed an ordinance outlawing certain types of symbolic expression likely to have deleterious effects on the community. "Whoever places on public or private property," read the ordinance,

> a symbol, object, appellation, characterization, or graffiti, including, but not limited to, a burning cross or Nazi swastika, which one knows or has reasonable grounds to know arouses anger, alarm or resentment in others on the basis of race, color, creed, religion or gender[8] commits disorderly conduct and shall be guilty of a misdemeanor.

The law was unanimously approved by the city council on March 9, 1982. At the time, one councilman proudly predicted St. Paul[9] would be a better place because of its passage. Yet Edward Cleary's initial hunch was right—the law had never been enforced until the Jones incident.

As lunchtime approached that day in June 1990, the busy public defender began to consider the issues before him. Like nearly everyone else, he abhorred the alleged actions of his client. But the sweeping breadth of the law that was used to arrest his client also troubled him. It was a law designed to punish hateful *expression*, even though St. Paul could have relied on more severe laws to punish the teenagers' threatening *conduct*. In other words, even though trespassing laws and the like already existed to prevent people from burning crosses in their neighbor's yards—some of which were felony offenses[10]—none of those laws addressed the hateful message at the center of the crime. That's where ordinance 292.02 came in. It seemed, Cleary later wrote, a clear attempt to "censor expression that others found objectionable, effectively mandating the 'proper political viewpoint' for the community of St. Paul."[11]

Russ Jones did not agree. "Having a cross burned in your yard is different from trespassing, and I think it should be identified as different," he later told a *New*

York Times reporter. "I don't see the free speech problem here, because burning a cross on someone's lawn is a direct threat, and how can a threat of violence be protected?"

Of course, that was partly Cleary's point, too—direct threats of violence *were already* unprotected forms of expression. But whereas Cleary believed the best way to handle such acts was by relying on existing content-neutral threat laws (and not by carving out free-speech exceptions), Russ Jones's question cut to the quick of the nexus of emotional and legal issues involved in the case. Cleary would need to fashion a legal argument that considered all of those issues at the initial hearing for his client. The date was set for July 13, 1990.

THE LAW OF THE LAND

Cleary had less than a month to research and write a short legal memorandum for the presiding judge, Charles Flinn, Jr. As he pored over past opinions and current standards of analysis, he kept coming back to his initial sense of the case: that ordinance 292.02 was too broadly written, and that it should be challenged *prima facie* ("on its face").

Typically, First Amendment claims are raised by challenging a law "as applied" to a particular person.[12] When this occurs, the law in question is evaluated on a case-by-case process. By challenging the St. Paul ordinance on its face, however, Cleary was asking Judge Flinn to consider the law *itself*, as opposed to the way the law was applied. In other words, Cleary focused on the fact that although his client was suspected of a heinous crime, R.A.V. still had the right to be charged under a constitutional law. Like any knowledgeable attorney, Cleary knew that overly broad laws are particularly threatening to the First Amendment, since constitutionally protected speech can get lumped in with unprotected expression. The legal standard judges use to prevent this inadvertent effect from occurring is known as the *overbreadth doctrine*, which the U.S. Supreme Court defined in *NAACP v. Alabama* (1958) as "a governmental purpose to control or prevent activities . . . by means which sweep unnecessarily broadly and thereby invade the area of protected freedoms." The overbreadth principle is designed not only to protect an individual's right to be charged under a constitutionally limited law but also the American public's right to become a party to the challenge—the idea being that overbroad laws have the potential to "chill" everyone's free expression rights, not just the rights of the accused.

Since 1958, however, the Court has restricted the scope of the overbreadth doctrine. In 1973, in *Broadrick v. Oklahoma*, the justices outlined a more stringent "substantial overbreadth" doctrine, which stated that a law could only survive a challenge on its face if its legitimate applications outweighed the potential effects of its misuse. And in 1984, in *Members of the City Council of the City of Los*

Angeles v. Taxpayers of Vincent, the Court ruled there "must be a realistic danger that the statute itself will significantly compromise recognized First Amendment protection of parties not before the Court for it to be challenged on overbreadth grounds." As Erwin Chemerinsky explains, the Court treats the overbreadth doctrine as such "strong medicine" because it "involves the facial invalidation of a law and because it permits individuals' standing to raise the claims of others not before the Court."[13] Yet the Court justifies the doctrine's continued use because, as Justice White wrote in the majority opinion for *Broadrick,* the "First Amendment needs breathing space."

Cleary felt confident Judge Flinn would rule that the ordinance used to arrest his client was dangerously overbroad. In fact, he felt 292.02 was the "mother of all hate-speech laws." But apart from the overbreadth question, there was also an important definitional question: What exactly is hate speech?

As constitutional law scholar Rodney Smolla[14] has discussed, "hate speech" is a general term "that has come to stand for verbal attacks based on race, ethnicity, religion, and sexual orientation or preference."[15] In practice, however, the phrase has become a lightning rod at the center of a much larger discussion of the extent to which open societies should tolerate intolerance. That debate was reaching its zenith just as Cleary was preparing his memorandum.

It was a clash of opposing good values. On one side, supporters of restrictive speech laws pointed out the ways such expression fails to contribute to a productive and open exchange of ideas. As Mary Ellen Gale explained it in 1990: "[S]omeone [who] is the target of racist speech . . . is silenced, frightened, and no longer able to participate fully in" society.[16] Others saw the laws as needed measures to shield members of minority groups from attacks that were designed to invoke the nation's painful legacy of slavery, inequality, and oppression. Mari Matsuda, a prominent race-hate-speech critic who was then teaching at UCLA Law School, noted in a 1989 *Michigan Law Review* article that the "emerging global standard prohibits . . . the kind of expression that most interferes with the rights of subordinated-group members to participate equally in society" and thereby to maintain "their basic sense of security and worth as human beings." To support that claim, Matsuda pointed to international standards and foreign laws that outlawed hate speech—measures such as article 4 of the International Convention on the Elimination of All Forms of Racial Discrimination, Britain's Race Relations Act, and similar laws in Canada, Australia, and New Zealand. Matsuda also spoke of the psychological pain experienced by victims of hate speech, pointing out that "victims of vicious hate propaganda have experienced physiological symptoms and emotional distress ranging from fear in the gut, rapid pulse rate and difficulty in breathing, nightmares, post-traumatic stress disorder, hypertension, psychosis, and suicide."[17]

In a much-discussed 1990 article on the topic, Charles R. Lawrence took a slightly different approach, arguing that the principle of equal citizenship that informed the famous 1954 school segregation case *Brown v. Board of Education* was equally applicable to issues of racist hate speech on campus. "Under that principle," he explained, "every individual is presumptively entitled to be treated by the organized society as a respected, responsible, and participating member." In Lawrence's estimation, this meant society must require "the affirmative disestablishment of societal practices that treat people as members of an inferior or dependent caste, as unworthy to participate in the larger community."[18] Lawrence's fellow law professor Richard Delgado agreed, arguing that "racial insults implicate powerful social interests in equality and equal personhood."[19] And a spokesman for the University of Massachusetts at Amherst defended his school's decision to adopt a speech code this way: "We have to realize that students come to the university having had driver's education and physical education but not multicultural education. Many students," he said, "from basically segregated communities come to college and encounter a level of diversity for which they are not properly prepared."[20]

The Matsuda-Lawrence-Delgado attack on race-hate speech represented far more than a mere academic attempt to tweak certain tenets of First Amendment doctrine. Their thought was part of a larger movement, what was then tagged "outsider jurisprudence." Its activist aim was to confront and combat racism, sexism, and other forms of injustice against minorities and the powerless. By that measure, a law's legitimacy hinged not on abstract notions of liberty, but on its ability to equalize unfair power relations between people so as to end bigotry and injustice. Hence, the practitioners of outsider jurisprudence rebelled against any exalted notions of the First Amendment that perpetuated the power of racism. Indeed, they took aim not only at conservatives but also at leftist liberals whose knee-jerk adherence to free-speech absolutism[21] blinded them to the oppressive impact of racism, be it in communities or on college campuses. Hate speech laws and speech codes were thus, in their eyes, constitutionally legitimate attempts to change America's legacy of racism.

On the other side, critics of hate-speech legislation urged states and universities to resist the temptation to outlaw certain types of expression. As First Amendment Center ombudsman Paul McMasters wrote in a 1999 article, all efforts to restrict speech "must focus on affirming the American tradition that no problem—even hate—is so intractable that we must censor words, images, and ideas to address it." Professor Nadine Strossen, then president of the ACLU, agreed. "The ACLU," Strossen argued in a 1990 article, "has never argued that harassing, intimidating, or assaultive conduct should be immunized simply because it is in part based on words." The problem with race-hate laws and speech codes proposed by Charles Lawrence and other like-minded advocates, she stressed, is that they are not "drawn narrowly" or "carefully applied" in ways to comport with basic free-speech liberties. In this respect, she argued that such measures (1) exceed the bounds of the fighting words doctrine; (2) chill protected speech; (3) are impermissibly content-based; and (4) "would justify sweeping prohibitions contrary to free speech principles." Moreover, she maintained that such laws would "not effectively counter racism"[22] and could even "aggravate" the problem because of "the discretion such laws inevitably vest in prosecutors, judges, and other individuals who implement them. One ironic, even tragic, result of this discretion," she added, "is that members of minority groups themselves—the very people whom the law is intended to protect—are likely targets of punishment."[23]

Columnist Nat Hentoff,[24] who shared Strossen's views, was equally troubled by the trend. "A principle has been set" on college campuses, he wrote in 1992, "that free speech is merely situational, merely relative to each administration's fears of the time. As times change, as college presidents and other administrators change, as the hegemony of the right replaces that of the left, so will the extent of free speech."[25] At the time Hentoff's words were published, all but four states had some type of statute dealing with hate crimes. Most of those laws, which were linked to common charges like trespass or assault, added more stringent penalties if the motives of the accused could be linked to prejudicial bias. But Cleary's contention was that the crime his client was accused of went even further by making the mere *expression* of hate a crime.

Looking back in his law books to see what the Court had said about such distinctions in the past, Cleary discovered that although the Court had never developed any official hate-speech doctrine, it had established some contours in a number of different (even conflicting) First Amendment categories of expression.

HURTFUL EXPRESSION

As he pored over the *Supreme Court Reports* that contained the High Court's opinions, Edward Cleary realized soon enough that his case involved several areas of First Amendment law, all of which he would need to consider before formulating his argument. In assessing his client's case, he considered the various doctrinal hurdles, the first of which was one that traced back a half century.

Fighting Words

In 1942, a unanimous Supreme Court (joined by Hugo Black) sustained the conviction of a Jehovah's Witness[26] named Walter Chaplinsky who caused a public disturbance by preaching that all religions were "rackets." Continuing his tirade in the midst of a hostile crowd, Chaplinsky called a city marshal, who had warned him earlier about inciting the crowd, a "God-damned racketeer" and "damned Fascist." Chaplinsky was prosecuted and convicted under a statute prohibiting language "plainly tending to excite the addressee to a breach of the peace." On appeal, the Supreme Court upheld the conviction. In a famous passage from *Chaplinsky v. New Hampshire*, Justice Frank Murphy (1890–1949) declared: "There are certain well-defined and narrowly limited classes of speech, the prevention and punishment of which has never been thought to raise any Constitutional problem. These include the lewd and obscene, the profane, the libelous, and the insulting or 'fighting' words."[27] His majority opinion defined the latter as utterances "which by their very utterance inflict injury or tend to incite an immediate breach of the peace" and which "are of [such] slight social value as a step to truth that any benefit that may be derived from them—is clearly outweighed by the social interest in order and morality."

"We are unable to say that the limited scope of the statute as thus construed contravenes the constitutional right of free expression," wrote Murphy. "It is a statute narrowly drawn and limited to define and punish specific conduct lying within the domain of state power, the use in a public place of words likely to cause a breach of the peace." On the basis of that language, one might think banning a symbol like a burning cross would be relatively simple. But as Jerome Barron and Thomas Dienes have noted, "labeling speech as fighting words has not been a dispositive ground of decision in very many Supreme Court cases since *Chaplinsky*." Far more likely, they explain, is for the Court to find "breach of the peace and disorderly conduct statutes that have been defended on a fighting words rationale to be facially overbroad." Indeed, although the Court has never explicitly overturned its ruling in *Chaplinsky*, neither has it upheld a single conviction under the fighting words doctrine since. Consequently, by 1990 the doctrine had been narrowed so much that Cleary could not be certain if it was still even considered good law.[28]

Hostile Audiences & Group Libel

Cleary found similar atrophy in the hostile audience doctrine, first articulated in *Feiner v. New York* (1951), a case in which a soapbox speaker was arrested for disorderly conduct after making inflammatory remarks about President Truman, the American Legion, and local officials. Irving Feiner also told the restless street corner crowd of supporters and opponents that "negroes...should rise up in arms and fight for their rights." Like *Chaplinsky*, that six-to-three decision—this time with Hugo Black in strong dissent[29]—was never overruled, but neither was it ever cited again by the Supreme Court to uphold a hostile audience conviction.

Another tenuous precedent came from a 1952 case, *Beauharnais v. Illinois*.
Joseph Beauharnais, president of the White Circle League, distributed racist literature at a January 1950 meeting that called for, among other things, "[o]ne million self respecting white people in Chicago to unite." He was subsequently
arrested and convicted of violating section 224a of the Illinois Criminal Code,
which read:

> It shall be unlawful for any person, firm or corporation to manufacture, sell,
> or offer for sale, advertise or publish, present or exhibit in any public place
> in this state any lithograph, moving picture, play, drama or sketch, which
> publication or exhibition portrays depravity, criminality, unchastity, or lack
> of virtue of a class of citizens, of any race, color, creed or religion which said
> publication or exhibition exposes the citizens of any race, color, creed or
> religion to contempt, derision, or obloquy or which is productive of breach
> of the peace or riots.

Arguing on his own behalf before the Illinois Supreme Court, Beauharnais—
with the words of Oliver Wendell Holmes in his mind—asked that the jury be
instructed to find him innocent unless it could be proven the leaflets were "likely
to produce a clear and present danger of a serious and substantive evil that rises
far above public inconvenience, annoyance or unrest." The Illinois court refused
to grant his request, and Beauharnais was convicted.

The U.S. Supreme Court affirmed the decision by a one-vote margin. Justice
Frankfurter wrote for the majority; and once again, Justice Hugo Black, the
Alabama-born former Klan member, wrote in strong dissent. In Frankfurter's
view, since the states already were able to punish the libel of individuals, they
should also retain the power to outlaw the same utterances when they were
directed against certain defined groups. Indeed, he claimed, there was a clear distinction between restricting explicitly political speech and restricting speech that
related to race, color, creed, or religion. Characterizing Beauharnais's speech as
clearly nonpolitical in nature, Frankfurter outlined the Court's major explanation
of *group libel*, or libel that defames a class of persons, especially because of their
race, national origin, and/or religious belief. "[W]hile this Court sits," he wrote,
"it retains and exercises authority to nullify action which encroaches on freedom
of utterance under the guise of punishing libel.... Certainly no one would contend that obscene speech, for example, may be punished only upon a showing of
[a clear and present danger]. Libel, as we have seen, is in the same class."

Hugo Black was livid: "the Court simply acts on the bland assumption that the
First Amendment is wholly irrelevant. It is not even accorded the respect of a
passing mention. This follows logically, I suppose, from recent constitutional
doctrine which appears to measure state laws solely by this Court's notions of

civilized 'canons of decency,' reasonableness, etc. ... Under this 'reasonableness' test, state laws abridging First Amendment freedoms are sustained if found to have a 'rational basis.'" And then, in a prescient passage, Black added:

> Unless I misread history the majority is giving libel a more expansive scope and more respectable status than it was ever accorded even in the Star Chamber. For here it is held to be punishable to give publicity to any picture, moving picture, play, drama or sketch, or any printed matter which a judge may find unduly offensive to any race, color, creed or religion. In other words, in arguing for or against the enactment of laws that may differently affect huge groups, it is now very dangerous indeed to say something critical of one of the groups. And any "person, firm or corporation" can be tried for this crime. "Person, firm or corporation" certainly includes a book publisher, newspaper, radio or television station, candidate or even a preacher.[30]

Were the *Beauharnais* opinion still sound law, it would have provided a special hate-speech exception to the First Amendment that might have made Cleary's job far more difficult. Yet much of Justice Black's mindset subsequently informed the Court's landmark 1964 ruling in *New York Times Co. v. Sullivan*, a case that took some of the doctrinal wind out of *Beauharnais*. And then in 1978, in the famous case that originated when a Nazi splinter group requested a permit to stage a demonstration in Skokie, Illinois—where roughly one in ten residents was a survivor of the Holocaust—the Court of Appeals for the Seventh Circuit ruled that although the U.S. Supreme Court had never explicitly overruled *Beauharnais*, its recent decisions protecting hateful speech had effectively done so.[31]

Clear and Present Danger

Cleary found clearer guidelines for understanding the extent to which racist speech must be protected in the 1969 case *Brandenburg v. Ohio*. Clarence Brandenburg, a kindred spirit with Joseph Beauharnais, was a Ku Klux Klan leader who organized a rally in Hamilton County, Ohio. At the rally, which was covered by local TV stations, Brandenburg delivered a racist speech: "Send the Jews back to Israel," he urged. "Bury the niggers," he demanded. He also stressed that if the U.S. government "continues to suppress the white, Caucasian race, it's possible that there might have to be some revengeance [*sic*] taken." Brandenburg was subsequently arrested and convicted for violating a criminal syndicalism statute that had been on the Ohio books since 1919. That conviction, however, was overruled by a unanimous U.S. Supreme Court, which concluded that there was no "imminent danger" of immediate harm in the actions taken by Brandenburg.

Although in past decisions the Court had held that mere advocacy of violent means to effect political and economic change was sufficient grounds for prosecution, the Court used the facts in *Brandenburg* to revise its stance on the issue. "[T]he constitutional guarantees of free speech and free press do not permit a State to forbid or proscribe advocacy of the use of force or of law violation," the Court wrote, "except where such advocacy is directed to inciting or producing imminent lawless action and is likely to incite or produce such action."[32]

Content-Based Discrimination

It was debatable whether or not the burning cross in the Joneses' lawn represented a type of advocacy that would produce "imminent lawless action." But Cleary was convinced that St. Paul ordinance 292.02 was a form of impermissible content discrimination. In that respect, it ran afoul of the three-prong test enunciated by the Court in *Ward v. Rock Against Racism* (1989), a case in which the Court held by a six-to-three margin that a New York City sound-amplification guideline was a "reasonable regulation of the place and manner" of public concerts.

Applying the Court's three-part test for judging the constitutionality of any governmental regulation of the time, place, and manner of protected speech, the Court explained that a challenged law must be justified "without reference to the content of the speech regulated"; it must be "narrowly tailored to serve a significant governmental interest"; and it must leave open "ample alternative channels for communication of the information." Judged by those criteria, Cleary thought, a court would have to rule for his client.

Although there were still other issues of law—for example, whether this was protected symbolic speech or unprotected conduct—those questions were more readily covered by existing precedent, a body of law that, Cleary thought, very much favored his client.

In the end, however, the public defender decided to take a more personal approach.

Cleary had appeared before Judge Flinn several times before, and as he read the concurring opinion in the 1989 flag-burning case *Texas v. Johnson*, it occurred to him that its author, Justice Anthony Kennedy, was a man Judge Flinn would greatly admire. "Born within a year of each other," Cleary later wrote, "both men were political conservatives and had come from small-town backgrounds."[33] So Cleary decided to conclude his argument by referring to Kennedy's opinion in *Johnson*, which acknowledged the difficulty of making decisions in such controversial cases. "The hard fact," Kennedy wrote, "is that sometimes we must make decisions we do not like. We make them because they are right, right in the sense that the law and the Constitution, as we see them, compel the result. And so great is our commitment to the process that, except in the rare case, we do not pause to express distaste for the result, perhaps for fear of undermining a valued principle that dictates the decision. This is one of those rare cases."[34]

Cleary's appeal worked. After taking the weekend to consider what was presented by the prosecution and the defense, the self-described conservative Judge Flinn agreed that St. Paul ordinance 292.02 was unconstitutional. Before the week was out, the Ramsey County Attorney's Office filed an appeal in the Minnesota Court of Appeals.[35]

Despite his round one victory, Edward Cleary had his first difficult choice to make. The public defender's office had no funds available for appeals. R.A.V. had no funds to hire a private counsel. Cleary was responsible for his other juvenile cases *and* the cases from his private practice. Taking on the appeal *pro bono* would be financially strenuous. Yet Cleary knew that if he didn't, the appeal would be dropped and the ordinance would remain on the books.

Cleary gave notice that, with the help of friend and fellow attorney Michael Cromett, he would handle the appeal. Shortly thereafter, the prosecutor's office petitioned for "accelerated review"—meaning the Minnesota Court of Appeals would be bypassed in favor of an expedited hearing before the Minnesota Supreme Court. On August 3, less than two weeks after Judge Flinn's order, the state's high court granted the request. A critical mass of its judges must have felt the matter was important enough to leapfrog its other cases.

Cleary, now set to argue before the state supreme court for the first time, did not take the news as a good sign. "We doubted this was a favorable development," he recalled. "By acting in such haste the court appeared to be taking issue with Judge Flinn's ruling."[36]

Oral arguments were scheduled for December 4, 1990.

"TERROR IN OUR NEIGHBORHOODS"

After receiving the government's brief in mid-September, Cleary learned that despite his challenge to the law itself, all attentions remained focused on the behavior of his defendant. "What the appellant actually hoped to establish," he wrote, "was that the majority could punish an unpopular viewpoint, since the 'behavior' itself could be punished by various provisions of the criminal code."[37]

In this sense the prosecution mirrored the sentiments of the many organizations that filed amicus briefs for the state. The NAACP filed a brief with an appendix, titled "Terror in Our Neighborhoods," that detailed acts and provided photographs of racist intolerance. And the Anti-Defamation League, relying heavily on *Beauharnais*, claimed that the First Amendment was not implicated in the case *at all*.

The emphasis on the factual allegations continued on the morning of December 4, when Ramsey County attorney Steven DeCoster rose to address the seven judges of the Minnesota Supreme Court. R.A.V.'s act of vandalism was also an act of terror, DeCoster claimed. But even if the court found the law to be overbroad, he argued, it should be narrowed to cover only "fighting words."

When Cleary's turn came, he tried to redirect the judges' attention to the language of the law itself. By leaving the ordinance intact, he argued, the court would signal to lawmakers that it was constitutional to restrict the right to free speech. When one of the judges then lectured him on the history of cross burning since the Civil War, Cleary knew he was doomed. It seemed the factual allegations in the case were too ugly to ignore, despite the significant implications such a ruling might have for the First Amendment.

Sure enough, even though it had months to review and issue its final decision, the Minnesota Supreme Court announced just six weeks later it had overturned Judge Flinn's order by a unanimous (seven-to-zero) vote. Although the ordinance "should have been more carefully drafted," the court, per associate justice Esther M. Tomljanovich, ruled that it was narrowly tailored enough to serve a "compelling governmental interest" in protecting the community against prejudicial threats to public safety and order. First Amendment claim denied.

"THE FIRST AMENDMENT IS BEING EMBATTLED FROM ALL SIDES"

Meanwhile, outside Minnesota, many colleges and universities continued responding to the intolerance on their campuses by enacting speech codes. The momentum did not even ebb when, in 1989, federal judge Avern Cohn delivered the first legal defeat of campus speech codes by ruling in *Doe v. Michigan* that the University of Michigan's antiharassment law was overbroad. (In response, the University simply revised its policy.)

As more colleges followed suit, the legality of the policies became a national debate. In a 1990 *New York Times* article, law professor and ACLU president Nadine Strossen commented on the odd alliances that were forming as a result. "Now we have minorities and feminists and the left allied with fundamentalists who believe some communitarian values take precedence," she said. "To them, group rights are more important than individual rights. The First Amendment is being embattled from all sides."[38]

Less than a month after the Minnesota Supreme Court's ruling, a Brown University student was expelled for shouting epithets in a public courtyard. It was, the *Times* reported, the first such expulsion in the country. Like the cross-burning case, the actions in question at Brown were indefensible and antisocial.

But not everyone agreed such behavior justified an expulsion. "As disgusting and disgraceful as the student's remarks were," wrote one citizen in a letter to the editor, "unless the circumstances under which he shouted them constituted a clear and present danger to his fellow students, his punishment represents a miscarriage of justice." The *Times* editors disagreed. "When bigots attack other students with ugly invective," they wrote, "universities, whether public or private, need not remain silent."[39]

The stakes of the debate had reached such heights that by March 1991 Congress had also entered the fray—in the form of House Resolution 1380, also known as the Collegiate Speech Protection Act. Introduced by Congressman Henry Hyde on March 12, the bill reflected the extent to which the debate over free speech on college campuses had consumed the attention of the nation. In short, it called for an amendment to the end of Title VI of the Civil Rights Act of 1964, by adding the following:

> A postsecondary educational institution that is a program or activity shall not make or enforce any rule subjecting any student to disciplinary sanctions solely on the basis of conduct that is speech or other communication protected from governmental restriction by the first article of amendment to the Constitution of the United States.[40]

Hearings had not even been scheduled, but already the bill had produced the strangest of bedfellows. Congressman Hyde, well known as one of the House's more conservative members, received a strong endorsement from the generally left-leaning ACLU. In his press release announcing the bill, the Illinois Republican, who had grown up an Irish-Catholic Democrat in Chicago until switching parties to support the presidential candidacy of Dwight D. Eisenhower, said the bill was drafted in order to stem the rising tide of campus intolerance. "The demands of political correctness," he said, "are casting a pall of intolerance over American universities."[41]

Later that year, more courts provided more opinions about the constitutionality of the campus codes. In August, a federal judge for the U.S. District Court for the Eastern District of Virginia overturned the suspension of the Sigma Chi fraternity at George Mason University, the fraternity responsible for the "ugly woman" contest. Initially, after numerous student complaints, university officials determined that Sigma Chi had created a hostile learning environment that was incompatible with the university's mission. When the fraternity claimed the sanctions violated their First Amendment rights, the university countered by claiming that the speech in question was not protected. But Judge Claude Hilton disagreed. "The First Amendment does not guarantee that other concepts virtually sacred to our Nation as a whole—such as the principle that discrimination based on race is odious and destructive—will go unquestioned in the market-place of ideas," he wrote.

Two months later, in October, a federal district judge voided the University of Wisconsin system's policy, which had been used to sanction at least nine students on various University of Wisconsin campuses. The policy forbade any comments, epithets, or other forms of expressive behavior that were: racist or discriminatory; directed at an individual; demeaning of an individual's race, sex, religion, color, creed, disability, sexual orientation, ancestry or age; and that created an intimidating, hostile, or demeaning environment for education, university-related work, or other university-authorized activity. Yet whereas Judge Robert W. Warren agreed that increasing diversity is "clearly a constitutionally permissible goal for an institution of higher education," he contended that the University of Wisconsin rule had "done as much to hurt diversity on Wisconsin campuses as it [has] to help it. By establishing content-based restrictions on speech, the rule limits the diversity of ideas among students and thereby prevents the 'robust exchange of ideas' which intellectually diverse campuses provide."

For Edward Cleary, it was a fascinating time to prepare a petition for review for the U.S. Supreme Court. Perhaps, he wondered, the growing national attention on hate speech would prompt the justices to accept his case. As he recalled, "our focus changed from traditional First Amendment case law to the debate over the repressive climate of a political-acceptability standard prevalent on campus.... Since the language of the ordinance reflected both student speech codes and a political standard set by a community, this phenomenon would be our focus, demonstrating the national significance of the issues we raised before the United States Supreme Court."[42]

Cleary knew the Court appreciated brevity in its petitions for certiorari. He also knew that the questions he posed, listed on the second page of the petition, usually determined whether or not the law clerk assigned to the initial review kept reading. So the Minnesota lawyer chose to ask just two:

1. May a local government enact a content-based, "hate-crime" ordinance prohibiting the display of symbols, including a Nazi swastika or a burning cross, on public or private property...without violating overbreadth and vagueness principles of the First Amendment to the United States Constitution?
2. Can the constitutionality of such a vague and substantially overbroad content-based restraint of expression be saved by a limiting construction, like that used to save the vague and overbroad content-neutral laws, restricting its application to "fighting words" and "imminent lawless action"?

Cleary's intention behind the first question, rather clearly, was to focus the Court's attention on the law itself instead of the Minnesota Supreme Court's narrow construction. Rewriting laws to make them narrower, Cleary suggested, was the role of the legislative—not the judicial—branch. And 292.02 was a classic example of an overbroad law.

With the second question, Cleary intended to suggest that any law that marked certain subjects and viewpoints for proscription could not be narrowly construed the same way as a law that was "content neutral." In other words, though it was permissible to enact a law that punishes expression that incites or produces immediate illegal activity,[43] it was equally unacceptable to enact a law that punishes certain types of expression simply because the message is undesirable. Indeed, he would argue, any laws that do not apply neutrally, without regard to content, pose the gravest threat to freedom of expression in all its forms. On this point Edward Cleary believed the law to be on his side, even if popular sentiment was not. It was up to the U.S. Supreme Court to decide that now.

A NEW COURT TO CONSIDER

On the morning of June 10, 1991, Cleary learned that the Supreme Court had accepted his petition. The Minnesota lawyer would have a chance to make his case before the nine most powerful jurists in the country. As of June, however, exactly who those justices would be and how they might interpret the facts of the case was uncertain. For one thing, Cleary was quite uncertain on how Justice David Souter would vote. President George H. W. Bush had nominated this obscure judge from New Hampshire to replace the retiring William Brennan, Jr. At the time, Souter, previously a state high court justice, had only just begun serving on the First Circuit Court of Appeals when Bush appointed him to the Court. Consequently, little was known of him,[44] leaving senators and court watchers to speculate on his ideological leanings and debate whether or not he would be confirmed. Then, three weeks after the R.A.V. case was accepted, the Court lost another member— Thurgood Marshall. The first African American Supreme Court justice, Marshall had been the lead attorney in the famous Brown case. With Brennan, he had also been one of the Court's strongest advocates of First Amendment rights.

Just like that, two of the votes that had comprised the majority in the 1989 and 1990 flag-burning cases were gone. One of the potential replacements was an enigma, and the other would not even be named until after the briefs for the case were filed. In the absence of reliable information on either the tendencies of Souter or the identity of the newest justice, Cleary began writing the summary of his legal brief. Hoping for the right balance between legal analysis and social context, he remembered an exchange from the movie about the lawyer and philosopher Sir Thomas More, A Man for All Seasons. Cleary had first seen the movie as a thirteen-year-old. As he considered the special issues at the center of the case, he remembered a dialogue between More and a young attorney that takes place after More says he would defend the Devil if asked. Remembering that the movie was based on a play of the same name, Cleary hurried out to a nearby bookstore to find a copy. In an old paperback, he found the scene. His hunch was right—it was a perfect crystallization of the issues before the Court:

> ROPER: So now you'd give the Devil benefit of law!
> MORE: Yes. What would you do? Cut a great road through the law to get after the Devil?
> ROPER: I'd cut down every law in England to do that!
> MORE: Oh? And when the last law was down, and the Devil turned round on you—where would you hide, the laws all being flat?...If you cut them down...d'you really think you could stand upright in the winds that would blow then? Yes, I'd give the Devil benefit of law, for my own safety's sake.

Cleary must have felt an affinity with More, a man who was executed by Henry VIII because he refused to compromise his principles. There was no danger of that for Cleary, although he had been publicly vilified for defending such undesirable behavior. His mother's friends had even confronted *her* about his decision. In fact, when by chance Cleary encountered his law school ethics professor the summer before the trial, his former mentor muttered bitterly, "It takes with some, and not with others."

Cleary concluded his brief[45] with a final call to focus on the central issue at hand:

> Restrictions might curtail some offensive expression but only at the cost of chilling a great deal of protected speech. The result may well be the silencing of political debate, the encouraging of orthodoxy, and the endangering of the individual's right to dissent. To enforce a notion of civility to the point of forbidding unpopular minority expression is to underestimate the citizens of this country at the cost of our basic right of self-expression.

Oral arguments were scheduled for December 4, 1991—exactly one year after Cleary's appearance before the Minnesota Supreme Court.

THE NOMINEE

Shortly after announcing its acceptance of the *R.A.V.* case, the U.S. Supreme Court became front-page news—for a different reason. On July 1, 1991,

President H.W. Bush nominated his candidate to replace the legendary Thurgood Marshall: Clarence Thomas. A conservative Republican who had served little more than a year as a federal appeals judge for the D.C. circuit,[46] Thomas's views on most major issues—like Souter's before him—were essentially unknown. What was known, however, was that he was a passionate opponent of affirmative action and that he was well regarded in conservative circles.

Cleary must have wondered how the candidate, if appointed, would interpret the facts of the *R.A.V.* case. Some of Thomas's past writings provided a partial window. In a 1987 letter to the editor of the *Wall Street Journal*, Thomas argued that if America hoped to establish a color-blind society, the Constitution had to be interpreted in a color-blind fashion. "Hence," he wrote, "I emphasize black self-help, as opposed to racial quotas and other race-conscious legal devices that only further and deepen the original problem." Later that year in a book review, this grandson of rural Georgia sharecroppers claimed that "the 'quest for racial justice,' as opposed to justice per se, is doomed, because American justice by definition cannot be race- or group-oriented."[47]

On the basis of the general drift of those writings, Thomas sounded like someone who *might* take issue with a racially motivated restriction on speech, even if the speech in question was a burning cross. But as the summer months wore on, a constellation of interest groups spoke out to oppose his nomination, casting his confirmation in doubt. Headlines and hearings followed, as the cultural wars escalated. The hearings nearly ended in a deadlock. On October 15, by a narrow margin,[48] Clarence Thomas won confirmation as an associate justice of the Supreme Court. He was sworn in as the nation's 106th Supreme Court Justice in a private ceremony on October 23.

"THE FOUNDATIONS OF AMERICA"

"He woke early, often by four o'clock, and arrived at the Court before five-thirty," wrote Ken Foskett, one of Thomas's biographers. Most mornings, Justice Thomas "was the only employee—other than the security guards—in the building. The quiet and solitude appealed to Thomas, and this was the only time he could fully concentrate and think."[49] One of the cases he needed to concentrate on was the one with docket number 90-7675—*R.A.V. v. City of St. Paul.*

The morning of December 4, 1991, was a bit chilly by Washington standards. Edward Cleary awoke at 5:30 A.M.—an hour after Clarence Thomas. Rain had steadily soaked the D.C. area for the past week, but there was sunshine that day. Feeling confident, Cleary reviewed the outline of his argument one last time at his hotel before setting off to the Supreme Court. As it turned out, other people awoke on December 4 intent on making racial history. At a packed news conference that morning at the National Press Club, former Klansman and neo-Nazi David Duke announced his candidacy for the presidency of the United States. Defeated a month earlier in a runoff for governor of Louisiana—in which he received 55 percent of the white vote—Duke warned that the nation was "unraveling. We're losing our way. This country is overwhelmingly European descent. It's overwhelmingly Christian. And if we lose our underpinning, I think we're going to lose the foundations of America."[50]

The timing was not a coincidence. But the Minnesota lawyer was undaunted— he had always been clear about the key issue at stake in his case, despite the series of compelling emotional appeals to the contrary. "Restrictions might curtail some offensive expression but only at the cost of chilling a great deal of protected speech," he wrote in the concluding paragraph of his brief. "To enforce a notion of civility to the point of forbidding unpopular minority expression is to underestimate the citizens of this country at the cost of our basic right of self-expression." Since penning those words, two prominent campus speech code opinions had been returned by lower courts. Cleary had always felt that St. Paul ordinance 292.02 mirrored the legal issues of the campus codes, so he requested that copies of the opinions be added as supplemental papers. He was less certain about how the nation's recent fascination with questions of race, speech, and censorship— Duke's presidential candidacy being the latest example—would impact his reception at the Court.

Sitting at his assigned table ten minutes before the scheduled start time of 10:00 A.M., Cleary scribbled "*Carpe diem*"—"Seize the day"—on the scratch pad next to the white quill pen that had been provided to him, as it had to countless other attorneys stretching back to the earliest days of the Court. The justices entered, and Cleary rose to deliver his opening remarks:

> Mr. Chief Justice, and may it please the Court. Each generation must reaffirm the guarantees of the First Amendment with the hard cases. The framers understood the dangers of orthodoxy and standardized thought and chose liberty.[51] We are once again faced with a case that will demonstrate whether or not there is room for the freedom for the thought that we hate, whether there is room for the eternal vigilance necessary for the opinions that we loathe.

Pointed questions from the justices followed, although not to the extent Cleary had anticipated. In fact, he recalls, "by giving me the opportunity to speak about the First Amendment in such broad terms, it appeared the members of the Court were sympathetic to our position."[52]

Clearly's opposing counsel, Thomas Foley, was less fortunate. The lawyerly duties of Foley, as the chief attorney for Ramsey County since 1978, did not involve trial or appellate practice. Almost immediately after beginning his opening remarks, Foley, perhaps out of practice, received a rough reception from the justices. A seemingly simple jurisdictional question from Justice Harry Blackmun forced Foley to quickly assume a concessionary stance, prompting an early admonition from Justice Antonin Scalia, who was well known for his pointed challenges of the lawyers who appeared before him. "Mr. Foley," Scalia chided, "if you are going to make all these concessions, you might as well sit down now." But the justice was not about to let that happen, as was evident in one exchange between Scalia and Foley about fighting words.

> SCALIA: If you want to prohibit fighting words, prohibit fighting words. But why pick only...fighting words for these peculiar purposes: race, color, creed, religion, and gender? What about other fighting words?
>
> FOLEY: I think the city has an absolute right and purpose to try to regulate the harm that goes on to its citizens. And certainly this bias-motivated conduct and violence is much more harmful and has more harmful impacts to its citizens—
>
> SCALIA: That's a political judgment. I mean, you may feel strongest about race, color, creed, religion, or gender. Someone else may feel strong as to about philosophy, about whatever. You picked out five reasons for causing somebody to breach the peace. But there are a lot of other ones. What's your basis for making that subjective discrimination?
>
> FOLEY: Your honor, the city of St. Paul is attempting to fashion responses to violence that it deems necessary to prohibit and will add additional harms to be regulated as it finds them.

By the time oral arguments concluded, Cleary felt cautiously optimistic. Although likely on different grounds, he felt confident he would receive the votes of Chief Justice William Rehnquist and of Scalia, Souter, and Byron White. Conversely, Justice Sandra Day O'Connor struck him as unsympathetic, and he had no clear read on Harry Blackmun, Anthony Kennedy, and John Paul Stevens. The newest Justice, Clarence Thomas, was even more of an enigma. During oral arguments, he had not asked a single question of either counsel.

Meanwhile, the media circus continued outside the courtroom. As Cleary left the building, he passed a hastily arranged press conference at which Gregory Johnson—the appellant in the seminal flag-burning case Cleary cited in his initial brief to Judge Flinn—was making a statement. While he was still in favor of flag burning, Johnson announced, he wished to publicly condemn the act of cross burning.

"WE HAVE BEEN COOL TOO LONG"

In the months that followed, Cleary did his best to carry on with his daily routines. After all, there was no way to accurately predict when the Court's decision would be announced. Toward the end of April, he agreed to participate in a forum at an inner-city high school, where he would discuss issues of intolerant behavior among adolescents. The date was April 28, 1992.

Since the date of the *R.A.V.* oral arguments, national news coverage of issues relating to racial tension and/or hate speech had subsided. David Duke's campaign for the presidency ended shortly after it started. The Thomas confirmation controversy was no longer front-page news. And the intensity of the university speech codes debate had begun to wane. And then on April 29, 1992, a jury acquitted four Los Angeles police officers who had been caught on an often-seen video beating and kicking black motorist Rodney King and tried for this offence. In the hours that followed, the sky around Los Angeles filled with smoke and the sound of police sirens. Angry rioters rampaged through the streets, looting stores, setting fires, and attacking passing motorists. It was the worst violence in that city since the Watts riots of 1965.

As the city burned, the rest of the nation watched the horror unfold on television. When asked by a *New York Times* reporter to share her reaction, white Chicagoan Linda Gits said, "I think this takes race relations back 30 years. We were getting somewhere in the 70s and it seems in the past 10 years we have started to slip back into the darkness and evilness of hate." James Buford, a black Republican from Missouri, agreed. "I have played by the rules," he sighed. "I have supported Clarence Thomas. I have supported the Bush administration and worked for it. I have tried through everything in my power to convince people the two-party system and the American dream can work out." But Buford, his confidence shaken, predicted the rioting would last for some time. "It's not a little weekend situation where we set up some job programs and a commission," he said. "Ain't none of that helped the people in that community before. There are Rodney Kings every night in major urban cities."[53] One of the looters was more to the point when asked why he was participating in the destruction: "We have been cool too long."[54]

The day after the verdict, President George Bush, Sr. addressed the nation. "Yesterday's verdict in the Los Angeles police case has left us all with a deep sense of personal frustration," he said. "Yet it is important that we respect the law and the legal processes that have been brought to bear on this case."[55] The question of race—with all its vestiges of cruel bigotry—was yet again in the public mind. What had been subtle before the L.A. riots was now manifest. Racism and injustice was alive and well in America.

"EACH MAN IS FREE"

Less than two months after the Rodney King verdict, on June 22, 1992, the U.S. Supreme Court handed down its opinion in *R.A.V. v. City of St. Paul.* Soon after the nation erupted in frustration over the historical inequities between white and black Americans, the nation's Supreme Court was now issuing an opinion about the legality of the nation's most iconic symbol of race-based hatred and intimidation. Depending on how the justices voted, Court watchers must have wondered how relevant President Bush's recent urging to "respect the law" might need to be.

The vote was nine to zero, a clear rebuke to the Minnesota Supreme Court's ruling. In so doing, commented Rodney Smolla, the Court "essentially laid to rest any prospect that 'hate speech' would be treated as an independent First Amendment category in which reduced levels of constitutional protection would be applied."[56] Yet despite the unanimous decision, the justices authored a total of four opinions, reflecting a deep philosophical split over how to analyze and resolve the core issues in the case.

Justice Scalia wrote for the majority; he was joined by Chief Justice Rehnquist and by Kennedy, Souter and Thomas. Confirmed unanimously by the Senate in 1986, Scalia, the son of Italian immigrants, had quickly established a reputation as a solid conservative. In the Court's civil liberties cases on which he sat with the recent retirees Brennan and Marshall, Scalia agreed with them less than half the time. On First Amendment issues, however, he was sometimes libertarian.[57] Hence, in *R.A.V.* he came down firmly—some would say too firmly—on the side of the First Amendment. From the vantage point of the champions of "outsider jurisprudence," it was unsurprising that Justice Scalia—a critic of the Court's liberal equal protection doctrines[58]—would write an absolutist-like First Amendment defense of hate speech. It was akin, in their minds, to what was happening with commercial speech and campaign financing laws: the First Amendment was being enlisted to buttress the rule of the powerful over the powerless. Others saw it differently, contending that the holding in *R.A.V.* and cases like it demonstrated that the First Amendment was not the ideological province of any single group. Its rules applied to *all* groups regardless of their ideological credentials.

What was not in dispute was that in his *R.A.V.* majority opinion, Justice Scalia, a former University of Chicago law professor, had reconfigured First Amendment law.[59] With analytical fervor, he rejected the two-tier theory of free speech advanced in *Chaplinsky v. New Hampshire*, which declared that certain categories of expression (e.g. fighting words, obscenity, defamation)[60] were entirely beyond the pale of First Amendment protection. Under that constitutional regime, content discrimination was permissible within specified categories, since such categories could otherwise be regulated by the state. But Scalia concluded "the government may proscribe libel; but it may not make the further content discrimination of proscribing only libel critical of the government." In other words, the government could not outlaw or regulate fighting words "based on hostility—or favoritism—towards the underlying message expressed." The new rule invalidated the St. Paul ordinance, which singled out bias-motivated messages "based on virulent notions of racial supremacy."

This new rule created a major problem for efforts to regulate hate speech. Such a rule and outcome were "indefensible" in the mind of Steven Shiffrin, one of the nation's leading First Amendment scholars. "[T]he Court simply bungled the First Amendment job in its most important encounter with racist speech in the last forty years," charged Shiffrin. He was especially troubled by the logic of Scalia's content-discrimination maxim. "The rationale of the general prohibition [against content discrimination]," Scalia explained, "is that content discrimination 'raises the specter that the Government may effectively drive certain ideas or viewpoints from the marketplace.'" But, Scalia concluded, "St. Paul has sufficient means at its disposal to prevent such behavior without adding the First Amendment to the fire." By Shiffrin's analytical measure, Scalia's rationale was "relentlessly simplistic." On the one hand, he explained, racial expression of the kind outlawed in the St. Paul ordinance offers, at best, "a slight contribution to truth." On the other hand, Justice Scalia's content-neutral alternative "would drive the very same ideas and viewpoints (along with others) from the marketplace."[61] That is, had the St. Paul law been upheld, Robert Viktora could have been criminally penalized. Then again, the same would have been true under Scalia's alternative. So, Shiffrin wondered, where's the gain?

Beyond analytical logic, there was something far more troubling to Shiffrin, who held the poetic vision of Ralph Waldo Emerson close to the center of his notion of the First Amendment.[62] That something had to do with the meaning of America itself. Scalia's view was of "a nation that spurns paternalism and tolerates different points of view, however hateful. It is a nation that is formally neutral in race relations." To Shiffrin's disapproval, that view did not take "seriously" the nation's history of racism and its concomitant commitment to constitutional and social equality. In that sense, the R.A.V. case was an ideological war between libertarianism and egalitarianism, and according to Shiffrin, the wrong side won.

Shiffrin was not alone in expressing such concerns. In their concurring opinions, White, Blackmun, and Stevens did what Scalia would not—they acknowledged the country's painful legacy of racist oppression. Justice White—joined by Blackmun, O'Connor, and Stevens—attempted to place the St. Paul law in a broader context. "This selective regulation reflects the city's judgment that harms based on race, color, creed, religion or gender are more pressing public concerns than the harms caused by other fighting words," he wrote. "In light of our nation's long and painful experience with discrimination, this determination is plainly reasonable."[63] But the main reason White's colleagues joined him was that there was another, far less controversial way, to resolve the case: "This case could easily be decided within the contours of established First Amendment law by holding, as petitioner argues, that the St. Paul ordinance is fatally overbroad because it criminalizes not only unprotected expression but expression protected by the First Amendment." He was unusually harsh in his closing assessment of Scalia's handiwork: "Its decision is an arid, doctrinaire interpretation, driven by the frequently irresistible impulse of judges to tinker with the First Amendment. The decision is mischievous at best, and will surely confuse the lower courts. I join the judgment, but not the folly of the opinion."[64]

Justice Blackmun strongly disagreed with the majority's decision to limit the categorical approach. "If we are forbidden from categorizing," he contended, "we shall reduce protection across the board. It is sad that, in its effort to reach a satisfying result in this case, the Court is willing to weaken First Amendment protections." In fact, although he concurred with the ultimate judgment because he felt ordinance 292.02 reached beyond "fighting words" to proscribe protected speech, Justice Blackmun disagreed strongly with the majority's belief that the speech in question was constitutional. "I see no First Amendment values that are compromised by a law that prohibits hoodlums from driving minorities out of their homes by burning crosses on their lawns," he wrote bitterly, "but I see great harm in preventing the people of Saint Paul from specifically punishing the race-based fighting words that so prejudice their community."[65]

Justice Stevens also felt the St. Paul law was impermissibly overbroad. But he felt compelled to say something regarding the recent riots in Los Angeles. "One need look no further," he wrote in a lengthy footnote, "than the recent social unrest in the Nation's cities to see that race-based threats may cause more harm to society and to individuals than other threats." Although he sympathized with the emotional intensity of the issue, Cleary felt the concurring justices' opinions had gone too far, "substituting vitriolic prose for constitutional analysis." Yet it was not hard to imagine why the justices felt compelled to editorialize. And Stevens wasn't done. "Just as the statute prohibiting threats against the President is justifiable because of the place of the President in our social and political order," he concluded, "so a statute prohibiting race-based threats is justifiable because of the place of race in our social and political order. Although it is regrettable that race occupies such a place and is so incendiary an issue, until the Nation matures beyond that condition, laws such as St. Paul's ordinance will remain reasonable and justifiable."[66]

Despite the impassioned rhetoric of some of the justices, Laura Jones, the woman whose family had been targeted by the cross, was not appeased. "It makes me angry that [my children] have to be aware of racism around them, that they notice it more and more," she told a *New York Times* reporter. "They're too young for that. That's one reason I'm so disappointed about the decision." Arthur Kroop, president of People for the American Way, shared in her disappointment. "The message from the Supreme Court," he said, "is that there's nothing you can do about hate crimes and nothing you should do."[67]

For Edward Cleary, the victory was bittersweet. Although resolute in his belief that the greater good of freedom was well served by the opinion, Cleary also knew it would be widely misunderstood. But as he recalled the words of the twenty-nine-year-old John F. Kennedy, speaking to the citizens of Boston on July 4, 1946, during his first campaign for public office, the Minnesota public defender remembered why he was willing, in the words of his client, to "march into hell for a heavenly cause":

> Conceived in Grecian thought, strengthened by Christian morality, and stamped indelibly into American political philosophy, the right of the individual against the State is the keystone of our Constitution. Each man is free. He is *free in thought*. He is *free in expression*. He is *free in worship*. To us, who have been reared in the American tradition, these rights have become a part of our very being. They have become so much a part of our being that most of us are prone to feel that they are rights universally recognized and universally exercised. But the sad fact is that this is not true. They were dearly won for us only a few short centuries ago and they were dearly preserved for us in the days just past. And there are large sections of the world today where these rights are denied as a matter of philosophy and as a manner of government. We cannot assume that the struggle has ended. It is never ending.[68]

PROTECTING FREEDOM FROM FEAR

So is it accurate to say that the concept of "hate speech" as a protected form of expression was really, as Rodney Smolla claimed, "laid to rest" with the *R.A.V.* decision?

Yes and no. As Smolla notes, the Court's refusal in its majority opinion to invoke the overbreadth doctrine as the basis for striking down the ordinance "largely closed the door on all hate speech regulation."[69] (By contrast, had any of the justices' concurring opinions been the primary voice of the Court, ordinance 292.02 *would* have been struck down as overbroad, leaving the door open to crafting more narrowly tailored hate speech laws.)

Justice Scalia's majority also rejected the proposition that 292.02 could be regulated under the secondary effects doctrine, ruling that "the emotive impact of speech on its audience is not a 'secondary effect'" that could be regulated under the First Amendment. The justices similarly took issue with the ordinance's narrowly defined interest in fighting words based on "race, color, creed, religion or gender." The First Amendment, Scalia instructed, "does not permit St. Paul to impose special prohibitions on those speakers who express views on disfavored subjects."[70]

What about the argument that *even if* the St. Paul ordinance targeted specific viewpoints for discrimination, the city was still justified in doing so because of a more overarching "compelling interest"? To this question, the Court conceded the point—to a degree. "We do not doubt that these interests are compelling, and that the ordinance can be said to promote them."[71] Nevertheless, "the Court treat[ed] strict scrutiny analysis as irrelevant to the constitutionality of the legislation."[72] "Under the majority's view," argued White, "a narrowly drawn, content-based ordinance could never pass constitutional muster if the object of that legislation could be accomplished by banning a wider category of speech."[73] Of course, the speech standards from the two cases that modernized Justice Holmes's famous "clear and present danger test"—*Brandenburg v. Ohio* and *Texas v. Johnson*—still stood, which meant expression "directed to inciting or producing imminent lawless action" could still be barred.

R.A.V.'s impact on the legal future of university speech codes seemed less in doubt. "This ruling certainly constitutes a warning shot across the bow of public institutions that currently have or are contemplating enacting such hate speech codes,"[74] said Sheldon Steinbach, counsel for the American Council on Education, an association of colleges and universities, two days after the result was announced. Sure enough, a year after the *R.A.V.* opinion was announced, the U.S. Court of Appeals for the Fourth Circuit upheld the initial ruling against George Mason University. "The University certainly has a substantial interest in maintaining an educational environment free of discrimination and racism," wrote Judge James M. Sprouse. "Yet it seems equally apparent that it has available numerous alternatives to imposing punishment on students based on the viewpoint they express."[75] And on February 27, 1995, Santa Clara County judge Peter G. Stone ruled in favor of a coalition of students and alumni who challenged the constitutionality of Stanford University's speech code and its legality under California state law.

The *R.A.V.* holding did not, by contrast, invalidate laws governing racial and sexual *harassment*. As Scalia wrote, perhaps with the recent travails of his newest colleague on his mind, "sexually derogatory 'fighting words,' among other words, may produce a violation of Title VII's general prohibition against sexual discrimination in employment practices." In other words, workplace provisions for sexual harassment and the like are distinguishable from attempts to regulate hate speech.[76]

So what *was* punishable? According to Smolla, it was still likely that "a verbal attack directed at a particular individual in a face-to-face confrontation that presents a clear and present danger may be penalized."[77] So, too, would it be legal to pass a statute that "does not single out any particular sub-class of fighting words, but is aimed at fighting words generally." In other words, the concept of "fighting words" might be *applied* to racially motivated incidents; it could not, however, be *limited* to such incidents.[78]

The justices elaborated on this concept in 1993, in the case of *Wisconsin v. Mitchell*. On October 7, 1989, in Kenosha, Wisconsin, Todd Mitchell and some friends were discussing the motion picture *Mississippi Burning* when, angered by a scene in which a young black boy is beaten by a white man, Mitchell and his friends, all of whom were black, talked about targeting a white person as retribution. When a young white boy approached the group, Mitchell asked them: "You all want to fuck somebody up? There goes a white boy; go get him." The group beat the boy severely, stole his tennis shoes, and left him unconscious. He remained in a coma for four days.

Mitchell was initially convicted of aggravated battery, an offense that carries a maximum sentence of two years' imprisonment. But because Mitchell selected his victim on the basis of the boy's race, the jury recommended increasing Mitchell's sentence to seven years under a state provision that allows for an enhancement of the maximum penalty for an offense whenever the defendant "intentionally selects the person against whom the crime...is committed...because of the race, religion, color, disability, sexual orientation, national origin or ancestry of that person."

Mitchell subsequently appealed, challenging the constitutionality of Wisconsin's penalty-enhancement provision on First Amendment grounds; the Wisconsin Court of Appeals rejected his challenge. The Wisconsin Supreme Court, relying directly on *R.A.V.*, reversed and ruled that the enhancement provision "violates the First Amendment directly by punishing what the legislature has deemed to be offensive thought."

But on June 11, 1993, in what must have been a shock to the Wisconsin Supreme Court judges, the U.S. Supreme Court disagreed by a *unanimous* vote. Duly intent on clarifying the extent to which state officials could sanction racially motivated crimes—and aware of the need to avoid contradicting the central tenets of the Civil Rights Act of 1964—Chief Justice Rehnquist explained that "the State's desire to redress what it sees as the greater individual and societal harm inflicted by bias-inspired conduct provides an adequate explanation for the provision over and above mere disagreement with offenders' beliefs or biases." According to Rehnquist, the key distinction between the two cases was this: "[W]hereas the ordinance struck down in *R.A.V.* was explicitly directed at expression (i.e., 'speech' or 'messages'), the statute in this case is aimed at conduct unprotected by the First Amendment."[79]

At this point, the justices may have hoped that the hate speech issue was settled. But in the months and years that followed, lower courts invoked the *R.A.V.* ruling both to uphold and to strike down speech restriction laws. Consequently, in 2002 the Court was forced to revisit the issue. And once again, the central symbol was a burning cross.

The first incident took place in May 1998, when two Virginia men, Richard J. Elliott and Jonathan S. O'Mara, burned a cross in the yard of an African American neighbor. Then, three months later, another man named Barry Black burned a thirty-foot cross in an open field at a Ku Klux Klan rally that, while on private property, was also in full view of passing motorists and nearby residents. The men were each charged with violating a Virginia statute that said: "It shall be unlawful for any person or persons, with the intent of intimidating any person or group of persons, to burn, or cause to be burned, a cross on the property of another, a highway or other public place. Any person who shall violate any provision of this section shall be guilty of a Class 6 felony."

All three lost their cases in trial court, and the convictions were upheld on appeal. But the Virginia Supreme Court, consolidating the cases, reversed by a four-to-three vote. Relying directly on *R.A.V.*, the state court held that the cross-burning statute was unconstitutional on its face; that it was indistinguishable from the St. Paul ordinance; that its narrow focus on cross burning was a clear example of viewpoint discrimination; and that the statute was overbroad because the enhanced probability of prosecution would have a "chilling effect" on free expression. The U.S. Supreme Court accepted the case and scheduled oral arguments for December 11, 2002. Apparently, the justices felt their standard as outlined in *R.A.V.* needed clarification in light of *other* doctrines not discussed in *R.A.V.*

Arguing on behalf of the petitioner, William H. Hurd defended the Virginia statute as the protector of a fundamental freedom in America—the "freedom from fear"—and attempted to explain why the cross deserved special scrutiny: "It says, 'we're close at hand. We don't just talk. We act. And it deliberately invokes the precedent of 87 years of cross-burning as a tool of intimidation."

Following Hurd was Michael Dreeben, a fellow supporter of the law and representative of the Office of the Solicitor General. Arguing on behalf of the United States, Dreeben tried to clarify the relationship between the current facts and those in *R.A.V.* Whereas in *R.A.V.* the Court was confronted with a statute prohibiting the use of language based on particularly undesirable messages, Dreeben explained that in the Virginia statute "the focus is not on any particular message, but on the effect of intimidation, and the intent to create a climate of fear."

Up to that point, the conversation had been standard fare—dry, doctrinaire, and largely dull. Then something unusual occurred. The typically silent and reserved Justice Clarence Thomas spoke. And he did so in an impassioned, bold baritone voice. "It was a gripping made-for-television moment," recounted Supreme Court reporter Linda Greenhouse of the *New York Times*. In a question directed at Dreeben, the justice from Pin Point, Georgia, leaned forward in his black leather chair. Almost scolding the government lawyer defending the Virginia law, Thomas stressed the nearly "100 years of lynching in the South," and then added pointedly: "You're actually understating the symbolism...of the burning cross." More emphatic still, he added: "I think that what you're attempting to do is to fit this into our jurisprudence rather than stating more clearly what the cross was intended to accomplish and, indeed, that it is unlike any symbol in our society."[80]

It had been eleven years since the Court's lone black member had endured the public humiliation of his confirmation hearings, hearings that were inextricably linked with the primary iconography of white mob violence—black male sexuality—and hearings that had prompted Thomas at one point to brand the experience a "high-tech lynching." Since being confirmed, Thomas had remained largely silent. He did not participate at all during the oral arguments in *R.A.V.* But now Thomas's decision to speak out, according to veteran Court reporter Lyle Denniston,[81] "changed both the mood and substance" of the argument, with justice after justice expressing "sympathy for the Virginia law."[82]

That tone shaped the reception given to the lawyer representing the respondents, constitutional law scholar Rodney Smolla. "At the heart of our argument," he began, "is that when the State targets a particular symbol or a particular symbolic ritual, it engages in content and viewpoint discrimination of the type forbidden by the First Amendment." Smolla faced a barrage of hypothetical questions from the bench. When the conversation returned to the debate about whether the burning cross possessed any particular danger as a symbol, Justice Scalia spoke up. "I dare say that you would rather see a man with a—with a rifle on your front lawn—if you were a black man at night...than see a burning cross on your front lawn."[83]

Feeding on the ethos Thomas had created, Michael Hurd elaborated on the unique status of the racist symbol in his rebuttal: Cross burning, he said,

is not just hate speech. It doesn't just say I don't like you because you are black. In the hands of the Klan, the message is the law cannot help you if you're black or Catholic or Jewish or foreign-born, or we just don't like you, and if you try to live your life as a free American, we are going to kill you....That's why it is especially virulent. And that's why under *R.A.V.*, this Court can allow us to proscribe it without having to pass any other law, or pretend it is the same as something quite different than what it is.

"We have not interfered with freedom of speech," Hurd concluded the emotionally packed hour of debate. "We have not tried to suppress any idea. All we have tried to do is protect freedom from fear for all of our citizens by guarding against this especially virulent form of intimidation."

For Edward Cleary, who watched the oral argument unfold, it was a "highly disappointing development." As soon as Thomas spoke, Cleary felt that "the questioning went from legitimate inquiry regarding viewpoint-based discrimination to a focus on the history of the burning cross." For the victorious lawyer in the *R.A.V.* case, this seemed to distract the Court from its central purpose. "Obviously, true threats are proscribable," he explained in a 2005 interview. "This was never an issue in *R.A.V.* or *Black*. The issue is how you proscribe those threats." Indeed, for the Minnesota attorney the chief legal question was a simple one: "Do you prosecute true threats under a content-neutral law or do you ban a symbol?"

On April 7, 2003, a six-person majority of the Court (joined by Justice Scalia) announced that it agreed—in part—with Hurd that cross burning fell outside the First Amendment's umbrella of protection as long as the state could prove that it was a "true threat"—made with the intent to intimidate. In a key passage in her plurality opinion, Justice O'Connor noted:

[T]he First Amendment permits a State to ban "true threats"...which encompass those statements where the speaker means to communicate a serious expression of an intent to commit an act of unlawful violence to a particular individual or group of individuals.... The speaker need not actually intend to carry out the threat. Rather, a prohibition on true threats protects individuals from the fear of violence and the disruption that fear engenders, as well as from the possibility that the threatened violence will occur.

Duly mindful of the history of cross burning, the Court's centrist jurist added:

Intimidation in the constitutionally proscribable sense of the word is a type of true threat, where a speaker directs a threat to a person or group of persons with the intent of placing the victim in fear of bodily harm or death. Respondents do not contest that some cross burnings fit within this meaning of intimidating speech, and rightly so. As the history of cross burning in this country shows, that act is often intimidating, intended to create a pervasive fear in victims that they are a target of violence.[84]

But didn't the Virginia law, as Professors Barron and Dienes ask, discriminate against a specific class of true threats by proscribing *only* cross burnings? While not openly denying that possibility, Justice O'Connor maintained that the *R.A.V.* holding nonetheless permitted content discrimination "based on the very reasons why the particular class of speech at issue...is proscribable." The logic of her argument was as follows: First, the state of Virginia can ban cross burnings done with the *intent to intimidate;* second, cross burning is a "particularly virulent form of intimidation"; and third, there exists a long and persistent history that cross burning is linked to impending racial violence.[85] In such circumstances, she concluded, there is no impermissible content discrimination with the Virginia cross-burning law.[86]

However, in a separate seven-to-two vote, the justices also ruled that the Virginia law was wrong to say that burning a cross is, *prima facie,* evidence of intimidation. "The act of burning a cross may mean that a person is engaging in constitutionally proscribable intimidation," said O'Connor, "or it may mean only that the person is engaged in core political speech. The *prima facie* evidence provision blurs the line between these meanings, ignoring all of the contextual factors that are necessary to decide whether a particular cross burning is intended to intimidate. The First Amendment does not permit such a shortcut."

On this point, Clarence Thomas felt his colleagues had gone too far. "In every culture," he began his dissent, "certain things acquire meaning well beyond what outsiders can comprehend. That goes for both the sacred and the profane. I believe that cross burning is the paradigmatic example of the latter." There was something special, even unique, about cross burning and its history of racial intimidation. "In our culture," Thomas added, "cross burning has almost invariably meant lawlessness and understandably instills in its victims well-grounded fear of physical violence." Given the painful history of racial violence, there could be no doubt that all the state was doing in outlawing cross burning was "penalizing conduct it must have viewed as particularly vicious."

It was a strange conclusion, in a new century, to a journey that had consumed the first three years of the previous decade. And yet as befits such a complex issue, opinions about how to interpret the outcome were mixed. "I'd do it all again to get the results we got," said James Jubilee, one of the targets of the Virginia crosses. "It's a small step, but a step forward."[87]

WHAT BECAME OF THEM?

The day after the *R.A.V* ruling, Laura Jones and her children stood in their front yard, mowing the lawn and cleaning up. It was a nice day in St. Paul: seventy-seven degrees, sunny, and serene. The sun was bright but not oppressive. It was, in short, a snapshot of life in middle America. A mere one hundred feet away from Jones and her children—on the other side of Earl Street—was a man who identified himself as a "white separatist." There he stood, wearing a baseball cap emblazoned with the image of old Dixie, and the words "Certified Southern Ass Kicker."

That day, the nineteen-year-old provocateur told a reporter from the *Star Tribune* that he was not a skinhead; he just shaved his head for "hygiene reasons."

James Walsh, the reporter, may have found that hard to believe, given the young man's manner and tattoos—a blue-green cross with a circle and a *P* on his left forearm, the Norse god Odin on his right biceps, and an eagle's head on his right shoulder. But Laura Jones knew who he was and what he stood for; he was Robert A. Viktora, "R.A.V.," standing at the home of Arthur Morris Miller III, his code-fendant in the cross-burning incident.

Although the case had just ended and Viktora's conviction had been reversed, the Dixie-capped teenager knew he could still face criminal charges under a different law. Maybe that explains why he tempered his comments as he spoke to Walsh. Was he sorry that it happened? "I'd rather not comment on that," he replied. But he could not hold his tongue for long. Black people and their like—those "minorities and stuff"—were responsible for the crime in the neighborhood.

In the end, Robert Viktora's infamy brought him little. After his case came down from the Supreme Court, he drove a truck and took factory work when he could find it. In the interim, he dreamed of a separatist America: "[W]hat if we had our own places in the country? he asked Walsh. "It's a big country. You wouldn't hear the yapping."

When Viktora returned to Laura Jones's neighborhood, she and her family did no yapping—they said nothing. Did she not feel threatened by the return of the man with the Dixie cap? "It hasn't made me feel that way," she told Walsh. "As long as he keeps to himself and doesn't bother us—fine."[88]

Within two months of the *R.A.V.* decision, Robert Viktora was back in trouble with the law, this time for a scuffle with a policeman. The incident that led to his arrest occurred after his companion allegedly yelled "White Power" to a white police officer. Viktora was fined $100 and sentenced to twenty hours of community service.

Whether or not Viktora thereafter kept to himself was of no great moment to federal prosecutors. Likewise, they were not troubled by the fact that he could not be retried under state law for what he been charged with in *R.A.V.* Relying on a federal law, they first charged and then convicted him of violating the Joneses' civil rights. He received a six-month sentence, which he appealed. On April 26, 1994, the U.S. Court of Appeals for the Eight Circuit ruled against him, leaving the conviction intact.

Meanwhile, Arthur Morris Miller III, Viktora's alleged accomplice, had been the only adult—then eighteen years old—involved in the cross-burning incident. He had initially pleaded guilty and received a thirty-day sentence. His conviction was voided as a result of the *R.A.V.* holding. The victory, however, was short-lived. Several months later, Miller (like Viktora) was indicted on federal charges of conspiring to interfere with the Jones family's housing rights by way of intimidation and threat of force. Again, he raised a First Amendment bar to his prosecution.

This time it failed, and Miller thereafter pleaded guilty to conspiring to violate the Joneses' right of access to housing. That charge alone carried a penalty of one year in prison and a $100,000 fine.

A month later, in December 1992, there was another cross-burning incident in Minnesota, this time at the home of Sam and Emelda Harris and their three children in the Minneapolis suburb Eden Prairie. There was more to that racist prank than cross burning. The two teenage boys had also left a letter with racial slurs and death threats in the Harris family's mailbox, and hung a pillowcase with a basketball in it from a tree, as if to imply a lynching.

The *R.A.V.* precedent was of no value to this pair. Charged with the felony of making terrorist threats, the two pleaded guilty. Meanwhile, the community rallied to the support of the Harris family. Flowers and gifts arrived at their door, as did hundreds of sympathetic letters. Solidarity banners flew, and concerned citizens posted green ribbons on trees as a part of the community's antiracism campaign.[89]

Shortly after *R.A.V.* came down, Edward Cleary the lawyer became Edward Cleary the author. He signed a contract with Random House in September 1992 to publish a memoir of the case and his involvement in it. By January 1994, the three-hundred-page book, *Beyond the Burning Cross*, was completed. Nat Hentoff, the syndicated columnist and First Amendment absolutist par excellence, wrote an introduction to the work. "The inflammatory case of *R.A.V. v. City of St. Paul*," he opined, "turned out to be an exceptional victory for everyone's First Amendment rights."

Cleary's career in First Amendment law did not end with *R.A.V.* Ten years later, he was involved in another First Amendment case that came before the Supreme Court. This time, however, he was on the side *opposing* the First Amendment claim. In *Republican Party, et al. v. White* (2002), a divided Court (five to four) struck down a Minnesota law that barred candidates in state judicial elections from announcing their views on disputed political issues. Once again, Justice Scalia wrote for the majority. Notably, the very law the Court struck down was the one Cleary had reviewed critically when he served as director of the Office of Lawyers Professional Responsibility. Though Cleary had real "doubts" about the constitutionality of the Minnesota law, he was nonetheless troubled by the broad sweep of Justice Scalia's opinion. "I just had hoped," he told a reporter for the *Minnesota Lawyer*, that the Supreme Court "would find a middle ground and it doesn't look to me like [it] did."[90]

Around the same time, former wrestler and Minnesota governor Jesse "the Body" Ventura nominated Cleary, then age forty-nine, to serve as a district court judge in Ramsey County. It had been a long time coming, but Edward J. Cleary was now "Honorable."

THE FUTURE OF HATE SPEECH

It is often and understandably surmised that Justice Scalia's *R.A.V.* ruling ended the constitutional battle over hate speech laws. Yet there also stands the ruling in *Virginia v. Black*, which, as Professors Barron and Dienes argue, indicates another means whereby states can constitutionally proscribe racist speech. Those additional means include any variety of criminal laws with stern penalties, ranging from trespassing to intimidation to interference with access to housing.

There remains the question of whether the *Black* holding, based on the historical link between cross burnings and "true threats," will be extended to other kinds of expression, such as the public display of swastikas. If so, the doctrine of hate speech could well be resurrected, at least in part. And while the *R.A.V.* Court seemed to have dispensed with the idea that there are categorical exclusions to the First Amendment (e.g., fighting words), the *Black* Court soundly recognized a category of low-value speech subject to regulation (e.g., true threats).

If he were still alive, the Court's ruling in *Virginia v. Black* might have proven acceptable to Justice Hugo Black. After all, as his 1942 *Chaplinsky* vote suggested,[91] the great absolutist did not believe fighting words were worthy of First Amendment protection. Given that, how likely is it that the First Amendment hero of the Warren Court would have taken exception to the notion that "true threats" are unprotected expression?

In the end, it may be that Justice William Brennan's belief, announced in a 1989 flag-burning case, holds equally true in the context of hate speech: "If there is a bedrock principle underlying the First Amendment, it is that the government may not prohibit the expression of an idea *simply* because society finds the idea itself offensive or disagreeable."[92]

Striking Back at the Birchers

Elmer Gertz and Defamation

Strange mix: Richard Nixon, Elmer Gertz, and Bebe Rebozo. In the spring of 1974, these three men—an embattled president, a civil liberties lawyer, and a wealthy businessman—shared a common goal: limiting the reach of a 1964 landmark First Amendment ruling. Richard Nixon directed his Justice Department to draft proposed legislation to make it easier for government officials to sue for defamation. Elmer Gertz urged the Supreme Court to reverse a federal ruling barring him from suing the publisher of *American Opinion*, a small monthly magazine. And Charles "Bebe" Rebozo was in a federal court suing the *Washington Post* for $10 million for libel. All three of these very different men hoped to protect themselves against press attacks on their respective reputations. And for all three, the First Amendment stood in their way.

Can an individual's interest in his or her good name be reconciled with society's interest in freedom of expression? How much leeway should the press have in commenting on political officials, celebrities, or public figures when such reporting strays from the truth? Does the First Amendment ever protect falsehoods? Should it? If so, why and to what extent?

These questions have plagued Americans ever since the Sedition Act of 1798, when President John Adams and his Federalist allies imprisoned their critics for engaging in "seditious libel"—that is, for disparaging or ridiculing Adams and his policies. That debate continued well into the middle of the twentieth century, when the Supreme Court rendered its momentous opinion in *New York Times Co. v. Sullivan* (1964), which altered the First Amendment landscape concerning both seditious libel and the common law of defamation.

By 1974, however, the law of free speech and defamation had not been settled entirely. Hence, Richard Nixon went to his Justice Department, Bebe Rebozo went to federal court, and Elmer Gertz went to the Supreme Court to preserve his reputation against slurs made against him by Robert W. Welch, Jr., a reactionary man dedicated to ridding the world of so-called Communists like Gertz. The liberal Gertz asked the Court to relax the First Amendment while the conservative Welch implored the justices to reinvigorate it. Here is their story, *Gertz v. Welch* (1974), which began in the 1960s and even before that—a few centuries earlier, to be precise.

FREE SPEECH AND THE "ABUSE" THEREOF: THE HISTORICAL BACKDROP

> Who steals my purse steals trash; 'tis something, nothing;
> 'Twas mine, 'tis his, and has been slave to thousands;
> But he that filches from me my good name
> Robs me of that which not enriches him
> And makes me poor indeed.
>
> —SHAKESPEARE, *Othello*

Elmer Gertz (1906–2000) knew the constitutional history better than most. He knew, as the noted First Amendment lawyer Bruce Sanford once observed, that "English legal systems have protected a remedy to defamed persons since pre-Norman times."[1] And he knew that anything that might diminish a person's good name, whether that person was a government official or a private citizen, had historically been held to be actionable either civilly (as in a defamation action) or criminally (as in seditious libel).

Gertz, a University of Chicago Law School graduate, also knew that the Delaware Declaration of Rights of 1776 proclaimed that "the liberty of the press ought to be inviolably preserved." He believed in that principle and spent a good measure of his career as a lawyer defending the colonial conception of freedom that prefigured the First Amendment. He knew, too, that the Delaware Declaration provided that "every freeman" shall have a "remedy" for "every injury done to him in his goods, lands, or person." That constitutional provision, which included a guarantee of a remedy for injury to one's reputation, never found a formal counterpart in the federal Constitution and its various amendments. As early as 1790 (a year before the First Amendment became the law of the land), the Pennsylvania Constitution's free-speech clause provided: "The free communication of thoughts and opinions is one of the invaluable rights of man, and every citizen may freely speak, write and print on any subject, being *responsible for the abuse of that liberty"* (emphasis added).

The limiting language at the end of the Pennsylvania free-speech clause found its way into many state constitutions, including that of Illinois[2]—the state in which *Gertz v. Welch* arose in 1969. Gertz had a lot of history on his side. Going back to the nation's founding, there was ample evidence that speech freedoms were to be constrained by the need to protect people's reputations against the "abuses of liberty." Elmer Gertz agreed with that history, and he could point to many respected free-speech liberals and others who shared that view.

Zechariah Chafee, the great World War I hero of the First Amendment (see chapter 5), once granted that "[w]e can all agree that the free speech clauses do not wipe out the common law as to . . . defamation of individuals."[3] That proposition, as Chafee explained in his *Free Speech in the United States,* was borne out in Supreme Court statements such as this one in the opinion of Chief Justice Edward Douglass White (1845–1921) in *Toledo Newspaper Co. v. United States* (1918): "However complete is the right of the press to state public things and discuss them, that right . . . is subject to restraints which separate right from wrong-doing." Those restraints included defamation laws.

Many years afterward, the liberal justice Frank Murphy (1890–1949) echoed that principle when he announced that defamation was *outside* the boundaries of the First Amendment. In a passage once known by every lawyer and law student, Justice Murphy spoke for the Court in *Chaplinsky v. New Hampshire* (1942) when he declared: "There are certain well-defined and narrowly limited classes of speech, the prevention and punishment of which has never been thought to raise any Constitutional problem. These include . . . *libelous"* expression. A decade later, Justice Frankfurter restated the point in his opinion for the Court in *Beauharnais v. Illinois* (1952): "Libelous utterances not being within the area of constitutionally protected speech, it is unnecessary, either for us or for the State courts, to consider the issues behind the phrase 'clear and present danger.' Certainly no one would contend that obscene speech, for example, may be punished only upon a showing of such circumstances. Libel, as we have seen, is in the same class." There was another passage in Frankfurter's *Beauharnais* opinion with which Gertz, a devoted Jew sensitive to the dangerous realities of anti-Semitism, would have surely agreed: "[I]f an utterance directed at an individual may be the object of criminal sanctions, we cannot deny to a State power to punish the same utterance directed at a defined group, unless we can say that this is a willful and purposeless restriction unrelated to the peace and well-being of the State." Thus, *group libel* laws were also permissible under the national Constitution.[4]

Historically, then, an ample body of federal and state constitutional and common law made it abundantly clear that one could not defame another—that is, one could not make disparaging or false statements that would subject a private or public person or government official or group to "hatred, ridicule or obloquy" (abuse). Elmer Gertz was quite familiar with that body of law, both as a scholar and a litigator. He was also familiar with the more recent changes in First Amendment law—changes that very much altered, but did not abandon the law of the past.

THE CIVIL LIBERTIES LIBEL LAWYER

Elmer Gertz was, by all measures, a civil liberties lawyer. He was a strong champion of Bill of Rights protections, be they the free-speech guarantees of the First Amendment or the Eighth Amendment prohibition against cruel and unusual punishments. He was opposed to capital punishment and believed firmly in the ideal of rehabilitation. Perhaps that explains why he represented Nathan Leopold—better known as the first half of "Leopold and Loeb," the two wealthy Jewish University of Chicago students who, in 1924, murdered a fourteen-year old boy for the "thrill" of committing the "perfect crime." Clarence Darrow originally represented the two and managed to spare their lives (they received life sentences) by delivering one of the most impassioned arguments ever made against capital punishment. Years later, in 1958, Gertz succeeded in getting Leopold, his onetime law school classmate, paroled, and in 1963 he persuaded the governor of Illinois to release Leopold and restore his full civil rights.[5] The case and his role in it, Gertz once wrote, "gave additional meaning to my life."[6]

Such unpopular clients were not foreign to Gertz's law practice. At one time, he also represented Jack Ruby—the Chicago nightclub owner who shot Lee Harvey Oswald. By the time Gertz came to the case, Ruby (his actual surname was Rubenstein) had already been convicted of murder. But Gertz appealed Ruby's death sentence and got a Texas court to overturn the conviction on the ground that excessive publicity had prejudiced the case. It was for naught, however; Ruby died in jail while waiting for a retrial.

There were scores of other cases as well. In all of them, Elmer Gertz remained a staunch defender of civil liberties. But his first love seemed to be the First Amendment. "I have represented authors, publishers, producers, distributors, and others in a vast variety of obscenity cases...almost invariably with success," he said. "I believe strongly in complete freedom of expression."[7]

One of the freedoms the mustached and spectacled lawyer defended vigorously was the freedom to print, publish, or distribute sexually explicit matter, what some called "obscene" materials. Perhaps Gertz's most famous defense of First Amendment freedoms came when he represented Henry Miller and his once controversial 1934 novel, *The Tropic of Cancer*, the American edition of which was published by Grove Press in 1961.

By the time Gertz came to the case, there was litigation involving Miller's novel in at least sixty other cases. In the Chicago area, police in eleven suburban communities confiscated all of the paperback copies of Miller's novel. As recounted by Edward de Gracia, a friend and noted First Amendment lawyer and scholar, Gertz had established close relations with several lawyers (including the late Stanley Fleishman, a noted obscenity lawyer) in other parts of the country who were involved in the case. He used those contacts to develop a trial strategy. It worked.

On February 21, 1962, the Cook County judge in the case handed down his ruling. It made for a banner headline for the next day's paper: "Tropic of Cancer Wins." Judge Samuel B. Epstein enjoined the police from interfering with the book's distribution. Some of the more memorable passages in Epstein's opinion included the following: "Censorship is a very dangerous instrumentality, even in the hands of a court." He also wrote: "Let not the government or the court dictate the reading matter of a free people." Henry Miller was impressed with Gertz's First Amendment performance: He called Gertz "one of the most amazing men I have ever met."[8]

What happened in the Miller case was pure Gertz; the decision represented a view of law and life in which the government, by and large, respected the rights of the people to read and view a wide variety of sexually oriented materials. If obscene speech was unprotected, then the definition of obscenity had to be given a narrow meaning. That maxim was reflected in several cases Gertz argued before Illinois appellate courts.

Gertz represented both authors and booksellers of so-called obscene books. In 1967, for example, he successfully represented Paul Romaine, a bookseller who sold *Memoirs of a Woman of Pleasure* (better known as *Fanny Hill*). The trial court fined Romaine $1,000 and placed him on probation for two years. But the state high court in *People v. Romaine* (1967) reversed, in an opinion by Justice Walter V. Schaefer—one of the giants in the history of the Illinois Supreme Court. The same year, however, Gertz lost an appeal in *Cusack v. Teitel Film Corporation*, in which the films *Rent-a-Girl* and *Body of a Female* were held to be obscene. But even in such difficult cases, Gertz could sometimes prevail as he did in *People v. Butler* (1971) and *People v. Sparks* (1974), two more film obscenity cases, both of which were decided by the Appellate Court of Illinois. His track record, then, was rather impressive when it came to defending the First Amendment rights of those who trafficked in "alternative" books or films.

The lion's share of First Amendment lawyers who litigate obscenity cases are Hugo Black absolutists—they tend to concede little, if any, power to government when it comes to regulating expression. By that measure, Elmer Gertz, the famed First Amendment lawyer, was no Hugo Black lawyer. That is, there was one area where he believed the government had an important role to play in limiting what he saw as the excesses of liberty.[9]

It is a catechism among First Amendment attorneys that under no circumstances do they represent a plaintiff in a libel case.

—Martin Garbus

Almost from the beginning of my career as a lawyer, in the early 1930's...I have handled one libel case after another. The subject is a recurring theme.

—Elmer Gertz[10]

Elmer Gertz was also a man very concerned about bigotry and smears against reputation. He was particularly concerned about slurs made by hate groups that sullied the reputations of good people. In that sense, Gertz was a civil liberties lawyer who, unlike some, had no qualms about representing a plaintiff in a slander (spoken words) or libel (print or broadcast) action. From that vantage point, Elmer Gertz's run-in with the John Birch Society seemed destined to happen.

In February 1964, the former president of the Chicago division of the American Jewish Congress spoke at 8:30 P.M. at Temple Beth Israel, on Bernard Street, in Chicago. The topic: "Hate Groups." The speaker: Elmer Gertz. For anyone who knew him, this kind of lecture at this kind of forum on this kind of topic was entirely what one would expect from a lawyer who had devoted so much of his life to the cause of civil rights. One of the tools in his arsenal of legal weapons against hate groups and others was the common law of defamation—a body of law with which Gertz had considerable familiarity.

Two decades earlier, in 1941, Gertz had filed actions in court to safeguard the reputations of those unfairly maligned. One of his early cases involved a husband who sued his wife's parents for saying false things about him to his spouse, who then left him. To the extent that state law had abolished such "alienation of affection" actions, Gertz argued, they ran afoul of the right-to-remedy guarantee (art. 1, sec. 12) of the Illinois Bill of Rights. In the years that followed, Gertz became a seasoned libel lawyer who also litigated appellate cases.

Gertz's involvement in *Parmelee v. Hearst Publishing Co.* (1950) foreshadows *Gertz v. Welch* in uncanny ways. The issue then before the Appellate Court of Illinois was whether a reputable economist and author had established sufficient facts to maintain a libel action against the *Chicago Herald-Tribune*. It seemed that the paper had published certain things about Maurice Parmelee that suggested to some that he was either a Communist or a Communist sympathizer and that he also was engaged in "depraved practices." If true, the appellate court declared, such accusations concerning his loyalty had to be considered against the backdrop of the fact that the "common belief in Cook County and elsewhere was that Communists and their 'fellow travelers' were not loyal citizens of the United States but were seeking unlawfully to overthrow the constitutional government of, and impose Communism on, the United States."[11] The three-judge appellate court concluded, however, that the plaintiff, Parmelee, had not made a case for libel and therefore affirmed the lower court judgment to dismiss the case. Though he lost the case, Gertz was even more determined to prevail in the future.

By the 1960s and 1970s, Gertz had become a familiar name in Illinois law circles as a formidable libel lawyer. In 1967, for example, the same lawyer who once defended Jack Ruby represented a man in a libel suit against the district attorney of New Orleans and *Playboy* for suggesting that the plaintiff, Gordon Novel, was involved in a conspiracy to assassinate President Kennedy. The following year, Gertz was in the Illinois Supreme Court representing Seymour Zeinfeld, an employee suing his former employer for defamation for implying that he had stolen money from that employer. The alleged libel occurred in a letter the former employer sent to a mortgage company to which the plaintiff had applied for a loan. The trial judge dismissed the case, and the appellate court sustained the dismissal. But the Illinois high court took its cue from Gertz and reversed. Five years later, Gertz and his young associate, Wayne B. Giampietro, secured a $25,000 judgment for their client, Gail H. Myers, in another case involving an allegedly libelous letter, this one involving a union member suing a local union and its executive board. This time, however, the appellate judges ruled against Gertz and his client.

There were, of course, other cases and other courts. But every one of the many defamation actions pointed to the complaint Gertz filed on his behalf on June 17, 1969, against Robert Welch, Inc. By that time, Gertz had mastered two bodies of law—defamation and First Amendment law. He also continued to lecture on the evils of hate groups. Notably, in a January 29, 1962, letter to his friend and client Henry Miller, Gertz wrote: "What you say about the American Nazi Party ... strikes a response in me, but I am too afraid of any abridgement of freedom of expression to feel comfortable about taking action against the John Birch Society or people like them. When they become a clear and present danger to the peace of the community, we can act."[12]

Apparently, by the summer of 1969 Elmer Gertz felt that the Birchers had become a real danger to his community. Then again, maybe it was no more than a case of the proverbial wolf having arrived at *his* door.

THE BIRCHERS

> Chief Justice Warren votes "92% in favor of Communists." President Eisenhower is "a dedicated, conscious agent of the communist conspiracy." Ronald Reagan is a "lackey" of Communist conspirators.
>
> —ROBERT WELCH, JR.[13]

Robert Henry Winborne Welch, Jr. (1899–1985) was a candy manufacturer; he was also the man who, in 1958, founded the ultraconservative John Birch Society.

Its aim: to rid the world of the menace of Communism. To that end, there seemed to be no lengths to which Welch and his fellow Birchers would not go to expose Communists. That extremism provided perfect fodder for leftist songwriters, like one ingenious twenty-two-year-old folksinger who was then busy launching his career as a musical maverick.

It was pure Bob Dylan—satirical, comical, whimsical, and political: "Talkin' John Birch Paranoid Blues" was Dylan's sardonic take on the Communist paranoia that had swept over America in the McCarthy era and afterward. In this 1963 ballad, Dylan fantasizes about secretly joining the John Birch Society to ferret out "Commies." The more he investigates, the more "Commies" he finds, until the unimaginable happens—"[I started] investigatin' myself!" Around that time, May 1963, Dylan was invited to appear on the *Ed Sullivan Show*, then the premier Sunday evening TV variety program. True to his contraire ways, the rebellious folksinger chose "Talkin' John Birch Paranoid Blues" as his song. While the great "Stone Face" Sullivan had approved the song, CBS-TV executives were of a different mind. Dylan was asked to play a noncontroversial ballad. He refused. And so an hour before live air time, he was canceled, leaving America's country darlin' Brenda Lee to sing "Losing You."

In the early 1960s, Brenda Lee was a far safer bet than Bob Dylan. The focus of Dylan's satire was a right-wing group with an estimated sixty to a hundred thousand members, a $5 million annual income, and 250 staff members. And thanks to Robert Welch, its notoriety far exceeded its numbers.

The gregarious Welch, born in North Carolina, knew how to attract people's attention with his prophet-like character. His background, both educational and professional, helped him along. Raised as a fundamentalist Baptist, Welch did a two-year stint at the Naval Academy at Annapolis before he went off to Harvard Law School, where he attended a class taught by Felix Frankfurter (who was soon to join the Supreme Court). The two men clashed constantly; for Welch's money, Frankfurter was a Marxist propagator. Fed up with such "indoctrination," the blue-eyed boy left Harvard in 1921 and changed careers.

Welch remained in Cambridge, Massachusetts, where he opened the Oxford Candy Company, which sold various candies, including a chocolate bar tagged "Tar Baby." Years later, Welch made big money when he went to work for his brother, who also owned a candy company. A talented, talkative entrepreneur, Welch helped boost his brother's candy sales from $200,000 in 1935 to $20 million in 1956. Soon, he would tap into his fundamentalist training, legal education, and wealth to embark on a new calling—one that would place his name in the history books.

His foray into politics flopped; in 1950 he ran unsuccessfully on the Republican ticket for lieutenant governor of Massachusetts. But fate had other plans for Robert Welch. His new day began in December 1958, when he met with eleven other men in Indianapolis and founded the John Birch Society, taking its name from an

American intelligence officer and Baptist missionary who was killed in 1945 by Chinese Communists. The Society grew and drew financial support from rich conservatives and organizational support from political holdovers once aligned with the Joseph McCarthy movement. Its catechism of political faith was:

- Less government, more individual responsibility
- Advancement of a "militant form of Americanism"
- Eradication, at home and abroad, of the "Communist menace"
- Public exposure of the "insider conspiracy" and its "diabolical" supporters (many of them Jewish) engaged in plots to overthrow America
- Opposition to "globalism"
- Abolition of the United Nations
- Abolition of income tax
- Repeal of certain "Communist inspired" civil rights laws
- Return of a "Christian-style civilization"[14]

To make his movement successful, Welch needed a national bullhorn. He got it when his society, based in Belmont, Massachusetts, launched its first official magazine, *One Man's Opinion*—later renamed *American Opinion*. That magazine, combined with fiery tracts by Welch (*The Politician* and *The Blue Book of the John Birch Society*) ignited the minds of many and instilled fear into the hearts of many others. (Chief Justice Warren, however, claimed never to have been intimidated by the Society's notorious billboard campaign to "impeach Earl Warren.")

On March 22, 1969, the long arm of the Birch Society touched Elmer Gertz. Actually, it had touched him earlier, but he was unaware of it until Mary Giampietro (the wife of Gertz's law partner, Wayne Giampietro) telephoned him one day. Mary had just finished shopping and was armed with bags of groceries when a woman approached her and dropped a pamphlet in one of her grocery bags. Curious, she later glanced at the pamphlet. Its banner read: "FRAME-UP— Richard Nuccio and the War on Police." Vaguely familiar with the local controversy concerning a Chicago policeman accused of shooting a young man, Mary kept on looking. What she saw next as she paged through the pamphlet horrified her: it was a picture of her husband's employer. Below his photograph was the caption: "Elmer Gertz of Red Guild Harasses Nuccio."[15] When Gertz heard the news, he asked Mary to hang up the phone and come to his law office immediately.

As Gertz reviewed the pamphlet, he noticed that it said "these reprints will be sent postpaid to any address in the United States." And who was paying the postage? The answer was also printed on the pamphlet: "This article first appeared in the April 1969 issue of the *American Opinion*, an internationally circulated Conservative journal."[16] That publication was the brainchild of Robert Welch; it was a John Birch Society publication.

Outraged by the slur on his reputation, Elmer Gertz filed a libel suit on June 17, 1969, in the federal district court in Chicago—*Gertz v. Robert Welch, Inc.* His lawyer was his partner,[17] Giampietro, a bright and hardworking lawyer but "not especially impressive in appearance," according to Gertz. Giampietro requested a jury trial. The case was tried before Judge Bernard Decker, who did not seem very sympathetic to the lawsuit. "It can only result in the repetition of the libel," he said in the very first in-chambers conversation, "and can do you no good. Money cannot compensate you for any harm to your reputation."[18] The judge was telling counsel early on that it was a mistake to pursue this case. But Gertz went ahead with it anyway...and won fifteen months later.

The jury found that Gertz was not a public figure, which meant that it was far more likely for him to prevail, since it was easier for a purely private person to win a defamation action. The jury awarded him $50,000, all of it in *punitive* damages, since no actual damages had been established. When the defense filed a motion for a judgment notwithstanding the verdict, Judge Decker granted it and then dismissed the suit. The reason: Judge Decker believed that Gertz was a public figure and that public issues were involved. On appeal to the U.S. Court of Appeals for the Seventh Circuit, two First Amendment issues presented themselves: (1) whether the rule of *New York Times Co. v. Sullivan* applied to the defendant's false and scurrilous statements about Gertz, and (2) if *Sullivan* did apply, whether there was insufficient evidence to support a finding that the statements had been published with actual malice.

The appellate tribunal considered the matter and rendered a two-to-one judgment in Welch's favor. Judge John Paul Stevens (soon thereafter to be nominated to the U.S. Supreme Court) wrote for the majority. Stevens ruled that *Sullivan* did apply to the facts of the case and that actual malice had not been established with "convincing clarity." He concluded his opinion with these words: "We cannot...apply a fundamental protection in one fashion to the *New York Times* and *Time* Magazine and in another way to the John Birch Society. Whether we are moved to applaud or to despise what is said, our duty to defend the right to speak remains the same."[19] Judge Roger Kiley concurred in the judgment, though he did so with "considerable reluctance." That reluctance was due, he added, to his fear that "we may have in this opinion pushed through what I consider the outer limits of the First Amendment protection against liability for libelous statements and have further eroded the interests of non–'public figures' in their personal privacy."[20]

Though heartening, Judge Kiley's opinion was of little help to Elmer Gertz. Now, four federal judges (one trial, three appellate) had ruled against him. It was time to take his case to the highest court in the land. His chances for success in that venue turned heavily on his and his lawyer's ability to convince a majority of the justices *not* to extend the rule of a seminal case—*New York Times Co. v. Sullivan.*

"DANCING IN THE STREETS": THE *SULLIVAN* RULING

It is an occasion for dancing in the streets.
—ALEXANDER MEIKLEJOHN TO HARRY KALVEN, JR.,
COMMENTING ON *New York Times Co. v. Sullivan*[21]

There is a story—true, no less—that speaks volumes about how different people think about free speech. Decades ago, four esteemed Harvard law professors—Paul Freund, Arthur Sutherland, Mark DeWolfe Howe, and Ernest Brown—published a then new edition of their highly esteemed casebook *Constitutional Law*. The edition followed on the heels of the famous First Amendment case *New York Times Co. v. Sullivan* (1964). In that famous opinion, there is this celebrated line: "[W]e consider this case against the background of a profound national commitment to the principle that debate on public issues should be uninhibited, robust, and wide-open."

That passage, that aphorism with its almost biblical staying power, was *deleted* from the text of the opinion reproduced in the casebook of the Harvard four. Fluff! Not the sort of stuff for the serious minded. Meanwhile, in Chicago, the gifted First Amendment scholar Harry Kalven was busy heralding the same passage his Cambridge colleagues viewed as superfluous. For Kalven, that passage amounted to a "strong major premise about freedom of discussion of public issues."[22] For its time, the *Sullivan* passage was a bold "characterization of American freedom,"[23] as columnist Anthony Lewis later observed. The characterization caught. Today, it represents one of the high ideals of our constitutional and cultural heritage. No casebook author would dare to omit it.

The constitutionally transformative character of *Sullivan* was made possible by its link to the civil rights movement. (see chapter 6) The case arose out of the defamation suit filed in an Alabama court by the Montgomery commissioner of public safety against the *New York Times* and four black clergymen. Sullivan sued them for statements published in a full-page ad entitled "Heed Their Rising Voices" that ran in the paper on March 29, 1960. The ad, which criticized how the police had handled the civil rights demonstrations in Montgomery, contained some inaccuracies. Though the ad made no explicit reference to Commissioner Sullivan, a jury in the Circuit Court of Montgomery County nonetheless awarded him damages of $500,000, the full amount claimed, against all of the defendants. The Supreme Court of Alabama affirmed that judgment. The defendants thereafter petitioned the Supreme Court. Review was accepted and the case set for oral argument on January 6, 1964.

Even though the *Times* and the clergymen were represented in the Supreme Court by the highly able counsel of Columbia University law professor Herbert Wechsler (1909–2000), a respected scholar, it was still a very difficult case to win.

After all, Sullivan could only lose if the Court were to overrule centuries of defamation law and ignore more recent pronouncements in its own opinions. And what was the chance of that happening? Two months later, however, the improbable happened: a unanimous Court reversed the judgment of the Alabama courts and established a vibrant new strand of First Amendment law. Justice Brennan authored the majority opinion with separate concurring opinions by Hugo Black (joined by William O. Douglas) and Arthur Goldberg (also joined by Douglas). History was being written anew.

Prior to *Sullivan*, the law of defamation had operated largely free of any First Amendment constraints. What the Supreme Court said in *Chaplinsky v. New Hampshire* (1942) and *Beauharnais v. Illinois* (1952) made that abundantly clear—defamation was outside the sphere of protected expression. Period. But with the *Sullivan* holding, the converse became true. "Libel can claim no talismanic immunity from constitutional limitations. It must be measured by standards that satisfy the First Amendment," wrote Brennan.

Such judicial thinking would obfuscate the Alabama commissioner's ability to sue the *Times* and the black clergymen. By the new constitutional measure, Sullivan would have a next to impossible chance of ever winning: "We...think the evidence was constitutionally defective [because] it was incapable of supporting the jury's finding that the allegedly libelous statements were made 'of and concerning' respondent." That is, a plaintiff like Commissioner Sullivan would have to prove that the libel alleged was about ("of and concerning") him *specifically*. Yet, as the *Sullivan* Court observed: "There was no reference to respondent in the advertisement, either by name or official position." Even if Commissioner Sullivan could satisfy the "of and concerning" requirement, he would still have to meet a high standard of proof if he were to collect any damages. According to the new national norm formulated in *Sullivan*:

> The constitutional guarantees require...a federal rule that prohibits a *public official* from recovering damages for a defamatory falsehood relating to his official conduct unless he proves that the statement was made with *"actual malice"*—that is, with *knowledge* that it was false or with *reckless disregard* of whether it was false or not.[24]

With such declarations, the *Sullivan* Court reconfigured the law of torts and constitutionalized it. Henceforth, "citizen-critics" of government officials could not be sued unless it was clear that (1) the allegedly defamatory words clearly pertained to a given official, and (2) those words were uttered or printed either with the actual knowledge that they were false or with reckless disregard of their falsity. Given that standard, certain false statements concerning public officials could now claim constitutional protection. The First Amendment demanded such breathing space, so the argument went, if "citizen-critics" were to speak their minds and freely participate in that experiment that was American constitutional democracy. In another key passage, Justice Brennan went on to put another nail in the coffin of the traditional law of defamation:

> Criticism of…official [government] conduct does not lose its constitutional protection merely because it is effective criticism and hence diminishes their official reputations. If neither factual error nor defamatory content suffices to remove the constitutional shield from criticism of official conduct, the combination of the two elements is no less inadequate. This is the lesson to be drawn from the great controversy over the Sedition Act of 1798, which first crystallized a national awareness of the *central meaning* of the First Amendment.

That "central meaning" meant that the troubling 166-year history of the Sedition Act could not be reconciled with the First Amendment. What had long been one of the great-unanswered questions had now been laid to rest: there could no longer be a crime of seditious libel.[25]

For Kalven, the *Sullivan* opinion was of watershed importance. As he put it in his posthumously published book *A Worthy Tradition:*

> The *New York Times* case is…of major significance on two levels. First, its underlying rationale makes a major contribution to [free] speech theory. By authoritatively declaring the unconstitutionality of seditious libel, it clears the air as to one of the key rationales underlying First Amendment policy. Second, by providing a constitutional dimension to what had been long regarded as a purely private law matter left to the common law of each state, *Times* and subsequent decisions have had a considerable impact on the tort law of defamation.[26]

Glorious as Meiklejohn and Kalven found the *Sullivan* opinion, two of their First Amendment heroes had a slightly different take on things. "We would," wrote Justice Black (joined by Justice Douglas), "more faithfully interpret the First Amendment by holding that at the very least it leaves the people and the press free to criticize officials and discuss public affairs with impunity."[27] Liberal as it was, the *Sullivan* test was, by Black's measure, inadequate to safeguard First Amendment freedoms. Only absolute protection could do that.

In post-*Sullivan* cases prior to *Gertz v. Welch* (1974), the Court further liberalized First Amendment law governing defamation. As Kalven put it in a famous 1964 law review article, the Court seemed likely "to follow a dialectic progression from [1] public official to [2] government policy to [3] public policy to [4] matters in the public domain."[28] But if *Sullivan* were to be extended that far, then what, if anything, would remain of the law of defamation? That question very much troubled Elmer Gertz. Such rulings, he wrote in his 1992 book about his case, "seemed to mark the end of defamation actions by anyone." This bothered him, both as a citizen and as a plaintiff litigant. "The burden of proof had simply become too great for the average person, and the media rejoiced," he wrote. "Almost smugly, they seemed to take the judicial rule protecting them as a matter of course."[29]

Others, such as constitutional scholar Bruce E. Fein, agreed that *Sullivan* had "raised a virtually insurmountable barrier to successful defamation actions by public officials." Quite apart from *extending Sullivan*, the specific holding in the case was highly problematic on its own terms, argued Fein in a 1984 monograph. "A legal system that offers only niggardly safeguards against false assaults on the reputations of public officials," he wrote, "encourages an atmosphere of suspicion and cynicism surrounding government. Such an atmosphere impairs the ability of government to undertake bold and decisive measures to address many vexing problems that confront contemporary society."[30]

As the future would unfold, these two men—Elmer Gertz and Bruce Fein—would both have unique opportunities to change the law of *Sullivan*. Meanwhile, Kalven and Meiklejohn "danced" with joy.

GERTZ AND NIXON—THE LIBERAL AND CONSERVATIVE THREATS TO *SULLIVAN*

In Elmer Gertz's mind, *Sullivan* and its progeny were anything but an occasion of joy. Something had to be done. To that end, on October 17, 1972, Gertz filed his petition for review in the U.S. Supreme Court. Given the facts of his case, surely the newly constituted Burger Court could see the wisdom of reconsidering either certain tenets of *Sullivan* or the excessively liberal applications of it. Speaking as a civil liberties advocate *and* a libel lawyer, Gertz seemed to be the ideal petitioner for the case in the high Court. The justices agreed and granted his petition, setting oral arguments for November 14, 1973.

"We had filed our petition *pro se*—that is, in my name as my own attorney—and in the name of Wayne B. Giampietro," Gertz recalled. But the clerk of the Court informed him that one name had to be removed. So Gertz chose to bow out, leaving Giampietro as the sole lawyer of record for the petitioner. Though he counseled his younger law partner, Giampietro alone argued the case in the High Court. It was his first appearance there. An Oklahoma City lawyer, General C. J. Watts, a former army general who had served as co-counsel in the Seventh Circuit phase of the case, represented Robert Welch. Unlike Giampietro, Watts was a seasoned appellate advocate.

The argument began at 10:48 A.M. on November 14, 1973, and ended fifty-nine minutes later. All of the justices participated in a lively and erudite exchange, except Justice Douglas, who remained silent. Meanwhile, Elmer Gertz was speaking at Southern Illinois University at Carbondale, addressing the faculty and students on censorship. "I gave scarcely a moment's thought," he recalled, "to what was happening in the case that meant so much to me. I felt that I had to contain my curiosity."[31]

Someone in power, however, *was* giving more than a moment's thought to the case. Unknown to him, Gertz had an undesired ally in Richard Nixon, who was likewise troubled by the constitutional regime created by the *Sullivan* rule. Nixon, like Gertz, especially hated the "smug" attitude he believed *Sullivan* created in the press. So, he, too, had some plans to curb *Sullivan's* reach. Those plans first took shape in 1966, before Nixon's presidency.

Prior to becoming president, Richard Nixon argued a "false-light privacy" case in the Supreme Court. He was the only president in American history who had argued a First Amendment case in the Supreme Court. The case was *Time, Inc. v. Hill* (1967).

The facts concerned a 1952 incident in which three escaped convicts took James Hill, his wife, and their five children hostage in their Whitemarsh, Pennsylvania, home. Nineteen hours later, the family was freed, unharmed. The police caught up with the three convicts, two of whom were killed in the clash. The family later moved away and discouraged further publicity about the incident, which had caused them extensive involuntary notoriety. In 1953, Joseph Hayes published *The Desperate Hours*, a novel inspired by the family's experience. That novel, in turn, was made into a play. Then, in February 1955, *Life* published an article entitled "True Crime Inspires Tense Play," with the subtitle "The ordeal of a family trapped by convicts gives Broadway a new thriller."

The *Life* article echoed many of the novel's inaccuracies concerning the Hill family and their experience. Though the inaccuracies were not defamatory, they were discomforting. So the Hill family sued under a New York statute that allowed for liability whenever oral or written statements place another in a "false light." The jury awarded the family $50,000 in compensatory damages and $25,000 in punitive damages. On appeal, the Appellate Division of the New York Supreme Court ordered a new trial as to damages but sustained the jury's verdict of liability.

Harold R. Medina, Jr.,[32] argued the matter for *Time*, and Richard Nixon represented the family. The case was first argued on April 27, 1966, and then reargued on October 18, 1966. It was decided some eleven weeks later. By a five-to-one-to-three margin (Justice Harlan both concurred and dissented in part), the Supreme Court reversed. Justice Brennan, the author of *Sullivan*, spoke for the majority.

He declared: "We have no doubt that the subject of the *Life* article, the opening of a new play linked to an actual incident, is a matter of public interest. The line between the informing and the entertaining is too elusive for the protection of... [freedom of the press]." As in *Sullivan*, certain kinds of false statements were entitled to First Amendment protection:

> Erroneous statement is no less inevitable in such a case than in the case of comment upon public affairs, and in both, if innocent or merely negligent, "it must be protected if the freedoms of expression are to have the 'breathing space' that they 'need...to survive.'..." As James Madison said, "Some degree of abuse is inseparable from the proper use of every thing; and in no instance is this [truer] than in that of the press."

The sixty-year-old jurist added a few more comments reminiscent of what he had penned in *Sullivan* about the need to foster a robust press:

> We create a grave risk of serious impairment of the indispensable service of a free press in a free society if we saddle the press with the impossible burden of verifying to a certainty the facts associated in news articles with a person's name, picture or portrait, particularly as related to non-defamatory matter....A negligence test would place on the press the intolerable burden of guessing how a jury might assess the reasonableness of steps taken by it to verify the accuracy of every reference to a name, picture or portrait.[33]

Accordingly, the majority concluded that the Hills had to satisfy the *Sullivan* "actual malice" standard if they were to prevail. "The fact that the Hills were private figures was of no moment to Justice Brennan," as Professors Jerome Barron and Thomas Dienes have observed. For Brennan, they added, "it was the public interest in the subject matter that was controlling."[34] The nature of the issue (was it a matter of public concern?) was what controlled and not the status of the person (was he or she a public figure?).

True to his constitutional convictions, Justice Black concurred but with his own absolutist twist: "The prohibitions of the Constitution were written to prohibit certain specific things, and one of the specific things prohibited is a law which abridges freedom of the press."[35] No balancing, no malice standard, just absolute protection in "false light" cases as in defamation ones.

Richard Nixon thought it an *awful* opinion, not only because of its adverse effect on people like the Hill family but also because of what its logic portended for public officials and public figures. His concerns were colorfully expressed a few years later in a taped October 16, 1972, White House conversation with John

Ehrlichman: "John, there is no libel anymore," Nixon said. "The goddamn press can do anything."[36]

In the years after *Sullivan* and prior to *Gertz*, the traditional tort law of defamation had been so revolutionized by *Sullivan* and subsequent cases that it seemed few political or public figures would ever entertain the idea of suing for libel. The First Amendment lawyer Bruce Sanford makes the point well:

> Nowhere is it written in modern American law that the media is supposed to win every case, although one could be forgiven for thinking so given the record over the [years] since the landmark *New York Times Co. v. Sullivan* revolutionized the law in 1964. During the 1960s, 1970s and [early] 1980s, winning libel plaintiffs could be counted on two hands. Most public officials and public figures resigned themselves to the glum reality that they didn't stand a chance in libel litigation. The legal deck was too heavily stacked against them.[37]

That legal reality tortured Richard Nixon and troubled Elmer Gertz. What happened in *New York Times Co. v. Sullivan*, *Time v. Hill*, and their progeny irked Nixon to no end. Like Gertz, he felt that the proper balance between press rights and reputational interests had not been struck. Something had to be done.

In October 1972, the *Washington Post* reported that FBI agents had concluded that the June 1972 break-in at the Watergate Hotel was connected to a massive political spying and sabotage effort conducted on behalf of Nixon's reelection operatives. Not long afterward, former Nixon aides James W. McCord, Jr. and G. Gordon Liddy were convicted of conspiracy, burglary, and wiretapping in the Watergate matter. Five other men also pleaded guilty, although the conspiratorial tracks had not yet led to the president. But the *Washington Post* and the *New York Times* were busy on the hunt. About the same time, the Senate had voted seventy-seven to zero to form a Select Committee on Presidential Campaign Activities. Sam Ervin (Democrat of North Carolina), the learned constitutionalist, chaired the committee.

Against that backdrop, the following conversation occurred between the president and his White House counsel, John Dean. As with many White House conversations, it was taped, though neither Nixon nor Dean had any idea that their words would one day become public. On February 28, 1973, the two men spoke of the law of libel:

PRESIDENT: Well, you of course know, that I said at the time of the Hills' case [*Time v. Hill*]—well, it is God-damned near impossible for a public figure to win a libel case any more.

DEAN: Yes sir. It is. To establish (1) malice, or reckless disregard of—no, they're both very difficult.

PRESIDENT: Yeah. Well, malice is impossible, virtually . . .

DEAN: Tough. That's a bad decision, Mr. President. It really is. It was a bad decision.

PRESIDENT: What the hell happened? What's the name of that—I don't remember the case, but it was a horrible decision.

DEAN: *New York Times v. Sullivan.*

PRESIDENT: *Sullivan* case.

DEAN: And it came out of the South on a civil rights—

PRESIDENT: Selma. It was talking about some, some guy that was—yea, he was a police chief or something. Anyway, I remember reading it at the time when—that's when we were suing *Life*, you know, for the *Hills* [case]. When *Life* was guilty as hell.[38]

At about the same time, things were heating up for the president and his men as the House and Senate attempted to obtain copies of the incriminating secret White House tapes. Of course, what Nixon and Dean said about *New York Times Co. v. Sullivan* was not of paramount interest to them. They were looking for "impeachable" evidence, as were the *Post* and the *Times*. The president and his legal counsel did what they could to keep Congress at bay. They also had an idea about what to do with the press—an idea that traced back all too naturally to Nixon's antipathy toward the *Sullivan* holding.

While *Gertz v. Welch* awaited a ruling in the Supreme Court, President Nixon took to the airwaves to deliver a national radio address calling on Congress to enact legislation to buttress libel laws, especially those involving government officials and political candidates. The embattled president said a change was needed to encourage "good and decent people" to engage in politics without fear of "slanderous attacks on them or on their families."[39] This change could occur if lawmakers enacted a federal libel law; to assist them, Nixon called on his Justice Department to draw up proposed legislation. Bruce Fein,[40] then a twenty-seven-year-old conservative whiz kid from Harvard Law School, was assigned to draft the proposed law. According to John MacKenzie's March 9, 1974, *New York Times* news account, the ideas under consideration included the following three suggestions:

1. "A federal libel law that would displace or supplement existing state laws where the person claiming he was libeled was a federal office holder or candidate. Such a plaintiff would have an easier time proving that the falsehood was malicious than he would under current Supreme Court doctrine."

2. "Guidelines to ease the burden of proof in libel cases tried in the federal courts. Such cases reach federal tribunals because the plaintiff and defendant are from different states."
3. "A national 'right-to-reply' law giving candidates access to space in news media whenever they are criticized there, whether the criticism is true or false." (A state law version of this proposal was then under First Amendment consideration by the Supreme Court in the *Miami Herald v. Tornillo* case.)

Admittedly, the specifics were far from finalized. And the president conceded that such proposed legislation presented a "constitutional problem." Nonetheless, "We'll try to be consistent with whatever the constitutional requirements are," Nixon told an Associated Press reporter. Meanwhile, Justice Department lawyers were "not sanguine about it, but they think it can be done," said one Nixon aide. When barraged by questions from reporters, White House spokesman Bryce Harlow emphasized that this was "not an effort to shaft the press." But something had to be done, in Nixon's mind, to curb the *Sullivan* rule that he thought gave the press a virtual "license to lie."[41]

By this time, the Nixon White House was under frontal attack from the Congress, the press, and the people. The Justice Department had more important things to do than work on draft legislation to weaken the powers of the press. Within a few months, a unanimous Supreme Court ruled that President Nixon had to turn over the tape recordings of the White House conversations, thereby rejecting the president's claim of "executive privilege." Three days later, the House Judiciary Committee passed the first of three articles of impeachment. And shortly afterward, Richard Nixon resigned.

Historical events had taken over Nixon's campaign to circumvent *New York Times Co. v. Sullivan*, and his proposed legislation died. But the threat to *Sullivan's* viability was not yet over; the Supreme Court was about to render other rulings that term. That's where Elmer Gertz and his case came back into the picture.

COMPROMISING THE FIRST AMENDMENT: THE COURT RULES

> The *Gertz* decision was a judicial compromise that attempted to accommodate the competing values of uninhibited, robust, and wide-open debate on public issues with society's need to protect reputation.
>
> —Rodney Smolla[42]

June 25, 1974, was a little-known milestone in the history of the First Amendment. On that day alone, the U.S. Supreme Court handed down *six* freedom-of-expression opinions:

- *Spence v. State of Washington* (flag desecration)
- *Miami Herald v. Tornillo* (newspapers and right to reply)
- *Lehman v. City of Shaker Heights* (public forum)
- *Saxbe v. Washington Post Co.* (press access to prisoners)
- *Letter Carriers v. Austin* (defamation)
- *Gertz v. Welch, Inc.* (defamation)

In four of those cases, the First Amendment claim was denied. *Gertz v. Welch, Inc.* was one of them.

It took the Court some seven months to decide the case. When it did, the margin of victory turned out to be far closer than the original vote in the justices' conference. After the justices heard oral arguments in *Gertz*, they retired to the Court's elegant conference room to cast their preliminary votes and to assign the writing of the majority opinion to a particular justice. At the outset, the vote was eight to one, with only Justice Douglas dissenting. But between that time and the date the *Gertz* ruling came down, three justices (Burger, Brennan, and White) changed their votes for differing reasons and, along with Douglas, dissented. Some (Brennan and Douglas) thought the majority opinion had read the First Amendment too narrowly; others (Burger and White) felt it had read the First Amendment too broadly. Still, the vote was five to four in Elmer Gertz's favor.[43] Justice Lewis Powell, the gentleman from Virginia, wrote for the majority.

Justice Powell had been appointed by Nixon to succeed Hugo Black. In some significant ways, Powell was the jurisprudential opposite of Black. He was the quintessential balancer, not like Black, the quintessential absolutist. Powell thought context controlling; Black thought general principles governed the law of the First Amendment. Powell was more in the Frankfurter camp (he was an L.L.M. student of Frankfurter at Harvard), whereas Black was well entrenched in the William O. Douglas camp.[44]

Cautious and conservative, Powell was known for his centrist positions in controversial cases, like the famous opinion he wrote and the decisive vote he cast in *University of California Regents v. Bakke* (1978), a landmark affirmative action case. True to his centrist orientation, in his Court career he wrote a relatively even number of majority opinions either affirming or denying a free-speech right. He was, in other words, not inclined to move the law, including the law of *New York Times Co. v. Sullivan*, in bold ways and with a broad stroke. Powell was a "balancer" (see chapter 1), a jurist in search of equitable compromises. In *Gertz*, he found such a compromise—one that won the approval of four justices (Stewart, Marshall, Blackmun, and Rehnquist) and the disapproval of four others (Burger, Brennan, Douglas, and White).

The sixty-seven-year-old justice set the tone for his majority opinion by way of two remarkable statements that cut in different directions. On the one hand, wrote Powell, "[u]nder the First Amendment there is no such thing as a false idea. However pernicious an opinion may seem, we depend for its correction not on the conscience of judges and juries but on the competition of other ideas." On the other hand, he continued,

> there is no constitutional value in false statements of fact. Neither the intentional lie nor the careless error materially advances society's interest in "uninhibited, robust, and wide-open" debate on public issues [*Sullivan*]. They belong to that category of utterances which "are no essential part of any exposition of ideas, and are of such slight social value as a step to truth that any benefit that may be derived from them is clearly outweighed by the social interest in order and morality." *Chaplinsky v. New Hampshire* (1942)[45]

Justice Powell's opinion both reaffirmed and challenged certain key tenets of *Sullivan* and its First Amendment progeny. Its holding attempted to strike a balance between free-speech liberties and reputational interests by way of three general rules:

1. When *public officials* or *public figures* sue for defamation concerning an issue of *public concern*, they must always prove *actual malice* as required by *Sullivan;*
2. Where *private* individuals are involved in a defamation action against a publisher or broadcaster pertaining to an issue of *public concern*,[46] there must, at a minimum, be proof of *negligence* (there can be no liability without fault) when "'the substance of the defamatory statement makes a *substantial* danger to reputation *apparent*'"; and
3. *Presumed or punitive damages* against a publisher or broadcaster cannot be recovered absent a *Sullivan* showing of *knowledge of falsity* or *reckless disregard for the truth.*[47]

Powell's public-versus-private-figure dichotomy was of great consequence, because a public figure suing for damages related to a matter of public concern could recover *only* if he or she established that the false statements were the product of "actual malice," whereas a private figure could recover compensatory damages by showing no more than that the false statements were the product of the defendant's negligence.

All of this was another way of saying that the primary First Amendment focus was now on the *status of the person* rather than the *nature of the issue*. To the extent that prior precedents, like *Rosenbloom v. Metromedia, Inc.* (1971), suggested otherwise, they were no longer controlling. But how are public figures to be distinguished from private ones? To that question, Justice Powell offered the following answer:

> In some instances an individual may achieve such *pervasive fame* or *notoriety* that he becomes a public figure for *all purposes* and in all contexts. More commonly, an individual *voluntarily injects* himself or is drawn into a *particular public controversy* and thereby becomes a public figure for a *limited* range of issues. In either case such persons assume special prominence in the resolution of public questions.[48]

Hence, an *all-purpose* public figure would be someone who is exposed to broad media exposure—someone like Tiger Woods, Jerry Falwell, or Sarah Palin. Such figures would be relatively few in number. By contrast, a *limited-purpose* public figure must be someone who, as Erwin Chemerinsky phrased it, "voluntarily, affirmatively, thrusts himself or herself into the limelight."[49]

Applying this standard, the Court found that Elmer Gertz was neither an all-purpose public figure nor a limited-purpose one, the latter being the case because he "plainly did not thrust himself into the vortex of this public issue, nor did he engage the public's attention in an attempt to influence its outcome." Accordingly, the majority reversed and remanded his case for a new trial consistent with the Court's new rules.[50]

While *Gertz* answered many questions, it left several open to subsequent determination. For example:

1. Is the identity of the defendant determinative in defamation actions?
2. Who is a public figure?
3. What is defamatory?
4. What is actual malice?

As in *Gertz*, the First Amendment claims *lost* in three of the Court's key post-*Gertz* decisions that spoke to the above questions. Indeed, *Gertz* was a turning point; the halcyon days of which Bruce Sanford had so blissfully spoken had passed. Even so, and again as in *Gertz*, the spirit of *Sullivan* survived, though it was not quite as robust as before. While *Gertz* focused heavily on the identity of the speaker, subsequent case law suggested that the defendant's identity was not the sole concern in defamation actions. Thus, in *Dunn & Bradstreet, Inc. v. Greenmoss Builders, Inc.* (1985), a badly divided Court, per Justice Powell for a plurality, declared that "permitting recovery of presumed and punitive damages in defamation cases absent a showing of 'actual malice' does not violate the First Amendment when the defamatory statements did *not involve matters of public concern*." Hence, when purely *private speech* is involved, the more rigorous rules of

Gertz need not apply. Chief Justice Burger and Justice White joined in the judgment but noted that *Gertz* should be "overruled."

The post-*Gertz* Court also tweaked the "public figure" question a bit by holding, in *Time, Inc. v. Firestone* (1976), that for a defendant to fall within the *limited-purpose public figure* category there must be a real "public controversy" *and* the alleged public figure must thrust himself or herself "to the forefront" of that controversy "in order to influence the resolution of the issues involved." By that measure, the Court later ruled in *Wolston v. Reader's Digest Association* (1979), a low-profile and relatively minor criminal prosecution does not render a defendant a limited-purpose public figure.

As to the question of "what is defamatory?" the Court in *Milkovich v. Lorain Journal Co.* (1990) made it clear that merely labeling a statement a matter of *opinion* does *not* render it immune from liability for defamation. That is, the First Amendment does not necessitate a separate "opinion" privilege restricting the application of defamation laws. As then Chief Justice Rehnquist put it in his majority opinion: "Simply couching such statements in terms of opinion does not dispel [defamatory] implications; and the statement, 'In my opinion Jones is a liar,' can cause as much damage to reputation as the statement, 'Jones is a liar.'" While the Court thus rejected a fact/opinion dichotomy, it nonetheless ruled that a plaintiff in a defamation action involving a public matter must prove *fault* and *falsity*—that is, that the allegedly defamatory statement was meant as a statement of fact rather than as hyperbole or satire or parody. Such a qualification, Professor Farber has observed, "provides the functional equivalent of [an opinion] privilege by careful tailoring of the plaintiff's duty to prove falsity."[51]

In *Harte-Hanks Communications v. Connaughton* (1989), the justices returned to the question of what constitutes "actual malice" in defamation actions. Justice Stevens (the author of the 1972 *Gertz* opinion in the Seventh Circuit) announced for the Court: "Although failure to investigate will not alone support a finding of actual malice ... the *purposeful avoidance* of the truth is in a different category."[52]

Just as *Gertz* had both limited and expanded *Sullivan*, the post-*Gertz* cases both limited and expanded *Gertz*, though there was more of the former than of the latter. But all of these subsequent developments were of little moment to Elmer Gertz, who was busy litigating his "victory" in the lower courts as his case was considered anew on remand.

GERTZ V. WELCH—YET ANOTHER EIGHT YEARS OF LITIGATION

Given the new standards announced by the Supreme Court, in order for Gertz to collect *compensatory* damages, he had to establish that Welch had *negligently* made false statements, whereas if he wanted to collect *punitive* damages, he had to offer proof of *actual malice*. Gertz amended his complaint and alleged *both* negligence and actual malice by Welch, and thus requested compensatory and punitive damages.

Though the defense had dragged things out to no end, Gertz and his counsel stayed their course. Seven years after the Supreme Court ruled, the second trial finally began on April 13, 1981, with federal judge Joel Flaum presiding. The trial lasted six days. When it ended, the jury awarded Gertz $100,000 in compensatory damages and $300,000 in punitive damages—a stark improvement over his original award of just $50,000 in punitive damages.

Predictably, Welch appealed. He argued, among other things, that Gertz had failed to prove liability under either a negligence or actual malice standard. The Court of Appeals for the Seventh Circuit took the case up for the second time— ten years after their original ruling that was reversed by the Supreme Court. Four months after the three-judge court—Jeffrey Sprecher, Richard Posner, and Dudley Bonsal—heard the case, they rendered a unanimous judgment in Elmer Gertz's favor. Judge Sprecher ended his opinion for the court on a firm note: "because we find no merit in the issues raised on appeal, the judgment of the trial court is AFFIRMED."[53]

Again, Welch appealed to the Supreme Court. This time, however, the Court declined review. It was over; the defense had run out of time, money, and legal arguments. The long winter of litigation finally ended. Elmer Gertz had fought a formidable fight and had likewise won a formidable victory. In bold relief, here is how the 166 months of on-and-off litigation ultimately played out:

- Robert Welch had to pay a judgment of $400,000 ($100,000 in compensatory and $300,000 in punitive damages).
- Welch had to pay an additional $81,808.08 in interest and court costs.
- Welch (and Gertz, too) had to bear the high costs of the lawyers' fees associated with fourteen years of litigation.
- Welch had to sell the building in which his magazine had its headquarters in order to pay for all of the litigation costs and damages.

For those who visited Elmer Gertz's home shortly thereafter, a picture was proudly displayed for all to see. It was a picture of two men with broad smiles— the older Gertz and the younger Giampietro. They were holding the check they had just received from Robert Welch, Inc. With that money, Elmer and Mamie Gertz (his second wife) took a cruise around the world. Elmer and Mamie made a pact: In each port in which they stopped, they would make a toast to the John Birch Society for making their trip possible.

Over the years Professor Gertz—he taught as an adjunct at John Marshall Law School—would instruct his students about his case. "I'm cited more now than *New York Times* against *Sullivan*," he would tell them with glee. And then, this self-described "humble" man would declare: "I'm no longer a person, I'm a legal landmark." Reflecting on that statement, he would then add: "I deserve the nice things people say about me."[54] And so, in the final seventy-two pages of his 1992 book about his landmark case, Elmer Gertz collected many of those "nice" statements and listed the numerous articles written about *Gertz v. Welch.*

As for Robert Welch, he stepped down as chairman of the Society not long after it paid out the damages award. Two months later, he suffered a stroke, and within a year, on January 6, 1985, he died in a nursing home in Winchester, Massachusetts. "By then his once-controversial group had faded into near political obscurity."[55] The voluble extremist and his group had been silenced by time, which was helped along by Elmer Gertz.

REBOZO V. THE WASHINGTON POST—THE TEN-YEAR LIBEL SUIT

> For Bebe Rebozo, 1973 was the beginning of an eighteen-month night-mare of harassment. He was investigated by the IRS, the GAO, and the Miami District Attorney, in addition to being scandalously hounded by the Erwin Committee itself.
>
> —RICHARD M. NIXON (1978)[56]

Richard Nixon and Elmer Gertz shared a common bond in their enmity for the world made possible by the *Sullivan* opinion—a world that made the life of Charles Gregory Rebozo (1912–1998) miserable.

Had Rebozo not befriended Nixon, the IRS, the Justice Department, and the Senate, among others, probably never would have investigated him. Likewise, the press might never have noticed him, in which case he never would have sued the *Washington Post* for $10 million for allegedly defaming him. But he did befriend Nixon, which put all the other wheels of fate in motion.

If loyalty is the measure of friendship, "Bebe" Rebozo may have been the best friend Richard Nixon ever had. For more than four decades, Rebozo was a devoted, generous, and understanding friend, both before and after Nixon became famous. Indeed, during the darkest days of the Watergate scandal and afterward, Rebozo lent unqualified personal and financial support.

On July 31, 1970, Rebozo was on the cover of *Life.* Next to the photo of him smiling against the backdrop of a golf course, the caption read: "Richard Nixon's Best Friend." And when he died, virtually every obituary had words such as "loyal," "faithful," "confidant," or "best buddy" in its headline.

"Bebe Rebozo is one of the kindest and most generous men I have ever known. He is a man of great character and integrity," the former president wrote in his memoirs. "Yet anyone who read only the press stories about him, his business dealings, or his friendship with me," Nixon added, "would have had to conclude that he combined the worst traits of Rasputin and Al Capone."[57]

Rebozo was an American success story. The son of a Cuban cigar maker, he grew up in Depression-era poverty and seemed certain to go nowhere, yet he became a self-made millionaire. He began his career in real estate and invested wisely. Then he went into banking and invested wisely again. By 1951, the year he met Senator Nixon, he was a successful businessman living comfortably in Key Biscayne, Florida. The two men met by chance, and not long afterward went cruising aboard Rebozo's ChrisCraft yacht, *Coco Lobo;* Rebozo fished, Nixon read. In time, their friendship flourished; they shared afternoons at sports arenas, evenings at the theatre, and charcoal-broiled steaks at the finest restaurants. The well-groomed bachelor taught the president-to-be how to make profitable land investments, which made their association ever stronger. In later years, Rebozo, forever giving, would pay to have a bowling alley installed in the basement of Nixon's White House, and this was, moreover, not the most gracious of his many gifts to Nixon and his family.

From the early days, "this good friend and necessary companion reinforced Nixon's worst prejudices about 'them'—the dreaded press." Rebozo "hated the press," recalled William Safire. He accused them of making "a bunch of prying, hostile threats to the privacy and the future of his friend," Dick Nixon. "In a sense," added Safire, "his distrust was not misplaced: some of the press proceeded to investigate Bebe, poking into the business affairs of this mysterious man so close to the President."[58]

That poking started with a series of *Newsday* articles in September and October 1971, articles that took detailed aim at certain business dealings of Bebe Rebozo. The six-part series of investigative reports—headed by Robert Greene—focused on alleged shady business investments by the president's successful banker friend.

When Nixon got wind of the probe, the flow of information from the General Services Administration and Departments of Defense and Interior to the *Newsday* reporters slowed down considerably. Here is how Joseph S. Spear recounts the Nixon White House response in his *Presidents and The Press: The Nixon Legacy:*

> Inside the White House John Dean supervised activities ... at one point they considered planting rumors that *Newsday* was looking into Rebozo's activities because some of its editors and reporters were "Kennedy loyalists." They toyed with the idea of filing antitrust charges against the *Los Angeles Times,* which was owned by the same publishing firm that owns *Newsday.*[59]

Meanwhile, Nixon instructed Ron Ziegler, his press secretary, that *Newsday* was to receive absolutely none of the courtesies commonly extended to other papers. As for the *Newsday* reporter who headed the series, Spear notes:

Robert Greene was called in for a tax audit by the New York State Internal Revenue Division, an act instigated by the White House. The tax authorities also went through the returns of *Newsday's* publisher, William Atwood, and its editor, David Laventhal, as well as the paper's fiscal records. *Newsday's* White House correspondent, Martin Schram, was denied the most routine privileges.[60]

If intimidation could bring the press in line, then Richard Nixon was more than willing to play that card, especially if a negative story concerned one of his closest friends.

For whatever reasons, Rebozo never took legal action against *Newsday*. But when he read Ronald Kessler's October 25, 1973, story on him in the *Washington Post*, the otherwise easy-going Rebozo could think of nothing but litigation.[61]

It was a bold front-page headline—"Bebe Rebozo Said to Cash Stolen Stock"— with a bold lead: "Charles G. (Bebe) Rebozo, President Nixon's close friend, cashed $91,500 in stolen stock in 1968 after he was told by an insurance investigator it was stolen, the investigator's sworn statement and other records in a Miami court file indicate." There was a head shot of Rebozo in the column next to the headline. It bore a small caption: "Bebe Rebozo: Denies He Knew."[62]

When it came to the press and their "gotcha" journalism, Nixon's response was simple: "Sue the sons of bitches." It didn't matter whether what they printed was truthful or not, because "in the public mind [a lawsuit] creates an impression that they lied."[63] Whether or not Rebozo ever knew or acted on that advice Nixon gave to Bob Haldeman in October 1972 is unknown. What is known, however, is that in 1973 Rebozo did sue the *Post* for libel, filing his case in a federal district court in Florida.

The complaint in *Rebozo v. The Washington Post* alleged that the lead sentence in Ronald Kessler's October 23, 1973, article was false in two respects: (1) the investigator did not tell Kessler *personally* the stocks were stolen, and (2) the stocks were cashed by the bank, not Rebozo. Once the case was filed, the parties engaged in protracted litigation over a variety of issues ranging from jurisdiction to the requirements of libel law.

At first, things looked good for the *Post* as when in September 1978 a federal judge dismissed Rebozo's $10 million libel suit. But good news changed to bad for the *Post* on February 19, 1981, when the U.S. Court of Appeals for the Fifth Circuit reversed that ruling. In his opinion for the Court, Circuit Judge Paul H. Roney wrote:

> There is...a material question of fact suggested by Kessler's October 6, 1973, memorandum to his editor, in which the reporter expressed uncertainty about whether the Key Biscayne Bank or Rebozo himself cashed the

stock. Kessler stated in that memorandum that if the bank, rather than Rebozo, had actually cashed the stock, [his] article's proposed lead paragraph would have to be modified.[64]

The case, in Judge Roney's eyes, was equally problematic for Kessler and the *Post* for still other reasons:

This memorandum, plus the fact that Kessler resolved the uncertainty expressed in it in such a way as to cast plaintiff Rebozo in the worst possible light and to make for Kessler a front-page story of an episode which otherwise might not have commanded any significant attention, when taken in a light most favorable to Rebozo, could amount to evidence of the reporter's reckless disregard for the truth or falsity of the assertion that "Charles G. (Bebe) Rebozo, President Nixon's close friend, cashed $91,500 in stolen stock."[65]

Rebozo v. The Washington Post Co. was thus sent back to the federal district court for "further proceedings." Since the Fifth Circuit had also concluded that Rebozo was a "public figure," that meant his attorneys had to prove that the *Post* published the Kessler story with either *malice* or *reckless disregard* of the truth. That was a difficult burden but one nonetheless made easier by the facts to which Judge Roney had alluded.

Some thirty-three months later, the parties settled out of court. As a part of the settlement, both parties agreed to make contributions to the Boys Clubs of America—the only monetary payouts in the settlement. The *Post* also agreed to the following statement, which appeared in the November 4, 1983 issue of the paper. In relevant part, it read:

(1) The *Post* did not intend its article to indicate that Mr. Rebozo in fact knew that the stock in his bank's possession had been stolen from a brokerage firm. It reported the insurance investigator's testimony that he notified Mr. Rebozo the stock was stolen, together with Mr. Rebozo's denial that he was ever told the stock was stolen. Mr. Rebozo has continued to deny that the insurance investigator told him the stock was stolen, and apart from the insurance investigator's recollection there is no evidence that Mr. Rebozo was in fact told that the stock was stolen.

(2) The article did not state that Mr. Rebozo committed a criminal act, and it was not intended to convey that implication.[66]

With that statement, the libel case of *Rebozo v. The Washington Post* ended... ten years after it began. Rebozo's reputation was spared, and the *Post's* money was spared (it never had to pay any damages). Even so, both parties paid a costly coin in attorneys' fees.

TO LIFE ("L'CHAIM") AND BEYOND

> He helped provide us with answers to who we are and what life requires.
> —RABBI VICTOR WEISSBERG, MEMORIAL TRIBUTE
> TO ELMER GERTZ (MAY 2, 2002)[67]

Elmer Gertz died on April 27, 2000. He was ninety-three. By any standard, this man whose legal career spanned seven decades lived a full life. As he described it in his autobiography (*To Life*) and elsewhere, Gertz had successfully represented Nathan Leopold, Henry Miller, and Jack Ruby; he played a major role in revitalizing the Illinois Bill of Rights; he fought for fair housing and championed the admission of African Americans to the Chicago Bar Association; he persuaded Illinois governor Otto Kerner to commute Paul Crump's death sentence and then got him paroled thirty years later. When he wasn't litigating, Gertz wrote books (ten of them) and articles (numerous) and taught law at John Marshall School of Law. And, of course, he defeated the Birchers—*Gertz v. Welch* stands as a great reputational-rights victory.

More than four hundred family members, friends, politicians, associates, and judges paid their final respects to the memory of Elmer Gertz. "He understood justice and pursued it for its own sake and those who needed its protection," said Rabbi Victor Weissberg of Temple Beth-El. Many were the accolades and awards that came to Gertz both during and after his life. In 1972, this son of Jewish immigrants received the State of Israel Prime Minister's Medal, an award he greatly treasured. After he died, the *Chicago Jewish News*'s list of Chicago's most important Jews in the twentieth century ranked him fifteenth. And the Illinois State Bar Association posthumously awarded him its highest honor, the Medal of Merit.

Gertz's long and illustrious career stands as a monument to freedom; he did not fear it. But he did fear what he saw as its excesses. In that regard, he felt that the First Amendment pendulum had swung too far and needed to be halted in the name of justice. By and large, there seemed to be some broad support for that position, at least as staked out in the *Gertz* case with its particular facts. Consider, for example, what Professor Rodney Smolla has observed:

> Although the *Gertz* decision was a defeat for the press, most media lawyers and First Amendment scholars actually praised the decision. Perhaps much of the praise came from the sympathy that many of them had for hapless Elmer Gertz, a respected lawyer and professor dragged into the mud by the

extremist John Birch Society. The "respectable press," after all, could hardly endorse what the editor of the *American Opinion* had done—it looked like a case of deliberate character assassination.[68]

Not a victory for the press, observed communications professor Richard Labunski, "but it clearly could have been worse."[69] Indeed. The "compromise" struck in *Gertz*, however, would have killed Hugo Black had he been alive when the case was decided. *Gertz* would have been more of a concession than he could bear. As he put it in an earlier separate opinion in *Curtis Publishing Co. v. Butts* (1967): "[I]t is time for this Court to abandon *New York Times Co. v. Sullivan* and adopt the rule to the effect that the First Amendment was intended to leave the press free from the harassment of libel judgments."[70] William O. Douglas, Black's First Amendment cohort, agreed: "Continued recognition of the possibility of state libel suits for public discussion of public issues leaves the freedom of speech honored by the Fourteenth Amendment a diluted version of First Amendment protection," he complained in his *Gertz* dissent. And William Brennan—the great champion of the landmark *Sullivan* ruling—also took strong exception to the *Gertz* "compromise": "The Court's holding...simply [denies] free expression its needed 'breathing space.' Today's decision will exacerbate the rule of self-censorship of legitimate utterance as publishers 'steer far wider of the unlawful zone.'"[71]

Had the views of Black, Douglas, and Brennan prevailed, Elmer Gertz would have lost his case, and Bebe Rebozo would never have settled his. Would that have pushed our First Amendment freedoms too far? If so, was it salutary, then, to have some modicum of sensible fear about too much free-speech freedom? However such questions are answered—and reasonable freedom-loving minds can disagree here—one thing seems clear: Richard Nixon's plans for restructuring the First Amendment were destined to die so long as *New York Times Co. v. Sullivan* remained the law of the land.

Saving Old Glory

Gregory Johnson and Flag Desecration

The flag is a bit of bunting to one who insists on prose. Yet…its red is our life blood, its stars our world, its blue our heaven. It owns our land. At will it throws away our lives.

—OLIVER WENDELL HOLMES, JR. (1901)[1]

For the great American jurist Oliver Wendell Holmes, the flag was a statement about who we are, were, and will be. Its message is transcendent, in much the same way the field at Gettysburg is, or the Iwo Jima Monument, or the memorial at Pearl Harbor. "We live by symbols," Holmes also said.

So much of our day-to-day life and expression involves symbols. And in the long-standing discussion and debate over the role of symbols in our national life, perhaps no symbol has generated more controversy than the flag. It is widely revered. It commands respect. To honor it is to show respect for those who have sacrificed life and liberty for the principles for which it stands. But what does it mean to honor it? And, most important, for what—and whom—does it stand?

The debate over such questions points to a larger legal question: What forms of symbolic expression should or should not be protected under the First Amendment? The question arises because *expression*, as we have seen in chapter 7 and will again see in chapter 10, is not always synonymous with *speech*. And unlike pure speech, expression involves an element of *conduct*, which can more readily be regulated.

Stories about our flag are a vital part of the history of the First Amendment. It is a history filled with rich stories and characters, and politics and religion, and the central challenge of a free people—learning how to live with our deepest differences, and creating unity in the *interest* of our diversity, not in spite of it.

FLAG DESECRATION AND THE EARLY AMERICAN EXPERIENCE

Though fights over flags and the flag heated up by the mid-nineteenth century, overall, as scholar Robert Goldstein has written, "the American flag's role in the life of the nation before the Civil War was remarkably unimportant."[2] First adopted as the symbol of the nation in 1777—after an American Indian sent the Continental Congress three strings of wampum to cover the cost of a flag that could protect Indian chiefs when they traveled to meet with representatives of Congress—the flag's primary purpose was largely limited to identifying federal buildings and American ships at sea. It was unthinkable to fly the flag outside a private home, and as late as 1847, representatives of the Dutch government were forced to ask, in all seriousness, "What *is* the American flag?"

A year later, in the war against Mexico, American military forces fought under the Stars and Stripes for the first time; previously, units had fought under distinct regimental emblems. As a symbol, however, the flag remained stationed in the minor leagues of America's patriotic pastimes—far more popular, Goldstein reports, were depictions and stories about George Washington, images of the American eagle, and "Columbia," an anthropomorphized representation of liberty (and the eventual namesake of the nation's capitol district).

So it was not until Confederate troops fired the first shots of the Civil War against a flag-bedecked Fort Sumter that the American flag became a national icon—at least to northerners—for the first time. In 1862, in fact, a man named William Mumford was publicly hanged for violating a new decree requiring that "the emblem of the United States must be treated with the utmost deference and respect by all persons."[3]

"Until now," wrote a woman in her Civil War–era diary, "we never thought about the flag being more than a nice design of red and white stripes." Before long, wartime songs like James Fields's "The Stars and Stripes" whipped public opinion into a jingoistic fervor with lines like "Their flag is but a rag—Ours is the true one / Up with the Stars and Stripes / Down with the new one!"[4]

Once the Civil War ended, the country's groundswell of patriotism led to a heightened sensitivity about respecting the flag. But that sentiment extended well beyond the use or desecration of the flag as an act of *political* expression or protest. Indeed, nearly every early law related to the flag aimed to prevent its misuse for *commercial* purposes.

In 1890, Congress introduced the first proposed federal flag-desecration law, which would have imprisoned anyone who "shall disfigure the national flag, either by printing on said flag, or attaching to the same ... any advertisement for public display."[5] (The law did not pass; although the flag had not yet become identified as an avenue for political *expression*, politicians had long since discovered its value as a rallying symbol for their political *campaigns*.) According to First Amendment lawyer and scholar Robert Corn-Revere,[6] an 1895 pamphlet listed more than one hundred ways the flag's image had been commercially exploited, ranging from cufflinks and draperies to paper napkins and fancy dog blankets. And in 1900, the newly-formed American Flag Association (AFA) proposed model legislation that prohibited placing "any words or marks or inscriptions or picture or design or device or symbol or token or notice or drawing or advertisement of any nature whatever upon any flag, standard, color, or ensign of the United States."[7] In other words, any and all forms of commercial exploitation sullied the sanctity of the flag.[8]

By 1912, more than thirty states and territories relied on the AFA's model legislation to formally ban any misuse of the national symbol. Yet some state courts went against the trend by declaring the laws to be unconstitutional, prompting the U.S. Supreme Court to address the special significance of the American flag for the first time, in 1907, in the case of *Halter v. Nebraska*.

The case revolved around a Nebraska law, enacted on April 8, 1903, that made it a misdemeanor to sell, expose for sale, or have in possession for sale any merchandise on which was printed a representation of the American flag. Expressly exempted from the law was any printing of the flag that was "disconnected from any advertisement." The "plaintiffs in error" in the case, two Omaha liquor salesmen named Nicholas Halter and Harry Hayward, were arrested for using the Stars and Stripes on a beer label. The pair admitted to the facts as charged, but contended the state law was null and void because it infringed on their personal liberty as protected by the Fourteenth Amendment to the Constitution ("nor shall any State deprive any person of life, liberty, or property, without due process of law"). A jury of their peers—and, later, the Supreme Court of Nebraska— disagreed, but the U.S. Supreme Court accepted review in the case, allowing the liquor salesmen to believe, at least for one more round, that their glass of legal hope was half full.

On March 4, 1907, however, the Court announced that it agreed, by an eight-to-one margin, with the lower courts' rulings. Because "Congress has established no regulation as to the use of the flag," wrote Justice John Marshall Harlan, the majority[9] concluded it could not "overlook certain principles of constitutional construction, long ago established and steadily adhered to, which preclude a judicial tribunal from holding as legislative enactment, Federal or State, unconstitutional and void, unless it be manifestly so. Guided by these principles, it would seem difficult to hold that the statute of Nebraska ... infringes any right protected by the Constitution of the United States." He added:

From the earliest periods in the history of the human race, banners, standards, and ensigns have been adopted as symbols of the power and history of the peoples who bore them. It is not, then, remarkable that the American people, acting through the legislative branch of the government, early in their history, prescribed a flag as symbolical of the existence and sovereignty of the nation. Indeed, it would have been extraordinary if the government had started this country upon its marvelous career without giving it a flag to be recognized as the emblem of the American Republic.[10]

For Halter and Hayward, it was a bearable burden of defeat—$50 fines each and the costs of the prosecution. But in a larger sense, the Court's inaugural opinion about the symbolic power of the flag set the stage for the next few decades, when tectonic shifts in the international political landscape, coupled with a sharp spike in the rate of immigration to the United States, transformed flag controversies from commerce to Communism, and raised new questions about the extent to which the United States was willing to honor its commitment to provide a true "marketplace of ideas."

THE BIRTH OF THE RED MENACE

By the dawn of the 1920s, it was clear that the end of the Great War, despite the hope brought by the November 1918 armistice, had not brought a lasting peace. Ever since 1917, when news spread across the globe of Vladimir Lenin's October Revolution—the first successful Marxist revolution of the twentieth century— U.S. officials were forced to admit that their twin beliefs in the power of free expression and free markets had perhaps found an equally seductive ideological foil.

The growing perception that the "Red Menace" threatened the American way of life helped shift popular concern about the flag away from commercial and toward ideological misuse. This new reverence protected the captains of commerce while imprisoning the comrades of Communism. During a 1923 Flag Day celebration, for example, secretary of labor James Davis warned an audience of American citizens that "disrespect for the flag" represented one of the "first steps" toward becoming a Communist sympathizer.[11] A year later, Congress passed the National Origins Act, which sharply limited the number of immigrants who could be admitted to the United States from any country—particularly those from southern or eastern Europe.

Although a decade earlier, amid the violence and fear of 1919, California had been one of thirty-two states to ban the display of red flags, no one from the Golden State had ever been arrested (let alone convicted) for violating the law. That was the case until Yetta Stromberg, a teenage daughter of Russian immigrants and a summer camp counselor, came along and raised a red flag at a

Communist camp for children. She was, along with a small group of fellow Communists, among the first people to be charged with violating section 403a of the California Penal Code, which provided:

> Any person who displays a red flag, banner or badge or any flag, badge, banner, or device of any color or form whatever in any public place or in any meeting place or public assembly, or from or on any house, building or window as a sign, symbol or emblem of opposition to organized government or as an invitation or stimulus to anarchistic action or as an aid to propaganda that is of a seditious character is guilty of a felony.

On October 24, 1929, Stromberg and four other female defendants were sentenced in superior court to serve terms of between six months and five years at San Quentin prison—the lone man to be arrested, Isadore Berkowitz, dodged earthly justice by hanging himself the Monday before sentencing.[12] As for Yetta, her bail pending appeal was set at $7,500—an enormous amount at the time.

On appeal, Stromberg's lawyers unsuccessfully restated their claim that the statute was an unwarranted limitation on the right of free speech.[13] "'It is inconceivable,'" reported the *Los Angeles Times*, quoting from the appeals court's decision, "'that the State has not the right to prohibit by penal laws the willful and deliberate training of traitors to itself under the guise of protection of the right to free speech, particularly, as in this case, among those who by reason of youth and inexperience have no chance to form an independent judgment.'"[14] The editorial board members of the *St. Louis Post-Dispatch* disagreed. "When a great and powerful country like the United States becomes so nervous over the activities of an obscure 19 year old teacher and the agitation of a few scattered communists as to send them to prison," they scolded, "then surely the mountain has labored and brought forth a mouse. These people did no violence; they are guilty only of expressing unpopular opinions, a right guaranteed by the constitution."[15]

Because of the constitutional questions involved, the U.S. Supreme Court agreed to hear the case. And because of a few recent legal developments, the defense's argument in *Stromberg*—that, under the Fourteenth Amendment, the red flag law was an impermissible limitation on the individual right to liberty—had a greater chance of success. The change in the legal landscape occurred in 1925 when, in the case of *Gitlow v. New York* (see chapter 2), the Court suggested for the first time that state governments were required to honor select First Amendment freedoms by way of the Fourteenth Amendment's guarantee of due process. "For present purposes," Justice Edward Sanford wrote, "we may and do assume that freedom of speech and of the press—which are protected by the First Amendment from abridgment by Congress—are among the fundamental personal rights and 'liberties' protected by the due process clause of the

Fourteenth Amendment from impairment by the States." It was just an assumption, as Sanford had explained, not a legally binding holding. Yet on April 15, 1931, when the lawyers for both sides delivered their oral arguments in the case of *Stromberg v. California*, all interested parties must have wondered how strongly Sanford's words would echo in the ears of the current High Court.

Little more than a month later, the justices provided their answer—and established a new category of First Amendment jurisprudence in the process. "It has been determined," wrote Chief Justice Charles Evans Hughes, citing *Gitlow*, "that the conception of liberty under the due process clause of the Fourteenth Amendment embraces the right of free speech." And although "the right is not an absolute one," said Hughes,

> [t]he maintenance of the opportunity for free political discussion, to the end that government may be responsive to the will of the people and that changes may be obtained by lawful means, an opportunity essential to the security of the Republic is a fundamental principle of our Constitutional system. A statute which upon its face, and as authoritatively construed, is so vague and indefinite as to permit the punishment of the fair use of this opportunity is repugnant to the guarantee of liberty contained in the Fourteenth Amendment.[16]

The relevant section of the California law was set aside, and Yetta Stromberg's conviction was reversed by a seven-to-two margin. Notably, as Corn-Revere has observed, "the Court found it unnecessary even to discuss whether the symbolic act in question [raising a red flag] constituted expression." The justices did, however, clearly indicate by their ruling that they believed one could express one's ideas by using a symbol instead of a speech. With those words, the legal concept that the First Amendment protected oral, written, *and* symbolic expression came into being.

In the decades to come, that distinction would demand further clarification from future Courts—and help stoke the fires of the ongoing debate about the role of the flag in American society. But first a different sort of ideological battle broke out. And once again, a child was at the center of the controversy.

"I PLEDGE ALLEGIANCE ..."

Billy Gobitas knew that refusing to salute the flag was not what fifth-graders did, especially fifth-graders in his hometown of Minersville, Pennsylvania. But four years after the *Stromberg* decision—on October 22, 1935—he stood on principle. "I do not salute the flag," he wrote to his local school board, "because I have promised to do the will of God." The next day, Billy's twelve-year-old sister, Lillian, followed suit. "This wasn't something my parents forced on us," she later explained. "I did a lot of reading and checking in the Bible and I really took my own stand."[17]

Although the Gobitas children were alone among Minersville's minors in their protests, they were unified in a much larger sense by their understanding of what deserved their primary allegiance. As Billy explained in his letter, members of his faith—Jehovah's Witnesses—believe that a flag salute is a form of idolatry, violating the biblical injunction not to "make unto thee any graven image, nor bow down to them." In short, to force the children of Witnesses to salute the flag was to compel them to participate in a form of symbolic expression antithetical to their religious convictions.

Despite the Gobitases' religious objections to the flag salute, the Minersville school board believed the Pledge of Allegiance should be considered an even higher calling, a sacred ritual in the service of helping fulfill the mission of public schools to instill a lifelong love of country. Besides, in a town where almost everyone was Roman Catholic, it was hard to find sympathy for such an antiestablishment stance. Billy and Lillian Gobitas were expelled from school.

The following year, with the help of the Watch Tower Society and the ACLU, the children's father, Walter Gobitas, filed suit. He argued that the Minersville school board had deprived his children of their constitutional rights to freedom of religion and speech. Surprisingly, the family won, first in the federal district court in Philadelphia and then again in the U.S. Court of Appeals for the Third Circuit—both times because the judges felt the children were exercising their inalienable rights to free speech and free exercise of religion.

The U.S. Supreme Court accepted the case for review, and on June 3, 1940, its opinion in *Minersville v. Gobitis*[18] was announced. By an overwhelming eight-to-one vote, and against the backdrop of the world's second global conflict, the Court decreed that the government had the authority to compel students to participate in the flag salute. Writing for the majority, Justice Frankfurter echoed some of the Court's language in *Halter*:

> The flag is the symbol of our national unity, transcending all internal differences, however large, within the framework of the Constitution. This Court has had occasion to say that "... the flag is the symbol of the nation's power, the emblem of freedom in its truest, best sense.... it signifies government resting on the consent of the governed; liberty regulated by law; the protection of the weak against the strong; security against the exercise of arbitrary power; and absolute safety for free institutions against foreign aggression."[19]

Justice Harlan Stone (1872–1946), alone in dissent, begged to differ. "The law which is thus sustained," Stone insisted, is unique in the history of Anglo-American legislation. It does more than suppress freedom of speech and more than prohibit the free exercise of religion, which concededly are forbidden by the First Amendment and are violations of the liberty guaranteed by the Fourteenth. For by this law the state seeks to coerce these children to express a sentiment which, as they interpret it, they do not entertain, and which violates their deepest religious convictions. The guaranties of civil liberty are but guaranties of freedom of the human mind and spirit and of reasonable freedom and opportunity to express them.

They presuppose the right of the individual to hold such opinions as he will and to give them reasonably free expression, and his freedom, and that of the state as well, to teach and persuade others by the communication of ideas. The very essence of the liberty which they guaranty is the freedom of the individual from compulsion as to what he shall think and what he shall say, at least where the compulsion is to bear false witness to his religion. If these guaranties are to have any meaning they must, I think, be deemed to withhold from the state any authority to compel belief or the expression of it where that expression violates religious convictions, whatever may be the legislative view of the desirability of such compulsion.

Within weeks of the Court's ruling, issued as it was during an American period of peace that was nearing its end, Jehovah's Witnesses across the country were targeted for their "unpatriotic" beliefs. By October 1940, fifteen Witnesses were victims of mob violence, spanning 355 communities and forty-four states. One was reportedly castrated for his act of resistance. Before World War II ended, over two thousand children of Jehovah's Witnesses were expelled from schools for refusing to salute the flag. Trying to make sense of it all, one federal official wrote that "the files of the Department of Justice reflect an uninterrupted record of violence and persecution of the Witnesses. Almost without exception, the flag and the flag salute can be found as the percussion cap that sets off these acts."[20]

In part because of the violence the *Gobitis* decision helped foment, three of the Court's members almost immediately began to rethink their votes. In fact, when Justice William O. Douglas told Frankfurter that Justice Hugo Black had apparently changed his mind on the case, Frankfurter asked if Black had been rereading the Constitution. "No," Douglas replied, "He has been reading the papers."[21]

Before long, Black, Douglas, and their colleagues—two of whom were new to the bench—got the chance to right their perceived wrong. On January 9, 1942, the West Virginia Board of Education, relying heavily on the Court's language in *Gobitis*, adopted a resolution that all teachers and pupils "shall be required to participate" in the Pledge of Allegiance. Refusing to do so would constitute "an Act of insubordination," possible expulsion, and perhaps even the prosecution of the child's parents or guardians.

Although certain modifications were made in response to the local PTA's concern that the Pledge as currently executed looked "too much like Hitler's" Nazi salute,[22] no concession was made to the Witnesses' religious objections. In response, the families of three young Witnesses—Walter Barnette, Lucy McClure, and Paul Stull—who had been expelled under the law brought suit in federal district court, alleging that the law amounted to an unconstitutional denial of the freedoms of religion and speech, and was therefore invalid under the 'due process' and 'equal protection' clauses of the Fourteenth Amendment.

This time, by a six-to-three vote—announced on Flag Day—the Court sided with the students, struck down the West Virginia flag-salute law, and overruled *Gobitis* in the process. Writing for the majority, Justice Robert Jackson[23] explored once again the issue of symbolic speech, delivering one of the Court's most celebrated opinions in its long history. "There is no doubt," Jackson conceded, "the flag salute is a form of utterance. Symbolism is a primitive but effective way of communicating ideas. The use of an emblem or flag to symbolize some system, idea, institution, or personality, is a short cut from mind to mind." Jackson cited the Court's earlier decision in *Stromberg* by referencing Chief Justice Charles Evans Hughes's contention that "the display of a red flag as a symbol of opposition" was constitutionally protected behavior. He then returned to the facts in West Virginia. "The question which underlies the flag-salute controversy is whether such a ceremony so touching matters of opinion and political attitude may be imposed upon the individual by official authority." In regard to this question, Jackson felt the nation's founding documents were clear:

> The very purpose of a Bill of Rights was to withdraw certain subjects from the vicissitudes of political controversy, to place them beyond the reach of majorities and officials and to establish them as legal principles to be applied by the courts. One's right to life, liberty, and property, to free speech, a free press, freedom of worship and assembly, and other fundamental rights may not be submitted to vote; they depend on the outcome of no elections.[24]

Making the case for minority rights in the face of majority will, Jackson continued: "Freedom to differ is not limited to things that do not matter much," he explained, before adding what would become one of the most celebrated lines in our First Amendment history: "If there is any fixed star in our constitutional constellation, it is that no official, high or petty, can prescribe what shall be orthodox in politics, nationalism, religion, or other matters of opinion or force citizens to confess by word or act their faith therein."[25]

The Court's decision in *Barnette* represented not just a monumental victory for Jehovah's Witnesses but also a remarkably fast turnaround—just three years—in the minds of a majority of the Court. When added to the Court's previous flag-related decisions, says Professor Chemerinsky, *Barnette* also raises two important and interrelated legal questions: First, "when should conduct be analyzed under the First Amendment?" And second, "what should be the test for analyzing whether conduct that communicates is protected by the First Amendment?"[26] Surprisingly, a quarter century would pass before the Court would provide any clear answers to those questions. And when it did, the conduct in question involved not the American flag, but a different symbol of the federal government.

FROM FLAGS TO DRAFT CARDS

David Paul O'Brien's military registration certificate was tiny and nondescript—on just two by three inches of white card paper. Inscribed on the small card, however, was all the vital information relating to O'Brien's military eligibility—not just his name and address but also his physical description, signature, and Selective Service number.

O'Brien, a nineteen-year-old philosophy major at Boston University, was well aware of both the utility and the significance of the card. So he decided to use it to make a larger point about the slowly escalating conflict in Vietnam. On March 31, 1966, before a sizable impromptu audience at the South Boston Courthouse, he and three companions set their draft cards on fire. The crowd, which included several FBI agents who were not receptive to the implied message behind the act, quickly closed in on the protesters. An FBI agent spirited O'Brien and the others away from the angry mob and into the safety of the courthouse. The young antiwar philosopher then followed up his symbolic act with a verbal explanation of his intent—to influence others to adopt his antiwar beliefs "so that other people would reevaluate their positions with Selective Service, with the armed forces, and reevaluate their place in the culture of today."[27]

O'Brien was indicted, tried, and convicted by a federal district court for violating a part of the Universal Military Training and Service Act—originally enacted in 1948 but then amended in 1965, just as America's involvement in Vietnam had begun to escalate. The Act subjected to criminal liability anyone who "forges, alters, or in any manner changes [or] knowingly destroys" or mutilates a registration certificate. On appeal, the Court of Appeals for the First Circuit held that the law was an unconstitutional abridgment of free speech because it singled out persons engaged in protests for special treatment.[28]

But the U.S. Supreme Court disagreed with the First Circuit and, in the case of *United States v. O'Brien*, found the language of the Act to be constitutional "both as enacted and as applied." Drawing a clear distinction between the facts in *O'Brien* and *Stromberg*—and using the phrase "symbolic speech" for the first time in a Supreme Court opinion—Chief Justice Earl Warren explained that the Act "does not distinguish between public and private destruction, and it does not punish only destruction engaged in for the purpose of expressing views."

"We cannot accept the view," Warren wrote on behalf of the seven-to-one majority,[29] "that an apparently limitless variety of conduct can be labeled 'speech' whenever the person engaging in the conduct intends thereby to express an idea." Then Warren formulated a test for evaluating the extent to which symbolic expression should be constitutionally protected:

> This Court has held that when "speech" and "nonspeech" elements are combined in the same course of conduct, a sufficiently important governmental interest in regulating the nonspeech element can justify incidental limitations on First Amendment freedoms.... [W]e think it clear that a government regulation is sufficiently justified if it is [1] within the constitutional power of the Government; if it [2] furthers an important or substantial governmental interest; if [3] the governmental interest is unrelated to the suppression of free expression; and if [4] the incidental restriction on alleged First Amendment freedoms is no greater than is essential to the furtherance of that interest.[30]

Applying this four-part test to the amended language of the Service Act, the Court felt all requirements were met, "and consequently...O'Brien can be constitutionally convicted for violating it." The majority was uninterested in the presumed legislative motive for amending the act—to outlaw draft card burning as a form of political protest—because of a principle of constitutional adjudication. "It is a familiar principle of constitutional law," Warren explained, "that this Court will not strike down an otherwise constitutional statute on the basis of an alleged illicit legislative motive."[31] Besides, whereas in *Stromberg* the law in question had specifically targeted dissent, in *O'Brien* the law was designed to assure "the smooth and proper functioning of the system that Congress has established to raise armies."

Notably, Hugo Black signed on to the majority's judgment and opinion. For the aging Alabama-born jurist, the decision was defensible because the expression in question involved *conduct*, not speech. Hence, consistent with his vote in the *Tinker* case (see chapter 10), Black felt no obligation to safeguard the rights of draft card burners.

Commenting on *O'Brien* years later, Professor Farber explains that the decision—and the test it articulated—has often been used to uphold government regulation. "Except for statutes that entirely foreclose a traditional channel of communication...the Court rarely invalidates a regulation once it has found it to be content-neutral."[32] Consequently, Farber contends, "the outcome of a given case often turns almost completely on whether the regulation is characterized as content-based." For Professors Jerome Barron and Thomas Dienes, that fact is important. "From a speech-protective point of view," they contend, "one of the surprises—maybe one of the disappointments—about *O'Brien* is that the Supreme Court took such a deferential approach to the government's assertion of its interests."[33] Laurence Tribe agrees, suggesting that the content-neutral distinction introduced a new, two-track system of First Amendment legal analysis. If the government regulates conduct without regard to the ideas being communicated, Tribe explains, it is acting in a content-neutral fashion, and the more government-friendly standard established in *O'Brien* will apply. If, however, the government regulates conduct because of some harm associated with the speaker's particular message, its law would be content-based and the standard in *O'Brien* would be inapplicable.[34]

David Paul O'Brien thought that such legal niceties were irrelevant. "Intellectually, I expected [the result]," he told an Associated Press reporter just after the Court announced its opinion. "But it was still a shock. I think this shows that the [Johnson] Administration and the courts are moving toward an oppressive state which will not tolerate dissent."[35] The young protester was not alone in his anger and frustration. Even as his case was making its way through the system, a second sort of conflagration had ignited the passions of everyday Americans, and required legal intervention as well. The nation's flag, far removed from the quaint days of its appearance on a Nebraska beer bottle, had become a potent symbol of political dissent. Just ask Sidney Street.

"WE DON'T NEED NO DAMN FLAG"

Across the globe—but particularly in the United States—1968 was a year of almost unprecedented upheaval, violence, and revolution. It began in late January, when North Vietnamese military forces used the Tet Nguyen Dan—the lunar New Year—as a diversion to surprise American and South Vietnamese troops across the country, including Saigon, where Ho Chi Minh's Communist fighters briefly captured the U.S. embassy. Although in time every attack was rebuffed, the symbolism of the Tet Offensive had a lasting effect on the psyche of the American public, and is considered by many to be the turning point of that war. A few months later, on April 4, Martin Luther King, Jr., was assassinated outside his hotel room in Memphis. Riots broke out across the country as a result, and significant sections of many major American cities—including Washington, D.C.—were set ablaze in anger and protest. Then, in early June, with the nation still mourning the loss of King, Robert F. Kennedy, Jr.—the presumptive Democratic nominee for president and a staunch antiwar advocate—was also gunned down.

As opposition to the war grew (1968 was also the year city police and anti-war protesters violently clashed outside the Democratic National Convention in Chicago), as social unrest widened, and as the nation's cultural vicissitudes grew more pronounced, Congress responded by enacting the first federal flag-desecration law. As Democratic congressman Hale Boggs put it, the federal law was designed to prevent "outrageous acts which go beyond protest and violate things which the overwhelming majority of Americans hold sacred." But the 1968 law did not have its desired effect. In fact, as a 1970 *Time* cover story reported, Old Glory had "become the emblem of America's disunity.... [The] defiant young blow their noses on it, sleep on it, set it afire or wear it to patch the seat of their trousers," while other Americans "wave it with defensive pride, crack skulls in its name and fly it from their garbage trucks, police cars and skyscraper scaffolds."[36]

Sidney Street was not one of the defiant young, nor was he out to crack skulls in its name. An African American World War II veteran and the recipient of a Bronze Star for his heroism, Street was a Brooklyn bus driver, not an antiwar activist. But on June 6, 1966, after hearing on the radio at his home that civil rights leader James Meredith had been shot by a sniper during a Mississippi march, the forty-seven-year-old veteran snapped. The proud owner of two American flags, Street took one from his drawer and carried it to the Brooklyn intersection of St. James and Lafayette avenues. As a small crowd—including at least one police officer—gathered around him, Street announced, "We don't need no damn flag," took a match and lit the flag on fire. The officer asked if the burning flag was his. "Yes," he replied, "that is my flag. I burned it. If they let that happen to Meredith, we don't need an American flag."[37] Shortly afterward, Street was arrested, tried, and convicted for violating a New York desecration law that made it a misdemeanor to "mutilate, deface, defile or defy, trample upon or cast contempt" on the American flag "either by words or act."

According to Robert Goldstein, during the bulk of Street's initial trial and subsequent state appeals court proceedings—all of which upheld his conviction—"virtually the entire focus of both prosecuting and defense attorneys was whether flag burning was a constitutionally-protected form of political protest."[38] Little attention was paid to Street's spoken criticisms. As the New York Court of Appeals made clear in its July 7, 1967, opinion, "[w]hile nonverbal expressions may be a form of speech within the meaning and protection of the First and Fourteenth Amendments, the State may, under its police powers, pro-scribe forms of conduct which threaten the peace, security or well-being of its inhabitants... [and] legitimately curb such activities in the interest of preventing violence and maintaining public order."[39] The ruling was appealed.

Two weeks after a strife-beset U.S. Supreme Court began its 179th year,[40] the justices sat to hear oral arguments in the case of *Street v. New York*. It was the first time since the *Halter* case in 1907 that the Court had formally considered the constitutionality of flag-desecration laws. There were, however, clear distinctions. *Halter* dealt with a commercial misuse of the flag and was argued and decided in terms of due process rights, not free speech rights. By contrast, Sidney Street's actions were a clear form of political protest, prompting his ACLU-affiliated lawyer, David Goldstick, to contend in his brief for the Court that flag burning was a legitimate form of political protest. "If we concede," Goldstick wrote, "that there are certain political symbols which are above desecration, we open the door to drastic suppression of our right to criticize the state. There is no logical differentiation between burning the flag and burning an effigy of the President. Our flag is really the effigy of a nation. As such, it is not immune from symbolic criticism." Interestingly, Goldstick also argued that "new, dramatic forms of communication" were needed in an increasingly visual society and a world in which it was harder to gain the attention of the mass media. "If, in fact, 'the medium is the message,'" he wrote, quoting Marshall McLuhan, "or at least an important ingredient of the message, this Court has [a] responsibility to insure that new, visual forms of communication receive the protection to which they are entitled."[41]

To counter, acting Brooklyn district attorney Elliott Golden cast the social turbulence of the nation as both a backdrop and a call to action. "We cannot afford to experiment by permitting all acts and words denigrating to our basic philosophies to freely reach the marketplace of ideas," he said. "The question of free expression must yield to the higher requirement"—that the nation "survive in the hostile atmosphere of a tumultuous present-day history."[42]

On October 25, 1968, in the justices' private conference about the case, a preliminary poll revealed a six-to-two majority[43] for reversing Street's conviction. Chief Justice Warren was one of the two holdouts. "The only question," he explained, "is whether New York can punish the public burning of an American flag. I think the state can do so to prevent riots and so forth. It is conduct, not pure speech or symbolic speech." Notably, Hugo Black agreed. For the First Amendment's great champion, the distinction between "speech" and "conduct" had been an essential determinant ever since the series of civil rights sit-in cases (see chapter 6) had crossed his desk. Initially, the other justices were inclined to follow the lead of John Harlan, who suggested they avoid "deal[ing] with the statute on its face." Since Street *could* have been convicted for his verbal expression and not his conduct, Harlan urged the Court to reverse on that narrow ground—even though Street's words had played little, if any, part in the arguments on either side.

It was a politically nuanced decision, designed to circumvent any direct ruling on the constitutionality of flag burning. But as the lull between the initial vote and the announcement of the decision dragged on, two of the justices who originally voted to overturn the conviction—Byron White and Abe Fortas—changed their minds. With an "apology to Brother Harlan for inconstancy," Fortas explained he had "finally concluded that it is sensible to accept the realities of the facts: that appellant was arrested for publicly burning the flag and that speech need not be considered part of the offense."[44] Despite the defections of Fortas and White, five justices still sided with Sidney Street and overturned his conviction—albeit on narrow grounds. Harlan's majority opinion had "resist[ed] the pull to decide the constitutional issues involved in this case on a broader basis than the record before us imperatively requires."[45]

Chief Justice Warren wrote a stinging dissent. Not only did the majority "strain to bring this trial within [the standard in] *Stromberg*," Warren began, "but more particularly it has declined to meet and resolve the basic question in the case.... The teaching of *Stromberg* is that, if there is any possibility the general verdict below rests on speech or conduct entitled to constitutional protection, then the conviction must be reversed. [But] the *Stromberg* analysis cannot be applied to appellant's conviction as... the record leaves no doubt that appellant did burn the flag." In more impassioned terms, he added: "In a time when the American flag has increasingly become an integral part of public protests, the constitutionality of the flag-desecration statutes enacted by all of the States and Congress is a matter of the most widespread concern.... I believe the States and the Federal Government do have the power to protect the flag from acts of desecration and disgrace."[46]

Justices White, Fortas, and Black, filing separate dissents, agreed with the chief justice's central complaint. "The Court has spun an intricate, technical web," wrote White, "but I fear it has ensnared itself in its own remorseless logic and arrived at a result having no support in the facts of the case or the governing law."[47] And true to his changed ways—since the tumult of the 1960s had made him reconsider his commitment to the First Amendment—Hugo Black was emphatic in dissent: "It passes my belief that anything in the Federal Constitution bars a State from making the deliberate burning of the American flag an offense. It is immaterial to me that words are spoken in connection with the burning. It is the burning of the flag that the State has set its face against."[48]

Although the case was decided on narrow grounds, the Court's decision in *Street* was, claims Goldstein, "something of a minor landmark, not only because it was the first High Court opinion on flag desecration laws in sixty years, but also because it clearly struck down the provisions contained in most state laws that outlawed remarks about the flag." Still, Goldstein believes the Court's refusal to directly address the constitutionality of physical desecration "fostered confusion and uncertainty in the lower courts."[49] And as the nation's involvement in the Vietnam War grew more and more unpopular, the justices would again be forced to confront, and dodge, the central question of whether the flag could constitutionally serve as "the effigy of the nation."

"I FELT THAT THE FLAG STOOD FOR AMERICA"

Despite desperate hopes for a respite, the end of the 1960s brought little change to the national political landscape. In fact, if anything, the ideological distinctions between Americans grew more pronounced. A good example of that chasm was the way different citizens viewed the significance of the American flag. In a 1971 news story, the *New York Times*'s Fred P. Graham recounted a few recent narratives to underscore the divide.[50] In Hauppauge, New York, "a young housewife was arrested for flying an American flag upside down to protest the Vietnam War." Further north in the state, in Claverack, "a bearded young man was arrested for driving a red, white and blue Volkswagen." At the same time, a New York American Legion post received no sanction for "invert[ing] its flag to protest the Government's dovish response" to a U.S. coastal freighter's attack and capture, and no arrests were made when "the state's agricultural products were advertised in a poster bearing a picture of Old Glory... with potatoes instead of stars."[51]

These and other examples of the flag's uneven treatment in the courts and proper use prompted Graham to pose the question the Supreme Court was artfully dodging: "Is the destruction or irreverent use of the American flag as an act of protest a form of 'symbolic speech' that is protected by the First Amendment's guarantee of freedom of expression?" On March 24, 1971, the country's nine most powerful legal minds again managed to sidestep that important question, this time because they were equally divided—Justice Douglas recused himself from considering the matter—in the case of *Radich v. New York.*

Stephen Radich, a Madison Avenue art gallery owner, had been arrested in 1967 for exhibiting antiwar sculptures that depicted the flag, among other things, as a noose hanging a human figure and an erect penis hanging from a cross. Initially sentenced to sixty days in jail and a $75 fine, Radich's conviction was upheld by New York's high court, which ruled that even if Radich had a sincere ideological viewpoint, he could not use "insults to the Flag" to express it.

In their private discussion of the case, the justices lined up as they had in *Street.* In conference, Chief Justice Burger, noting that *Street* had been "written to avoid the present issue," asked John Harlan, the author of that opinion, to speak first. "This is an emotional field," Harlan began. "If Congress or the states want to pass an act that the American flag can't be used for a protest meeting, that is one thing—but here there is no such law. There is only a judicial rule that the flag can't be used in a protest against government action." Harlan thus voted to reverse Radich's conviction. Justice Potter Stewart agreed with his colleague—and explained his reasoning with the issue of symbolic speech in mind. "There is only conduct here in the exhibition," he said. "However, the conduct here is 'First Amendment conduct'—it is no different from talking. Radich did not destroy or burn the flag. I would reverse on *Street.*" Not surprisingly, Burger, Black, and

White (and, later, Blackmun) disagreed. "Making a male penis out of a flag is desecration," said Burger. "If any act on flag desecration can be supported, this is it." As other conference notes indicate, White then explained why he was unconcerned that Radich, and not the sculptor, was the one on trial. "The essence of the crime was casting contempt on the flag," opined the former college football star. "The act of exhibition is as execrable as creating the work of art." Black, too, was unshakeable. "I have had bouts with my clerks about this issue. The government can create a symbol and protect it. One can speak against the flag, but he can't use the flag to desecrate it. That is true here," he said. "I affirm."[52]

That left the deciding vote in the hands of the Court's most liberal defender of First Amendment freedoms—William O. Douglas. But Douglas had already recused himself; the same law firm that was representing Radich had once represented him.[53] That left the Court deadlocked at four to four, thus affirming the lower court's ruling.[54]

Three years later—just a few months before President Richard Nixon was forced to step down in disgrace—the Court again confronted the issue of flag desecration, this time via the case of Valerie Goguen, a twenty-one-year-old Massachusetts resident arrested in January 1970 for violating a 1899 state statute that made it a crime, punishable by a one-year prison sentence and a $100 fine, to "publicly...treat contemptuously the flag of the United States." Local police arrested Goguen for sewing a small cloth version of the flag to the seat of his pants. Although the opening words of the state statute outlawed publicly mutilating, trampling on, or defacing the flag, Goguen was not charged with any act of physical desecration. The state supreme court then upheld his six-month sentence. When the matter was taken to federal courts on a habeas corpus appeal, the Court of Appeals for the First Circuit held that the contempt provision of the statute was unconstitutionally vague and overbroad.

For a still skittish U.S. Supreme Court, that initial oversight by local police proved useful. "We affirm [the First Circuit's ruling] on the vagueness ground," wrote Justice Lewis Powell[55] on behalf of the six-to-three majority, before clarifying that he and his colleagues did "not reach the correctness of the holding below on overbreadth or other First Amendment grounds." It was another in a line of narrowly won victories.

Justice Rehnquist, the newest member of the Court after assuming Harlan's seat on January 7, 1972, was unconvinced. "The issue of the application of the First Amendment to expressive conduct, or 'symbolic speech,' is undoubtedly a difficult one," wrote the future chief justice, who saw no reason why the Government could not protect the physical integrity of the flag. "For what they have purchased is not merely cloth dyed red, white and blue, but also the one visible manifestation of two hundred years of nationhood—a history compiled by generations of our forebears and contributed to by streams of immigrants from the four corners of the globe."[56] Despite Rehnquist's passionate discontent, the majority opinion, confined as it was to the "treats contemptuously" phrase of the Massachusetts law, left standing the remaining sections that made it a crime to mutilate or deface the flag. By implication, that meant that similar laws across the country, similarly worded, also remained good law.

And so the conflict continued, with the next battle breaking out in the state of Washington, and the next decision being announced just three months after *Smith v. Goguen*, in the case of *Spence v. Washington*.

Just six days after an exchange between national guardsmen and student protesters on the campus of Kent State University left four students dead, Harold Spence displayed outside his Seattle apartment window an upside-down U.S. flag with a peace symbol. According to Court records, Spence indicated that his private act of protest was about not just the killings at Kent State but also the U.S. government's recent invasion of Cambodia, and that his purpose "was to associate the flag with peace instead of war and violence. I felt there had been so much killing," Spence explained, "and that this was not what America stood for. I felt that the flag stood for America and I wanted people to know that I thought America stood for peace."

When three Seattle police officers noticed the altered flag, they entered the apartment building and spoke to Spence, who said: "I suppose you are here about the flag. I didn't know there was anything wrong with it. I will take it down."[57] Despite Spence's willingness to remove the flag, he was charged under the state's flag-desecration statute, which prohibited placing "any word, figure, mark, picture, design, drawing or advertisement of any nature upon any flag" and/or to "expose to public view any such flag." Found guilty by a jury of his peers, Spence was sentenced to ten days in jail (suspended) and a $75 fine. On appeal, however, the Washington Court of Appeals reversed the conviction, finding that the "improper use" statute was both overbroad and invalid on its face under the First and Fourteenth amendments. The state supreme court disagreed, reinstating Spence's conviction.

This time, the U.S. Supreme Court, recognizing the confusion of the lower courts, attempted to clarify the legal concept of "symbolic speech" by establishing when conduct could be considered communicative. In a six-to-three *per curiam* opinion (with Burger, White, and Rehnquist in dissent), the justices reversed the conviction and found that the First Amendment in fact protected Spence's symbolic speech.

"The Court for decades has recognized the communicative connotations of the use of flags," wrote the justices, citing *Stromberg* and *Barnette*. "Moreover, the context in which a symbol is used for purposes of expression is important, for the context may give meaning to the symbol.... It may be noted, further, that this was not an act of mindless nihilism. Rather, it was a pointed expression of anguish by [Spence] about the then-current domestic and foreign affairs of his government."[58]

As Professor Chemerinsky has noted, the *Spence* Court emphasized two factors in concluding that the conduct was communicative: "conduct is analyzed as speech under the First Amendment if, first, there is the intent to convey a particularized message, and second, there is a substantial likelihood that the message would be understood by those receiving it." Professors Barron and Dienes also note that the *Spence* decision "provides a guide for identifying symbolic speech."[59] Nonetheless, Chemerinsky believes that

> problems in applying this test are inevitable. How is it to be decided whether a person intended an act to communicate a message? Is it subjective, in which case a person always can claim such an intent in a hope to avoid punishment, or is it objective from the perspective of the reasonable listener, in which case it collapses the first part of the test into the second? How is it to be decided whether the message is sufficiently understood by the audience? Moreover, why should protection of speech depend on the sophistication and perceptiveness of the audience?[60]

In a 1995 *Stanford Law Review* article, Robert Post shared Chemerinsky's sense of the opinion.[61] "The fundamental difficulty with the *Spence* test is that it locates the essence of constitutionally protected speech exclusively in an abstract triadic relationship among a speaker's intent, a specific message, and an audience's potential reception of that message."[62] Despite the lingering questions of what constituted communicative conduct, by the time of its decision in *Spence* the Court had granted First Amendment protection to a steadily expanding list of expressive acts, from peaceful parades in favor of civil rights to black antiwar armbands. Yet the Court's then recent flag-desecration cases (*Radich, Goguen, Spence*), decided as narrowly as they were, provided no real guidance on the question of whether physically damaging flags to express a political idea was a constitutionally protected form of expression.

Still, the justices looked as though they might receive a reprieve from the cultural conflict that produced the flag-desecration cases. On August 8, 1974— six weeks after the *Spence* decision was announced—President Richard Nixon resigned. Eight months later, on April 23, 1975, President Gerald Ford announced the end of the Vietnam War. A week later, scores of U.S. helicopters struggled to airlift Americans out of Saigon, providing a final painful image of the country's shocking military defeat. The following year, Americans celebrated the two hundredth anniversary of the Declaration of Independence. And in the years that followed, according to Goldstein, incidents of flag desecration "virtually disappeared."

Despite the public's understandable desire to seek respite from the intensity of the Vietnam era, the nation's courts, "left legally adrift by the Supreme Court," struggled to identify a consistent approach to flag desecration. "Some courts," Goldstein writes, relied on *O'Brien* "to bolster their contention that flag desecration laws were unconstitutional, but others leaned upon *O'Brien* to reach the opposite conclusion."[63] In fact, between 1970 and 1980 nearly twenty state legislatures revised their flag-desecration laws, marking the first major overhaul of the statutes since the end of the nineteenth century.

Texas was among the states to do so. In 1973, its lawmakers passed a venerated objects law that made it a class A misdemeanor, punishable by up to one year in jail and a $2,000 fine, to "intentionally or knowingly desecrate" a public monument, a place of worship or burial, or a state or national flag. "For purposes of this section," the statute read, " 'desecrate' means deface, damage, or otherwise physically mistreat in a way that the actor knows will seriously offend one or more persons likely to observe or discover his action." Like many such laws, for years after its passage the Texas venerated objects law served a largely symbolic purpose. But unlike its forbears, which were primarily concerned with commercial misuse of the flag, the Texas law targeted only acts of political dissent.

For eleven years, that bit of legislative revisionism faded into the annals of state law books. But things changed in 1984, when a twenty-seven-year-old member of the Revolutionary Communist Youth Brigade helped bring the state law into sharp focus, forced the U.S. Supreme Court to finally rule on the constitutionality of flag desecration, and set off a new wave of ideological gamesmanship that has continued to the present day.

"A SYMBOL OF INTERNATIONAL PLUNDER AND MURDER"

Sixty years after the Red Scare of 1919, and just months after images of Iranian students burning American flags helped inspire the unexpected overthrow of the Shah of Iran, a small Maoist organization called the Revolutionary Communist Party (RCP) began to glorify flag burning in its newspaper, *Revolutionary Worker*, by publishing pictures of miniature flag-burning kits. "Burn the flag," the magazine encouraged its readers, and "then pin it proudly on your chest." Between the 1979 Iranian revolution and the 1984 Republican National Convention, Goldstein reports that RCP members were implicated in at least eight separate flag-burning incidents, "but they generally attracted only local media attention and most Americans were undoubtedly completely unaware of them."[64]

That changed on a stiflingly hot August day in Dallas when ninety-nine protesters, many of them members of the RCP's youth group, the Revolutionary Communist Youth Brigade (RCYB), staged a series of antagonistic demonstrations to protest the renomination of President Ronald Reagan. Marching across town to City Hall in triple-digit heat, the protesters—described by a *Chicago Tribune* reporter as "largely punk rockers and disheveled-looking, long-haired folks"[65]—made about ten stops along the way. According to Goldstein, the protesters "repeatedly held 'die-ins' to portray the effects of nuclear war, chanted obscenities such as 'Fuck America,' pounded on windows with their fists, overturned newspaper racks, spray-painted building walls and windows," and entered a Neimann-Marcus department store long enough to antagonize shoppers with chants of "Eat the rich, feed the poor."[66]

Despite their behavior (which included entering one restaurant and eating food off customers' plates), the protesters caused only minor damage, and no one was injured. But when the march concluded at City Hall with the group burning an American flag—and then beating the heat by jumping into the fountain outside—a phalanx of Dallas police surrounded and arrested the demonstrators.

Each person was charged with disorderly conduct, a class C misdemeanor that carried a $200 fine. Eventually, all of the disorderly conduct charges were dropped, and nine of the protesters were brought up on different charges. Four of the newly charged were alleged to have violated the state's 1973 venerated objects law, a class A misdemeanor. Two of the four failed to appear for trial and forfeited their bonds. A third pled guilty on July 20, 1986. The fourth, an ex–military brat named Gregory Lee Johnson, showed up to fight the charges. Before the decade was over, every elected official in the United States would know his name.

Johnson, who spent part of his childhood on army bases in the United States and in West Germany, remembers the origins of his anger as a twelve-year-old talking to "radical GIs who went against the masters of war." When, as a young man, he came into contact with the RCYB, he felt he'd "been looking my whole life for something like that." Johnson became increasingly involved with the movement; according to information introduced at his Dallas trial, he was arrested nearly twenty times during RCP protests. And although he denied the flag-burning charge in a December 1984 press release, the young radical proudly announced his support of the August protests, and of the image of "the American flag [going] up in flames, a symbol of international plunder and murder reduced to ashes."[67]

In early December 1984, Johnson's case came to trial in Dallas County Criminal Court before a jury of one man and five women. Because the evidence about Johnson's role in the actual flag burning was so scanty, the attorney representing the city, Michael Gillett, focused on the disorderliness of the demonstrators. "Our theory," Gillett explained during a pretrial hearing, "is that by his conduct and participation [Johnson] would be responsible for acts of co-conspirators and was acting as a party by aiding and encouraging this type of conduct." Gillett also stressed the inherent need of governments to regulate certain forms of expression.

Even the "expression of an idea" must be balanced against the public's right to "order, decency and morality," he explained. If the country can't legislate against that, then "what is this country about?"

Gillett's legal argument was based, as Goldstein has noted, on Texas's "law of parties," which holds that "a person is criminally responsible for an offense committed by the conduct of another if, acting with intent to promote or assist the commission of the offense, he solicits, encourages, directs, aids, or attempts to aid the other person to commit the offense."[68] In his closing argument, Gillett emphasized this point by saying that although he was convinced Johnson had indeed burned the flag, at any rate he "was guilty as sin as far as the law of parties was concerned."

After four days of testimony, Johnson—arriving at court each day wearing an RCYB t-shirt and frequently engaging others in the courtroom in political debates—was found guilty of the charges and assessed the maximum punishment, one year in jail and a $2,000 fine.[69] A little over a month later, a unanimous three-judge panel of the state Court of Appeals for the Fifth District sustained that conviction. Though the court conceded that flag burning was a form of "symbolic speech," it nonetheless accepted the city's contention that the state's interest in "preventing breaches of the peace" and protecting "the flag as a symbol of national unity" outweighed any "infringement of Johnson's constitutional rights."

On March 26, 1986, Johnson's two ACLU lawyers, Stanley Weinberg and Doug Skemp, requested that the Texas Court of Criminal Appeals hear the case. The court agreed to schedule oral arguments on September 16, 1987. Seven months later, in a five-to-four decision that relied heavily on the U.S. Supreme Court's 1943 ruling in *Barnette*, the state criminal appeals court declared that Texas's venerated objects law violated Johnson's First Amendment right to engage in political protest, and rejected the Fifth District's contention that Texas's interest in preventing such behavior was more compelling than Johnson's constitutional right to symbolic speech. For Texas to legally censor Johnson, Judge Charles Campbell explained, the state would need to prove that Johnson's behavior posed a "grave and immediate danger" to the flag's ability to "rouse feelings of unity and patriotism.... We do not believe such a danger is present" here.

Judge Campbell's opinion—and the court's razor-thin majority in favor of the young radical—was a surprise, given the court's general reputation for conservative decisions. But as Campbell explained later, his sense at the time was that "Supreme Court precedent in this area was crystal clear, and to write it in any other way was just to completely ignore precedent with everything the Supreme Court has ever said about the First Amendment." Campbell, who became the author of the ruling when he was randomly selected to write the majority opinion, continued, "As a judge, what I feel about the law personally cannot enter into how I interpret it from an objective standpoint."[70]

The city of Dallas tried to get the Court of Criminal Appeals to rehear the case, but again, by a five-to-four vote, the court declined to reconsider its decision. Dallas had one last chance; on July 26, 1988, it filed its petition for certiorari with the U.S. Supreme Court.

It had been over eighty years since its *Halter* decision, and fifteen since its trio of Vietnam-era decisions, yet the Court's repeated efforts to put the flag controversy to rest had failed. On October 17, 1988—just weeks before the nation would elect its forty-first president—the Court announced it would revisit the issue. The case was *Texas v. Johnson*, docket number 88-155.

"I RESPECTFULLY DISSENT"

"At first glance," wrote *Washington Post* reporter Al Kamen on March 19, 1989, "the case to be argued Tuesday at the Supreme Court seems strangely anachronistic."[71] Yet despite the many years since the end of the Vietnam era, Kamen reported that "emotional disputes over the respect owed the nation's symbol seem to be increasing" again. Partly, the flag's resurgence onto the national scene was due to its major role in the recently concluded presidential contest between George H. W. Bush and Michael Dukakis. "Much like the McKinley campaign of 1896 that had helped fuel the original flag protection movement," Goldstein reports, "Bush surrounded his campaign stops and advertisements with flags, as well as habitually leading his audiences in mass recitals of the Pledge of Allegiance and even visiting a flag factory." Indeed, the month before the election a *Time* reporter noted that "five weeks after the Republican convention, the public can be certain of two things about George Bush: he loves the flag and he believes in pledging allegiance to it every morning. But some voters may wonder what he would do with the rest of his day if he became president."[72]

Of course, the senior Bush did become president, and flag salutes and controversies continued. In particular, Kamen referenced the Senate's recent ninety-seven-to-zero vote—passed without hearings and after only fifteen minutes of debate—in support of a bill that would make it a crime to "knowingly display" the flag on the floor or the ground.

Sponsored by Senate minority leader Robert Dole (Republican from Kansas) and thirty-six other senators, the bill was passed as a swift and angry response to an exhibit at the Art Institute of Chicago entitled "What Is the Proper Way to Display the U.S. Flag?" A young student named "Dread" Scott Tyler provided his answer by mounting a collage of images of flag burnings and flag-draped coffins, and by placing a flag on the floor in front of a book in which visitors were encouraged to write their answers to the exhibit's central question—although they would have to stand on the flag to do so. That was enough for the Chicago City Council, which denounced the exhibit and passed an ordinance to make such desecration a crime. It was also enough to prompt a unanimous U.S. Senate to propose amending the 1968 federal flag-desecration law.

Despite Congress's resolute actions, it was still anyone's guess how the Supreme Court would decide *Texas v. Johnson*. Since the Court's last flag-related ruling in 1974, three of the justices who had voted in the majority—Douglas, Powell, and Stewart—had retired. Rehnquist, a staunch believer in laws prohibiting flag desecration, had become the nation's chief justice. And former president Ronald Reagan had appointed three new figures to the bench—Scalia, O'Connor, and Kennedy. If Rehnquist and White could convince their three newest colleagues to join them, Kamen speculated, they "might be able to restrict use of the flag in the political or artistic arenas." Judge Campbell read the Court's decision to grant certiorari the same way. "I thought that they had decided that they were gonna change the rules and reinterpret the whole concept of what speech was under the First Amendment,"[73] he recalled. Either way, court watchers agreed, it was sure to be an extremely close vote.

To prepare for the battle, Johnson decided to shake up his legal team by hiring the radical civil liberties lawyer William Kunstler. Arguably the most famous leftist lawyer in the country, Kunstler had helped found the Center for Constitutional Rights (CCR), an organization committed to providing *pro bono* representation in civil liberties cases. In his career, the long-haired, side-burned, and baritone-voiced Kunstler had defended the rights of the Chicago Seven, provided legal counsel to Martin Luther King, defended the ribald comedian Lenny Bruce, and established a reputation for bringing to his clients not just legal acumen but also a flair for publicity. He and the incendiary Johnson were an ideal fit.

Behind the scenes, the legal mover was a bright young attorney at CCR named David Cole.[74] Cole was particularly adept at writing briefs, prompting Kunstler to say later, "Cole did three-fourths of the brief. I was like Charlie McCarthy—he handed it to me [at oral argument] and said, 'Go!' " Goldstein reports that Cole's strategy with the brief was to present the Court with a "number of ways in which this case could be resolved in our favor without reaching the ultimate question as to whether flag burning was protected by the Constitution."[75] Cole outlined the ways the language of the Texas statute was "particularly vulnerable." Recognizing the Court's decision in *Street* as focusing on Sidney Street's words instead of his behavior, Cole emphasized that Johnson, too, could have been convicted for his words alone. The one angle Cole believed the justices were least likely to pursue was a direct confrontation of the constitutionality of flag desecration laws.

Shortly after oral argument began, on March 21, 1989, Cole and others realized they might have been wrong. Almost immediately after Dallas assistant district attorney Kathi Drew began arguing that the state of Texas had interests more compelling than Johnson's First Amendment rights, two of the Court's newest members—Scalia and Kennedy—interrupted her to suggest that the Texas law was an unconstitutional form of content discrimination. Scalia, in particular, demonstrated the type of pointed questioning from the bench that has unnerved countless attorneys who have appeared before him:

SCALIA: Could Texas prohibit the burning of copies of the Constitution, state or federal?

DREW: Not to my knowledge, Your Honor.

SCALIA: Well, how do you pick what to protect? I mean, you know, if I had to pick between the Constitution and the flag, I might well go with the Constitution.

Later, the exchange between Drew and Scalia took another unexpected turn.

DREW: Your Honor, we believe that if a symbol over a period of time is ignored or abused, that it can, in fact, lose its symbolic effect.

SCALIA: I think not at all. I think when somebody does that to the flag, the flag becomes even more a symbol of the country. I mean, it seems to me you're running quite a different argument—not that he's destroying its symbolic character, but that he is showing disrespect for it, that you not just want a symbol, but you want a venerated symbol, and you don't make that argument because then you're getting into a sort of content preference. I don't see how you can argue that he's making it any less of a symbol than it was.

Other justices were less hostile to the legislation. World War II veteran John Paul Stevens asked Kunstler if he believed the federal government had "any power at all to regulate" how the flag could be "displayed in public places." When Kunstler replied that he did not see "any state interest whatsoever," Stevens, his face visibly red, responded tersely, "I feel quite differently."

Three months later, a divided Court announced its decision in *Texas v. Johnson.* "In a decision virtually certain to be a First Amendment landmark," wrote the *New York Times* Court reporter Linda Greenhouse, "the Supreme Court ruled today that no laws could prohibit political protesters from burning the American flag."[76] At the announcement, William Brennan, representing the five-justice majority, read extensively from his opinion. "To conclude that the government may permit designated symbols to be used to communicate only a limited set of messages would be to enter territory having no discernible or defensible boundaries," Brennan explained. "In evaluating these choices under the First Amendment, how would we decide which symbols were sufficiently special to warrant this unique status? To do so, we would be forced to consult our own political preferences, and impose them on the citizenry, in the very way that the First Amendment forbids us to do."

For Brennan, the Texas law failed because the two interests asserted by the state in defense of the law failed. First, the facts of the case did not involve any breach of the peace. Second, the interest in protecting the flag as a national symbol was related to the suppression of protected expression—a violation of the third part of the *O'Brien* test. Following that logic, Johnson's conviction was set aside. As Brennan declared: "If there is a bedrock principle underlying the First Amendment, it is that the government may not prohibit the expression of an idea simply because society finds the idea itself offensive or disagreeable."[77]

Another of the new justices, Anthony Kennedy, concurred, but not before explaining the personal challenges he faced in deciding the case. "The hard fact is that sometimes we must make decisions we do not like," he wrote. "[T]hough symbols often are what we ourselves make of them, the flag is constant in express-ing beliefs Americans share, beliefs in law and peace and that freedom which sus-tains the human spirit." This case, Kennedy explained, "forces recognition of the costs to which those beliefs commit us. It is poignant but fundamental that the flag protects those who hold it in contempt."[78]

For Chief Justice Rehnquist, whose dissent was joined by justices White and O'Connor, Kennedy's logic had gone one step too far. "The flag is not simply another 'idea' or 'point of view' competing for recognition in the marketplace of ideas," he lectured. "Millions and millions of Americans regard it with an almost mystical reverence regardless of what sort of social, political, or philosophical beliefs they may have. I cannot agree that the First Amendment invalidates the Act of Congress, and the laws of 48 of the 50 States, which make criminal the public burning of the flag." The chief justice concluded, "The Court's role as the final expositor of the Constitution is well established, but its role as a Platonic guardian admonishing those responsible to public opinion as if they were truant schoolchil-dren has no similar place in our system of government."[79]

The otherwise liberal Justice Stevens, also in dissent, read a lengthy portion of his opinion from the bench. "The ideas of liberty and equality have an irresistible force in motivating leaders like Patrick Henry, Susan B. Anthony, and Abraham Lincoln," read Stevens, his voice bearing the timbre of emotion, his face flushed, and his eyes on the verge of tears. "If those ideas are worth fighting for—and our history demonstrates that they are—it cannot be true that the flag that uniquely symbolizes their power is not itself worthy of protection from unnecessary dese-cration. I respectfully dissent."[80]

As Professor Chemerinsky has observed, the majority's logic was based on its belief that, unlike in *O'Brien*, "the government's interest was not unrelated to suppression of the message; to the contrary." Chemerinsky explains that "the law's purpose was to keep the flag from being used to communicate protest or dissent."[81] Brennan's opinion also stressed that the Texas law "did not prevent all flag destruction, but rather applied only when there would be an offense to others." Furthermore, as Professors Barron and Dienes make clear, the state's claim that it needed the law to maintain order was simply "not implicated" by the facts of the case, since "no disturbance of the peace actually occurred or threatened to occur because of Johnson's burning of the flag."[82] Citing the Court's 1969 decision in *Brandenburg v. Ohio*, Brennan reminded his readers that the mere *potential* for disturbance was insufficient cause for action, and that only a clear showing of "imminent lawless action" would justify such suppressive measures.

Brennan did make a concession of sorts. "It is not the State's ends," he wrote, "but its means to which we object." Then the aging Justice offered an alternative course of action. "We can imagine no more appropriate response to burning a flag than waving one's own," he said, and "no better way to counter a flag-burner's message than by saluting the flag that burns." The United States, Brennan concluded, does "not consecrate the flag by punishing its desecration, for in doing so we dilute the freedom that this cherished emblem represents."[83]

CONGRESS AND THE SUPREME COURT REVISIT THE ISSUE

In the days and weeks that followed the decision, Americans witnessed what *Newsday* termed a "firestorm of indignation" and what Goldstein characterized as a "greater, more immediate, and more negative [reaction] than to any other Supreme Court ruling in American history." Congressman Douglas Applegate (Democrat from Ohio) called the decision "the greatest travesty in the annals of jurisprudence." Conservative columnist Pat Buchanan referred to the Court as a "renegade tribunal." And Senate Republican leader Bob Dole warned that "if [the justices] don't like our flag, they ought to go and find one they do like."[84]

Before long, angry rhetoric gave way to reactive legislation. Within a week, 172 representatives and 43 senators had sponsored nearly forty separate resolutions calling for a federal amendment to the U.S. Constitution that would outlaw flag desecration. And two days after the *Johnson* decision was announced, Senate Judiciary Committee chairman Joe Biden (Democrat from Delaware) proposed to amend the 1968 federal flag desecration law to punish anyone, regardless of motive, who "knowingly and publicly mutilates, burns, displays on the floor or ground or tramples upon any flag." After ten minutes of debate, Biden's proposal passed ninety-seven to three. In time, Biden's proposal[85] became the foundation for the Flag Protection Act (FPA), which was overwhelmingly passed by both houses of Congress in October 1989 and which decreed up to one year in jail and/ or a $1,000 fine for anyone who "knowingly mutilates, defaces, physically defiles, burns, maintains on the floor or ground, or tramples upon any flag of the United States." For the purposes of the FPA, a "flag" was defined as "any flag of the United

States, or any part thereof, made of any substance, of any size, in a form that is commonly displayed." The FPA did not provide any definition of what constituted "mutilation" or "defacement." It did, however, exempt the ceremonial burnings of worn flags, apparently in direct contradiction of the Court's ruling in *Johnson*.

There were doubts everywhere about the legality of the FPA. As one Senate source told Goldstein in 1990, "If you were on the Senate floor that Friday night [after the ruling] as I was, you would know the speed that train had. The Constitution was about to be amended on the floor of the U.S. Senate with no hearings, no nothing."[86] Accordingly, on October 12, 1989, Congress sent the FPA to the White House. The next day, President Bush announced that although he would not sign the bill, he would allow it to become law. In theory, this was because Bush preferred a constitutional amendment as the "most lasting and legally correct" response. In reality, it was because he was in a politically awkward situation, and he knew that any bill passed by Congress can become law even without a presidential signature.[87] Meanwhile, Congress debated whether or not to go beyond the scope of the FPA and propose an amendment to the Constitution. On October 19, however, the Senate fell fifteen votes shy of the required two-thirds majority.

Why would so many politicians sign on to such a legally dubious—and constitutionally precarious—piece of legislation as the FPA? According to a key House Democratic leadership aide at the time, it was because a critical mass of the representatives and senators believed that "if time was allowed to work, the pressure [to outlaw flag burning] would decrease, the hysteria would decrease and the atmosphere would get more normal." At the same time, "it wasn't just a delay strategy because lots of folks felt that" the FPA would be held constitutional, and "clearly it warranted a try because there was a very good argument that you don't go to the Constitution if you can achieve the goal through other means."[88]

At midnight on October 27, the moment the FPA became law, a spate of flag burnings took place across the country. At one of these protests, in Seattle, leaflets passed out ahead of time invited readers to attend a "Festival of Defiance":

> On October 28 it becomes illegal to desecrate the flag. This fascist law is not an "exception" to the concept of free speech but an attack on political protest and dissent, and a precedent for the future. Blind patriotism must not be the law of the land. Unlike the flag-kissers, we will not whine, we will Rock and Roll in a Festival of Defiance.[89]

After setting ablaze a flag belonging to the local post office, seven of the Seattle protesters (including three "John Does" who were never located) were charged with destroying federal property and violating the FPA. Two days later, a second group of protesters—including Gregory Lee Johnson, a young self-described "revolutionary artist" named Shawn Eichman, and the young Chicago art student, "Dread" Scott Tyler—desecrated several flags on the steps of the U.S. Capitol. (Johnson was not one of the three individuals arrested for the act; ironically, his flag would not ignite.) Commenting on the arrests, William Kunstler told reporters, "Here you have it. Congress wanted a swift case. They're going to get it." And *Time* observed that until the FPA was enacted, "flag burning had virtually gone out of style as a means of radical protest." Now, however, "desecrating the Stars and Stripes has become a bit of a fad."[90] The Supreme Court was not free of the issue yet.

Promptly, federal district courts in both the District of Columbia and the state of Washington struck down the FPA. According to one well-informed Justice Department source, this was not exactly bad news at the Department. As Goldstein reports, "the [Justice Department] briefs did not provide a 'vigorous' defense of the FPA and anyone reading them would conclude, 'You can't expect to win with this.'...[T]hey seemed to be saying, 'We [the Justice Department] agree it's unconstitutional.'"[91] By contrast, Kunstler's and Cole's briefs maintained that *Johnson* made clear that any governmental interest in protecting the flag against physical attacks that might "somehow dilute its 'symbolic value'" was "necessarily related to the suppression of expression." Consequently, they claimed, the standard in *O'Brien*, which would have provided greater protection for the government's actions, was irrelevant.

On February 23, 1990, two days after the Seattle district court ruling, the Justice Department announced it would ask for expedited mandatory Supreme Court review of the decision, thanks to a provision that had been written into the FPA. And on March 13, Solicitor General Kenneth Starr[92] asked the Court to hear a consolidated appeal from the two district court cases. Interestingly, the primary argument advanced by Starr in the government's brief[93] was that the Court should reconsider its opinion in *Johnson*, since the "people's elected representatives" had expressed their "considered decision that the physical desecration of the flag is—uniquely—anathema to the nation's values." Starr also outlined a slightly different angle to the case. In the same way that obscenity, libel, and fighting words have "demonstrable destructive effects" that outweigh their value as categories of free speech, so, too, Starr claimed, does flag burning, especially since "suitable alternative means" are available to any protester who wishes to put forth "whatever protected expression may be part of the intended message."

The question of when the Court would hear oral arguments was crucial, given that 1990 was an election year. Any preelection ruling would almost guarantee a renewed drive for a constitutional amendment and make the issue a rallying cry across the country, a development that was more likely to benefit the Republicans. A post-election ruling was the preference of Democrats and amendment opponents. On March 30, 1990, the Court announced it would consolidate the Seattle and Washington, D.C., flag-burning cases—under the name *U.S. v. Eichman*—and hear oral argument at a special session on May 14.[94] Almost immediately afterward, Linda Greenhouse reported: "Republican Party strategists predicted that a renewed debate over a constitutional amendment will help keep Democratic candidates on the defensive in the fall Congressional campaign."[95]

Three days after hearing the arguments of both sides, the justices' preliminary vote at their private conference suggested the same five-to-four split as in *Johnson*. And less a month later, on June 11, the Court announced its opinion in *U.S. v. Eichman*. Once again, Justice Brennan read from his majority opinion before a hushed, crowded courtroom. Finding a content-based purpose for the FPA, Brennan wrote:

> [I]t is clear that the Government's asserted interest in protecting the "physical integrity" of a privately owned flag in order to preserve the flag's status as a symbol of the Nation and certain national ideals is related to the suppression, and concerned with the content, of free expression. The mere destruction or disfigurement of a symbol's physical manifestation does not diminish or otherwise affect the symbol itself. The Government's interest is implicated only when a person's treatment of the flag communicates a message to others that is inconsistent with the identified ideals.[96]

This time, Justice Stevens chose not to read parts of his dissent from the bench, opting instead to simply record his disagreement for the official record. "The symbolic value of the American flag is not the same today as it was yesterday," wrote Stevens, whose dissent was joined by Rehnquist, White, and O'Connor. He added:

> Events during the last three decades have altered the country's image in the eyes of numerous Americans, and some now have difficulty understanding the message that the flag conveyed to their parents and grandparents— whether born abroad and naturalized or native born. Moreover, the integrity of the symbol has been compromised by those leaders who seem to advocate compulsory worship of the flag even by individuals whom it offends, or who seem to manipulate the symbol of national purpose into a pretext for partisan disputes about meaner ends. And, as I have suggested, the residual value of the symbol after this Court's decision in *Texas v. Johnson* is surely not the same as it was a year ago.[97]

Senator Dole was among the first to give voice to the losing side's displeasure. "There are no options left," he told Greenhouse. "It's either do nothing or have a constitutional amendment. I think we ought to do something."[98] President Bush agreed, urging Congress to pass the amendment by July 4. "Honest and patriotic

Americans may differ on this issue," the president explained, but "I am absolutely convinced this is the proper course for our country."

Shortly after the Court's decision in *Eichman*, and despite the president's urging, a Senate resolution to authorize a flag amendment failed to pass by the required two-thirds vote. President George Bush never mentioned the amendment again during his term, and he referenced it only once during his unsuccessful re-election campaign against Arkansas governor Bill Clinton. Then, for a few years at least, the issue faded from the headlines.

The political landscape changed dramatically in 1994, however, when the Republican Party assumed control of both houses of Congress, spurred in large part by its "Contract with America." Since that time, the issue has steadily resurfaced, only to be beaten back by an ever-increasingly narrow margin. The House voted overwhelmingly to authorize a flag amendment in 1995, 1997, 1999, 2001, 2003, and 2005. Twice the measure came to a vote in the Senate, in 1995 and 2000, and twice it failed to receive enough votes. And then in 2006, the Senate came within one vote of securing the sixty-seven needed for the approval of Senate Judicial Resolution 12—"The Congress shall have power to prohibit the physical desecration of the flag of the United States." Had one more senator voted for its passage (and when one considers that all fifty states have already passed resolutions supporting a flag-protection amendment), Senate Judicial Resolution 12 would have become the first amendment to the First Amendment in American history.

Shortly after learning of the narrow defeat, Senate majority leader Bill Frist (Republican of Tennessee) expressed his disappointment. "Countless men and women have died defending that flag," he said. "It is but a small humble act for us to defend it." Frist's colleague Senator Daniel Inouye (Democrat of Hawaii) took a different perspective. "Our country's unique because our dissidents have a voice," said the World War II veteran and Medal of Honor recipient. "While I take offense at disrespect to the flag, I nonetheless believe it is my continued duty as a veteran, as an American citizen, and as a United States senator to defend the constitutional right of protesters to use the flag in nonviolent speech."[99] With that as the bare majority sentiment, the principle of freedom trumped that of fear.

As of 2006, the matter seemed settled. But there were other battles, other forms of protest, and other kinds of expression in which the law of the First Amendment was not as settled. One such area was that of *student* protests. As fate had it, the first such case to reach the Supreme Court involved symbolic expression.

Count-Me-Ins and Count-Me-Outs

Mary Beth Tinker and Student Speech

America's public schools were founded in order to educate students to be active and informed citizens. That, at least, was part of their original mission.

The nation's public schools, more than any other public institution in our country, were to be laboratories for future generations' learning about their rights and responsibilities as members of a democracy. But just how much of the freedom that was promised to them could (or should) students practice during the school day? More specifically, how much First Amendment freedom did they have as students? It took 178 years before the U.S. Supreme Court directly answered that important question. And the courts and public continue to debate that answer to this day.

On February 17, 2003, the American war against Taliban forces in Afghanistan was nearly a year and a half old. The war in Iraq was imminent. And Bretton Barber, a high school junior from Dearborn, Michigan, was angry about it. At one point in the conflict, Barber voiced his dissent on a student Web site: President George W. Bush, he wrote, "had managed to instill fear into the hearts of countless Americans....Now he was going to do this in the international community, with an unjust pre-emptive war." The seventeen-year-old felt he had only one choice. "It was time to speak up." He received his opportunity earlier that week, when his English teacher assigned a "compare and contrast" essay, after writing which the students would present their observations to the class. Barber compared President Bush and Iraqi dictator Saddam Hussein. "Bush has already killed over 1,000 people in Afghanistan," he later told a reporter. "That's terrorism in itself."[1]

It was a strong (some would say inflammatory) stance, especially in the Dearborn public school district, where many students had family members serving in the U.S. armed forces. But the teenage activist decided his presentation would also benefit from a visual aid, so he upped the ante—he wore a t-shirt with a picture of the president and the words "International Terrorist." Barber wore the shirt "to emphasize the message, 'no war.' High school can be a pretty apathetic place." His plan was "to generate some discussion about what was then the brewing war in Iraq." Yet, the shirt had little effect. "After presenting my essay with the shirt on," he added, "I was sure someone else would want to speak up about the situation in the country. But no one did. In fact, I wore the shirt for three hours, and there was little said about it. No one engaged me; no one wanted to talk. It seemed as though apathy was omnipresent in my high school, and no t-shirt could change that. But then it did, in a different form."[2]

During lunch that day, Barber was approached by the school's vice principal, Michael Shelton, and told he must either turn the shirt inside out or go home. According to local and national news reports, when Barber asked why, Shelton told him the shirt promoted terrorism. Barber refused and was sent home. He returned to school later that day to meet with the principal, Judith Coebly. "She immediately asked if I was familiar with the Supreme Court case, *Tinker v. Des Moines*," Barber recounted to the *New York Times*. "I said I was very familiar with it. She said it happened in 1969. "And I said no, it happened in 1965."[3]

TINKERING WITH THE WAR EFFORT

Young Barber had it right—at least in principle—on the basis of that case: *Tinker v. Des Moines Independent School District* (1969).

The *Tinker* controversy began in the final month of 1965. The United States was in the early stages of its war against the Communist forces in Vietnam. Senator Robert F. Kennedy had urged for a Christmas truce. Almost two thousand American soldiers had been brought home in caskets. (The next year alone, over six thousand more would join them.) Across the country, the first signs of a widening civil unrest were beginning to appear.

It was even happening in Des Moines. Founded in 1834, that city proudly claimed to be the third largest insurance center in the world, as well as the city with a greater number of skywalks per capita "than any other city of comparable size in the U.S." It was, and is, not exactly the type of place one would expect citizens to be sowing seeds of dissent and civil disobedience. Even less likely was the fact that the source of this unrest was the city's youngest citizens. Although it's hard to fathom from a modern perspective, the notion of student protest was a relatively new phenomenon in the United States in 1965. But the war in Vietnam, coupled with the stirring bravery of the young protesters of the civil rights movement, had awakened in scores of other young Americans a more active yearning for a different type of government, and a different type of world order. And so, in December, some students in Des Moines began to plot their own protest. In time, their actions would require the intervention of the U.S. Supreme Court and result in the most significant student rights free-speech case in American history.

The story started when a small number of high school and college students from the area organized a response to U.S. policy in Vietnam. One of the students, in a proposed article for his high school's student newspaper, explained the plan:

> Some high school and college students in Iowa who are interested in expressing their grief over the deaths of soldiers and civilians in Vietnam will fast on Thursday, December 16th. They will also wear black arm-bands starting on that same day. The National Liberation Front (Vietcong) recently proposed a 12-hour truce on Christmas Eve. The United States has not yet replied to their offer. However, Senator Robert Kennedy has suggested that the truce be extended indefinitely pending negotiations.[4]

If their demands were not met, the young journalist warned that the students were prepared to be persistent:

> If the United States takes this action the arm-bands will be removed. If it does not the bands will be worn throughout the holiday season and there will be a second fast on New Year's Day. High school and college students are also encouraged to forego their usual New Year's Eve activities and meet together to discuss this complex war and possible ways of ending the killing of Vietnamese and Americans.... All students interested in saving lives and ending the war in Vietnam are urged [to participate].[5]

School administrators barred the article's publication. Yet word of the plan got around anyway. A small number of Des Moines students—including sixteen-year-old Christopher Eckhardt, fifteen-year-old John Tinker, and his thirteen-year-old sister Mary Beth—decided to participate in the protest. As John said later in official court records, "I hoped such a truce would stop the killing and...lead to a peaceful settlement in the war."[6]

The day before their scheduled protest, the students read an article in the local newspaper. The school district had just passed a new policy forbidding students from wearing black armbands. "The schools are no place for demonstrations," said Raymond Peterson, the district's director of secondary education. "We allow for free discussion of these things in the classes... [but] the educational program would be disturbed by students wearing arm-bands." The policy grew out of an emergency meeting of all district principals on Tuesday, December 14, in response to the rumor that students were planning to stage a protest during school hours later that week. According to Peterson, it "was based on a general school policy against anything that was a disturbing situation within the school."[7]

It was an extremely broad policy (*"anything* that was a disturbing situation") with a decidedly specific target (arm-bands). Yet in 1965, the law favored the school district's censorial actions. The Supreme Court had never decided a case that mapped out the First Amendment rights of students in a public school setting, so the students had no real precedent on their side.[8] Indeed, whenever lower courts had ruled on the rights of students in the past, they almost always echoed a refrain that formed the backbone of the Des Moines school district's proposed policy on student conduct—that "one of the most important responsibilities of a building principal is to help establish and maintain an atmosphere... which will allow teachers to achieve the primary purpose of public school education—that of educating each person to his maximum potential. Since the best interests of the school may be served only through the establishment and maintenance of an orderly, disciplined faculty and student body," the school policy emphasized, "it is deemed essential that school administrators... assume the responsibility of establishing and maintaining such an environment."[9]

The Iowa students had a difficult choice to make. Should they go through with their protest, believing that their First Amendment right to freedom of expression outweighed the certain suspensions and disciplinary actions they would suffer at school? Or did they have a greater responsibility to abide by the rules of their school district, and reserve their protest for an appropriate time outside the school day?

In all, seven students protested. Mary Beth and Christopher wore their arm-bands[10] to school on the originally scheduled day, Thursday, December 16. In court documents, Mary Beth recalled the morning progressing uneventfully, save for a few boys making "smart remarks" during lunch. But, she added, "they always do that to us [girls], about anything."

Things changed after lunch, when she arrived for Richard Moberly's math class. The day before, the class had spent the entire period discussing the new policy and the wave of demonstrations that were then happening across the country. According to court papers, Moberly recalled telling the class that "if there was going to be a demonstration in my class, it would be for or against something in mathematics and if they wanted to demonstrate in my school, they better be demonstrating about something that was in my class."[11] When he saw Mary Beth's narrow strip of black ribbon, held together around her arm by a single safety pin, Moberly laid a pass on her desk telling her to go to the office. There, the school's assistant principal told her to remove the ribbon and return to class. Mary Beth obliged. Shortly after returning to class, however, she was retrieved by the school's adviser, who informed Mary Beth she was suspended.

The morning unfolded differently for Christopher Eckhardt, a young man with the dubious distinction of being voted by his classmates the student with the cleanest locker. As befits such conscientious behavior, Eckhardt went to the principal's office as soon as he arrived at school. "I knew I was breaking a rule," he said, although "I didn't expect exactly to be suspended...I didn't know exactly what they would do." Eckhardt met with the school's vice principal, Donald Blackman, who asked that he remove his arm-band. Eckhardt politely refused. At this point, Blackman assumed a different strategy. Eckhardt remembers:

> Mr. Blackman had told me that I had a good record with the school, and asked me if I was looking for a busted nose, and I told him I wasn't, and he said something to the effect that that is what it was going to look like on my record for being suspended from school, and Mrs. Cross informed me that the colleges didn't accept demonstrators and protestors, and they told me this and asked me to remove my arm-band and I told them I was going to keep it on, and...they let me know while I was going to be out of school that I could probably have plenty of time to find a new school to go to and I told them I liked [my school] and I wanted to come back, and they said that if I did anything like this again that I wouldn't come back.[12]

Similar stories unfolded for other Des Moines students who wore arm-bands that day. Fifteen-year-old John Tinker was not among them. "I didn't feel that I should just wear [the arm-band] against the will of the principals without even trying to talk to them first," he said. When John learned there was a school board meeting the evening of December 16, he decided he would try to speak to them first. "We thought if it was brought to the school board's attention," he said, "they would change their decision" to enforce the new policy.[13]

School board president Ora Niffenegger recalled receiving a flurry of calls that night from several students. They each told him "they had been denied a constitutional right to wear arm-bands and they wanted to call an emergency meeting of the school board." Niffenegger told them "formalities and custom and common courtesy" forbade him from calling such a meeting. They were free to present their concerns at the next meeting. In the interim, Niffenegger offered some free advice: "I told them they were taking the wrong way out, that we had in this country of ours a well-defined way in which to handle this matter and that was that if they didn't like the way our elected officials were handling things, it should be handled with the ballot box and not in the halls of our public schools."[14]

Perhaps Niffenegger forgot the students were not yet eligible to vote. In any case, John Tinker, unconvinced and thwarted in his attempt to resolve the matter outside school property, had heard enough. He staged his silent protest the next day, Friday, December 17. For him, it was a matter of conscience. "I do not consider this a trivial matter," he said. "It is important to me because I morally think it is wrong, and when people are getting killed, I guess that's important to me." Despite his strongly held beliefs, Tinker remembered feeling "self-conscious about wearing the arm-band.... Some of the students were making fun of me for wearing it...but they thought I should have the right to if I wanted to." After lunch, Tinker was told the principal wanted to see him immediately. "When I told him I was not going to take the arm-band off he told me I would have to leave school."[15] So he did.

In all, despite the protests, the two days passed peacefully and quietly. There was no violence; just seven students in the entire district participated; and those who did quietly left their schools when they were asked to do so. A few days later, however, at the first school board meeting after the suspensions, local journalists reported that the meeting room was "filled to overflowing" with advocates on both sides of the issue. Some people spoke of the importance of maintaining discipline in a school setting. Others claimed that the policy denied the school children of Des Moines their First Amendment right to free speech.

After a contentious two-hour meeting in which the board struggled to maintain order, it was decided by a four-to-three vote that the arm-band policy would remain in effect...for the time being. Conveniently, it was winter break, which meant the students of Des Moines would not have their school buildings as stages for at least the next two weeks.

While the students vacationed, other citizens of Des Moines joined the debate. Resident Melvin Hall, in a January 1 letter to the editors of the *Des Moines Register*, feared a dangerous precedent if students were allowed to wear arm-bands. "If they have this right," he wrote, "then let's forget about using our schools for learning and make them halls for demonstrators." Another writer doubted that the arm-band wearing could even be characterized as a *student* protest. Does anyone really believe, he wrote, that "the children had access to and had the intellectual maturity to understand the significance of the complicated Viet Nam problem? Is it not more reasonable to suppose they were being used by their parents to publicize and foster the parents' opinions?" Conversely, one of the most moving letters to defend the students was written by Lance Corporal Harry Corry:

> I am appalled at what I consider not only an infringement upon the civil liberties of U.S. citizens but also at the seeming lack of concern for my

friends and fellow Marines who are fighting and dying in Viet Nam for this very cause. To me this is not just a great injustice but the height of hypocrisy. Why defend a society that cannot even allow its citizens to honor the very people who keep it free?[16]

Clearly, the issue was not going to just go away. And when classes resumed, on January 4, 1966, the legal battle began.

MAKING A CASE FOR STUDENT RIGHTS

According to the Tinkers' father, Leonard, bringing a suit against the school district was not a decision his family entered into lightly. But as they spent the winter break discussing the issue, the Tinker and Eckhardt families "became convinced that this was very definitely a matter of conscience for [the students], that they were not lightly defying authority... but they had a conviction.... I had to make a choice as to whether or not I would stand by my children... in saying something that I thought was true [and] honorable."

In their lawsuit, which named twenty-three defendants in all, the families asked for the following: an injunction—or temporary suspension—of the armband policy; the coverage of all costs associated with bringing the case to trial; and $1.00 for "nominal" damages.[17] They sued under Section 1983 of Title 42 of the laws of the United States. It was a law originally enacted almost a century earlier, as part of Section 1 of the 1871 Civil Rights Act, which made it a crime to unfairly use one's authority to deprive people of their civil rights.

The first trial began in July 1966, in the courtroom of Chief Judge Roy Stephenson of the U.S. District Court for the Southern District of Iowa. The lead attorney for the families, Dan Johnston, was a twenty-eight-year-old volunteer lawyer for the Iowa Civil Liberties Union. He had just graduated from Drake University Law School. Johnston argued that the students' wearing of black arm-bands was a protected form of free expression, and that the hastily passed policy prohibiting the arm-bands constituted a "prior restraint" on expressive activity. To bolster his claim in his legal papers, Johnston cited several Supreme Court cases. In *Stromberg v. California* (1931) (see chapter 9), the Court ruled seven to two in favor of nineteen-year-old Communist camp counselor Yetta Stromberg, who had been arrested for violating California's "red flag" law by leading her campers in a morning salute of the Soviet flag. "The [right to] display a flag 'as a sign, symbol or emblem of opposition to organized government'... is a fundamental principle of our constitutional system," wrote Chief Justice Charles Evans Hughes.

Another case Johnston relied on was *Thornhill v. Alabama* (1940). Byron Thornhill and other employees of the Brown Wood Preserving Company had been arrested for picketing their employer. Despite the seemingly clear unconstitution-ality of such an arrest, the state of Alabama had made picketing illegal in 1923, and the state supreme court ruled against Thornhill's First Amendment claim. But the U.S. Supreme Court disagreed. In an eight-to-one vote, it reaffirmed that "freedom of speech...embraces at the least the liberty to discuss publicly and truthfully all matters of public concern without previous restraint or fear of subsequent punish-ment." The most useful case for Johnston was *West Virginia State Board of Education v. Barnette* (1943), in which the Court affirmed the constitutional right of students to refuse to participate in mandatory school exercises on grounds of conscience. That case began when the West Virginia Board of Education, motivated by the patriotic fervor sweeping the country during World War II, adopted a measure requiring all public school students to salute the flag and recite the Pledge of Allegiance. Students who did not participate could be expelled. Remarkably, their parents could even lose custody of them. But, a group of Jehovah's Witnesses chal-lenged the law on First Amendment grounds. A majority of the court (six to three) agreed with the Witnesses. "There is no doubt that, in connection with the pledges, the flag salute is a form of utterance," wrote Justice Robert Jackson. And the state could not compel such utterances of school children, especially when such compul-sion conflicted with sincerely held religious beliefs.

Despite this precedent, Johnston knew *Barnette* had a limited application to the Iowa arm-band protest. The students had not, for example, been forced to profess allegiance to something they did not believe. And *Barnette* provided no standard for judging the constitutionality of other types of student speech, like black arm-bands. It did, however, reinforce a principle by which Johnston could suggest that the students' chosen form of expression qualified for First Amendment protection. It was a principle first introduced in *Stromberg*, and it instructed that nonverbal or symbolic communication could qualify as protected speech. In other words, Johnston could claim that just as the act of pledging allegiance was a form of *expressive conduct*, or *symbolic speech*, so, too, was wearing a black arm-band for peace.

In addition to the Supreme Court cases, Johnston referenced two decisions handed down by the Fifth Circuit Court of Appeals earlier that year. In the first case, *Burnside v. Byars*, the right of Mississippi students to protest racial segrega-tion by wearing "freedom buttons" was upheld. "Wearing buttons," wrote Judge Walter Gewin, "is certainly not in the class of those activities which inherently distract students and break down the regimen of the classroom such as carrying banners, scattering leaflets, and speechmaking, all of which are protected methods of expression, but all of which have no place in an orderly classroom." Gewin con-cluded by outlining a standard of sorts, one Johnston hoped Stephenson would adopt. "School officials cannot infringe on their students' right to free and unre-stricted expression," Gewin wrote, as long as the expression does "not materially or substantially interfere with the requirements of appropriate discipline in the operation of the school."[18]

Five weeks later, on September 1, 1966, Judge Stephenson ruled against the students.[19] "The reactions and comments of other students as a result of the arm-bands," he wrote, "would be likely to disturb the disciplined atmosphere required for any classroom.... School officials must be given a wide discretion and if, under the circumstances, a disturbance in school discipline is reasonably to be anticipated, actions which are reasonably calculated to prevent such a disruption must be upheld."[20] Judge Stephenson was also uninterested in the logic of the Supreme Court cases Johnston cited. Curiously, he chose instead to base his reasoning on a case neither legal team had even mentioned, a case that was substantially restricted by subsequent rulings and that had fallen into disfavor among some leading constitutional scholars—*Dennis v. United States* (1951; see chapter 5).

The same day the judge issued his opinion, Johnston appealed the decision to the Eighth U.S. Circuit Court of Appeals, the federal appeals court responsible for reviewing lower court decisions in Iowa and six other midwestern states. He argued that the lower court judge had improperly considered facts outside the official record—in this case, the tense atmosphere across the country as a result of the war. School officials countered by claiming they had a responsibility to maintain an orderly environment and pointing out that the students had other means of opposing the war.

Meanwhile, some members of the Des Moines community reacted in anger to the students' continuing legal fight. According to Professor Peter Irons, Mary Beth Tinker remembered that people "threw red paint at our house, and we got lots of calls." Some of the people who called offered words of support; others delivered threats. "We got all kinds of threats to our family," said Mary Beth, including one person who called the Tinker house "on Christmas Eve and said the house would be blown up by morning."

But the families remained resolute in their determination to continue the legal fight. "I thought the school authorities had to obey the Constitution," said Leonard Tinker. "It was my position that my children were involved in a matter of their conscience and that they have both a right to conscience and a right to speak, and these rights are very primary rights in my mind." Despite their principled stance, the Tinkers and Eckhardts received more bad news on November 3, 1967—almost two years after they first wore their arm-bands to school. The full panel of the Eighth Circuit issued a brief, unrevealing *per curiam* opinion. Judge Stephenson's judgment, they announced, "is affirmed by an equally divided court."

The setback in the Eighth Circuit notwithstanding, Dan Johnston took his final appeal to the U.S. Supreme Court with a sense of hope. A number of lower courts had recently issued opinions regarding student speech, many of which contradicted each other in their logic. That suggested to Johnston that the Court might feel the need to step in and address the issue directly. What the young Iowa attorney couldn't have known was that by 1968, several justices were already addressing it—behind closed doors.

COUNT-ME-OUTS AND COUNT-ME-INS

In his 1968 book *Concerning Dissent and Civil Disobedience*, Supreme Court Justice Abe Fortas (1910–1982) reflected on the society that was changing around him. The young people of the country were leading a large-scale revolt, he wrote, a revolt that typified "a fairly new phenomenon for this country." In the past, young Americans "accepted the leadership of their elders, not uncritically, but passively.... Now this has drastically changed. Young people have suddenly taken on distinctive character and quality. They are not merely junior-size editions of their elders.... They are no longer predictably proceeding in a straight line behind their parents and grandparents, preparing to receive the torch from their elders and run the next lap in the old relay race."[21]

The son of immigrant Jews, Abe Fortas first distinguished himself by successfully representing Clarence Earl Gideon before the U.S. Supreme Court in *Gideon v. Wainwright* (1963), the case that established the system whereby state courts provide lawyers in criminal cases for defendants unable to afford their own. Named to the Court the same year the Iowa protest first took place—1965—Fortas was a protégé of fellow Justice William O. Douglas, a socially progressive jurist. Not surprisingly, therefore, Fortas spoke positively of the new breed of student activists. They were becoming, he wrote, "a positive, differentiated factor in American life"—some of them, at least. Fortas characterized two kinds of young people in his book: count-me-outs and count-me-ins. The count-me-outs, Fortas explained, were "immersed in the warm fluid of me-ness." These young people had "quietly divorced themselves from the mainstream of life" and declined "to join in the agony and activity of their time." By contrast, the count-me-ins had "ideas, programs, convictions, energy, and initiative. Some of them were significant participants in the freedom rides and the early struggle to end discrimination against Negroes. They organize and participate in mass activities to achieve their objectives and to defeat governmental and university actions which they oppose." And most of all, he wrote, they "found impetus, reason and outlet in the opposition to the war in Vietnam."[22]

Whereas Fortas was hopeful about the new generation of young people, one of his colleagues on the Court, the venerable Hugo Black, was skeptical. "I find it difficult to believe that students from the kindergarten on through college have a constitutional right to use the schools for advertising their political views," he wrote to his friend Charles Reich (see epilogue). "There are some things in our society that...are not exclusively controlled by constitutional provisions." As a result, Black believed "it would be best for those in charge of the schools to establish the rules for the students to follow."

They were conservative words and thoughts. Were they really coming from the First Amendment stalwart Hugo Black—the man who had, in the words of biographer Roger Newman, "until recently...held up the Bill of Rights like the Holy Grail"? What had happened to the absolute defender of First Amendment freedoms, the man who had first stated that "no law" means no law?

In one sense, the aging justice had begun to lose his faith in the system. Black's more recent opinions, Newman observed, "expressed deep apprehensions about the ability of the judicial system to handle the new cases that would arise." It was a strange new world, a world where everywhere, it seemed, the young generation was flouting the authority of its elders. And so, in a greater sense, Black's heroic defense of freedom had begun to ebb in the face of his steadily increasing fear of the way the world was changing. As Black aged and his tendons shrank, Newman wrote, "so did the joints in his Constitution lose their elasticity." Consequently, the man who "had formerly aspired to determine the soul of a document intended to endure for ages"[23] now spent nights at home with his wife watching the nation sink further into a social civil war on the evening news. It troubled him greatly.

By the time the *Tinker* case was up for review, Hugo Black had someone besides the student protesters to bear the brunt of his fearful rage—Abe Fortas. In fact, in 1968 one of Chief Justice Warren's clerks characterized the tension between the two men as "one of the most basic animosities on the Court." In nearly every case that had mattered to Fortas since he joined the Court, Black was on the other side. This was largely the result of their differing approaches to jurisprudence. Black had always been a man of formal principles; Fortas was a crusader for social policy. But it was also because when the two men sought to give a name to the changing face of the new generation, Fortas saw the spirit of the count-me-ins, whereas Black saw an angry sea of count-me-outs.

Despite their differences, when the case first came before the Court for review on March 4, 1968, the two justices, for a brief moment, agreed; neither wanted to hear the case. Black's rationale was clear. Fortas was less certain about whether the First Amendment required the Court to intervene in issues of school discipline. Five other justices, however, voted to accept the students' case. That meant Dan Johnston and the Tinker and Eckhardt families would have one more day in court. Oral arguments were scheduled for November 12, 1968.

ORAL ARGUMENTS IN TROUBLING TIMES

As the troublesome and tragic months of 1968 wore on, antiwar protests on college campuses across the country sparked violent exchanges like those at the University of Washington, where students danced by the light of a burning ROTC building to the chant "This is number one, and the fun has just begun, burn it down, burn it down, burn it down." It was a difficult time to be making the claim that students in America's high schools deserved more—not less—free expression rights. Dan Johnston was willing to make that claim. But which strategy would best serve his clients' interests?

Although the Court had never established any standard for determining the constitutionality of student speech, Johnston had already followed a small trail of jurisprudence he could use in constructing his argument. With the help of national ACLU attorney David Ellenhorn, the Iowa upstart also asked the Court in his brief to resolve the split decisions in the Eighth and Fifth circuits, given that these two circuits had ruled on student expression cases but came to different conclusions.

Oral arguments began exactly one week after the election of Richard Nixon. Johnston emphasized in his opening remarks that the students wore the arm-bands "as a matter of conscience to express the views that they had." Before long, an intellectual swordfight broke out between the young Iowa attorney and Justice Byron White (1917–2002) over just how symbolic—and disruptive—those arm-bands were. "While [students are] studying arithmetic or mathematics, they're supposed to be taking in this message about Vietnam?" White interrupted. "Well," replied Johnston, "the method the students chose in this particular instance was specifically designed in such a way that it would not cause that kind of disruption." White was unconvinced. "They intended the students to think about it outside of class but not in class?" he asked. "I think perhaps," Johnston conceded, "it might for a few moments have…distracted some students, just as many other things do in the classroom, which are allowed, from time to time." But the students' contention, he continued, "is that the policy as it was adopted…will not stand the test of freedom of expression under the First Amendment."[24]

To strengthen this claim, Johnston pointed to passages in policy statements of some district administrators, who conceded that the arm-band policy was content-specific. Donald Blackman, Eckhardt's principal, recalled "students wearing religious symbols such as crosses and things of that sort," and political buttons involving student campaigns. Yet he confessed in official court records that "there is no regulation against this sort of political demonstration." Mary Beth's math teacher spoke of seeing students wearing the symbol of Nazi Germany—the Iron Cross. Yet even that symbol, he said, "never caused a disruption in my class," and it, too, "was not included in the policy involving the arm-bands." And when Raymond Peterson, the district's director of secondary education, was asked by Johnston if the policy was directed solely at the students who were planning to wear black arm-bands, Peterson replied candidly: "Not at the students; at the principle of it."

Despite these potentially damning admissions, the school district's attorney, Alan Herrick, returned in his opening remarks to a familiar refrain. The issue before the Court, he said, was determining "how far it wants to go under the constitutional amendments for free speech in reviewing every decision of every school district made in good faith, in its reasonable discretion and judgment, as necessary to maintain order and a scholarly, disciplined atmosphere within the classroom." To support his claim, Herrick referenced a 1966 Supreme Court case, *Adderley v. Florida*, in which hundreds of students were arrested for trespassing while protesting the arrests of fellow students in a jail driveway. The Court had ruled in the case that the state has the power to control its own property for lawful, nondiscriminatory purposes. Herrick saw convenient parallels to the Iowa public school protest. Notably, the author of that opinion was none other than Hugo Black.

Next, it was Justice Marshall's turn to interrupt. He asked how many students had been involved in the *Adderley* case. "It was quite a large number," Herrick replied. "How many were involved in this one?" said Marshall. "Well," Herrick said, "there were five suspended for wearing arm-bands." Marshall pressed further. "Were any wearing arm-bands who were not suspended?" he pressed. "Yes," said Herrick, "I think there were two."[25] "Seven out of eighteen thousand," Marshall pronounced, "and the school board was afraid that seven students wearing armbands would disrupt eighteen thousand?" To counter Marshall's claim, Herrick referred to a soldier who had been a student in the Des Moines school system and then died in Vietnam. Some of his friends were still students at the time of the student protest, Herrick explained, before reminding Marshall of the original reason given for the hastily enacted policy. "It was felt that if any kind of a demonstration existed, it might evolve into something that would be difficult to control."

But Herrick was barking up the wrong tree. "Do we have a city in this country that hasn't had someone killed in Vietnam?" Marshall asked. "No, I think not," Herrick admitted. "But if someone is going to appear in court with an arm-band here," he countered, "protesting the thing, then it could be explosive. That is the situation we find ourselves in." "It *could* be," Marshall bellowed. "Is that your position? And there is no evidence that it *would* be? Is that the rule you want us to adopt?"[26] Without a material or substantial disruption of the school environment, Marshall had implied, the constitutional rights of students must be honored.

It was clear Hugo Black would reject that premise. It was less clear how Fortas and the other justices would feel about it.

Three days later, during the conference of the case, Chief Justice Warren began by saying he would reverse the lower court decisions, but only "on the narrow ground of equal protection." The board singled out a specific type of conduct in its policy, Warren explained, and although he was willing to concede that schools could sometimes abolish such discussions, the clear viewpoint discrimination in this case—"they allowed the wearing of fascist crosses and so forth"—could not be overlooked. Justices Douglas and Brennan agreed. Potter Stewart joined them, but he qualified his support. "School authorities have the power to discipline students," he said, "and I would not want to see anything written that questions that power." Justices Harlan and Black, conversely, voted to affirm.

Then Justice White redirected the conversation. Despite his verbal sparring with the young Iowa attorney, White announced that he, too, was willing to vote for the students. He was less sure, however, of the reasoning. "If school authorities are empowered to maintain order and protect discipline," he explained, "the school must be allowed to classify what disrupts communication among students. . . . The arm-band communicates in competition with the teacher. But," he continued, "they did not ban this badge only from the classroom, but from the entire school." White outlined the standard he suggested the Court use in deciding the case. "The state does not defend the arm-band prohibition on that ground but on a physically disruptive ground, of which there is no evidence. They can ban some communication but not others."

It was just the angle Fortas needed to justify voting to reverse. "I am closer to Byron than to the Chief," he said. "School authorities can and must control the schools, but they must show some shred of a justification in the sense of the prohibition being necessary to carrying on school functions." Fortas then made the distinction that moved the Court's decision away from an equal protection issue, as Warren had originally recommended. "The justification," he said, "must be in terms of school functions, not equality."[27]

The other votes quickly followed. When Chief Justice Warren counted them up, he found a seven-to-two split in favor of the students. Mary Beth and John Tinker, Chris Eckhardt, and their attorney wouldn't know it for another three months, but they had scored a historic victory for student rights. School officials could no longer censor student expression simply in the name of school discipline and order. They, too, were bound by the First Amendment.

It was Hugo Black's nightmare, all over again. He immediately began work on his no-holds-barred dissent. Abe Fortas, Black's bitter colleague, would write for the majority.

CHILDREN ARE TO BE SEEN AND NOT HEARD?

In his book on civil disobedience, Abe Fortas admitted that, like Hugo Black, he was uncertain about the future of the nation. "I do not know how profound in intensity or how lasting the current youth revolt may be," he wrote.

> It may presage a new and welcome era of idealism in the nation. It may forecast the development of greater maturity and independence of outlook among our young people, and this may be productive of much good. It may

even bring about the development of increased maturity in the educational and living rules of our colleges. In any event, it presents a challenge to the older generations as well as to youth to reconsider the goals of our society and its values, and urgently to reappraise the distribution of function and responsibility among the generations.[28]

Despite his uncertainty, Fortas believed the older generation was required to take the *risk* of freedom in order to honor and light the path of the next generation. Otherwise, how would future Americans learn what it means to be a free and responsible member of a democracy? Justice Jackson had said it decades earlier in his *Barnette* opinion: "One's right to life, liberty and property, to free speech, a free press, freedom of worship and assembly, and other fundamental rights may not be submitted to vote; they depend on the outcome of no elections."

Fortas wrote Jackson's spirit of rightfulness and hope into his *Tinker* majority opinion. He cited Jackson's call for "scrupulous protection of Constitutional freedoms of the individual, if we are not to strangle the free mind at its source and teach youth to discount important principles of our government as mere platitudes." And, he announced, "[i]t can hardly be argued that either students or teachers shed their constitutional rights to freedom of speech or expression at the schoolhouse gate." More important, in a nod to the Fourteenth Amendment, Fortas characterized students "in school as well as out" as "'persons' under our Constitution. They are possessed of fundamental rights which the state must respect." He also characterized the student arm-bands as a type of expression that was virtually "pure speech," which he said the Court had repeatedly held "is entitled to comprehensive protection under the First Amendment."[29]

The problem, Fortas continued, "lies in the area where students in the exercise of First Amendment rights collide with the rules of the school authorities." So he offered a standard to use in balancing those competing interests. Noting that a student's rights do not embrace merely classroom hours, Fortas wrote that "when he's in the cafeteria, or on the playing field, or on the campus during the authorized hours, he may express his opinions, even on controversial subjects like the conflict in Vietnam, if he does so without '*materially and substantially interfer[ing] with the requirements of appropriate discipline in the operation of the school*' *and without colliding with the rights of others*" (italics added). "Any word spoken," he continued, "that deviates from the view of another person may start an argument or cause a disturbance. But our Constitution says we must take this risk."[30]

For the aging Hugo Black, it was a bad omen. "The Court's holding in this case," his dissent began, "ushers in what I deem to be an entirely new era in which the power to control pupils by the elected 'officials of state supported public schools...' in the United States is in ultimate effect transferred to the Supreme

Court....It may be that the Nation has outworn the old-fashioned slogan that 'children are to be seen and not heard,' but one may, I hope, be permitted to harbor the thought that taxpayers send children to school on the premise that at their age they need to learn, not teach." The depth of Black's resentment was palpable in his words. So, too, was his fear of the future. "Change has been said to be truly the law of life," he wrote, "but sometimes the old and tried and true are worth holding."[31] Then he wrote a sentence one might have expected to flow from the pen of J. Edgar Hoover, not from one of FDR's most liberal constitutional stewards. "Uncontrolled and uncontrollable liberty," he wrote, "is an enemy to domestic peace." After reading this line, an incredulous Abe Fortas scribbled in the margin of his copy, "Hugo Black!!" Earl Warren was more to the point. "Old Hugo really got hung up in his jock strap on that one."[32]

What had happened? Had Black lost his abiding faith in the constitutional principles of freedom and democracy? Not exactly. But he had certainly lost faith in the ability of the nation's young people to exercise that freedom in a productive way. "One does not need to be a prophet or the son of a prophet," he proclaimed, "to know that after the Court's holding today some students in Iowa schools and indeed in all schools will be ready, able, and willing to defy their teachers on practically all orders. This is the more unfortunate for the schools since groups of students all over the land are already running loose, conducting break-ins, sit-ins, lie-ins, and smash-ins."

To be fair, it was 1969, and the country was approaching the end of one of its most tumultuous decades since, arguably, the American revolution itself. Yet Black had gone further than anyone could ever have predicted for him—in effect, he decided America had become a country of count-me-outs. And *Tinker v. Des Moines*, he believed, had set up the nation's schools "to the whims and caprices of their loudest-mouthed, but maybe not their brightest, students." Maybe. But Black's characterization was not demonstrably true in Iowa. Despite her historic victory, Mary Beth Tinker was hardly interested in returning to her state to foment revolution. "I didn't want to be a big star," she said, "because I was a teenager. [And] teenagers never want to stand out in a crowd. They just want to blend in."

BACK TO THE FUTURE

Bretton Barber didn't want to blend in. He also didn't fit Abe Fortas's decades-old description of a count-me-out. He was an honors student. He was not making waves simply to cause trouble. And, as he demonstrated in his conversation with the principal, he knew his First Amendment law. Or did he? It was, after all, 2003. Practically speaking, was *Tinker* still the law of the land? Bretton Barber certainly thought it was. But as Professor Erwin Chemerinksy pointed out during a 2000 symposium looking back at the *Tinker* decision, "in the thirty years since *Tinker*, schools have won virtually every constitutional claim involving students' rights." Chemerinsky added that the Court had never directly overruled *Tinker*. Yet as all constitutional scholars know, Fortas's "material and substantial disruption" standard has been significantly narrowed since 1969, so much so that today there are fourt major standards of student expression, not one. *Tinker* was the first.

The *Fraser* Standard

The first major retreat from *Tinker* occurred in 1986, in the case of *Bethel School District No. 403 v. Fraser*. The trouble began when high school student Matthew Fraser decided to give a speech nominating classmate Jeff Kuhlman for a student government office. Fraser decided to deliver a speech laced with sexual metaphors. Among other things, he described his friend Jeff as "a man who is firm— he's firm in his pants, he's firm in his shirt … [and] most … of all, his belief in you, the students of Bethel, is firm." Fraser then completed his clever wordplay by letting the student body know that Jeff Kuhlman was "a man who will go to the very end—even the climax, for each and every one of you."

Asked later about the speech, Fraser confessed that he had written it about an hour before the assembly. "One teacher told me it would 'raise eyebrows,'" he said. "But no teacher told me that it violated school policy." A day later, however, he was presented with the policy. Clearly written with the *Tinker* standard in mind, the policy read: "Conduct which materially and substantially interferes with the educational process is prohibited, including the use of obscene, profane language or gestures." Applying their own glass to the policy, school officials promptly suspended Fraser.

Fraser sued in federal court, claiming his suspension violated his First Amendment rights. Two lower courts agreed, ruling that his speech was in fact protected by the *Tinker* standard. But on July 7, 1986, the Supreme Court held differently. "Surely," wrote Chief Justice Warren Burger, on behalf of the seven-to-two majority,[33] "it is a highly appropriate function of public school education to prohibit the use of vulgar and offensive terms in public discourse. A high school assembly or classroom is no place for a sexually explicit monologue directed towards an unsuspecting audience of teenage students." More significantly, Burger wrote that "the marked distinction between the political 'message' of the armbands in *Tinker* and the sexual content of respondent's speech in this case seems to have been given little weight by the Court of Appeals." The chief justice continued, "the undoubted freedom to advocate unpopular and controversial views in schools and classrooms must be balanced against the society's countervailing interest in teaching students the boundaries of socially appropriate behavior."[34]

Burger then crafted a second standard for student expression, one in which he gave clear reference to the *Tinker* case. Because school officials have an *"interest in teaching students the boundaries of socially appropriate behavior,"* he wrote, *"they can censor student speech that is vulgar or indecent, even if it does not cause a 'material or substantial disruption.'"*[35] (emphasis added)

Despite the ruling in the case, David Hudson, an attorney with the First Amendment Center in Nashville, says many courts are still divided in how they apply the *Fraser* standard. "Some courts apply *Fraser* to all vulgar or lewd student speech...if the speech is student-initiated," maintains Hudson. "Other courts only apply *Fraser* to vulgar student speech that is in some way school-sponsored." The distinction is significant, Hudson argues, because it gives school officials the ability to characterize some student speech as offensive or vulgar even if the expression contains a political message.

Lower courts also disagree over what types of speech are subject to censorship under the *Fraser* standard. For example, the Eleventh U.S. Circuit Court of Appeals has ruled that school districts can ban the Confederate flag because it is plainly offensive to students. And another court confronted this issue when a junior high school student wore a t-shirt to class bearing the words, "Drugs Suck!" The student in the case argued that the shirt conveyed an important "antidrug message" and did not disrupt the school environment. The school countered that the shirt was inappropriate because the word "suck" has a vulgar connotation. The federal district court in Virginia sided with the school and based its decision on a broad application of the *Fraser* standard:

> Teachers and administrators must have the authority to do what they rea-
> sonably believe is in the best interest of their educational responsibilities, as
> we cannot abandon our schools to the whims or proclivities of children.
> The Court finds that ... [s]chool [o]fficials had an interest in protecting their
> young students from exposure to vulgar and offensive language.[36]

This case and a host of others like it illustrate how the *Fraser* standard has come to limit the reach of *Tinker.* Yet, just as the *Fraser* decision altered the landscape of student rights, the Court's 1988 decision in *Hazelwood School District v. Kuhlmeier* added a third standard of expression for school officials to consider.

The *Hazelwood* Standard

In *Hazelwood*, the Court ruled that students' First Amendment rights were not violated when a high school principal censored two student articles on contro-versial topics (pregnancy and divorce) in the school newspaper. The principal barred the stories after reviewing the galleys. He believed the piece about teen pregnancy was inappropriate for some of the younger students at the school, on the basis of its discussion of sexual activity and birth control. In addition, he decided to censor the divorce article because the writers did not afford the parent of one of the students mentioned in the article a chance to respond to certain comments. Several of the paper's staff members challenged the principal's action in federal court, claiming a violation of their First Amendment rights. The district court sided with the school, finding that the principal's concerns were reasonable and legitimate. A federal appeals court disagreed, ruling that under the *Tinker* standard there was "no evidence in the record that the principal could have reasonably forecast that the censored articles or any materials in the censored articles would have materially disrupted class work or given rise to substantial disorder in the school."

Once the case reached the Supreme Court, the justices focused heavily on the First Amendment concept of a *public forum*—places such as a public park or street where the government has less leeway to regulate speech than in others— and asked themselves whether the school officials had by policy or practice opened up a public "forum for student expression" by allowing students to make content decisions.

On January 13, 1988, the Court ruled five to three that it had not. "The public schools do not possess all of the attributes of streets, parks, and other traditional public forums that 'time out of mind, have been used for purposes of assembly, communicating thoughts between citizens, and discussing public questions,'" wrote Justice White. "Hence, school facilities may be deemed to be public forums only if school authorities have 'by policy or by practice' opened those facilities 'for indiscriminate use by the general public,' or by some segment of the public, such as student organizations. If the facilities have instead been reserved for other intended purposes," White concluded, "then no public forum has been created, and school officials may impose reasonable restrictions on the speech of students, teachers, and other members of the school community."[37]

It was an ironic development. Byron White, the justice who had helped make the *Tinker* ruling possible, had now helped to curtail it. By this ruling, the Court created the *Hazelwood* standard, which states that *"educators do not offend the First Amendment by exercising editorial control over the style and content of student speech in school-sponsored expressive activities so long as their actions are reasonably related to legitimate pedagogical concerns* (emphasis added)."[38]

Justice William Brennan disagreed. "The young men and women of Hazelwood East expected a civics lesson," he wrote in his dissent, "but not the one the Court teaches them today." What troubled the justice was that the school was picking and choosing among viewpoints, censoring those it found too controversial for a high school audience. Brennan felt the school had a responsibility to go farther. "The mere fact of school sponsorship does not," he argued, "license such thought control in the high school, whether through school suppression of disfavored viewpoints or through official assessment of topic sensitivity. The former would constitute unabashed and unconstitutional viewpoint discrimination, as well as an impermissible infringement of the students' " 'right to receive information and ideas.' " He added, "The State's prerogative to dissolve the student newspaper entirely (or to limit its subject matter) no more entitles it to dictate which viewpoints students may express on its pages, than the State's prerogative to close down the schoolhouse entitles it to prohibit the non-disruptive expression of antiwar sentiment within its gates."[39]

The promise of *Tinker* had been breached, or so thought Justice Brennan: "The case before us aptly illustrates how readily school officials (and courts) can camouflage viewpoint discrimination as the 'mere' protection of students from sensitive topics."

The "Bong Hits 4 Jesus" Standard

Nearly twenty years passed between the Court's ruling in *Hazelwood* and its decision to accept another student speech case for review. In the years between 1988 and 2007, most lower courts divided student speech into three categories:

1. Vulgar, lewd, obscene, and plainly offensive student speech (*Fraser* standard)
2. School-sponsored student speech (*Hazelwood* standard)
3. All other student speech (*Tinker* standard)

Then, on June 25, 2007, the Court added a fourth standard for courts to consider. School officials have the authority, announced Chief Justice John Roberts, to restrict student speech that may promote illegal drug use—even if the speech takes place off-campus on a public street across from the school.

The case began on January 24, 2002, as the Olympic torch was traveling through Juneau, Alaska. When Juneau-Douglas High School principal Deborah Morse learned that the torch would pass directly by the school, she decided to excuse staff and students to participate in the celebration. Joseph Frederick, an eighteen-year-old senior, never made it to school that day. But he and some fellow students had an idea. Setting themselves up directly across from the school on public property, they waited for the torch-bearers—and the accompanying TV cameras—to pass in front of them. At that moment, they unfurled a fourteen-foot-banner with the cryptic message "Bong Hits 4 Jesus."[40] When Morse saw the banner, she left school property and crossed the street to confront Frederick. He countered the principal's order to take down the banner by asking, "What about the Bill of Rights and freedom of speech?"

Morse later explained that she thought the banner encouraged illegal drug use, a clear violation of an established school policy. Frederick countered in a court affidavit that his "message" carried no deeper meaning whatsoever. "We thought we had a free-speech right to display a humorous saying," he said. "The content of the banner was less important to us than the fact that we were exercising our free-speech rights to do a funny parody."

Frederick sued in district court, alleging that the school board and Morse had violated his First Amendment rights. He also sought declaratory and injunctive relief, compensatory and punitive damages, and attorney's fees. The district court decided in favor of Morse and the board, ruling that they were entitled to *qualified immunity*—a legal defense that requires courts to enter judgment in favor of a government employee unless the employee's conduct violates "clearly established statutory or constitutional rights of which a reasonable person would have known."[41]

But the Ninth Circuit Court of Appeals reversed. Although Frederick's speech essentially took place at a "school-authorized activit[y]," school officials had not demonstrated that his speech gave rise to the "risk of substantial disruption" that *Tinker* requires. Perhaps of greater interest to the Court, however, was the Ninth Circuit's decision to refuse Morse the defense of qualified immunity. This meant the principal could be held liable for monetary damages. As Chief Justice Roberts later explained on behalf of the six-justice majority, the Supreme Court "granted certiorari on two questions: whether Frederick had a First Amendment right to wield his banner, and, if so, whether that right was so clearly established that the principal may be held liable for damages."

"The question thus becomes whether a principal may, consistent with the First Amendment, restrict student speech at a school event, when that speech is reasonably viewed as promoting illegal drug use," wrote Roberts. "We hold that she may." Although the message itself was little more than "gibberish," Morse "had to decide to act—or not act—on the spot.... Failing to act would send a powerful message to the students in her charge, including Frederick, about how serious the school was about the dangers of illegal drug use." So Frederick was not entitled to seek any damages from his former principal after all.

Chief Justice Roberts then distinguished Frederick's case from the Court's past decisions in *Bethel v. Fraser* and *Hazelwood v. Kuhlmeier*. "*Kuhlmeier* does not control this case because no one would reasonably believe that Frederick's banner bore the school's imprimatur," the chief justice explained. And in response to an argument by Kenneth Starr, representing the school official pro bono, that Frederick's speech was, per *Fraser*, "plainly offensive," Roberts wrote: "We think this stretches *Fraser* too far; that case should not be read to encompass any speech that could fit under some definition of 'offensive.' After all," he opined, "much political and religious speech might be perceived as offensive to some."[42]

Because of the narrowness of the Court's ruling—highlighted by a concurring opinion from Justice Samuel Alito, who underscored that the decision "goes no further than to hold that a public school may restrict speech that a reasonable observer would interpret as advocating illegal drug use"—the long-term impact of *Morse* may be limited. Justice Anthony Kennedy agreed. But Justice John Paul Stevens, joined by justices Souter and Ginsburg, still felt passionate enough to write a dissent. "In my judgment," he wrote, "the First Amendment protects student speech if the message itself neither violates a permissible rule nor expressly advocates conduct that is illegal and harmful to students."[43]

Adding another layer to the ruling was Justice Stephen Breyer, concurring in part and dissenting in part, who felt that both sides got it half wrong. "This Court need not and should not decide this difficult First Amendment issue on the merits," he wrote. "Rather, I believe that it should simply hold that qualified immunity bars the student's claim for monetary damages and say no more." As Breyer explained, "although the dissent avoids some of the majority's pitfalls, I fear that, if adopted as law, it would risk significant interference with reasonable school efforts to maintain discipline." In addition, the majority's decision to weigh in on the First Amendment issue was problematic:

> In resolving the underlying constitutional question, we produce several differing opinions. It is utterly unnecessary to do so. Were we to decide this case on the ground of qualified immunity, our decision would be unanimous, for the dissent concludes that Morse should not be held liable in damages for confiscating Frederick's banner. And the cardinal principle of judicial restraint is that "if it is not necessary to decide more, it is necessary not to decide more."[44]

Perhaps the most unexpected part of the ruling, however, was the concurring opinion of Justice Clarence Thomas. "I write separately to state my view that the standard set forth in *Tinker v. Des Moines Community School District* is without basis in the Constitution." Like Justice Black before him, Thomas seemed to think that what was at stake here involved an important constitutional principle. "In my view," Thomas continued, "the history of public education suggests that the First Amendment, as originally understood, does not protect student speech in public schools" at all. "In short," wrote Thomas, echoing Hugo Black's dissent in *Tinker*, "in the earliest public schools, teachers taught, and students listened. Teachers commanded, and students obeyed. Teachers did not rely solely on the power of ideas to persuade; they relied on discipline to maintain order." He then added a yet bolder statement: "I join the Court's opinion because it erodes *Tinker*'s hold in the realm of student speech, even though it does so by adding to the patchwork of exceptions to the *Tinker* standard. I think the better approach is to dispense with *Tinker* altogether, and given the opportunity, I would do so."[45]

MODERN-DAY COUNT-ME-INS

When Bretton Barber decided to wear his t-shirt to school, of course, the *Morse* decision was still four years away; only three student speech standards then existed. Which standard should have applied? It was clearly not school-sponsored speech. One could, however, make an argument that it was plainly offensive. Even if a court ruled that it wasn't offensive, was the Bush "terrorist" t-shirt likely to cause a "material or substantial disruption"?

Dave Mustonen, spokesman for Dearborn public schools, certainly thought so. "It was felt that emotions are running very high," Mustonen said in a February 19, 2003, article in the *Detroit News*. "The shirt posed a potential disruption to our learning environment at the school. Our number one obligation is to make sure that we have a safe learning environment for all of our students." It sounded a lot like Iowa and 1965. And in the end, despite the weakening of the *Tinker* decision in the years since, the Tinker and Eckhardt victory then remained relevant enough to support Bretton Barber's victory in 2003. "There is no evidence," wrote U.S. district judge Patrick J. Duggan, "that the t-shirt created any disturbance or disruption" at the school, and "the record does not reveal any basis for [the assistant principal's] fear aside from the fact that the t-shirt conveyed an unpopular political message."

Fresh from his victory, Barber had a message he wanted to share with other students across America. Although one imagines Justice Thomas disagreeing—and Justice Black shouting from his grave—the Michigan teenager's words provide another example of why men like Abe Fortas had reason to be optimistic: "My hope is that you, too, will have a defining moment," he wrote. "Perhaps, like with me, your defining moment will come as a result of your decision to become involved. And all I can tell you is this: When it comes, truly live that moment. Take it all in, and let it become a part of who you are. Because if you do, you will not only better yourself, but you will touch the lives of countless others, in ways that you never could have imagined."[46]

Epilogue

Hugo Black and Beyond

The Future of Freedom

We end where we began, with Justice Hugo Black. In the arc of his long life, we have seen him facing everything from the old clear and present danger battles to the new battles over symbolic speech. At points, as in the case of student expression and the tumult of the 1960s, he strayed quite a bit from his proud absolutism. Then again, he did hold onto a good measure of his beloved First Amendment absolutism, as his opinions in the *Pentagon Papers* case and in obscenity cases make clear.[1]

Quite apart from the soundness of his First Amendment jurisprudence, one cannot dismiss his impact on both the law and culture of free speech in America. That impact had far less to do with his majority opinions for the Court in free-speech cases (there were only thirteen of them) than with the mood he created in the Court and country about the importance of defending the principle of free speech. In that world, Black's absolutism made it easier for the Court to accept the near absolutism of Justice Brennan and his constitutional successors.

In his own singular way, Hugo Black also contributed to what came to be known as the "Warren Court Revolution." That revolution brought an unprecedented measure of liberty to this nation. By the late 1960s, that liberty challenged the military establishment, condemned the excesses of capitalism, rebuked compromise politics, confronted racism, and questioned conventional values (among other things). It was a time of protest, and the First Amendment had come alive— too alive for some people.

In that swirl of social revolution, Justice Black agreed to a national television interview. It was a highly unusual decision for any sitting Supreme Court justice. In that remarkable interview, we see the two sides of Hugo Black, the side that welcomed freedom and the side that feared it. Here was the great Justice Black both invigorating the First Amendment as never before—while at the same time diminishing its value as a symbol of liberty.

The year was 1968, one of the most tumultuous in American history. That interview and what followed is a portrait of a man reflecting back on the past that he made present. In that sense, it is a cautionary tale... but with what moral?

MADE FOR TV

The camera crews pulled up to 619 South Lee Street, the location of a beautiful home in the Old Town section of Alexandria, Virginia. It was September 1968, and they were there to film an interview that had been more than a decade in the planning. Martin Agronsky, a CBS reporter, had approached Justice Black as early as 1957 about doing an on-camera interview. The request fell on deaf ears until years later, when Fred Friendly (1915–1998),[2] then president of CBS News, spoke to his black-robed friend and made it happen. As a condition for airing the interview, Black reserved the right to review the recording and to correct misstatements, or even to deny permission to air the broadcast entirely.

The interview was filmed in Black's upstairs study. His comfortable quarter with an air of the Enlightenment was full of shelves brimming with books of all sorts. Livy's *History of Rome* was in one section, Holmes's *Common Law* in another. When the agreed-upon time came, Agronsky was joined by Eric Sevareid (1912–1992)[3] to ask questions.[4] Agronsky posed the first substantive question to the eighty-two-year-old Justice:

AGRONSKY: Mr. Justice, you have dedicated your life... on the Court toward the application of the Bill of Rights to all of the states. Now you said once, "It's my belief that there are absolutes in our Bill of Rights, and that they were put there on purpose by men who knew what words meant—and meant their prohibitions to be absolutes." What are your reasons for saying that?

BLACK: Well, I'll read you the part of the First Amendment that caused me to say that there are absolutes in our Bill of Rights. I did not say that our entire Bill of Rights is an absolute. I said there are absolutes in our Bill of Rights. Now, if a man were to say this to me on the street, "Congress shall make no law respecting an establishment of religion"— that's the First Amendment—I would think: Amen, Congress should pass no law. Unless they just didn't know the meaning of words. That's what they mean to me. Certainly they mean that literally.

As the interview continued, Black periodically reached into his suit coat to pull out, and then read from, a dog-eared pocket copy of the Constitution. The moment turned out to be a made-for-TV event that only the old populist senator from Alabama could pull off. Maybe that explains why so many forgot that Justice Black had cast his absolutism aside when it came to student protests, certain types of picketing, draft-card burning, and even commercial speech, among other things. Later, Sevareid asked the following question having to do with political protests in public places:

> SEVAREID: Justice Black, on [the] matter of free speech and assembly, and the rights of the people to have order, I think you wrote a dissent[5] a couple of years ago, it involved a small public library in Louisiana, and you said that no group, however just their cause, has a constitutional right to use other people's property, even the property of the government—
>
> BLACK: That's right.
>
> SEVAREID: —as a stage to express their dissent. If protestors or demonstrators don't have any inherent right to use streets or any public places, then aren't you really infringing the right of protest itself? How can they do it? Where do they do it?
>
> BLACK: Well that assumes that the only way to protest anything is to go out and do it in the streets. That is not true. That is simply not true in life. It never has been true.

It was a peculiar response, colored more by fear than logic. In 1951 Black wrote in defense of a young college student (Irving Feiner) who went into the streets of Syracuse to lock tempers with a hostile crowd. And in 1949 it was Black who rallied to the defense of Charles Kovacs when he rolled his truck armed with loud amplifiers onto the streets of Trenton to complain about labor disputes. But those cases were many years ago.

> BLACK: I've never said that freedom of speech gives people the right to tramp up and down the streets by the thousands, either by saying things that threatened others, with real literal language, or that threatened them because of the circumstances under which they do it. I've never said that.

Here was Hugo Black, the great First Amendment absolutist, defending a cramped view of freedom of speech, assembly, and petition. And he did so in the context of a nation of civil rights and antiwar activists taking to the public streets to speak their minds and "vote" with the collective assembly of their bodies. Black's position was out of sync with what Justice Douglas—Black's First Amendment ally—had just written in his book *Points of Rebellion:* "the basic right of public protest may not be abridged." For Justice Douglas, that right included taking to the streets in robust ways. Oblivious to Douglas's more absolute form of First Amendment absolutism, Justice Black continued:

> BLACK: [The First Amendment does not protect] a man's right to walk around and around my house, if he wants to; [threaten] my people, [confine] my family [within] the house, make them afraid to go out of doors, afraid that something will happen.... That's conduct [not speech].

Was this a sign of cracks in the liberty bell of Black's absolutism? Or did it reflect a sober appreciation of where to draw the First Amendment line—between speech and conduct, between demonstrations in public places versus those in front of private homes? If the latter, does this mean that Justice Black would permit the government to close off all access for protests in front of the homes of the town mayor, or a convicted pedophile, or of an abortion doctor? Take it a slight step further: what about protests in front of abortion clinics?[6] Could they be banned, too?

Agronsky persisted—What about the "demonstrators who gathered before the hotels in Chicago and Grant Park?" The "contemporary example" he selected referred to the antiwar demonstrations that occurred just a month prior in August 1968. Protestors, radicals, and flower children of all kinds (numbering ten to twenty thousand) came to Chicago en masse to protest the Vietnam War as the Democratic Convention was being held. Mayor Richard Daley, a power-holding man accustomed to having his way, refused to grant the protesters parade or park permits; instead, he brought in five thousand national guardsmen and seven thousand federal troops to meet them head on. During the melee, demonstrators and police clashed in gory exchanges while TV cameras broadcast the bloody scenes around the world. As police batons swung wildly, protesters screamed: "The whole world is watching; the whole world is watching; the whole world..." With those images fresh in mind, the interview with Justice Black continued:

> AGRONSKY: Do you think that the demonstrators in this instance were right to assemble the way they did, or the police were right in not permitting them to assemble and charging them and breaking up the demonstration?
>
> BLACK: Well, that gets right on the cases we have. We're liable to have that very case. I don't want to say what my view would be, because I don't

know what the evidence would show. I don't know what they were doing. I don't know how far they went. [Mayor] Daley says they did so-and-so, and the other side says they're just a group of nice young idealists who should not be noticed. Now, the Constitution doesn't say that any man shall have a right to say anything he wishes, [go] anywhere he wants to go. That's agreed, isn't it? Nothing in there says that. All right. It doesn't say people shall have a right to assemble on other people's property. It just doesn't say it. It says they shall have a right to assemble, if they're peaceable, but it doesn't say how far you can go in using other's people's property.

AGRONSKY: You mean even government property—

BLACK: Why, certainly, that's not theirs.

SEVAREID: You can't assemble in mid-air.

BLACK: That's not theirs.

SEVAREID: Well, whose is it—it is government property—

BLACK: It belongs to the government as a whole. Just exactly as a corporation's property belongs to the corporation as a whole. And just as an individual owns it. Now, the government would be in a very bad fix, I think, if the Constitution provided that the Congress was without the power to keep people from coming into the Library of Congress and spending the day there, demonstrating or singing because they wanted to protest the government. They have a right to talk where they have a right to be, under valid laws.

Black's response was remarkable for its candor. It was equally remarkable coming from the lips of this reputed First Amendment absolutist. While the justice formally declined to pass judgment on the facts before him, could there be any doubt where he stood on this matter of protest concerning a group of not so "nice young idealists"? His view of the public forum concept barely recognized public streets and public parks as legitimate places of protest. Contrast this with what Justice Douglas said around the same time, again in *Points of Rebellion:*

While violence is not protected by the Constitution, lawful conduct, such as marching and picketing, often boils over into unlawful conduct because people are emotional, not rational, beings. So are the police; and very often they arrest the wrong people. For the police are an arm of the Establishment and view protestors with suspicion. Yet American protestors need not be submissive. A speaker who resists arrest is acting as a free man. The police do not have *carte blanche* to interfere with his freedom. They do not have the license to arrest at will or silence people at will. This is one of many instances showing how *the Constitution was designed to keep government off the backs of the people.*[7]

Where Black was timid, evasive, or hesitant when it came to the First Amendment public protests, Douglas was daring, outspoken, even provocative in spirit. But while the aging Hugo was gun-shy on some First Amendment issues, he was certainly not so on others, as the following exchange reveals.

> AGRONSKY: Do you think there are any times at all when obscenity can be restricted, prohibited, and not come into conflict with the freedom of the press guarantee? The freedom of speech guarantee in the Constitution?
>
> BLACK: I've said they couldn't. Of course, I understand that pornography sounds bad. It really sounds bad. But I've never seen anybody say what it is. Nobody... If the idea is to keep people from learning about the facts of life, as between the sexes, that's a vain task. It's a vain task. How in the world can you keep people from learning, who mix with others out on the street, and around the various places? They're going to learn. But that's not the reason I take that view."

The senior justice then paused and continued with his constitutional gospel:

> BLACK: The reason I take the view is that it's an expression of opinion. It refers to one of the strongest urges in the human race. Something that people have not failed to talk about, and they will not fail to talk about. People are... going to say, "You're letting my children suffer." There's plenty of argument for the idea. But they ought to take their children and warn them against things themselves rather than try to pass a law."

He then reaffirmed his noncompromising commitment to freedom of expression:

> BLACK: Obscenity is wholly ambiguous. It means one thing to you, and another thing to you, and another thing to these people, and another thing to me. I don't like it. I don't use it. I never have; I've always detested it. But that's no reason, I think, that it's not speech on an important subject. Let them talk."

For First Amendment purposes, Justice Black spoke about obscenity—the rude, ribald, and raunchy—much as he would speak about Plato's *Symposium* or Oscar Wilde's *Salomé*. But could the two really be equated? And what about other concerns like obscenity on television, or indecency on radio, or XXX-rated movies on the Internet, or child pornography, or racy websites on computers in public libraries? Would Justice Black, had he lived long enough, have protected these, too, with absolute confidence?

The interview went on for an hour. The justice and his interlocutors discussed *Brown v. Board of Education* (1954), crime, the role of the Court, the judicial nomination process, and how to interpret the Constitution.[8] Then the justice closed with these words:

> BLACK: It's intended to be a government of the people, by the people and for the people. It's failed at various times and in various localities. But it's done mighty well, compared with the other nations of the world. It's certainly better than the empire Augustus had. I think this country has lived because of its Constitution and its law and its ideals of liberty and equality and freedom, I think every time we take a move in that regard, to make it what they said, to improve the public tranquility under law, that it moves another step toward lasting a longer time.
>
> AGRONSKY: Thank you, Mr. Justice.
>
> SEVAREID: Thank you, Mr. Justice.

Americans must have sensed the uniqueness of the opportunity to gain such far-ranging insight into the mind of a sitting justice, given the warm and wide reception the interview received. At the end of the program, CBS announced it would mail a pocket copy of the Constitution to anyone who requested one. Soon thereafter, over 128,000 copies were sent out. While the editors of the *New York Times* took respectful exception to the justice's views on the First Amendment and the right to protest in the streets, they nonetheless raised their glasses to his constitutional idealism: "Long live the Constitution!"[9] they wrote.

"A REVOLUTION IS COMING"

> I want to bring down this system, and replace it with one more responsive to human needs.
>
> —CHARLES A. REICH, *The Greening of America* (1970)

Charles A. Reich was a modern-day Walt Whitman, a man with a keen and open mind and a fervent compassion for the powerless. Before he "dropped out" and moved to San Francisco in the early 1970s, he was a distinguished Yale Law School professor, the author of a seminal law review article ("The New Property"), and a man who in the late 1960s was changing the face of American law and life. He was also a Hugo Black law clerk during the landmark 1953–54 Court term.

The two men had a special, almost paternal, bond. The justice was proud of his protégé, and the professor lovingly admired his constitutional godfather...so much so that he dedicated an article in the *Harvard Law Review* to "Mr. Justice Black and the Living Constitution."[10] And then in 1970, Charles Reich took the nation by storm with the publication of *The Greening of America*. Its cover proclaimed boldly:

> There is a revolution coming. It will not be like revolutions of the past. It will originate with the individual and with culture, and it will change the political structure only as its final act. It will not require violence to succeed, and it cannot be successfully resisted by violence. This is the revolution of the new generation.[11]

It was a book about and to the youth culture: "The whole emerging pattern," Reich wrote, "from ideals to campus demonstrations to beads and bell bottoms to the Woodstock Festival, makes sense and is part of a consistent philosophy. It is both necessary and inevitable, and in time it will include not only youth, but all people in America."[12] The history and future of the nation were neatly described in a tripartite construction:

- *Consciousness I* is the traditional outlook of the American farmer, small businessman, and worker who is trying to get ahead.
- *Consciousness II* represents the values of an organizational society.
- *Consciousness III* is the new generation.

This new generation rejected many of the old ideas that had so often been championed in Norman Rockwell–like depictions of American values. The aim of the new generation was to change America from the "vast and terrifying anti-community" it was charged to be. The emerging consciousness would drive the nation away from "disorder, corruption, hypocrisy, and war," away from enforced poverty, away from the "destruction of the environment," away from the unconstitutional assertion of government power, and away from meaningless work. "Consciousness III can make a new society," Reich stressed.

As much as he loved Charlie, Hugo could not abide this rejection (if it was that) of his beloved America. Black dissented, as reflected in what he wrote in the margin of a page in *Greening*: "I do not agree."[13] For him, the American dream had not yet been destroyed. He still *believed* in his nation, as created, as handed down to him, and as preserved. For Justice Black, the rebelliousness of the 1960s, with its student unrest, race riots, and antiwar demonstrations, was tearing this nation apart. He feared that, deeply. For Charles Reich, by stark contrast, these same actions were signs that America had finally come of age, thanks in good measure to the Warren Court's steadfast commitment to the Bill of Rights and the First Amendment. Reich welcomed that, openly.

True to that sentiment of uninhibited freedom, at the end of *Greening* Reich acknowledged that his "greatest individual debt" was not to Hugo Black but to "Thomas I. Emerson." For it was Emerson, also a Yale law professor, who had long defended an expansionist interpretation of the First Amendment.[14] In his highly influential book *The System of Freedom of Expression* (1970), Emerson expressed his disapproval of Black's view on public protests.

By the time he left the Court on September 17, 1971 (Constitution Day), Hugo Black had *in some respects* come to fear the freedom he once championed. While he would proudly hold his ground in the *Pentagon Papers* case, by the end of his career he began to backpedal on things like the right to assembly, flag burning, the public forum doctrine, and symbolic expression. By that measure, had he lived, he probably would have joined Justice Clarence Thomas, who in 2003 argued that cross burning (see chapter 7) was not protected expression. One can only imagine how the events of 9/11 might also have affected his First Amendment jurisprudence.

Granted, Justice Black had his justifications. But in the end, they seemed wooden. His absolutism seemed fearful of the potential of a First Amendment unbound, the kind of First Amendment hailed by Reich, Emerson, and Justices Douglas and Brennan, among others.

If you do not fear freedom, you cannot defend it. That idea is peculiar precisely because there is something strange about tolerating that which we fear. And yet that is as good as any conceptual touchstone. If we fear it, we must protect it. Why? There are many answers—because we are uncertain about truth; because we need to self-realize; because we yearn to improve the common good; because we need to check government power; because we believe in an open society; because we value dissent; because we are willing to trust our collective fate to social Darwinism; or even because we have certain sentiments about freedom.

But this is a touchstone, not a tablet of an all-encompassing truth. There are other considerations. Questions of the legitimacy of judicial review very much affect First Amendment decision-making as they affect all kinds of constitutional interpretation. Thus text and history matter, as do the justifications tendered for valuing one kind of expression over others. And certain kinds of expression are, within a narrow confine, believed to be so immediately injurious that they are today jettisoned outside the universe of First Amendment protection. By the same token, ours is a tradition that frowns on prior restraints on freedom of expression, even when national security is at stake. At times, the free-speech and equality principles work hand in hand; at other times, they war with one another. All such considerations are, to be sure, tempered by the real-life and imminent consequences of protecting expression in this or that context.

Behind every view or theory or justification for protecting expression under the First Amendment is a sentiment about freedom. That sentiment, like dye poured into a beaker of water, colors everything. It explains why the Jehovah's Witnesses' lawyer, Hayden Covington, argued as he did, why Justice Robert Jackson ruled as he did, and why Justice Felix Frankfurter dissented as he did in the flag-salute case. It explains why the moderate Alexander Bickel argued for the right to publish the Pentagon Papers, while the moderate Justice John Harlan II voted against that claim. And, it helps explain why the liberal Justice John Paul Stevens dissented in the flag desecration cases, while the otherwise conservative Antonin Scalia joined in defending those free-speech claims. Likewise, that sentiment about freedom *might* help to explain why a conservative Justice like Samuel Alito paused[15] when it came to giving school officials the kind of unbridled power over student expression that Justice Black might well have given them in the "Bong Hits for Jesus" case.

Granted, most sitting judges would assuredly deny that any such sentiments influence their rulings at all—but that is to be expected. It is part of the mystique of judging. Even so, if one studies a judge's opinions with any degree of rigor, it soon enough becomes apparent how and to what extent the dye of this sentiment has colored his or her view of the First Amendment. Surely, the constitutional legacy of Hugo Black demonstrates this. For though he had a strong sentiment wed to a bold and courageous form of freedom, he too had his breaking point— and it was the point at which fear overcame him.

The more open the society, the more it will strive to nourish—in classrooms, in courtrooms, and in the culture—a generous sentiment about freedom. It is a sentiment, as we have noted, that does not stand alone. It must be informed by other considerations. And yet it remains that "fixed star in our constitutional constellation,"[16] that point of light in a dark universe that directs our journey.

Steven Shiffrin, a longtime friend of the First Amendment, once said that "we need not trade freedom for destiny or destiny for freedom."[17] Perhaps. Then again, a truly free people may change their destiny, for better or worse. The First Amendment enshrines that right, a right grounded in the Declaration of Independence. It is a right premised on the possibility of *change*. And everyone, including Hugo Black, fears change *at some point*.

Clearly, change is not *always* better. And yet we can afford to take a few more chances in order to live in a world where, to the greatest extent reasonably possible, First Amendment freedom is our collective default position. It is a risk worthy of a free people. In that spirit, then, and with that sentiment at heart, we enthusiastically echo Willa Cather: "Coraggio, Americano!"[18]

Free-speech Timeline

The following historical events, court cases, and ideas have significantly shaped our current system of First Amendment freedom of expression, assembly, petition, and association jurisprudence.[i]

1215   Abuses by England's King John cause a revolt by nobles, who compel him to recognize rights for both noblemen and ordinary Englishmen. This document, known as the Magna Carta, establishes the principle that no one, including the king or a lawmaker, is above the law, and establishes a framework for future documents such as the American Declaration of Independence and the Bill of Rights.

1628   The English legal-reform movement occurs and states its objectives in the Petition of Right, which leads to civil war and the deposing of King Charles I in 1649. This important document sets out the rights and liberties of the common man as opposed to the prerogatives of the Crown and expresses many of the ideals that later led to the American Revolution.

1641   The Massachusetts General Court formally adopts the first broad statement of American liberties, the Massachusetts Body of Liberties. The document includes a right to petition and a statement about due process.

1735   New York publisher John Peter Zenger is tried for libel after publishing criticism of the royal governor of New York. Zenger is defended by Andrew Hamilton and acquitted. His trial establishes the principle that

[i] This timeline is a revised and expanded version of a timeline prepared by the First Amendment Center and posted on its website: www.firstamentcenter.org

truth is a defense to libel and that a jury may determine whether a publication is defamatory or seditious.

1776   Virginia's House of Burgesses passes the Virginia Declaration of Rights, the first bill of rights to be included in a state constitution in America.

The Continental Congress adopts the final draft of the Declaration of Independence on July 4.

1787–88   The *Federalist Papers*, a unique collection of eighty-five essays written by Alexander Hamilton, James Madison, and John Jay urging ratification of the Constitution, are originally published in New York newspapers as the *Federalist* and widely reprinted in newspapers throughout the nation. In *Federalist* no. 84, Alexander Hamilton writes on the subject of the liberty of the press, declaring that "the liberty of the press shall be inviolably preserved."

1787   The U.S. Constitution is adopted into law on September 17 by the Federal Constitutional Convention; it is later ratified by the states on June 21, 1788.

1791   On December 15, Virginia becomes the eleventh state to approve the first ten amendments to the Constitution, thereby ratifying the Bill of Rights.

1798   President John Adams oversees the passage of the Alien and Sedition Acts. In response, Thomas Jefferson introduces the "Kentucky Resolution" and James Madison issues the "Virginia Resolution" to give states the power to determine the constitutionality of the Alien and Sedition Acts. On September 12, newspaper editor Benjamin Franklin Bache, the grandson of Benjamin Franklin, is arrested under the Sedition Act for libeling President John Adams.

1801   Congress lets the Sedition Act of 1798 expire, and President Thomas Jefferson pardons all persons convicted under it. Among other things, the Act punished those who uttered or published "false, scandalous, and malicious" writings against the government.

1836   The House of Representatives adopts gag rules preventing discussion of antislavery proposals. The House repeals the rules in 1844.

1859   John Stuart Mill publishes the essay *On Liberty*. The essay expands John
        Milton's argument that if speech is free and the search for knowledge
        unfettered, then eventually the truth will rise to the surface.

1863   General Ambrose Burnside of the Union Army orders the suspension of
        publication of the *Chicago Times* on account of repeated expression of
        disloyal and incendiary sentiments. President Abraham Lincoln rescinds
        Burnside's order three days later.

1864   By order of President Lincoln, General John A. Dix, a Union commander,
        suppresses the *New York Journal of Commerce* and the *New York World*
        and arrests the newspapers' editors after both papers publish a forged
        presidential proclamation purporting to order another draft of four hun-
        dred thousand men. Lincoln withdraws the order to arrest the editors,
        and the papers resume publication two days later.

1868   The Fourteenth Amendment to the Constitution is ratified. The amend-
        ment, in part, requires that no state shall "deprive any person of life, lib-
        erty, or property, without due process of law; nor deny to any person
        within its jurisdiction the equal protection of the laws."

1873   Antiobscenity reformer Anthony Comstock successfully lobbies
        Congress to pass the Comstock Law, the first comprehensive antiobscen-
        ity statute enacted at the federal level. The law targets the "Trade in and
        Circulation of, obscene literature and Articles for immoral use" and
        makes it illegal to send any "obscene, lewd or lascivious" materials or any
        information or "any article or thing" related to contraception or abortion
        through the mail.

1897   The U.S. Supreme Court hands down *Davis v. Massachusetts*, an early
        public forum case.

1907   In *Patterson v. Colorado*—its first free-press case—the U.S. Supreme
        Court determines it does not have jurisdiction to review the "contempt"
        conviction of U.S. senator and Denver newspaper publisher Thomas
        Patterson for articles and a cartoon that criticized the state supreme
        court. The Court writes that "what constitutes contempt, as well as the
        time during which it may be committed, is a matter of local law." Leaving
        undecided the question of whether First Amendment guarantees are
        applicable to the states via the Fourteenth Amendment, the Court holds
        that the free-speech and press guarantees only guard against prior
        restraint and do not prevent "subsequent punishment."

1917   Congress passes the Espionage Act, making it a crime "to willfully cause or attempt to cause insubordination, disloyalty, mutiny, or refusal of duty, in the military or naval forces of the United States," or to "willfully obstruct the recruiting or enlistment service of the United States."

        The Civil Liberties Bureau, a forerunner of the ACLU, is formed in response to passage of the Espionage Act.

1918   Congress passes the Sedition Act, which forbids spoken or printed criticism of the U.S. government, the Constitution, or the flag.

1919   In *Schenck v. U.S.*, U.S. Supreme Court Justice Oliver Wendell Holmes, Jr., sets forth his "clear and present danger" test: "whether the words used are used in such circumstances and are of such a nature as to create a *clear and present danger* that they will bring about the substantive evils that Congress has the right to prevent." Charles T. Schenck and others were accused of urging draftees to oppose the draft and "not submit to intimidation." Justice Holmes also writes that not all speech is protected by the First Amendment, citing the now famous example of falsely crying "Fire" in a crowded theater.

        In *Frohwerk v. United States*, a unanimous Court, per Justice Holmes, upholds the conviction under the Espionage Act of 1917 of a German-language newspaper editor who in a series of articles denounced the government's involvement in foreign wars.

        In *Debs v. U.S.*, the U.S. Supreme Court upholds the conviction of socialist and presidential candidate Eugene V. Debs under the Espionage Act for making speeches opposing World War I. Justice Holmes claims to apply the "clear and present danger" test; however, he phrases it as requiring that Debs's words have a "natural tendency and reasonably probable effect" of obstructing recruitment.

        The U.S. Supreme Court upholds the convictions of five individuals charged with violating the Espionage Act in *Abrams v. United States*. The individuals circulated pamphlets critical of the U.S. government and its involvement in World War I. In a dissenting opinion, Justice Holmes writes that "the ultimate good desired is better reached by free trade in ideas—that the best test of truth is the power of the thought to get itself accepted in the competition of the market." This passage forms the foundation of the "marketplace of ideas" theory of the First Amendment.

1920   Roger Baldwin and others start up a new organization dedicated to pre-
        serving civil liberties, the American Civil Liberties Union (ACLU).

1921   Congress repeals the Sedition Acts.

        President Warren Harding commutes Eugene Debs's sentence to time
        served.

1925   In *Gitlow v. New York*, the U.S. Supreme Court upholds, under the New
        York criminal anarchy statute, Benjamin Gitlow's conviction for writing
        and distributing the *Left Wing Manifesto*. The Court assumes, however,
        that the free-speech clause of the First Amendment applies to the states
        through the due process clause of the Fourteenth Amendment.

        New York governor Al Smith pardons Benjamin Gitlow on December 11.

1926   H. L. Mencken is arrested for distributing copies of *American Mercury*.
        Censorship groups in Boston contend the periodical is obscene.

1927   The U.S. Supreme Court upholds California's criminal syndicalism law in
        Whitney v. California. The case involves Charlotte Anita Whitney, a
        member of the Socialist Party and former member of the Communist
        Labor Party. Justice Louis Brandeis writes in his concurring opinion a
        passage that becomes a fundamental First Amendment principle: "If
        there be time to expose through discussion the falsehood and fallacies, to
        avert the evil by the processes of education, the remedy to be applied is
        more speech, not enforced silence."

        Anita Whitney is pardoned on June 27 by California governor Clement
        Calhoun Young.

1928   In *People of State of New York ex rel. Bryant v. Zimmerman*, the U.S.
        Supreme Court upholds a New York law that mandates that organiza-
        tions requiring their members to take oaths file certain organizational
        documents with the secretary of state. The Court writes: "There can
        be no doubt that under that power the state may prescribe and apply
        to associations having an oath-bound membership any reasonable
        regulation calculated to confine their purposes and activities within
        limits which are consistent with the rights of others and the public
        welfare."

1931   In *Stromberg v. California*, the U.S. Supreme Court reverses the state court
        conviction of Yetta Stromberg, a nineteen-year-old member of the Young
        Communist League, who violated a state law prohibiting the display of a
        red flag as "an emblem of opposition to the United States government."
        Legal commentators cite this case as the first in which the Court recognizes
        that protected speech may be nonverbal, or a form of symbolic expression.
        In addition, the Court formally holds that the free-speech guarantee of the
        First Amendment applies to the states. Since the text of the First Amendment
        refers to only "Congress," rulings such as the *Stromberg* one were necessary
        to extend the protections of the guarantee to the states.

        In *Near v. Minnesota*, the U.S. Supreme Court invalidates a permanent
        injunction against the publisher of the *Saturday Press*. The Court rules
        that the Minnesota statute granting state judges the power to enjoin as a
        nuisance any "malicious, scandalous and defamatory newspaper, maga-
        zine or other periodical" is "the essence of censorship." The Court con-
        cluded that the primary aim of the First Amendment was to prevent prior
        restraints of the press

1933   President Franklin D. Roosevelt pardons those convicted under the
        Espionage and Sedition Acts.

        California repeals its red flag law, ruled unconstitutional in *Stromberg*.

1936   In *Grosjean v. American Press Co.*, the U.S. Supreme Court invalidates a
        state tax on newspaper advertising applied to papers with a circulation
        exceeding twenty thousand copies per week as a violation of the First
        Amendment. The Court finds the tax unconstitutional because "it is seen
        to be a deliberate and calculated device in the guise of a tax to limit the
        circulation of information to which the public is entitled in virtue of the
        constitutional guaranties."

1937   In *DeJonge v. Oregon*, the U.S. Supreme Court reverses the conviction of
        an individual under a state criminal syndicalism law for participation in a
        Communist Party political meeting. The Court writes that "peaceable
        assembly for lawful discussion cannot be made a crime. The holding of
        meetings for peaceable political action cannot be proscribed."

1938   *Life* is banned in the U.S. for publishing pictures from the public health
        film *The Birth of a Baby*.

1939   Georgia, Massachusetts, and Connecticut finally ratify the Bill of Rights.

1940   Congress passes the Smith Act, Title I of the Alien Registration Act of 1940, which makes it a crime to advocate the violent overthrow of the government.

1940   In *Thornhill v. Alabama*, the U.S. Supreme Court strikes down an Alabama law prohibiting loitering and picketing "without a just cause or legal excuse" near businesses. The Court writes: "The freedom of speech and of the press guaranteed by the Constitution embraces at the least the liberty to discuss publicly and truthfully all matters of public concern without previous restraint or fear of subsequent punishment."

The Court upholds a Pennsylvania flag salute law in *Minersville School District v. Gobitis* by a vote of eight to one. A Jehovah's Witness family that had two children in the public schools challenged their expulsion on First Amendment grounds. "National unity is the basis of national security," Justice Felix Frankfurter writes for the majority. Only Chief Justice Harlan F. Stone dissents from the Court's ruling, which is overruled three years later in *West Virginia State Board of Education v. Barnette*.

1941   Congress authorizes President Franklin D. Roosevelt to create the Office of Censorship.

1942   The U.S. Supreme Court determines "fighting words" are not protected by the First Amendment. In *Chaplinsky v. New Hampshire*, the Court defines "fighting words" as "those which by their very utterance inflict injury or tend to incite an immediate breach of peace." The Court states that such words are "no essential part of any exposition of ideas, and are of such slight social value as a step to truth that any benefit that may be derived from them is clearly outweighed by the social interest in order and morality."

1943   In *West Virginia State Board of Education v. Barnette*, the U.S. Supreme Court rules that a West Virginia requirement to salute the flag violates the free-speech clause of the First Amendment.

In *National Broadcasting Co. v. United States*, the U.S. Supreme Court states that no one has a First Amendment right to a radio license or to monopolize a radio frequency.

1948   Publication of Alexander Meiklejohn's *Free Speech and Its Relation to Self-Government.*

1949   In *Terminiello v. Chicago*, the U.S. Supreme Court limits the scope of the "fighting words" doctrine. Writing for the majority, Justice William O. Douglas says that the "function of free speech...is to invite dispute. It may indeed best serve its high purpose when it induces a condition of unrest, creates dissatisfaction with conditions as they are, or even stirs people to anger."

1951   In *Dennis v. United States*, the U.S. Supreme Court upholds the convictions of twelve Communist Party members convicted under the Smith Act of 1940. The Court finds that the Smith Act, a measure banning speech that advocates the violent overthrow of the federal government, does not violate the First Amendment. The case has yet to be overruled.

1952   In *Burstyn v. Wilson*, the U.S. Supreme Court, for the first time, finds that motion pictures are included within the free-speech and free-press guaranty of the First Amendment. The Court finds a New York statute that permits the banning of motion pictures on the ground that they are "sacrilegious" to be unconstitutional after the New York State Board of Regents rescinds the license of the distributor of the film *The Miracle* to show the film in the state.

1957   The U.S. Supreme Court determines that "obscenity is not within the area of constitutionally protected speech or press." In *Roth v. United States*, the Court determines that obscenity is a category of speech not protected by the First Amendment. In his opinion, Justice William Brennan writes: "Obscene material is material which deals with sex in a manner appealing to prurient interest." He explains that the determination of whether material is obscene should be judged by "contemporary community standards."

        California municipal judge Clayton Horn rules in *People v. Ferlinghetti*, decided on October 3, 1957, that the poem Howl is not obscene.

1958   The U.S. Supreme Court allows the NAACP of Alabama to withhold its membership list from Alabama lawmakers. In *NAACP v. Alabama*, the Court states that the demand by Alabama officials for the NAACP to provide them a membership list violates members' associational rights.

1959   The U.S. Supreme Court upholds the conviction of a college professor who refuses, on First Amendment grounds, to answer questions before the House Un-American Activities Committee. In *Barenblatt v. United States*, the Court states that "where First Amendment rights are asserted to bar governmental interrogation, resolution of the issue always involves a balancing by the courts of the competing private and public interests at stake in the particular circumstances shown." The Court concludes that the investigation is for a valid legislative purpose and that "investigatory power in this domain is not to be denied Congress solely because the field of education is involved."

In *Bates v. City of Little Rock*, the U.S. Supreme court strikes down a Little Rock city license tax ordinance that required the compulsory disclosure of any local organization's membership list in order to verify its tax-exempt status.

1961   The U.S. Supreme Court denies First Amendment claims of two applicants for admission to the Illinois and California bars, respectively, in the cases *In Re Anastaplo* and *Konigsberg v. State Bar of California*.

Comedian Lenny Bruce is arrested in San Francisco for obscenity. A San Francisco jury acquits him.

1962–63   Lenny Bruce arrested is for obscenity in Chicago and Los Angeles.

In *NAACP v. Button* (1963), the U.S. Supreme Court strikes down an Alabama antisolicitation law as applied to the NAACP's civil rights litigation activities.

1964   In *New York Times Co. v. Sullivan*, the U.S. Supreme Court overturns a libel judgment against the *New York Times*. The Court rules that public officials may not recover damages for a defamatory falsehood relating to their conduct unless they prove the statement was made with actual malice. The Court defines actual malice as "with knowledge that it was false or with reckless disregard of whether it was false or not." In what will become one of the most famous passages in First Amendment history, Justice Brennan announces that the nation's First Amendment freedoms represent a "profound national commitment to the principle that debate on public issues should be uninhibited, robust, and wide-open."

Lenny Bruce is arrested in New York for obscenity and convicted after an eight-month trial. His Illinois obscenity conviction is overturned by the Illinois Supreme Court.

1965   In *Lamont v. Postmaster General*, the U.S. Supreme Court declares for the first time a federal law unconstitutional on First Amendment grounds. It is also the first case in which the precise phrase "marketplace of ideas" is employed, albeit by Justice Brennan in his concurrence.

In *Freedman v. Maryland*, the Court strikes down a Maryland law requiring that all films be submitted to a board of censors before being shown.

The Court in *Cox v. Louisiana* overturns disturbance of the peace and obstruction of public passageways convictions for peaceful demonstrations and concludes that the petitioners' First Amendment rights to freedom of speech and assembly were violated.

1966   The U.S. Supreme Court invalidates a Massachusetts court decision that found the 1750 book *Memoirs of a Woman of Pleasure* (commonly known as *Fanny Hill*) obscene. In *Memoirs v. Massachusetts*, Justice William Brennan writes that a book cannot be declared obscene unless it is found to be "utterly without redeeming social value."

In *Elfbrant v. Russell*, the Court invalidates an Arizona statute requiring the dismissal of any state employee who knowingly becomes a member of the Communist Party or any party whose intentions include overthrowing the government.

In *Sheppard v. Maxwell*, the Court reverses the murder conviction of Dr. Sam Sheppard because the trial judge failed to quell publicity surrounding the trial. In its opinion, the Court recognizes gag orders as a legitimate means of controlling pretrial and trial publicity.

1967   The U.S. Supreme Court invalidates a New York law prohibiting the employment of public school and university teachers who belong or have belonged to "subversive" groups such as the Communist Party. The Court in *Keyishian v. Board of Regents* emphasizes the importance of academic freedom, writing: "Our Nation is deeply committed to safeguarding academic freedom, which is of transcendent value to all of us and not merely to the teachers concerned."

1968   Adoption of Federal Flag Desecration Law (18 U.S.C. 700 et seq.):
        Congress approves the first federal flag-desecration law in the wake of a
        highly publicized Central Park flag-burning incident in protest of the
        Vietnam War. The federal law makes it illegal to "knowingly cast "con-
        tempt" on "any flag of the United States by publicly mutilating, defacing,
        defiling, burning or trampling upon it." The law defines "flag" in an expan-
        sive manner, similar to most states.

        In *United States v. O'Brien*, the U.S. Supreme Court upholds the conviction
        of David Paul O'Brien, an antiwar protester accused of violating a federal
        statute prohibiting the public destruction of draft cards. O'Brien claims
        that the burning of draft cards is "symbolic speech" protected by the First
        Amendment. The Court concludes that conduct combining "speech" and
        "nonspeech" elements can be regulated if the following four requirements
        are met: (1) the regulation is within the constitutional power of the
        government; (2) it furthers an "important or substantial" government
        interest; (3) the interest is "unrelated to suppression of free expression";
        and (4) "incidental restriction" on First Amendment freedoms is "no
        greater than is essential to the furtherance" of the government interest. The
        Court concludes that all requirements were satisfied in this case.

        The Court rules that school board officials violated the First Amendment
        rights of Illinois public school teacher Marvin Pickering, who was fired
        for writing a letter critical of the school administration to a local news-
        paper. The Court writes in *Pickering v. Board of Education* that the
        "problem in any case is to arrive at a balance between the interests of the
        teacher, as a citizen, in commenting upon matters of public concern and
        the interest of the State, as an employer, in promoting the efficiency of
        the public services it performs through its employees."

1969   The U.S. Supreme Court rules in *Tinker v. Des Moines Independent School
        District* that Iowa public school officials violated the First Amendment
        rights of several students by suspending them for wearing black arm-
        bands to protest U.S. involvement in Vietnam. The Court determines
        that school officials may not censor student expression unless they can
        reasonably forecast that the expression will cause a substantial disruption
        of school activities.

        In *Street v. New York*, the Court holds that New York could not convict a
        person on the basis of his verbal remarks disparaging the flag. Street was
        arrested after he learned of the shooting of civil rights leader James

Meredith and reacted by burning his own flag and exclaiming to a small crowd that if the government could allow Meredith to be killed, "we don't need no damn flag."

In *Brandenburg v. Ohio,* a leader of a Ku Klux Klan group is convicted under Ohio law and sentenced to prison primarily on the basis of a speech he made at a Klan rally. The Court unanimously rules that speech advocating the use of force or crime is not protected if (1) the advocacy is "directed to inciting or producing imminent lawless action," and (2) the advocacy is also "likely to incite or produce such action."

In *Stanley v. Georgia,* the Court rules that the First and Fourteenth amendments protect a person's "private possession of obscene matter" from criminal prosecution. The Court notes that the state, although possessing broad authority to regulate obscene material, cannot punish private possession of such in an individual's own home.

In *Red Lion Broadcasting Co. v. Federal Communication Commission,* the Court finds that Congress and the Federal Communications Commission did not violate the First Amendment when it required a radio or television station to allow response time to persons subjected to personal attacks and political editorializing on air.

1971   In *New York Times v. United States,* the U.S. Supreme Court allows continued publication of the Pentagon Papers. The Court holds that the central purpose of the First Amendment is to "prohibit the widespread practice of governmental suppression of embarrassing information." This case establishes that the press has almost absolute immunity from pre-publication restraints.

In *Cohen v. California,* the Court reverses the breach-of-peace conviction of an individual who wore a jacket with the words "Fuck the Draft" in a courthouse. The Court concludes that offensive and profane speech are protected by the First Amendment.

In *Baird v. State Bar of Arizona,* the Court, in a five-to-four ruling, concludes that a state's power to inquire about a person's beliefs or associations is limited by the First Amendment, which prohibited a state from excluding a person from a profession solely because of membership in a political organization or because of his or her beliefs.

In *Law Students Civil Rights Research Council v. Wadmond,* by contrast, another divided Court concludes that a requirement that an applicant furnish proof that he or she "believes in the form of government of the United States and is loyal to such government," is not constitutionally invalid.

1972   The U.S. Supreme Court rules in *Branzburg v. Hayes* that the First Amendment does not exempt reporters from "performing the citizen's normal duty of appearing and furnishing information relevant to the grand jury's task." The Court rejects a reporter's claim that the flow of information available to the press will be seriously curtailed if reporters are forced to release the names of confidential sources for use in a government investigation.

In *Lloyd Corp. v. Tanner,* the Court rules that owners of a shopping center may bar antiwar activists from distributing leaflets at the center. The Court finds that citizens do not have a First Amendment right to express themselves on privately owned property.

1973   The U.S. Supreme Court in *Miller v. California* defines the test for determining if speech is obscene: (1) whether the "average person applying contemporary community standards" would find that the work, taken as a whole, appeals to the prurient interest; (2) whether the work depicts or describes, in a patently offensive way, sexual conduct specifically defined by the applicable state law; and (3) whether the work, taken as a whole, lacks serious literary, artistic, political, or scientific value.

The Court rules in *Paris Adult Theatre I v. Slaton* that a state may constitutionally prohibit exhibitions or displays of obscenity, even if access to the exhibitions is limited to consenting adults.

1974   In *Miami Herald Publishing Co. v. Tornillo,* the U.S. Supreme Court invalidates a state law requiring newspapers to give free reply space to political candidates the newspapers criticize. The Court rules that the right of newspaper editors to choose what they wish to print or not to print cannot be infringed to allow public access to the print media.

In *Spence v. Washington,* the Court holds that the state of Washington could not convict a person for attaching removable tape in the form of a peace sign to a flag.

1976   In *Buckley v. Valeo*, the U.S. Supreme Court rules that certain provisions of the Federal Election Campaign Act of 1976, which limits expenditures to political campaigns, violate the First Amendment.

The Court rules that the First Amendment does not apply to privately owned shopping centers. In *Hudgens v. National Labor Relations Board*, the Court holds that as long as the state does not encourage, aid, or command the suppression of free speech, the First Amendment is not subverted by the actions of shopping center owners.

The Court finds that an appropriately defined zoning ordinance, barring the location of an "adult movie theatre" within one hundred feet of any two other "regulated uses," does not violate the First Amendment—even if the theater is not showing obscene material. In *Young v. American Mini Theatres*, the Court concludes that the ordinance is not a prior restraint and is a proper use of the city's zoning authority.

The Court rules that the public has a First Amendment right to the free flow of truthful information about lawful commercial activities. In *Virginia State Board of Pharmacy v. Virginia Citizens Consumer Council*, the Court invalidates a Virginia law prohibiting the advertisement of prescription drug prices.

The Court invalidates a gag order imposed on the press in *Nebraska Press Association v. Stuart*. The Court writes that "prior restraints on speech and publication are the most serious and the least tolerable infringement on First Amendment rights."

1977   In *Abood v. Detroit Board of Education*, the U.S. Supreme Court declares that a state may require a public employee to pay dues to organizations such as unions and state bars, as long as the money is used for purposes such as collective bargaining and contract and grievance hearings. The Court notes that, pursuant to the First Amendment, state workers may not be forced to give to political candidates or to fund political messages unrelated to their employee organization's bargaining function.

1978   The Illinois Supreme Court rules in *NSPA v. Skokie* that the National Socialist Party of America, a neo-Nazi group, can march through Skokie, Illinois, a community where by a number of Holocaust survivors reside.

The Court upholds the power of the Federal Communications Commission to regulate indecent speech broadcast over the air. In *FCC v. Pacifica*, the Court allows Commission regulation because the broadcast media are a "uniquely pervasive presence" and easily accessible to children. The Court, however, does make clear that, although the government can constitutionally regulate indecent speech in the broadcast media, it does not have power to enforce a total ban on such speech.

In *First National Bank of Boston v. Bellotti*, the Court rules that a state criminal statute that forbids certain expenditures by banks and business corporations for the purpose of influencing the vote on referendum proposals violates the First Amendment.

1980   In *Central Hudson Gas & Electric Corporation v. Public Service Commission*, the U.S. Supreme Court sets forth a four-part test for determining when commercial speech may or may not be regulated by states. The test states that (1) the commercial speech must not be misleading or involve illegal activity; (2) the government interest advanced by the regulation must be substantial; (3) the regulation must directly advance the asserted government interest; and (4) the government regulation must not be more extensive than is necessary to serve the government interest at stake.

In *Richmond Newspapers, Inc. v. Virginia*, the Court rules that the right of the public and press to attend criminal trials is guaranteed under the First and Fourteenth amendments.

1982   The U.S. Supreme Court rules in *New York v. Ferber* that child pornography is not protected by the First Amendment.

In *NAACP v. Claiborne Hardware*, the Court holds that while states have broad power to regulate economic activities, there is no comparable right to prohibit peaceful political activity such as that found in peaceful political boycotts.

The Court rules in *Board of Education v. Pico* that school officials may not remove books from school libraries because they disagree with the ideas contained in the books. The Court states that "the right to receive ideas is a necessary predicate to the recipient's meaningful exercise of his own rights of speech, press, and political freedom" and makes clear that "students too are beneficiaries of this principle."

1983   The U.S. Supreme Court rules in *Connick v. Myers* that the First Amendment rights of a former assistant district attorney were not violated when she was dismissed for distributing a questionnaire criticizing workplace practices. The case, along with the Court's 1968 *Pickering* decision, forms the basis of much public employee First Amendment law.

1984   Congress passes the Equal Access Act, which prohibits secondary schools that are receiving federal financial assistance from denying equal access to student groups on the basis of religious, political, or philosophical beliefs or because of the content of their speech.

1985   The U.S. Supreme Court upholds a zoning law regulating the location of adult businesses. The Court determines in *City of Renton v. Playtime Theatres, Inc.* that the law does not discriminate on the basis of the expression of the adult businesses because it focuses on the harmful secondary effects allegedly associated with such businesses.

1986   The U.S. Supreme Court case *Bethel School District v. Fraser* curtails the protections established in *Tinker*. Bethel School District in Spanaway, Washington, suspended seventeen-year-old Matthew Fraser, an honors student, for two days after what was considered a lewd spring election campaign speech he gave at a school assembly with six hundred students present. His candidate won. However, the courts held that the manner of speech, delivered before a captive audience, rather than the content, was disruptive and contrary to the values the school intended to promote.

1987   The U.S. Supreme Court upholds a Missouri regulation limiting inmates' mail correspondence, while striking down a regulation prohibiting inmates from marrying. The Court in *Turner v. Safley* establishes the following standard in inmate cases: "when a prison regulation impinges on inmates' constitutional rights, the regulation is valid if it is 'reasonably related' to legitimate penological interests."

1988   In *Hazelwood School District v. Kuhlmeier*, the U.S. Supreme Court rules that school officials may exercise editorial control over content of school-sponsored student publications if they do so in a way that is reasonably related to legitimate pedagogical concerns.

In *Hustler Magazine, Inc. v. Falwell*, *Hustler* publishes a parody of a liquor advertisement in which Jerry Falwell is depicted in a lewd manner. A unanimous Court rules that a public figure must show that the offending publication was written with actual malice in order to recover money for intentional infliction of emotional distress. The Court rules that political cartoons and satire "have played a prominent role in public and political debate."

1989   Congress passes the Flag Protection Act, which punishes anyone who "knowingly mutilates, defaces, physically defiles, burns, maintains on the floor or ground, or tramples upon any U.S. flag."

In *Texas v. Johnson*, the U.S. Supreme Court rules that burning the American flag is a constitutionally protected form of free speech.

1990   The U.S. Supreme Court in *United States v. Eichman* invalidates the Flag Protection Act of 1989. The Court finds that the statute violates free speech.

Following the *Eichman* decision, Congress considers and rejects a constitutional amendment specifying that "the Congress and the States have the power to prohibit the physical desecration of the flag of the United States." The amendment fails to muster the necessary two-thirds congressional majorities, as it is supported by only a 254–177 margin in the House (290 votes were necessary) and a 58–42 margin in the Senate (67 votes were necessary).

The U.S. Supreme Court determines in *Milkovich v. Lorain Journal* that there is no wholesale exemption from libel for all statements alleged to be opinions. The Court writes: "We are not persuaded that, in addition to these protections, an additional separate constitutional privilege for 'opinion' is required to ensure the freedom of expression guaranteed by the First Amendment."

1991   In *Simon & Schuster, Inc. v. Members of the New York State Crime Victims Board*, the U.S. Supreme Court invalidates the New York "Son of Sam" law that requires accused or convicted persons to turn over to the state proceeds from any work describing their crimes. Justice Sandra Day O'Connor finds that the law is overbroad and that it regulates speech on the basis of content.

The Court in *Rust v. Sullivan* upholds a federal program that prevents those receiving federal funding for reproductive health services from discussing abortion as a method of family planning. The Court explains: "The Government can, without violating the Constitution, selectively fund a program to encourage certain activities it believes to be in the public interest, without at the same time funding an alternative program which seeks to deal with the problem in another way."

1992   In *R.A.V. v. City of St. Paul*, the U.S. Supreme Court invalidates a St. Paul, Minnesota, hate-speech ordinance, saying it violates the First Amendment.

1995   In *Rosenberger v. Rector and Visitors of the University of Virginia*, the U.S. Supreme Court invalidates a policy denying funds to a Christian student newspaper on free-speech grounds. The Court finds that the university committed viewpoint discrimination by denying funding on the basis of the religious ideas expressed in the publication.

President Bill Clinton orders the Department of Education to send guidelines on religious expression to every public school district in the United States.

1996   The U.S. Supreme Court in *44 Liquormart, Inc. v. Rhode Island* invalidates a state law forbidding advertising of liquor prices.

Congress passes the Communications Decency Act. It is immediately challenged on First Amendment grounds.

1997   The U.S. Supreme Court in *Reno v. ACLU* rules that the Communications Decency Act of 1996 is unconstitutional. The Court concludes that the Act, which makes it a crime to display indecent or patently offensive material on the internet where a child may find it, is too vague and tramples on the free-speech rights of adults.

1998   The Child Online Protection Act, which attaches federal criminal liability to the online transmission for commercial purposes of material considered harmful to minors, is enacted by Congress.

The Court rules in *National Endowment for the Arts v. Finley* that a federal statute requiring the Endowment to consider general standards of decency before awarding grant monies to artists does not infringe on First Amendment rights.

In *Arkansas Educational Television Commission v. Forbes*, the Court rules that a public television station's exclusion of a political candidate from its televised debate does not violate the First Amendment. The Court declares the station-sponsored debate to be a nonpublic forum, ruling that exclusion of the candidate for reasonable and viewpoint-neutral reasons is allowed.

2000   In *Boy Scouts of America v. Dale*, the U.S. Supreme Court rules that application of a public accommodation law to force the Boy Scouts to accept a gay scoutmaster is a violation of the private organization's freedom of association guaranteed by the First Amendment.

In *United States v. Playboy Entertainment Group*, the Court rules that a federal law requiring cable operators to "fully scramble" indecent and sexually explicit programming on adult stations violates the First Amendment.

2001   The U.S. Supreme Court rules in *Bartnicki v. Vopper* that a federal law prohibiting the publication of illegally intercepted wire communications violated the First Amendment rights of those who published the communications, though they were not the ones who intercepted them. The Court reasons that application of the law to the defendants in this case "implicates the core provision of the First Amendment because it imposes sanctions on the publication of truthful information of public concern."

2002   The U.S. Supreme Court rules in *Republican Party of Minnesota v. White* that a provision prohibiting judicial candidates from announcing their views on disputed legal or political issues violates the First Amendment.

2003   The U.S. Supreme Court rejects constitutional challenges (including one based on the First Amendment) to the Copyright Term Extension Act, which extended the copyright protection term by twenty years. The Court reasons in *Eldred v. Ashcroft* that copyright law already has built-in First Amendment protections in the fair use doctrine and the expression-idea dichotomy principle (providing that copyright protects expressions, not ideas).

The Court rules in *Virginia v. Black* that a state law banning cross burning largely passes constitutional muster. The Court reasons that many cross burnings are so intimidating that they constitute true threats. The Court invalidates a part of the Virginia law that presumed that all cross burnings were done with the intent to intimidate.

The Court upholds the Children's Internet Protection Act in *United States v. American Library Association, Inc.* The law requires public libraries and public schools to install filtering software on computers to receive federal funding.

The Court upholds the vast majority of the federal campaign finance law, the Bipartisan Campaign Reform Act, against First Amendment challenge in *McConnell v. Federal Election Commission.*

In *Nike v. Kasky,* Court considers whether Nike can be charged with violating a state consumer protection law concerning allegedly false advertising when it made statements in response to charges made by its critics. Though argued, the case is dismissed on jurisdictional grounds.

On December 23, New York governor George Pataki posthumously pardons the comedian Lenny Bruce. It is the first such pardon in the state's history.

2004   The U.S. Supreme Court rejects a First Amendment–based challenge to a government program that calls for mandatory assessments from beef producers to fund generic advertising. The Court in *Johanns v. Livestock Marketing Association* said the program constituted government speech and, thus, was immune from First Amendment scrutiny.

The Court upholds a lower court's preliminary injunction preventing enforcement of the Child Online Protection Act. The Court reasons in *Ashcroft v. ACLU II* that "filtering software is an alternative that is less restrictive than COPA, and, in addition, likely more effective as a means of restricting children's access to materials harmful to them."

2006   In *Garcetti v. Ceballos,* a divided U.S. Supreme Court holds that when public employees make statements pursuant to their official duties, they are not speaking as citizens for First Amendment purposes, and the Constitution does not insulate their communications from employer discipline.

2007   In *Morse v. Frederick,* the U.S. Supreme Court rules that principal Deborah Morse did not violate the First Amendment rights of high school student Joseph Frederick when she punished him for displaying a "Bong Hits 4 Jesus" banner on a public street directly across from his school while the Winter Olympic Torch Relay passed through Juneau, Alaska. The Court creates a "drug speech" exception to the Court's landmark student-speech case, *Tinker v. Des Moines Independent Community School District.*

2008   In *Davis v. Federal Election Commission,* the U.S. Supreme Court sets aside a federal campaign finance law—the so-called Millionaire's Amendment—that relaxed campaign finance limits for opponents of congressional candidates spending more than $350,000 of their own money.

2010   In *Citizens United v. Federal Election Commission,* the U.S. Supreme Court concludes that restrictions on broadcast of ads to promote a campaign film critical of presidential candidate Hillary Rodham Clinton violated the First Amendment.

In *United States v. Stevens,* the Court sets aside a federal law banning the knowing sale of depictions of animal cruelty with the intention of placing such depictions in interstate commerce for commercial gain.

Acknowledgments

No book is written alone...there are always others who, in any variety of ways, helped out, and pitched in. We happily recognize those who lent a hand to bring this book to fruition.

The origin of this book goes back many years, to a time when Dedi Feldman made magic as an editor at Oxford University Press. This book would have been impossible without her encouragement and support. Dedi, as many authors can attest, represents much of what is best in book publishing, and we are confident that in the days to come her star will rise still higher in that universe. Thanks as well to our new editor at Oxford, David McBride. We are also indebted to Neeti Madan of Sterling Lord Literistic, who moved the first mountain for us.

We are grateful to our friends for their comments on various chapters: George Anastaplo, Seth Berlin, Edward Cleary, Robert Corn-Revere, David Hudson, Lee Levine, Christopher May, Martin Redish, David Skover, Geoffrey Stone, David Vladeck, and Jeremy Zucker. Thanks go out as well to Judge Louis H. Pollak, who helped us bring the story of his father, Walter Pollak, back to life. Thanks, too, to Judge Robert L. Carter, who assisted us in telling his remarkable free-speech story. We also benefited from the research assistance of Hannah Bergman and Mike Darner. Special thanks to Lindsey Davis for her remarkable assistance.

Paul McMasters, our former colleague, was always generous with his help, and this book is the better for it. Thanks Paul.

Finally, to our spouses, Susan Cohen and Sarah Margon: thanks for standing behind us and allowing us to live our dreams as writers.

Ronald Collins: And what of Sam Chaltain? Well, he's one hell of a coauthor. While others idle, Sam is full throttle. Oh how I've enjoyed the ride with him—those late nights of writing and editing, those seemingly endless years of research, and all those dialogues about law and life and all sorts of other things that matter, including poetry. It's been a long haul, but I've enjoyed the thrill of it—watching all those deadline signposts zoom by as we traveled to this point in our shared journey. So to you, Sam, this: May your ride be long, may your highway lead to wondrous places, may the top be down and the stars bright, and may you always remember Kerouac's saw—Gun it, my man, gun it! (If Jack Kerouac or Dean Moriarty didn't say that, they should have.)

Sam Chaltain: And what of Ron Collins? Ron is a worker, a researcher, a student, and a dreamer—but above all else, Ron is a writer. Through this process I have learned from him how to prepare, how to work in tandem, and how to dream big. If this book effectively strikes the delicate balance between legal scholarship and narrative arc, it is because of him. If it has introduced the serious scholar to new insights about these cases or characters, it is because of him. And if in the future I am able to continue writing and publishing in this field of scholarship, it is because of the skills and the self-discipline I have learned from him. Thank you for the opportunity, professor. I'll see you down the road.

About the Authors

Ronald Collins is the Harold S. Shefelman scholar at the University of Washington School of Law and a fellow at the First Amendment Center. He writes and lectures on freedom of expression. Collins served as a law clerk to Justice Hans A. Linde on the Oregon Supreme Court, and thereafter as a Fellow under Chief Justice Warren Burger at the U.S. Supreme Court. Collins has taught constitutional law and commercial law at Temple Law School and George Washington Law School. He has written constitutional briefs that were submitted to the Supreme Court and various other federal and state high courts. His journalistic writings on the First Amendment have appeared in *Columbia Journalism Review*, the *New York Times*, and the *Washington Post*, among other publications. He is the coauthor (with David Skover) of *The Death of Discourse* (1996, 2nd ed., 2005). He is also the editor of *The Fundamental Holmes: A Free Speech Chronicle and Reader* (2010), *The Death of Contract* (1995), and *Constitutional Government in America* (1980). His scholarly articles have appeared in *Harvard Law Review, Stanford Law Review, Michigan Law Review* and in the *Supreme Court Review*, among other places. In 2003, he successfully petitioned New York Governor George Pataki to posthumously pardon the comedian Lenny Bruce. In 2010 he was selected to be a resident fellow in fiction writing at the Norman Mailer Writers Colony in Provincetown, Massachusetts.

Sam Chaltain (www.samchaltain.com) is a DC-based writer, educator, and strategic consultant. Formerly the National Director of the Forum for Education and Democracy, an education advocacy organization, Sam was also the founding director of the Five Freedoms Project, a national program that helps K-12 principals create more democratic learning communities. Sam spent five years at the First Amendment Center as the co-director of the First Amendment Schools program. He came to the Center from the public and private school systems of New York City, where he taught high school English and History. Sam's writings about his work have appeared in both magazines and newspapers, including the *Washington Post, Education Week,* and *USA Today*. A periodic contributor to

CNN and MSNBC, Sam is also the author or co-author of four other books: *The First Amendment in Schools* (ASCD, 2003); *First Freedoms: A Documentary History of First Amendment Rights* (Oxford University Press. 2006); *American Schools: The Art of Creating A democratic Learning Community* (Rowman & Littlefield, 2009); and *Faces of Learning: 50 Powerful Stories of Defining Moments in Education* (Wiley, 2011). Sam has a Master's degree in American Studies from the College of William & Mary, and an M.B.A. from George Washington University, where he specialized in non-profit management and organizational theory. He received his undergraduate degree from the University of Wisconsin at Madison, where he graduated with a double major in Afro-American Studies and History.

Notes

Prologue

1. The text of the 1791 amendment reads: "Congress shall make no law respecting an establishment of religion, or prohibiting the free exercise thereof; or abridging freedom of speech, or of the press; or the right of the people peacefully to assemble, and to petition the Government for a redress of grievances."

2. There are, to be sure, other collections of free-speech stories. In this regard, our aim is more illustrative than comprehensive. Moreover, many of the stories we recount have long been forgotten and/or little noticed. For other free-speech stories, *see First Amendment Stories* (Andrew Koppelman & Richard Garnett, eds., 2011); *Free Speech on Trial* (Richard A. Parker, ed., 2003); Randall P. Bezanson, *Speech Stories: How Free Can Speech Be?* (1998); Fred W. Friendly & Martha J. H. Elliott, *The Constitution: That Delicate Balance* (1984); and *Constitutional Law Stories* (Michael C. Dorf, ed., 2004). Additional examples are listed in the Sources at the end of the book.

Chapter 1

1. 366 U.S. 82, 116 (1961) (Black, J., dissenting).
2. Quoted in George Anastaplo, *Human Being and Citizen* (1975), at p. 106.
3. 366 U.S. 82, 115–116 (1961) (Black, J., dissenting).
4. Anastaplo did his doctoral work under Leo Strauss (1899–1973), the noted political philosopher sometimes associated with conservative causes.
5. In 1950 Joseph McCarthy (1909–1957), a congressman from Wisconsin, became infamous when he accused the State Department of harboring 205 prominent Communists, a charge he never substantiated. In 1953 he became chairman of the Permanent Subcommittee on Investigations, before which he called numerous citizens and accused them of being disloyal Americans. The Smith Act, proposed by Congressman Howard W. Smith of Virginia, was introduced in 1939 and modified in 1940. It provided a fine of up to $10,000 and a penalty of ten years in prison for anyone who attempted to undermine the morale of military forces or for anyone who "advocates, abets, advices, or teaches" the violent overthrow of the government or who publishes or organizes for that purpose. It was upheld in the controversial case of *Dennis v. United States*, 341 U.S. 494 (1951). *See* chapter 5, *infra*.

6. *Human Being and Citizen*, pp. at 105–114; Cornelia Grumman, "Wrong Question," *Chicago Tribune Magazine*, November 26, 2000, at pp. 14–18, 20, 22, 24.

7. See sources cited in note 6, *supra*.

8. See sources cited in note 6, *supra*.

9. Collins phone interview with Mrs. Anastaplo, June 12, 2008.

10. There were, to be sure, exceptions as evidenced by Harlan's opinion for the majority in *Cohen v. California* (1971), wherein he sustained a First Amendment claim to wear a "fuck the draft" jacket in a public courthouse corridor. Justice Black joined in the dissent.

11. *Barenblatt v. United States*, 360 U.S. 109, 126 (1959).

12. *Konigsberg v. State Bar*, 353 U.S. 252, 311 (1957) (Harlan, J., dissenting).

13. *Dennis v. United States*, 342 U.S. 494, 580 (Black, J., dissenting).

14. 365 U.S. 399, 422 (1961) (Black, J., dissenting).

15. At the time he was a powerful senator from Alabama. On April 26, 1935, the senator's photograph was on the cover of *Time*.

16. Hugo Black, "The Bill of Rights," 35 *New York University Law Review* 865, 879 (1960).

17. 357 U.S. 513, 531 (1958) (Black, J., concurring).

18. His grandfather, Justice John Marshall Harlan (1833–1911), was noted for his dissents, especially in *Plessy v. Ferguson*, 163 U.S. 537 (1896), wherein he forcefully opposed the "separate but equal" doctrine.

19. He was not always that way. Prior to coming to the Court, Frankfurter worked with Louis Brandeis on progressive cases and in the 1920s was openly supportive of Sacco and Vanzetti, the two infamous Italian-born laborers and anarchists who were tried, convicted, and executed for murdering two men during a payroll robbery of a shoe company. *See* Felix Frankfurter, *The Case of Sacco and Vanzetti: A Critical Analysis for Lawyers and Laymen* (1927).

20. 366 U.S. 82, 115–116 (1961) (Black, J., dissenting).

21. 366 U.S. at 88.

22. *Ibid.* at 89.

23. 366 U.S. at 114–116 (Black, J., dissenting).

24. Quoted in Roger K. Newman, *Hugo Black: A Biography* (1994), at p. 507.

25. 315 U.S. 568, 571 (1942).

26. John Paul Stevens, "The Freedom of Speech," 102 *Yale Law Journal* 1293, 1301 (1993).

CHAPTER 2

1. Lewis E. Lawes, *Twenty Thousand Years in Sing Sing* (1932), at p. 182.

2. But for the assassination, Oliver Wendell Holmes (1841–1935) might never have been nominated to the Supreme Court since President McKinley then had no intention of nominating Holmes to fill the vacancy created by Justice Horace Gray's announced resignation.

3. New York Penal Code 161 (1902).

4. *New York Times*, January 5, 1920; *Washington Post*, November 21, 1919.

5. Arthur Garfield Hays, *Trial by Prejudice* (1933), p. 260; cited in Blanchard at p. 117.

6. Lewis E. Lawes, *Twenty Thousand Years in Sing Sing* (1932), at p. 219.

7. Chafee (1885–1957), a Harvard law professor, became a noted and highly influential free-speech scholar. His first book was titled *Freedom of Speech* (1920) and was thereafter expanded into *Free Speech in the United States* (1941).

8. In a March 13, 1789, letter to Francis Hopkinson, Jefferson complained: "What I disapproved of from the first moment...was the want of a bill of rights to guard liberty against the legislative *as well as the executive branches* of the government, that is to say to secure freedom in religion, freedom of the press" and other freedoms. (emphasis added)

9. The final text of the First Amendment notwithstanding, in time the First Amendment was applied as against the *executive* branch. See, e.g., *New York Times Co. v. United States* (1971) (the Pentagon Papers Case) (*see* ch. 4). In other cases, the First Amendment was likewise held binding on the judicial branch. See, e.g., *Nebraska Press Association v. Stuart* (1976).

10. This has jurisprudential implications, as Oregon Supreme Court Justice Hans Linde has observed: "If government acts without a basis in valid law, the court need not find facts or weigh circumstances in the individual case. When a constitutional prohibition is addressed to lawmakers, as the First Amendment is, the role that it assigns to courts is the censorship of laws, not participation in government censorship of private expression." Quoted in Robert Nagel, *Intellect and Craft* (1995) at p. 63.

11. A detailed account of this history and what followed is set out in Charles Warren, "The New 'Liberty' under the Fourteenth Amendment," 39 *Harvard Law Review* 431 (1925–26).

12. Margaret A. Blanchard, *Revolutionary Sparks* (1992), at p. 112.

13. "Red Bombs Palmer's House; Dies Himself; Family Is Not Injured," *Washington Post*, June 3, 1919, p. 1.

14. "Attempt to Terrorize Has Failed, Says Palmer," *Washington Post*, June 4, 1919, p. 1.

15. Christopher M. Finan, *From the Palmer Raids to the Patriot Act* (2007).

16. Zechariah Chafee, Jr., *Free Speech in the United States* (1941), at p. 319.

17. "Socialists Assail 'Left Wing' Party," *New York Times*, June 24, 1919, p. 5.

18. "Drastic Penalties Planned for Reds," *New York Times*, November 12, 1919, p. 1.

19. The National Civil Liberties Bureau later became the American Civil Liberties Union. And Nelles's pamphlets on wartime prosecutions helped to shape Zechariah Chafee's views on the First Amendment, which played an important role in the history of free speech in America. Nelles would later be co-counsel for the rights claimant in *Whitney v. California* (1927), the free speech case in which Justice Brandeis issued his famous concurrence.

20. Arthur and Lila Weinberg, *Clarence Darrow: A Sentimental Rebel* (1980), at p. 290.

21. *Ibid.* at 291.

22. Albert Fried, *Communism in America: A History in Documents* (1997), at p. 51.

23. "Gitlow Convicted in Anarchy Trial," *New York Times*, February 6, 1920, p. 17.

24. Lawes, *Twenty Thousand Years in Sing Sing*, at p. 220.

25. Benjamin Gitlow, *I Confess: The Truth about American Communism* (1939).

26. Section 8 of article 1 of the New York state Constitution reads as follows: 'Every citizen may freely speak, write and publish his sentiments on all subjects, being responsible for the abuse of that right; and no law shall be passed to restrain or abridge the liberty of speech or of the press.'

27. Benjamin Gitlow *I Confess* (1939).

28. Such laws were not called into constitutional question by a majority of the Court until the ruling in *New York Times Co. v. Sullivan* (1964). For a contemporary discussion of the historical backdrop of all of this, see Geoffrey R. Stone, *Perilous Times: Free Speech in Wartime—From the Sedition Act of 1798 to the War on Terrorism* (2004). *See also* Leonard W. Levy, *Emergence of a Free Press* (1985).

29. See Ronald Collins, "Benjamin Bache and the Fight for a Free Press," July 14, 2008, www.firstamendmentcenter.org/analysis.aspx?id=20296.

30. Incredibly, Thomas Cooper declined the pardon and served his full sentence.

31. In relevant part, the text of the Fourteenth Amendment provides: "No State shall make or enforce any law which shall abridge the privileges or immunities of citizens of the United States; nor shall any State deprive any person of life, liberty, or property, without due process of law; nor deny any person within its jurisdiction the equal protection of the laws." Even though the Fourteenth Amendment was passed in 1868 to protect the rights of recently freed slaves, Howard Zinn has observed that of the 307 Fourteenth Amendment cases brought before the Court between 1890 and 1910, just nineteen dealt with the rights of minorities; the other 288 dealt with the rights of *corporations*.

32. But according to Charles Warren, in at least "twenty cases between 1877 and 1907 the Court was required to rule upon" the wisdom of John Marshall's 1833 ruling in *Barron v. Baltimore*. In all, he stressed, the Court followed the *Barron* precedent. Recently, the Court applied the Second Amendment's right to bear arms guarantee to the states in *McDonald v. City of Chicago*, 561 U.S. ___ (2010).

33. As early as 1916, another progressive, Theodore Schroeder, advanced that same view. See his *Free Speech for Radicals* (1916). Schroeder was a key figure in the early progressive movement to safeguard free speech, especially related to obscenity.

34. See *Schenck v. United States* (1919), *Frohwerk v. United States* (1919), *Debs v. United States* (1919), and *Abrams v. United States* (1919) (Holmes, J., & Brandeis, J., dissenting). *See* chapter 5, *infra*.

35. As Holmes declared in *Schenck:* "The question in every case is whether the words used are used in such circumstances and are of such a nature as to create a clear and present danger that they will bring about the substantive evils that Congress has a right to prevent."

36. At the time of the *Gitlow* case, the Supreme Court welcomed one-hour arguments from counsel on both sides of the case. Today, that time has been reduced to thirty minutes for each side.

37. Pollak's son, federal judge Louis Pollak, recounted this story to us in June 2003.

38. A few years later, Justice Sanford wrote the majority opinion in *Whitney v. California* (1927), in which Justice Brandeis authored his famous concurrence.

39. This "bad tendency" test applied a less protective gloss to the "clear and present danger" line of First Amendment cases. In time, the Court moved beyond such a restricted interpretation and wooden application of the First Amendment. *See* chapter 5, *infra*.

40. Liva Baker, *The Justice from Beacon Hill* (1991), at p. 589.

41. The First Amendment's right to *petition* was later inferred as applying to the states in *Edwards v. South Carolina* (1963), and the right of *association* was deemed to be binding on the states in *NAACP v. Alabama ex rel. Patterson* (1958).

42. Walter Pollak would later argue (with Walter Nelles) *Whitney v. California* (1927), a famous First Amendment case known for Brandeis's concurrence. Pollak also argued *Powell v. Alabama* (1932), one of the famous Scottsboro cases in which nine black youths were arrested and convicted for allegedly raping a white woman. See Roger K. Newman, ed., *The Yale Biographical Dictionary of American Law* (2009), at p. 430 (entry by Louis H. Pollak).

43. The governor pardoned Benjamin Gitlow on December 11, 1925, arguing that he had already been punished enough for a "political crime." Moreover, the governor halted further prosecutions under the Criminal Anarchy Act.

44. "Gitlow, Set Free, Rejoins Radicals," *New York Times*, December 13, 1925, p. 18.

45. *See Bridges v. California* (1941).

46. *See* Melvin Urofsky, *A Voice That Spoke for Justice: The Life and Times of Stephen S. Wise* (1982).

47. Walter Nelles, one of the founders of the ACLU and a professor at Yale Law School, died in 1937. His last book, *A Liberal in Wartime* (1940), was published posthumously. *See* "Prof. Walter Nelles of Yale Law School; An Expert on Labor Injunction and Former Lawyer Here Is Dead at Age of 53," *New York Times*, April 1, 1937, p. 23.

CHAPTER 3

1. The epigraph to this chapter is from Cynthia Stokes Brown, ed., *Alexander Meiklejohn: Teacher of Freedom* (Cynthia Stokes Brown, ed., 1981), at p. 14.

2. "Meiklejohn Defiant, Urges Amherst Men to Abolish Trustees," *New York Times*, June 21, 1923, p. 1.

3. *Ibid.*

4. *Ibid.*

5. Zechariah Chafee, Jr., is known in some circles as "the scholar of modern free speech law." His scholarly writings and books were highly influential, especially in the development of Justice Holmes's First Amendment thought.

6. Adam R. Nelson, *Education and Democracy: The Meaning of Alexander Meiklejohn, 1872–1964* (2001), at p. 119.

7. "Sees Test for America," *New York Times*, January 21, 1923, p. 6.

8. *Milk Wagon Drivers Union of Chicago, Local 753. v. Meadowmoor Dairies, Inc.*, 312 U.S. 287, 293 (1941).

9. *Abrams v. United States*, 250 U.S. 616, 630 (1919) (Holmes, J., dissenting).

10. The precise phrase, though often attributed to Holmes, was not of his exact making. *See* Ronald Collins, *The Fundamental Holmes: A Free Speech Chronicle and Reader* (2010), at pp. 282–283.

11. "The Path of the Law," 10 *Harvard Law Review* 457, 465–466 (1897).

12. In later years Meiklejohn would expand it with additional essays, letters, and petitions, all published under the title *Political Freedom: The Constitutional Powers of the People* (1960).

13. Tom C. Clark later served as an associate justice on the Supreme Court from 1949 to 1967. Though he was not known for any special expertise in the area of free-speech law, he did, nonetheless, author the opinion for the Court in *Joseph Burstyn, Inc. v. Wilson* (1952), wherein the First Amendment was applied to motion pictures for the first time.

14. Congressman Richard M. Nixon would later vigorously urge the case against Hiss.

15. "'Everything Worth Saying Should Be Said,'" *New York Times Magazine*, July 18, 1948, p. 8.

16. *Free Speech and Its Relationship to Self-Government* (1948), at pp. x–xiv.

17. *Ibid*.

18. *Ibid*. at p. 91 (emphasis added).

19. Editorial, "Abridging Freedom," *New York Times*, July 18, 1948. E, p. 8.

20. *Free Speech and Its Relation to Self-Government*, at pp. 57–107

21. Consistent with this, Meiklejohn found the "'liberties' of what we call "'Free Enterprise'…destructive of the freedoms of a self-governing society." Thus, he believed that "privately sponsored television" and commercial advertising could (and should) be heavily regulated by the government. Modern free-speech doctrine, of course, does not permit such intrusive restrictions on broadcast and commercial expression.

22. *Free Speech and Its Relation to Self-Government*, at pp. 22–27.

23. *Ibid*. at p. 27.

24. Quoted in Meiklejohn, *Political Freedom* (1960), at p. 101. In a footnote to his concurring opinion in *Dennis*, Frankfurter wrote: "Professor Meiklejohn is a leading exponent of the absolutist interpretation of the First Amendment. Recognizing that certain forms of speech require regulation, he excludes those forms of expression entirely from the protection accorded by the Amendment."

25. In 1947 and afterward, HUAC investigated Hollywood "radicals." The charge was that Communists had taken over major control of the movie industry. As such, Communists were said to be placing subversive messages and negative images of the United States into Hollywood films. The Hollywood Ten was a group of American screenwriters and directors, all current or former members of the Communist Party, who were convicted of contempt of Congress for refusing to cooperate with HUAC's investigations.

26. See *Education and Democracy*, at pp. 296–306 (general discussion).

27. *Political Freedom*, at pp. 156–158.

28. In 1943, Lerner published *The Mind and Faith of Justice Holmes*, a collection of Holmes's writings.

29. Book Review, *The New Republic*, September 13, 1948, p. 21, quoted in *Education and Democracy*, at p. 243.

30. Quoted in Donald L. Smith, *Zechariah Chafee, Jr.: Defender of Liberty and Law* (1986), at p. 90.

31. Chafee, Book Review, 62 *Harvard Law Review* 891–901 (1949).

32. Hugo L. Black, *A Constitutional Faith* (1969) at p. 46 (emphasis added).

33. Meiklejohn, "The First Amendment Is an Absolute," 1961 *Supreme Court Review* 245.

34. *The Tolerant Society* (1986), at pp. 147–148.

35. *The First Amendment* (1998), at p. 7.

36. *American Constitutional Law* (2nd ed., 1988), sec. 12–2, at p. 789.

37. See Ronald Collins and David Skover, *The Death of Discourse* (1996, 2nd ed., 2005).

38. *Procunier v. Martinez*, 416 U.S. 396, 427 (1974).

39. *The First Amendment* (1998), at p. 4.

40. "The Checking Value in First Amendment Theory," 1977 *American Bar Foundation Research Journal* 521.

41. *New York Times Co. v. United States*, 403 U.S. 713, 717 (1971) (Black, J., concurring).
42. Emerson was a law professor at Yale Law School and the author of the seminal book *The System of Freedom of Expression* (1970). He was once also a young associate in Walter Pollak's law firm. Pollak, recall (chapter 2), argued *Gitlow v. New York* (1925), and later argued *Whitney v. California* along with Walter Nelles.
43. Harvey Zuckman, Robert Corn-Revere, et al., *Modern Communications Law* (1999), at p. 87.
44. *Milk Wagon Drivers Union of Chicago, Local 753. v. Meadowmoor Dairies, Inc.,* 312 U.S. 287, 294 (1941).
45. *The Tolerant Society* (1986), at p. 141.
46. Stephen H. Shiffrin, *The First Amendment, Democracy, and Romance* (1990), at pp. 5–8.
47. *Whitney v. California,* 274 U.S. 357, 375 (1927) (Brandeis, J., concurring) (emphasis added).
48. "The Supreme Court and the Meiklejohn Interpretation of the First Amendment," 79 *Harvard Law Review* 1 (1965).
49. Harry Kalven, Jr. (1914–1974), a law professor at the University of Chicago, was a noted First Amendment scholar. His books include *The Negro and the First Amendment* (1965) and *A Worthy Tradition: Freedom of Speech in America* (1974). His law review articles, like his 1964 *Supreme Court Review* one on the *Sullivan* case, were quite influential. According to Professor Bollinger: "This triumvirate of *New York Times Co. v. Sullivan,* Harry Kalven, and Alexander Meiklejohn spawned a major idiom for talking about freedom of speech and press."
50. "The Supreme Court and the Meiklejohn Interpretation of the First Amendment," 79 *Harvard Law Review* 1 (1965).
51. On February 20, 1943, the *Saturday Evening Post* ran on its cover Norman Rockwell's now famous painting *Freedom of Speech*. The work, which is pure Meiklejohn, features a man clad in working clothes rising up to speak his mind amid a group of quizzical figures clad in business attire.
52. Editorial, "Alexander Meiklejohn," *Washington Post*, December 18, 1964, sec. A, p. 16.
53. "Dr. Alexander Meiklejohn Dead," *New York Times*, December 17, 1964, p. 41. See also "Gentle Iconoclast," *New York Times*, June 9, 1957, p. 84.

CHAPTER 4

1. Daniel Ellsberg, *Secrets* (2002), at p. 209.
2. In 2004, Errol Morris produced an Academy Ward–winning documentary *The Fog of War*, which consisted of an extended interview with McNamara and explored his role in the Vietnam conflict.
3. Cited in Rudenstine *The Day the Presses Stopped* (1996), at p. 40.
4. Ellsberg *Secrets*, at p. 268.
5. Hedrick Smith & Neil Sheehan, "Westmoreland Requests 206,000 More Men, Stirring Debate in Administration," *New York Times*, March 10, 1968, p. 1.
6. Ellsberg, *Secrets*, at pp. 204–206.
7. *Ibid.* at pp. 206–207.

8. *Ibid.* at pp. 220.
9. *Ibid.* at pp. 289–290.
10. Rudenstine, *The Day the Presses Stopped*, at p. 67.
11. *Ibid.* at p. 72.
12. William Hubbs Rehnquist (1924–2006), a Nixon appointee, joined the Court as an associate justice in 1972. In 1986, President Reagan named him chief justice. Selected by Nixon for his conservatism, his view on criminal justice, and his favoring of a more limited role for the Court, Rehnquist was known as the most conservative member of the Burger Court.
13. Laurence H. Tribe *American Constitutional Law* (1988), sec.12.34–36.
14. Michael Kent Curtis, *Free Speech: The People's Darling Privilege* (2000), at p. 29.
15. Leonard W. Levy, *Legacy of Suppression* (1960), at p. 10.
16. Quoted in Leonard W. Levy, *Emergence of a Free Press* (1985), at p. 90.
17. John Milton, *Aeropagetica and Education* (George H. Sabine, ed., 1951), at p. 40.
18. Thomas I. Emerson, *The System of Freedom of Expression* (1970), at p. 504.
19. Quoted in *Emergence of a Free Press*, at pp. 12–13.
20. Emerson, *The System of Freedom of Expression*, at p. 506
21. Fred Friendly, *Minnesota Rag* (1981), at p. 99.
22. 283 U.S. 697, 713 (1931).
23. At the time Rehnquist conducted his research, the Court had outlined three requirements that must be met in order for a licensing scheme to be valid. First, the licensing scheme must indicate an important reason for the licensing (see *Cox v. New Hampshire* (1941)); second, it must have clear standards that leave almost no arbitrary discretion to the licensing authority (see *Saia v. New York* (1948) and *Kunz v. New York* (1951)); and third, it must have clear procedural safeguards in place (*see Teitel Film Corp. v. Cusack* (1968), and *Carroll v. President and Commr. of Princess Anne County* (1968)). For a more detailed analysis, see Erwin Chemerinsky, *Constitutional Law: Principles and Policies* (2006), at pp. 964–968.
24. 394 U.S. 147, 151 (1969).
25. 283 U.S. at 716.
26. *Near v. State of Minnesota Ex Rel. Olson*, 283 U.S. 697, 716 (1931). In this opinion Hughes outlined two other scenarios in which prior restraints may be constitutional: First, to enforce the primary requirements of decency…against obscene publications, and second, to protect against incitements to acts of violence and the overthrow by force of orderly government.
27. Rudenstine, *The Day the Presses Stopped*, at p. 80.
28. Ellsberg, *Secrets*, at p. vii.
29. Floyd Abrams (1936–), a 1960 graduate of Yale Law School, is the most noted First Amendment lawyer of our time. He has argued the following cases, among others, in the Supreme Court: *Nebraska Press Assoc. v. Stuart* (1976) and *Herbert v. Lando* (1979).
30. Alexander Bickel (1924–1974) was born in Bucharest, Romania. He arrived in the United States with his parents in 1938. A *summa cum laude* graduate of Harvard Law School, Bickel later clerked for Supreme Court justice Felix Frankfurter, who influenced Bickel's belief in the importance of judicial restraint in constitutional law. Bickel gained the reputation of being a liberal in politics and a constitutional conservative in legal philosophy. He taught at Yale Law School from 1956 until his death.

31. Floyd Abrams *Speaking Freely* (2005), at pp. 1–31.

32. *Ibid.* at p. 7.

33. Loeb had been advising the *Times* since 1929; Brownell had been attorney general under President Eisenhower. Both men worked for Lord, Day & Lord, the law firm that had represented the newspaper for over six decades.

34. Susan E. Tifft & Alex S. Jones, *The Trust* (1999), at p. 482.

35. Rudenstine, *The Day the Presses Stopped*, at p. 103.

36. Abrams, *Speaking Freely*, at p. 7.

37. Rudenstine *The Day the Presses Stopped*, at p. 106.

38. *United States v. New York Times Co. et al.*, 328 F. Supp. 324, 325 (S.D.N.Y. 1971).

39. In later years, Bagdikian became a media critic, and then the dean of the Graduate School of Journalism at the University of California at Berkeley. He is the author of the widely acclaimed book *The Media Monopoly*.

40. Ellsberg, *Secrets*, at p. 394.

41. *Ibid.* at p. 401.

42. 328 F. Supp. at 331.

43. Rudenstine, *The Day the Presses Stopped*, at p. 213.

44. Erwin N. Griswold *Ould Fields, New Corne*, quoted in *The Lanahan Readings in Civil Rights and Civil Liberties* (David M. O'Brien, ed., 1999), at p. 72.

45. Rudenstine, *The Day the Presses Stopped*, at p. 143.

46. Quoted in O'Brien, *Lanahan Readings*, at p. 74.

47. Rudenstine, *The Day the Presses Stopped* at p. 9.

48. Roger K. Newman, *Hugo Black: A Biography* (1994), at p. 615.

49. Sanford J. Ungar *The Papers and the Papers* (1972), at p. 228.

50. Quoted in O'Brien, *Lanahan Readings*, at p. 77.

51. Newman *Hugo Black: A Biography*, at p. 614.

52. Quoted in Abrams, *Speaking Freely*, at p. 40.

53. Justice Stewart (1915–1985) later came to be a strong defender of press rights as evidenced by what he wrote in his famous article "Or of the Press," 26 *Hastings Law Journal* 631 (1975). His view was that the press clause of the First Amendment created a special status for the press in our system of constitutional government. "The primary purpose of the constitutional guarantee of a free press," he wrote there, was to "create a fourth institution outside the government as an additional check on the three official branches."

54. Quoted in *The Supreme Court in Conference* (Dell Dickson, ed., 2001), at p. 270.

55. Quoted in *ibid.* at p. 371.

56. Although nineteen newspapers published parts of the Pentagon Papers, the government only pursued TROs for *The New York Times*, *The Washington Post*, *The Boston Globe*, and *The St. Louis Post-Dispatch*.

57. Isaac Clarke Prey, *Memoirs of James Gordon Bennett and His Times* (1855), at p. 119.

58. Newman, *Huge Black: A Biography*, at p. 617.

59. 403 U.S. 713, 714 (1971).

60. Laurence Tribe *American Constitutional Law* (1988), at p. 730.

61. Tifft & Jones, *The Trust*, at pp. 492–493.

62. 403 U.S. at 717 (Black, J., concurring).

63. *Ibid.* at 717 (Black, J., concurring).

64. *Ibid.* at 727 (Brennan, J., concurring).

65. *Ibid.* at 730 (Stewart, J., concurring) (emphasis added).

66. *Ibid.* at 731–732 (White, j., concurring in judgment) (emphasis added).

67. *Ibid.* at 737 (White, J., concurring in judgment).

68. *Ibid.* at 742–743 (Marshall, J., concurring).

69. *Ibid.* at 751 (Burger, C. J., dissenting).

70. *Ibid.* at 758–759 (Harlan, J., dissenting).

71. Justice Blackmun (1908–1994) is best known for his majority opinion in *Roe v. Wade* (1972), the controversial abortion case. Perhaps his most important First Amendment majority opinions were his opinions in *Bigelow v. Virginia* (1975) and *Virginia Pharmacy Bd. v. Virginia Consumer Council* (1976), both commercial speech cases. In the biography *Becoming Justice Blackmun*, Linda Greenhouse reports that Blackmun's vote in the Pentagon Papers case "solidified his reputation as a close ally of the new Chief Justice (Warren Burger), prompting Burger to send him a handwritten letter at the conclusion of the term. "You did not know what the President was getting you into but I am sure you have no regrets," he wrote. "Far from it, you have flowered under the combination of the pressures and the challenge and every friend is happy and proud. It has been a 'hard' year with more 'great cases' than any year in the memory of Court watchers. Yet I will immodestly say we have carried our share. Others must decide how well we have done it," Burger concluded, "but I am not worried."

72. 403 U.S. at 761 (Blackmun, J., dissenting).

73. *Ibid.*

74. *Ibid.* at p. 620.

75. "Guilty: The Government," *New York Times*, May 12, 1973, p. 32.

76. David Rudenstine, *The Day the Presses Stopped* (1994), at p. 90.

77. *Ibid.* at p. 344.

78. See *Vance v. Universal Amusement Co.* (1980), *Freedman v. Maryland* (1965), and *Joseph Burstyn, Inc. v. Wilson* (1952).

79. See *Bantam Books, Inc. v. Sullivan* (1963).

80. See *Southeastern Promotions, Ltd. v. Conrad* (1975).

81. See *National Socialist Party v. Skokie* (7th Cir., 1977). This was the famous case in which Nazi adherents applied for a permit to stage a rally in Skokie, Illinois, the home of an extremely large number of Holocaust survivors.

82. *Snepp v. United States* (1980).

83. *Pickering v. Board of Education* (1968).

84. *United States v. Progressive, Inc.* (1979).

85. *Madsen v. Women's Health Center* (1994) and *Schenck v. Pro-Choice Network of Western New York* (1997).

86. *Paris Adult Theatre I. v. Slaton* (1973) and *Alexander v. United States* (1993).

87. *Thomas v. Chicago Park District* (2002).

88. *Nebraska Press Association v. Stuart* (1976).

89. *United States v. Noriega* (11th Cir., 1990).

90. Sometimes it may be necessary to permit prior restraints in order to protect certain commercial interests or property rights. Thus, courts have allowed restraints barring the disclosure of information relating to trade secrets, or to prevent copyright

infringement, or to protect commercially sensitive employment information. By the same logic, injunctions may issue to safeguard property rights related to trade names or artistic rights. Similarly, there is no right to disseminate patently false and misleading information about a consumer product.

91. "Rethinking Prior Restraint," 92 *Yale Law Journal* 409, 437 (1983).

92. Tribe, *American Constitutional Law* (1988), at p. 1040.

93. Smolla, *Smolla and Nimmer on Freedom of Speech* (1994), sec. 15.2.

94. *Top Secret* (2007), at pp. 19–26. According to Stone, "to justify the criminal punishment of the press for publishing classified information, the government must prove that the publisher knew (a) it was publishing classified information, (b) the publication of which would result in likely, imminent, and serious harm to the national security, and (c) the publication of which would not meaningfully contribute to public debate. In practical effect, this has been the law of the United States for more than a half century." *Ibid.* at p. 26.

95. Quoted in Abrams, *Speaking Freely*, at p. 31.

CHAPTER 5

1. Quoted in Ellen Schrecker, *The Age of McCarthyism* (2nd ed., 2002), at p. 132.

2. His birth name was Francis Xavier Waldron. He was born in Seattle on August 10, 1905.

3. Quoted in Schrecker, *The Age of McCarthyism*, at p. 203.

4. *1947–48 Hearings, Eightieth Congress, first session, Pt. IV*, at p. 2826.

5. *Dennis v. United States*, 341 U.S. 494, 581 (1951) (Black, J., dissenting).

6. An African American lawyer, Davis was a Harvard Law School graduate and, among other things, secretary of the *Daily Worker.*

7. Born Arno Gust Halberg, Hall had attended the Lenin Institute in Moscow. He had been tried in Minneapolis in the 1930s for attempting to overthrow the government and in 1937 pleaded guilty to charges of possessing explosives during a labor strike. He was fined $5,000.

8. Potash, who never became an American citizen, was born in Russia. In 1920, he was convicted and sentenced to serve three years in jail for criminal anarchy. Later, he was also convicted of conspiracy to obstruct justice. At the time of the *Dennis* trial, he was on bail in a deportation case.

9. Winston, also an African American, had attended the Lenin Institute in Moscow.

10. There were actually twelve defendants. William Z. Foster, however, was too ill to attend that trial, so it proceeded against the other eleven named defendants.

11. The reference—synonymous with a gross miscarriage of justice—is to the 1931 trial of nine black youths who were indicted in Scottsboro, Alabama. They were charged with raping two white women and thereafter found guilty. The young men were sentenced to death or to prison terms of seventy-five to ninety-nine years. The U.S. Supreme Court reversed their convictions in 1932.

12. "Accused Reds Protest Use of 400 Police," *Washington Post*, January 18, 1949, p. 1.

13. Wiecek, *The Birth of the Modern Constitution* (2006), at p. 543.

14. Of course, this assumes that the "clear and present" danger test, however applied, was the only applicable test—a questionable assumption, as we will show later in this chapter.

15. In all, some 141 persons were prosecuted under the Smith Act, though only twenty-nine went to jail. The law, now amended, remains on the books (18 U.S. Code sec. 2385).

16. The first epigraph to this section is quoted in Hawthorne Daniel, *Judge Medina: A Biography* (1952), at p. 310. The second epigraph is quoted in Belknap, *Cold War Political Justice* (1977), at p. 77.

17. At the trial level, the *Dennis* case went by the name *United States v. Foster*, as in William Foster.

18. They were: Harry Sacher (of New York; chief counsel for defense, a lawyer who had long represented Communists); Richard Gladstein (of Los Angeles; he once represented Harry Bridges, a West Coast labor leader); Louis F. McCabe (he had represented Dennis re contempt of Congress); Abraham J. Isserman (had represented Communists in high-profile cases); George W. Crockett, Jr. (of Detroit; an African American lawyer); Mrs. Yetta Land (of Cleveland; a labor lawyer); and Maurice Sugar ("adviser for defense").

19. *Cold War Political Justice* (1977), at p. 80.

20. According to Belknap, during an uproar in the courtroom one of the defendants, Gus Hall, "screamed at the bench that he had seen more law and constitutional rights in a kangaroo court. 'Mr. Hall,' the judge replied, 'you are hereby remanded [to the House of Detention] for the balance of the trial.'" *Ibid.* at p. 98.

21. *Ibid.* at p. 69.

22. Quoted in Martin Redish, *The Logic of Persecution* (2005), at pp. 86–87.

23. *Ibid.*

24. *Cold War Political Justice* (1977), at p. 111.

25. Hawthorne Daniel, *Judge Medina: A Biography* (1952), at p. 285.

26. *Ibid.* at pp. 285–286.

27. *Ibid.* at p. 292 (emphasis added).

28. *Ibid.* at pp. 287–291.

29. The epigraph to this section is from Gerald Gunther, *Learned Hand: The Man and the Judge* (1994), at p. 605.

30. Quoted in Geoffrey Stone, *Perilous Times: Free Speech in Wartime* (2004), at p. 401.

31. 183 F.2d at 206.

32. *Learned Hand: The Man and the Judge* (1994), at p. 600.

33. There were, to be sure, some First Amendment controversies and cases before 1917. *See* David M. Rabban, *Free Speech in Its Forgotten Years* (1997).

34. The New York City postmaster, Thomas G. Patten, who was the official defendant in this action, held identical views.

35. The following standard fare from *The Masses* riled Burleson: Four cartoons, entitled "Congress and Big Business," "Making the World Safe for Capitalism," "Conscription," and "Liberty Bell"; a poem sympathetic to Emma Goldman and Alexander Berkman, who had been jailed for draft resistance; and three articles that applauded the "sacrifice" of conscientious objectors and hailed Goldman and Berkman, those "friends of American freedom."

36. Stone, *Perilous Times* (2004), at p. 164.

37. *Ibid.* at p. 145.

38. *Ibid.* at p. 170.

39. Quoted in "Cartoon Caused Ban on 'Masses,'" *Washington Post*, July 23, 1917, p. 5.

40. Quoted in *Ibid.*

41. Quoted in Stone, "The Origins of the 'Bad Tendency' Test: Free Speech in Wartime," 2002 *Supreme Court Review* 411.

42. *Masses Publishing Co. v. Patten*, 244 F. 535, 540 (S.D.N.Y., 1917) (emphasis added).

43. "Freedom of Speech, " 17 *The New Republic* 66, 67 (1918), reprinted in 32 *Harvard Law Review* 932, 956–57 (1919).

44. A few years after *The Masses* case, the Supreme Court declared that the postmaster general had broad powers to regulate the uses of mail in time of war. *United States ex rel Milwaukee Social Democrat Publishing Co. v. Burleson* (1921) (Holmes and Brandeis dissenting). In his *Free Speech in the United States*, Professor Chafee was highly critical of the ruling, especially given the prior restraints imposed by the postmaster.

45. Like Benjamin Gitlow (see chapter 2), Max Eastman came to reject the cause he once defended. By the 1950s, he became a strong supporter of Senator Joseph McCarthy and the HUAC. His anti-Communist articles were published in *Reader's Digest* and in the *National Review*, among other publications.

46. Quoted in Liva Baker, *The Justice from Beacon Hill* (1991), at p. 516.

47. *In Holmes and Frankfurter: Their Correspondence: 1912–1934* (Robert M. Mennel & Christine L. Compston, eds., 1996), at pp. 69–70.

48. *The Common Law* (1951), at p. 37.

49. Quoted in Stone, *Perilous Times* (2004), at p. 198.

50. *The Justice from Beacon Hill* (1991), at p. 516.

51. The Court had recently heard and ruled on the *Selective Draft Law Cases* (1918) and *Goldman v. United States* (1918), among other such cases. The rights-claims were denied in all of them. First Amendment free-speech issues were not, however, crystallized in those cases the same way they were in the four Espionage Act cases the Court agreed to review in 1918.

52. One side of one of the circulars bore the following banner: "LONG LIVE THE CONSTITUTION OF THE UNITED STATES / Wake Up, America! Your Liberties are in Danger!" The full text of the circular is reproduced in *The Fundamental Holmes: A Free Speech Chronicle and Reader* (Ronald K. L. Collins, ed. 2010), at pp. 237–241.

53. *Free Speech in Its Forgotten Years* (1999), at p. 279 (emphasis added).

54. 249 U.S. 47, 52 (emphasis added).

55. *Ibid.* (emphasis added).

56. *Perilous Times* (2004), at p. 193.

57. 249 U.S. at 52.

58. *Free Speech in Its Forgotten Years* (1999), at p. 344.

59. *Ibid.* at p. 342.

60. Quoted in 250 U.S. at 620.

61. 250 U.S. 616, 629 (1919) (Holmes, J., dissenting).

62. 250 U.S. at 628 (Holmes, J., dissenting).

63. 250 U.S. at 630 (Holmes, J., dissenting).

64. *Ibid.* (emphasis added).

65. *Ibid.* (emphasis added).

66. *The First Amendment* (1998), at p. 61.

67. 268 U.S. 652, 670 (1925).

68. 268 U.S. at 669.

69. In *Schaefer* (1920), the publishers of a German-language newspaper that glorified German forces and attacked the sincerity of the American involvement in the war were convicted of violating the Espionage Act. The Court sustained some of the convictions by a six-to-three margin, with Holmes and Brandeis dissenting on constitutional grounds and Justice Clarke on statutory grounds.

70. 268 U.S. at 673 (Holmes, J., dissenting).

71. *Ibid.*

72. *The Morality of Consent* (1975), at p. 77.

73. *Free Speech in the United States* (1941), at p. 325.

74. 274 U.S. 357, 376 (1927) (Brandeis, J., concurring).

75. *Ibid.* at 376.

76. *Ibid.* at 377.

77. *Ibid.*

78. "Originally, Brandeis intended to dissent on the basis that the 'clear-and-present danger' standard had not been met, that the supposed overthrow was too far removed from the meeting. Statements 'however reprehensible moral,' he said in an early draft, 'are not ordinarily a justification for denying free speech; because where the element of incitement is lacking the danger is remote." Leonard Baker, *Brandeis and Frankfurter* (1984). For an account of the entire matter, *see* Collins and Skover, "Curious Concurrence," 2005 *Supreme Court Review* 333.

79. Writes Rabban: "*Herdon v. Lowry*, a 1937 opinion reversing the conviction of a Communist Party organizer who had been attempting to recruit Southern blacks, marked the reappearance of clear and present danger. [The majority opinion], after unconvincingly attempting to distinguish *Gitlow*, applied a rigorous definition of the clear and present danger test to reject, for the first time in the history of Supreme Court adjudication, the bad tendency theory...." *Free Speech in Its Forgotten Years*, at p. 375.

80. *United States v. Dennis*, 183 F.2d. 201, 212 (2nd Cir., 1950).

81. *Ibid.*

82. *Ibid.* at 212–213.

83. In his concurring opinion, Judge Chase argued that the Court's *Gitlow* ruling was "controlling" and therefore should be used to resolve the case.

84. 274 U.S. at 376 (Brandeis, J., concurring).

85. *The Birth of the Modern Constitution: The U.S. Supreme Court, 1941–1953* (2006), at p. 558.

86. Editorial, "'Clear and Present Danger,'" *New York Times*, August 4, 1950, p. 20.

87. When Judge Hand retired, none other than Harold Medina succeeded him in 1951.

88. The Court's grant of certiorari was limited to one issue, namely, the constitutionality of the Smith Act. Professor Martin Redish, among others, has been highly critical of the Court for ignoring the issue of whether the *Dennis* defendants actually committed any acts that "presented a danger that was 'clear and present' in any coherent sense of that phrase." *The Logic of Persecution* (2005), at p. 90.

89. Russell Porter, "High Court Hears Appeal of 11 Reds," *New York Times*, December 5, 1950, p. 20.

90. Solicitor General Perlman intervened on behalf of the United States to file an amicus brief in *Shelley v. Kraemer* (1948), wherein his office argued against judicial enforcement of racially discriminatory restrictive covenants. In 1952, however, he declined the request by then NAACP lawyer Thurgood Marshall and others to file a supportive brief in *Brown v. Board of Education.*

91. Porter, "High Court Hears Appeal of 11 Reds," *New York Times*, December 5, 1950, p. 20.

92. See Belknap, *Cold War Political Justice*, at p. 136; "Court Gets Appeal of Reds," *Washington Post*, December 5, 1950, p. 22; and Porter, "High Court Hears Appeal of 11 Reds," *New York Times*, December 5, 1950, p. 20.

93. Attorney General Tom Clark (1899–1977) had prosecuted Smith Act cases. Thus, the most junior justice did not participate in the case.

94. "Fourteen times during the period 1937–48," observes Belknap, "the Supreme Court had decided cases on the basis of the clear-and-present-danger test, always ruling against the challenged governmental action, but in the summer of 1949 death claimed Frank Murphy and Wiley Rutledge, half of the four-man liberal phalanx around which majorities in those cases had formed. As replacements Truman had named [the far more conservative] Sherman Minton…and Tom Clark.…" *Cold War Political Justice*, at p. 133.

95. Quoted in *The Supreme Court in Conference (1940–1985)* (Dell Dickson, ed., 2001), at p. 279.

96. The same day, the Court rendered an opinion in *Garner v. Board of Public Works* (1951) in which it upheld a law compelling Los Angeles city employees to swear under oath that they had never belonged to any organization advocating the unlawful overthrow of the government.

97. The epigraph to this section is from *Perilous Times* (2004), at p. 395.

98. It was, however, cited approvingly by the Court, though in another context, namely the law of prior restraints bearing on lawyers' remarks concerning judicial proceedings. See *Gentile v. State Bar of Nevada* (1991). The *Dennis* holding has never been formally overturned. *See* Collins and Skover, "What Is 'War'? Reflections on Free Speech in Wartime," 36 *Rutgers Law Journal* 833 (2005).

99. 341 U.S. 494, 507 (1951).

100. *Ibid.*, at 510 (emphasis added).

101. *Learned Hand: The Man and the Judge* (1994), at p. 599.

102. *The System of Freedom of Expression* (1970), at p. 115.

103. 341 U.S. 494 at 550–551 (Frankfurter, J., concurring).

104. *Ibid.*, at 551 (Frankfurter, J., concurring).

105. *Ibid.*, at 525 (Frankfurter, J., concurring).

106. *Ibid.*, at 549 (Frankfurter, J., concurring).

107. *Ibid.*, at 550–551 (Frankfurter, J., concurring).

108. *Ibid.*, at 580 (Black, J., dissenting).

109. *Ibid.*, at 581 (Black, J., dissenting). In 1995, the U.S. National Security Agency released translations of Soviet cables decrypted in the 1940s by the Venona Project, a top-secret U.S. endeavor in the 1940s to gather and decrypt messages sent by agents of Soviet military intelligence. Some of these documents (and the Comintern documents, too) suggest that American Communists at the time of the *Dennis* case had ties to, and worked in tandem with, Soviet forces. "One can persuasively argue,"

writes Professor Redish in his *The Logic of Persecution,* that "on the basis of the evidence revealed by both the Venona and Comintern documents... that many of the allegations leveled at American communists by conservatives during the 1940s and 1950s were absolutely true." Nonetheless, he added, "the improprieties of the American communists during the McCarthy era in no way automatically validate the government's treatment of those communists." *Ibid.* at p. 99.

110. "Frightened America," April 1952, reproduced in *The Progressive,* April 2009, p. 59.

111. A divided Supreme Court also upheld Judge Medina's contempt sentences against Dennis and the other defense lawyers.

112. *Judge Medina Speaks* (1954), at p. 239.

113. 354 U.S. 298, 325 (1957).

114. *Ibid.* at 203, 210 (1961).

115. *Ibid.* at 262–263 (Douglas, J., dissenting).

116. *The Court Years: 1939–1975: The Autobiography of William O. Douglas* (1980), at p. 101.

117. 367 U.S. at 262 (Black, J., dissenting).

118. *Ibid.* at 262 (Black, J., dissenting).

119. *Ibid.* at 290, 302 (Black, J., concurring). There was one other related opinion that term, *Communist Party v. Control Board* (1961). There, the Court, per Justice Frankfurter, upheld a section of the Internal Security Act of 1950 requiring "Communist-action" organizations to register with the government. Chief Justice Warren and justices Black, Douglas, and Brennan filed spirited dissents.

120. "High Court Puts Curb on U.S. Reds in 2 Major Cases," *New York Times,* June 6, 1961, p. 1.

121. Journalist I. F. Stone (1907–1989) was one of the six founders of the group. He served as an associate editor of *The Nation* and founded his own paper, *I. F. Stone's Weekly.* He was an outspoken critic of the Smith Act, the HUAC, and Senator Joseph McCarthy.

122. Quoted in Marquese, *Chimes of Freedom: The Politics of Bob Dylan's Art* (2003), at p. 88.

123. *Ibid.* at p. 90.

124. The *Brandenburg* facts involved a Ku Klux Klan leader who had been convicted under Ohio's criminal syndicalism law of advocating violence as a means of political change. During the course of a rally in an open farm field, a cross was burned as a crowd of hooded and a few armed figures watched. Not very versant in the English language, the Klan leader declared: "We're not a revengent organization, but if our President, our Congress, our Supreme Court, continues to suppress the white, Caucasian race, it's possible that there might have to be some revengeance taken." For bad measure, he then added a bit more race-hate speech: "I believe the nigger should be returned to Africa, the Jew returned to Israel." *Brandenburg,* 395 U.S. 444, 446.

125. *First Amendment Law* (2009), at p. 74.

126. Recall Judge Hand's free-speech test in *The Masses* case was grounded in *statutory* interpretation and was not based on the First Amendment. Tellingly, in his 1958 Holmes Lecture at Harvard, the eighty-seven-year-old defender of judicial restraint declared: "I do not think the interests mentioned in the First Amendment are

entitled in point of constitutional interpretation to a measure of protection differ-ent from other interests...." Learned Hand, *The Bill of Rights* (1963), at p. 56.

127. According to Professor Tinsley Yarbrough, the *per curiam* opinion was probably authored by Justice Fortas. *John Marshall Harlan: Great Dissenter of the Warren Court* (1992), at p. 323. The justice's most notable First Amendment opinion was *Tinker v. Des Moines Independent Community School District* (1969) (see chapter 10).

128. 395 U.S. 444, 448 (1969).

129. *Speech, Crime and the Uses of Language* (1989), at p. 206.

130. Justice Douglas also issued a concurring opinion, which Justice Black joined. Essentially, Douglas believed that only *overt* forms of expression—"brigaded with action"—could be regulated or banned.

131. 395 U.S. at 449–450 (Black, J., concurring).

132. Of course, the Court has recognized that "true threats" are not protected expres-sion. See *Virginia v. Black* (2003). And the Court has never applied *Brandenburg* in an actual war-time case, which is important, since *Schenck* has never been formally overruled.

133. *The Birth of the Modern Constitution* (2006), at p. 563.

134. *Abrams v. United States*, 250 U.S. 616, 630 (Holmes, J., dissenting).

135. *The First Amendment* (1998), at p. 71.

CHAPTER 6

1. " 'Evasive,' or 'He Satisfied Me,' U.S. Says, as Justice Explains," *Washington Post*, October 2, 1937.

2. Richard Kluger, *Simple Justice* (1977), at p. 396.

3. *Missouri ex rel Gaines v. Canada*, 305 U.S. 337 (1938). The Court announced its ruling in the case in December 1938. Writing for the six-justice majority, Chief Justice Charles Evans Hughes ruled that Gaines "was entitled to the equal protec-tion of the laws, and the State was bound to furnish him within its borders facilities for legal education" that were commensurate with what its white students could expect.

4. "Freedom to Petition and Freedom to Assemble: A Public Interview with Judge Robert L. Carter and Professor Geoffrey R. Stone," C-SPAN, November 30, 2005.

5. Robert L. Carter, *A Matter of Law* (2005), at p. 29.

6. Langston Hughes, *Fight for Freedom: The Story of the NAACP* (1962), at p. 16.

7. *Ibid.* at pp. 17–18.

8. Among the signers were Jane Addams, founder of Hull House; William Lloyd Garrison, the famous Boston abolitionist; John Dewey, the educational scholar from Columbia University; Ida Wells Barnett, the anti-lynching activist; and W. E. B. Du Bois.

9. Hughes, *Fight for Freedom*.

10. In that year, Carter authored an amicus brief for a case in the federal district court in California in which separate schools for children of Mexican ancestry were chal-lenged as a violation of the Fourteenth Amendment. The District Court held that separate-but-equal schools were unconstitutional, but the Ninth Circuit ruled that the Mexican-American children deserved to win the case not because the Court's 1896 decision in *Plessy v. Ferguson* was invalid, but because there was no California

statute authorizing segregated schools. Nonetheless, as Richard Kluger has observed, "Carter's brief was a useful dry run…[because] it tested the temper of the courts without putting the NAACP itself directly in the field and, as important, it drew added attention to the case in a number of the leading law reviews across the country." Kluger, *Simple Justice*, at p. 400.

11. Unfortunately, the story did not end well. Once Texas's Law School admitted Sweatt, he was forced to endure endless intimidation tactics from his white classmates, including a burning cross next to his car, and the slashing of his tires. In time, Sweatt grew ill from the stress and dropped out.

12. Kluger, *Simple Justice*, at p. 400.

13. *Congressional Record*, 84th Congress, Second Session, vol. 102, pt. 4 (March 12, 1956).

14. City officials were equally determined to resist all efforts toward integration. In "Lies, Lies, Lies" (2004), Kermit Hall reports that in January 1959 the city ordered the Montgomery zoo and all thirteen public parks to be sold "as a way of evading a federal court order mandating their integration." Kermit L. Hall, "Cultural History and the First Amendment: *New York Times v. Sullivan* and its Times," in *Constitutionalism and the American Culture: Writing the New Constitutional History*, Sandra F. Vanurkkleo, Kermit L. Hall, and Robert J. Kaczorowski, eds. (2002), at p. 267.

15. Carter, *Matter of Law*, at pp. 147–148.

16. Mark V. Tushnet, *Making Civil Rights Law* (1994), at p. 283.

17. Carter, *Matter of Law*, at p. 154.

18. Walter Jones, "What Is Left of the Confederacy in the South Today?" address to the New England Oto-Laryngological Society, Boston, February 9, 1955.

19. The Alabama Supreme Court essentially encouraged the NAACP to seek a writ of certiorari, and then rejected its petition by ruling that a writ of mandamus, not certiorari, was the only appropriate way to challenge a contempt order in Alabama.

20. Carter, *Matter of Law*, at p. 155.

21. After the conference, a sharp divergence occurred between Black and Douglas, who wanted to decide the case on First Amendment grounds, and Frankfurter, who wanted to decide the case on due process grounds. In the end, Harlan's unanimous opinion came closer to Frankfurter's line of thinking than to that of Black or Douglas.

22. Writing in 1970, legal scholar Thomas Emerson predicted that the historical significance of the Court's ruling in *NAACP v. Alabama* would be mixed. Its "creation of an independent constitutional 'right of association' is an important development," he begins, "but its value as constitutional doctrine is highly questionable. There can be no doubt that freedom of association, as a basic element in the democratic process, must receive constitutional protection. But the freedom to be safeguarded is so inclusive, appears in so many forms, and is subject to such varied restrictions, that the rules for protection cannot be capsuled into a single doctrine called the 'right of association.'" Writing in *First Amendment Law in a Nutshell* (2008), law professors Jerome Barron and C. Thomas Dienes supported Emerson's forecast. "Supreme Court response to the implied rights [of association] has traveled a vacillating course," they explained. "Today, however, the Court generally applies a heightened standard of scrutiny when reviewing government burdens on the right to associate for purposes of political expression." *First Amendment in a Nutshell*, at p. 273.

23. "Plan to Combat NAACP Urged," *Washington Post*, October 3, 1958, p. B4.

24. Tushnet, now a Harvard law professor, was a law clerk to Justice Thurgood Marshall during the 1972–73 Court term.

25. "Official Puts Little Rock Onus on Reds," *Washington Post*, May 22, 1959, p. A17.

26. We explore the law of defamation and its relationship to the First Amendment in great detail in chapter 8.

27. Harrison E. Salisbury, "Fear and Hatred Grip Birmingham," *New York Times*, April 12, 1960, p. 1.

28. Anthony Lewis, *Make No Law* (1991), at p. 35.

29. Dell Dickson, ed., *The Supreme Court in Conference: 1940–1985* (2001).

30. In *Shelton v. Tucker*, B. T. Shelton's case was combined with two other teachers' cases with similar facts.

31. On February 25, 1963, the Court announced its decision in the case of *Edwards v. South Carolina*. Writing for the eight-to-one majority, Justice Stewart wrote: "These petitioners were convicted of an offense so generalized as to be, in the words of the South Carolina Supreme Court, 'not susceptible of exact definition.' And they were convicted upon evidence which showed no more than that the opinions which they were peaceably expressing were sufficiently opposed to the views of the majority of the community to attract a crowd and necessitate police protection." But, Stewart elaborated, "[t]he Fourteenth Amendment does not permit a state to make criminal the peaceful expression of unpopular views." Arguing successfully on behalf of the students was Jack Greenburg. Greenburg later won two other civil rights–era First Amendment cases before the Court: *Walker v. City of Birmingham* (1967) and *Shuttlesworth v. City of Birmingham* (1969).

32. Tom Clark (1899–1977), associate justice on the U.S. Supreme Court from 1949 to 1967, grew up in Dallas in a family of lawyers. Appointed attorney general in 1945 by President Harry S. Truman, Clark served in that capacity until 1949, when Truman nominated him to succeed Justice Frank Murphy. Known as an ideological independent, the moderately conservative Clark later became a champion for judicial reform toward the end of his career, and helped establish the Federal Judicial Center after his retirement.

33. Dickson, *Supreme Court in Conference*, at pp. 317, 318.

34. White, the former valedictorian and all-American football player at the University of Colorado, had been an active supporter during Kennedy's presidential campaign; both had served during World War II as naval officers. Although the new president had already named White deputy attorney general, it took just four days after Whittaker's retirement for Kennedy to name the "Whizzer" as his first nominee to the Court. Eight days after that, the Senate confirmed the former professional football player and Rhodes scholar by a voice vote. And on April 16, Byron White was sworn in as the ninety-third justice in the history of the Supreme Court. It was slower going for Goldberg, whom Kennedy had chosen to be his first secretary of labor. The Chicago-born and educated son of Russian immigrants was known as one of the country's preeminent labor mediators; indeed, he was largely responsible for the 1955 merger of the AFL and CIO. But whereas Kennedy had swiftly placed White in Whittaker's vacant seat, the nation's first Catholic president was forced to spend the summer wondering if the Court's second Jewish justice would return from his stroke in time for the Court's new term in October. On August 29, however, Frankfurter

made it official. "I need hardly tell you, Mr. President, of the reluctance with which I leave the institution whose concerns have been the absorbing interest of my life," wrote the ailing justice. But "[t]he Court should not enter its new term with uncertainty as to whether I might later be able to return to unrestricted duty." Kennedy nominated Goldberg later that day.

35. "Bars NAACP Permanently from Alabama," *Chicago Daily Tribune*, December 30, 1961, p. 7.

36. Thomas I. Emerson, *The System of Freedom of Expression* (1970), at p. 429.

37. Carter, *Matter of Law*, at pp. 162–163.

38. As Tushnet has observed, the *Button* decision did more than save the NAACP from extinction in Virginia—it also endorsed a new form of legal practice, one in which lawyers could make "contact with people who were not yet clients but might become plaintiffs" and deliver "speeches publicizing the organization's willingness to support lawsuits." This style of barratry, Tushnet writes, "tested the limits of traditional standards." But the Court's decision in Carter's favor gave "a stamp of constitutional approval to the kind of lawyering that the Legal Defense Fund developed." *Making Civil Rights Law* (1996), at p. 282.

39. Jones, "What Is Left of the Confederacy in the South Today?"

40. Kermit L. Hall, " 'Lies, Lies, Lies': The Origins of *New York Times v. Sullivan*," 9 *Communication Law and Policy* (2004), at p. 421.

41. Decades later, in 2000, Nachman published a tribute in the *Alabama Law Review* to a noted civil rights jurist, Frank Johnson of Alabama. In it he wrote: "Judge Johnson has been a constant hero of mine."

42. While *New York Times v. Sullivan* was not a case in which Bob Carter had a direct hand, it was one in a long line of cases involving—as legal scholar Harry Kalven, Jr., put it- "the Negro and the First Amendment." These cases, championed mainly by Carter, expanded the reach of First Amendment protection in unprecedented ways. Yet it is a fair assumption that, absent the civil rights component, the advent of freedom of association and the revision of libel law might never had developed the way they did.

43. The case originated out of Mississippi when state NAACP president Aaron Henry, following his arrest and release on a charge of disturbing the peace, accused local officials of hatching a "diabolical plot" against him and his organization. Henry was thereafter successfully sued for civil libel, a ruling the Mississippi Supreme Court later affirmed. But the Court reversed in a short *per curiam* opinion. Basing its decision largely on the precedent established by *New York Times v. Sullivan*, the justices ruled that the conviction "violate[d] the First and Fourteenth Amendments" because it subjected Henry to punishment "solely because of his publication of criticisms against respondents' performance of their public duties." 380 U.S. 356, 358 (1965).

44. Carter, *Matter of Law*, at p. 227.

45. As quoted in "Ideals of Klan Extolled by Black in 1926 Speech," *Los Angeles Times*, September 15, 1937, at p. 1.

46. The Court issued two separate opinions in *Cox v. Louisiana*. In the first, a seven-to-two judgment, the justices reversed breach-of-peace and obstructing-public-passages convictions against Cox. In the second, they ruled by a five-to-four margin that a statute prohibiting picketing "near" a courthouse with the intent to obstruct justice, despite being "a precise, narrowly drawn regulatory statute which proscribes certain

specific behavior," nonetheless allowed public officials "a type of entrapment violative of the Due Process Clause" of the Fourteenth Amendment.

47. *Cox v. Louisiana II*, 379 U.S. 559 (1965). Kalven later characterized the decision as a
    low point for the Court, because of the way the opinion reflected an "irritation and
    anxiety in confronting one of the most difficult practical issues of the moment."

48. Fred P. Graham, "The Law: At 80, Hugo Black Looks Ahead," *New York Times*,
    February 27, 1966, p. E7.

49. *Mr. Justice Black, Absolutist on the Court* (1980), at p. 146.

50. *The System of Freedom of Expression* (1970), at p. 298.

51. 379 U.S. 559, 578 (Black, J., concurring).

52. *Mr. Justice Black, Absolutist on the Court* (1980), at pp. 177-179.

53. *The System of Freedom of Expression* (1970), at p. 298.

54. 379 U.S. 559, 584 (Black, J., concurring and dissenting in part).

55. 383 U.S. 131, 142 (Black, J., dissenting).

56. *Ibid.* at 168.

57. 385 U.S. 39, 48.

58. Quoted in Tinsley Yarbrough, *John Marshall Harlan: Great Dissenter of the Warren
    Court* (1992), at p. 241.

59. 385 U.S. 39, 55 (Douglas, J., dissenting).

60. 395 U.S. 444, 446.

61. *Ibid.* at 448.

62. *Ibid.* at 447.

63. *Only Words* (1993), at. p. 71.

64. *Ibid.* at pp. 85–86. MacKinnon was also referring to a later civil rights case by the
    Court, *NAACP v. Claiborne Hardware* (1982), but her words seem equally appro-
    priate when considering some of the civil rights free speech cases of the 1960s.

65. It also bears noting that the right of freedom of association vouchsafed by Carter in
    the civil rights context has now become a weapon in the arsenal of those challenging
    limits on campaign expenditures. See, e.g., *Randall v. Sorrell* (2006).

66. Carter, Robert L. "The Three Freedoms," graduate thesis, Columbia University Law
    School, August 1, 1941.

67. The quoted materials that follow are from that event. Ronald Collins conducted the
    interview.

68. Quoted in Jon Panish, *The Color of Jazz: Race and Representation in Postwar American
    culture* (2007), at p. 86 (originally in James Baldwin's *Going to Meet the Man* (1965)).

CHAPTER 7

1. Tamar Lewin, "Hate-Crime Law Is Focus of Case on Free Speech," *New York Times*,
   December 1, 1991, at pp. 1, 32.

2. In addition to the cross burned at the Jones house, several other crosses were burned
   in the same neighborhood that night.

3. Edward J. Cleary, *Beyond the Burning Cross* (1994), at p. 10.

4. Felicity Barringer, "Campus Battle Pits Freedom of Speech against Racial Slurs,"
   New York Times, April 25, 1989, p. A20.

5. "University Panel Votes to Prohibit Harassing Words," *New York Times*, May 27,
   1990, p. 40.

6. In his 1991 book *Illiberal Education*, social critic Dinesh D'Souza explains that the term "seems to have originated in the early part of this century, when it was employed by various species of Marxists to describe and enforce conformity to preferred ideological positions." Eventually, however, the term faded from public use, "only to be revived in the 1980s, when it came to apply to the assorted ideologies of the late 1960s and early 1970s: black consciousness and black power, feminism, homosexual rights, and, to a lesser degree, pacifism, environmentalism, and so on." According to D'Souza, the first article about political correctness in a national publication was Richard Bernstein's *New York Times* feature "The Rising Hegemony of the Politically Correct," October 29, 1990.

7. Anthony DePalma, "Battling Bias, Campuses Face Free-speech Fight," *New York Times*, February 20, 1991, sec. B, p. 9.

8. City Ordinance 292.02 was unanimously approved on March 9, 1982, although it was not until April 1990 that "gender" was added—also by unanimous approval—to the list of protected subjects.

9. About this time, the city council of Minneapolis also approved of an antipornography ordinance, though the mayor ultimately vetoed the measure.

10. The main Minnesota law that would have addressed the alleged conduct, according to Cleary, was a felony provision of terroristic threats, Minnesota Statute §609.713 ("Whoever threatens, directly or indirectly, to commit any crime of violence with purpose to terrorize another…").

11. Cleary, *Beyond the Burning Cross*.

12. Current First Amendment law, as announced by the Roberts Court, generally frowns on facial challenges. *See, e.g., Washington State Grange v. Washington State Republican Party* (2008) and *United States v. Williams* (2008). *But see United States v. Stevens*, 559 U.S.—(2010) (striking down a federal law by way of a facial challenge).

13. Erwin Chemerinsky, *Constitutional Law: Principles And Policies* (2002), at p. 979.

14. In 1997, Rodney Smolla, a First Amendment scholar and now the president of Furman University, successfully argued *Rice v. Paladin Enterprises, Inc.* (4th Cir.), in which the court held that the publisher of the book *Hit Man: A Technical Manual for Independent Contractors* (1983) was not immune from civil liability when one of its purchasers employed the advice given and murdered three people. See Smolla, *Deliberate Intent: A Lawyer Tells the True Story of Murder by the Book* (1999).

15. Rodney Smolla, *Smolla and Nimmer on Freedom of Speech* (1994), at p. 6.01[2].

16. Neil Lewis, "Friends of Free Speech Now Consider Its Limits," *New York Times*, June 29, 1990, sec. B, p. 7.

17. Mari J. Matsuda, "Public Response to Racist Speech" (1989).

18. Charles R. Lawrence III, "If He Hollers Let Him Go" (1990). Cited in *First Amendment Anthology* (Donald Lively et al., eds., 1994), at p. 251.

19. Richard Delgado, "Campus Antiracism Rules" (1991). Cited in Lively et al., *First Amendment Anthology*, at p. 251.

20. Anthony DePalma "Battling Bias, Campuses Face Free Speech Fight" (1991), p. B9.

21. In this regard the thinking of the likes of Matsuda, Lawrence, and Delgado in the race-hate context very much tracked that of Andrea Dworkin and Catharine MacKinnon in the antipornography context.

22. In his book *Hate Speech, Pornography, and the Radical Attack on Free Speech Doctrine* (1999), Professor James Weinstein observed that "the most important benefits that banning hate speech...might produce are extremely speculative. Because proof of the relationship between [hate speech and illegal discrimination] is sparse, there is no guarantee that a ban would alleviate [the various] harms." *See also Extreme Speech and Democracy* (Ivan Hare and James Weinstein, eds., 2009).

23. Strossen continued: "For example, among the first individuals prosecuted under the British Race Relations Act of 1965, which criminalized the incitement of racial hatred, were black power leaders.... Rather than curbing speech offensive to minorities, the British law instead has been regularly used to curb speech of blacks, trade unionists, and antinuclear activists. In perhaps the ultimate irony, this statute, which was intended to restrain the neo-Nazi National Front, instead has barred expression by the Anti-Nazi League." *Defending Pornography*, at p. 221.

24. Hentoff, now a senior fellow at the Cato Institute, is a nationally renowned defender of free speech. *See his Free Speech for Me—but not for Thee* (1993), *Speaking Freely: A Memoir* (1997), and *The First Freedom* (1980).

25. Nat Hentoff, *Free Speech for Me—But Not for Thee* (1992).

26. Mr. Chaplinsky was represented by Hayden C. Covington, who argued more First Amendment cases (and all on behalf of Jehovah's Witnesses) in the Supreme Court than any other nongovernment lawyer in American history.

27. *Chaplinsky v. New Hampshire*, 315 U.S. 568 (1942).

28. As Erwin Chemerinsky explains, "[t]he Court has used three techniques in overturning [fighting words] convictions. First, the Court has narrowed the scope of the fighting words doctrine by ruling that it applies only to speech directed at another person that is likely to produce a violent response. Second, the Court frequently has found laws prohibiting fighting words to be unconstitutionally vague or overbroad. Third, the Court has found laws that prohibit some fighting words—such as expression of hate based on race or gender—to be impermissible content-based restrictions of speech." *Constitutional Law: Principles and Policies* (2006), at p. 1002.

29. In the dissent for *Feiner v. New York* 340 U.S. 315, 328 (1951), Black wrote: "In my judgment, today's holding means that as a practical matter, minority speakers can be silenced in any city. Hereafter, despite the First and Fourteenth Amendments, the policeman's club can take heavy toll of a current administration's public critics. Criticism of public officials will be too dangerous for all but the most courageous."

30. 343 U.S. 250, 273 (Black., J., dissenting).

31. A panel of judges for the Seventh Circuit in *Collin v. Smith* (1978) expressed "doubt" about the doctrine's contemporary relevance in light of *Sullivan* and subsequent cases. Among the cases the Circuit court cited were: *New York Times Co. v. Sullivan* (1964); *Garrison v. Louisiana* (1964); *Gertz v. Welch* (1974); *Cohen v. California* (1971); *Gooding v. Wilson* (1972); and *Brandenburg v. Ohio* (1969).

32. 395 U.S. 444, 447.

33. Cleary, *Beyond the Burning Cross*, at p. 37.

34. 491 U.S. 397, 421 (Kennedy, J., concurring).

35. The other teenager arrested for the cross burning, Arthur Miller III, was scheduled for his own hearing on July 23, 1990. Yet even after Judge Flinn ruled that the law was

unconstitutional, Miller pleaded guilty to violating section 292.02, and was sentenced to thirty days of incarceration.

36. Cleary, *Beyond the Burning Cross*, at p. 39.

37. *Ibid.* at p. 53.

38. Neil Lewis. "Friends of Free Speech Now Consider Its Limits," (1990), p. B7.

39. "How Much Hate to Tolerate," *New York Times*, February 21, 1991, p. A20.

40. If it had become a law, HR 1380 would also have permitted students to obtain "appropriate injunctive and declaratory relief."

41. Although the bill never became law, the proposal was discussed in Henry Hyde and George Fishman, "The Collegiate Speech Protection Act of 1991: A Response to the New Intolerance in the Academy," 37 *Wayne Law Review* 1469 (1991).

42. Cleary, *Beyond the Burning Cross*, at p. 69.

43. Here, Cleary was referring to *Brandenburg v. Ohio*, 395 U.S. 444, 447 (1969), in which the Court ruled that even speech advocating violence was a protected form of expression *unless* it could be proven that the speech was "directed to inciting or producing imminent lawless action and is likely to incite or produce such action."

44. Born in Melrose, Massachusetts, on September 17 (what later became Constitution Day), 1939, and raised in a small town in New Hampshire, David Souter studied philosophy, and then law, at Harvard. In his senior honors thesis he examined the legal philosophy of Oliver Wendell Holmes, Jr. He announced his retirement from the Court in the spring of 2009 and was succeeded by Sonia Sotomayor.

45. In his 1994 book on *R.A.V., Beyond the Burning Cross* (p. 112), Cleary wrote that Harvard Law School professor and former solicitor general Charles Fried spoke to him about the possibility of Fried arguing the case, *pro bono*. Cleary declined the offer. Similarly, Cleary notes a conversation he had with Professor Geoffrey Stone, then dean of the University of Chicago Law School. (*Ibid.*) As Stone recalled it in mid-June 2005: "Cleary asked if I would be willing to help on the brief. I told him I would, but that it was important for someone to argue the case who had lots of Supreme Court experience. I said this is going to be a close case, and we would need every edge we could get. I suggested several experienced Supreme Court advocates, including Mike McConnell and David Strauss. Cleary said he wanted to argue the case himself. I strongly objected, saying that could not be in the best interest of either his client or the development of the law. 'Nothing personal, but there's no principled reason why someone who's never argued before in the Supreme Court should choose to take this on himself.' Cleary was adamant on this score." According to Cleary, "the four law professors I contacted directly [for guidance] were Phil Frickey (then at Minnesota, now at Berkeley), Cass Sunstein (at Chicago), who then led me to Kathleen Sullivan (then at Harvard), and John Siliciano, a friend of mine who was a law professor at Cornell and who had clerked for Thurgood Marshall. Of those, only Sullivan and Siliciano agreed to help." (Collins phone interview, June 15, 2005).

46. Clarence Thomas, who was born in 1948, attended the College of the Holy Cross and thereafter took his law degree from Yale Law School. He served as an assistant attorney general in Missouri and then as a legislative assistant to Republican senator John Danforth of Missouri. In 1981, Thomas was appointed assistant secretary for civil rights at the U.S. Department of Education. The following year, Thomas became chairman of the Equal Employment Opportunity Commission.

47. Cited in "Clarence Thomas in His Own Words," *New York Times*, July 2, 1991, sec. A, p. 14.
48. Thomas was confirmed by a vote in the Senate of fifty-eight to forty-two. Eleven Democrats joined forty-one of the forty-three Republicans in supporting him.
49. *Judging Thomas: The Life and Times of Clarence Thomas* (2005), at p. 258.
50. Robin Toner, "Duke Takes His Anger into 1992 Race," *New York Times*, December 5, 1991, sec. A, p. 1.
51. As Cleary granted, this line was a paraphrase of what Justice Douglas wrote in dissent in his 1952 *Beauharnais v. Illinois* opinion: "The Framers of the Constitution knew human nature as well as we do. They too had lived in dangerous days; they too knew the suffocating influence of orthodoxy and standardized thought. They weighed the compulsions for restrained speech and thought against the abuses of liberty. They chose liberty." 343 U.S. 250, 287 (1952).
52. Cleary, *Beyond the Burning Cross*, at p. 160.
53. Isabel Wilkerson, "Acquittal in Beating Raises Fears over Race Relations," *New York Times*, May 1, 1992, sec. A, p. 23.
54. Michel Marriott, "The Sacking of a Neighborhood: An Orgy of Looting, a Carnival of Chaos," *New York Times*, May 1, 1992, sec. A, p. 21.
55. Seth Mydans, "Verdicts Set Off a Wave of Shock and Anger," *New York Times*, April 30, 1992, sect. D, p. 22.
56. Rodney Smolla, *Smolla and Nimmer on Freedom of Speech* (1994).
57. This was readily apparent during oral arguments in *United States v. Stevens* (2010), in which Scalia was openly hostile to a federal law that made it illegal to commercially disseminate depictions of animal cruelty.
58. In *Justice Antonin Scalia and the Conservative Revival* (1997), Richard Brisbin contends: Former "Professor Antonin Scalia once remarked that it was an 'embarrassment' to teach Supreme Court opinions about the Fourteenth Amendment's Equal Protection Clause. Finding a 'trivialization' of the Constitution, he thought the Court had neglected "hard-minded, reasoned analysis" in an effort to provide experimental and discriminatory remedies for racial and gender discrimination. His remedy was simple: "the application of neutral rules of law would leave persons to rise or fall on their own merit."
59. Scalia's opinion was, according to Yale Law School professor Akhil Reed Amar, "an ambitious reconceptualization and synthesis of First Amendment doctrine." In a 1992 article for the *Harvard Law Review* titled, "The Case of the Missing Amendments," Amar suggested that the *R.A.V.* majority focused too exclusively on the First Amendment, and failed to consider whether the Reconstruction Amendments "might provide a principled basis for such distinctions." 106 Harv. L. Rev. 124, 126 (1992).
60. The last time the Court had created an express exception to the First Amendment was in the 1982 case of *New York v. Ferber* (child pornography). In 2009, the Court was asked by then Solicitor General Elena Kagan to create another exception to the First Amendment in the case of *United States v. Stevens* (commercial depictions of animal cruelty).
61. Steven H. Shiffrin *Dissent, Injustice, and the Meanings of America* (1999), at p. 63.
62. See Steven Shiffrin, *The First Amendment, Democracy and Romance* (1990).

63. *R.A.V.*, 505 U.S. at 407 (White, J.).

64. *Ibid.* at 415 (White, J.).

65. *Ibid.* (Blackmun, J.).

66. *Ibid.* at 425, 433, n. 9 (Stevens, J.).

67. Don Terry, "Rights Advocates Uncertain About Ruling's Impact," *New York Times*, June 23, 1992, sec. A, p. 16.

68. Cited in Cleary, *Beyond the Burning Cross*, at p. 189.

69. Smolla, Rodney. *Smolla and Nimmer on Freedom of Speech* (1994), at p. 6.02[4].

70. 505 U.S. 377, 391.

71. *Ibid.* at 395 (Scalia, J.).

72. *Ibid.* at 403 (White, J.).

73. *Ibid.* at 404 (White, J.).

74. William Celis, "Universities Reconsidering Bans on Hate Speech," *New York Times*, June 24, 1992, p. A13.

75. *Iota Xi Chapter of Sigma Chi Fraternity v. George Mason University*, 993 F.2d 386 (4th Cir. 1993).

76. Akhil Reed Amar, for one, found this logic curious. Why, he wondered, had Scalia "all but ignored this concession and offered no detailed explanation of how the St. Paul ordinance differed from the 'incidental' regulation of speech under Title VII"? Apparently, he concluded, "the Scalia Five thought it obvious that, unlike the federal statutes, the local ordinance targeted only 'speech' and not 'conduct.'" ("The Case of the Missing Amendments, 106 *Harvard Law Review* 124, 129 (1992)). Cleary added in a June 15, 2005 interview with Collins that "one obvious difference between the St. Paul Ordinance and Title VII, which should not be overlooked, is that Title VII is applicable to the workplace environment. The St. Paul Ordinance had no such limitation."

77. "Rethinking First Amendment Assumptions About Racist Speech and Sexist Speech," 47 *Washington and Lee law Review* 171, 198 (1990).

78. Smolla & Nimmer, *Smolla and Nimmer on Freedom of Speech*, at p. 6.02[4].

79. *Mitchell*, 508 U.S. 476, 487, 488. Commenting on the case later, Edward Cleary, who had sat on a moot court and attended the *Mitchell* oral argument, believes that the "distinction between hate speech and hate crimes" was a fundamental part of his argument in *R.A.V.*, and explains his decision not to challenge the count charging Viktora with an enhancement law violation. "I suspected," he explains, "that the Rehnquist Court would see a major distinction between hate speech and hate crime enhancement laws. So while the Wisconsin Supreme Court might have been shocked, I certainly wasn't, and anyone who had attended the *Mitchell* oral argument would not have been surprised either." Phone Interview with Collins, June 12, 2007.

80. Linda Greenhouse. "Court Choice Puts Nation's Racial Legacy on Table," *New York Times*, July 8, 1991, sec. A, p. 9. See also "Clarence Thomas in His Own Words," *New York Times*, July 2, 1991, sec. A, p. 14.

81. Denniston, who now writes for SCOTUSblog, has been covering the Court for a half century.

82. "Thomas Breaks Silence to Denounce Klan: Court Weighs Cross Burning," *Boston Globe*, December 12, 2002, sec. A, p. 2. One can only wonder if the result in *R.A.V.*

would have been the same had Thomas spoken out the same way there as he had done in *Virginia v. Black*.

83. Quoted in H.L. Pohlman, *Constitutional Debates in Action* (2004), at p. 191.

84. 538 U.S. 343 (2003).

85. Barron and Dienes, *First Amendment Law* (2000), at pp. 213–214.

86. Barry Black's conviction (cross burning performed with owner's consent on private property and located in an open field) was thus overturned, while criminal proceedings against Richard Elliott and Jonathan O'Mara (cross burning on private property without owner's consent) were allowed to proceed on remand to the Virginia Courts.

87. Quoted in "Virginia High Court Throws Out Part of Cross-burning Law," Associated Press, March 8, 2004. See also James Walsh, "Cross-burning Victim, Suspect Discuss Feelings," Minneapolis *Star Tribune*, June 24, 1992, sec. B, p. 1.

88. *Ibid.* (James Walsh).

89. Then there is the case of *Virginia v. Black*, 538 U.S. 343 (2003), and the three men accused of unlawful cross burnings. Recall that Barry Black burned a thirty-foot cross in an open field at a Ku Klux Klan rally, whereas Richard Elliott and Jonathan O'Mara attempted to burn a cross in the yard of James Jubilee, an African American neighbor. The Supreme Court reversed Barry's conviction on First Amendment grounds. The judgments against Elliott and O'Mara, by contrast, were "vacated" and sent back to the Virginia courts "for further proceedings." In March 2004, the Virginia Supreme Court rendered its judgments in the two cases, ruling that the convictions of Richard Elliott and Jonathan O'Mara could stand since their particular acts of cross burning were intentional and constituted "true threats." 262 Va. 764, 553 S. E. 2d 738 (2001). Both men were sentenced to ninety days in jail, and ordered to pay a $2,000 fine—although O'Mara's penalty and fine were later cut in half. "Virginia has clearly declared that if you burn a cross with the intent to intimidate someone, we will prosecute you," said state attorney general Jerry Kilgore in the wake of the state court's latest ruling. Associated Press, "Virginia high court throws out part of cross-burning law," March 8, 2004. On that score, even Kent Willis, executive director of the Virginia chapter of the ACLU, agreed: "This puts the cross-burning law where it should be—that is, if someone is going to be prosecuted for cross burning there must be evidence there was intent to intimidate someone based on their race or religion." *Ibid.*

90. Commenting on the *Republican Party* case in 2007, Cleary added: "I believed then, and I believe now, that judicial campaigns are distinguishable from campaigns for legislative or executive elected office, and that speech-sensitive restrictions can be adopted that will survive constitutional scrutiny." Phone interview with Collins, July 12, 2007.

91. In his book *Mr. Justice Black and His Critics* (1988), Tinsley Yarbrough has observed: "Shortly before his death,…[Black] said that he had not fully formulated his First Amendment views when *Chaplinsky* was decided and that, in any event, he had joined the decision because he saw the case as one in which the speech in question was merely part of a course of conduct." At p. 165.

92. *Texas v. Johnson*, 491 U.S. 397, 414 (1989).

CHAPTER 8

1. Bruce W. Sanford, *Libel and Privacy: The Prevention and Defense of Litigation* (1991), at p. 1.

2. Gertz was elected to the Sixth Illinois Constitutional Convention in 1969 and chaired the Illinois Bill of Rights Committee.

3. Zechariah Chafee, Jr., *Free Speech in the United States* (1941), at p. 14.

4. *Beauharnais v. Illinois*, 343 U.S. 250, 266. In *Collin v. Smith* (7th Cir., 1978), a panel of judges of the U.S. Court of Appeals for the Seventh Circuit expressed "doubt" about whether "*Beauharnais* remains good law after the constitutional libel cases."

5. The Leopold case and Gertz's involvement in it are discussed at length in Gertz's book *A Handful of Clients* (1965).

6. Elmer Gertz, *To Life* (1974), at p. 187.

7. The epigraph to this section is from *ibid.* at p. 246.

8. "Tropic of Cancer Wins," *New York Times*, February 22, 1962, p. 23, and see Elmer Gertz & Felice F. Lewis, *Henry Miller: Years of Trial and Triumph, 1962–1964: The Correspondence of Henry Miller and Elmer Gertz* (1978).

9. In a June 27, 1962, letter to Henry Miller, Gertz wrote: "Although I did not agree with what Justice Black said [recently at New York University] on the subject of libel, I found almost everything else he that he said true and inspiring." Reproduced in Elmer Gertz and Felice Flanery Lewis, editors, *Henry Miller: Years of Trial and Triumph, 1962–1964: The Correspondence of Henry Miller and Elmer Gertz* (1978).

10. The epigraphs to this section are from Martin Garbus with Cohen, Stanley, *Tough Talk: How I Fought for Writers, Comics, Bigots, and the American Way* (1998), at p. 242, and Gertz, *To Life*, at p. 217.

11. Gertz, *To Life*, at pp. 217–246.

12. Gertz & Lewis, *Henry Miller*, at p. 27.

13. The epigraph to this section is from Elmer Gertz, *Gertz v. Robert Welch, Inc.: The Story of a Landmark Libel Case* (1992), at pp. 7, 211.

14. See Elmer Gertz, *Gertz v. Welch, Inc.: The Story of a Landmark Case* (1992), Gene Grove, *Inside the John Birch Society* (1961), and *The Blue Book of the John Birch Society* (1961).

15. *Ibid.* at pp. 1–2.

16. *Ibid.* at p. 2.

17. He is a partner in the Rolling Meadows, Illinois law firm of Stitt, Klein, Daday, Aretos & Giampietro.

18. Gertz, *Gertz v. Robert Welch, Inc.*, at pp. 43, 44.

19. *Gertz v. Robert Welch, Inc.*, 471 F.2d 801, 818 (7th Cir., 1972).

20. 471 F.2d. at 818–819 (Kiley, J., concurring).

21. The epigraph to this section is from Harry Kalven, Jr., "The New York Times Case: A Note on 'The Central Meaning of the First Amendment,'" 1964 *Supreme Court Review* 191, n. 125.

22. *Ibid.* at text accompanying n. 43.

23. *Make No Law: The Sullivan Case and the First Amendment* (1991), at p. 143.

24. 376 U.S. 254, 279–280 (emphasis added).

25. *Ibid.* at 273 (emphasis added).

26. *A Worthy Tradition: Freedom of Speech in America* (1988), at p. 63.

27. 376 U.S. at 296 (Black, J., concurring).

28. "The New York Times Case: A Note on 'The Central Meaning of the First Amendment,'" 1964 *Supreme Court Review* 221.

29. Gertz, *Gertz v. Robert Welch, Inc.*, at p. 28.

30. Bruce E. Fein, *New York Times v. Sullivan: An Obstacle to Enlightened Public Discourse and Government Responsiveness to the People* (1984). Much of the same concern was later expressed by Justice Byron White in his concurrence in *Dunn & Bradstreet, Inc. v. Greenmoss Builders, Inc.* (1985) wherein White wrote: "I have... become convinced that the Court struck an improvident balance in the *New York Times* case between the public's interest in being fully informed about public officials and public affairs and the competing interest of those who have been defamed in vindicating their reputation." White then added: "The *New York Times* rule... countenances two evils: first, the stream of information about public officials and public affairs is polluted and often remains polluted by false information; and second, the reputation and professional life of the defeated plaintiff may be destroyed by falsehoods that might have been avoided with a reasonable effort to investigate the facts. In terms of the First Amendment and reputational interests at stake, these seem grossly perverse results." 472 U.S. 749, 792 (1985) (White, J., concurring in judgment).

31. Gertz, *Gertz v. Robert Welch, Inc.*, at p. 92.

32. He was the son of Judge Medina (see chapter 5).

33. 385 U.S. 374, 389 (1967).

34. *First Amendment Law* (3rd ed., 2004), at p. 155.

35. 385 U.S. at 399 (Black, J., concurring).

36. Quoted in *Abuse of Power: The New Nixon Tapes* (Stanley I. Cutler, ed., 1997), at p. 164.

37. *Don't Shoot the Messenger: How Our Growing Hatred of the Media Threatens Free Speech for Us All* (1999), at p. 176.

38. Quoted in Lewis, *Make No Law*, at p. 188.

39. Quoted in John P. MacKenzie, "Libel Changes; Nixon Urges Changes in Libel Laws," *Washington Post*, March 9, 1974, sec. A, p. 1.

40. At this time Fein was a Justice Department lawyer. Later he served as an associate deputy attorney general under Ronald Reagan and then as general counsel to the Federal Communications Commission. Later still, he was a partner in Fein & Fein in Washington, D.C. More recently, he offered the following advice to the president: "President George W. Bush should pack the U.S. Supreme Court with philosophical clones of justices Antonin Scalia and Clarence Thomas and defeated nominee Robert H. Bork." *See* "Taking the Stand: Pack the Supreme Court," *Washington Lawyer*, February 2005.

41. In a monograph published a decade later—"*New York Times v. Sullivan:* An Obstacle to Enlightened Public Discourse and Government Responsiveness to the People" (1984)—Bruce Fein argued: "Fidelity to the First Amendment and other constitutional aspirations would be best harmonized if the Supreme Court authorized public officials to initiate defamation actions bottomed on the *negligent* publication of falsehoods" (emphasis added).

42. The epigraph to this section is from Rodney A. Smolla, *Suing the Press: Libel, Media, and Power* (1986), at p. 58.

43. Actually, seven of the nine justices voted to reverse the Seventh Circuit judgment against Gertz with only Brennan and Douglas dissenting on that count.

44. During his tenure on the Court (1972–1988), Lewis Powell authored seventeen First Amendment freedom-of-expression majority opinions, the most noticed being *Central Hudson Gas & Electric Corp. v. Public Service Commission* (a 1980 commercial speech case).

45. 418 U.S. 323, 340.

46. When a *private* individual is involved in a defamation action against a publisher or broadcaster pertaining to an issue of merely *private* concern, there may be liability without fault.

47. For a thoughtful critique of *Gertz*, and a proposed restructuring of its public figure standard, *see* Lee Levine, "The Editorial Function and the Gertz Public Figure Standard," 87 *Yale Law Journal* 1723 (1978).

48. 418 U.S. at 351.

49. *Constitutional Law: Principles and Policies* (2002), at p. 1014.

50. Writing in forceful dissent, Chief Justice Warren Burger and Justice Byron White voted to reverse the judgment of the Court of Appeals and reinstate the jury's verdict. Justice White's lengthy dissent, with which Gertz agreed, was especially critical of the majority opinion:

    For some 200 years—from the very founding of the Nation—the law of defamation and right of the ordinary citizen to recover for false publication injurious to his reputation have been almost exclusively the business of state courts and legislatures.... But now, using [the First] Amendment as the chosen instrument, the Court, in a few printed pages, has federalized major aspects of libel law by declaring unconstitutional in important respects the prevailing defamation law in all or most of the 50 States.... I fail to see how the quality or quantity of public debate will be promoted by further emasculation of state libel laws for the benefit of the news media. If anything, this trend may provoke a new and radical imbalance in the communications process.

51. *Milkovich*, 497 U.S. 1, 19; Daniel Farber, *The First Amendment* (1998), at pp. 90–91.

52. 491 U.S. 657, 692.

53. *Gertz v. Robert Welch, Inc.*, 680 F.2d 527 (7th Cir., 1982).

54. Quoted in Peter Irons, *The Courage of Their Convictions: Sixteen Americans Who Fought Their Way to the Supreme Court* (1989), at p. 353.

55. Michael Seiler, "Robert Welch, Founder of Birch Society, Dies at 85," *Los Angeles Times*, January 8, 1985, sec. 1, p. 1.

56. The epigraph to this section is from *RN: The Memoirs of Richard Nixon* (1978), at p. 964.

57. *Ibid.*

58. William Safire, *Before the Fall: An Inside View of the Pre-Watergate White House* (1975), at p. 614.

59. *Presidents and The Press: The Nixon Legacy* (1984).

60. *Ibid.*

61. Ronald Kessler was a well-regarded investigative reporter. In subsequent years, he used those skills to become a best-selling author who wrote books on George W. Bush, the FBI, the CIA, and Congress, among other topics.

62. Ronald Kessler, "Bebe Rebozo Said to Cash Stolen Stock; Stock Stolen by the Mafia Was Cashed by Rebozo Denies Knowing Stock He Cashed Was Stolen," *Washington Post*, October 25, 1973, sec. A, p. 1.

63. Cutler, *Abuse of Power*, at p. 165.

64. *Rebozo v. The Washington Post Co.*, 637 F.2d 375, 382 (5th Cir., 1981), *cert. den.* 454 U.S. 964 (1981).

65. 637 F.2d at 382.

66. "Charles (Bebe) Rebozo, Post Settle 10-Year-Old Libel Suit," *Washington Post*, November 4, 1983, sec. A, p. 4.

67. The epigraph to this section is quoted in Maura Kelly, "400 Honor Life, Ideals of Elmer Gertz," *Chicago Tribune*, May 2, 2000, sec. 2, p. 6.

68. *Suing the Press*, at pp. 59–60.

69. *Libel and the First Amendment: Legal History and Practice in Print and Broadcasting* (1987), at p. 158.

70. 388 U.S. 130, 172 (Black, J., concurring & dissenting in part).

71. *Curtis*, 388 U. S. 130, 172, (Black, J.); *Gertz*, 418 U.S. 323, 358 (Douglas, J.); *ibid.* at 364 (Brennan, J.).

CHAPTER 9

1. The epigraph to this chapter is from Oliver Wendell Holmes, Jr., "John Marshall," February 4, 1901, reproduced in *The Collected Works of Justice Holmes*, edited by Sheldon M. Novick (Chicago: University of Chicago Press, 1995), vol. III 3, at p. 509.

2. Robert Justin Goldstein, *Flag Burning and Free Speech* (2000), at p. 1.

3. *Ibid.* at p. 6.

4. *Ibid.* at p. 5.

5. HR 10475, *To Prevent Desecration of the United States Flag*, 51st Congress, 1st Session (1890). Cited in Robert Corn-Revere, "Implementing a Flag-Desecration Amendment to the U.S. Constitution," *First Amendment Center: First Reports* (vol. 6, no. 1, July 2005), at p. 8.

6. Corn-Revere is a noted First Amendment lawyer who, among other things, successfully argued *United States v. Playboy Entertainment Group* (2000) and thereafter, in 2003, authored a petition to Governor George E. Pataki of New York to posthumously pardon the comedian Lenny Bruce, which Pataki did.

7. Corn-Revere (2005), at p. 9.

8. It is a sign of our times that the commercial exploitation of the flag is no longer seen, by and large, as socially objectionable.

9. Justice Holmes was a part of that majority. Justice Peckham dissented.

10. 205 U.S. 34, 41.

11. Goldstein, *Flag Burning and Free Speech*, at p. 11.

12. Although seven people were initially arrested, one of the defendants, Sarah Cutler, was acquitted after testifying she was merely a visitor to the camp.

13. The state appeals court reversed Judge Charles Allison's judgments against the defendants in all cases except Stromberg's, whose petition to the state supreme court was denied.

14. "State Red Flag Law Supported," *Los Angeles Times*, July 1, 1930, sec. A, p. 1.

15. Cited in "Editorial of the Day," *Chicago Daily News*, December 5, 1929, p. 14.
16. 283 U.S. 359, 369.
17. Charles Haynes et al., *First Freedoms* (2006).
18. Due to a printer's error, the Gobitas family name is misspelled in legal records.
19. 310 U.S. 586, 596.
20. Victor W. Rotnem and F. G. Folson, "Recent Restrictions upon Religious Liberty" (1942), at p. 1053.
21. Sidney Fine, *Frank Murphy: The Washington Years* (1984), at p. 187.
22. At that time, students did not cover their hearts; instead, they raised their right arm out stiffly in front of them, making the act of pledging allegiance to the American flag very much resemble the Nazi fascist salute.
23. In 1945, President Harry Truman appointed Jackson to serve as U.S. chief of counsel for the prosecution of Nazi war criminals. Jackson took a leave of absence from the Supreme Court to do so.
24. 319 U. S. 624, 638.
25. In *Barnette*, the Court established that students have a First Amendment right to opt out of the Pledge of Allegiance. But conflicts were far from over. On Flag Day, 1954, eleven years after the *Barnette* decision, Congress changed the phrase "one nation indivisible" to "one nation, under God, indivisible." As Charles Haynes has written in *First Freedoms*:

    Anxious to distinguish atheistic communism from the United States, many in Congress sought to reaffirm what they believed were the religious roots of the nation. A congressional report accompanying the "under God" legislation stated that "from the time of our earliest history our people and our institutions have reflected the traditional concept that our nation was founded on a fundamental belief in God." Over the years, some civil liberties groups and others have objected to "under God" in the Pledge as a violation of the establishment clause of the First Amendment. But not until 2002 did a court agree. In June of that year, a three-judge panel of the Ninth Circuit Court of Appeals ruled that the 1954 law was unconstitutional. The case was brought by Michael Newdow, a California atheist, who sued because he did not want his elementary school–age daughter subjected to what he saw as state-imposed religion. On appeal to the U.S. Supreme Court, *Elk Grove Unified School District v. Newdow* focused solely on whether or not the recitation of the Pledge of Allegiance in public schools violates the establishment clause of the First Amendment. Once again, the Court issued its opinion on Flag Day—June 14, 2004. Without ruling on the constitutional question, the Court held that Newdow lacked standing to bring the case because the child's mother had primary legal custody and could make final decisions involving the child. By deciding not to decide, the Supreme Court left the door open to future establishment clause challenges to the Pledge of Allegiance.

26. Erwin Chemerinsky, *Constitutional Law* (1997), at p. 868.
27. *United States v. O'Brien*, 391 U.S. 367, 370 (1968).
28. 376 F.2d 538 (1st Cir., 1967). The First Circuit also felt that the section of the Training and Service Act used to indict O'Brien—the section that had been amended in 1965—imposed a separate requirement that obligated registrants to keep their certificates in their "personal possession at all times."

29. Justice William O. Douglas was the lone dissenter. Justice Thurgood Marshall did not participate in the case.

30. 391 U.S. 367, 377. In a concurring opinion, Justice Harlan suggested that an additional requirement be added—that the regulation avoid "entirely preventing a 'speaker' from reaching a significant audience with whom he could not lawfully communicate." *Ibid* at 389 (Harlan, J.)

31. *Ibid*. at 383. Warren grounded the Court's belief in the principle of constitutional adjudication by quoting a 1904 opinion, *McCray v. United States*: "The decisions of this court from the beginning lend no support whatever to the assumption that the judiciary may restrain the exercise of lawful power on the assumption that a wrongful purpose or motive has caused the power to be exerted."

32. Daniel Farber, *The First Amendment* (1998), at p. 26. As Barron and Dienes explain it, a "content-based regulation involves government regulation of expression based on what is being said—the content of the message." By contrast, a content-neutral regulation "involves restrictions which may burden First Amendment expression but without regard to the message being communicated." *First Amendment Law in a Nutshell* (2000), at pp. 250–254.

33. Jerome Barron and Thomas C. Dienes, *First Amendment Law in a Nutshell* (2000), at p. 251.

34. Laurence Tribe, *American Constitutional Law* (2n ed., 1988), sect. 12-7.

35. "Decision Shocks O'Brien," *New York Times*, May 28, 1968, p. 32.

36. "Who Owns the Stars and Stripes?," *Time*, June 6, 1970.

37. *Street v. New York*, 394 U.S. 576, 579 (1969).

38. *Saving Old Glory* (1995), at p. 103.

39. *Street v. New York*, 20 N. Y. 2d 231, 229 N. E. 2d 187 (1967).

40. The Court's second most junior member, Abe Fortas, failed to receive confirmation from the Senate after being nominated to succeed Earl Warren as chief justice, largely because his nomination sparked a broad-scale attack on the perceived liberalism of the Warren Court. Fortas remained on the Court, however, until May 14, 1969.

41. Quoted in *Saving Old Glory*, at p. 104.

42. *Ibid.*, at p. 105.

43. According to Goldstein in *Flag Burning and Free Speech* (2000), at p. 107, it was really a seven-to-two majority, since Justice Douglas abstained at the Court conference, "apparently for tactical reasons, although his papers deposited at the Library of Congress make clear he strongly favored the preliminary majority view."

44. Laura Kalman, *Abe Fortas: A Biography* (1990), at p. 286.

45. *Street*, 394 U.S. 576, 581.

46. *Ibid*. at 604 (Warren, C.J., dissenting).

47. *Ibid*. at 610 (White, J., dissenting).

48. *Ibid*. (Black, J., dissenting).

49. Robert Justin Goldstein, *Flag Burning and Free Speech* (2000), at p. 39.

50. A quarter of a century later, Fred Graham served as the chief anchor and managing editor of COURT TV.

51. See Robert Goldstein, editor, *Desecrating the American Flag* (1996), at p. 96.

52. *The Supreme Court in Conference* (Dell Dickson, ed., 2001), at pp. 349–350.

53. A year before the *Radich* case, House minority leader (and future U.S. president) Gerald Ford unsuccessfully attempted to impeach the sitting Justice Douglas.

54. Three years after *Radich v. New York*, a federal district court quashed Radich's conviction in *United States ex rel Radich v. Criminal Court* (S.D.N.Y., 1974).

55. Powell was Black's successor on the Court. Black died on September 25, 1971.

56. *Smith*, 415 U.S. 566, 602–603.

57. *Spence v. Washington*, 418 U.S. 405, 406 (1974).

58. *Ibid.* at p. 410.

59. *First Amendment Law in a Nutshell* (2004), at p. 249.

60. Chemerinsky, *Constitutional Law*, at p. 868.

61. Post, who has written extensively on the First Amendment, became the dean of Yale Law School in 2009. During the 1978–79 Court term, he was a law clerk to Justice Brennan.

62. Robert Post, "Recuperating First Amendment Doctrine," 47 *Stanford Law Review* 1249 (1995). Because of the confusion generated by the *Spence* test, Barron and Dienes, in *First Amendment Law in a Nutshell* (2000), report that the Court "has vacillated in using the test" in the years since.

63. Goldstein *Flag Burning and Free Speech*, at pp. 41–42.

64. Goldstein reports further that prosecutions took place in at least five of the incidents, "and as a result almost a dozen people spent a total of about ten years in jail for actions the Supreme Court would ultimately declare in *Texas v. Johnson* (1989) were protected by the First Amendment." *Ibid.* at p. 30.

65. Cited in Goldstein, *Flag Burning and Free Speech*, at p. 47.

66. *Ibid.*

67. *Ibid.* at pp. 50–52.

68. *Ibid.* at p. 56.

69. Speaking about the case years later, trial judge John Hendrik admitted to Goldstein that, in large part because he worked in a state where judges were elected, he never considered declaring the state law to be unconstitutional. "There's no doubt," he said, "any judge who's elected would have to think long and hard" about making such a political statement." Hendrik added that most of the judges he knows "regularly pay attention" to public opinion and either "give it a whole lot of weight or not depending upon how courageous they are or how strong they feel about the individual position." *Ibid.* at p. 46.

70. *Ibid.* at p. 65.

71. Al Kamen,"Emotional Disputes Flare Over Flag Desecration," *Washington Post*, March 19, 1989, sec. A, p. 9.

72. Cited in Goldstein, *Flag Burning and Free Speech*, at pp. 88–89.

73. Cited in, *Flag Burning and Free Speech*, at p. 83.

74. Today, David Cole is a noted author and a professor of law at Georgetown University.

75. Goldstein, *Flag Burning and Free Speech*, at pp. 86–87.

76. Linda Greenhouse, "Justices, 5–4, Back Protesters' Right to Burn the Flag," *New York Times*, June 22, 1989, sec. A, p. 1. Greenhouse is a Pulitzer Prize –winning reporter who covered the Court for nearly three decades for the *New York Times*. Currently, she is a senior fellow at Yale Law School.

77. 491 U.S. 397, 409.
78. *Ibid.* at p. 421 (Kennedy, J.).
79. *Ibid.* at p. 435 (Rehnquist, C.J.).
80. *Ibid.* at p. 439 (Stevens, J.).
81. Chemerinsky, *Constitutional Law: Principles and Policies* (3rd ed., 2006), at p. 1067.
82. Jerome Barron & Thomas C. Dienes *First Amendment Law in a Nutshell* (2008), at pp. 255–260.
83. 491 U.S. at 420.
84. Cited in Goldstein, *Flag Burning and Free Speech*, at pp. 111–112.
85. Later, then Senator Biden, now vice president, filed an amicus brief in the Supreme Court in the case of *United States v. Eichman* (1990). The brief supported the position of the Appellant.
86. Goldstein, *Flag Burning and Free Speech*, at p. 115.
87. If Congress is in session, and the president either fails to sign a piece of legislation passed by both houses of Congress—or fails to veto it within ten working days of its transmission to him—the bill becomes law anyway.
88. Goldstein, *Flag Burning and Free Speech*, at p. 148.
89. Cited in Rod Smolla, *Free Speech in an Open Society* (1992), at p. 90.
90. Goldstein, *Flag Burning and Free Speech*, at pp. 172–173.
91. *Ibid.* at p. 179.
92. In the 1990s Kenneth Starr, a former court of appeals judge and solicitor general, and current president of Baylor University, served as the independent counsel who investigated the alleged misconduct of President Clinton, including alleged sexual misconduct with Monica Lewinsky and other women. Starr later successfully argued *Morse v. Frederick* (2008), a student expression case (see chapter 10). He represented the school district. In 1975, he served as a law clerk to Chief Justice Burger.
93. That brief was coauthored with John G. Roberts, the current chief justice of the United States.
94. All nine justices agreed to take the appeal; four (Blackmun, Brennan, Marshall, and Stevens) voted to affirm the lower court rulings without any further proceedings, while five (Kennedy, O'Connor, Rehnquist, Scalia, and White) chose to request legal briefs and hear oral argument.
95. Linda Greenhouse. "High Court to Rule Quickly on Flag-burning Law," *New York Times*, March 31, 1990, p. 1.
96. 496 U.S. 310, 317.
97. *Ibid.* at 323–324 (Steves, J.).
98. Linda Greenhouse, "Supreme Court Voids Flag Law; Stage Set for Amendment Battle," *New York Times*, June 12, 1990, at p. A1.
99. "Flag-protection group vows continued fight," www.firstamendmentcenter.org/news.aspx?id=17082 (Associated Press, June 28, 2006).

CHAPTER 10

1. Karen Bouffard, "Student gets sent home over his anti-Bush T-shirt," *Detroit News*, February 19, 2003.
2. Bretton Barber, "One Year Ago: Notes from a Student Activist." Posted on www.yfen.org. Accessed on October 29, 2004.

3. Tamar Lewin, "High School Tells Student to Remove Antiwar Shirt," *New York Times*, February 26, 2003.

4. Quoted in John W. Johnson, *The Struggle for Student Rights* (1997), at p. 38.

5. *Ibid.* at p. 5.

6. Charles Haynes, et al., *First Freedoms* (2006), at p. 86.

7. *Ibid.*

8. As mentioned in chapter 9, Justice Jackson's famous language in the flag salute case of *West Virginia v. Barnette* (1943) provided that students have some level of First Amendment protection, but the Court did not provide a test or explain when school officials couldn't punish students for their expression.

9. *First Freedoms*, at p. 86.

10. One of the arm-bands is on display at the Newseum in Washington, D.C.

11. Leah Farish, *Tinker v. Des Moines: Student Protest* (1997), at p. 13.

12. Doreen Rappaport, *Tinker v. Des Moines: Student Rights on Trial* (1994), at p. 62.

13. *Ibid.*

14. *Ibid.*

15. *Ibid.*

16. Cited in John W. Johnson, *The Struggle for Student Rights* (University Press of Kansas, 1997), at p. 53.

17. The Tinker family's attorney, Dan Johnston, asked for nominal damages because he thought the passage of time might erode the significance of the issues in his case. In other words, by the time the case could be settled, the students might have graduated, or decided they were no longer interested in wearing an arm-band in protest. Hence, he added the count for nominal damages to ensure that the case could not be declared "moot."

18. Burnside v. Byars, 363 F. 2d 744—(5th Cir. 1966).

19. In February 1966, Judge Stephenson found a former University of Iowa student guilty of a federal charge of mutilating his draft card.

20. *Tinker v. Des Moines Independent Community School District*, 258 F.Supp. 971 (1966).

21. Abe Fortas, *Concerning Dissent and Civil Disobedience* (1968), at p. 86.

22. *Ibid.* at pp. 88–89.

23. Roger K. Newman, *Hugo Black: A Biography* (1994), at pp. 593–594.

24. Transcript of oral argument. Cited in Peter Irons, ed. *Courts, Kids and the Constitution* (2000), at pp. 24–25.

25. The two in question were also from the Tinker family—their ten-year-old sister and eight-year-old brother. Since the policy did not extend to the elementary schools, no disciplinary action was taken.

26. Cited in Peter Irons, ed., at pp. 28–31.

27. Dell Dickson, ed. *The Supreme Court in Conference* (2001), at pp. 337–338.

28. Abe Fortas, *Concerning Dissent and Civil Disobedience*, at p. 93.

29. *Tinker v. Des Moines Independent Community School District*, 393 U.S. 503, 512 (1969).

30. 393 U.S. at 514.

31. 393 U.S. at 525 (Black, J. dissenting).

32. Laura Kalman, *Abe Fortas: A Biography* (1990), at p. 290.

33. Surprisingly, the liberal justice William Brennan joined in the judgment of the Court.

34. *Bethel School Dist. No. 403 v. Fraser*, 478 U.S. 675, 686 (1986).

35. 478 U.S. at 682.

36. *Broussard v. School Board of the City of Norfolk*, 801 F. Supp. 1526 (E.D. Virg. 1992).

37. *Hazelwood School District v. Kuhlmeier*, 484 U.S. 260, 268 (1988).

38. Further, the Court ruled that "a school must be able to set high standards for the student speech that is disseminated under its auspices—standards that may be higher than those demanded by some newspaper publishers or theatrical producers in the 'real world.'" In addition, the ruling contains broad language on what type of speech school officials may censor, including any speech that might "associate the school with any position other than neutrality on matters of political controversy." The Court then defined school-sponsored expression equally broadly, including "school-sponsored publications, theatrical productions, and other expressive activities that students, parents and members of the public might reasonably perceive to bear the imprimatur of the school…whether or not they occur in a traditional classroom setting, so long as they are supervised by faculty members and designed to impart particular knowledge or skills to student participants and audiences." 484 U.S. at 271–272.

39. *Hazelwood School District v. Kuhlmeier* 484 U.S. 260, 287 (1988), (Brennan, J. dissenting).

40. The banner is currently on display at the Newseum in Washington, D.C.

41. See *Harlow v. Fitzgerald*, 457 U.S. 800 (1982).

42. *Morse v. Frederick*, 551 U.S. 393 (2007). Many amicus briefs—from both liberal and conservative groups—had urged the Court to constrain the ability of school officials to censor any student speech deemed controversial.

43. *Morse v. Frederick*, 551 U.S. 393 (2007), Alito, J. concurring.

44. *Ibid.* (Breyer, J. concurring in the judgment in part and dissenting in part).

45. *Ibid.* (Thomas, J. concurring).

46. Bretton Barber, "One Year Ago: Notes from a Student Activist." Posted on www.yfen. org. Accessed on October 29, 2004.

Epilogue

1. *See, e.g.,* his concurrence in *Smith v. California* (1959), and his dissent in *Ginsburg v. United States* (1966). In *Ginsburg* Black wrote: "For myself I would follow the course which I believe is required by the First Amendment, that is, recognize that sex at least as much as any other aspect of life is so much a part of our society that its discussion should not be made a crime." 383 U.S. 463, 481 (Black, J., dissenting).

2. Among other things, Friendly worked with the famed Edward R. Murrow to create *See It Now*, a news magazine show that won four Emmy Awards. *See generally* Ralph Engelman and Morley Safer, *Friendlyvision: Fred Friendly and the Rise and Fall of Television Journalism* (2009).

3. Sevareid had also worked with Murrow.

4. The exchange that follows is set out in "Justice Black and the Bill of Rights: CBS News Special," 9 *Southwestern University Law Review* 937 (1977).

5. *See Cox v. Louisiana* (1965) (Black, J., concurring & dissenting in part).

6. *See Hill v. Colorado* (2000) (restrictions on approaching patients within one hundred feet of an abortion clinic or other health-care facilities to hand out leaflets or display protest signs upheld); *Schenck v. Pro-Choice Network of Western New York* (1997) (no-protest "floating buffer zone" within a fifteen-foot radius of abortion clinics held to violate First Amendment); *Madsen v. Women's Health Center, Inc.* (three-hundred-foot buffer zone around staff residences of abortion providers struck down on First Amendment grounds); *Carey v. Brown* (1980) (statute prohibiting picketing in front of residences struck down on equal protection grounds).

7. William O. Douglas, *Points of Rebellion* (1969), at pp. 5–6.

8. A question was also raised about the justice's pre-Court ties to the Klan. That segment was edited out.

9. Editorial, "In the Nation: How Far Does Free Speech Go?" *New York Times*, December 5, 1968, p. 46.

10. Charles A. Reich, "Mr. Justice Black and the Living Constitution," 76 *Harvard Law Review* 673 (1963).

11. *The Greening of America*, at pp. 13–14.

12. *Ibid.* at p. 14.

13. Quoted in Roger K. Newman, *Hugo Black: A Biography* (1994), at p. 599.

14. Thomas Emerson was a young associate in Walter Pollak's law firm. Pollak was one of the lawyers who represented Benjamin Gitlow in the Supreme Court (see chapter 2).

15. We refer to Justice Alito's concurrence in *Morse v. Frederick* (2008), wherein he wrote: "I join the opinion of the Court on the understanding that (a) it goes no further than to hold that a public school may restrict speech that a reasonable observer would interpret as advocating illegal drug use and (b) it provides no support for any restriction of speech that can plausibly be interpreted as commenting on any political or social issue, including speech on issues such as 'the wisdom of the war on drugs or of legalizing marijuana for medicinal use." 551 U.S. 393 (2007).

16. *West Virginia State Board of Education v. Barnette*, 319 U.S. 624, 642 (1943).

17. *The First Amendment, Democracy and Romance* (1990), at p. 169.

18. *Death Comes for the Archbishop* (reprint, 2008), at p. 205.

Sources

CHAPTER 1. FEAR AND FREEDOM

Baird v. State Bar of Arizona, 401 U.S. 1 (1971).
Barenblatt v. United States, 360 U.S. 109 (1959).
Dennis v. United States, 341 U.S. 494 (1951) (Black, J., dissenting).
In re Anastaplo, 366 U.S. 82 (1961) (Black, J., dissenting).
In re Anastaplo, 18 Ill.2d 182, 163 N.E.2d 429 (1959).
In re Anastaplo, 3 Ill.2d 471, 121 N.E.2d 826 (1954).
In re Stolar, 401 U.S. 23 (1971).
Konigsberg v. State Bar, 353 U.S. 252 (1957).
Konigsberg v. State Bar, 366 U.S. 36 (1961) (Black, J., dissenting).
Law Students Civil Rights Research Council v. Wadmond, 401 U.S. 154 (1971).
Schware v. Board of Bar Examiners, 352 U.S. 232 (1957).
Speiser v. Randall, 357 U.S. 513 (1958).
Wilkinson v. United States, 365 U.S. 399 (1961).

Anastaplo, George. *Human Being and Citizen: Essays on Virtue, Freedom and the Common Good* (Chicago: Swallow Press, 1975).
——— . *The Constitutionalist* (Dallas: Southern Methodist University Press, 1971).
Black, Hugo Lafayette. *A Constitutional Faith* (New York: Knopf, 1968).
Dunne, Gerald. *Hugo Black and the Judicial Revolution* (New York: Simon and Schuster, 1977).
Kalven, Harry, Jr. *A Worthy Tradition: Free Speech in America*, edited by Jamie Kalven (New York: Harper and Row, 1988).
Magee, James. *Mr. Justice Black: Absolutist on the Court* (Charlottesville: University of Virginia Press, 1980).
Newman, Roger K. *Hugo Black: A Biography* (New York: Pantheon, 1994).

Anastaplo, George. "Mr. Justice Black, His Generous Common Sense, and the Bar Admission Cases," 9 *Southwestern University Law Review* 977 (1977).
Black, Hugo L. "The Bill of Rights," 35 *New York University Law Review* 865 (1960).
——— ."Justice Black and First Amendment 'Absolutes': A Public Interview," 37 *New York University Law Review* 549 (1962).

Collins, Ronald. Book Review Essay on George Anastaplo, *Human Being and Citizen,* 50 *Southern California Law Review* 337 (1977).

Dillard, Irving. "Mr. Justice Black and *In Re Anastaplo,*" 9 *Southwestern University Law Review* 953 (1977).

Grumman, Cornelia. "Wrong Question," *Chicago Tribune Magazine,* November 26, 2000, p. 14. *Memorial Address and Other Tributes in the Congress of the United States on the Life and Contributions of Hugo LaFayette Black* (Washington, D.C., 92nd Congress, First Session, 1972).

Stevens, John Paul. "The Freedom of Speech," 102 *Yale Law Journal* 1293 (1993).

Chapter 2. "Everybody Is against the Reds"

Adamson v. California, 332 U.S. 46 (1947).

Fiske v. Kansas, 274 U.S. 380 (1927).

Gilbert v. Minnesota, 254 U.S. 325 (1920).

Gitlow v. New York, 268 U.S. 652 (1925).

Palko v. Connecticut, 302 U.S. 319 (1937).

People v. Gitlow, 195 A.D. 773, 187 N.Y.S. 783 (N.Y. App. Div., 1921).

People v. Gitlow, 234 N.Y. 132, 136 N.E. 317 (New York: 1922).

Pierce v. United States, 255 U.S. 398 (1921).

Powell v. Alabama, 287 U.S. 45 (1932) (Scottsboro case).

Prudential Insurance Company v. Cheek, 259 U.S. 530 (1922).

Stromberg v. California, 283 U.S. 359 (1931).

Whitney v. California, 274 U.S. 357 (1927).

Amar, Akhil Reed. *The Bill of Rights* (New Haven, Conn.: Yale University Press, 2000).

Baker, Liva. *The Justice from Beacon Hill* (New York: HarperCollins, 1991).

Blanchard, Margaret. *Revolutionary Sparks: Freedom of Expression in Modern America* (New York: Oxford University Press, 1992).

Brant, Irving. *The Bill of Rights: Its Origin and Meaning* (New York: New American Library, 1965).

Chafee, Zechariah, Jr. *Free Speech in the United States* (New York: Atheneum, 1969).

Cogan, Neil. *The Complete Bill of Rights: The Drafts, Debates, Sources, and Origins* (Oxford: Oxford University Press, 1997).

Cushman, Clare, ed. *The Supreme Court Justices: Illustrated Biographies, 1789–1995,* 2nd ed. (Washington, D.C.: Congressional Quarterly, 1995).

Emerson, Thomas I. *The System of Freedom of Expression* (New York: Vintage, 1970).

Feldman, Stephen M. *Free Expression and Democracy in America* (Chicago: University of Chicago Press, 2009).

Finan, Christopher M. *From the Palmer Raids to the Patriot Act: A History of the Fight for Free Speech in America* (New York: Houghton Mifflin, 2007).

Fried, Albert. *Communism in America: A History in Documents* (New York: Columbia University Press, 1997).

Gitlow, Benjamin. *I Confess: The Truth about American Communism* (New York: Dutton, 1939).

———. *The Whole of Their Lives: Communism in America* (New York: Scribner's, 1948).

Hall, Kermit, ed. *The Oxford Companion to the Supreme Court of the United States* (New York: Oxford University Press, 1992).

Kaufman, Andrew L. *Cardozo* (Cambridge, Mass.: Harvard University Press, 1998).

Lawes, Lewis E. *Life and Death in Sing Sing* (New York: Doubleday, Doran, 1928).

——— . *Twenty Thousand Years in Sing Sing* (New York: Ray Long and Richard Smith, 1932).

Levy, Leonard W. *Emergence of a Free Press* (New York: Oxford University Press, 1985).

——— . *Origins of the Bill of Rights* (New Haven, Conn.: Yale University Press, 1999).

Mennel, Robert M., and Compston, Christine L., eds. *Holmes and Frankfurter: Their Correspondence, 1912–1934* (Hanover, NH: University of New Hampshire Press, 1996).

Murphy, Paul L. *The Constitution in Crisis Times: 1918–1969* (New York: Harper and Row, 1972).

Posner, Richard, ed. *The Essential Holmes: Selections from Letters, Speeches, Judicial Opinions, and Other Writings of Oliver Wendell Holmes, Jr.* (Chicago: University of Chicago Press, 1992).

Rabban, David M. *Free Speech in Its Forgotten Years* (New York: Cambridge University Press, 1997).

Tierney, Kevin. *Darrow: A Biography* (New York: Crowell, 1979).

Wagman, Robert J. *The First Amendment Book* (New York: Pharos Books, 1991).

Weinberg, Arthur and Lila. *Clarence Darrow: A Sentimental Rebel* (New York: Putnam, 1980).

"Benjamin Gitlow: 1891–1965," in *Dictionary of American Biography*, supp. 7: 1961–1965 (American Council of Learned Societies, 1981).

Chafee, Zechariah, Jr. "Walter Heilprin Pollak," *Nation*, October 12, 1940, pp. 318–319.

Hale, Swinburne. "Criminal Anarchy," 21 *New Republic* 270 (January 28, 1920).

Josephson, Harold. "Political Justice during the Red Scare: The Trial of Benjamin Gitlow," in *American Political Trials*, edited by Michal R. Belknap (Westport, Conn.: Greenwood Press, 1981).

Linde, Hans A. "Courts and Censorship," 66 *Minnesota Law Review* 171 (1981).

Pollak, Louis H. "Advocating Civil Liberties: A Young Lawyer before the Old Court," 17 *Harvard Civil Rights-Civil Liberties Law Review* 1 (1982).

"Pollak." In *The Dictionary of American Biography*, vol. 22, supp. 2 (New York: 1958), pp. 534–535.

Stevens, John Paul. "The Freedom of Speech," 102 *Yale Law Journal* 1293 (1993).

"Palmer and Family Safe," *New York Times*, June 3, 1919, p. 1.

"Red Bombs Palmer's House; Dies Himself; Family Is Not Injured," *Washington Post*, June 3, 1919, p. 1.

"Attempt to Terrorize Has Failed, Says Palmer," *Washington Post*, June 4, 1919, p. 1.

"Flynn Prepares Big Haul of Reds," *New York Times*, June 19, 1919, p. 13.

"Reds in Garden Urge Revolution and Soviets Here," *New York Times*, June 21, 1919, p. 1.

"Socialists Assail Left Wing Party, *New York Times*, June 24, 1919, p. 5.

"Nation-wide Bomb Plot Unearthed," *New York Times*, October 30, 1919, p. 1.

"Larkin and Gitlow Held," *New York Times*, November 11, 1919, p. 1.

"Drastic Penalties Planned for Reds," *New York Times*, November 12, 1919, p. 1.

"A Terrorist Plot," *Washington Post*, November 21, 1919, p. 6.

"Gitlow Convicted in Anarchy Trial," *New York Times*, February 6, 1920, p. 17.

"A Criminal Anarchist," *New York Times*, February 7, 1920, p. 10.

"A Real Menace," *Washington Post*, February 8, 1920, p. 24.

"Gitlow, Anarchist, Gets Limit Sentence," *New York Times*, February 12, 1920, p. 15.

"Gitlow's Anarchy Sentence Affirmed," *New York Times*, April 21, 1921, p. 4.

"Communists Name Gitlow for Mayor," *New York Times*, August 27, 1921, p. 4.

"Gitlow Wins Plea for Liberty on Bail," *New York Times*, April 23, 1922, p. 5.

"Gitlow Is Paroled on Second Charge," *New York Times*, April 27, 1922, p. 7.

"Gitlow and Larkin Must Serve Terms," *New York Times*, July 13, 1922, p. 19.

"Larkin Pardoned, Leaves Sing Sing; Others May Follow," *New York Times*, January 18, 1923, p. 1.

"'Free Speech' Case Up in the Supreme Court," *New York Times*, November 24, 1923, p. 3.

"Gitlow Loses Fight in Highest Court to Annul Anarchy Law," *New York Times*, June 9, 1925, p. 1.

"The Gitlow Decision," *Washington Star*, June 9, 1925.

"The Gitlow Case," *New Republic*, July 1, 1925.

"Gitlow Is Pardoned by Governor Smith as Punished Enough," *New York Times*, December 12, 1925, p. 1.

"Gitlow, Set Free, Rejoins Radicals," *New York Times*, December 13, 1925, p. 18.

"W. H. Pollak Dies; Leader at Bar, 53," *New York Times*, October 3, 1940, p. 25.

"Black's Practice Upheld by Judges," *New York Times*, May 15, 1947, p. 28.

"Board Overrules Reds' Challenge," *New York Times*, April 24, 1951, p. 13.

"Soviet Set Up Here in '21, Gitlow Says," *New York Times*, April 25, 1951, p. 14.

"$50 Per Day Paid Ex-Communist as U.S. Witness," *Washington Post*, May 11, 1951, p. 16.

"Registration of Communists Up Monday," *Washington Post*, September 9, 1951, p. 2.

"Heated Exchanges Mark Final Hearing to Record U.S. Reds as Stalin-Bossed," *Washington Post*, January 8, 1953, p. 2.

"2 Rabbis Denounce Red Label on Wise," *New York Times*, September 14, 1953, p. 2.

"Benjamin Gitlow Is Dead at 73," *New York Times*, July 20, 1965, p. 33.

"Benjamin Gitlow, 74," *Washington Post*, July 21, 1965, sec. C, p. 4.

CHAPTER 3. CALLING DR. MEIKLEJOHN

Abrams v. United States, 250 U.S. 616 (1919).

Cohen v. California, 403 U.S. 12 (1971).

Dennis v. United States, 341 U.S. 494 (1951).

Garrison v. Louisiana, 379 U.S. 64 (1964).

Landmark Communications, Inc. v. Virginia, 435 U.S. 829 (1978).

Milk Wagon Drivers Union v. Meadowmoor Dairies, Inc., 312 U.S. 287 (1941).

Parker et al v. City of Los Angeles, 338 U.S. 327 (1949).

Procunier v. Martinez, 416 U.S. 396 (1974).

Baker, C. Edwin. *Human Liberty and Freedom of Speech* (New York: Oxford University Press, 1989).

Barron, Jerome, and C. Thomas Dienes. *First Amendment Law*, 4th ed. (St. Paul: West Group, 2008).

Bollinger, Lee C. *The Tolerant Society* (New York: Oxford University Press, 1986).

Brown, Cynthia Stokes, ed. *Alexander Meiklejohn: Teacher of Freedom* (Berkeley: Meiklejohn Civil Liberties Institute, 1981).

Canavan, Francis. *Freedom of Expression: Purpose as Limit* (Durham, N.C.: Carolina Academic Press, 1984).

Chafee, Zechariah, Jr. *Free Speech in the United States* (Cambridge, Mass.: Harvard University Press, 1941).

Emerson, Thomas I. *The System of Freedom of Expression* (1970).

Farber, Daniel A. *The First Amendment* (New York: Foundation Press, 1998).

Feldman, Stephen M. *Free Expression and Democracy in America* (Chicago: University of Chicago Press, 2009).

Garvey, John H. and Schauer, Frederick, eds. *The First Amendment: A Reader*, 2nd ed. (St. Paul: West Group, 1996).

Gunther, Gerald. *Learned Hand: The Man and the Judge* (New York: Knopf, 1994).

Hill, Walker H., ed. *Learning and Living. Proceedings of an Anniversary Celebration in Honor of Alexander Meiklejohn, Chicago, May 8–10, 1942* (Chicago: W. H. Hill, 1942).

Hirsch, H. N. *The Enigma of Felix Frankfurter* (New York: Basic Books, 1981).

Meiklejohn, Alexander. *Free Speech and Its Relation to Self-Government* (New York: Harper, 1948).

———. *Political Freedom: The Constitutional Powers of the People* (New York: Oxford University Press, 1965).

———. *What Does America Mean?* (New York: Norton, 1935).

Mill, John Stuart. *On Liberty*, edited by David Bromwich and George Kateb (New Haven, Conn.: Yale University Press, 2003).

Milton, John. *Areopagitica*, with commentary by Sir Richard C. Jebb (Cambridge: Cambridge University Press, 1918).

Nelson, Adam R. *Education and Democracy: The Meaning of Alexander Meiklejohn, 1872–1964* (Madison: University of Wisconsin Press, 2001).

Newman, Roger K. *Hugo Black: A Biography* (New York: Pantheon, 1994).

Redish, Martin. *Freedom of Expression: A Critical Analysis* (Lexis Law, 1984).

Schauer, Frederick. *Free Speech: A Philosophical Inquiry* (New York: Oxford University Press, 1982).

Shiffrin, Steven. *The First Amendment, Democracy, and Romance* (Cambridge, Mass.: Harvard University Press, 1990).

Smith, Donald L. *Zechariah Chafee, Jr.: Defender of Liberty and Law* (Cambridge, Mass.: Harvard University Press, 1986).

Smolla, Rodney. *Smolla and Nimmer on Freedom of Speech* (New York: Matthew Bender, 1994).

Sunstein, Cass. *Democracy and the Problem of Free Speech* (New York: Free Press, 1993).

Tribe, Laurence. *American Constitutional Law*, 2nd ed. (Mineola, N.Y.: Foundation Press, 1988).

Zuckman, Harvey, Corn-Revere, Robert, et al. *Modern Communication Law* (St. Paul: West Group, 1999).

Baker, C. Edwin. "Scope of the First Amendment Freedom of Speech," 25 *U.C.L.A. Law Review* 964 (1978).

BeVier, Lillian R. "The First Amendment and Political Speech," 30 *Stanford Law Review* 316 (1978).

Blasi, Vincent. "The Checking Value in First Amendment Theory," 1977 *American Bar Foundation Research Journal* 521.

Bork, Robert. "Neutral Principles and the First Amendment," 47 *Indiana Law Review* 1 (1971).

Brennan, William J., Jr. "The Supreme Court and the Meiklejohn Interpretation of the First Amendment," 79 *Harvard Law Review* 1 (1965).

Chafee, Zechariah, Jr. Book Review, 62 *Harvard Law Review* 891 (1949).

Emerson, Thomas. "Toward a General Theory of the First Amendment," 72 *Yale Law Journal* 877 (1963).

Holmes, Oliver Wendell. "Natural Law," 32 *Harvard Law Review* 40 (1918).

Kalven, Harry, Jr. "Mr. Alexander Meiklejohn and the *Barenblatt* Opinion," 27 *University of Chicago Law Review* 315 (1960).

———. "The *New York Times* Case: A Note on 'The Central Meaning of the First Amendment,'" 1964 *Supreme Court Review* 191.

Kauper, Paul. Book Review, 58 *Michigan Law Review* 619 (1960).

Meiklejohn, Alexander. "The Balancing of Self-Preservation against Political Freedom," 49 *California Law Review* 4 (1961).

———. "The First Amendment and Evils That Congress Has a Right to Prevent," 26 *Indiana Law Review* 477 (1951).

———. "The First Amendment Is an Absolute," 1961 *Supreme Court Review* 1.

———. "Freedom to Hear," *Lawyers Guild Review*, 1950, p. 26.

———. "What Does the First Amendment Mean?" 20 *University of Chicago Law Review* 461 (1953).

"Sees Test for America: Amherst President Says Our Democracy Is Only at Beginning," *New York Times*, January 21, 1923, p. 6.

"Amherst in Clash over Meiklejohn," *New York Times*, June 15, 1923, p. 1.

"Amherst Dispute Divides Faculty," *New York Times*, June 16, 1923, p. 2.

"Meiklejohn Meets with Trustees Today," *New York Times*, June 18, 1923, p. 3.

"Expect Meiklejohn Will Resign Today," *New York Times*, June 19, 1923, p. 1.

"Meiklejohn Quits Amherst: Trustees Urge Retirement," *Washington Post*, June 20, 1923, p. 1.

"Meiklejohn Resigns Amherst Leadership, Gets Year's Leave," *New York Times*, June 20, 1923, p. 1.

"Meiklejohn Defiant, Urges Amherst Men to Abolish Trustees," *New York Times*, June 21, 1923, p. 1.

"Meiklejohn Stirring Figure in American College Life," *New York Times*, June 24, 1923, sect. XXX, p. 3.

Alexander Meiklejohn. "A New College with a New Idea," *New York Times Magazine*, May 29, 1927, sec. 4, p. 1.

Alexander Meiklejohn. "In Memoriam: An Address Delivered in Boston on the Anniversary of the Execution of Sacco and Vanzetti," *New Republic*, September 5, 1928, p. 69.

Alexander Meiklejohn. "Liberty for What?" *Harper's*, August 1935, p. 364.

Florence Finch Kelly. "What America Means to Dr. Meiklejohn," *New York Times*, January 5, 1936, sec. BR, p. 3.

Editorial. "Abridging Freedom," *New York Times*, July 18, 1948, sec. E, p. 8.

Alexander Meiklejohn. " 'Everything Worth Saying Should be Said,' " *New York Times Magazine*, July 18, 1948, p. 8.

Max Lerner, Book Review, *New Republic*, September 13, 1948, p. 21.

Alexander Meiklejohn. "Should Communists Be Allowed to Teach?" *New York Times Magazine*, March 27, 1949, p. 10.

"Meiklejohn Hails Rights of People," *New York Times*, May 7, 1950, p. 85.

"Dr. Meiklejohn Denounces Anti-Red Campaign as Idiocy," *Washington Post*, October 8, 1951, sec. B, p. 1.

Alexander Meiklejohn. "The Crisis in Freedom," *Progressive*, June 16, 1952, p. 15.

"Meiklejohn Hits High Court Policy," *New York Times*, Feb. 1, 1953, p. 65.

"Complaint Right Urged at Inquiry," *New York Times*, Nov. 15, 1955, p. 14.

Harold Taylor. "Meiklejohn: The Art of Making People Think," *New York Times, Magazine*, May 5, 1957, p. 243.

"Amherst Relives Meiklejohn Era," *New York Times*, June 9, 1957, p. 84.

"Gentle Iconoclast: Alexander Meiklejohn," *New York Times*, June 9, 1957, p. 84.

"Ex-Amherst Head Feted on '23 Step," *New York Times*, Nov. 3, 1957, p. 122.

"House Group Attacked: Meiklejohn Asks Abolition of Un-American Activity Unit," *New York Times*, December 17, 1957, p. 25.

Editorial. "A Plea to the House," *Washington Post*, December18, 1957, sec. A, p. 14.

Alexander Meiklejohn. Letter to the Editor. "A Plea to the House," *Washington Post*, December 18, 1957, sec. A, p. 14.

"Medals Galore," *Washington Post*, July 7, 1963, sec. E, p. 6.

"Alexander Meiklehohn, Former Amherst Head," *Washington Post*, December 18, 1964, sec. C, p. 7.

Obituary, *Washington Post*, December 18, 1964, sec. A, p. 16.

Obituary, *Nation*, December 28, 1964, p. 506.

"Tribute Planned for Meiklejohn," *Washington Post*, January 10, 1965, sec. B, p. 9.

Robert F. Levey. "Press Freedom Talks Honor Scholar," *Washington Post*, March 26, 1972, sec. D, p. 1.

CHAPTER 4. "THE FINAL JURY OF THE NATION"

Alexander v. United States, 509 U.S. 544 (1993).

Bantam Books, Inc. v. Sullivan, 372 U.S. 58 (1963).

Cox v. New Hampshire, 312 U.S. 569 (1941).

Freedman v. Maryland, 380 U.S. 51 (1965).

Gitlow v. New York, 268 U.S. 652 (1925).

Joseph Burstyn, Inc. v. Wilson, 343 U.S. 495 (1952).

Kovacs v. Cooper, 336 U.S. 77 (1949).

Lovell v. City of Griffin, 303 U.S. 444 (1938).

Madsen v. Women's Health Center, 512 U.S. 753 (1994)

National Socialist Party of America v. Village of Skokie, 432 U.S. 43 (1977).

Near v. State of Minnesota Ex Rel. Olson, 283 U.S. 697 (1931).

Nebraska Press Assn. v. Stuart, 427 U.S. 539 (1976).

New York Times Co. v. Sullivan, 376 U.S. 254 (1964).

New York Times Co. v. United States, 403 U.S. 713 (1971).

Paris Adult Theater I v. Slaton, 413 U.S. 49 (1973).

Patterson v. Colorado, 205 U.S. 454 (1907).

Pickering v. Board of Education, 391 U.S. 563 (1968).

Pittsburgh Press Co. v. Pittsburgh Commission on Human Relations, 413 U.S. 376 (1973).

Saia v. New York, 334 U.S. 558 (1948).

Schenck v. Pro-Choice Network of Western New York, 519 U.S. 357 (1997).

Shuttlesworth v. City of Birmingham, 394 U.S. 147 (1969).

Snepp v. United States, 444 U.S. 507 (1980).

Southeastern Promotions Ltd. v. Conrad, 420 U.S. 546 (1975).

Stromberg v. California, 283 U.S. 353 (1931).

Terminiello v. Chicago, 337 U.S. 1, 37 (1949).

Thomas v. Chicago Park District, 534 U.S. 316 (2002).

United States v. Macintosh, 283 U.S. 605 (1931).

United States v. New York Times Co. et al., 328 F. Supp. 324 (S.D.N.Y. 1971).

United States v. New York Times Company et al., 444 F.2d 544 (2d Cir. 1971).

United States v. Washington Post, 446 F.2d 1322 (D.C. Cir. Ct. 1971).

Vance v. Universal Amusement Co., 445 U.S. 308 (1980).

Walker v. City of Birmingham, 388 U.S. 307 (1967).

Abrams, Floyd. *Speaking Freely* (New York: Viking Press, 2005).

Barron, Jerome A., and Dienes, C. Thomas. *First Amendment Law in a Nutshell*, 4th ed. (Minneapolis: West Group, 2008).

Bickel, Alexander. *The Morality of Consent.* (New Haven, Conn.: Yale University Press, 1975).

Black, Hugo, Jr. *My Father: A Remembrance* (New York: Random House, 1975).

Blackstone, William. *Commentaries on the Law of England* (Chicago: University of Chicago Press, 1975).

Chafee, Zechariah, Jr. *Free Speech in the United States* (New York: Atheneum, 1969).

Chemerinsky, Erwin. *Constitutional Law: Principles and Policies* (Aspen, Colo.: Aspen Law and Business, 2nd ed., 2002).

Curtis, Michael Kent. *Free Speech: The People's Darling Privilege* (Durham, N.C.: Duke University Press, 2000).

Dickson, Dell, ed. *The Supreme Court in Conference (1940–1985)* (New York: Oxford University Press, 2001).

Dunne, Gerald T. *Hugo Black and the Judicial Revolution* (New York: Simon and Schuster, 1977).

Ellsberg, Daniel. *Secrets: A Memoir of Vietnam and the Pentagon Papers* (New York: Viking Press, 2002).

Emerson, Thomas I. *The System of Freedom of Expression* (New York: Vintage Books, 1970).

Farber, Daniel A. *The First Amendment: Second Edition* (New York: Foundation Press, 2003).

Fraleigh, Douglas M., and Tuman, Joseph S. *Freedom of Speech in the Marketplace of Ideas* (New York: St. Martin's Press, 1997).

Frey, Isaac Clarke. *The Memoirs of James Gordon Bennett and His Times* (New York: Stringer & Townsend, 1855).

Greenhouse, Linda. *Becoming Justice Blackmun* (New York: Times Books, 2005).

Griswold, Erwin N. *Ould Fields, New Corne: The Personal Memoirs of a Twentieth-Century Lawyer.* St. Paul: West Group, 1992).

Friendly, Fred. *Minnesota Rag.* Minneapolis: University of Minnesota Press, 1981).

Hall, Kermit, ed. *The Oxford Companion to the Supreme Court of the United States* (New York: Oxford University Press, 1992).

Levy, Leonard W. *Freedom of Speech and Press in Early American History* (New York: Harper Torchbooks, 1963).

Nagel, Robert F., ed. *Intellect and Craft: The Contributions of Justice Hans Linde to American Constitutionalism* (New York: Westview Press, 1995).

Newman, Roger K. *Hugo Black: A Biography* (New York: Pantheon Books, 1994).

Prados, John, and Porter, Margaret Pratt, eds. *Inside the Pentagon Papers.* Lawrence: University of Kansas Press, 2004).

Rudenstine, David. *The Day the Presses Stopped.* Berkeley: University of California Press, 1996).

Smolla, Rodney A. *Smolla and Nimmer on Freedom of Speech: A Treatise on the First Amendment* (New York: Times Mirror Books, 1994).

Stone, Geoffrey. *Top Secret* (Lanham, Md.: Rowman and Littlefield, 2007).

Strum, Phillipa. *When the Nazis Came to Skokie.* Lawrence: University of Kansas Press, 1999).

Tift, Susan E., and Jones, Alex S. *The Trust: The Private and Powerful Family behind the New York Times* (New York: Little Brown, 1999).

Tribe, Laurence H. *American Constitutional Law*, 2nd ed. (Mineola, N.Y.: Foundation Press, 1988).

Ungar, Sanford J. *The Papers and the Papers* (New York: Dutton, 1972).

Zinn, Howard. *A People's History of the United States: 1492–Present* (New York: HarperCollins, 1995).

Blasi, Vincent. "Toward a Theory of Prior Restraint: The Central Linkage," 66 *Minnesota Law Review* 11 (1981).

Jackson, Robert H. "Wartime Security and Liberty under Law," 1 *Buffalo Law Review* 103 (1951).

Jeffries, John Calvin, Jr. "Rethinking Prior Restraint," 92 *Yale Law Journal* 409 (1983).

Linde, Hans A. "Courts and Censorship," 66 *Minnesota Law Review* 171 (1981).

Stewart, Potter. "Or of the Press," 26 *Hastings Law Journal* 631 (1975).

"Press-gag Statute Assailed by Editor," *Washington Post*, April 19, 1929, p. 5.

"To Appeal on 'Free Press,'" *New York Times*, January 12, 1930, p. 26.

"Brandeis Criticizes Minnesota Gag Law," *New York Times*, January 31, 1931, p. 6.

"Highest Court Gets Press Liberty Case," *Washington Post*, January 31, 1931, p. 7.

"Press Gag Barred by Supreme Court; Minnesota Law Hit," *New York Times*, June 2, 1931, p. 1.

"Editor's Killers Hired by 'Reds,' Friend Charges, *Washington Post*, September 8, 1934, p. 10.

"Declares Reds Hired Guilford's Assassin," *New York Times*, September 8, 1934, p. 30.

"J. M. Near, Editor, Dies, Gag Law Case Figure," *New York Times*, April 19, 1936, sec. N, p. 10.

Hedrick Smith and Neil Sheehan. "Westmoreland Requests 206,000 More Men, Stirring Debate in Administration," *New York Times*, March 10, 1968, p. 1.

"The Covert War," *New York Times*, June 13, 1971, p. 38.

Neil Sheehan. "Vietnam Archive: Pentagon Study Traces 3 Decades of Growing U.S. Involvement," *New York Times*, June 13, 1971, p. 1.

Neil Sheehan. "Vietnam Archive: A Consensus to Bomb Developed before '64 Election, Study Says," *New York Times*, June 14, 1971, p. 1.

Frankel, Max. "Court Step Likely," *New York Times*, June 15, 1971, p. 1.

Neil Sheehan. "Vietnam Archive: Study Tells How Johnson Secretly Opened Way to Ground Combat," *es*, June 15, 1971, p. 1.

David S. Broder. "Humphrey Says He, LBJ Didn't Lie," *Washington Post*, June 17, 1971, sec. A, p. 1.

Bernard Gwertzman. "Soviet Seizes on Secret Papers to Criticize Policies of Nixon," *New York Times*, June 18, 1971, p. 15.

Stanley Karnow. "A Fundamental Question," *Washington Post*, June 19, 1971, sec. A, p. 21.

William L. Ryan. "Hanoi Evidently Knew Much about Escalation Plans," *Washington Post*, June 19, 1971, sec. A, p. 13.

Max Frankel. "A Great Test—'This, Too, Vietnam Wrought,'" *New York Times*, June 20, 1971, sec. E, p. 1.

James Reston. "Back to the Congress," *New York Times*, June 20, 1971, sec. E, p. 13.

Robert B. Semple, Jr. "Secrecy Backed," *New York Times*, June 20, 1971, p. 1.

"Study Said to Show Bomb Lulls Were Meant to 'Placate' Public," *New York Times*, June 20, 1971, p. 27.

"What They Said in Public and in Private," *New York Times*, June 20, 1971, sec. E, p. 1.

Carroll Kilpatrick. "White House Says It Aims to Back Law, Not Aid Democrats," *Washington Post*, June 20, 1971, p. 15.

Lacey Fosburgh. "Reactions Focus on Security Rules," *New York Times*, June 21, 1971, p. 1.

Hobart Rowen. "LBJ's Economic Aides Were Misled," *Washington Post*, June 23, 1971, sec. A, p. 24.

Elsie Carpenter. "Part of Study in Hand Months Ago, Fulbright Seeking Rest," *Washington Post*, June 23, 1971, sec. A, p. 10.

Fred P. Graham. "Times Series Is Delayed Again; Paper to Appeal to High Court," *New York Times*, June 24, 1971, p. 1.

"Language v. Thought: The Documents," *Washington Post*, June 25, 1971, sec. A, p. 20.

Stuart Auerbach. "U.S. Declines to Curb L.A. Times and Knight," *Washington Post*, June 25, 1971, sec. A, p. 1.

"Agnew Sees Press in 'Cheap Operation,'" *New York Times*, June 26, 1971, p. 11.

"N.A.B. Board Backs CBS on 'Pentagon,'" *New York Times*, June 26, 1971, p. 58.

Murray Illson. "Paper in St. Louis Defends Articles," *New York Times*, June 26, 1971, p. 10.

Henry Giniger. "Pentagon Study Prominently Reported in Europe," *New York Times*, June 26, 1971, p. 10.

Fred P. Graham. "Supreme Court Agrees to Rule on Printing of Vietnam Series," *New York Times*, June 26, 1971, p. 1.

John P. Mackenzie. "Immediate End of Ban Denied, 5–4," *Washington Post*, June 26, 1971, sec. A, p. 1.

"Government Plea to Supreme Court," *Washington Post*, June 26, 1971, sec. A, p. 11.

Sanford J. Ungar. "Papers Defer on Printing Cleared Data," *Washington Post*, June 26, 1971, sec. A, p. 1.

John Field. "Ellsberg Arrest Is Ordered," *Washington Post*, June 26, 1971, sec. A, p. 1.

Rep. John Culver. "The Papers and the Role of Congress," *Washington Post*, June 26, 1971, sec. A, p. 14.

James Reston. "A Troubled Friend," *New York Times*, June 27, 1971, sec. E, p. 15.

"Detroit News Criticizes Papers for Publishing Study," *New York Times*, June 27, 1971, p. 27.

James M. Naughton. "The Impact," *New York Times*, June 27, 1971, sec. p. 1.

Fred P. Graham. "Two-Hour Debate," *New York Times*, June 27, 1971, p. 1.

Fred P. Graham. "U.S. v. Press," *New York Times*, June 27, 1971, sec. E, p. 1.

"Transcript of Oral Argument in Times and Post Cases before the Supreme Court," *New York Times*, June 27, 1971, p. 24.

Christopher Lydon. "Supreme Court Decision on Vietnam Study Awaited," *New York Times*, June 28, 1971, p. 1.

"A State Department History of the Vietnam War," *Washington Post*, June 28, 1971, sec. A, p. 20.

Jack Anderson. "Deception on Vietnam Still Goes On," *Washington Post*, June 28, 1971, sec. B, p. 13.

Tom Wicker. "A Man to Be Trusted," *New York Times*, June 29, 1971, p. 37.

"Decision Delayed on Vietnam Study," *New York Times*, June 29, 1971, p. 1.

"U.S. Pullout Plan in 1962 Reported," *New York Times*, June 29, 1971, p. 9.

Letters to the Editor, *Washington Post*, June 29, 1971, sec. A, p. 19.

Joseph Kraft. "The Ellsberg Case," *Washington Post*, June 29, 1971, sec. A, p. 19.

Barry Zorthian. "It Was and Is the Most Open of Wars," *New York Times*, June 30, 1971, p. 41.

Sanford J. Ungar and George Lardner, Jr. "War File Articles Resumed," *Washington Post*, July 1, 1971, sec. A, p. 1.

"Australian Reds Sell War Articles of Times," *New York Times*, July 1, 1971, p. 16.

Fred P. Graham. "Burger Dissents," *New York Times*, July 1, 1971, p. 1.

"The Pentagon Papers—Free at Last," *Washington Post*, July 1, 1971, sec. A, p. 22.

Robert Reinhold. "Ellsberg Asserts Others Aided Him," *New York Times*, July 2, 1971, p. 1.

Alvin Shuster. "Saigon Networks Shun Disclosures," *New York Times*, July 2, 1971, p. 13.

Betty Medsger. "Dean Assails 'Abuse of Truth' Revealed in War Documents," *Washington Post*, July 3, 1971, sec. A, p. 21.

Max Frankel. "Presses Roll—But the Conflict Remains," *New York Times*, July 4, 1971, sec. E, p. 1.

"The Court's Decision," *New York Times*, July 4, 1971, sec. E, p. 10.

Max Frankel. "The Lessons of Vietnam," *New York Times*, July 6, 1971, p. 1.

Dean Acheson. "The Purloined Papers," *New York Times*, July 7, 1971, p. 37.

David E. Rosenbaum. "Cooper Acts to Force C.I.A. to Report to Congress, "*New York Times*, July 8, 1971, p. 14.

Stephen S. Rosenfeld. "National Security: The Public's Affair," *Washington Post*, July 9, 1971, sec. A, p. 20.

Nona B. Brown. "Pentagon Papers," *New York Times*, July 11, 1971, sec. E, p. 4.

Arthur L. Gavshon. "Some Allies Comparing Briefings by U.S. with Pentagon Papers," *Washington Post*, July 11, 1971, p. 18.

"Agnew: Papers Issue Appalls World Heads," *Washington Post*, July 12, 1971, sec. A, p. 17.

Judith Kinnard. "Air of Expectancy, Then Tears, Shouts, Embraces," *New York Times*, May 12, 1973, p. 69.

"Guilty: The Government," *New York Times*, May 12, 1973, p. 32.

CHAPTER 5. FIGHTING TIMES AND FIGHTING FAITHS

Note: The articles and stories relating to Eugene Dennis and his cases are so voluminous that space does not permit us to list all of the sources we consulted. The sources from which we quoted are, however, all listed here. Two particularly notable works about the *Dennis* case and its history are Michal R. Belknap's exhaustively documented *Cold War Political Justice: The Smith Act, the Communist Party, and American Civil Liberties* (1977) and David Caute's informative work *The Great Fear: The Anti-Communist Purge under Truman and Eisenhower* (1978). A detailed account of the trial—perhaps unduly slanted toward Judge Medina—can be found in Hawthorne Daniel, *Judge Medina: A Biography* (1952). J. Woodford Howard's long-awaited biography of Judge Medina is still unpublished. Legal historian William Wiecek offers an instructive account of the *Dennis* case and the politics of the day in *The Birth of the Modern Constitution* (2006). Martin Redish's book *The Logic of Persecution* (2005) provides an informative description and analysis of the McCarthy era and the legal relevance of the Venona documents. The leading work on Judge Hand's role in all of this is Gerald Gunther's authoritative biography, *Learned Hand: The Man and the Judge* (1994). David Rabban's *Free Speech in Its Forgotten Years* (1997) provides a meticulous and invaluable account of the history of the free-speech cases prior to 1930. The definitive work on free speech in wartime is Geoffrey Stone's *Perilous Times: Free Speech in Wartime* (2004). A More recent and likewise valuable work is Stephen Feldman's *Free Expression and Democracy in America: A History* (2009).

Abrams v. United States, 250 U.S. 616 (1919).

Brandenburg v. Ohio, 395 U.S. 444 (1969).

Bridges v. California, 314 U.S. 252 (1941).

Communist Party v. Control Board, 367 U.S. 1 (1961).

Debs v. United States, 249 U.S. 211 (1919).

DeJonge v. Oregon, 299 U.S. 353 (1937).

Dennis v. United States, 339 U.S. 162 (1949).

Dennis v. United States, 340 U.S. 887 (1950).

Dennis v. United States, 341 U.S. 494 (1951).

Fox v. Washington, 236 U.S. 273 (1915).

Frohwerk v. United States, 249 U.S. 204 (1919).

Garner v. Board of Public Works, 341 U.S. 716 (1951).

Gentile v. State Bar of Nevada, 501 U.S. 1030 (1991).

Gitlow v. New York, 268 U.S. 652 (1925).

Goldman v. United States, 245 U.S. 366 (1918).

Herndon v. Lowry, 301 U.S. 242 (1937).

Hess v. Indiana, 414 U.S. 105 (1973).

Keyishian v. Board of Regents, 385 U.S. 589 (1967).

NAACP v. Claiborne Hardware Co., 458 U.S. 886 (1982).

Noto v. United States, 367 U.S. 290 (1961).

Patterson v. Colorado, 205 U.S. 454 (1907).

Scales v. United States, 367 U.S. 203 (1961).

Selective Draft Law Cases, 245 U.S. 366 (1918).

Schaefer v. United States, 251 U.S. 466 (1920).

Schenck v. United States, 249 U.S. 47 (1919).

Shelley v. Kraemer, 334 U.S. 1 (1948).

Speiser v. Randall, 357 U.S. 513 (1958).

Stromberg v. California, 283 U.S. 359 (1931).

Tinker v. Des Moines Independent County School District, 393 U.S. 503 (1969).

United States ex rel Milwaukee Social Democrat Publishing Co. v. Burleson, 255 U.S. 407 (1921).

Virginia v. Black, 123 S. Ct. 1536 (2003).

Watts v. United States, 394 U.S. 705 (1969).

Whitney v. California, 274 U.S. 357 (1927).

Yates v. United States, 354 U.S. 298 (1957).

Masses Publishing Co. v. Patten, 244 F. 535 (S.D.N.Y. 1917).

Masses Publishing Co. v. Patten, 245 F. 102 (2d Cir. 1917).

Williamson v. United States, 184 F.2d 280 (2d Cir. 1950).

United States v. Dennis, 183 F.2d. 201 (2d Cir. 1950).

Joint Appendix to Brief for Appellants and Brief for Respondent, *United States v. Dennis*, 183 F.2d. 201 (2d Cir. 1950).

First Amendment Center, Advocacy of Violence Cases, www.firstamendmentcenter.org/faclibrary/libraryexpression.aspx?topic=violence.

Alschuler, Albert W. *Law without Values: The Life, Work, and Legacy of Justice Holmes* (Chicago: University of Chicago Press, 2000).

Baker, Leonard. *Brandeis and Frankfurter: A Dual Biography* (New York: Harper and Row, 1984).

Baker, Liva. *The Justice From Beacon Hill: The Life and Times of Oliver Wendell Holmes* (New York: HarperCollins, 1991).

Barron, Jerome, and Dienes, C. Thomas. *First Amendment Law*, 4th ed. (St. Paul: West Group, 2009).

Belknap, Michal R. *Cold War Political Justice: The Smith Act, the Communist Party, and American Civil Liberties* (Westport, Conn.: Greenwood Press, 1977).

Berns, Walter F. *Freedom, Virtue and the First Amendment* (Chicago: H. Regnery, 1965).

Bickel, Alexander. *The Morality of Consent* (New Haven, Conn.: Yale University Press, 1975).

Bollinger, Lee C. *The Tolerant Society* (New York: Oxford University Press, 1986).

Buhle, Mari Jo, Buhle, Paul, and Georgakas, Dan, eds. *Encyclopedia of the American Left* (Urbana: University of Illinois Press, 1992).

Chafee, Zechariah, Jr. *Free Speech in the United States* (Harvard University Press, 1941).

Caute, David. *The Great Fear: The Anti-Communist Purge under Truman and Eisenhower* (New York: Simon and Schuster, 1978).

Daniel, Hawthorne. *Judge Medina: A Biography* (New York: Wilfred Funk, 1952).

Dennis, Eugene. *Eugene Dennis Indicts the Wall Street Conspirators* (New York: New York National Office, Communist Party, 1948).

——. *Ideas They Cannot Jail* (New York: International, 1950).

——. *Is Communism Un-American?* (New York: New Century, 1947).

——. *Letters from Prison* (New York: International, 1956).

Dickson, Dell, ed. *The Supreme Court in Conference (1940–1985): The Private Discussions. Behind Nearly 300 Supreme Court Decisions* (New York: Oxford University Press, 2001).

Douglas, William O. *The Court Years: 1939–1975: The Autobiography of William O. Douglas* (New York: Random House, 1980).

Emerson, Thomas I. *The System of Freedom of Expression* (New York: Vintage Books, 1970).

Farber, Daniel. *The First Amendment* (New York: Foundation Press, 1998).

Foster, William Z., and Dennis, Eugene. *The Menace of American Imperialism* (New York: New Century, 1945).

Garvey, John H., and Schauer, Frederick, eds. *The First Amendment: A Reader*, 4th ed. (St. Paul: West Group, 2008).

Greenawalt, Kent. *Speech, Crime and the Uses of Language* (New York: Oxford University Press, 1989).

Gunther, Gerald. *Learned Hand: The Man and the Judge* (New York: Knopf, 1994).

Hall, Kermit, ed. *The Oxford Companion to the Supreme Court of the United States* (New York: Oxford University Press, 1992).

Hand, Learned. *The Bill of Rights: The Oliver Wendell Holmes Lectures, 1958* (Atheneum, 1972).

Herman, Arthur. *Joseph McCarthy: Reexamining the Life and Legacy of America's Most Hated Senator* (New York: Free Press, 1999).

Hirsch, H. N. *The Enigma of Felix Frankfurter* (New York: Basic Books, 1981).

Kalven, Harry, Jr. *A Worthy Tradition*, edited by Jamie Kalven (New York: Harper and Row, 1988).

Holmes, Oliver Wendell, Jr. *The Common Law* (New York: Little Brown, 1951).

Marion, George. *The Communist Trial: An American Crossroads* (New York: Wilfred Funk, 1952).

Marquesse, Mike. *Chimes of Freedom: The Politics of Bob Dylan's Art* (New York: Free Press, 2003).

Medina, Harold. *Judge Medina Speaks* (New York: Mathew Bender, 1954).

Meiklejohn, Alexander. *Free Speech and Its Relation to Self-Government* (New York: Harper, 1948).

——. *Political Freedom: The Constitutional Powers of the People* (New York: Oxford University Press, 1965).

Mennell, Robert M., and Compston, Christine L., eds. *Holmes and Frankfurter: Their Correspondence, 1912–1934* (Hanover: University of New Hampshire Press, 1996).

Newman, Roger K. *Hugo Black: A Biography* (New York: Pantheon, 1994).

Novick, Sheldon M. *Honorable Justice: The Life of Oliver Wendell Holmes* (New York: Bantam Doubleday Dell, 1989).

O'Brien, David M. *Storm Center: The Supreme Court in American Politics*, 6th ed. (New York: Norton, 2003).

Pohlman, H. L. *Justice Oliver Wendell Holmes: Free Speech and the Living Constitution* (New York: New York University Press, 1991).

Rabban, David M. *Free Speech in Its Forgotten Years* (Cambridge: Cambridge University Press, 1997).

Redish, Martin. *Freedom of Expression: A Critical Analysis* (San Francisco, CA: Lexis Law, 1984).

———. *The Logic of Persecution: Free Expression and the McCarthy Era* (Stanford: Stanford University Press, 2005).

Shick, Marvin. *Learned Hand's Court* (Baltimore, MD: Johns Hopkins Press, 1970).

Schrecker, Ellen. *Many are the Crimes: McCarthyism in America* (Princeton: Princeton University Press 1998).

Schubert, Glendon. *Dispassionate Justice: A Synthesis of the Judicial Opinions of Robert H. Jackson* (Indianapolis: Bobbs-Merrill, 1969).

Simon, James F. *Independent Journey: The Life of William O. Douglas* (New York: Penguin, 1980).

Smolla, Rodney. *Smolla and Nimmer on Freedom of Speech* (New York: Matthew Bender, 1994).

Steinberg, Peter L. *The Great "Red Menace": United States Prosecution of American Communists, 1947–1952* (Westport, CT: Greenwood Press, 1984).

Stone, Geoffrey R. *Perilous Times: Free Speech in Wartime* (New York: Norton, 2004).

Tribe, Laurence. *American Constitutional Law*, 2nd ed. (Foundation Press, 1988).

White, G. Edward. *Justice Oliver Wendell Holmes: Law and the Inner Self* (New York: Oxford University Press, 1995).

Wiecek, William M. *The Birth of the Modern Constitution: The United States Supreme Court, 1941–1953* (New York: Cambridge University Press, 2006).

Yarbrough, Tinsley. *John Marshall Harlan: Great Dissenter of the Warren Court* (New York: Oxford University Press, 1992).

Zuckman, Harvey, and Corn-Revere, Robert, et al. *Modern Communication Law* (St. Paul: West Group, 1999).

Blasi, Vincent. "The Checking Value in First Amendment Theory," 1977 *American Bar Foundation Research Journal* 521.

Boudin, Louis. "'Seditious Doctrines' and the 'Clear and Present Danger' Rule," 38 *Virginia Law Review* 178 (1952).

Chafee, Zechariah, Jr. *Freedom of Speech in War Time*, 32 *Harvard Law Review* 932 (1919).

Corwin, Edward S. "Bowing Out 'Clear and Present Danger,'" 27 *Notre Dame Law Review* 358 (1952).

"*Dennis v. United States*, Trial Excerpts," available at the website of The Center for Programs in Contemporary Writing, University of Pennsylvania, http://www.writing.upenn.edu/~afilreis/50s/dennis-opening.html.

Dow, David R., and Shieldes, R. Scott. "Rethinking the Clear and Present Danger Test," 73 *Indiana Law Journal* 1217 (1998).

Dylan, Bob. "Transcript of Bob Dylan's Remarks at the Bill of Rights Dinner at the Americana Hotel on 12/13/63," available at the website of Corliss Lamont, http://www.corliss-lamont.org/dylan.htm.

"Max Eastman Internet Archive," available at the website of Marxists Internet Archive, www.marxists.org/history/etol/writers/eastman/index.htm.

Emerson, Thomas. "First Amendment Doctrine and the Burger Court," 68 *California Law Review* 422 (1980).

Gorfinkel, John A., and Mack, Julian W., II. "*Dennis v. United States* and the Clear and Present Danger Test," 39 *California Law Review* 475 (1951).

Gunther, Gerald. "Learned Hand and the Origins of Modern First Amendment Doctrine," 27 *Stanford Law Review* 719 (1975).

Howard, J. Woodford, Jr. "Judge Harold R. Medina," 69 *Judicature* 126 (1985).

Linde, Hans. "Clear and Present Danger Reexamined," 22 *Stanford Law Review* 1163 (1970).

McCloskey, Robert. "Free Speech, Sedition, and the Constitution," 45 *American Political Science Review* 168 (1951).

"Medina, Harold R.," in *Great American Judges: An Encyclopedia* (Santa Barbara, Calif.: ABC-CLIO, 2003), vol. 2, pp. 519–529.

Harold Medina Papers, Princeton University Library, catalog available at Mudd Manuscript Library, Princeton University, http://infoshare1.princeton.edu/libraries/firestone/rbsc/finding_aids/medina/.

Mendelson, Wallace. "Clear and Present Danger from *Schenck* to *Dennis*," 52 *Columbia Law Review* 313 (1952).

Mollan, R. "Smith Act Prosecutions: The Effect of the *Dennis* and *Yates* Decisions," 26 *University of Pittsburgh Law Review* 705 (1965).

Oakes, James L. "Memorial to Harold R. Medina," 90 *Columbia University Law Review* 1459 (1990).

O'Brian, John Lord. "Civil Liberty in War Time," 62 *Reports of the New York Bar Association* 275 (January 17, 1919).

"Profile of Eugene Dennis," available at the website of Spartacus Educational, www.spartacus.schoolnet.co.uk/U.S.AdennisE.htm.

"Prosecution and Defense Statements, 1949 Trial of American Communist Party Leaders, available at the website of History Matters, http://historymatters.gmu.edu/d/6446/.

Ragan, Fred D. "Justice Oliver Wendell Holmes, Jr., Zechariah Chafee, Jr., and the Clear and Present Danger Test of Free Speech: The First Year, 1919," 58 *Journal of American History* 24 (1971).

Redish, Martin H. "Advocacy of Unlawful Conduct and the First Amendment: In Defense of Clear and Present Danger," 70 *California Law Review* 1159 (1982).

Richardson, Elliot. "Freedom of Expression and the Function of the Courts," 65 *Harvard Law Review* 1 (1951).

Rohr, Mark. "Communists and the First Amendment: The Shaping of Freedom of Advocacy in the Cold War Era," 28 *San Diego Law Review* 1 (1991).

Stone, Geoffrey R. "Judge Learned Hand and the Espionage Act of 1917: A Mystery Unraveled," 70 *University of Chicago Law Review* 335 (2003).

————. "The Origins of the 'Bad Tendency' Test: Free Speech in Wartime," 2002 *Supreme Court Review* 411.

Wiecek, William M. "The Legal Foundations of Domestic Anticommunism: The Background of *Dennis v. United States*," 2001 *Supreme Court Review* 375.

"Socialists to Test the Espionage Act," *New York Times*, July 10, 1917, p. 7.

"The Masses Wins Fight for Mails," *New York Times*, July 25, 1917, p. 11.

"Cartoon Caused Ban on 'Masses,'" *Washington Post*, July 23, 1917, p. 5.

Russell Porter. "Publisher Is Indicted," *Washington Post*, November 20, 1917, p. 9.

"O'Leary Indicted on Sedition Charge," *New York Times*, November 24, 1917, p. 3.

"Radical's View of Outlook Here," *New York Times*, February 24, 1918, p. 44.

"Wilson Wrote to Eastman," *New York Times*, April 19, 1918, p. 11.

"Eastman Goes to the Jury Today," *New York Times*, November 4, 1918, p. 10.

Zechariah Chafee, Jr. "Freedom of Speech," *New Republic*, November 16, 1918, p. 67.

"Masses Defendants Free," *New York Times*, January 11, 1919, p. 22.

"Fate of Eastman in the Jury's Hands," *New York Times*, April 25, 1918, p. 20.

"Judge Dismisses the Masses Jury," *New York Times*, April 28, 1918, p. 5.

Ernst Freund. "The Debs Case and Freedom of Speech," *New Republic*, May 3, 1919, p. 13.

"Bans on Reds Urged by Schwellenbach," *New York Times* (AP story), March 12, 1947, p. 12.

"12 Leaders "Dennis Concedes in Changed Name," *New York Times*, March 31, 1947, p. 25.

"Would Prosecute Communist Party: Thomas Urges Clark to Act," *New York Times*, April 2, 1947, p. 32.

"Dennis Asks U.S. to Protect Communists," *Washington Post*, April 7, 1947, p. 2.

"Dennis Is Cited, Contempt Charged," *New York Times*, April 10, 1947, p. 29.

"Two Contempt Actions Voted against Dennis," *Washington Post*, April 10, 1947, p. 1.

"Dennis Is Indicted on Congress Charge," *New York Times*, May 1, 1947, p. 36.

"Deny Congress Contempt," *New York Times*, May 6, 1947, p. 21.

Samuel Tower. "FBI Head Brands Communist Party a 'Fifth Column,'" *New York Times*, May 27, 1947, p. 1.

"Dennis Chooses Jail and Fine Instead of Answering Queries," *Washington Post*, June 9, 1947, p. 1.

"Counsel for Dennis Hits Un-American Affairs Committee," *Washington Post*, June 24, 1947, p. 6.

"Dennis, Communist Aide, Guilty of Contempt over House Inquiry," *New York Times* (AP story), June 27, 1947, p. 1.

Russell Porter. "Jury Examination in Red Trial Begun: Court Is Picketed," *New York Times*, March 1, 1948, p. 1.

"12 Leaders Are Indicted: U.S. Starts Roundup," *Washington Post*, July 21, 1948, p. 1.

"Text of Indictment of 12 Communists," *New York Times*, January 17, 1949, p. 9.

"11 Communists Fail to Halt Trial Here," *New York Times*, January 18, 1949, p. 1.

"Accused Reds Protest Use of 400 Police," *Washington Post*, January 18, 1949, p. 1

Russell Porter. "Contempt Appeal of 2 Reds Argued," *New York Times*, January 18, 1949, p. 7.

"Communist Trial Is Set for Nov. 15," *New York Times*, November 2, 1948, p. 18.

Milton Lehman. "White Knight or False Prophet?" *New York Times*, August 1, 1948, Sunday Mag., p. 11.

"Medina Excuses 86 on Red Jury Panel," *New York Times*, March 9, 1949, p. 3.

Russell Porter. "Challenges Take 7 Off Red Trial Jury," *New York Times*, March 15, 1949, p. 8.

Russell Porter. "One Challenge Left Defense in Reds' Trial," *Washington Post*, March 16, 1949, p. 2.

"U.S. Reds Ordered to Revolt in 1945, Budenz Tells Court," *New York Times*, March 25, 1949, p. 1.

"The Trial of Communist Leaders," *Time*, April 4, 1949, p. 24.

Time, April 25, 1949 (cover).

"Little Commissar," *Time*, April 25, 1949, p. 22.

"'Rumpuses' of Reds, Scored by Medina," *New York Times*, April 28, 1949, p. 1.

Russell Porter. "Medina Threatens to Put Davis in Jail," *New York Times*, May 27, 1949, p. 1.

Russell Porter. "Medina Rules Out Mass of Evidence," *New York Times*, June 1, 1949, p. 17.

Quentin Roosevelt. "Sketchbook of Communists' Trial," *New York Times*, June 19, 1949, Sunday Mag., p. 8.

Russell Porter. "Davis Denies Reds Advocated Force," *New York Times*, July 6, 1949, p. 1.

Russell Porter. "Davis Admits Lies, Appear in Records," *New York Times*, July 13, 1949, p. 19.

"FBI Is Main Target at Rights Session," *New York Times*, July 17, 1949, p. 10.

Jack B. Alexander. "The Ordeal of Judge Medina," *Saturday Evening Post*, August 12, 1949, p. 18.

Russell Porter. "Red Trial Defense Preparing to Rest," *New York Times*, September 2, 1949, p. 11.

"Communists: Fizzled Firecracker," *Newsweek*, September 5, 1949, p. 22.

Russell Porter. "Red Defense Rests; Rebuttal Waived," *New York Times*, September 24, 1949, p. 1.

"Both Sides Rest Cases in Red Trial," *Washington Post*, September 24, 1949, p. 7.

Russell Porter. "Judge Chides Reds on 'Open' Activities," *New York Times*, September 29, 1949, p. 16.

Russell Porter. "Jury Due to Get Red Case on October 13," *New York Times*, October 5, 1949, p. 18.

"Red Trial Is Laid to Truman Order," *New York Times*, October 11, 1949, p. 18.

Russell Porter. "Jury Holds Fate of 11 Reds; Judge in His Charge Warns Communism Is Not on Trial," *New York Times*, October 14, 1949, p. 1.

"Text of Judge Medina's Charge to the Jury at the Trial of the Communist Leaders," *New York Times*, October 14, 1949, p. 14.

"Brief Biographies of Accused Reds," *New York Times*, October 15, 1949, p. 2

Russell Porter. "11 Communists Convicted of Plot; Medina to Sentence Them Friday; 6 of Counsel Jailed in Contempt," *New York Times*, October 15, 1949, p. 1.

"11 Top Reds Found Guilty and Medina Jails Counsel," *Washington Post*, October 15, 1949, p. 1.

"Verdict Received by Tense Audience," *New York Times*, October 15, 1949, p. 4.

"10 Top Reds of U.S. Get Maximum 5-Yr. Terms," *Washington Post*, October 22, 1949, p. 1.

Russell Porter. "Communists: Guilty as Charged," *Newsweek*, October 24, 1949, p. 25.

Russell Porter. "Million Bail Asked for Red Leaders," *New York Times*, November 2, 1949, p. 5.

Russell Porter. "Communist Freed in Bail of $260,000 to Press Appeals," *New York Times*, November 4, 1949, p. 1.

"Violent Outbreak in Harlem Marks Jail Release Celebration for Davis," *New York Times*, November 4, 1949, p. 1.

Russell Porter. "Government Argues That 'Intent' Convicts the Communist Leaders," *New York Times*, June 24, 1950, p. 2.

Editorial. "'Clear and Present Danger,'" *New York Times*, August 4, 1950, p. 20.

Chalmers M. Roberts. "Judge Hand Echoes a Famous Opinion," *Washington Post*, August 6, 1950, sec. B, p. 1.

Irwin Ross. "Harold Medina—Judge Extraordinary," *Reader's Digest*, February 1950, p. 85.

Russell Porter. "Lack of Evidence Argued for 11 Reds," *New York Times*, June 22, 1950, p. 4.

Lewis Wood. "President Praises Solicitor General," *New York Times*, June 26, 1950, p. 17.

Russell Porter. "High Court Hears Appeal of 11 Reds," *New York Times*, December 5, 1950, p. 20.

"Jail of 11 Reds Is Sought by U.S. as Security Step," *New York Times*, August 14, 1950, p. 1.

"Red Leader Dennis, Freed from U.S. Jail; Eager to Wage a 'Red Crusade for Peace,'" *New York Times*, March 13, 1951, p. 14.

"Bricker Asks Probe of Judges Who Have Freed Communists," *Washington Post* (UPI story), March 30, 1951.

"Reds' Lawyers Seek a Stay in Contempt," *New York Times*, June 8, 1951, p. 17.

"4 Reds Missing as 7 Are Jailed; Hunted by FBI," *Washington Post*," July 3, 1951, sec. B, p. 10.

Clayton Knowles. "11 Top Reds Lose High Court Plea for Rehearing on Their Conviction," *New York Times*, October 9, 1951, p. 1.

"6 Lawyers for Reds to Get Review of Contempt Terms by High Court," *New York Times*, October 23, 1951, p. 1.

Charles M. Roberts. "Reds' Lawyers Win Hearing by High Court," *Washington Post*, October 23, 1951, p. 13.

"Top Court Upholds Contempt Jailing," March 3, 1952, p. 11.

Russell Porter. "Red Counsel Begin Contempt Terms," *New York Times*, April 25, 1952, p. 8.

Harry Schwartz. "Communists Meet without Dennis," *New York Times*, December 11, 1959, p. 12.

"Philip B. Perlman, 70, Ex-Solicitor General," *Washington Post*, August 1, 1960, sec. B, p. 1.

"Eugene Dennis, 56, Red Leader, Dies," *New York Times*, February 1, 1961, p. 35.

"1,000 Attend Rites for Eugene Dennis," *New York Times*, February 6, 1961, p. 23.

Anthony Lewis. "High Court Puts Curb on U.S. Reds in 2 Major Cases," *New York Times,* June 6, 1961, p. 1.

Robert D. McFadden. "J. Parnell Thomas, Anti-Red Crusader, Is Dead," *New York Times,* November 20, 1970, p. 44.

Stephen Caplan. "J. Parnell Thomas Dies," *Washington Post,* November 20, 1970, sec. C, p. 12.

John T. McQuiston. "Ex-Rep. Smith Dies at Home in Virginia," *New York Times,* October 4, 1976, p. 24.

"Harold Medina, U.S. Judge, Dies at 101," *New York Times,* March 16, 1990, sec. B, p. 7.

Jacob Weisberg. "Cold War without End," *New York Times Magazine,* November 28, 1999, p. 121.

Bob Baird. "Hurley Faces Justice at Foley Square," New York, NY: *Journal News,* January 15, 2004.

William O. Douglas. "Frightened America," April 1952, reproduced in *Progressive,* April 2009, p. 59.

Chapter 6. Saving the NAACP

Note: Some of the biographical material concerning Robert Carter we drew from his book *A Matter of Law: A Memoir of Struggle in the Cause of Equal Rights* (2005).

Adderley v. Florida, 385 U.S. 39 (1966).

Bates v. City of Little Rock, 229 Ark. 819, 319 S.W.2d 37 (1958).

Bates v. City of Little Rock, 361 U.S. 516 (1960).

Brandenburg v. Ohio, 395 U.S. 444 (1969).

Brown v. Board of Education of Topeka, 347 U.S. 483 (1954).

Brown v. Louisiana, 383 U.S. 131 (1966).

Bryant v. Zimmerman, 278 U.S. 63 (1928).

Cameron v. Johnson, 381 U.S. 741 (1965).

Cox v. Louisiana, 379 U.S. 536 (1965).

Cox v. Louisiana, 379 U.S. 559 (1965).

Edwards v. South Carolina, 372 U.S. 229 (1963).

Gibson v. Florida Legislative Investigation Committee, 372 U.S. 539 (1963).

Gregory v. City of Chicago, 394 U.S. 111 (1969).

Henry v. Collins, 380 U.S. 356 (1965).

Louisiana ex rel Gremillion v. NAACP, 366 U.S. 293 (1961).

NAACP v. Alabama, 265 Ala. 349, 91 So.2d 214 (1956).

NAACP v. Alabama, 357 U.S. 449 (1958).

NAACP v. Alabama, 360 U.S. 240 (1959).

NAACP v. Alabama, 360 U.S. 240 (1959).

NAACP v. Alabama, 377 U.S. 288 (1964).

NAACP v. Button, 371 U.S. 415 (1963).

NAACP v. Overstreet, 384 U.S. 118 (1966).

National Association v. Gallion, 368 U.S. 16 (1961).

New York Times v. Sullivan, 376 U.S. 254 (1964).

Randall v. Sorrell, 548 U.S. 230 (2006).

Shelton v. Tucker, 364 U.S. 479 (1960).
Shuttlesworth v. Birmingham, 394 U.S. 147 (1969).
Walker v. City of Birmingham, 388 U.S. 307 (1967).

Barron, Jerome A., and Dienes, C. Thomas. *First Amendment Law in a Nutshell*, 4th ed. (St. Paul: West Group, 2008).

Branch, Taylor. *Parting the Waters: America in the King Years, 1954–1963* (New York: Simon and Schuster, 1988).

———. *Pillar of Fire: America in the King Years, 1963–1965* (New York: Simon and Schuster, 1998).

Breton, Marcela, ed. *Hot and Cool: Jazz Short Stories* (New York: Penguin Books, 1990).

Carter, Robert L. *A Matter of Law: A Memoir of Struggle in the Cause of Equal Rights* (New York: The New Press, 2005).

Dickson, Dell, ed. *The Supreme Court in Conference (1940–1985)* (New York: Oxford University Press, 2001).

Eastland, Terry, ed. *Freedom of Expression in the Supreme Court: The Defining Cases* (New York: Rowman and Littlefield, 2000).

Emerson, Thomas I. *The System of Freedom of Expression* (New York: Vintage Books, 1970).

Fein, Bruce E. *New York Times v. Sullivan: An Obstacle to Enlightened Public Discourse and Government Responsiveness to the People* (Washington, D.C.: American Legal Foundation, 1984).

Hall, Kermit, ed. *The Oxford Companion to the Supreme Court of the United States* (New York: Oxford University Press, 1992).

Hamilton, Virginia Van der Veer. *Hugo Black: The Alabama Years* (Baton Rouge: Louisiana State University Press, 1972).

Hughes, Langston. *Fight for Freedom: The Story of the NAACP* (New York: Berkley, 1962).

Kalven, Harry, Jr. *The Negro and the First Amendment* (Chicago: University of Chicago Press, 1965).

———. *A Worthy Tradition: Freedom of Speech in America* (New York: Harper and Row, 1988).

Kluger, Richard. *Simple Justice: The History of Brown v. Board of Education and Black America's Struggle for Equality* (New York: Vintage Books, 1977).

Lewis, Anthony. *Make No Law: The Sullivan Case and the First Amendment* (New York: Vintage Books, 1991).

Lively, Donald E., Roberts, Dorothy E., and Weaver, Russell L., eds. *First Amendment Anthology* (Cincinnati: Anderson, 1994).

MacKinnon, Catharine A. *Only Words* (Cambridge, Mass.: Harvard University Press, 1993).

Magee, James J. *Mr. Justice Black: Absolutist on the Court* (Charlottesville: University of Virginia Press, 1980).

Matsuda, Mari J., et al. *Words That Wound: Critical Race Theory, Assaultive Speech and the First Amendment* (Boulder, Colo.: Westview Press, 1993).

Newman, Roger K. *Hugo Black: A Biography* (New York: Pantheon Books, 1994).

Suitts, Steve. *Hugo Black of Alabama: How His Roots and Early Career Shaped the Great Champion of the Constitution* (Montgomery, Ala.: New South Books, 2005).

Tushnet, Mark V. *Making Civil Rights Law: Thurgood Marshall and the Supreme Court, 1936–1961* (New York: Oxford University Press, 1994).

VanBurkleo, Sandra F., et al., eds. *Constitutionalism and American Culture* (Lawrence: University Press of Kansas, 2002).

Yarbrough, Tinsley E. *Mr. Justice Black and his Critics* (Durham, N.C.: Duke University Press, 1988).

———. *John Marshall Harlan: Great Dissenter of the Warren Court* (New York: Oxford University Press, 1992).

Carter, Robert L. "The Three Freedoms," graduate thesis, Columbia University Law School, August 1, 1941.

———. *Freedom to Petition and Freedom to Assemble: A Public Interview with Judge Robert L. Carter and Professor Geoffrey R. Stone*, moderated by Ronald Collins, C-SPAN, November 30, 2005; C-SPAN product ID no. 190077-1).

Hall, Kermit L. " 'Lies, Lies, Lies': The Origins of *New York Times v. Sullivan*," 9 *Communication Law and Policy* (4, autumn 2004).

Jones, Walter B. "What Is Left of the Confederacy in the South Today?" Speech to the New England Oto-Laryngological Society (Boston, February 9, 1955).

Kalven, Harry, Jr. "Upon Rereading Mr. Justice Black on the First Amendment," 14 *U.C.L.A. Law Review* 428 (1967).

Nachman, Roland M., Jr. "Memorial to Frank M. Johnson, Jr.," 51 *Alabama Law Review* 1381, 1406 (2000).

"The Southern Manifesto," *Congressional Record*, 84th Congress, 2nd sess., vol. 102, pt. 4 (March 12, 1956).

Sullivan, Patricia. "Judge Carter and the *Brown* Decision," available at the website of the Organization of American Historians, www.oah.org/pubs/nl/2004feb/sullivan.html (February 2004).

Franklyn Waltman. " 'Dark-Horse' Nomination of Alabaman Facing Study," *Washington Post*, August 13, 1937, p. 1.

Franklyn Waltman. "Politics and People," *Washington Post*, August 14, 1937, p. 2.

"Inquiry into Black on the Klan Urged," *New York Times*, August 17, 1937, p. 9.

Russell B. Porter. "South Learns Jurist's Pact," *Los Angeles Times*, September 13, 1937, p. 7.

Ray Sprigle. "Records Disclose Justice Black Life Member of Ku Klux Klan," *Los Angeles Times*, September 13, 1937, p. 1.

Ray Sprigle. "How Order Made Black Life Member Told," *Los Angeles Times*, September 14, 1937, p. 1.

"Black Ouster Now Is Held Impossible," *New York Times*, September 14, 1937, p. 18.

Ray Sprigle. "Ideals of Klan Extolled in 1926 Speech," *Los Angeles Times*, September 15, 1937, p. 1.

"Press Demands Black Charges Be Investigated," *Chicago Daily Tribune*, September 15, 1937, p. 3.

"Roosevelt Named Black Unaware of Link to Klan," *New York Times*, September 15, 1937, p. 1.

Ray Sprigle. "Steam Roller Charged in Black Confirmation," *Los Angeles Times*, September 16, 1937, p. 1.

Ray Sprigle. "Black Hears How Klan Seeks White Supremacy," *Los Angeles Times*, September 17, 1937, p. 6.

Ray Sprigle. "Black's Membership Sworn to by Klansmen," *Los Angeles Times*, September 18, 1937, p. 2.

"Klan to Defend Roosevelt for Naming Black," *Chicago Daily Tribune*, September 19, 1937, p. 2.

"On the Air Today," *Washington Post*, October 1, 1937, p. 26.

"Cross Burned in Jersey as Black Makes Speech," *New York Times*, October 2, 1937, p. 2.

"Black Makes History Casually in Atmosphere of Friendliness," *Washington Post*, October 2, 1937, p. 1.

" 'Evasive,' or 'He Satisfied Me,' U.S. Says as Justice Explains," *Washington Post*, October 2, 1937, p. 1.

"Weight of Press against Black in Radio Plea," *Washington Post*, October 2, 1937, p. 3.

"Glass Still Believes Black Unfit for Bench," *Los Angeles Times*, October 2, 1937, p. 3.

"Terror in Florida," *Washington Post*, December 29, 1951, p. 8.

"Judge Orders Bus Line to End Integration Rule," *Los Angeles Times*, May 10, 1956, p. 12.

"Court Order Bans NAACP in Alabama," *Washington Post*, June 2, 1956, p. 39.

"NAACP Ponders Reply to Alabama Injunction," *Washington Post*, June 5, 1956, p. 37.

"Injunction in Alabama Challenged by NAACP," *Washington Post*, June 27, 1956, p. 17.

"Alabama Fines NAACP $10,000," *Washington Post*, July 26, 1956, p. 20.

"Alabama Judge Refuses to Set Aside $100,000 Fine Levied against NAACP," *Washington Post*, July 31, 1956, p. 1.

"Florida Bill Seeks Probe of NAACP," *Washington Post*, July 31, 1956, p. 24.

"NAACP Loses Its Plea for $100,000 Fine Stay," *Washington Post*, August 1, 1956, p. 9.

"The Nation," *New York Times*, August 5, 1956, Section E, p. 1.

"The Jones Law," *New Republic*, August 6, 1956, p. 4.

"Florida Law Calls for Probe of NAACP," *Chicago Daily Tribune*, August 22, 1956, sec. A, p. 7.

"Bills Aimed at NAACP Stir Va. Assembly Fight," *Washington Post*, September 11, 1956, p. 28.

"Arlington Civic Group Raps Anti-NAACP Bills," *Washington Post*, September 12, 1956, p. 31.

Editorial. "Extremism at Richmond," *Washington Post*, September 12, 1956, p. 10.

"Va. Session Redrafts Bills to Control NAACP," *Washington Post*, September 14, 1956, p. 18.

"NAACP Head Urges Negroes to Fight Hard," *Washington Post*, September 17, 1956, p. 30.

"High Court to Review NAACP Fine," *Washington Post*, May 28, 1957, sec. A, p. 9.

Philip Benjamin. "Little Rock Moves to Seize Officers of the NAACP," *New York Times*, November 1, 1957, p. 1.

"Little Rock Council Hits at NAACP," *Washington Post*, November 1, 1957, sec. A, p. 1.

"City's Curb of NAACP Up in Court," *Washington Post*, November 5, 1957, sec. A, p. 19.

Lawrence O'Kane. "Impasse Remains for Little Rock," *New York Times*, November 18, 1957, p. 19.

"Mrs. Bates Is Fined $100 In Little Rock," *New York Times*, December 4, 1957, p. 47.

"NAACP Penetration Charged," *New York Times*, February 11, 1958, p. 11.

Gertrude Samuels. "The Silent Fear in Little Rock," *New York Times*, March 30, 1958, SM, p. 11.

"Letters to the Times," *New York Times*, May 9, 1958, p. 22.

"Judge Refuses to Bar Himself," *Washington Post*, June 21, 1958, sec. B, p. 8.

Richard L. Lyons. "Secret NAACP Lists Upheld by High Court," *Washington Post*, July 1, 1958, sec. A, p. 1.

Editorial. "Freedom of Association," *Washington Post*, July 3, 1958, sec. A, p. 12.

"NAACP Asks Ban on Florida Probe," *Washington Post*, September 3, 1958, sec. A, p. 1.

"Plan to Combat NAACP Urged," *Washington Post*, October 3, 1958, sec. B, p. 4.

"Faubus Friends and Foes Divide School Vote," *Los Angeles Times*, December 7, 1958, p. 1.

"Florida Court Orders NAACP Records Opened," *Washington Post*, December 20, 1958, sec. A, p. 10.

"Arkansas High Court Upholds NAACP Fines," *Chicago Daily Tribune*, December 23, 1958, p. 5.

"Alabama Fine Stands For NAACP," *Washington Post*, February 13, 1959, sec. A, p. 13.

"Alabama Backs Fine on NAACP," *New York Times*, February 13, 1959, p. 16.

"Virginia NAACP Laws to Be Tested Today," *Washington Post*, March 23, 1959, p. 2.

"Teachers Resent 2 Arkansas Laws," *New York Times*, April 26, 1959, p. 55.

"Official Puts Little Rock Onus on Reds," *Washington Post*, Washington Post, May 22, 1959, sec. A, p. 17.

"Arkansas Loses in NAACP Case," *New York Times*, June 9, 1959, p. 31.

"Virginia Bar Seeks Ban on NAACP," *Washington Post*, June 30, 1959, sec. B, p. 2.

"NAACP Units Deny Inciting School Suits," *Washington Post*, July 31, 1959, sec. B, p. 10.

"State Court to Hear Three NAACP Suits," *Washington Post*, October 15, 1959, B10.

"Two Refuse to Bare Lists of NAACP," *Washington Post*, November 5, 1959, sec. A, p. 18.

"Probe of Negroes' Lawyers Urged," *Washington Post*, December 20, 1959, sec. B, p. 19.

"Louisiana Rebuffed on NAACP Curb," *New York Times*, February 7, 1960, p. 18.

"Court in Arkansas Backs Teacher Law," *New York Times*, February 9, 1960, p. 17.

Anthony Lewis. "Court Backs NAACP on Secrecy in Little Rock," *New York Times*, February 24, 1960, p. 1.

Harrison E. Salisbury. "Fear and Hatred Grip Birmingham," *New York Times*, April 12, 1960, p. 1.

"Teacher Affidavits Face 2d Court Test," *New York Times*, June 21, 1960, p. 19.

"The Times Argues Case," *New York Times*, July 26, 1960, p. 13.

"Suit against Times Argued in Alabama," *New York Times*, July 27, 1960, p. 18.

"Libel Issue Argued," *New York Times*, August 2, 1960, p. 26.

"NAACP Case Pushed," *New York Times*, August 6, 1960, p. 8.

"Times Loses Point in Alabama Suits," *New York Times*, August 6, 1960, p. 8.

"Louisiana's Attorney General Bolts US Integration Hearing," *New York Times*, August 27, 1960, p. 1.

Elsie Carper. "Split Decision Is Won by Virginia NAACP in Segregation Suit," *Washington Post*, September 3, 1960, sec. B, p. 1.

Editorial. "Contempt for Freedom," *Washington Post*, September 8, 1960, sec. A, p. 22.

"Suits in Alabama Raise Press Issue," *New York Times*, September 25, 1960, p. 87.

"Convict State Atty. General of Contempt," *Chicago Daily Tribune*, October 8, 1960, sec. W, p. 3.

"NAACP in Fight," *New York Times*, October 25, 1960, p. 18.

"Times, 4 Clerics Lose Libel Case," *New York Times*, November 4, 1960, p. 67.

"Teachers Upheld in Arkansas Test," *New York Times*, December 13, 1960, p. 28.

"S.C. Jails 188 Negro Protesters," *Washington Post*, March 3, 1961, sec. A, p. 5.

"Jail Negroes for March on S.C. Capitol," *Chicago Daily Tribune*, March 3, 1961, p. 14.

"150 Negroes Held in Racial Demonstration," *Los Angeles Times*, March 3, 1961, p. 28.

"'Mississippism' Fought," *New York Times*, April 8, 1961, p. 10.

James E. Clayton. "NAACP Member List Case Review Slated," *Washington Post*, May 9, 1961, sec. A, p. 2.

"High Court Upholds NAACP against Two Louisiana Statutes," *New York Times*, May 23, 1961, p. 33.

Editorial. "Confrontation in Vienna," *New York Times*, June 4, 1961, sec. E, p. 10.

James E. Clayton. "High Court Hears Race Law Argued," *Washington Post*, November 9, 1961, sec. D, p. 11.

Anthony Lewis. "High Court Considers NAACP Membership Case," *New York Times*, December 6, 1961, p. 28.

"Tear Gas Quells Negroes' Protest," *New York Times*, December 16, 1961, p. 1.

"Louisiana Moves to Curb Students," *New York Times*, December 17, 1961, p. 45.

"Bars NAACP Permanently from Alabama," *Chicago Daily Tribune*, December 30, 1961, p. 7.

"NAACP Aide Jailed," *New York Times*, March 15, 1962, p. 27.

Anthony Lewis. "Ailing Justice Whittaker Leaving Supreme Court," *New York Times*, March 30, 1962, p. 1.

Anthony Lewis. "Supreme Court Defers 12 Cases," *New York Times*, April 3, 1962, p. 1.

"Supreme Court, Divided 4–4, Shelves 12 Cases," *Los Angeles Times*, April 3, 1962, p. 16.

Nate Haseltine. "Justice Frankfurter's Collapse Laid to Brief Halt of Blood Flow to Brain," *Washington Post*, April 7, 1962, sec. A, p. 1.

James E. Clayton. "Doctors Bar Return of Frankfurter to Work on Supreme Court Till Fall," *Washington Post*, May 1, 1962, sec. A, p. 1.

Edward T. Pollard. "Frankfurter Retiring; Goldberg to Be Named," *Washington Post*, August 30, 1962, sec. A, p. 1.

James E. Clayton. "Bench Loses Brilliant and Controversial Gadfly for Legal Precision," *Washington Post*, August 30, 1962, sec. A, p. 20.

"Text of Frankfurter-Kennedy Letters," *New York Times*, August 30, 1962, p. 14.

Paul M. Yost. "Goldberg's Arrival May Herald Shift in Court Sentiment," *Washington Post*, September 30, 1962, sec. A, p. 4.

"Leader Denies NAACP Incited Ole Miss Clash," *Los Angeles Times*, December 13, 1962, sec. L, p. 1.

"High Court Lifts Barrier for NAACP," *Los Angeles Times*, January 15, 1963, p. 17.

Editorial. "Championing Rights," *Washington Post*, January 20, 1963, sec. E, p. 6.

Anthony Lewis. "187 Negroes Win Voided Sentences," *New York Times*, February 26, 1963, p. 1.

Editorial. "Protecting Speech," *Washington Post*, February 27, 1963, sec. A, p. 16.

James E. Clayton. "High Court Ruling Limits Authority of Legislative Investigators," *Washington Post*, March 26, 1963, sec. A, p. 2.

"Supreme Court Puts Limit on Red Activity Inquiries," *Los Angeles Times*, March 26, 1963, p. 2.

"Negro Congressman Is Unhurt in Clarksdale, Miss., Bombing," *New York Times*, April 13, 1963, p. 35.

"Mississippi Blast Rips NAACP Aide's Store," *New York Times*, May 5, 1963, p. 82.

"Blast in Negro Store Blamed on Lightning," *Los Angeles Times*, May 6, 1963, p. 26.

"Home of Negro Leader Is Hit by 3 Bullets," *Chicago Tribune*, June 9, 1963, p. 3.

Claude Sitton. "Governor Leaves," *New York Times*, June 12, 1963, p. 1.

Anthony Lewis. "A New Racial Era," *New York Times*, June 13, 1963, p. 14.

Claude Sitton. "Negroes Request Federal Troops," *New York Times*, September 17, 1963, p. 1.

Tom Wicker. "President in Plea," *New York Times*, June 12, 1963, p. 1.

Carroll Kilpatrick. "Rights Plan Is Outlined in Speech," *Washington Post*, June 12, 1963, sec. A, p. 1.

"Recall That Negro Leader Defied Peril," *Chicago Tribune*, June 13, 1963, sec. S, p. 5.

"Kennedy, Eisenhower Tackle Race Problem," *Los Angeles Times*, June 13, 1963, p. 1.

"Eisenhower Meets Kennedy on Rights," *New York Times*, June 13, 1963, p. 1.

Joseph Hearst. "Urges Enacting Law to Protect Negroes," *Chicago Tribune*, June 14, 1963, p. 8.

"Negro's Conviction Upheld," *New York Times*, July 13, 1963, p. 7.

"Sit-in to Be Held in Daley's Office," *New York Times*, July 20, 1963, p. 9.

Paul West. "75 Marchers Hold School Protest Rally," *Chicago Tribune*, July 20, 1963, p. 3.

"Clarksdale Jails NAACP Leader," *New York Times*, July 31, 1963, p. 13.

"W. B. Jones Dies; Judge in Alabama," *New York Times*, August 2, 1963, p. 27.

Tom Wicker. "Kennedy Decries Racial Bombings; Impugns Wallace," *New York Times*, September 17, 1963, p. 1.

"Lawyer in Birmingham Blames Whites, Saying 'We All Did It,'" *New York Times*, September 17, 1963, p. 24.

Robert E. Baker. "Miss. Negroes Plan 'Private' Election," *Washington Post*, October 27, 1963, sec. E, p. 3.

"Rules Negro Libeled Cop in Mississippi," *Chicago Tribune*, December 3, 1963, p. 14.

"Negro Leader Fails in Libel Case Plea," *New York Times*, December 3, 1963, p. 36.

"Threat to Burn Self Voiced by Negro Leader," *Los Angeles Times*, February 3, 1964, p. 16.

"Negro Clergyman Denies He Would Burn Himself," *New York Times*, February 7, 1964, p. 60.

E. W. Kenworthy. "Civil Rights Bill to Be Law Tonight," *New York Times*, July 2, 1964, p. 16.

Homer Bigart. "Dr. King Outlines Rights Law Tests," *New York Times*, July 2, 1964, p. 1.

"Mississippi Search Slows Rights Drive," *New York Times*, July 2, 1964, p. 17.

"Two Put Rights Law to the Test in a Cafeteria," *Chicago Tribune*, July 3, 1964, p. 1.

Joseph Hearst. "Rights Bill Becomes Law," *Chicago Tribune*, July 3, 1964, p. 1.

Editorial. "A National Victory," *New York Times*, July 3, 1964, p. 20.

"Johnson's Address on Civil Rights Bill," *New York Times*, July 3, 1964, p. 9.

"South's Leaders Hold Bill Illegal," *New York Times*, July 3, 1964, p. 9.

"Rights Reaction Varied," *Chicago Tribune*, July 4, 1964, p. 1.

Editorial. "Enlarging Freedom," *Washington Post*, July 4, 1964, sec. A, p. 6.

Humbert Tosi. "Civil Rights: The Long Road to Enactment," *Los Angeles Times*, July 5, 1964, sec. J, p. 4.

"Civil Rights Act," *New York Times*, July 5, 1964, sec. E, p. 1.

Claude Sitton. "Graves at A Dam," *New York Times*, August 5, 1964, p. 1.

"F.B.I. and Sailors Join Wide Hunt," *New York Times*, August 5, 1964, p. 37.

"No Common Grave," *New York Times*, August 5, 1964, p. 37.

"3 Bodies Found at Mississippi Dam Where Rights Workers Disappeared," *Washington Post*, August 5, 1964, sec. A, p. 1.

Richard Reston. "Melee Set Off by 'Freedom' Unit," *Los Angeles Times*, August 26, 1964, sec. B, p. 1.

John D. Pomfret. "High Court Clears a Racial Protester," *New York Times*, January 19, 1965, p. 21.

Joseph Hearst. "Court Rejects Estes' Appeal on Mail Fraud," *Chicago Tribune*, January 19, 1965, p. 4.

Editorial. "Mass Protests," *Washington Post*, January 21, 1965, sec. A, p. 16.

John D. Pomfret. "The News of the Week in Law," *New York Times*, January 24, 1965, sec. E, p. 9.

"Rights Aide Freed of Libel Payment," *New York Times*, March 30, 1965, p. 27.

"Klan Planning a Drive in North for Summer," *New York Times*, June 6, 1965, p. 77.

Fred P. Graham. "Supreme Court, in 5 Decisions, Provided Clue to Its Future Role," *New York Times*, June 14, 1965, p. 38.

"Klan's Inside Story Told to House Probers," *Los Angeles Times*, September 24, 1965, p. 6.

"Johnson Orders Reorganization of Federal Civil Rights Program," *New York Times*, September 25, 1965, p. 1.

Carroll Kilpatrick. "Federal Rights Setup Revamped by President," *Washington Post*, September 25, 1965, sec. A, p. 1.sec. A, p. 5.

Fred P. Graham. "At 80 Hugo Black Looks Ahead," *New York Times*, February 27, 1966, sec. E, p. 7.

"3 in Klan Robes Near Rights Event," *Washington Post*, May 1, 1967, sec. B, p. 10.

"Ku Klux Klan Rally Blocked in Louisville," *Chicago Tribune*, August 12, 1967, sec. D, p. 12.

"Court Voids Law on Using Violence," *New York Times*, June 10, 1969, p. 24.

CHAPTER 7: CROSSES AND CRISES

Note: In writing and researching this chapter, we benefited greatly from Edward Cleary's book *Beyond the Burning Cross* (1994). Our discussion of what happened to R.A.V. after his Supreme Court case also draws heavily on James Walsh, "Cross-burning Victim, Suspect Discuss Feelings," Minneapolis, MN: *Star Tribune*, June 24, 1992, sec. B, p. 1.

American Bookseller Association v. Hudnut, 771 F.2d 1197 (1985), *affirmed mem.*, 475 U.S. 1001 (1986).

Berger v. Battaglia, 779 F.2d 992 (4th Cir. 1985), *cert. den.*, 476 U.S. 1159 (1986).

Barnes v. Glen Theatre, Inc., 501 U.S. 560 (1991).

Beauharnais v. Illinois, 343 U.S. 250 (1952).

Black v. Virginia, 262 Va. 764, 553 S.E.2d 738 (2001).

Boos v. Barry, 485 U.S. 312 (1988).

Brandenburg v. Ohio, 395 U.S. 444 (1969).

Broadrick v. Oklahoma 413 U.S. 601 (1973).

Cantwell v. Connecticut, 310 U.S. 296 (1940).

Chaplinsky v. New Hampshire, 315 U.S. 568 (1942).

City Council of Los Angeles v. Taxpayers for Vincent, 466 U.S. 789 (1984).

Cohen v. California, 403 U.S. 15 (1971).

Collin v. Smith, 578 F.2d 1197 (7th Cir. 1978), *cert. den.*, 439 U.S. 916 (1979).

Corry v. Leland Stanford University, No. 740309, Superior Court of Santa Clara County, California (1995).

Dambrot v. Central Michigan University, 839 F. Supp. 477; (E.D. Mich. 1993).

Dawson v. Delaware, 503 U.S. 159 (1992).

Doe v. Michigan, 721 F. Supp. 852 (E.D. Mich. 1989).

Elliott v. Commonwealth, 593 S.E.2d 263 (Va. 2004)

Feiner v. New York, 340 U.S. 315 (1951).

Gay Alliance of Students v. Matthews, 544 F.2d 162 (4th Cir. 1976).

Gooding v. Wilson, 405 U.S. 518 (1972).

Healy v. James, 408 U.S. 169 (1972).

In the Matter of Welfare of R.A.V., 464 N.W.2d 507 (Minn. 1990).

Iota Xi Chapter of Sigma Chi Fraternity v. George Mason University, 773 F. Supp. 792; (E.D. Va. 1991).

Iota Xi Chapter of Sigma Chi Fraternity v. George Mason University, 993 F.2d 386 (4th Cir. 1993).

Keyishian v. Board of Regents, 385 U.S. 585 (1967).

Lewis v. New Orleans, 415 U.S. 123 (1974).

NAACP v. Alabama, 357 U.S. 449 (1958).

O'Mara v. Commonwealth, 535 S.E.2d 175 (Va. 2001).

O'Mara v. Commonwealth, 93 S.E.2d 263 (Va. 2004).

Papish v. University of Missouri, 410 U.S. 667 (1973).

People v. Spielman, 149 N.E. 466 (Ill. 1925).

Piarowski v. Illinois Community College, 759 F.2d 625 (7th Cir. 1985), *cert. den.*, 474 U.S. 1007 (1985).

R.A.V. v. St. Paul, 505 U.S. 377 (1992).

Republican Party, et al. v. White, 536 U.S. 765 (2002).

Rice v. Paladin Enterprises, 128 F.3d 233 (4th Cir. 1997), *cert. den.* 523 U.S. 1074 (1998).

Roth v. United States, 354 U.S. 476 (1957).

Schad v. Borough of Mt. Ephraim, 452 U.S. 61 (1981).

Spence v. Washington, 418 U.S. 405 (1974).

Street v. New York, 394 U.S. 576 (1969).

Stromberg v. California, 283 U.S. 359 (1931).

Terminiello v. Chicago, 337 U.S. 1 (1949).

Texas v. Johnson, 491 U.S. 397 (1989).

UMW Post v. Board of Regents of the University of Wisconsin, 774 F. Supp. 1163 (E.D. Wisc. 1991).

United States v. Eichman, 496 U.S. 310 (1990).

United States v. O'Brien, 391 U.S. 367 (1968).

United States v. Williams, 128 S. Ct. 1830 (2008).

University of California Regents v. Bakke, 438 U.S. 265 (1978).

Ward v. Rock Against Racism, 491 U.S. 781 (1989).

Washington State Grange v. Washington State Republican Party, 128 S. Ct. 1184 (2008).

West Virginia State Board of Education v. Barnette, 319 U.S. 624 (1943).

Whitney v. California, 274 U.S. 357 (1927).

Wisconsin v. Mitchell, 508 U.S. 47 (1993).

Barron, Jerome A., and Dienes, Thomas C. *First Amendment Law in a Nutshell*, 3rd ed. (St. Paul: West Group, 2004).

Brisbin, Richard A. *Justice Antonin Scalia and the Conservative Revival* (Baltimore: John Hopkins University Press, 1997).

Chemerinsky, Erwin. *Constitutional Law: Principles and Policies* (Aspen, Colo.: Aspen Law and Business, 1997).

Delgado, Richard, and Stefancic, Jean. *Must We Defend Nazis?* (New York: New York University Press, 1997).

D'Souza, Dinesh. *Illiberal Education: The Politics of Race and Sex on Campus* (New York: Free Press, 1991).

Eastland, Terry, ed. *Freedom of Expression in the Supreme Court: The Defining Cases* (New York: Rowman and Littlefield, 2000).

Emerson, Thomas I. *The System of Freedom of Expression* (New York: Vintage Books, 1970).

Farber, Daniel A. *The First Amendment*, 2nd ed. (New York: Foundation Press, 2003).

Foskett, Ken. *Judging Thomas: The Life and Times of Clarence Thomas* (New York: Morrow, 2004).

Freedman, Monroe, and Freedman, Eric M., eds. *Group Defamation and Freedom of Speech* (Westport, Conn.: Greenwood Press, 1995).

French, David, et al., eds. *FIRE's Guide to Free Speech on Campus* (Philadelphia: Foundation for Individual Rights Education, 2005).

Gates, Henry L., et al. *Speaking of Race, Speaking of Sex: Hate Speech, Civil Rights and Civil Liberties* (New York: New York University Press, 1994).

Greenawalt, Kent. *Fighting Words: Individuals, Communities, and Liberties of Speech* (Princeton: Princeton University Press, 1995).

Haiman, Franklyn S. *"Speech Acts" and the First Amendment* (Carbondale: Southern Illinois University Press, 1993).

Hall, Kermit, ed. *The Oxford Companion to the Supreme Court of the United States*, 2nd ed. (New York: Oxford University Press, 2005).

Hentoff, Nat. *Free Speech for Me—But Not for Thee* (New York: HarperCollins, 1992).

Heumann, Milton, and Church, Thomas W., eds. *Hate Speech on Campus: Cases, Case Studies and Commentaries* (Boston: Northwestern University Press, 1997).

Holzer, Henry Mark, ed. *Speaking Freely: The Case against Speech Codes* (Ventura, Calif.: Second Thoughts Books, 1994).

Irons, Peter, ed. *May It Please the Court: The First Amendment* (New York: New Press, 1997).

Kalven, Harry, Jr. *The Negro and the First Amendment* (Chicago: University of Chicago Press, 1965).

Lively, Donald E., Roberts, Dorothy E., and Weaver, Russell L., eds. *First Amendment Anthology* (Cincinnati: Anderson, 1994).

Matsuda, Mari J., et al. *Words That Wound: Critical Race Theory, Assaultive Speech, and the First Amendment* (Boulder, Colo.: Westview Press, 1993).

Nowak, John E., and Rotunda, Ronald D. *Principles of Constitutional Law* (St. Paul: Thompson/West, 2004).

Posner, Richard A. *The Essential Holmes* (Chicago: University of Chicago Press, 1992).

Shiell, Timothy C. *Campus Hate Speech on Trial* (Lawrence: University of Kansas Press, 1998).

Shiffrin, Steven H. *Dissent, Injustice, and the Meanings of America* (Princeton, N.J.: Princeton University Press, 1999).

Smolla, Rodney A. *Deliberate Intent: The Behind-the-scenes Story of the Infamous Hit-man Case* (New York: Crown, 1999).

——. *Smolla and Nimmer on Freedom of Speech: A Treatise on the First Amendment* (New York: Times Mirror Books, 1994).

Tribe, Laurence H. *American Constitutional Law*, 2nd ed. (Mineola, N.Y.: Foundation Press, 1988).

Walker, Samuel. *Hate Speech: The History of an American Controversy* (Lincoln: University of Nebraska Press, 1994).

Weinstein, James. *Hate Speech, Pornography, and the Radical Attack on Free Speech* (Boulder, Colo.: Westview Press, 1999).

Whillock, Rita Kirk, and Slayden, David, eds. *Hate Speech* (Thousand Oaks, Calif.: Sage, 1995).

Yarbrough, Tinsley E. *Mr. Justice Black and His Critics* (Durham, N.C.: Duke University Press, 1988).

Amar, Akhil Reed. "The Case of the Missing Amendments: *R.A.V. v. City of St. Paul*," *106 Harvard Law Review* 124 (1992).

Bell, Jeannine. "O Say, Can You See: Free Expression by the Light of Fiery Crosses," *39 Harvard Civil Rights-Civil Liberties Law Review* 335 (2004).

Cleary, Edward J. Telephone interview, June 22, 2005.

Delgado, Richard. "Campus Antiracism Rules: Constitutional Narratives in Collision," *85 Northwestern University Law Review* 343 (1991).

"Hate Crimes," *MacNeil/Lehrer NewsHour*, February 20, 1992 (transcript 4274).

Hyde, Henry J., and Fishman, George. "The Collegiate Speech Protection Act of 1991: A Response to the New Intolerance in the Academy," *37 Wayne Law Review* 1469 (1991).

Karst, Kenneth L. "Boundaries and Reasons: Freedom of Expression and the Subordination of Groups," *1990 University of Illinois Law Review* 95.

Lawrence, Charles R. "If He Hollers Let Him Go: Regulating Speech on Campus," *Duke Law Journal* 431 (1990).

Lively, Donald E. "Reformist Myopia and the Imperative of Progress: Lessons for the Post-Brown Era," 46 *Vanderbilt Law Review* 865 (1993).

Matsuda, Mari J. "Public Response to Racist Speech: Considering the Victim's Story," 87 *Michigan Law Review* 2320 (1989).

Mauro, Tony. "Policing Hate Speech: Not the Government's Job," May 2009, www.tjcenter.org/wp-content/uploads/Spkng%20Frly%20Mauro%204-27-09.pdf.

McMasters, Paul. "Must a Civil Society Be a Censored Society?" 26 *Human Rights*, No. 4 (1999).

Schauer, Frederick. "Intentions, Conventions, and the First Amendment: The Case of Cross-Burning," 2003 *Supreme Court Review* 197.

Strossen, Nadine. "Regulating Racist Speech on Campus: A Modest Proposal?" *Duke Law Journal* 484 (1990).

Barringer, Felicity. "Campus Battle Pits Freedom of Speech against Racial Slurs," *New York Times*, April 25, 1989, sec. A, p. 1.

"Regents Approve a Disputed Ban on Discrimination," *New York Times*, June 18, 1989, p. 36.

Bernstein, Richard. "On Campus, How Free Should Speech Be?" *New York Times*, September 10, 1989, sec. E, p. 5.

"University Panel Votes to Prohibit Harassing Words," *New York Times*, May 27, 1990, p. 40.

"Student at Brown Is Expelled under a Rule Barring 'Hate Speech,'" *New York Times*, February 12, 1991, sec. A, p. 1.

"Kicked Out," *New York Times*, February 17, 1991, sec. E, p. 7.

Anthony DePalma. "Battling Bias, Campuses Face Free Speech Fight," *New York Times*, February 20, 1991, sec. B, p. 9.

"How Much Hate to Tolerate," *New York Times*, February 21, 1991, sec. A, p. 20.

Harvard Hollenberg. "Brown Blurs Line between Speech and Action," *New York Times*, March 16, 1991, p. 22 (letter to the editor).

Linda Greenhouse. "Justices to Decide If Hate Crime Law Illegally Curbs Freedom of Expression," *New York Times*, June 11, 1991, sec. A, p. 20.

Andrew Rosenthal. "Marshall Retires from High Court; Blow to Liberals," *New York Times*, June 28, 1991, sec. A, p. 1.

Neil Lewis. "Friends of Free Speech Now Consider Its Limits," *New York Times*, June 29, 1990, sec. B, p. 7.

"Clarence Thomas in His Own Words," *New York Times*, July 2, 1991, sec. A, p. 14.

Maureen Dowd. "Bush's 'Best Man,'" *New York Times*, July 2, 1991, sec. A, p. 1.

Linda Greenhouse. "Bush Picks a Wild Card," *New York Times*, July 2, 1991, sec. A, p. 1.

Steven A. Holmes. "Black Quandary over Court Nominee," *New York Times*, July 4, 1991, sec. A, p. 12.

Richard L. Berke. "Judge Thomas Faces Bruising Battle with Liberals over Stand on Rights," *New York Times*, July 4, 1991, sec. A, p. 12.

Linda Greenhouse. "A Remade Court Shifts the Fulcrums of Power," *New York Times*, July 7, 1991, sec. E, p. 1.

Linda Greenhouse. "Court Choice Puts Nation's Racial Legacy on Table," *New York Times*, July 8, 1991, sec. A, p. 9.

Roberto Suro. "NAACP Defers Stance on Court Pick," *New York Times*, July 9, 1991, sec. A, p. 1.

Roberto Suro. "Jackson Assails Thomas," *New York Times*, July 11, 1991, sec. A, p. 17.

Richard L. Berke. "Black Caucus Votes to Oppose Thomas for High Court Seat," *New York Times*, July 12, 1991, sec. A, p. 1.

Neil Lewis. "As Hearings on Thomas Approach, Attention Focuses on Foes' Strategy," *New York Times*, July 29, 1991, sec. A, p. 12.

Anthony DePalma. "U.S. Judge Upholds Speech on Campus," *New York Times*, August 29, 1991, sec. A, p. 25.

"Lessons in Protest and Tolerance," *New York Times*, September 3, 1991, sec. A, p. 22.

Neil Lewis. "Law Professor Accuses Thomas of Sexual Harassment in 1980's," *New York Times*, October 7, 1991, sec. A, p. 1.

Linda Greenhouse. "Justices Return to Work," *New York Times*, October 7, 1991, sec. A, p. 1.

"Anita Hill and the Senate's Duty," *New York Times*, October 8, 1991, sec. A, p. 24.

Anna Quindlen. "An American Tragedy," *New York Times*, October 12, 1991, p. 29.

Jane Gross. "Americans Riveted by Lesson in Civics," *New York Times*, October 12, 1991, p. 1.

Anthony DePalma. "Taboo Issues of Sex and Race Explode in Glare of Hearing," *New York Times*, October 13, 1991, p. 1.

"Court Voids Wisconsin U's Ban on Hate Speech," *New York Times*, October 13, 1991, p. 25.

R. W. Apple, Jr. "Court's 2D Black," *New York Times*, October 16, 1991, sec. A, p. 1.

Orlando Patterson. "Race, Gender, and Liberal Fallacies," *New York Times*, October 20, 1991, sec. E, p. 15.

Kathleen Quinn. "Joe McCarthy, Back in Style," *New York Times*, November 2, 1991, p. 23.

"Taking Sides against Ourselves," *New York Times*, November 17, 1991, sec. A, p. 1.

Tamar Lewin. "Hate-crime Law Is Focus of Case on Free Speech," *New York Times*, December 1, 1991, p. 1.

"Running for President: Hate and Fear," *New York Times*, December 5, 1991, sec. A, p. 32.

Linda Greenhouse. "Justices Weigh Ban on Voicing Hate," *New York Times*, December 5, 1991, sec. B, p. 19.

Bishop, Katherine. "Ads on Holocaust 'Hoax' Inspire Campus Debates," *New York Times*, December 23, 1991, sec. A, p. 1.

Seth Mydans. "Since Beating, Little Change for Los Angeles Police," *New York Times*, March 29, 1992, p. 12.

Seth Mydans. "Verdicts Set Off a Wave of Shock and Anger," *New York Times*, April 30, 1992, Sect D, p. 22.

Seth Mydans. "900 Reported Hurt," *New York Times*, May 1, 1992, sec. A, p. 1.

Isabel Wilkerson. "Acquittal in Beating Raises Fears over Race Relations," *New York Times*, May 1, 1992, sec. A, p. 23.

Andrew Rosenthal. "Bush Says Verdict 'Stunned' Him; He Vows to Put an End to Rioting," *New York Times*, May 2, 1992, p. 1.

Richard W. Stevenson. "Calm Is Tenuous," *New York Times*, May 2, 1992, p. 1.

Don Terry. "Decades of Rage Created Crucible of Violence," *New York Times*, May 3, 1992, p. 2.

"Excerpts from the U.S. Supreme Court's Decision on Speech and Crimes of Bias," *New York Times*, June 23, 1992, sec. A, p. 16.

Linda Greenhouse. "Opinions Are Split," *New York Times*, June 23, 1992, sec. A, p. 1.

Don Terry. "Rights Advocates Uncertain about Ruling's Impact," *New York Times*, June 23, 1992, sec. A, p. 16.

"Loosing Hateful Speech," *New York Times*, June 24, 1992, sec. A, p. 20.

James Walsh. "Cross-burning Victim, Suspect Discuss Feelings," Minneapolis *Star Tribune*, June 24, 1992, sec. B, p. 1.

Linda Greenhouse. "The Court's 2 Visions of Free Speech," *New York Times*, June 24, 1992, sec. A, p. 13.

William Celis. "Universities Reconsidering Bans on Hate Speech," *New York Times*, June 24, 1992, sec. A, p. 13.

Floyd Abrams. "Right Way to Read 'Hate Speech' Opinion," *New York Times*, July 3, 1992, sec. A, p. 24 (letter to the editor).

"A 2d Hate-crime Charge for Man after High Court Voided the First," *New York Times*, October 23, 1992, sec. B, p. 16.

"Man Who Had Role in Hate-crimes Case Enters a Guilty Plea," *New York Times*, November 6, 1992, sec. A, p. 13.

Randy Furst. "Black Family Gets Strong Support after Cross-Burning," Minneapolis *Star Tribune*, December 24, 1992, sec. B, p. 1.

Neal Goldfarb. "No Legal Defense Left to Those Who Give Instructions for Murder," *Legal Times*, November 17, 1997, p. 23.

"Supreme Court Allows Lawsuit against Hit Man Publisher," Associated Press, April 20, 1998.

"*Hit Man* Publisher Settles Oregon Lawsuit," Associated Press, February 27, 2002.

Michelle Lore. "Office of Lawyers Professional Responsibility Director Returns to Courtroom," *Minnesota Lawyer*, August 12, 2002.

Linda Greenhouse. "An Intense Attack by Justice Thomas on Cross Burning," *New York Times*, December 12, 2002, p. 1.

Jan Crawford Greenburg,. "Emotional Court Weighs Cross Burning," *Chicago Tribune*, December 12, 2002, p. 10.

Lyle Denniston. "Thomas Breaks Silence to Denounce Klan: Court Weighs Cross Burning," *Boston Globe*, December 12, 2002, sec. A, p. 2.

David G. Savage. "Thomas Assails Cross Burning as Terror Tactic," *Los Angeles Times*, December 12, 2002, p. 41.

Joan Biskupic. "Cross Burning Case Agitates Thomas," *U.S.A. Today*, December 12, 2002, sec. A, p. 3.

"Justice Thomas Speaks Out—Against Free Speech," *Newsday*, December 13, 2002, sec. A, p. 52.

Glod, Maria. "Fire Long Gone, Intimidation Still Smolders," *Washington Post*, April 11, 2003, sec. B, p. 5.

"Virginia High Court Throws Out Part of Cross-burning Law," Associated Press, March 8, 2004.

Jon Frank. "Jail Time Finally Given for Cross Burning," *Virginian-Pilot*, July 1, 2004, sec. B, p. 2.

CHAPTER 8: STRIKING BACK AT THE BIRCHERS

Note: We relied heavily on Elmer Gertz, *Gertz v. Welch, Inc.: The Story of a Landmark Case* (1992) and *To Life: The Story of a Chicago Lawyer* (1974). Extensive bibliographical material concerning the *Gertz* case is stored in the special collection of the Morris Library, Southern Illinois University at Carbondale. An abbreviated account of the *Gertz* case is presented in Peter Irons, *The Courage of Their Convictions: Sixteen Americans Who Fought Their Way to the Supreme Court* (1989).

Beauharnais v. Illinois, 343 U.S. 250 (1952).
Chaplinsky v. New Hampshire, 315 U.S. 568 (1942).
Curtis Publishing Co. v. Butts, 388 U.S. 130 (1967).
Dunn & Bradstreet, Inc. v. Greenmoss Builders, Inc., 472 U.S. 749 (1985).
Garrison v. Louisiana, 379 U.S. 64 (1964).
Cusack v. Teitel Film Corp., 230 N.E.2d 241 (Ill. 1967).
Farnsworth v. Chicago Tribune, 253 N.E.2d 408 (Ill. 1969).
Gertz v. Robert Welch, Inc., 306 F. Supp. 310 (N.D. Ill. 1969).
Gertz v. Robert Welch, Inc., 322 F. Supp. 997 (N.D. Ill. 1971).
Gertz v. Robert Welch, Inc., 418 U.S. 323 (1974).
Gertz v. Robert Welch, Inc., 459 U.S. 1226 (1983) (cert. denial).
Gertz v. Robert Welch, Inc., 471 F.2d 801 (7th Cir. 1972).
Gertz v. Robert Welch, Inc., 680 F.2d 527 (7th Cir. 1982).
Herbert v. Lando, 441 U.S. 153 (1979).
Hutchinson v. Proxmire, 443 U.S. 111 (1979).
Leopold v. Levin, 259 N.E.2d 250 (Ill. 1970).
Miami Herald Publishing Co. v. Tornillo, 418 U.S. 241 (1979).
Myers v. Spohnholtz, 297 N.E.2d 183 (Ill. App. 1973).
Nelson v. Nuccio, 131 Ill. App. 2d 2611 (Ill. 1st Dist. 1971).
New York Times Co. v. Sullivan, 376 U.S. 254 (1964).
Old Dominion Branch No. 46, National Ass'n of Letter Carriers, AFL-CIO v. Austin, 418 U.S. 264 (1974).
Parmelee v. Hearst Publishing Co., 93 N.E.2d 512 (1950).
People v. Butler, 275 N.E.2d 400 (Ill. 1971).
People v. Nuccio, 253 N.E.2d 353 (Ill. 1969).
People v. Nuccio, 294 N.E.2d 276 (Ill. 1973).
People v. Romaine, 231 N.E.2d 413 (Ill. 1967).
People v. Sparks, 321 N.E.2d 33 (Ill. App. 1974).
Rebozo v. The Washington Post Co., 637 F.2d 375 (5th Cir. 1981), *cert. den.* 454 U.S. 964 (1981).
Rebozo v. The Washington Post Co., 515 F.2d 1208 (5th Cir. 1975).
Rosenblatt v. Baer, 383 U.S. 75 (1966).
Rosenbloom v. Metromedia, Inc., 403 U.S. 29 (1971).
Rubenstein v. State, 407 S.W.2d 793 (Crim. App. Tex. 1966).

St. Amant v. Thompson, 390 U.S. 727 (1968).

Time, Inc. v. Firestone, 424 U.S. 448 (1970).

Toledo Newspaper Co. v. United States, 247 U.S. 402 (1918).

University of California Regents v. Bakke, 438 U.S. 265 (1978).

Zeinfeld v. Haynes Freight Lines, Inc, 243 N.E.2d 217 (Ill. 1968).

Barron, Jerome, and Dienes, Thomas. *First Amendment Law,* 3rd ed. (St. Paul: West Group, 2000).

Beason, Randall, Cranberg, Gilbert, and Soloski, John. *Libel Law and the Press: Myth and Reality* (New York: Free Press, 1987).

Chafee, Zechariah, Jr. *Free Speech in the United States* (Cambridge, Mass.: Harvard University Press, 1942).

Chemerinsky, Erwin. *Constitutional Law: Principles and Policies,* 2nd ed. (New York: Aspen, 2002).

de Gracia, Edward. *Girls Lean Back Everywhere: The Law of Obscenity and the Assault on Genius* (New York: Random House, 1992).

Dickson, Dell, ed. *The Supreme Court in Conference (1940–1985)* (New York: Oxford University Press, 2001).

Emerson, Thomas I. *The System of Freedom of Expression* (New York: Vintage, 1970).

Farber, Daniel A. *The First Amendment,* 2nd ed. (New York: Foundation Press, 2003).

Fein, Bruce. *New York Times v. Sullivan: An Obstacle to Enlightened Public Discourse and Government Responsiveness to the People* (Washington, D.C.: American Legal Foundation, 1984).

Freund, Paul, Sutherland, Arthur, DeWolfe Howe, Mark, and Brown, Ernest. *Constitutional Law: Cases and Other Problems,* 3rd ed. (New York: Little, Brown, 1967).

Garbus, Martin, with Cohen, Stanley. *Tough Talk: How I Fought for Writers, Comics, Bigots, and the American Way* (New York: Times Books, 1998).

Gertz, Elmer. *A Handful of Clients* (Chicago: Follett, 1965).

Gertz, Elmer, and Lewis, Felice F. *Henry Miller: Years of Trial and Triumph, 1962–1964: The Correspondence of Henry Miller and Elmer Gertz* (Carbondale: Southern Illinois University Press, 1978).

Hall, Kermit, ed. *The Oxford Companion to the Supreme Court of the United States,* 2nd ed. (New York: Oxford University Press, 2005).

Hedin, Benjamin, ed. *Studio A: The Bob Dylan Reader* (New York: Norton, 2004).

Hentoff, Nat. *The First Freedom: The Tumultuous History of Free Speech in America* (New York: Delacorte Press, 1980).

Kutler, Stanley I., ed. *Abuse of Power: The Nixon Tapes* (New York: Simon and Schuster, 1997).

Labunski, Richard. *Libel and the First Amendment: Legal History and Practice in Print and Broadcasting* (New Brunswick, N.J.: Transaction Books, 1987).

Levy, Leonard W. *Emergence of a Free Press* (New York: Oxford University Press, 1985).

Lewis, Anthony. *Make No Law: The Sullivan case and the First Amendment* (New York: Random House, 1991).

Marqusee, Mike. *Chimes of Freedom: The Politics of Bob Dylan's Art* (New York: New Press, 2003.

Nixon, Richard. *The Memoirs of Richard Nixon* (New York: Simon and Schuster, 1990).

O'Neil, Robert M. *The First Amendment and Civil Liability* (Bloomington: Indiana University Press, 2001).

Porter, William E. *Assault on the Press: The Nixon Years* (Ann Arbor: University of Michigan Press, 1976).

Rosenberg, Norman L. *Protecting the Best Men: An Interpretive History of the Law of Libel* (Durham, N.C.: University of North Carolina Press, 1986).

Sack, Robert D. *Sack on Defamation: Libel, Slander, and Related Problems* (New York: Practicing Law Institute, 2001), Vol. 1.

Safire, William. *Before the Fall: An Inside View of the Pre-Watergate White House* (New York: Doubleday, 1975).

Sanford, Bruce W. *Don't Shoot the Messenger: How Our Growing Hatred of the Media Threatens Free Speech for All of Us* (New York: Free Press, 1999).

———. *Libel and Privacy: The Prevention and Defense of Litigation*, 2nd ed. (New York: Harcourt Brace Jovanovich, 1999).

———. *Sanford's Synopsis of Libel and Privacy*, 4th ed. (Mahwah, N.J.: World Almanac Books, 1991).

Schwartz, Bernard. *Super Chief: Earl Warren and His Supreme Court—a Judicial Biography* (New York: New York University Press, 1983).

Shiffrin, Steven. *The First Amendment, Democracy, and Romance* (Cambridge, Mass.: Harvard University Press, 1990).

Smith, James Morton. *Freedom's Fetters: The Alien and Sedition Laws and American Civil Liberties* (Ithaca, N.Y.: Cornell University Press, 1956).

Smolla, Rodney A. *Law of Defamation* (New York: C. Boardman, 1986).

———. *Smolla and Nimmer on Freedom of Speech: A Treatise on the First Amendment* (New York: Times Mirror Books, 1994).

———. *Suing the Press: Libel, the Media, and Power* (New York: Oxford University Press, 1986).

Spear, Joseph C. *Presidents and the Press* (Cambridge, Mass.: MIT Press, 1984).

Tedford, Thomas L., and Herbeck, Dale A. *Freedom of Speech in the United States* (State College, Pa.: Strata, 2005).

Tribe, Laurence H. *American Constitutional Law, Second Edition* (Mineola, N.Y.: Foundation Press, 1988).

Citrine, Charlie. "Watergate Timeline," available at the website of Bjørnetjenesten, www.bjornetjenesten.dk/teksterdk/watergate.htm.

Emerson, Thomas I. "Freedom of the Press under the Burger Court," in *The Burger Court: The Counter-REVOLUTION That Wasn't* (New Haven, Conn.: Yale University Press, 1983), 1–28.

Fein, Bruce. "Taking the Stand: Pack the Supreme Court," *Washington Lawyer*, February 2005, www.dcbar.org/for_lawyers/washington_lawyer/february_2005/stand.cfm.

Fiss, Owen. "Kalven's Way," 43 *University of Chicago Law Review* 4 (1975) (re Freund casebook).

Kalven, Harry, Jr. "The *New York Times* Case: A Note on 'The Central Meaning of the First Amendment,'" 1964 *SupremeCourt Review* 191.

———. "'Uninhibited, Robust, and Wide-Open': A Note on Free Speech and the Warren Court," 67 *Michigan Law Review* 289 (1968).

Levine, Lee J. "Judge and Jury in the Law of Defamation: Putting the Horse before the Cart," 35 *American University Law Review* 3 (1985).

———. Note. "The Editorial Function and the *Gertz* Public Figure Standard," 87 *Yale Law Journal* 1723 (1978).

"Shaping the Law with a Fein Touch; Profile of Bruce Elliott Fein," *Broadcasting*, June 11, 1984, vol. 106, p. 111.

Stang, Alan. "As I See It: A Brief Memoir," www.alanstang.com/.

"Watergate 25: Timeline, the Details," www.washingtonpost.com/wp-srv/national/longterm/watergate/chronology.htm.

"Doctor Defies Alienation Law in $50,000 Lawsuit," *Chicago Tribune*, September 17, 1941, p. 24.

"Leopold Asks for Sentence Commutation," *Chicago Daily Tribune*, July 8, 1957, p. 1.

Clay Gowran. "Set Leopold Free, His Friends Urge," *Chicago Daily Tribune*, July 10, 1957, p. 1.

"Thrill Slayer Leopold Gets Parole," *Los Angeles Times*, February 21, 1958, p. 1.

"Tropic of Cancer Wins," *New York Times*, February 22, 1962, p. 23.

Herb Lyon. "Tower Ticker," *Chicago Tribune*, May 15, 1963, p. 14 [re Ed Sullivan and Bob Dylan].

"Hate Groups Are Topic for Temple Men's Club," *Chicago Tribune*, February 20, 1964, sec. N, p. 3.

"Sues Playboy and Garrison for 10 Million," *Chicago Tribune*, November 2, 1967, p. 22.

"Cop Sued for $350,000 in Police Killing," *Chicago Tribune*, July 4, 1968, p. 3.

"Lawyer Loses Suit against Birchers," *Washington Post*, December 10, 1970, sec. A, p. 5.

John Hanrahan. "Watergate Probers to Hold Hearings on $100,000 Hughes Paid Rebozo," *Washington Post*, October 25, 1973, sec. A, p. 19.

Ronald Kessler. "Bebe Rebozo Said to Cash Stolen Stock; Stock Stolen by the Mafia was Cashed by Rebozo—Denies Knowing Stock He Cashed Was Stolen," *Washington Post*, October 25, 1973, sec. A, p. 1.

"Rebozo's Bank Hired Barred Broker," *Washington Post*, October 25, 1973, sec. A, p. 1.

"Nixon Aims to Tighten Libel Laws," *Washington Post*, March 7, 1974, sec. A, p. 8 (AP story).

John MacKenzie. "Libel Challenges," *Washington Post*, March 9, 1974, sec. A, p. 1.

Linda Matthews. "The Miami Herald Case," *Washington Post*, April 15, 1974, sec. A, p. 1.

"Rebozo Suits against Post Still Stands," *Washington Post*, May 9, 1974, sec. A, p. 4 (AP story).

"Ordinary Citizen Given Right to a Libel Suit over False Report," *New York Times*, June 26, 1974, p. 89.

John MacKenzie. "High Court Makes Private Person's Libel Suit Easier," *Washington Post*, June 26, 1974, sec. A, p. 8.

"Court Rules for Rebozo against Post," *Washington Post*, July 17, 1975, sec. A, p. 2 (UPI story).

"Rebozo Suit against Post Dismissed," *Washington Post*, September 19, 1978, sec. A, p. 7 (AP story).

"Rebozo Suit vs. Post Ordered Reopened," *Washington Post*, February 20, 1981, sec. A, p. 16 (AP story).

"Charles (Bebe) Rebozo, Post Settle 10-year-old Libel Suit," *Washington Post*, November 4, 1983, sec. A, p. 4.

"Rebozo and Paper Settle Suit," *New York Times*, November 5, 1983, p. 32 (AP story).

"John Birch Society Founder Robert Welch," *Chicago Tribune*, January 8, 1985, sec. C, p. 6 (obit.).

Robert D. McFadden. "Robert Welch Jr. Dead at 85; John Birch Society's Founder," *New York Times*, January 8, 1985, sec. B, p. 6.

Michael Seiler. "Robert Welch, Founder of Birch Society, Dies at 85," *Los Angeles Times*, January 8, 1985, sec. 1, p. 1.

Allison Klein. "Bebe Rebozo, President Nixon's Best Buddy, Dies at 85," Knight Ridder, May 9, 1998.

"Bebe Rebozo, Confidant of President Nixon, Dies at 85," Associated Press, May 9, 1998.

David Binder. "Bebe Rebozo, Loyal Friend in Nixon's Darkest Days, Dies at 85," *New York Times*, May 10, 1998, p. 36.

David Binder. "Charles (Bebe) Rebozo, 85; Longtime Nixon Confidant," *New York Times*, May 10, 1998, p. 12.

Maura Kelly. "400 Honor Life, Ideals of Elmer Gertz," *Chicago Tribune*, May 2, 2000, sec. 2, p. 6.

CHAPTER 9: SAVING OLD GLORY

Note: No one writing on flag desecration can do any reliable or informed work without relying, even heavily so, on the many works of Robert Justin Goldstein. We gratefully recognize our own debt to Professor Goldstein. In addition, the best analytical work yet done on flag desecration constitutional amendments is Robert Corn-Revere, "Implementing a Flag-Desecration Amendment to the U.S. Constitution," *First Amendment Center: First Reports* (vol. 6, no. 1, July 2005).

Goguen v. Smith, 471 F.2d 88 (1st Cir. 1972).

Halter v. Nebraska, 205 U.S. 34 (1907).

Hoffman v. United States, 445 F.2d 226 (D.C. Cir. 1971).

Minersville School District v. Gobitis, 310 U.S. 586 (1940).

New York v. Radich, 294 N.Y.S.2d 285 (N.Y. S. Ct., 1969).

New York v. Radich, 308 N.Y.S.2d 846 (N.Y. 1970).

Radich v. New York, 401 U.S. 531 (1971).

R.A.V. v. City of St. Paul, 505 U.S. 377 (1992).

Smith v. Goguen, 415 U.S. 566 (1974).

Spence v. Washington, 418 U.S. 405 (1974).

Street v. New York, 20 N. Y. 2d 231, 229 N. E. 2d 187 (1967).

Street v. New York, 394 U.S. 576 (1969).

Stromberg v. People of State of California, 283 U.S. 359 (1931).

Texas v. Johnson, 491 U.S. 397 (1989).

United States ex rel Radich v. Criminal Court, 385 F. Supp. 165 (S.D.N.Y. 1974).

United States v. Eichman, 496 U.S. 310 (1990).

United States v. Eichman, 731 F. Supp. 1123 (D.D.C. 1990).

United States v. Haggerty, 731 F. Supp. 415 (Wa. Dist. Ct., 1990).
United States v. O'Brien, 391 U.S. 367 (1968).
West Virginia State Board of Education v. Barnette, 319 U.S. 624 (1943).

Barron, Jerome, and Dienes, C. Thomas. *First Amendment Law in a Nutshell*, 4th ed. (St. Paul: West Group, 2008).

Chemerinsky, Erwin. *Constitutional Law: Principles and Policies*, 2nd ed. Aspen, Colo.: Aspen Law and Business, 2002).

Curtis, Michael Kent. *The Constitution and the Flag* (New York: Garland Press, 1993).

Dickson, Dell, ed. *The Supreme Court in Conference: 1940–1985* (New York: Oxford University Press, 2001).

Emerson, Thomas, I. *The System of Freedom of Expression* (New York: Random House, 1970).

Farber, Daniel A. *The First Amendment*, 2nd ed. (New York: Foundation Press, 2003).

Gitlin, Todd. *The Intellectuals and the Flag* (New York: Columbia University Press, 2006).

Goldstein, Robert J. *Burning the Flag: The Great 1989–90 American Flag Desecration Controversy*. Kent, Ohio: Kent State University Press, 1996).

———, ed. *Desecrating the American Flag*. Syracuse, N.Y/: Syracuse University Press, 1996).

———. *Flag Burning and Free Speech*. Lawrence: Kansas University Press, 2000).

———. *Saving Old Glory: The History of the American Flag Desecration Controversy*. Boulder, Colo.: Westview Press, 1995).

Haynes, Charles C., Chaltain, Sam, and Glisson, Susan. *First Freedoms: A Documentary History of First Amendment Rights in America* (New York: Oxford University Press, 2006).

Irons, Peter, ed. *May it Please the Court: The First Amendment* (New York: New Press, 1997).

Kalman, Laura. *Abe Fortas: A Biography*. New Haven, Conn.: Yale University Press, 1990).

Leepson, M. *Flag: An American Biography* (New York: St. Martin's Press, 2005).

Marty, Martin E. *Modern American Religion*, vol. 3, *Under God, Indivisible 1941–1960* (Chicago: University of Chicago Press, 1999).

The Misuse of the Flag of the United States: An Appeal to the Fifty-Fourth Congress of the United States (Chicago: National Flag Committee of the Society of Colonial Wars in the State of Illinois, 1895).

Robinson, M., and Simoni, C. *The Flag and the Law: A Documentary History of the Treatment of the American Flag by the Supreme Court and Congress*, vols. 1–4 (Buffalo: W. S. Hein, 1993).

Schwartz, Bernard. *Super Chief: Earl Warren and His Supreme Court*. New York: New York University Press, 1983).

Smolla, Rodney, A. *Free Speech in an Open Society* (New York: Knopf, 1990).

———. *Smolla and Nimmer on Freedom of Speech: A Treatise on the First Amendment* (New York: Times Mirror Books, 1994).

Welch, M. *Flag Burning: Moral Panic and the Criminalization of Protest* (New York: de Gruyter, 2000).

Yarborough, Tinsley. *John Marshall Harlan: Great Dissenter of the Warren Court*. New York: Oxford University Press, 1992).

"Constitutional Amendment to Prohibit Physical Desecration of U.S. Flag," S. Rpt. 108–334, 108th Congress, 2nd Session 17 (July 22, 2004).

Conyers, J. "Desecrating the Constitution," 8 *Seton Hall Constitutional Law Journal* 1 (1997).

Corn-Revere, Robert. "Implementing a Flag-Desecration Amendment to the U.S. Constitution," *First Amendment Center: First Reports*, vol. 6, no. 1 (July 2005).

Dorsen, Norman. "Flag Desecration in Courts, Congress and Country," 17 *Thomas M. Cooley Law Review* 417 (2000).

Dyer, J. R. "*Texas v. Johnson*: Symbolic Speech and Flag Desecration under the First Amendment," 25 *New England Law Review* 895 (1991).

Ely, John Hart. "Flag Desecration: A Case Study in the Roles of Categorization and Balancing in First Amendment Analysis," 88 *Harvard Law Review* 1482 (1975).

Gey, Steven G. "This Is Not a Flag: The Aesthetics of Desecration," *Wisconsin Law Review* 1549 (1990).

Goldstein, Robert J. "The Great 1989–1990 Flag Flap: An Historical, Political and Legal Analysis," 19 *University of Miami Law Review* 106 (1990).

Greenawalt, Kent. "O'er the Land of the Free: Flag Burning as Speech," 37 *U.C.L.A. Law Review* 925 (1990).

Harpaz, Leora. "Justice Jackson's Flag Salute Legacy: The Supreme Court Struggles to Protect Intellectual Individualism," 64 *Texas Law Review* 817 (1986).

Henderson, M. A. "Today's Symbolic Speech Dilemma: Flag Desecration and the Proposed Constitutional Amendment," 41 *South Dakota Law Review* 533 (1996).

Loewy, Arnold H. "The Flag Burning Case: Freedom of Speech When We Need It Most," 68 *North Carolina Law Review* 165 (1989).

"Measures to Protect the American Flag, 1990: Hearing before the Senate Comm. on the Judiciary," 101st Congress, 2nd sess., 113 (June 21, 1990).

Michelman, Frank. "Saving Old Glory: On Constitutional Iconography," 42 *Stanford Law Review* 1337 (July 1990).

Post, Robert, "Recuperating First Amendment Doctrine," 47 *Stanford Law Review* 1249 (1995).

Rosen, Jeffrey. "Was the Flag Burning Amendment Unconstitutional?" 100 *Yale Law Journal* 1073 (1991).

Rotnem, Victor W., and Folson, F. G., Jr. "Recent Restrictions upon Religious Liberty," *American Political Science Review*, Vol. XXXVI, No. 6 (1942).

Stone, Geoffrey R. "Flag Burning and the Constitution," 75 *Iowa Law Review* 111 (1989).

Taylor, R. N., III. "The Protection of Flag Burning as Symbolic Speech and the Congressional Attempt to Overturn the Decision *Texas v. Johnson*," 58 *University of Cincinnati Law Review* 1477 (1990).

Vergobbi, David J. "*Texas v. Johnson*," in *Free Speech on Trial*, edited by Richard A. Parker (Tuscaloosa: University of Alabama Press, 2003), pp. 281–297.

"Flag Must Be Respected—Advertising on National and State Emblems to Be Stopped," *New York Times*, July 22, 1900.

"Court Protects Flag," *Washington Post*, March 5, 1907, p. 13.

"Asserted Reds Arraigned in Redlands Court," *Los Angeles Times*, August 6, 1929, sec. A, p. 14.

"Red Paraders Arrested," *Los Angeles Times*, September 7, 1929, sec. A, p. 1.

"Children Bare Red Camp Talk," *Los Angeles Times*, October 4, 1929, p. 12.

"Red Flag Flying Punished," *Los Angeles Times*, October 10, 1929, p. 10.

"Sentence Given to Women Reds," *Los Angeles Times*, October 24, 1929, p. 6.

"Editorial of the Day," *Chicago Daily News*, December 5, 1929, p. 14.

"Five Reds Held for Jury Trial," *Los Angeles Times*, April 30, 1930, sec. A, p. 3.

"Boy Reveals Red Tactics," *Los Angeles Times*, May 8, 1930, sec. A, p. 12.

"Red Riot Charges Denied," *Los Angeles Times*, May 9, 1930, sec. A, p. 9.

"Reds Get Jail Sentences," *Los Angeles Times*, May 14, 1930, sec. A, p. 1.

"State Red Flag Law Supported," *Los Angeles Times*, July 1, 1930, sec. A, p. 1.

"Will Test Red Flag Laws," *New York Times*, July 9, 1930, p. 18.

"Yetta Stromberg in Appeal to Supreme Court," *Los Angeles Times*, October 9, 1930, p. 20.

"California Law Placing Curb on Reds Attacked," *Los Angeles Times*, December 10, 1930, p. 1.

"State's Red Flag Law Attacked," *Los Angeles Times*, March 29, 1931, p. 5.

"State to Fight Red Case Plea," *Los Angeles Times*, April 3, 1931, sec. A, p. 3.

"Supreme Court Rules Red Flag Is Not Sedition," *Chicago Daily Tribune*, May 19, 1931, p. 8.

"Red Banner Law Upset," *Los Angeles Times*, May 19, 1931, p. 3.

"Legion Swats Communism," *Los Angeles Times*, May 22, 1931, p. 12.

"Plan Salute Ruling Fight," *New York Times*, December 3, 1937, p. 25.

Lewis Wood. "Supreme Court Ends Compulsion of Flag Salute," *New York Times*, June 14, 1943, p. 1.

"Court Upholds N.Y. Ban on Flag Burning," *Los Angeles Times*, July 8, 1967, p. 3.

"Court Ruling Backs Ban on Flag Burning," *Washington Post*, July 8, 1967, sec. A, p. 4.

"Decision Shocks O'Brien," *New York Times*, May 28, 1968, p. 32.

"Draft Card Burning," *Washington Times*, May 28, 1968, p. 20.

Fred P. Graham. "High Court Backs Ban on Burning of Draft Cards," *New York Times*, May 28, 1968, p. 1.

Ronald J. Ostrow. "Court Upholds Ban on Burning of Draft Cards, *Los Angeles Times*, May 28, 1968, p. 1.

"Students and the Draft," *New York Times*, May 28, 1968, p. 46.

Claudia Levy. "Women Burn Draft Cards at Court," *Washington Post*, June 18, 1968, sec. A, p. 1.

Fred P. Graham. "Strife-Beset Supreme Court Begins Term Today," *New York Times*, October 7, 1968, p. 50.

"High Court is Asked to Upset State Ban on Flag Mutilation," *New York Times*, October 22, 1968, p. 21.

"Court Upholds Right to Denounce Flag," *New York Times*, April 22, 1969, p. 22.

"Chaos Over the Issue of Its Abuse," *New York Times*, January 10, 1971, sec. E, p. 10.

"High Court Backs Law Against Flag Contempt," *Los Angeles Times*, March 25, 1971, p. 4.

"Conviction Upheld for Flag Patch," *Washington Post*, February 4, 1972, sec. C, p. 2.

"Wearing Flag on Seat of Pants Ruled No Crime," *Los Angeles Times*, May 30, 1972, p. 2.

Linda Mathews. "High Court Voids Statute Covering 'Contemptuous Treatment' of Flag," *Los Angeles Times*, March 26, 1974, p. 5.

Warren Weaver, Jr. "Court Voids Law Barring Contemptuous Use of Flag," *New York Times*, March 26, 1974, p. 21.

"Court Curbs State Law on Flag Use," *Washington Post*, June 26, 1974, sec. A, p. 8.

"99 Arrested in Dallas Protest," *New York Times*, August 23, 1984, sec. A, p. 26.

Al Kamen. "Emotional Disputes Flare Over Flag Desecration," *Washington Post*, March 19, 1989, sec. A, p. 9.

Nina Pillard and David Cole. "Defenders of the Flag," *New York Times*, March 23, 1989, sec. A, p. 28.

Linda Greenhouse. "Justices, 5–4, Back Protesters' Right to Burn the Flag," *New York Times*, June 22, 1989, sec. A, p. 1.

"New Glory for Old Glory," *New York Times*, June 23, 1989, sec. A, p. 28.

George F. Will. "Far Out with the First Amendment," *Washington Post*, June 23, 1989, sec. A, p. 23.

John P. MacKenzie. "The Hard Case of the Flag: Apologies and Surprises," *New York Times*, June 25, 1989, sec. E, p. 4.

William Raspberry. "Protecting a Hateful Act," *Washington Post*, June 26, 1989, sec. A, p. 11.

"Wrapped Up in the Flag," *New York Times*, June 27, 1989, sec. A, p. 22.

James J. Kilpatrick. "The Flag Will Survive," *Washington Post*, June 28, 1989, sec. A, p. 23.

Nat Hentoff. "A Frenzy of Flag Waving," *Washington Post*, July 1, 1989, sec. A, p. 17.

Linda Greenhouse. "High Court to Rule Quickly on Flag-burning Law," *New York Times*, March 31, 1990, p. 1.

Linda Greenhouse. "Supreme Court Voids Flag Law; Stage Set for Amendment Battle," *New York Times*, June 12, 1990, sec. A, p. 1.

Dan Balz and Tom Kenworthy. "Bush Again Calls for Flag Amendment," *Washington Post*, June 13, 1990, sec. A, p. 9.

Tom Kenworthy. "Panel Reluctantly Clears Flag Amendment," *Washington Post*, June 14, 1990, sec. A, p. 4.

Robert J. Goldstein. "Snuffing Out Symbolic Speech: This Flag Is Not for Burning," *Nation*, July 18, 1994, p. 84.

Phillip Taylor. "Amendment Backers, Foes Clash over Flag-desecration History," www.firstamendmentcenter.org (Associated Press, July 14, 1998).

Phillip Taylor. "Members of Congress ready to unfurl latest plan for flag amendment," www.firstamendmentcenter.org (Associated Press, February 23, 1999).

Phillip Taylor. "2 Harvard Professors Challenge Constitutionality of Flag-protection Statute," www.firstamendmentcenter.org (Associated Press, May 12, 1999).

Phillip Taylor. "House Prepared for Flag-amendment Vote," www.firstamendmentcenter.org (Associated Press, June 4, 1999).

Phillip Taylor. "State Officials Seldom Give Up on Flag-desecration Laws," www.firstamendmentcenter.org (Associated Press, March 13, 2001).

"Indiana Man Charged with Burning U.S. Flag," www.firstamendmentcenter.org (Associated Press, October 2, 2001).

"Flag-Burning Suspect Ordered Not to Touch, Handle or Possess Any U.S. flag," www.firstamendmentcenter.org (Associated Press, October 9, 2001).

"House Again OKs Changing Constitution to Ban Flag-Burning," www.firstamendment-center.org (Associated Press, June 4, 2003).

Ken Paulson. "Patriotism and Politics: The Rush to Rewrite the Constitution," www.firstamendmentcenter.org (June 15, 2003).

"Senate Subcommittee Approves Flag Amendment," www.firstamendmentcenter.org (Associated Press, June 3, 2004.

"Leave the Flag Alone," *Eugene (OR) Register-Guard*, June 14, 2004, sec. A, p. 8.

Orrin Hatch. "Desecration Is Not 'Speech,'" *U.S.A Today*, June 24, 2004, sec. A, p. 12.

L. J. Korb. "Flag Desecration Fissure," *Washington Times*, June 29, 2004, sec. A, p. 17.

"Senate Panel OKs Flag-burning Amendment," www.firstamendmentcenter.org (Associated Press, July 20, 2004).

Paul McMasters. "Burning the Bill of Rights to save the flag," www.firstamendmentcenter.org/commentary.aspx?id=14012, September 10, 2004.

"County Won't Prosecute Veteran for Upside-down U.S. Flag," www.firstamendmentcenter.org (Associated Press, November 13, 2004).

"63% Oppose Flag-burning Amendment, New Survey Shows," www.firstamendmentcenter.org (June 10, 2005).

"House Again Passes Flag-burning Amendment," www.firstamendmentcenter.org (Associated Press, June 22, 2005).

"10th Circuit Panel Hears Arguments in Utah Flag Case," www.firstamendmentcenter.org (Associated Press, August 18, 2005).

"Flag-protection Group Vows Continued Fight," www.firstamendmentcenter.org/news.aspx?id=17082 (Associated Press, June 28, 2006).

CHAPTER 10. COUNT-ME-INS AND COUNT-ME-OUTS

Note: Two particularly useful resources for the *Tinker* case and its history are John W. Johnson, *The Struggle for Student Rights* (1997) and the Supreme Court Appendix, no. 1034, for the case. U.S. casualty information was derived from the Combat Area Casualty File of 11/93 and the Adjutant General's Center (TAGCEN) file of 1981, available from the National Archives.

Adderley v. State of Florida, 385 U.S. 39 (1966).

Bethel School District No. 403 v. Fraser, 478 U.S. 675 (1986).

Blackwell v. Issaquena County Board of Education, 363 F.2d 749 (CA 5th Cir. 1966).

Broussard v. School Board of the City of Norfolk, 801 F. Supp. 1526 (E.D. Virg. 1992).

Burnside v. Byars, 363 F.2d 744 (5th Cir. 1966).

Dennis v. United States, 341 U.S. 494 (1951).

Desilets v. Clearview Board of Education, 630 A.2d 333 (S. Ct. N.J. 1993), *aff'd*, 137 N.J. 585 (1994).

Hazelwood School District v. Kuhlmeier, 484 U.S. 260 (1988).

Stromberg v. California, 283 U.S. 359 (1931).

Thornhill v. Alabama, 310 U.S. 88 (1940).

Tinker v. Des Moines Independent County School District, 393 U.S. 503 (1969).

West Virginia State Board of Education v. Barnette, 319 U.S. 624 (1943).

Barron, Jerome, and Dienes, C. Thomas. *First Amendment Law*, 2nd ed. (St. Paul: West Group, 2000).

Dickson, Dell, ed. *The Supreme Court in Conference (1940–1985): The Private Discussions behind Nearly 300 Supreme Court Decisions* (New York: Oxford University Press, 2001).

Farish, Leah. *Tinker v. Des Moines: Student Protest* (Springfield, N.J.: Enslow, 1997).

Fortas, Abe. *Concerning Dissent and Civil Disobedience* (New York: Signet Books, 1968).

Hall, Kermit, ed. *The Oxford Companion to the Supreme Court of the United States* (New York: Oxford University Press, 1992).

Haynes, Charles C., et al. *The First Amendment in Schools* (Alexandria, Va.: ASCD, 2003).

Hudson, David L. *The Silencing of Student Voices* (Nashville: First Amendment Center, 2003).

Irons, Peter. *The Courage of Their Convictions: Sixteen Americans Who Fought Their Way to the Supreme Court* (New York: Penguin, 1990).

Kalman, Laura. *Abe Fortas: A Biography* (New Haven, Conn.: Yale University Press, 1990).

Newman, Roger K. *Hugo Black: A Biography* (New York: Pantheon, 1994).

Yarbrough, Tinsley E. *Mr. Justice Black and His Critics* (Durham, N.C.: Duke University Press, 1988).

Amar, Akhil Reed. "A Tale of Three Wars: Tinker in Constitutional Context," 48 *Drake Law Review* 507 (2000).

Barber, Bretton. "One Year Ago: Notes from a Student Activist," available at the web site of Youth Free Expression Network: http://yfen.org/pages/opeds/oped-bretton.htm.

Chemerinsky, Erwin. "Students Do Leave Their First Amendment Rights at the Schoolhouse Gate: What's Left of *Tinker*?" 48 *Drake Law Review* 527 (2000).

Des Moines, city of. Official web site, www.ci.des-moines.ia.us/departments/AC/Information/AChistoricalinfo.htm.

Johnson, John W. "Behind the Scenes in Iowa's Greatest Case," 48 *Drake Law Review* 473 (2000).

Strossen, Nadine. "Keeping the Constitution inside the Schoolhouse Gate," 48 *Drake Law Review* 445 (2000).

"Ban on Armbands Upheld," *New York Times*, January 5, 1966, p. 6.

"Children, Says the Court, Should be Seen *and* Heard," *New York Times*, November 17, 1968, sec. E, p. 5.

"Court to Rule on Students' Right to Hold War Protests in School," *New York Times*, March 5, 1968, p. 26.

"High School Tells Student to Remove Antiwar Shirt," *New York Times*, February 26, 2003.

"High Court Upholds a Student Protest," *New York Times*, February 25, 1969, p. 1.

"Peaceful Protests in Schools Upheld" *Washington Post*, February 25, 1969, sec. A, p. 1.

"Student Gets Sent Home Over His Anti-Bush T-shirt," *The Detroit News*, February 19, 2003.
"T-shirt Fight Tests Free Speech in Schools," *Detroit News*, September 18, 2003.
"War 'Mourning' Pressed," *New York Times*, January 18, 1968, p. 50.

EPILOGUE. HUGO BLACK AND BEYOND

Buckley v. Valeo, 421 U.S. 1 (1976).
Cox v. Louisiana, 379 U.S. 536 (1965).
Cox v. Louisiana II, 379 U.S. 559 (1965).
FCC v. Pacifica, 438 U.S. 726 (1978).
Feiner v. New York, 340 U.S. 315 (1951).
Ginsburg v. United States, 383 U.S. 463 (1966).
Morse v. Frederick, 127 S. Ct. 2618 (2007).
Reno v. ACLU, 521 U.S. 844 (1997).
Smith v. California, 361 U.S. 147 (1959).

Black, Hugo, Jr. *My Father: A Remembrance* (New York: Random House, 1975).
Douglas, William O. *Points of Rebellion* (New York: Random House, 1970).
Dunne, Gerald. *Hugo Black and the Judicial Revolution* (New York: Simon and Schuster, 1977).
Emerson, Thomas I. *The System of Freedom of Expression* (New York: Vintage, 1970).
Newman, Roger K. *Hugo Black: A Biography* (New York: Pantheon, 1994).
Reich, Charles A. *The Greening of America* (New York: Random House, 1970).
———. *Opposing the System* (New York: Crown, 1995).
———. *The Sorcerer of Bolinas Reef* (New York: Random House, 1976).
Shiffrin, Steven. *The First Amendment, Democracy and Romance* (Cambridge, Mass.: Harvard University Press, 1990).

Hutchinson, Dennis. Book Review Essay, "Hugo Black among Friends," 93 *Michigan Law Review* 1885 (1995).
"Justice Black and the Bill of Rights: CBS News Special," 9 *Southwestern University Law Review* 937 (1977).
Kalven, Harry, Jr. "The Concept of the Public Forum: *Cox v. Louisiana* (1965)," in *Free Speech and Association*, edited by Philip B. Kurland (Chicago: University of Chicago Press, 1975).
Reich, Charles A. "Foreword: Mr. Justice Black as One Who Saw the Future," 9 *Southwestern University Law Review* 845 (1977).
———. "Mr. Justice Black and the Living Constitution," 76 *Harvard Law Review* 673 (1963).
———. "The New Property," 73 *Yale Law Journal* 733 (1964).

Editorial. "In the Nation: How Far Does Free Speech Go?" *New York Times*, December 5, 1968, p. 46.
Wolf Von Eckardt. "Charles Reich, Kids, and the 'New Consciousness,'" *Washington Post*, November 10, 1970, sec. A, p. 18.

John P. MacKenzie. "'All Deliberate Speed' Was Unwise Policy, Black Feels," *New York Times*, December 4, 1968, sec. A, p. 28.

Herbert Marcuse. "Charles Reich—A Negative View," *New York Times*, November 6, 1970, p. 35.

Charles A. Reich. "The Rebirth of the Future: I," *New York Times*, October 21, 1970, p. 47.

———. "The Rebirth of the Future: II," *New York Times*, October 22, 1970, p. 47.

Index

Abernathy, Ralph, 156
Abood v. Detroit Board of Education, 316
abortion, 319–20, 366n6
Abrams, Floyd, 70–71
Abrams, Jacob, 101, 110
Abrams, Mary, 101
Abrams v. United States, 110–11, 128,
    131, 306
abstention concept, 150
Ackerman, Kenneth, 22, 23, 24
actual malice standard, 163, 219, 223,
    229–32, 235, 319
Adams, John, 29, 208–9, 304
Adamson v. California, 36
Adderley v. Florida, 167, 281
advertising, 50
affirmative action, 227
Afghanistan War, 269
Agronsky, Martin, 293–98
Alabama. *See NAACP v. Alabama*
Alabama Pleading and Practice at Law
    (Jones), 153
Alabama Supreme Court, 147–49, 151,
    156, 159, 162, 218, 346n19
Alexander Meiklejohn Lecture, 57
Ali, Muhammad, 14
Alien and Sedition Acts, 28–29, 304
Alien Registration Act, 89, 92–93, 309
Alito, Samuel, 290, 301, 366n15
Amar, Akhil Reed, 353n59, 354n76
amendment proposals, 264–65, 319

American Civil Liberties Union (ACLU):
    and flag desecration cases, 251;
    founded, 307;
    and Gitlow pardon, 37;
    and Internet regulation, 320;
    and Meiklejohn, 48;
    origins of, 306, 331n19;
    and Pledge of Allegiance cases, 244;
    and speech codes, 176, 186–87;
    and student expression, 280
American Council on Education, 199
American Flag Association (AFA), 240
American Jewish Congress, 213
American Mercury, 307
American Nazi Party, 214
American Opinion, 208, 216, 237
American Revolution, 303
American Socialist Party, 107
Amherst College, 40
amicus briefs, 48, 141, 185, 343n90,
    345n10, 365n42
Amsterdam News, 142
Anastaplo, George, 4–16, 57, 128.
    See also *In Re Anastaplo*
Anastaplo, Sara, 7
animal cruelty, 323, 353n60
Anthony, Susan B., 263
Anti-Defamation League, 175, 185–86
Anti-Federalists, 20
antirevolution laws, 21
anti-Semitism, 175, 210